CITIZENSHIP IN CLASSICAL ATHENS

What did citizenship really mean in classical Athens? It is conventionally understood as characterised by holding political office. Since only men did so, only they have been considered to be citizens, and the *polis* has appeared primarily as the scene of men's political actions. However, Athenian law defined citizens not by political office, but by descent. Religion was central to the *polis* and in this domain women played prominent public roles. Both men and women were called 'citizens'. On a new reading of the evidence, Josine Blok argues that for the Athenians their *polis* was founded on an enduring bond with the gods. Laws anchored the *polis*'s commitments to humans and gods in this bond, transmitted over time to male and female Athenians as equal heirs. All public offices, in various ways and as befitting gender and age, served both the human community and the divine powers protecting Athens.

JOSINE BLOK is Professor of Ancient History and Classical Civilisation at Utrecht University and a member of the Royal Dutch Academy of Sciences. She has won wide acclaim for her innovative work on archaic and classical Greece, notably on the Greek *polis*, and is a winner of the prestigious VICI award for groundbreaking research issued by the Netherlands Organisation for Scientific Research. She has been a Visiting Fellow at various universities including Oxford and Paris Sorbonne, and is the founder and current chair of the European Network for the Study of Ancient Greek History.

CITIZENSHIP IN CLASSICAL ATHENS

JOSINE BLOK

CAMBRIDGE
UNIVERSITY PRESS

CAMBRIDGE
UNIVERSITY PRESS

University Printing House, Cambridge CB2 8BS, United Kingdom

One Liberty Plaza, 20th Floor, New York, NY 10006, USA

477 Williamstown Road, Port Melbourne, VIC 3207, Australia

314-321, 3rd Floor, Plot 3, Splendor Forum, Jasola District Centre, New Delhi - 110025, India

79 Anson Road, #06-04/06, Singapore 079906

Cambridge University Press is part of the University of Cambridge.

It furthers the University's mission by disseminating knowledge in the pursuit of education, learning and research at the highest international levels of excellence.

www.cambridge.org
Information on this title: www.cambridge.org/9781108702430
DOI: 10.1017/9781139017916

First published 2017
First paperback edition 2019

A catalogue record for this publication is available from the British Library

ISBN 978-0-521-19145-6 Hardback
ISBN 978-1-108-70243-0 Paperback

Contents

Tables

Preface

> First, we should give our city a name,
> something grand and notable;
> and then sacrifice to the gods.
>
> Peisetairos creates a new *polis*, in Aristophanes, *Birds*, 809–11[1]

This book investigates the nature of citizenship in classical Athens: how the Athenians thought about citizenship and how they put it into practice. The questions underlying this study emerged when I noticed that the ancient Greek ideas about citizenship that have most influenced modern conceptions have been those of Aristotle in the *Politics*, and that, conversely, modern conceptions influenced the way scholars read Aristotle and approached citizenship in Athens. Yet, when we compare Aristotle's views with evidence on the historical reality of classical Athens, we find that he painted a very partial picture of what it was to be a citizen. The aim of this book is to arrive at a picture of citizenship in Athens that comes closer to what the ancient evidence tells us. Before actually trying to do so, I should like to explain in a few words why I think this matters.

In *Politics*, Aristotle offers a famous definition of a citizen as a member of a community (*polis*) who is in a position to participate in political office. Athenian law, however, defined citizens on the criterion of their descent from an Athenian parent. Women were excluded from political office, but the vocabulary for citizens at Athens shows symmetrical words for male and female citizens. This evidence implies that in some way women and men were both considered to be citizens, despite women's exclusion from politics. And while cult was an important domain of public roles for women citizens, it was demonstrably equally so for men. All

[1] Πρῶτον ὄνομα τῇ πόλει / θέσθαι τι μέγα καὶ κλεινόν, εἶτα τοῖς θεοῖς / θῦσαι μετὰ τοῦτο. Transl. J. Henderson (Loeb ed.).

of this is not easily compatible with the Aristotelian notion of citizenship. What did scholars make of this discrepancy?

Since in the 1980s classical studies, in line with the humanities and social sciences, developed a strong focus on the cultural foundations of society, classical scholars are more or less agreed that in ancient Greece religion was deeply intertwined with all aspects of the *polis*. 'Embeddedness' – a term typically gaining currency since the 1980s – captures the anchorage of societal institutions in the values, practices and beliefs of the community, an approach changing the perception of religion and politics both as domains in their own right and in their mutual relationship. François de Polignac argued (1984) that the *polis* was based, socially and spatially, on the organisation of its cults and the location of its sanctuaries. The concept '*polis* religion', coined by Christiane Sourvinou-Inwood (1990), highlights the embeddedness of religion in the social structures of the Greek *polis*. Although recent critiques emphasise the autonomy of Greek religious experience also beyond that framework, they do not invalidate the significance of the concept for understanding the *polis* itself. Given that religion was so central to the *polis*, it is difficult to believe that citizenship was only a political and not at all a religious concept. Nonetheless, that is the picture that still prevails even in the best work in the field. In the study of ancient Greece, the *conceptual* disengagement between the domains of politics and religion remains, ultimately, profound.

A second problem I encountered in classical scholarship are the prevalent views of women's roles in ancient Greece and in classical Athens in particular. Although there is plenty of evidence for women taking public roles alongside men in cult and speaking in public on occasions when men were present, scholars have persistently assumed that women in ancient Greece were essentially outsiders of their society, not merely because separation of male and female spheres and a domestic life for women were highly valued, but primarily because women were excluded from political participation. Where citizen women are reported to be involved in *polis* activities, such evidence is usually understood as the exception proving the rule, while the rule itself is not questioned. Where the evidence highlights women's participation in cult, the significance of this fact for the *polis* more broadly tends to be undervalued. Of course, this perspective is not mistaken *in toto*. Politics *were* eminently important in ancient Greece, and so was the possibility to participate in them. Women *did* have a societal scope on average more limited than that of the men of their class. What is wrong, in my view, is the absolute weight these elements have acquired in the prevailing perceptions, leading to a distorted view of female citizens' lives and of the ancient *polis* in general.

Looking critically, I realised that the Aristotelian conception of citizenship was a central tenet in both strands of classical scholarship and that the fact that they held this view played an essential role in the problems I just described. Most ancient historians, including myself, were 'raised' on this view of Greek citizenship, and apparently this conception is tenacious. But it is definitely not the only way to understand citizenship at Athens, and the extant evidence elicits also quite different questions from those we usually ask. Cult clearly was essential to Athenian citizenship, so what does this mean for the conception and organisation of public office at Athens and for the meaning of gender for such roles? If citizenship was a matter of participation in the first place, why was it based on descent? In other words, what exactly did descent 'mean' for citizenship?

In the introductory chapter, my first objective is to deconstruct current approaches to Athenian citizenship by identifying their constitutive elements, notably different estimation of sources, the impact of modern ideas of citizenship and problems of vocabulary and definitions of citizenship. Important literary evidence on Athenian notions and practices of citizenship will be compared to Aristotle's definition of the citizen in *Politics*. I shall analyse this text quite extensively, to clarify why I think using his conception for understanding the historical situation at Athens is misleading, despite the significance of *Politics* as a philosophical analysis of the *polis* and despite much excellent historical scholarship that is primarily drawing on the *Politics*. Following this discussion, evidence on descent, cults, politics and gender as components of Athenian citizenship will be used to formulate new, elementary questions about citizenship at Athens and to outline the ways in which this book will attempt to answer those questions in the subsequent chapters.

Given that the *polis* was the defining framework of classical Greek society, comprehending the principles of citizenship, i.e. membership of and participation in the *polis*, is essential for our understanding of ancient Greece more widely. Classical Athens is a particularly significant but also an exceptional case, both for its democratic constitution and for the wealth of evidence that allows us to study it in detail. This book is meant primarily for ancient historians and classicists working on ancient Greece; the Greek evidence is cited in the footnotes to facilitate critical engagement with my arguments. Translations are provided in the main text, either my own or following the most recent translations in the Loeb Classical Library (Harvard University Press, Cambridge, MA/London, indicated as

Loeb ed.). In this way, I also hope to reach an audience beyond the circle of professional Hellenists. In modern debates on citizenship, democratic Athens plays an important role for historical comparison. Our notion of citizenship at Athens therefore has a substantial impact also on how we think about citizenship today.

Acknowledgements

On finishing this book, I deeply appreciate the opportunity to express my gratitude to all those who have supported me in the many years of its gestation. Many people gave me generously the gifts of their friendship, their time, their attention, their critical faculties, their encouragement and, let me not forget, their money. I wish to thank here all of them and some in particular.

Parts of this book were presented as papers to audiences in Europe and the United States; I thank my hosts warmly for inviting me and the audiences for their comments. Some of these papers provided the groundwork for this book, but since they were written and published my views have developed, and I have revisited the evidence or reconsidered the arguments. More importantly, the argument developed in this book brings it all together in a whole that is more than the sum of its parts. This book thus largely supersedes these earlier publications, but it is useful to explain here briefly how they are connected. For parts of the research for this book, furthermore, I collaborated with others, whose contributions I would gladly acknowledge.

A lecture on 'gender' in Oxford (1998) was the first try-out of some of my questions about Greek citizenship, a paper that Hans-Joachim Gehrke translated into German for a presentation, first in Freiburg-im-Breisgau and next elsewhere in Germany (published in *Historische Zeitschrift* 2004). In 2000, the Netherlands Organisation for Scientific Research (NWO) granted me a so-called Aspasia award for a pilot project on Greek citizenship, consisting of my own work on citizenship vocabulary (published in *Klio* 2005, revised here), Olaf Borgers's investigation of the visual representation of citizenship on Attic vases (published in *BABesch* 2008) and a conference on Solon, which André Lardinois and I organised together in December 2003 (published volume at Brill, Leiden/Boston 2006, paperback edition 2011).

Appointed in 2001 to the chair of Ancient History at Utrecht University, my inaugural lecture in 2002 (published Utrecht 2002 and in *Lampas* 2003, all in Dutch) presented some of the ideas underlying this book in a nutshell: citizenship based on *hiera kai hosia*, the congruencies between citizen roles of men and women in cult, modes of participation of citizens and metics, the fundamental role of the *gene* as models of 'pure' citizen descent and the transmission of eligibility for priesthood among them, and the meaning of all of this for Pericles' Citizenship Law. At that time, these ideas were hardly more than a hypothesis.

A large grant from NWO (the so-called VICI award, 2004–9) allowed me to develop these ideas with four PhD students and with Stephen Lambert, who in 2005 joined our forces. I am immensely grateful to all of them for their collaboration and to NWO for giving us the opportunity to do so. Floris van den Eijnde explored the creation of the socio-cultural landscape of Attica between 1000 and 600. Covering the prehistory of this book, he shows (in diss. Utrecht 2010; book to appear shortly) that the nucleus of what was to become citizenship based on cult emerged and spread in the early archaic age around the practice of dining, especially on sacrificial meat. Sara Wijma investigated the participation of metics in Athenian cults, on which I had done some preliminary work (published in *Historische Anthropologie* 2007). In her book, *Embracing the immigrant: The participation of metics in Athenian polis religion (5th–4th century BC)* (Stuttgart 2014) she shows in detail how participation in *hiera kai hosia* as the defining model of participation in the *polis* accommodated and integrated non-Athenians to a significant extent, both at *polis* level and in the demes. In a series of articles, Evelyn van 't Wout argues that *atimia* was not a fixed legal penalty, but entailed the exclusion of the *atimos* person from the position in the *polis* that should be his or her due. She demonstrates that citizenship as community membership depended on social acceptance and was always negotiable. Saskia Peels has explored the semantics of the adjective *hosios* in depth. Analysis of *hosios* was a part of my work right from the start and my results are laid down in several articles (2009–14) and reconsidered in this book, but I only describe the essential elements. As a linguist, Saskia Peels explains *why* the semantics of *hosios* work the way they do and how the value term *hosios* was used in persuasive discourse and sacred laws, commending certain behaviour because the gods valued it, in her book *Hosios: A semantic study of Greek piety* (Leiden/Boston 2015). For all of them as PhD students, my approach to citizenship was their point of departure, their results helped testing its validity and provided useful material to which I recurrently refer here, but in all essential respects their works are their own.

No one has contributed to this book and supported my efforts on it as much as Stephen Lambert. It was *agathe tyche* in the shape of our mutual friend Adele Scafuro that brought Stephen, whose work on the phratries and the *gene* I admired, to Utrecht at the right moment. On joining the project, he contributed to it in many ways, but especially by an investigation of the structures and practices of priesthood at Athens before and after Pericles' Citizenship Law, to see if my hypothesis on the connection between this law and priesthood was valid (published in *Historia* 2010). Besides our individual work for the project and other topics, we co-authored one publication. The material I had gathered on the Attic *gene* and the case for allotment as the means of selection for *genos* priests was so vast, joined with his work on Attic prosopography and priesthoods, that we decided to write the article together (published as Blok and Lambert in the *Zeitschrift für Papyrologie und Epigraphik* 2009). Stephen and I have read and commented on each other's work intermittently, especially concerning the citizenship project, but also subsequently. Last but not least, he has helped me tremendously with the final text of this book. I am deeply grateful for everything I learned from him, notably on epigraphy, and most of all for the friendship we developed over the years.

Friendship and collegiality are also the hallmark of the European Network for the Study of Ancient Greek History, an academic haven and breeding ground of new ideas rolled into one. In papers at our annual meetings since 2000, I tried out many of the ideas for this book and always received constructive criticism. I thank Kostas Buraselis, Gunnel Ekroth, Lin Foxhall, Hans-Joachim Gehrke, Maurizio Giangiulio, André Lardinois, Nino Luraghi, Irad Malkin, Christian Mann, Oswyn Murray, Christel Müller, Thomas Heine Nielsen, Vinciane Pirenne-Delforge, François de Polignac, Kurt Raaflaub, Robert Rollinger, Rosalind Thomas and Marek Węcowski for all they have given me over the years.

Many colleagues and friends read parts of this book or otherwise gave me helpful advice, some of whom even despite disagreement with my views for which, of course, no one but I carries any responsibility. I am especially grateful to Karen Bassi, Bas van Bavel, Jaap Mansfeld, Glenn Most, Maarten Prak, Scott Scullion, Violaine Sebillotte Cuchet, Ineke Sluiter and Henk Versnel for giving my work their time and attention. A special word of thanks I owe to Robert Parker for recurrent discussions of *hosios*, and to P.J. Rhodes for generously giving his comments on passages of this book or matters of evidence. Robin Osborne's critical comments did much to improve the final text. Floris Cohen kindly read the drafts and offered supportive advice.

A special tribute I owe to the Fondation Hardt at Vandoeuvres and to all who make working there so wonderful. The Fondation, where much of the material for this book was collected and drafts of the text were made, has been a hospitable refuge from my increasingly demanding academic duties in the past years. I am also grateful to the Netherlands Institute at Athens for hosting me so wonderfully when I visited Athens. Emmy Mestropian-Makri was of invaluable help in getting permissions from Greek institutions, notably for the photo of the relief in the National Archaeological Museum at Athens adorning the cover of this book.

I can hardly find words to express my love for and gratitude to Wessel, Julia and Matthijs Krul, who truly 'share in everything' and whose warm loyalty encouraged me time and again. Wessel and Matthijs read parts of this book and gave their constructive comments. I dedicate this book to my husband, my daughter and my son, all three my fellow historians, and to the loving memory of my father, who so much enjoyed to see my work growing.

Abbreviations

Abbreviations of classical authors and texts follow those in S. Hornblower and A. Spawford, *Oxford Classical Dictionary* (3rd ed.; Oxford 2003), supplemented by those in LSJ; abbreviations of epigraphical corpora not included below follow those of the Packard Humanities Institute (www.epigraphy.packhum.org); abbreviations of journals follow *L'année philologique* (www.annee-philologique.com).

Ag. 16	A.G. Woodhead (ed.), *Agora* XVI: *Inscriptions*: *The decrees* (Princeton 1997)
Ag. 19	G.V. Lalonde, M.K. Langdon, M.B. Walbank (eds), *Agora* XIX: *Inscriptions*: *Horoi, poletai records, and leases of public lands* (Princeton 1991)
AIO	Attic Inscriptions Online (www.atticinscriptions.com)
APF	J.K. Davies, *Athenian propertied families, 600–300 B.C.* (Oxford 1971)
DAA	A.E. Raubitschek, *Dedications from the Athenian Acropolis: Catalogue of the inscriptions of the sixth and fifth centuries B.C.* (Cambridge, MA 1949)
FRA	M.J. Osborne, S.G. Byrne, *The foreign residents of Athens: An annex to the lexicon of Greek personal names: Attica* (Leuven 1996)
FGrH	F. Jacoby, *Die Fragmente der griechischen Historiker* (Berlin 1923–30; Leiden 1940–58)
FHG	C. Müller, *Fragmenta Historicorum Graecorum* I–IV (Paris 1841–70)
Harrison	A.R.W. Harrison, *The law of Athens* (2nd ed.) I–II (Oxford 1968–71, repr. London/Indianapolis 1998)
IG I^3	*Inscriptiones Graecae* I: *Inscriptiones Atticae Euclidis anno anteriores*. 3rd edn (Berlin 1981, 1994). Fasc. 1, D. Lewis (ed.), *Decreta et tabulae magistratuum* (nos 1–500); fasc. 2, D. Lewis, L. Jeffery (eds), *Dedicationes. Catalogi. Termini. Tituli sepulcrales. Varia. Tituli Attici extra Atticam reperti. Addenda* (nos 501–1517)

IG II²	*Inscriptiones Graecae* II and III: *Inscriptiones Atticae Euclidis anno posteriores*, 2nd edn, Joh. Kirchner (ed.) (Berlin 1913–40)
IG II³	*Inscriptiones Graecae* II, III³: *Inscriptiones Atticae Euclidis anno posteriores*; I: *Leges et decretae*; S.D. Lambert (ed.) (nos 292–572), V.N. Bardani and S.V. Tracy (eds) (nos 1135–1461) (Berlin 2012)
K-A	R. Kassel, C. Austin, *Poetae Comici Graeci* (Berlin 1983–)
LfgrE	*Lexicon des frühgriechischen Epos* (Hamburg 1955–2010)
LGPN	M.J. Osborne, S.G. Byrne, *A lexicon of Greek personal names*, II: *Attica* (Oxford 1994) supplemented with *Athenian Onomasticon Search* (www.seanb.org)
LIMC	*Lexicon Iconographicum Mythologicum Classicum* (Zürich 1981–)
LR	D.F. Leão, P.J. Rhodes (eds) *The laws of Solon: A new edition with introduction, translation and commentary* (London/New York 2015)
LSCG	F. Sokolowski, *Lois sacrées des cités grecques* (Paris 1969)
LSJ	H.G. Liddell, R. Scott, H.S. Jones, R. McKenzie, *A Greek–English lexicon, with a supplement* (9th edn; Oxford 1996)
LSS	F. Sokolowski, *Lois sacrées des cités grecques: Supplément* (Paris 1962)
ML	R. Meiggs, D. Lewis, *A selection of Greek historical inscriptions to the end of the fifth century B.C.* (Oxford 1969)
NGSL	E. Lupu, *Greek sacred law: A collection of new documents* (Leiden/Boston 2005; Religions in the Graeco-Roman World, vol. 152)
Nomima	H. van Effenterre, F. Ruzé, *Nomima : Receuil d'inscriptions politiques et juridiques de l'archaisme grec* I–II (Rome 1994–5)
OCT	*Oxford Classical Texts*
OR	R. Osborne, P.J. Rhodes, *Greek historical inscriptions* (in press)
Osborne I–IV	M.J. Osborne, *Naturalization in Athens* I–IV (Brussels 1981–3)
Parker, *PS*	R.T.C. Parker, *Polytheism and society at Athens* (Oxford 2005)
PHI	The Packard Humanities Institute – Searchable Greek Inscriptions (www.epigraphy.packhum.org)

Rhodes, *CAAP*	P.J. Rhodes, *A commentary to the Aristotelian Athenaion Politeia* rev. edn (Oxford 1993)
RO	P.J. Rhodes, R. Osborne, *Greek historical inscriptions 404–323 BC* (Oxford 2003)
Schwenk	C.J. Schwenk, *Athens in the age of Alexander: The dated laws and decrees of 'the Lykourgan era' 338–322 B.C.* (Chicago 1985)
SEG	*Supplementum Epigraphicum Graecum*
Syll.^{3}	W. Dittenberger, *Sylloge Inscriptionum Graecarum* 3rd ed., F. Hiller von Gaertringen, J. Kirchner, H.R. Pomtow, E. Ziebarth (eds) I–IV (Leipzig 1915–24)
TLG	*Thesaurus Linguae Graecae* (www.stephanus.tlg.uci.edu)

I

Rethinking Athenian Citizenship

'What I have to say about myself is, I think, the simplest and most just: that because I am born from *astos* parents on both sides and have received my *kleros* of the property and of the family, I am a citizen (*polites*).'[1]

Euxitheos, in *Against Euboulides*, Dem. 57.46

In Athenian law, a citizen was someone born from citizen parents. Until the mid-fifth century, one parent of citizen birth, usually the father, sufficed for citizen status, but since Pericles' Citizenship Law of 451/0 only those born from two citizen parents could participate (*metechein*) in the Athenian *polis*.[2] What did this *metechein* entail? Going through the rich documentation on classical Athens, we find many areas of public and private life where Athenians were active *as citizens*, usually organised according to gender and age. All the citizens, male and female, participated in religion in a wide variety of ways. For male citizens over eighteen, furthermore, participation in political office and its concomitant financial administration was an important domain of citizen activities, beside military duties. In sum, we find that descent is the fundamental qualification for citizenship in Athenian law, and that participation in religion and other fields are the typical ways of acting as a citizen.

[1] Dem. 57.46: λοιπὸν δέ μοι περὶ ἐμαυτοῦ πρὸς ὑμᾶς εἰπεῖν, τὸ μὲν ἁπλούστατον οἶμαι καὶ δικαιότατον, ἐξ ἀμφοτέρων ἀστῶν ὄντα με, κεκληρονομηκότα καὶ τῆς οὐσίας καὶ τοῦ γένους, εἶναι πολίτην. This speech is dated shortly after 346/5. All dates are BCE, unless otherwise indicated.

[2] *Ath.Pol.* 26.3: καὶ τρίτῳ μετ᾽ αὐτὸν ἐπὶ Ἀντιδότου διὰ τὸ πλῆθος τῶν πολιτῶν Περικλέους εἰπόντος ἔγνωσαν, μὴ μετέχειν τῆς πόλεως ὃς ἂν μὴ ἐξ ἀμφοῖν ἀστοῖν ᾖ γεγονώς. 'And in the third year after this, when Antidotos was archon, they decided owing to the large number of citizens on the proposal of Pericles that no one who was not born from both *astos* parents would participate (*metechein*) in the *polis*.' Cf. Ael. *VH*. 13.24, Plut. *Per.* 37.3. For *metechein* in citizenship law, cf. Schol. Aeschin. 1.39. Coşkun's arguments (2014) for a date close to 445/4, when a scrutiny of the citizen body took place in connection to a gift of grain by Psammetichos of Egypt (Philochoros, *FGrH* 328 F 119; Plut. *Per.* 37.3) and for the law being retroactive, do not answer the many questions they raise, so I retain here the date, the text and the contents of Pericles' Citizenship Law proposed in Blok (2009b).

When ancient historians discuss Athenian citizenship, however, strange things happen. Let me give one example, an article by John Davies entitled 'Athenian citizenship: the descent group and the alternatives' (1977).[3] It is not very recent, but it is concerned precisely with the qualification of descent and it offers a lucid analysis of crucial moments when the Athenians debated how it should be used as a criterion for citizenship. Used and quoted extensively since its publication, the article expresses what is in many respects the prevailing view. Its first lines are as follows:

> Classical Athens defined membership of its citizen body, and thereby its civic space, rigorously in terms of descent. Citizens were those who were male; were sons of a citizen father; were born from a woman who was the daughter of a citizen father; were born from a woman who was 'pledged' (ἐγγυητή); and had been accepted as members of their father's (phratry and) deme.[4]

The statement in the first sentence is clearly founded in Athenian law. But why, having first correctly identified Athenian insistence only on descent, does he proceed with the *non sequitur* that 'citizens were those who were male'? To understand this, we have to bring in a further text, Aristotle's *Politics*, book III, the most extensive ancient theory of citizenship. Here, Aristotle states:

> Who [or what], therefore, is a citizen (*polites*) is clear from these considerations: we can now say that he who is in a position to share in political or [and] judicial office, is a citizen of that *polis*, and a *polis* is a group of such people large enough in number to maintain a self-sufficient life, speaking generally.[5]

Aristotle does not claim that his argument in the *Politics* applies to Athens, nor to any other specific *polis*, although he observes that his definition of a citizen works best in a democracy.[6] Nonetheless, many historians have used Aristotle's *Politics* and in particular his definition of a citizen as a guideline in their analysis of real Greek *poleis*, notably of

[3] Davies (1977).

[4] Davies (1977) 105. On 106, Davies states that the rules on descent as laid down in Pericles' law themselves are clear, but his handling of them shows that statement to be too optimistic.

[5] Arist. *Pol.* 1275b17–22: τίς μὲν οὖν ἐστιν ὁ πολίτης, ἐκ τούτων φανερόν· ᾧ γὰρ ἐξουσία κοινωνεῖν ἀρχῆς βουλευτικῆς ἢ (*OCT*: καὶ) κριτικῆς, πολίτην ἤδη λέγομεν εἶναι ταύτης τῆς πόλεως, πόλιν δὲ τὸ τῶν τοιούτων πλῆθος ἱκανὸν πρὸς αὐτάρκειαν ζωῆς, ὡς ἁπλῶς εἰπεῖν. For ἐξουσία as 'to be in a position', Ostwald (1996) 55. 'βουλευτικῆς' means 'deliberative' rather than 'legislative', although presumably the former is seen as a component of the latter. In Aristotle's definitions ἁπλῶς usually means 'without further qualifications' (see e.g. 1275a19 below), but here ὡς ἁπλῶς εἰπεῖν is not a part of the formal definition.

[6] Arist. *Pol.* 1275a33–1275b17.

Athens. This also applies to Davies's argument. The reason for his at first sight illogical phrase 'citizens were those who were male' becomes clear when he characterises citizenship as holding elected or allotted political office and the concomitant right to own property.[7] Descent now turns out to be no more than the condition for and therefore the means of access to political office; the emphasis is entirely on the latter, and women, who do not share these functions of citizenship, are not even considered members of the descent group 'citizens' in their own right anymore, but are only 'daughters of citizen fathers'. This conception of citizenship is fundamentally at odds with the Athenian citizenship laws, which do not limit participating in the *polis* to political office and refer explicitly to both men and women as citizens by legitimate birth (*astos*, *aste*, with contrastive counterparts *nothos*, *nothe*), making legitimacy emphatically dependent on birth from a citizen woman.[8] In fact, the Athenian laws approach the issue from the other side: male and female are both citizens when legitimately descended from Athenian parents, and this status is conditional for participation in the *polis* for both. Political office is not mentioned, let alone used as a means to conceptualise the rules of descent. Looking for the reason why Davies makes this fundamental turn away from the very laws the use of which he sets out to clarify, we find that he derives his conception of a citizen not from these laws, but from Aristotle.[9]

More examples of this use of the *Politics* in some of the best historical work on Athens will appear later in this chapter. It is remarkable that in all of them, as in Davies's article, the choice of Aristotle's definition as the leading concept by which to interpret the evidence is not really explained. One among several reasons might be that the passage from the *Politics* is virtually unique in the ancient Greek record in that it offers criteria on which citizenship is defined in general terms, abstracted from specific *polis*

[7] Davies (1977) 105. He gives no references for this conception, but I assume that 'were sons of a citizen father; were born from a woman who was the daughter of a citizen father; and had been accepted as members of their father's (phratry and) deme' combines *Ath.Pol.* 42.1: 'Those who are born from *astos* parents on both sides share in the *politeia*, and they are enrolled in the demes when they are eighteen years of age', with *Ath.Pol.* 55.3, a part of the questions to the candidates for the archonship: 'Who is your father and to what deme does he belong, and who is your father's father, and who your mother, and who her father and what his deme?'; the phrase 'born from a woman who was "pledged" (ἐγγυητή)' is derived from citizenship law, Is. 6.47; law *ap.* Dem. 43.51.

[8] Is. 6.47; law *ap.* Dem. 43.51; Ath. 13.577b; Schol. Aeschin. 1.39. For the full texts and discussion, see Chapters 2.1; 3.1; 6.1.

[9] Davies (1977) 114: the difference between the inhabitants of the area or community and those 'who are citizens of that community in Aristotle's sense of sharing the holding of office and the administration of justice'. Also Whitehead (1991) 137–8.

laws.[10] Such a use of general characteristics is what we expect a definition to be like. For some historians, furthermore, the relevance of Aristotle's *Politics* to Athens seems to be grounded not so much on the *Politics* itself, but rather on the *Athenaion Politeia* (henceforth *Ath.Pol.*). Written by an unknown author belonging to Aristotle's circle in the 330s and revised in the 320s as a part of the project of the *Politics*, the text contains both a historical and a systematic account of the *politeia* (societal and political organisation or 'constitution') of Athens. Here we need to ask if *Ath.Pol.*'s testimony on historical Athens was collected independently of the *Politics* or rather drafted with the conception of citizenship proposed in the philosophical work in mind.

Whatever the reason of their choice, Aristotle's focus on political office has led historians to take only, or primarily, this element into account when studying citizenship at Athens. No one will contest the importance of politics to the self-conception of the *polis* as a citizen community, but we may ask if other aspects were not equally important, if not more so. Surveying the evidence, one other essential aspect is the role of the divine world in the Athenian conception of the *polis* and of religion broadly conceived as central domain of the actions typical of citizens. Current scholarship, as I will discuss in more detail below, is investigating the *polis* as the platform of religion, but tends to underestimate religion as a crucial element of *citizenship*. Concomitantly, many activities of women taking place in the domain of religion have not been sufficiently understood as acts of citizenship, nor, on the other hand, have religious actions been sufficiently understood as integral to men's civic roles. Only when these elements are given their full due can we attain a more comprehensive understanding of what politics, in the sense of running the *polis*, really meant at Athens.

What means do we have to attempt a different approach to citizenship in classical Athens? Among the numerous texts documenting ideas about citizenship and the ways it was practised, some stand out for their length and wealth of details. One of them is a speech written by Demosthenes in or shortly after 346/5 (Dem. 57) for the defence of a certain Euxitheos, a man from the deme Halimous on the western coast of Attica who had been deleted from the list of citizens in his deme, because allegedly he was not of citizen descent on both sides. The speech is not a theoretical or

[10] τίς in the first line can be translated either as 'what?' or as 'who?', in the first case leading to a description of what a citizen *typically* does or is, and in the second case asking who fulfil this role. Both readings are possible: H. Rackham (Loeb ed.) 'What constitutes a citizen is therefore clear'; T.A. Sinclair and T.J. Saunders (Penguin Classics): 'From these considerations it has become clear who a citizen is.'

historical account of Athenian citizenship, but it shows what Athenians expected a citizen to be and to do.

We begin our enquiry into Athenian citizenship by examining in greater depth the three contemporary ancient accounts introduced above – Demosthenes 57, Aristotle's *Politics* and the *Ath.Pol.* – to see what each of them tells us about what it meant to be a citizen and what the relationship between their conceptions of citizenship might be. To that end we need to break down the complex concept of citizenship into its major components by asking some fundamental questions. *What* was a citizen in the view of the author, that is to say, which activities or attitudes did the author identify as typical of a citizen? *Who* were the citizens, that is to say, what were the qualifications or criteria according to which one was a citizen? Some of the answers are stated explicitly in these texts, others are merely implied. This vocabulary will here serve only to chart the writer's perceptions of citizenship, but we need to look into the precise meaning of these words at a later stage. We begin with Demosthenes 57, Euxitheos' defence speech before the Athenian court.

1.1 Euxitheos' Appeal

In 346/5, the Athenian *polis* decided to hold a scrutiny (*diapsephismos*) of all its citizens. Details on the motives for this decision are lacking, but the pressure of the military conflicts with Philip of Macedon played an important role as in Athens itself tensions ran high, even if the peace of Philocrates in 346 gave a temporary relief. The *diapsephismos* created an ideal opportunity to settle old scores. The speech written by Demosthenes for Euxitheos is our main source for the procedure. In every deme a meeting was held of the demesmen – that is of those who had previously been recognised at age eighteen as having two citizen parents – and each individual demesman was re-examined to consider again whether both his parents did have good claims to citizen status.[11] Euxitheos was one among many who were ejected from the list of citizens in the course of this scrutiny.[12] He appealed to the people's court to revise the deme's decision.

[11] For the regular procedure of *dokimasia* (assessment) of a young adult male on entering the deme, *Ath.Pol.* 42.1.

[12] Cf. Is. 12 (*Euphiletos*) of 344/3; Is. 3.37 (*Pyrrhos*), the date of which is unknown, but the occasion referred to may well have been the same *diapsephismos* of 346/5; references in the speech to Diophantos of Sphettos (*LGPN* no. 54) and Dorotheos of Eleusis (*LGPN* no. 52) suggest a date in the 340s. Euxitheos himself refers to 'many who with justice have been expelled from all the demes' (Dem. 57.2), of course in contrast to himself, 'a victim of political rivalry'; note also his claim that many members of his own deme have been cast out unjustly (57.58), whereas several *xenoi* have bought their way in (57.59).

Much was at stake: if Euxitheos failed to convince the *dikastai*, he could be sold into slavery. His speech had to be cast in terms in which the *dikastai* would recognise their own conceptions and expectations. Only in this way could he win their understanding and sympathy.[13]

Demosthenes deploys several lines of argument to persuade the jury. First, he shows how the speaker himself and his witnesses acted in accordance with, and his opponents contrary to, the laws which the collective of citizens had to uphold and were read out aloud during the trial. Moreover, he appeals to the expectations among his audience as to what in all probability the conduct of plaintiff and defendant would be in situations with which the jury were familiar. Demosthenes encapsulates these arguments in compelling character sketches of plaintiff and defendant, a textbook example of Athenian forensic method.[14] In this speech, Euxitheos is portrayed as the victim of a certain Euboulides, a man keen to harm his fellow citizens, who out of malice had manipulated his fellow demesmen to vote against Euxitheos, who presents himself as a man devoted to the common good. In sum, Demosthenes needed to convince the court that Euxitheos was indeed legally qualified to be a citizen, in terms of *who* he was and *what* he was and did. To do so he both brought arguments that directly bore on the legal criteria for citizenship (two citizen parents) and arguments that depended on matching Euxitheos' past behaviour to what the court would have expected of a citizen, and only of a citizen. Let us first look at the contents of Euxitheos' argument.

The accusations that Euboulides had put forward were false, and now it was up to him, Euxitheos, to tell what was true and just (*dikaios*) and to show that he was truly a citizen (1). Since the *dikastai* feel passionately about just claims to citizenship (1–3) and about the necessity to observe the *nomoi* (laws) and *dike* (justice; 4–6), they need to know that Euboulides' actions were motivated by malice, arising from Euxitheos' support of a woman previously prosecuted by Euboulides for impiety. (We may note here that Euboulides will have been fined 1,000 drachmae for this failed prosecution in what is bound to have been a high-profile case; the loss of face incurred in losing a trial like this was severe.) Now, Euboulides had used the *polis*'s scrutiny of its citizens – a legitimate exercise for the public good – as an opportunity to take his private revenge (8–16). No doubt had

[13] On social knowledge involved in legal procedures Humphreys (1983a); Humphreys (1985); Humphreys (2007 (orig. 1985)).

[14] References to the laws and witnesses are 'external' persuasive arguments, according to Arist. *Rhet.* 1375a21–1377b11, whereas the drawing of character is an 'internal' argument.

ever been raised about whether any of his relatives had been true Athenians. Owing to his *eugeneia* (good birth) on his father's side, i.e. membership of a *genos* (23–8), he was elected by his fellow demesmen to be a candidate for allotment for the deme's priesthood of Heracles.[15] Had he been selected by the lot, it would have been his duty to sacrifice on behalf of the very men who now tried to prevent him even from sharing sacrifice with them (46–7; 62). The schemes of his fellow demesmen and their unjust decision (59–66) were caused by his time of office as demarch, when he had pressed them to pay their overdue debts to the treasuries of the deme and of the sanctuaries (63). Finally, he performed a new scrutiny of himself, testified to his citizen status and ended with a passionate plea to be allowed to bury his mother in the ancestral tomb, and not to be cut off from the *polis* and his relatives, but to be buried in his fatherland (67–70).

After disqualifying the actions of the deme against him, Euxitheos devotes the largest part of his speech to persuading the *dikastai* of his citizen status. He does so with two strands of evidence. One aims at demonstrating the citizen status of his father and of his mother, and similarly of his grandparents. Euxitheos claims that although his father was born before the re-enactment of the law on citizen status and therefore only needed one parent of citizen birth to be a citizen himself (29–30), nonetheless his father was in fact an Athenian of citizen descent on both sides (23). The same holds true for his mother. Witnesses are produced to testify to all family relations on both sides (17–54). The other strand of evidence consists of showing that he himself, his parents and other relatives all participated in the group activities typical of Athenian citizens, namely the cults and religious rituals marking Athenian kinship. The two strands are tightly woven together, because participation in such rituals was a sign of being a born Athenian, i.e. citizen status. By going through all of these group activities, so familiar to his audience, the impression is reinforced that because Euxitheos' parents and he himself had always participated without anyone protesting, every one of them and he, Euxitheos, too, must have been truly qualified to do so. Crucial in demonstrating his status are the solemn giving-in-marriage of the women according to the law (54), the sacrifices with the *phrateres* (*polis* subgroup supervising legitimacy), sacrifice with his kin to Apollo Patroios (protector of patrimony) and Zeus Herkeios (protector of the *oikos* fence), and sharing ancestral tombs (*patroia mnemata*) with them (54). He had passed the scrutiny of

[15] For *genos*, see Chapter 3.

Athenian birth for offices (46). In other words, there never had been and could not be any doubt that Euxitheos was born an Athenian citizen.[16]

We must not only look closely at the arguments but also at the words and expressions (as crafted by Demosthenes) in which Euxitheos cast his plea to be acknowledged as a citizen. The first instance of such vocabulary occurs very early in the speech, where Euxitheos proclaims:

> [There were many occurrences of injustice towards citizens who were victimised in this scrutiny and lost their status . . .] I will tell you at once what I consider to be just (*dikaia*) in these matters. I hold it to be your duty to treat harshly those who are proven to be *xenoi* (strangers), and who, without persuading you or asking for it, have come with stealth and violence to participate (*metechein*) in your *hiera* (things of the gods, cults and rituals) and *koina* (common things), but to help and save those who have met with misfortune and who demonstrate that they are *politai*.[17]

Here, a contrast is made between *xenoi*, who do not share the privilege of participating in the *hiera* and *koina* of the *polis*, and others who do. Implied in the latter group are *politai* who may seem to be *xenoi* but nonetheless can demonstrate their status. The speaker reminds the *dikastai* that the demesmen took their oaths on the *hiera* (sacrifices (26)) and recounts how he went to all the *hiera* (sacred places (54)) where only born Athenians were expected to be. Throughout the speech, Euxitheos' account of his sharing in the *hiera* of his family, of the deme and of the *polis* builds on this initial distinction between those who are members of the *polis* and those who are not, filling in the picture of himself as someone who from his youth participated in these *hiera* without anyone objecting. The implied conclusion is clear: he was a *polites*. The concept of 'sharing' recurs in the vocabulary used: *meteinai tes poleos* (to be a member of the *polis*) occurs at the beginning (1), the middle (23) and three-quarters of the way through (55) the speech; and the same idea is present in *metechein tes poleos* (to participate in the *polis*), which occurs in a cluster at 51.6 and 51.10, soon followed by *meteinai* in 55.

A frequently recurring verb (nineteen times) is *proseko*, 'it is befitting, it belongs to'.[18] Demosthenes uses it to indicate that something should be

[16] MacDowell (2009) 293: 'If in truth Euxitheos was not the son of Thoukritos, Demosthenes has shown great skill in obscuring the fact.'

[17] Dem. 57.3: . . . ἃ νομίζω περὶ τούτων αὐτῶν πρῶτον εἶναι δίκαια, ἐρῶ πρὸς ὑμᾶς. ἐγὼ γὰρ οἴομαι δεῖν ὑμᾶς τοῖς μὲν ἐξελεγχομένοις ξένοις οὖσιν χαλεπαίνειν, εἰ μήτε πείσαντες μήτε δεηθέντες ὑμῶν λάθρᾳ καὶ βίᾳ τῶν ὑμετέρων ἱερῶν καὶ κοινῶν μετεῖχον, τοῖς δ᾽ ἠτυχηκόσι καὶ δεικνύουσι πολίτας ὄντας αὐτοὺς βοηθεῖν καὶ σῴζειν.

[18] Dem. 57.1 (2×), 2, 4 (2×), 5 (2×), 6, 24, 25, 30, 32, 34, 36, 44, 46, 56, 69 (2×).

the case, either because it is typical of a situation or person, or because something ought to belong to someone. He begins the speech with this word to make his client's position clear: the slanders of Euboulides do not 'befit' him, Euxitheos (1); instead, he is confident of showing that it befits him to belong to the *polis* (2). The *dikastai* should not take the deme's vote as a sign that membership of the *polis* would not befit him (6). Even if his father had only one citizen parent, it would still befit him to be a *polites*, because he was born before the archonship of Eukleides (30) – an implicit reference to an apparently well-known law on legitimacy.

In all these passages with *proseko* claims are made to everything that belongs to the status of a citizen, by drawing on what people know as a solid convention or what is to be expected considering what everyone knows, or on which the *polis* is entirely agreed and what therefore ought to be the case, but never to a notion that in modern terms is called a *right*. The string of *proseko* constructions throughout the speech weaves an argument strongly claiming that citizen status has been part of Euxitheos' life just as it has been of all who are like him – Athenian citizens – and that it ought to belong to him here and now and in the future. After hearing the witnesses testify to the legitimacy of his descent on both sides and his participation in the *hiera*, just over half way through his speech, he sums up what must be the clearest statement of his citizen status:

> What I have to say about myself is, I think, the simplest and most just: that because I am born from *astos* parents on both sides and have received my *kleros* (allotted part) of the property and of the family, I am a citizen (*polites*).[19]

Note that Euxitheos calls both his parents *astos* (born citizen) and mentions that he has received his *kleros* (share in the inheritance) of property and family; receiving this *kleros* is presented as the ground for being a citizen (*polites*) and therefore serves as a sign of being one. Throughout the speech, 'citizen' is designated *polites* in case of a man and *politis* of a woman, or *astos* of a man and *aste* of a woman.[20] To the exact meaning of these words we need to return at a later stage, but here we may note that being a *polites* means to belong to the *polis* with all that entails and *astos* indicates being born of citizen parents, unlike, for instance, someone made a citizen by a decree.

19 Dem. 57.46.

20 Dem. 57: πολίτης male citizen, in sing. or plur.: 3, 11, 17, 20, 26, 29, 30, 44, 45, 46, 48, 51, 59, 61; πολῖτις female citizen, in sing. or plur.: 30, 43; ἀστός male (born) citizen, sing. or plur. 24, 25, 30, 46, 54. ἀστή female (born) citizen, sing. or plur. 35, 36, 40, 43, 45, 46, 54.

Apart from a *polites*, Euxitheos calls himself an *Athenaios* (Athenian). The first time, he does so as a statement:

> [What I hold to be just] I am going to demonstrate to you: that I am an Athenian, both from my father's and from my mother's side, and offer witnesses of all this, who you will judge to be truthful.[21]

This designation of himself and his father as *Athenaios*, one of eight occasions in the speech where 'being *Athenaios*' expresses their citizen status, resonates with the way the members of the court are addressed as *Athenaioi*, nineteen times in all.[22] The implication, that he is an *Athenaios* as much as they are, is made explicit once he has produced all the witnesses and their accounts:

> As to me, gentlemen *dikastai* (and by Zeus I beg you that no one starts shouting or being angry at what I want to say), I consider myself an *Athenaios* on the same grounds as each one of you, because I have from the beginning regarded her as my mother whom I present as such to you, and I do not pretend that I am hers while in reality I am not but someone else's. And the same holds true, gentlemen *Athenaioi*, for my father.[23]

Now that it will come to a decision, Euxitheos makes a distinction (56) between the *dikastai* on the one hand, and the deme, the *boule* and the assembly on the other: only the decisions of the first are eminently concerned with *dike*. In this way, he conjures up the image of a group of *Athenaioi* consisting of the *dikastai* and himself, who by virtue of their commitment to justice distinguish themselves from the rest of the citizens.

Finally, when stating the grounds of his citizen status, Euxitheos uses the verb *kleronomeo*, receiving one's part (*kleros*) of the inheritance.[24] The noun *kleros* is the root of the verb *kleroo*, to allocate or select by lot. Euxitheos uses *kleros* words in relation to his birth and inheritance (46.6), and when he recounts he was elected to stand for selection by lot for the priesthood of Heracles (46.10). He returns to his qualification for allotment several times closely following on the same passage (48.3; 48.4; 49.3; 53.3; 62.9).

[21] Dem. 57.17: δεῖξαι πρὸς ὑμᾶς ἐμαυτὸν Ἀθηναῖον ὄντα καὶ τὰ πρὸς πατρὸς καὶ τὰ πρὸς μητρός, καὶ μάρτυρας τούτων, οὓς ὑμεῖς ἀληθεῖς φήσετ᾽ εἶναι.

[22] Sing. Ἀθηναῖος: 17, 19, 22, 23, 27, 29, 50, 61; plur. ὦ ἄνδρες Ἀθηναῖοι: 6, 7, 8, 22, 30, 32, 35, 37, 43, 44, 45, 47, 48, 50, 56, 58, 59, 60, 62; used in other cases: 14, 31.

[23] Dem. 57.50: ἐγὼ δ᾽, ὦ ἄνδρες δικασταί (καί μοι πρὸς Διὸς καὶ θεῶν μηδεὶς θορυβήσῃ, μηδ᾽ ἐφ᾽ ᾧ μέλλω λέγειν ἀχθεσθῇ), ἐμαυτὸν Ἀθηναῖον ὑπείληφ᾽ ὥσπερ ὑμῶν ἕκαστος ἑαυτόν, μητέρ᾽ ἐξ ἀρχῆς νομίζων ἥνπερ εἰς ὑμᾶς ἀποφαίνω, καὶ οὐχ ἑτέρας μὲν ὢν ταύτης δὲ προσποιούμενος· πατέρα πάλιν, ὦ ἄνδρες Ἀθηναῖοι, τὸν αὐτὸν τρόπον.

[24] He does so twice, once referring to his own inheritance (46), once concerning his mother's first husband who received an inheritance through an *epikleros* he could marry (41).

Although in both cases composite verbs are used, not the single root *kleros*, it is plausible that here again Demosthenes aimed at an echo effect, joining the status of citizen due to inheritance to the qualification to stand for allotment for a public office, here in cult.[25]

Some elements immediately catch the eye. Citizenship is articulated by two verbs, *meteinai* (*being* a citizen) and *metechein* (*acting* as a citizen), both verbs with the prefix *meta-* indicating belonging to a larger whole; this larger whole is here 'the *polis*'. The status of being a citizen is indicated by *polites*, *astos* and *Athenaios* and depends on birth from citizen parents on both sides. Euxitheos demonstrates his acting as a citizen most conspicuously by reference to his participation in sacrifice and other religious actions (*hiera*). He refers to the cults of the phratry, the *genos* and the deme in which he took part, but he also reminds the *dikastai* and the entire audience at the trial that the gods are engaged in the oaths taken and in the performance of justice.[26] Thirteen times in the course of his speech, he refers to the oaths that members of the *boule* (council), the *dikastai* and witnesses took to fulfil their duty to justice and the laws, and to the impiety breaking these oaths would entail; twice he supplicated the *dikastai* in the name of Zeus and the gods to act righteously.[27]

By contrast, participation in political office is not portrayed as a significant feature of citizenship. Euxitheos mentions the fact that he had passed the *dokimasia* (scrutiny) to hold office primarily to underscore previous acceptance by the deme of his citizen birth (46). He devotes more words to his eligibility for the office of priest and the prospective role in the ritual if he had been selected than to his office as demarch. He only refers to the latter when describing how it had negatively affected his position among the demesmen, when he did his duty in collecting the arrears of debts on behalf of the community. No other political function that an average male citizen might hold by virtue of having been accepted among the demesmen, notably in the *boule* and the *dikasterion*, features in his portrayal of himself as a citizen.

Furthermore, in the vocabulary of this speech male and female citizens are not distinguished in any other way than by the gendered morphology

[25] LSJ *s.v.* κλῆρος lists 'lot', 'what is acquired by lot' before 'estate, inheritance'. For a Greek audience these meanings of the word must have been closely associated. On *kleros*, see further Chapters 3.5; 5.7.

[26] At a trial not only the *dikastai* but also many onlookers were present and exerted their influence, see Lanni (1997) and Thomas (2011) for the broad audience in and around the courts and the effects of *thorybos* (shouting and other noise during public sessions).

[27] Oaths: Dem. 57.8, 22, 26, 36, 39, 44, 53, 56, 59, 61, 62, 63, 69. Supplication: 57.50, 59.

of the words referring to them. *Astos* and *aste* (born citizens), *polites* and *politis* (*polis* members) are used symmetrically, as are their opposites, *xenos* and *xene* (51, strangers).[28] On the basis of this document, then, we may assume that in some fundamental way, men and women were both citizens. Owing to the crucial importance of citizen mothers in this case and similar ones dealing with legitimate descent, *aste* occurs even more frequently than its masculine counterpart. *Athenaios* is used for Euxitheos and his father, creating, as I suggested, an association between himself and the *dikastai*. Finally, it seems that allusions are made to the connection between the inheritance of one's part of the family property and being eligible for allotment to office in the use of verbs with the root *kleros*.

There is some support for the view that Demosthenes' case here is representative of Athenian views generally in that Isaeus uses the same kinds of arguments to demonstrate legitimate birth and citizen status of his clients. The last part of a speech by Isaeus from a citizenship trial similar to that of Euxitheos, and dating probably to 344/3, is extant, and it deals with the witnesses to the defendant's parentage and his acceptance by the phratry (12.8).[29] The speaker is the defendant's half-brother. Neither political office nor *hiera* (except those implied in the oaths) are described in this fragment. We cannot know what appeared in the lost parts, but the train of the argument and the terminology are the same as in Dem. 57: citizen status is to be an *Athenaios* (12.2, 7); the father had legitimate sons, so no need to smuggle a non-Athenian into his family, and to the brother it was of no benefit to share the inheritance with yet another (12.3); the father introduced the son to the phratry (12.3); it was not to the benefit of the kinsmen to witness to Euphiletos' status as they did (12.6–8); the mother swore an oath in the Delphinion that Euphiletos was her son (12.9; her status as *aste* was apparently uncontested) and the father swore that his son was born by this *aste* in a marriage by pledge (*engye*; 12.9). Former arbitrators likewise had judged that Euphiletos was the brother and fellow-citizen (*polites*) of the speaker. Defending the citizen status of his half-brother, the speaker dares the opponents to name any other kind of evidence by which one could prove one's status as a citizen (12.6–7). In his trials on legitimacy with the purpose of gaining an inheritance, Isaeus advanced similar arguments, showing the legitimacy of the claimants by depicting the family relationships (*engye*, birth, phratry) and the

[28] For the precise meanings of these words, see Chapter 4.

[29] Is. 12 (*Euphiletos*); for the date, Wyse (1904) 715–16.

hiera they shared.[30] All these cases therefore show that birth from an *astos* and an *aste*, legitimacy and inheritance rights, confirmed by uncontested participation in *hiera*, were at the heart of citizen status and laid down in citizenship law.

1.2 Aristotle's 'Citizen': a Philosophical Definition

Aristotle's definition of a citizen in *Politics*, book III, is the single extant definition in the classical Greek record of 'a citizen' in general terms.[31] To understand why he created this particular definition and what kind of citizenship it relates to, we need to examine it in the overall argument of the *Politics*, a treatise on which Aristotle worked between 335 and 323. A large part of the work comprises an analysis of the *polis* as a social, economic and political community and of the principles in a *politeia* (political system) that may further justice. Classifications of different types of *politeiai* and the mechanisms of political change are an important component of this analysis. A smaller section is devoted to a design of the best possible *polis* and its *politeia*. In what order Aristotle wrote the various parts is a topic of debate, since it is clear that he returned to his arguments time and again. In the standard editions I follow here, the larger part with the analysis of the *politeiai* is labelled books I to VI, the shorter one with the design of the best *politeia* is books VII to VIII. The overall aim of the treatise, however, weaves all parts loosely into a whole.

Aristotle recurrently mentions this aim in the *Politics*, namely to establish which conditions may create the best possible *politeia*, one that may guarantee a good life, a life of happiness, to the citizens of the *polis*:

> the object of our present study is the best *politeia* and that is the one under which the *polis* is most happy, and as we stated before, this happiness cannot prevail without virtue ....[32]

An essential condition of such a *polis* is a *politeia* that conforms to the sense of justice of its citizens. What exactly Aristotle understands a *politeia* to be is not consistent: at one point he describes the *politeia* as the order

30 Is. 9.10–13; Is. 8.15–16; and see Chapter 3.

31 That Aristotle regards his definition as such, and not merely as a practical description, is clear from his explicit reference to it as διορισμός (e.g. 1275b13–14), from the way he introduces it (see below) and from the way he uses it in his analysis of *politeiai*.

32 Arist. *Pol.* 1328b33–9: ἐπεὶ δὲ τυγχάνομεν σκοποῦντες περὶ τῆς ἀρίστης πολιτείας, αὕτη δ' ἐστὶ καθ' ἣν ἡ πόλις ἂν εἴη μάλιστ' εὐδαίμων, τὴν δ' εὐδαιμονίαν ὅτι χωρὶς ἀρετῆς ἀδύνατον ὑπάρχειν εἴρηται πρότερον ...; cf. 1260b27–9; 1288b3–6; 1323a14–22. *EN* 1097b30–1098a20: happiness is a life in accordance with *arete*.

(*taxis*) of those who live together in the *polis*, but elsewhere he states that a *politeia* is the order (*taxis*) of the various *archai* (offices) of a *polis*.[33] We will come back to this issue shortly, but here we note that Aristotle concurs with one of the main tenets of Greek political thought, that in order to attain happiness the relations between the members of a *polis* should be based on justice. Unlike Plato, however, for whom the relationship between humans and the divine was essential to the notion of a just society, Aristotle focuses almost exclusively on human actions and conduct.

Given the aim of the *Politics*, Aristotle needs a definition of citizenship that serves this purpose. Following his rules of logic, a proper definition must fulfil criteria fitting the general system of which it is to be a part. Such a definition must be valid in all circumstances, and in the context of the *Politics* the definition of a citizen must fit the goal of the overall argument, that is to designate the foundations of a just society.

First, one needs to know what a *polis* is. In book I, Aristotle discusses the *polis* as a *koinonia* (community), with the resources necessary for its independent economic existence. The *polis* is both a natural phenomenon – human beings need to live together by nature – and a man-made construction. An essential aspect of the nature of a *koinonia* is leadership (*arche*): someone needs to be in charge if the whole is to survive. By nature, man leads woman and master rules over slave. But among free men the matter cannot be resolved so easily. Nature, moreover, is not enough: without virtue, humans would be the most lawless (*anhosios*) creatures on earth. If a *polis* is to survive, it needs to be just: justice, that is passing judgement (*krisis*) on what is just, is the order (*taxis*) of the *polis*.[34] A *polis*, in other words, is a *koinonia* (of those who have a common goal) in a *politeia*. Book II focuses on sharing (*metechein*) as an essential and typical element of a *polis*. Aristotle outlines in which respects members of a *polis* should share – for instance, they need to share the same *politeia* to be an effective unity – and in which respects they should not; for instance, to share all the women and children and all property between men will not work.[35] A *polis* needs a balance between variety and unity, between equality and inequality.

In book III, Aristotle begins by characterising the citizen as a part of this whole – the *polis* determines what its constituent part, a *polites*, is.[36] Next, he reviews various qualities to see if they apply to all citizens and characterise all citizens, and to do so he looks for elements in which they

[33] *Pol.* 1274b38–9; 1278b9–10.
[34] *Pol.* 1253a36–40.
[35] *Pol.* 1261a–1262b: disagreement with Plato's communism.
[36] *Pol.* 1274b42–1275a2.

actively share (*metechein*). He notes disagreement on what a citizen is; for some, this depends on the *politeia*, because democracies and oligarchies work differently in this respect.[37] Shared domicile also will not do as a criterion, because slaves also share this, but they are not citizens. Just sharing the same legal system (*dike*) will not do either, because foreigners, who by definition are not citizens, also appear in the courts of a *polis*. And there is the problem of those who are citizens but no longer have an active share in the *polis*, for instance when they face *atimia* (enforced inability to participate properly) or are forced into exile.

At this point, Aristotle somewhat unexpectedly launches his own definition. He introduces it with the statement, 'We are looking for "the citizen" without further qualifications (*haplos*)',[38] and next offers this definition here for the first time in a succinct form:

> A citizen without further qualifications (*haplos*) is defined by nothing more than sharing actively (*metechein*) in judicial office (*krisis*) and political office (*arche*).[39]

After examining various types of political office, in which he briefly considers whether a *dikastes* and a member of the assembly are *archai* and decides that this is merely a matter of terminology, he reaffirms his previous statement in the more extensive definition quoted above. Aristotle's definition does not follow logically from the preceding arguments; indeed, it is offered as if out of the blue.[40] How did he get here?

At first, he was looking for characteristics that all citizens share without any further qualifications, and tried to eliminate such criteria that are not relevant to *all* citizens.[41] In the following passage, where he offers his own

[37] *Pol.* 1275a3–5: 'For there is often a difference of opinion about a citizen: people do not all agree that the same person is a citizen; someone who would be a citizen in a democracy is often not a citizen in an oligarchy'; cf. 1278a15–27.

[38] *Pol.* 1275a19: ζητοῦμεν γὰρ τὸν ἁπλῶς πολίτην καὶ μηδὲν ἔχοντα τοιοῦτον ἔγκλημα διορθώσεθς δέομενον ...

[39] *Pol.* 1275a22–4: πολίτης δ' ἁπλῶς οὐδενὶ τῶν ἄλλων ὁρίζεται μᾶλλον ἢ τῶι μετέχειν κρίσεως καὶ ἀρχῆς.

[40] For other conflicting aspects of his reasoning in the *Politics*, see Keyt (1991). Morrison (1999) points out several inconsistencies in Aristotle's definition of the citizen, among others that it cannot work for monarchy and oligarchy as *politeiai* and that the tension between the conception of the *polis* as a political community working towards the common good (the object of the *Politics*) and the wider, social meaning of the *polis* (the common notion in Greek practice, reverberating in Aristotle's text) is never resolved (152). Johnson (1984) follows Aristotle's logic in his definition of a citizen by its elimination of alternatives, but does not seem to notice the break in Aristotle's discourse when introducing his definition. For the relation between Aristotle's definition and political theory more broadly, see Piepenbrink (2001) 15–67.

[41] *Pol.* 1275a19–20.

solution, his reasoning remains implicit, so we cannot be entirely sure. Yet his tacit argument here seems to be that all who hold office (*arche* and *krisis*) are citizens, therefore that holding political office is distinctive of a citizen and therefore that holding office defines a citizen. Strictly speaking, where he states that he who has the right to participate in political and judicial office is a citizen of that *polis* in which he has that right, his observation is correct.[42] But when he next implies that *only* those who participate in office are citizens, his reasoning takes the form of an inverted syllogism. It is not the outcome of his earlier arguments. If he had stuck to his own logic, he would have found that all who are considered citizens *all share their qualification by birth*.[43] Aristotle adds explicitly that this is the case and that his definition differs from what the Greeks normally take a citizen to be:

> But in practice they [the Greek *poleis*] define as a citizen someone from two citizen (*astos*) parents and not just from one side only, that is from the father or from the mother; and some others follow this principle even further, that is to two or even more generations.[44]

In the *Politics* as a whole, Aristotle considers descent from citizen parents a necessary condition, insisting on intermarriage and shared rituals as indispensable ingredients for a coherent, self-sufficient life of the *polis*.[45] As a criterion of citizenship, however, he finds descent insufficient, firstly because the way it is applied differs from *polis* to *polis*:

> But in many constitutions the law draws (its citizens) even from foreigners (*xenoi*); for in some democracies he who is born from a female citizen (*politis*) is a citizen (*polites*), and the same rule is valid in many places also with regard to bastards (*nothoi*). Nevertheless, since they make such people into

[42] *Pol.* 1275b18–22.

[43] According to Schütrumpf (1991) 396–7, Aristotle does not deny the validity of descent as a criterion of citizenship, but regards it as a necessary but not a sufficient criterion. This view seems to me only partly correct. To make room for his own approach, Aristotle seems intent to prove that not all citizens are so by birth, when he points out that some people are *made* citizens by decree and others have become citizens when a colony was founded (1275b25–33). His argument is unconvincing in light of the fact, surely known to him, that usually the founders of Greek colonies were citizens by descent of the mother city and that laws and rituals made both them and newcomers citizens *as if* by birth of the new *polis*. Citizens-by-decree were likewise *as if* by birth and their children were so in fact (see Chapter 6.1). Similar objections could be raised against Aristotle's own definition and apparently came to his mind, where he observes that some people were *made* citizens by holding an *arche* due to a revolution changing the *politeia*. He contends, however, that in such cases it only matters whether these new citizens got citizenship wrongly or rightly (1275b34–1276a3). These inconsistencies suggest that he does not argue systematically here, but towards a preconceived definition fitting his wider argument.

[44] *Pol.* 1275b22–4, Ὁρίζονται δὲ πρὸς τὴν χρῆσιν πολίτην τὸν ἐξ ἀμφοτέρων πολιτῶν καὶ μὴ θατέρου μόνον, οἷον πατρὸς ἢ μητρός, οἱ δὲ καὶ τοῦτ᾽ ἐπὶ πλέον ζητοῦσιν, οἷον ἐπὶ πάππους δύο ἢ τρεῖς ἢ πλείους.

[45] *Pol.* 1280b15–1281a9.

> citizens because of a lack of citizens of legitimate birth (*gnesios*) – because they make use of such laws due to under-population – as soon as they are doing well in the mass of their population, then they gradually rid themselves first of those born of a male or female slave, and next of those from women [only]; in the end, they only make those citizens (who are) born from both citizen (*astos*) parents.[46]

Secondly, and this is surely the decisive reason, descent is inadequate as a criterion to understand what sharing means at the level of the *politeia*, that is to say for the construction of the just *polis* and its *arche* that are the objects of his treatise.

In this argument, Aristotle first shifts the focus from the *polis* (the community) to the *politeia* (the organisation of the community) as the significant framework of citizenship: he moves from a *polis* as a collection of citizens (*politai*), to the *politeia* as the order of those who live together in the *polis*, and next describes a *polis* as a kind of *koinonia*, in fact a *koinonia* in a *politeia*. Next, he slides from a *politeia* being the order (*taxis*) of those who live together in the *polis* to a more specific and restricted meaning of the *politeia* as the order in a *polis* of its various *archai* and especially of the *arche kyria* (supreme *arche*).[47] Defining sharing in the *politeia* thus as sharing in *arche* (and *krisis*), he then inverts this argument, stating that those who share in *arche* under a particular *politeia* are citizens.[48]

The move away from sharing in the *polis* on the qualification of birth from citizen parents towards his own conception of the citizen marks the deliberate distinction between his theoretical system and the practices Aristotle observed in Greece.[49] Selecting sharing in political office as the defining element of being a *polites*, and declaring holding such office the

[46] *Pol.* 1278a26–34. ἐν πολλαῖς δὲ πολιτείαις προσεφέλκει τινὰς καὶ τῶν ξένων ὁ νόμος· ὁ γὰρ ἐκ πολίτιδος ἔν τισι δημοκρατίαις πολίτης ἐστίν, τὸν αὐτὸν δὲ τρόπον ἔχει καὶ τὰ περὶ τοὺς νόθους παρὰ πολλοῖς. οὐ μὴν ἀλλ᾽ ἐπεὶ δι᾽ ἔνδειαν τῶν γνησίων πολιτῶν ποιοῦνται πολίτας τοὺς τοιούτους (διὰ γὰρ ὀλιγανθρωπίαν οὕτω χρῶνται τοῖς νόμοις), εὐποροῦντες δὴ ὄχλου κατὰ μικρὸν παραιροῦνται τοὺς ἐκ δούλου πρῶτον ἢ δούλης, εἶτα τοὺς ἀπὸ γυναικῶν, τέλος δὲ μόνον τοὺς ἐξ ἀμφοῖν ἀστῶν πολίτας ποιοῦσιν. However, he does not consider the fact that on his own definition in different *politeiai* citizens will be different (1275b4–8) an objection to his own logic (see also note 43).

[47] *Pol.* 1274b42–75a: a *polis* is a collection of citizens (*politai*); 1274b38–9: the *politeia* is the order of those who live together in the *polis*; 1276b1–5: a *polis* is a kind of *koinonia*, and in fact a *koinonia* in a *politeia*; 1278b9–10: a *politeia* is an ordering (*taxis*) of a *polis* of its various *archai* and especially of the *arche kyria* of all (supreme *arche*).

[48] *Pol.* 1277b33–1278a25.

[49] Davies (2004) draws a similar conclusion (21): 'the development of the state and of the idea of citizenship set out by Aristotle, though still influential among historians of political theory, tells us a great deal about Aristotle and about the activity of reflection about political practice which culminates in his work, but virtually nothing about the actual historical processes which engendered the Greek concept of citizenship'. Davies seems here to take up a position different from his article (1977).

typical virtue (*arete*) of a citizen, Aristotle bypasses (legitimate) descent from citizen parents as the primary criterion of citizen status. He takes it for granted as a fundamental qualification, but assigns it no role on the most significant level of analysis. If this choice is understandable given his focus on citizens' actions, it is striking that he excludes holding *religious* office from his analysis of citizens' participation. In the *Politics* overall, the relationship of the *polis* with its gods seems to play a minor role. Aristotle's conceptions pose a stark contrast to Euxitheos' account of himself as a citizen: holding religious office and sharing in *hiera* with his relatives, his *phrateres* and his demesmen were essential for demonstrating his citizen status, due to his legitimate birth from two Athenian parents.

Why did Aristotle leave those components largely outside his conception of citizenship, which an Athenian like Euxitheos regarded as vital? As a citizen of Stagira in Chalcidice, Aristotle had been living in Athens for a long time. He was well acquainted with this *polis* and its political system, as is unmistakable from the *Politics*. But for the purposes of his philosophical treatise, he disengaged his arguments and his vocabulary from the common practices and values around him. His reasons for doing so are sometimes stated explicitly, and sometimes must be deduced from allusions to the basic assumptions of his work.

In his philosophy in general, Aristotle directs his analysis to those parts of life that lend themselves to observation, notably of the mechanisms shaping natural and human life. His emphasis on such observations and his sharp, if selective, eye for real phenomena have earned him the reputation of an empiricist philosopher, notably in contrast to Plato's idealism. But this label can easily be misunderstood. It certainly does not mean that his work takes empirical reality simply as a point of departure. Instead, according to the current scholarly consensus, Aristotle's philosophy presents a perception, interpretation and evaluation of reality within his own philosophical framework.[50] His analysis is intrinsically embedded in his

[50] For this method and reasoning in Aristotle's scientific work generally, see Solmsen (1970; orig. 1960), who shows clearly how Aristotle makes use of concepts current at the time, expanding and refining them to accommodate observed phenomena, and introducing new concepts; but also how he marshals the phenomena to fit his ever more intricate network of concepts. Useful concepts, for Aristotle, need to be generally applicable and as few in number as possible. Solmsen demonstrates this particularly clearly for Aristotle's meteorology (393–439). Cf. Cohen (2010) 4–10: 'the fundamental principles he [Aristotle] derived from comparative analysis (notably, change conceived as the actualization of what is potentially there) lead one to assign to sense data their fitting place inside an overall scheme of things.' Likewise, in his political theory, including the notion *politeia*, Aristotle used and adjusted the concepts of his predecessors: Bordes (1980), Bordes (1982) 435–54. For the same effects in the *Poetics*, see below.

logic, his metaphysics and his system of classification. Since phenomena are to be classified according to generally valid parameters, things that are essentially different need to be excluded from a particular domain of inquiry. In other words, Aristotle's works do not entail an empirical approach to reality, in order to describe and interpret it in a particular way, but offer something substantially different: a theoretical construction pertaining to observable phenomena, which are selected by and adjusted to the criteria and aims of Aristotelian philosophy.[51]

In the domain of social life, this epistemology restricts the topics of inquiry and the analysis of cause and effect to the field of *human* agency. The gods are altogether superior to humans, and although we can perceive what the gods do, we cannot investigate why and how they do it. These epistemological principles have a specific bearing on the analysis of human society: the gods may be drawn into the analysis, for instance by way of contrast, but they cannot play a structural role in an inquiry into human society.[52] Aristotle defines the *polis* as a community, the members of which need each other to exist; this basic need is generally the major factor explaining social relations.[53] The gods, however, do not need humans to exist and therefore are not part of the *polis*.[54] In the domain of politics, Aristotle is particularly concerned with the causes of institutional change. Change can only be due to human agency; the gods, being eternal, have no part in change. More specifically, Aristotle argues that a *polis*, if it is to satisfy the norms of virtue and justice, requires taking turns in ruling and

[51] A comparable case to Aristotle's definition of *polites* is that of *doulos* (slave), as Vlassopoulos (2011) shows: modern scholarship has followed Aristotle (*Pol.* 1253b33) in his conception of slavery as a form of property, a 'minority position' (116) that Vlassopoulos explains from the 'polemical aims' of the *Politics* where he construes a conception of slavery in distinction to Plato and other Greek thinkers (121), which 'necessitated a redefinition of *doulos* as a form of property', whereas the contemporary usage of *doulos* and cognates shows more varied meanings all referring to domination.

[52] This point of view, which he usually touches upon only briefly, underlies Aristotle's major works on human society, *Nicomachean Ethics* (*EN*) and *Politics*. *EN*: 1099b11–14: if happiness is a gift from the gods, it belongs to a different type of inquiry (ἀλλὰ τοῦτο μὲν ἴσως ἄλλης ἂν εἴη σκέψεως οἰκειότερον) – Aristotle continues with the human capacity to create happiness; 1101b18–27: the gods are beyond the measure of humans, praising them is an undue comparison; 1145a25–7: the parameters of human conduct make no sense for gods; 1158b29–1159a7: friendship is based on a certain type of equality; gods are too unequal to be friends; 1177a12–1177b31: what is divine is essentially superior, and the mind is the superior = divine aspect of man.

[53] *Philia*, human bonding underlying the *polis*, based on utility: Arist. *EE* 1242a1–1243a34; as a source of coherence of the *polis*, *Pol.*1262b8–25.

[54] *Pol.*1253a25–29: 'It is clear then that the *polis* is also by nature prior to the individual; for if an individual, when separated, is not fully self-sufficient, he will have the same relationship to the whole as the other parts do. But someone who is incapable of being part of a community (for example an animal) or who does not need to do so because he is entirely self-sufficient (for example a god) is no part of a *polis*.'

being ruled among those considered fit to do so. The gods, however, never take turns within the *polis* – in the world beyond the confines of human existence, their reign is eternal.[55] In sum, since divine actions are beyond the realm of philosophical knowledge and the gods do not share in human society on congruent terms, they are not to be included in an inquiry into human society (*Politics*).

Similar principles guide Aristotle's views in the *Poetics*: in his analysis of Athenian tragedy, neither the role of the gods within the plays nor the Dionysian context of drama itself is taken into consideration.[56] In this case, too, Aristotle's exclusion of divine involvement does not mean that the role of the gods was not vital to the Greeks in real life. Neither does it mean that Aristotle supposes humans can live without the gods. His outline of an ideal *polis* in *Politics*, books VII and VIII, begins with a comparison of human and divine happiness: humans are essentially different from the gods, who need no external things and actions but only their own nature to be happy and good.[57] Humans, however, do need external things and acts. In order to exist, the *polis* needs food, crafts, arms, money and 'fifth but first of all, the care of the divine, what is called a priesthood' and an institution deciding *dike* among the people.[58] In his ideal *polis*, one half of the soil is to be used in common, half of which again is to serve the gods.[59] Human society thus needs its exchange with the divine, but in his philosophical works, Aristotle takes the existence of the gods and their significance to human society for granted; they are not liable to inquiry, they only expect proper worship.

In sum, for these reasons, Aristotle leaves the gods almost entirely out of his analysis of human society and in so doing deviates implicitly from Greek practice. His definition of a citizen explicitly and deliberately moves away from the historical reality of Greek *poleis*. He finds the common Greek practices wanting as a satisfactory basis for a definition that meets his criteria. After eliminating alternatives, he proposes his famous definition of a citizen as someone who participates in political and judicial

55 Priesthoods therefore are different from *archai*, although both are offices instituted by the *polis*; *Pol.* 1299a17–19; 1322b18–30. See Chapter 5.1 for both types of office as *timai* of the *polis*.

56 I owe this observation to Glenn W. Most.

57 *Pol.* 1323b21; 1325b23.

58 *Pol.* 1328b12–15: πέμπτον δὲ καὶ πρῶτον τὴν περὶ τὸ θεῖον ἐπιμέλειαν, ἣν καλοῦσιν ἱερατείαν. Priesthood assigned to the citizen class, not to farmers or artisans, in advanced age of wisdom: 1329a28–34.

59 *Pol.* 1330a13–14.

office (*arche* and *krisis*). It works best in a democracy, he notes; in other *politeiai*, the body of *politai* will be different.[60]

1.3 Contrasting Views

Aristotle's definition of a citizen and Euxitheos' self-description by Demosthenes coincide in some important respects: both characterise citizenship as sharing, as participating in a common enterprise (*metechein*). Aristotle derives his conception from his analysis of the *polis* as a *koinonia* and of citizens as members of this composite body, rather than as individuals assembled into a group. Demosthenes presumably drew in the first place on the vocabulary of the Athenian citizenship laws and the discourse of fourth-century Athens. Concerning *metechein*, his concept of citizenship is not at odds with Aristotle's. Conversely, where Aristotle writes about descent as the fundamental qualification in the *poleis* that he knows of, he uses the words *astos*, *polites* and *politis* in much the same way as Euxitheos does. But here the similarities end.

In his definition of a *polites* as someone who shares (*metechein*) in political and judicial office, Aristotle assigns to the word a meaning of his own that fits his argument in the *Politics*. The purposeful distinction he makes between his own vocabulary and that of the Greeks in general is connected to the shift at this point of his argument from the *polis* to the *politeia* as the decisive framework of citizenship. Since he further restricts the *politeia* here to the most important *archai*, his definition of citizenship is in effect limited to men. In Euxitheos' account, by contrast, *metechein* is realised in the first place in religion: sharing in the ancestral cults of the *polis* more than anything shows him acting as a citizen. Furthermore, the symmetrical terminology in his discourse indicated that both men and women were considered citizens. This classification of citizens in terms of gender as stated by Euxitheos and Aristotle respectively thus reflects their distinct conceptions of citizenship.

If we look more closely, a better explanation may be arrived at for the differences between the ontology of Athenian citizenship in Euxitheos'

[60] *Pol.* 1275a33–1275b17. *Pol.* 1293a1–11: in a democracy all persons of citizen birth can participate because the *polis* is wealthy enough to enable the poor to do so; in this case not the laws rule, but the mass of the poor. 1298a29–33: in some democracies deliberation is up to the assembled citizens, while the magistrates only prepare the agenda; this is a system that resembles a tyranny of the masses. Aristotle refers in both cases to 'democracies that have developed to their ultimate form' and that exist in his lifetime. Athens had much in common with both models, but its *politeia* also fell into categories of democracy where deliberation is mainly done in a smaller body of the citizens, while all citizens have access to these offices by rotation (1298a10–29).

appeal and Aristotle's logic. Euxitheos' appeal shows that, in the classical age, a citizen was conceptualised as *being* part of a social entity: an inhabitant of A, a member of group B, or a child of C and D. Birth from citizen parents was the normal way in which this 'being a citizen' came about; in this respect, citizenship as presented in Euxitheos' speech had a physical dimension. Furthermore, citizenship was an existence that depended on social recognition and was valued in its social context – a condition often defined as 'status'. Rules on all these elements – criteria by which one belonged to the group, ways in which social recognition should come about – were laid down in law or maintained by convention. In no way was citizenship abstracted from the person; quite the reverse, abstract and concrete elements were all essentially connected in the ways in which a citizen put his or her status into action and in which s/he was valued. Fine-tuning such a system took the form of specifying the conditions and procedural rules regulating access to the relevant groups and forms of participation. Aristotle, by contrast, aimed at a definition of a phenomenon in general terms, based on the qualities observed in particular cases and eliminating elements that would not cover all examples. His method in logic conceived of things as *having the quality* X or Y, by recognising a particular quality as a common element in various cases and thus abstracting this quality from each case. In this system, fine-tuning entailed a more precise definition of quality X, discarding aspects of X not relevant for all cases, asking why a particular thing would or would not have X and what the consequences of having X would be. This logic implies an essentially different view of the connection between a thing and its qualities than the ontological identity between a person and the status of citizenship as expressed in Demosthenes' text for Euxitheos.

In practical terms, Aristotle's criticism of the Greek conception of citizenship was not entirely unjustified. That descent was an inadequate criterion of citizenship for the construction of a just and stable *polis* could be inferred from the centuries of recurrent strife between groups favouring either wider or more limited access to political office.[61] The word *polites* indicates that the person it refers to is a member of the *polis*, but it does not indicate at all whether he or she is eligible for *polis* office or not.[62] Throughout Greek history, many free men were citizens of their *polis* but not entitled to political office. This is obvious in all aristocracies, oligarchies or tyrannies, but it is most poignantly illustrated in classical Athens

[61] Piepenbrink (2001) 41.
[62] See Chapter 4.

during the oligarchic revolutions. Under the oligarchy of 411, all citizens of Athens were citizens (a), but only 5,000 could be politically active citizens (b), and 400 among these were to fulfil the legislative and executive duties (c). The distinction between the groups depended, as usual, on procedural rules, namely quality of descent for (a), a property and experience test for (b) and internal election to get into (c). All people belonging to (a), (b) and (c) were still *Athenaioi* and *politai*, citizens born from citizen parents and with a claim to sharing in the rites of *oikos* and *polis*, even if only (b) or (c) were involved in political office and all others not.[63] Indeed, as Aristotle observed, common usage of Greek citizenship vocabulary provided no immediately perceptible difference between citizens with and without active political participation.[64]

Such a difference, however, was precisely what Aristotle needed for his definition. Among the words used for a citizen, *polites* and *astos* describe the social fact that someone is a member of a *polis*, and meeting certain criteria, notably of descent.[65] As such, these words indicate a quality that may be used in the Aristotelian manner, to be generalised from particular cases – person A is a *polites* of Corinth, person B is a *polites* of Argos, and this would allow us to define what a *polites* is. Although *polites* was a common Greek word, citizens usually conceived themselves as belonging by birth to a *particular polis*, physically and socially: Euxitheos and the *dikastai* called themselves *Athenaioi* rather than *politai* of Athens. The ethnic indicates citizenship as a specific condition that cannot be abstracted into a generalised quality with relevance in other cases, for instance a quality of Athenian-ness, that may also be recognised in a Corinthian. On the contrary, a Corinthian can only share in 'being an Athenian' when the *demos* has made him an Athenian *as if* by birth. The ethnic thus covers the notion of citizen status in classical Greece most pertinently. For Aristotle's purposes, however, this would not do; he needed terms which captured the phenomenon in its general (here: *polites*), not specific aspects (here: *Athenaios*, *Korinthios* et al.), and which isolated what he considered the essential quality (here: not descent as qualification or sharing in

63 Historical accounts looking back at this episode use the normal words for Athenian citizens: *Ath. Pol.* 29.4: *Athenaioi* – all Athenians; 29.5 the 5,000 *Athenaioi* with certain qualities (in 411); 35.2: the Thirty at first act moderately towards the *politai* = the citizens without political office (in 404). Sharing in rites: Xen. *Hell.* 2.4.20–2. The analysis of citizenship vocabulary (Chapter 4) gives no indication that we should expect them to have been called anything else but *Athenaioi* or *politai*.

64 Cf. Arist. *Pol.* 1278a15–25, where he refers to those 'other' citizens as the citizens who are only ruled and do not belong to the group who rules.

65 See Chapters 3 and 4.

religion but political participation). Thus, he created terms deliberately distinct from the usual vocabulary. *This is precisely what he says he is doing in his definition.*[66] In connection with political office, the underlying criterion of descent is no longer discussed. As mentioned before, one must assume that Aristotle took this for granted, for it was inconceivable that a non-*polites* would have access to political office in a Greek *polis*.

In this argument, Aristotle moved the concept of citizenship to a level of abstraction only partially related to what his contemporaries took the notion to be. Again a comparison with the *Poetics* is instructive, where his descriptions of tragedy and historiography, serving certain philosophical purposes, are raised to such a level of abstraction that neither Euripides nor Thucydides are qualified to be representative of their genres.[67] Indeed, the level of abstraction of Aristotle's definition is such that we may wonder whether it was applicable to real, historical *poleis* at all. If we suppose that as a 'general conception of citizenship in a *polis*' it *ought* to work for most *poleis*, at least where access to *archai* was concerned, even a quick glance shows clearly that it often did not.[68] In the multi-layered *politeia* of Sparta, for instance, many Spartiatai never made it to the ephorate, the main *archai*. [69] In Thebes, which in the course of the fifth and fourth centuries changed from an oligarchy to a system with less restricted political access and then back again, many *politai* were not admitted to leading offices but were still considered *politai*. Even in Athens, where a wide section of the male citizen population was involved in political office, Aristotle's definition did not cover the real-life situations. But the *Politics* does not claim to describe any particular existing *polis*, it tries to establish what the best possible *polis* should be like.

1.4 The *Athenaion Politeia*

The third text with a detailed account of Athenian citizenship is the *Athenaion Politeia*, the only extant representative of the 158 *politeiai*

[66] Note the μὲν – δὲ construction in *Pol.* 1275b17–24, marking the contrast between Aristotle's own conception and the practices of the Greeks.

[67] De Ste. Croix (1992), expounding the relation between Aristotle's genre descriptions and his focus on *general* patterns. Funke (1998) 70–1, pointing to Aristotle's failure to notice new developments in political structures, also compares the *Politics* with the *Poetics*.

[68] Aristotle's own *caveat* that his definition worked best in a democracy (1275b5) is not maintained in the arguments throughout the *Politics*; Rhodes (2009a) 61–3 notices that there is a problem here; see also below.

[69] In the fourth century, however, according to Rhodes (1981), over 50 per cent of the male Spartiates served as ephors due to the decreased number of full citizens.

drafted in the Aristotelian school to serve as material for the *Politics*.[70] Clearly Aristotle did not write all of the *politeiai*. Although some scholars have thought that because of the importance of Athens Aristotle might have written this particular one himself, on stylistic grounds most scholars nowadays think the author was not Aristotle; yet the close connection with the *Politics* is clear at various points.[71] Differences in detail in the historical accounts of Athens indicate that parts of *Politics* were written before the *Ath.Pol.*[72]

It is useful here to consider briefly how Aristotle meant the various *Politeiai* such as the *Ath.Pol.* to be composed and read. The *Politics*, as mentioned before, follow on from the *Ethics*, where Aristotle discusses how human happiness depends on virtue and how in most people virtue depends on the laws of the *polis*.[73] For the well-being of the *polis*, much depends therefore on those who make the laws. Like doctors, they need to know what the art of lawmaking is in order to keep people healthy and cure diseases. Effective laws emanate from wisdom and intelligence.[74] Intelligent individuals can certainly study existing laws with profit, but wisdom needs a type of knowledge of legislation bound by clear conditions:

> doubtless it would be agreed that it would be best for a man who wants to be a professional and a man of science (*theoretikos*) to advance to general principles, and acquaint himself with these by the proper method; because that, as we said, is what real science (*episteme*) is about.[75]

What the science of politics needs, therefore, is not just a collection of laws, but the right method of studying these laws. Previous philosophers have left the topic of legislation (*nomothesia*) largely uninvestigated, according to Aristotle, so it is better if he and his students occupy themselves in their own manner

> with the whole question of the *politeia*, to make our philosophy of human affairs complete as far as possible. First, we shall try to go through everything of value by our predecessors on this or that part, and next investigate

[70] Arist. *EN* 1180b20–1181b24, esp. 1181b15–24, and see below.

[71] For the debate on the authorship of the *Ath.Pol.*, Rhodes, *CAAP*, 61–3. The last date mentioned in *Politics* is the murder of Philip of Macedon in 336 (1311b1–3); for the date of the *Ath.Pol.* in the 330s and its revision in the 320s, Rhodes, *CAAP*, 51–8.

[72] Rhodes, *CAAP*, 58–61.

[73] *EN* 1179a33–1180a6.

[74] *EN* 1180a22–3: ὁ δὲ νόμος ἀναγκαστικὴν ἔχει δύναμιν, λόγος ὢν ἀπό τινος φρονήσεως καὶ νοῦ.

[75] *EN* 1180b20–3: οὐδὲν δ' ἧττον ἴσως τῷ γε βουλομένῳ τεχνικῷ γενέσθαι καὶ θεωρητικῷ ἐπὶ τὸ καθόλου βαδιστέον εἶναι δόξειεν ἄν, κἀκεῖνο γνωριστέον ὡς ἐνδέχεται· εἴρηται γὰρ ὅτι περὶ τοῦθ' αἱ ἐπιστῆμαι. Transl. H. Rackham (Loeb ed.) slightly modified. Cf. 1181a24–1181b2.

> scientifically (*theoresai*) on the basis of our collection of *politeiai* what sort of things preserve or destruct *poleis* and what sort of things (do so in) each of the *politeiai* in particular, and what the causes are that some *poleis* are well organised and others the reverse. For once we have investigated (*theoresai*) these issues, we are perhaps in a better position both to establish which *politeia* is the best and how each type of *politeia* is constituted by its own laws and customs.[76]

In these passages, Aristotle states clearly that the collection of *politeiai* is meant to instruct his students in the science of politics following his own philosophical methods (*theoresai*): the *politeiai* are compiled to serve as evidence enabling an investigation of how to attain the best *politeia* and to exemplify the general principles of legislation and the habits on which such a *politeia* should rest. He resumes this argument in the *Politics*, book IV: the duty of those who devote themselves to the science (*episteme*) of the *politeia* must study the general principles of the best *politeia* that may be valid in all *poleis* and to that end they must study all varieties of *politeiai*.[77]

The text of the *Ath.Pol.* is divided into two parts. The first part, now consisting of some fragments preserved in the writings of other authors and the extant chapters 1–41 of the surviving papyrus of the *Ath.Pol.* itself, offers an historical account of Athens from its (mythical) origins to the constitution of 403/2, including some minor revisions that remained in force until the author's day.[78] The second part, chapters 42–66, contains a systematic but not exhaustive description of the Athenian *politeia* of the 330s and 320s.

The historical account traces the development of the Athenian *politeia* from the ancient kings (fr. 1, 2, 7), through an oligarchy (2.2, 5.1) to Solon's system based on four property classes balanced by the people's influence on jurisdiction by the right to appeal to a people's court, and then to the first steps towards democracy (9); it continues with the time of the tyrants (13–19), the constitution of Cleisthenes (20–22.1) which laid the foundation of the

76 *EN* 1181b14–23: καὶ ὅλως δὴ περὶ πολιτείας, ὅπως εἰς δύναμιν ἡ περὶ τὰ ἀνθρώπεια φιλοσοφία τελειωθῇ. πρῶτον μὲν οὖν εἴ τι κατὰ μέρος εἴρηται καλῶς ὑπὸ τῶν προγενεστέρων πειραθῶμεν ἐπελθεῖν, εἶτα ἐκ τῶν συνηγμένων πολιτειῶν θεωρῆσαι τὰ ποῖα σῴζει καὶ φθείρει τὰς πόλεις καὶ τὰ ποῖα ἑκάστας τῶν πολιτειῶν, καὶ διὰ τίνας αἰτίας αἳ μὲν καλῶς αἳ δὲ τοὐναντίον πολιτεύονται. θεωρηθέντων γὰρ τούτων τάχ᾽ ἂν μᾶλλον συνίδοιμεν καὶ ποία πολιτεία ἀρίστη, καὶ πῶς ἑκάστη ταχθεῖσα, καὶ τίσι νόμοις καὶ ἔθεσι χρωμένη.

77 *Pol.* 1288b10–1289a12.

78 The fragments are numbered differently in various editions; I follow here the Loeb edition (ed. and transl. H. Rackham), which is based on F. Kenyon's *OCT* but arranges the fragments in a narrative order before *Ath.Pol.* 1.

democracy, the ensuing extension of the democracy in the following decades and notably under Ephialtes and Pericles (22.2–28), the oligarchy of 411 and its planned *politeia* (29–33), the subsequent restoration of the democracy (34.1–2), the oligarchy of the Thirty Tyrants and its fall (34–8) and finally the reconciliation and new democratic *politeia* of 403/2 (39–41). Chapter 41 rounds off the historical survey with a retrospective assessment, marking eleven steps in the development of the Athenian *politeia* towards the fourth-century democracy.

True to its title, the *Ath.Pol.* does not claim to be a history of the Athenian *polis*, but of its *politeia*, its system of office holding in the domain of the *polis*, especially the offices with *arche*, authority over others, including other citizens. The *politeia* is characterised by the rules of access to the main *archai*, notably the archonships, the access of the common people to legal protection and jurisdiction and by the influence of the common people in the main political bodies, notably the *boule* and *dikasteria*, but eventually also the assembly, among other things through the institution of payment for holding office (27.4; 41.3). The author makes the focus on the *politeia* explicit at every stage, for instance in his description of the 'old *politeia*' before Draco (3.1), where he argues that the original royal prerogatives were invested in the archons known as the Basileus and the Polemarchos, and that the Archon (*sc.* Eponymous) was the last to be instituted, proof of which is that he does not perform ancestral rites (*patria*) like the other two. In this era, '*politeia* had been given to those who could provide themselves with armour' (4.2), and the common people were subordinated in this *politeia* (5.1). Solon made a new *politeia* and other laws (7.1), and his *politeia* had 'three democratic features' (9.1).

The second part likewise does not claim to give a full account of Athenian citizenship, but only of its *politeia*. It opens as follows:

> The present structure of the *politeia* is the following. Those who are born from two citizen parents (*astoi*) share (*metechein*) in the *politeia*, and they are registered among the demesmen when they are eighteen years old.[79]

Next, all the major and many of the more modest administrative offices are listed, with the ways in which selection for them took place at the time of *Ath.Pol.*: by election or by lot or a combination of both (*klerosis ek prokriton*) and the way in which this manner of selection had changed

[79] *Ath.Pol.* 42.1: Ἔχει δ᾽ ἡ νῦν κατάστασις τῆς πολιτείας τόνδε τὸν τρόπον. μετέχουσιν μὲν τῆς πολιτείας οἱ ἐξ ἀμφοτέρων γεγονότες ἀστῶν, ἐγγράφονται δ᾽ εἰς τοὺς δημότας ὀκτωκαίδεκα ἔτη γεγονότες.

over time. All offices discussed are those at *polis* level, occasionally prepared by pre-selection in the demes; the offices at deme level and those in other subgroups (phratries, *gene*) are not included. Neither does eligibility for the *polis* priesthoods appear in the historical or systematic account of the *polis*. But religious officials and duties feature quite prominently in the systematic part. Especially, chapters 56–8 discuss fairly extensively the selection procedure of the three most venerable and prestigious *archai* of Athens, the archonships of the Basileus, the Archon Eponymous and the Polemarchos, and their main duties. The latter are almost entirely in the sphere of religion: offering sacrifice, leading processions, overseeing religious festivals. Each of the three archons, furthermore, had particular responsibilities in the sphere of jurisdiction.[80]

The *Ath.Pol.* focuses clearly on participation in the *polis* offices, whereas the qualifications for membership of the *polis* and changes in the composition of the citizen body are addressed quite summarily: the original four Ionian tribes (fr. 1, 5), the policy of Solon to restore enslaved Athenians to citizen status (6), Cleisthenes' inclusion of newly made citizens into his new ten-tribe system (21.4) and Pericles' Citizenship Law of 451/0 that made *metechein tes poleos* dependent on two Athenian parents (26.3). The temporary abandonment of this law and its reinstitution in 403/2, which featured in Euxitheos' defence, are not mentioned. The expression *metechein tes poleos* occurs only twice: in the passage on Pericles' Law just mentioned, and in a passage (2.3) on a law ascribed to Solon, which threatened those who would not take up their arms in a civil strife with being *atimos* and ceasing to *metechein tes poleos*.[81] A comparable condition pertained before Solon, when the *politeia* was such that the common people 'so to speak were in a situation that they did not have a share (*metechein*) in anything' (2.3).[82] *Metechein tes poleos* apparently indicates the possibility or capacity to take an active part in the *polis* in whatever way.

The *hiera* of the *polis* in which Euxitheos was so keen to demonstrate his participation to convince the *dikastai* of his citizen status appear in several ways. Oaths are taken on the *hiera* (1.1, 29.5), here meaning sacrificial victims. *Hiera* are also the sanctuaries of the *polis*, which are visited by the ephebes in the year of their training (42.3) and in some of

80 For the selection and duties of the archons, see Chapter 5.4.

81 For an explanation of this puzzling law as in fact requiring citizens *not* to take sides in civil strife and a possible dating of (a redaction of) the law to the early fourth century, Van 't Wout (2010a). For *atimos*, see below, Chapter 5.6.

82 *Ath.Pol.* 2.3: οὐδενὸς γὰρ ὡς εἰπεῖν ἐτύγχανον μετέχοντες.

which money and archives of the *polis* are kept (44.1); special officials are appointed by lot to see to their upkeep and repair (50.1–2). The sanctuary (*hieron*) of Eleusis played a crucial role in the reconciliation of 403 (39). In the *hieros* place of the Areopagus court cases are held on homicide when presided over by the Basileus (57.4), but until that moment a man accused of homicide has to stay away from the *hiera* (public sacred places and cults). The *hiera* are also the private household cults, crucial in the *dokimasia* of the archons (55.3). *Hiera* (sacrifices and festivals) of all sorts are the responsibility of many *polis* office holders, among whom the archons (56, 57, 58) play the most prominent roles, but also others who have to perform *polis* sacrifices and oversee festivals (54.6–7). *Hiera* – all things of the gods: sacrifices, festivals, temples, divine property – not surprisingly are listed as a special item on the agenda of *boule* and assembly (30.5; 43.6).

As a historical and systematic account, the *Ath.Pol.* is inevitably selective, as it would be impossible to provide a complete overview of Athens's history and its laws. What matters here is the nature of this selection. After a short account of the origins of the *polis*, the focus shifts firmly to the *politeia*. Membership by descent is discussed perfunctorily and participation is conceived almost exclusively in terms of *archai* and jurisdiction. It is particularly striking that in the extensive list of *polis* offices those related to cults are far under-represented.[83] In these respects, the selection the *Ath.Pol.* made of the historical events and of the contemporary *politeia* of Athens matches the programme of *Politics*; it is not an independent source confirming the historical validity of Aristotle's philosophical project in *Politics*, but serves this project and was conceived on the same theoretical principles.

However, *Ath.Pol.* also offers details on aspects of the *polis* that entered into the framework of the *Politics* only summarily or not at all. Although their significance for the *polis* is taken for granted in the *Ath.Pol.*, just as in the major part of the *Politics*, the *hiera* come to the surface of the text when they play a role in historical events concerning the *politeia*, as a topic on the agenda of the main political bodies, and most extensively in connection with offices responsible for them. Compared, however, with the wealth of other sources on the *hiera* of Athens, their presence in *Ath. Pol.* is not very abundant. In other words, behind *Ath.Pol.*'s account of the Athenian *politeia* is a world of ideas and practices of which occasionally we get a glimpse. One such glimpse is *Ath.Pol.*'s account of the three

[83] Hansen (1980); see below, Chapter 5.

archons. The primarily religious nature of these offices and the special kinds of jurisdiction they were responsible for do not play any notable part in *Politics*: we do not get the impression that Aristotle would regard these elements as incompatible with his analysis, but neither does he take them into account in any significant way. The Athenian archonships had little in common with the deliberative office and regular jurisdiction that Aristotle presents as the typical features of citizenship.

1.5 Ancient Greek Citizenship in Modern Scholarship

We may infer from the above that, for an understanding of the *historical practices* of Athenian citizenship, Demosthenes' plea for Euxitheos as a true Athenian citizen appears a more adequate guide than Aristotle's conceptions in *Politics*. Legitimate descent with concomitant inheritance rights, confirmed by participation in *hiera*, was the core of citizenship, as laid down in the laws of Athens. Participation in political office, important though it certainly was in the lives of male Athenians, did not feature in either the laws or the legal contests over citizenship, even of male Athenians, as a primary sign of citizenship. Aristotle's project is quite far removed from these laws and practices, and deliberately so.

Nonetheless, modern historiography has followed Aristotle rather than Euxitheos in its studies of the *polis* Athens, and has generally adopted Aristotle's definition as an adequate representation of historical Greek citizenship. On reflection, this is a remarkable state of affairs, considering the specific nature of Aristotle's definition. It is not inconceivable that due to the similarities between the *Ath.Pol.* and *Politics* scholars have taken the first to be a more complete account and the second to be more historical-descriptive than these texts themselves claim to be. At all events, the impact of *Politics* is notable on historical studies of citizenship at Athens that in other respects follow quite different approaches. They show the same switch of perspective exemplified above in Davies's article. Whereas Athenian law begins with legitimate descent of male and female citizens and leads, on this condition, to participation (*metechein*) in the *polis*, phrased in a general way without specifying a domain of life for this participation, the leading historical scholarship begins with participation in the *polis* defined as *holding political office* and next argues towards descent as a prerequisite, interpreting the latter by way of the first. A clear sign of the difference between the two views is the role assigned to Athenian women: in Athenian law, women are citizens and in other evidence are shown participating in the *polis* in religion as citizens; in modern historiography they are considered only as wives of male citizens and their cultic roles are not perceived as civic activities (if perceived as significant at all).[84] A few representative examples may illustrate the main lines of argument.

One current in scholarship approaches the *polis* primarily as a state identified by its formal political institutions. A prominent example of this view is the Copenhagen Polis project led by Mogens Hansen for over thirty years. Although in his multi-volume oeuvre Hansen refers to the fact that the *polis* included the territory and the cults of a Greek community, his point of departure is that the *polis* was defined by its political institutions. His conception of citizenship follows that of Aristotle without reservation, which he regards as representative of Greek historical conceptions of citizenship generally.[85] Hansen notes that citizenship depended on descent and in this context he mentions female citizens occasionally, but overall they play no role in his analysis.[86] Why this is so becomes clear when Hansen states: 'The principal privilege of an Athenian citizen was his political rights; in fact, they were more than just a "privilege": they constituted the essence of citizenship,' a statement that in the footnote he founds on the definition in Aristotle's *Politics*.[87] In this perception, women have no share in the 'essence' of citizenship. P.J. Rhodes, in his work on civic ideology and institutions, has a similar conception of the the *polis* as a state, adopting a perspective on citizenship from the political centre:

> In an extended sense the children and wives of adult male citizens were a part of the citizen body, because the male children would grow up to become full citizens and the wives would give birth to the next generation of full citizens.[88]

[84] That on the political definition of 'citizen' scholars find it difficult to classify women as citizens is illustrated by the tendency of removing the conundrum to a footnote, for instance Finley (1981) 13: 'Throughout this brief account of social structure, the status of women is not considered. Politically excluded everywhere, their "citizenship" or "non-citizenship" was nevertheless essential in the transmission of status and property to the succeeding generations.' Likewise Todd (1993) 171, a footnote to a chapter on 'Status relationships: citizen, metic, slave': 'Athenian women (or at least, citizen women: female slaves are not so readily distinguished from their male counterparts) could perhaps be seen as a fourth and separate group. But on balance, and with some misgivings, I shall stick here with the pattern of three groups, and discuss the position of women in the context of family law.'

[85] Hansen (1991) 58: 'According to the Greek conception, most clearly formulated by Aristotle, a *polis* was "a community [*koinonia*] of citizens [*politai*] with regard to the constitution [*politeia*]"'; 64–5. Hansen (1998); Hansen (2000); Hansen (2007); political institutions: Hansen (1993); summary in Hansen (2006) 109–5.

[86] Hansen (1991) 94–7, female citizens 96.

[87] Hansen (1991) 97 and n. 119.

[88] Rhodes (2009a) 60.

Full citizenship is conceived here as political participation and again female citizens only feature here as mothers of male citizens; their own participation in the *polis* does not appear under the umbrella of citizenship. Rhodes notes, however, that in many *poleis* the definition of Aristotle does not work for sections of the male citizen population; how to account for the many male citizens without access to office in oligarchies in Aristotelian terms? Despite these reservations, Rhodes does not appear to question the validity of the definition in the *Politics* for historical analysis.[89]

The historical debate on the ancient *polis* took a different turn when scholars observed that individual, abstract rights defined in law, which form the backbone of present-day citizenship, were unknown in ancient Greek law, as semantic analysis of legal terms clearly shows.[90] Using anthropological methods, scholars have begun to highlight the social-structural dimensions of ancient Greek societies behind political institutions and the differences between the ancient *polis* and (modern) states. In this scholarship, citizenship in classical Athens appears as a political status embedded in values and social practices in the widest sense.[91]

An influential work, one that in fact contributed much to the success of this approach, is Philip Manville's *The origins of citizenship in ancient Athens* (1990).[92] He notes that 'what we would call the state was always represented as *hoi Athenaioi,* meaning the political community of citizens.... To be an Athenian citizen, as an Athenian himself might say, was to be someone who *metechei tes poleos*: someone who shares in the

89 Rhodes (2009a) 61–3.

90 Since 'rights' is not an ancient concept (Ostwald (1996)), the meaning of political and legal terms formerly translated almost inadvertently into modern terminology is now being reconsidered. Important examples are *ta dikaia* (and cognate expressions), once translated as 'rights' and now circumscribed by Bolmarcich (2007) 36 as 'what is right' and by Mirhady (2007) 55 as 'what is relevant to justice'. Carter (2004): freedom of speech not a 'right' but a quality belonging to persons who should speak without fear; Carter (2007): a concept of 'contract' only visible in the later fourth century.

91 Manville (1990); Walter (1993); Manville (1994); Ostwald (1996); Cartledge (2000); Carter (2004); Hall (2007); Liddel (2007); Hammer (2009). Mann (2008), in response to amongst others Blok (2004), advocates the system theory of sociologist Niklas Luhmann to arrive at an integrated perspective on politics and society at Athens; the problem how women (and metics) were related to the political system, which Mann keeps firmly as the defining element of citizenship with reference to Pericles' funerary oration (Thuc. 2.40.2) and Aristotle's definition in *Politics* (Mann (2008) 4, n. 10), is a matter of 'classifying the sources [relevant to women and metics] to different parts of the system' to be followed by 'analysis of structural connections between the political and the social systems' (32–3; my transl.). Mann thus in fact postpones this integrative analysis to the future, while the system theory of Luhmann does not inspire confidence that a solution be attained.

92 Manville (1990), who states his intention to move away from a teleological conception of the *polis*'s history as an organic development towards the classical democracy, by adopting 'anthropological-style' methods (34, n. 104).

polis.' Manville's phrase recalls Euxitheos' rendering of his own position as a citizen; and Manville adds the pertinent question: 'What did this really mean in the classical age?'[93] A systematic exploration of this question would have revealed that the same terminology of *meteinai* and *metechein tes poleos* applied to female citizens.[94] However, only one page after this passage Manville excludes women from the inquiry: 'the citizens of the polis were the native Athenian males who had reached the age of eighteen.' Here, Manville follows the *Ath.Pol.* to the letter, apparently without noticing that in 42.1 the text does not speak of *metechein tes poleos* but of *metechein tes politeias* and clearly is concerned here with admission to the political body of the *polis*. Next, Manville states (12–13) that 'other Athenian groups, women and children, deserve a brief mention because of their ambiguous position in the society'; a sign of this is that 'Athenian women, and a fortiori Athenian girls, could not own or inherit property'. The latter statement is incorrect, as we shall see in more detail in Chapter 3: women's inheritance rights were a vital component of the conception of citizenship and its transmission. After this, Manville no longer refers to female citizens, nor do we hear much about the participation in the *hiera* so crucial to Euxitheos' self-definition as a citizen.[95] Why Manville's potentially wider view of citizenship is narrowed down to the conventional topics of male political office holding becomes clear when he adopts Aristotle's *Politics* as a searchlight, not only Aristotle's definitions of a *polis* and of a citizen (40–2), but also the philosophical premises of the *Politics* without any qualification: '[c]itizens are not taxpayers but rather shareholders in a corporation whose profits are moral excellence' (45). Although Manville observes that the *Politics* is 'not a history of those specific states', Aristotle's conceptions guide the rest of his argument on Athens, including the historical development of the *polis*.[96]

93 Manville (1990) 6–7; and 34: '"I am Athenian," said the proud citizen of classical Athens; "I share in the polis."'

94 Citizenship law valid for men and women: Is. 6.47; law *ap.* Dem. 43.51; Schol. Aesch. 1.39: ἐκεῖ μὲν γὰρ ἔστι νόθῳ μηδὲ νόθῃ μὴ εἶναι ἀγχιστείαν μήθ' ἱερῶν μήθ' ὁσίων ἀπ' Εὐκλείδου ἄρχοντος, 'for according to the law no male or female bastard has any claim, based on kinship, to *hiera kai hosia*, as of the archonship of Eukleides'. Participation of women *as* citizens: [Dem.] 59.111: 'At this point the most virtuous of women will be angry at you that you have considered this woman worthy to participate equally with themselves in the *polis* and the *hiera*' (ὁμοίως αὐταῖς ... μετέχειν τῶν τῆς πόλεως καὶ τῶν ἱερῶν).

95 Manville (1990) 60–9 for phratries and cults of the *oikos* as part of 'early society'.

96 Manville (1990) 35–54; 38; 40–2. An approach comparable to Manville's is adopted by Walter (1993): *An der polis teilhaben* focuses on participation as the major feature of ancient citizenship, not only in Athens but in various *poleis*. Walter shows more interest in cult and inheritance than Manville does (e.g. 126–32 on the decree of Naupaktos, see also Chapter 6.3) but likewise fails to take female citizens into account. Aristotle's definition of citizenship is an important influence here (23–7).

A third approach to the Greek *polis*, which a group of scholars in Paris developed from the 1960s onward, was likewise grounded in anthropological methods, but with a very different theoretical basis. The so-called Paris school, among whom Jean-Pierre Vernant, Marcel Detienne and Pierre Vidal-Naquet played a formative role, adopted the methods of Claude Lévi-Strauss's structuralist anthropology and applied them to ancient Greek society. Structuralist analysis is essentially synchronic, focusing on the relationship of key notions within a culture in its entirety instead of on (individual) agency and historical change.[97] Not (legal) institutions, but the classificatory order by which each culture construes itself is the key to understanding a society. This order is shaped by binary oppositions: culture versus nature, male versus female, self versus other, creating a structure of polar relationships that does not alter fundamentally over time.[98]

Despite this crucially different point of departure, however, the Paris school retained the Aristotelian idea of the citizen prevailing in classical scholarship and incorporated it within the framework of structuralist methodology. Modelled into the comprehensive structure of binary opposites, the male citizen became the defining figure not just of the political system, but of the entire culture of the Greek *polis*, its myths, cults, rituals, literature and visual works of art, whereas woman was by definition the opposite, anything but the male citizen, the ultimate other, part of nature, outside the cultural order of society.[99] Some Paris scholars proposed interpretations which seemed to be driven primarily by the force of this theoretical model, but could hardly be maintained in the face of the evidence. Marcel Detienne, for instance, argued that ancient Greek women, because they (allegedly) were non-citizens, were normally excluded from active participation in animal sacrifice, a view that is demonstrably untenable.[100] Nicole Loraux developed a highly influential notion of Athenian

97 Graeber (2001) 13–22 notes that structuralist models are very helpful to chart structural differences and connections between various elements of a culture, but are incapable of accounting for human actions in terms of purposes and agency, because the structuralist model cannot provide a hierarchy of more or less valued elements.

98 Vernant (2006) 174: 'Each stage of this analysis has shown the polarity between the static and the mobile, the open and the enclosed, the interior and the exterior: a polarity that is not only evident in the interplay of domestic institutions (division of labor, marriage, consanguinity, meals) but also inscribed even in the nature of man and woman' (orig. 1965).

99 Structuralist thought applied in ancient Greek scholarship, for instance Vernant (1985); Vidal-Naquet (1986); Detienne (1989); Goldhill (1994); Zeitlin (1996). On the differences between the institutional-legal tradition and the Parisian holistic-cultural approach to the *polis*, Murray (1990).

100 Detienne (1989); refutation by Osborne (1993).

citizenship in two large monographs, published in 1981. She argued that women in Athens were not only non-citizens, but more poignantly non-Athenians, because the word *Athenaia* for an Athenian female citizen did not exist. This exclusion of 'the feminine' from the notion 'citizen' had its counterpart in the imagined unity of the *polis* of male Athenian citizens, envisioned in the Athenian myth of autochthony that was especially fostered in Athenian funerary orations.[101] Loraux's point of departure, however, that the word *Athenaia* did not exist in Athens, is unfounded.[102] Although Loraux later admitted this fact, she did not revise her views.[103]

Nonetheless, by assigning a pivotal role to myth and ritual in the understanding of *polis* culture in the widest sense, the Paris school had a profound impact on the study of ancient Greek societies, reinforcing anthropological approaches in classical studies within the wider 'cultural turn' of the 1980s and 1990s. Since the mid-1990s, moreover, the model of binary opposites has lost some of its force. Many classical scholars productively combine elements of the various methodologies, interpreting both the political and the religious aspects of the *polis* as 'embedded' in society in a broad sense. However, because the Paris school consolidated the conventional notion that Greek – or Athenian – citizenship was 'defined by holding political office' within their own methodology, they did not affect any change in that direction.

This observation might even be put more strongly. On finding that prominent scholars made inexplicable errors against the available evidence (for instance Manville's assumption that girls had no inheritance rights in Athens and Loraux's contention that the word *Athenaia* did not exist) and that other scholars widely accepted these errors (and interpretations developed on them), it would seem that the Aristotelian definition of citizenship was so authoritative that scholars, in approaching the evidence with it firmly in mind, were inclined to read the evidence in this light and did not notice what did not fit. Conversely, scholars who argued that the evidence

101 Loraux (1986); Loraux (1993). Loraux contended that instead of *Athenaiai*, Athenian women were called *Attikes gynaikes*, but this expression occurs even less frequently than *Athenaia* and could hardly have figured as the current alternative. See also Chapter 4.6. That Loraux's views were based on weak evidence was noted quite soon after publication of her work by Brulé (1987); see also Jacquemin (2005).

102 For instance, Ion of Chios (*FGrH* 392 F 11 (ca. 480–420) and the comedy writers Cantharos (F 5, K-A) and Pherecrates (F 39, K-A) of the fifth, and Philemon (F69, K-A) and Diphilus (F 10, K-A) of the late fourth century all use *Athenaia* for a female Athenian citizen. Ar. Byz. notes (*Nom.aet.* F 1): Ἀθηναία, ἀστή: ὅτι ἐστὶ Ἀθηναία γυνή, ὥσπερ καὶ Ἀθηναῖος. '*Athenaia*, an *aste* [female citizen]: because *Athenaia* is a woman, just like *Athenaios* [a man]'. See further below, Chapter 4.6.

103 Loraux (1993) 247–8; Loraux (2000).

points in quite different directions exerted little or no influence. In 1986, for instance, Cynthia Patterson drew attention to the similarity between masculine and feminine forms of *Attikos*/*Attike* and *astos*/*aste*, which she argued should be brought to bear on the understanding of the Athenian *polis* and of its citizenship vocabulary, but her arguments had little impact.[104] In a volume on the Greek city (1990), Christiane Sourvinou-Inwood published an article showing how in Athens participation in religion was anchored in *polis* structures and vice versa. Creating the quintessential link between the institutional and structuralist-religious approaches to the *polis*, her work immediately became highly influential in the study of Greek religion.[105] A few years later she published an equally incisive article on women's public roles as citizens in a volume on women in antiquity (1995).[106] Reviewing various models of comparative ethnography commonly used to assess women's roles in ancient Greece, Sourvinou-Inwood argued that at Athens women were subordinate to men in the *oikos*, which was defined by kinship relations and property interests, but that women and men both operated as citizens in the public sphere, and in public cult women acted on an equal footing with male citizens. Priestesses exemplified the participation in the public domain of women in general.[107] This article, however, had no impact on the current debate about citizenship.

In sum, the scholarship reviewed so far shows the influence of a paradigm in which citizenship at classical Athens is conceived as a male status characterised by holding political office. This conception, based on Aristotle's definition in *Politics* and reinforced by passages from the *Ath. Pol.*, assigns to 'citizen' a very specific, limited meaning that is at odds with the vocabulary at Athens, precisely as is the case with Aristotle's own usage of the word *polites*. The evidence on citizenship represented in Demosthenes' speech for Euxitheos is not sufficiently or systematically taken into account. With the political aspects of citizenship centre stage, scholars are inclined to mistake this part for the whole and to overlook that the lives of the men and women involved encompassed many more domains where they acted as citizens. More specifically, the evidence points to a notion of citizenship in which religion played a key role and women were involved in essential ways.

104 Patterson (1986) 63. The remarkable non-reception of Patterson's arguments is also noted by Jacquemin (2005) 338, n. 7.

105 Sourvinou-Inwood (1990); on the main tenets of this article and its reception, Parker (2011) 57–61; Kindt (2012) 13–35.

106 Sourvinou-Inwood (1995).

107 Cf. Connelly (2007).

1.6 Ancient Greek Citizenship: After the Enlightenment

At this point, we should like to ask why scholars preferred Aristotle's definition to Euxitheos' account, in spite of all the evidence supporting the latter as a more plausible historical picture. Could it be that, besides the intellectual attraction of the conceptions laid out in *Politics*, modern conceptions of citizenship contributed to this predilection for the 'political' citizen? Our modern vocabulary, as we just saw, is not an innocent instrument. Contemporary meanings and connotations inherent in our terminology may influence our view of the past without our being aware of it. In present-day discourse 'citizenship' implies not only being a free and equal bearer of individual rights in civil society, but also specifically using such rights for active participation in the political sphere.[108] This conception of citizenship is a relatively recent one, and so is a tendency to associate the typical 'political citizen' with ancient Greece, especially with democratic Athens. A quick tour through the genealogy of the modern use of 'citizen' may clarify the causes and impact of this association.

In early modern Europe citizenship consisted primarily of a status held in a city or state which entailed enjoyment of certain rights in the judicial, economic and religious spheres, often restricted to the city where one lived.[109] In some regions (German free towns, Italian republics, the Dutch Republic) citizens were called precisely that ('burgers'), in other countries they were not. In monarchies such as Great Britain, France and Spain, the inhabitants were subjects of the monarch, but in other respects the legal regime was similar to that which applied in other regions and strongly focused on city life. Citizen status afforded some legal protection and economic rights, which, in the case of citizens in cities, usually depended on residence. Formal political participation at the level of cities, or beyond at the level of the kingdom or republic in which they resided, was only open

[108] Faulks (2000) 3–4: 'Citizenship contains an internal logic that demands that its benefits necessarily become ever more universal and egalitarian.' '[Citizen status] recognises the contribution a particular individual makes to that community, while at the same time granting him or her individual autonomy. This autonomy is reflected in a set of rights which . . . always imply recognition of political agency on the part of the bearer of those rights.'

[109] A bibliography for this vast subject is beyond the scope of my argument; see for instance Peyrou (2006) for citizenship models in early modern Europe; Prak (1997) for early modern citizenship in (Dutch) towns; Fahrmeier (2007) for the concepts and practices of citizenship in modern Europe, showing the shift from legal rights, social (national, ethnic) and economic citizenship to the prevailing conception of political rights as constitutive of citizenship; Scott (1996) for the gender aspects of the political citizen since the French Revolution.

to a tiny minority (the majority made itself heard indirectly or through rioting) and hence was not a defining feature of 'citizenship'.[110] A prominent sign of being a citizen of a city was membership of local groups such as guilds, charities and the militia. In most states and cities, an individual had to embrace the prevailing religious faith to be recognised as a citizen. In monarchies the sovereign determined the faith of his or her subjects, including the level of tolerance of others. Ideally, a state was united in one (prevailing) creed and in every state political institutions and religion – in practice the Christian church of the prevailing denomination – were intrinsically bound together, with the religious establishment often holding the dominant authority. Objection to this entanglement between religious and political institutions became a leading principle of Enlightened political thought.

When political thinkers began looking for models to support citizens' legal protection against, and economic autonomy in the face of, state authority, it was first and foremost to the Roman Republic that civic republicanism looked for its political principles. In Rome the sovereignty of the citizens was firmly anchored in status distinctions, with a concomitant distance between the ruling political elite and the people at large.[111] In the eighteenth century, classical Greece came to be regarded as a wellspring of Western art and literature and provided models of individual virtue (notably exemplified in Plutarch's *Lives*), but neither the ideology nor the practice of democratic Athens suited the current political climate.[112] Some intellectuals admired ancient Sparta for what they saw as its austere, masculine virtue, but Sparta was not regarded as a model of political institutions. Drawing on Enlightened principles under which rights were separated from any religious tradition, the American Declaration of Independence and the French Revolution still drew mainly on Roman models in their political terms and aims.

Interest in ancient Greece as a political model emerged from two sources. On the one hand, the Romantic urge for freedom in the decades

[110] Around 1780, the electorate in Great Britain was ca. 4% of the population, but those who actually made use of their prerogative ca. 1%; in Prussia and Austria the electorate was ca. 0.1%; in France it was nominally less than 10% but active 0% – those who assembled as *citoyens* in 1789 claimed to revive an ancient right. In the French Revolution and its aftermath until 1810, the active electorate varied between 6% (1789) to 24% (1792) and 8% (1804) of the population; see Fahrmeier (2007) 15, 38.

[111] The Roman model, which distinguished on principle between those with a right to vote and those elected to represent the people, was central to Enlightened political thought and formed the basis of the American and French constitutions, see Manin (1997) 94–131.

[112] On the unsuitability of democratic Athens as a political model to early modern Europe and its rise to prominence in nineteenth-century England, see Roberts (1994).

of the French Revolution and the Napoleonic wars, together with the Greek War of Independence (1821–32), entrenched a perception of ancient Greece as the origin of liberty. On the other hand, ideals of education in civic virtue drew on the revolutionary concept that liberty entailed the right to political participation in the state, alongside the notion that it also entailed individual autonomy vis-à-vis the state. Claims to political participation based on individual rights as the cornerstone of civic liberty came to be at the heart of the liberal notion of citizenship and became the quintessential feature of citizenship in the nineteenth and twentieth century. Who this citizen with individual civic rights might be in terms of gender, race and class was a contested issue. The notion of primary right for every human being eventually brought about the abolition of slavery. Romantic ideas about national culture merged with political aspirations for a wider basis of the body politic. Moreover, in many countries political pressures sought to effectuate a separation of church and state, or at least control over the first by the second. These movements forged a path towards the creation of constitutions in many European states (1830, 1848, 1870) and converged in giving rise to the concept of the nation state.

With political empowerment thus becoming the hallmark of modern citizenship, classical Greece grew in significance and gradually replaced Republican Rome as the key model of ancient – and modern – citizenship in Europe and North America.[113] For nineteenth-century liberalism in particular, Aristotle's conception of the citizen fitted the modern image of the political citizen very well. That in many ancient *poleis* only free men of some wealth would fall into the category of the citizen suited the current liberal principle of a restricted electorate. For the men of the ruling classes, the idea of citizenship as political participation shared by free equals and exercised by taking turns in ruling and being ruled matched their own experience. This view of Greece as a source of specifically *political* inspiration first became prominent particularly in Great Britain, with its strong liberal movement. By the later nineteenth and the early twentieth century, some elements of this view needed revision. A strong movement emerged claiming universal suffrage, first for men only and next also for women, in other words full and equal political citizenship, and succeeded in this goal in the course of the twentieth century. While many Western nation states had extended their colonial empires into tributaries of the political and

[113] Greece as a general political model for Europe, Funke (2002) 13–16; early nineteenth-century political philosophy based on comparison with ancient Greece, Liddel (2007) 4–10; ancient Athens as a model for 'modern gentlemen' in Britain, Roberts (1994) 229–55. For a critical appraisal of political entitlement as the core of citizenship, Isin (2002), on Greece 53–92.

economic power of the citizens in the mother country, the same democratic ideals of political citizenship in the context of autonomous statehood prevailed in the ideology of decolonisation.

In effect, in the twentieth century Aristotle's citizen seemed to resemble the citizens of modern states who identified with their individual, political rights on the basis of legal equality. After the Second World War, intensifying democratisation in Western Europe and the United States shifted attention overwhelmingly to bringing about the intended equality in legal and political entitlement as the defining feature of citizenship. Communitarian aspects, that is to say the awareness of community membership in social and religious terms and the obligations for citizens arising from that membership, seemed typical of an old-fashioned *Gemeinschaft* that a free, secular and democratic society could leave behind. One of the most prominent questions for citizenship in the present day concerns the balance between individual rights and communitarian aspects.

In sum, 'citizen' means a great variety of things, always with some reference to a certain qualification to belong to the community, to some legal protection and to claims to some participation, but with an enormous divergence of scope and application. The idea that citizenship entails the free exercise of (political) rights emerged in the later seventeenth century, that it should be so on the basis of equality, though on a restricted basis, in the later eighteenth century, and has been realised for all adult male and female citizens in many, but not all, nations of the world only in the last century. Nowadays, political agency is an essential feature of citizenship, beside many other rights and duties belonging to it.

Drawing on these values in contemporary politics, the politically entitled citizen became the central figure in the perception of the ancient *polis* prevailing in ancient historical scholarship in the twentieth century. Classical scholars, we must conclude, for a long time have embraced this modern conception of the citizen and its apparent congruence with Aristotle's, which they saw reflected with particular clarity in the citizen of democratic Athens. This convergence of values rendered the appreciation of the non-political elements of Athenian citizenship very difficult.[114] Following the rapid secularisation of states as well as academia in the West in the later twentieth century, many historians saw the prominence of democratic politics in classical Athens also as a form of, or related to,

[114] Vlassopoulos (2007) 68–96 seeks to introduce a new approach to the Greek *polis*, moving away from the 'liberal' tradition anchored in the European nation state, again based on Aristotle, not on his political citizen, but on his idea of the *koinonia*.

secularisation, a form of rationalism connected to a decline in traditional faith in the gods. In many currents of ancient historical scholarship, 'the political' was conceived as a human sphere of rational thought and action that might be tied to social-economic interests but owed its very existence to its separation from religion in its ideas and institutions.[115] The results of this approach in the historical analysis of political institutions, economic practices and law are impressive, but by identifying the *polis* primarily with its political structures, major parts of its existence were insufficiently understood as essentially belonging to it. Even recent approaches drawing on comparative and anthropological methods or concerned with the socio-religious foundations of the *polis* do not seem very much inclined to question the meaning of 'citizenship' as such, as we just saw. But citizenship at Athens meant much more than activities in the political sphere alone. If we want to investigate what all the notions and practices of Athenian citizenship entailed, how can we use the modern word 'citizen' without introducing its modern and inappropriate connotations?

1.7 Defining Citizenship

To find a way to do so, I propose to look for a definition of citizenship which clarifies the picture that emerges from the evidence for classical Athens that we have encountered so far. Some parameters of the term 'citizenship' are both clear and inescapable. The context of citizenship is a political community, often labelled a state: all questions as to who belongs to the community and what the members are entitled to do to put their citizenship into practice derive their answer and meaning ultimately from this context.[116] In the current development of global citizenship, the role of states for the legal conditions and social identity of citizens is quite different from that in which states were the most salient entities, whereas in the late medieval and early modern eras in many regions of Europe citizenship was defined by cities before being an aspect of states. Political participation in the state in some form by at least some citizens is a necessary condition to speak of citizens, rather than of subjects. In many states

[115] Prominent examples of this view, though with different approaches, are Meier (1980), the political work of M.I. Finley, and the studies by M.H. Hansen. Even Parker (1983) 125–8 assumes a process of secularisation in the fourth century, doubting the impact of pollution by murder in homicide cases; for a revision of Parker's reading of this topic, Harris (2015).

[116] Berent (2004) calls into question that classical Athens was a 'state' due to the virtually non-existent distance between the Athenian state and its citizens; his argument is persuasively rebutted by Anderson (2009).

in history, only a small number of citizens were entitled to political office, but since they were considered to represent the community and its varied interests, their political citizenship would encompass the citizenship of all. Other kinds of entitlements to legal status or participation are equally relevant to identifying community members as citizens. Let us review some current definitions of citizenship that claim to be applicable more widely than only to modern nation states, to see whether they may provide help in understanding citizenship in ancient Athens.

Charles Tilly, whose work on the socio-economic history of the (early) modern period has had a major impact on historical scholarship, defines citizenship as the

> continuing series of transactions between persons and agents of a given state in which each has enforceable rights and obligations by virtue of 1) the person's membership in an exclusive category and 2) the agent's relation to the state rather than any authority the agent may enjoy.[117]

'Transactions', as well as 'persons and agents' can refer to more than political participation, i.e. civil society in a wider sense, yet the emphasis on political and legal rights is clear. Moreover, there is no agreement on the question if, or in which, domains of life citizens of classical Athens enjoyed what we would call enforceable rights in respect of the *polis*. The vocabulary Euxitheos used to put forward his claims – all in terms of what was 'fitting', never in terms of 'rights' – corroborates the findings discussed above that for his status as a citizen this was not really the case. Finally, Tilly's definition presupposes a distinction and distance between the citizens and the state, which is a crucial factor in concepts of citizenship of the (early) modern period but makes less sense in the case of classical Athens.

Michael Walzer, a sociologist with a great interest in citizenship in its historical varieties, offers the following: 'a citizen is a member of a political community, entitled to whatever prerogatives and encumbered with whatever responsibilities are attached to membership'.[118] This definition is far more flexible, by virtue of an open classification of the 'political community' and an equally open indication of the prerogatives and

117 Tilly (1995) 8. Prak (1997) 403 criticises Tilly's definition, in that it 'makes it difficult to distinguish between various types of ties between state officials and inhabitants of the state'; cf. Faulks (2000) 10.

118 Walzer (1988) 211; he relates the positive (entitlement to political participation) and negative (freedom from interference) notions of liberty to the dual features of citizenship, i.e. political office and membership of the community.

responsibilities – 'rights' and 'political office' are avoided here. Finally, in the words of political scientist Will Kymlicka, citizenship entails 'liberal ideas of individual rights and entitlements on the one hand, and communitarian ideas of membership in and attachment to a particular community on the other'.[119] Although Kymlicka's modern term 'liberal ideas of rights' does not suit ancient Greece, his description reinforces the useful features of Walzer's definition, in that both connect the perspective of the individual to the communitarian aspects of citizenship. Citizenship, in their view, consists of two elements, membership of a political community to which an individual feels connected in some ways and a claim to participation in that community in a variety of ways; the two parts are not identical but are still tightly connected.

Compared with the terms in which Euxitheos described himself, this definition of citizenship works very well: Euxitheos construes himself as *Athenaios* and *polites*, a member of the Athenian *polis*, a status based on his descent from two Athenian parents. He describes claims to participation in terms of participation in *hiera* and in *koina*, designating the offices of priest and demarch as specific examples of participatory roles. More generally, membership of the community tallies fairly well with *meteinai*, the claims to participation with *metechein*. I shall therefore use the following as a working definition of citizenship: 'citizenship consists of membership of a political community, in which an individual holds claims to whatever prerogatives and is encumbered with whatever responsibilities are attached to this membership, with communitarian ideas of membership in and attachment to this particular community'. When discussing particular texts and cases, for practical reasons I shall reduce this rather long definition by referring to its main constituent parts, 'membership' and 'participation'. Likewise, for the sake of brevity I continue using the English words 'citizen' and 'citizenship'. We need, however, to explore more fully what it meant to 'be a citizen' in classical Athens and how this was expressed.

1.8 Athenian Citizenship: Towards a New Perspective

This book aims at finding new answers to the elementary questions of citizenship in classical Athens, by following the signs Euxitheos flagged

[119] Kymlicka (2002) 284; he describes these features of citizenship in his discussion of a controversy among political scientists about the frictions between liberalism, utilitarianism and communitarianism, and the capacity of the notion 'citizenship' to transcend these antagonistic political conceptions.

up in his defence speech for the Athenian court. We need to investigate how far his notions were representative of Athenian norms and practices generally, and what the connections might be between his conception of citizenship and the information provided by the *Ath.Pol.* and other documents on the Athenian *polis*. This line of enquiry will help to reconnect the political and religious aspects of the classical *polis* more systematically in our historical analysis, taking current debates on citizenship in ancient Athens a step further.

This inquiry is laid out in the next five chapters, each addressing an elementary question of citizenship at Athens. Finding that citizenship means sharing in a community, we ask in Chapter 2, *in what* is a citizen expected to share? If this is not by definition the Aristotelian 'political and judicial office', then what is it? Taking the citizenship laws and the law on legitimacy, to which Euxitheos refers, as a starting point, we find that to be a citizen is to share in '*hiera* and *hosia*'. Tracing this more or less fixed expression in a variety of sources and historical circumstances, *hiera kai hosia* turn out to refer to the bond between humans and gods, their reciprocal relationship established at and continued since the beginning of the *polis*. It is a metaphysical notion, but many obligations and rewards implied in it were tangible and real in daily life. Man-made laws on *polis* life and in particular on citizenship were grounded in this bond with the gods. Chapter 3 addresses the *criteria* for citizenship. Finding that legitimate birth was conditional for membership of the *polis*, why is that so? The crucial notion at work here will appear to be *inheritance*, and we shall seek to find out how it worked for male and female citizens. Furthermore, we need to see where the new structure of 508/7 set up by Cleisthenes interfered with the existing system and where it was in fact built upon it. In Chapter 4, the question *who is a citizen* is approached from the angle of language and its anchorage in society. Since a single equivalent of the modern word 'citizen' did not exist in ancient Greek, we look into the Greek vocabulary to find terms for members of the *polis* and what was meant by them. Special attention will be paid to similarities and differences in words for male and female citizens, to see what this vocabulary may reveal about symmetries and asymmetries in gender roles in the *polis*. Chapter 5 looks into the rules for *participation*, that is, how the citizens *put their citizenship into practice*. I will argue that *time* (value) was the core notion guiding the access of individual citizens to roles in the public sphere. All citizens participated in religious activities, male citizens in addition were active in the political bodies, while both spheres were tightly connected. We need to inquire, furthermore, what conduct citizens were expected to display in this context, and how *timai* (honours and public offices) were distributed among them. In a concluding, brief Chapter 6, I discuss some consequences of the Athenian model of citizenship for outsiders who were closely tied to the Athenian community, both before and after Pericles' Citizenship Law of 451/0. How did Athenian practice work out for those made into citizens by decree, and how and why came the status of *metoikos* into being? Finally, I briefly address with all due caution the question whether the results gained for Athens are of some validity for other *poleis*. Only classical Athens has left sufficient evidence to look into the details of citizenship as I will do in this book, but democratic Athens was not representative of 'the' Greek *polis*, neither in political terms nor in many other respects. In fact, no single *polis* can be taken to be 'representative' of the whole of Greece without further qualifications. Can, however, the *model* of citizenship that is the outcome of this study illuminate the conceptions and practices of citizenship in other, politically different and less well-documented *poleis*?

Among the methods used for this book, a few need to be clarified briefly. Semantic analysis of the Greek vocabulary for citizenship is employed fairly frequently. Understanding key concepts and values expressed in the language and discourse of the society in question is an indispensable method for anthropologists and historians, who need to find a way into a culture very different from their own. Even if no method can provide access to the past in a way immune to the effect of contemporary notions, some methods are deliberately aimed at minimising such effects. They are of crucial importance in areas of research that are vulnerable to such influences, and citizenship is demonstrably such an area. The semantic method I use here may be dubbed 'historical-philological', as distinct from the far more sophisticated methods developed in modern linguistics.[120] Collecting all passages with the lexeme in question, each passage is interpreted as much as possible without a preconceived notion of the meaning of the word, which to that end is transliterated rather than translated.[121] Translation into our modern languages is not avoided, but deferred as long as possible. Systematic comparison finally charts the range of meanings of the word in context, obviously with due respect to the types of

[120] Modern semantic theories illuminate, for instance, the relative meaning of cognates to one another and are especially productive to study ancient value terms and their use in persuasive contexts; cf. Rademaker (2005); Sluiter (2008); Peels (2015) 3–26.

[121] Passages from literary sources were collected by lemma search in the *TLG* taken at various dates; from epigraphical evidence, searches were made in the PHI, section Attica, of lexemes in various cases and spellings.

texts involved. This semantic research has a distinguished pedigree in classical studies and ties in with the important strand of *Begriffsgeschichte* in historical scholarship.[122] Epigraphic evidence, furthermore, will play quite a large role in this study; technical issues are addressed where strictly relevant in footnotes.

A further methodological element that may need an introduction is the concept of institutions developed by economic historian Douglass North. It belongs to an extensive discussion on the relationship between institutions and market economy that is not of immediate concern here, but I think that his notion of the 'rules of the game', which will appear succinctly in Chapter 3 and more extensively in Chapter 5, helps to clarify how certain aspects of Athenian society worked. The difference between his view of institutions and the conventional notion of institutions as formal organisations, as used by most political historians, will, I trust, become clear in my discussion.

The set-up of this book is primarily synchronic, but historical change will be taken into account throughout, since structural features are often clarified precisely by their transformation. The historical period under consideration will take us roughly from Solon to the late fourth century, but the focus will be mainly on the classical fifth and fourth centuries.

[122] The historical-philological method in classical studies is developed and used by, among others, J. Chadwick in lexical analysis more generally, by A.W.H. Adkins, K.J. Dover, N.R.E. Fisher and D. Cairns for ancient value terms, J. Bordes, K.A. Raaflaub, A. Fouchard and D. Carter for political vocabulary, and by J. Rudhardt and V. Pirenne-Delforge for religious terminology. For *Begriffsgeschichte*, developed in modern cultural history by Koselleck (1979), see Busse (1994); Bleicken (1994) 461–70; Richter (1995); Hampshire-Monk (1998).

2

A Bond between Polis *and Gods*

> In your presence, men of Athens, I now invoke all the gods and goddesses that hold the land of Attica, and Apollo Pythios, who is ancestral (*patroios*) for the *polis* ... that if I speak the truth they will grant me prosperity and salvation, but if I ... accuse him falsely, they may dispossess me of all *agatha* (good things).
>
> Demosthenes, *On the crown*, 141[1]

> O city, o land, and clear water,
> Gods in the sky and gods deep in the earth who keep their graves,
> and Zeus Soter, as third, guarding the homes of *hosios* men,
> receive this group of women suppliants with the respectful spirit of this land.
>
> Chorus of Danaids, Aesch. *Suppl.* 22–30[2]

Citizens of Athens were characterised by sharing in the *polis,* but what exactly was it that they shared? Only citizens could hold political office, but many male and all female Athenians, though they lacked the possibility of doing so, were citizens nevertheless. When Euxitheos had to demonstrate what was essential for his citizenship, he advanced his descent from two Athenian parents and his participation in the *hiera*, an argument with which Demosthenes expected to convince the *dikastai* and that recurs in other court cases on citizen status.[3] But what exactly did the *hiera* represent for sharing in the *polis* more widely? And what had descent to do with it?

[1] Dem. 18.141: τοὺς θεοὺς πάντας καὶ πάσας ὅσοι τὴν χώραν ἔχουσι τὴν ᾿Αττικήν, καὶ τὸν Ἀπόλλω τὸν Πύθιον, ὃς πατρῷός ἐστι τῇ πόλει. Parts of this chapter revisit arguments published as Blok (2010), Blok (2011), Blok (2014a).

[2] Aesch. *Suppl.* 22–30: ὦ πόλις, ὦ γῆ καὶ λευκὸν ὕδωρ / ὕπατοί τε θεοὶ καὶ βαρυτίμους χθόνιοι θήκας κατέχοντες / καὶ Ζεὺς σωτὴρ τρίτος, οἰκοφύλαξ / ὁσίων ἀνδρῶν, δέξασθ' ἱκέτην / τὸν θηλυγενῆ στόλον αἰδοίωι / πνεύματι χώρας.

[3] Is. 9.7–13; Is. 8.15–16, and below, Chapter 3.

2.1 Citizens by Birth

In his defence of his citizenship before the Athenian court, Euxitheos set out to prove he was born from two Athenians, providing evidence that both his parents were Athenian citizens. This took the form of witnesses who confirmed that his grandparents on either side were born Athenians (57.20–30, 37–45). Regarding his father, however, he added that

> it will be made clear that he was born at a time when, even if he were an *astos* on one side only, it would befit (*proseko*) him to be a *polites*; for he was born before the archonship of Eukleides.[4]

Euxitheos refers here to one of a set of laws instituted immediately after the Peloponnesian War, to be effective from the archonship of Eukleides (403/2).[5] Three surviving fragments show the gist of these laws. One of them is cited in two sources, Isaeus (6) and Demosthenes (43):

> a) For according to the law no male or female *nothos* (bastard) has any claim, based on kinship on either side (*anchisteia*), to *hiera kai hosia*, as of the archonship of Eukleides.[6]

The context of this clause was probably a law on the role of the *anchisteia* (relatives both on the paternal and maternal side) in succession.[7] A remark in Athenaeus seems to refer to the same or a related law:

> b) The orator Aristophon, the same who proposed in the archonship of Eukleides that he, who was not born from an *aste*, was a *nothos*.[8]

A third passage refers to a law making legitimacy a condition of sharing in the *polis*:

> c) Eumelos the Peripatetic says in the third book on Old Comedy that Nikomenes passed a decree that as of the archonship of Eukleides no one was to participate (*metechein*) in the *polis*, who could not prove that both

4 Dem. 57.30: τοῖς χρόνοις τοίνυν οὕτω φαίνεται γεγονὼς ὥστε, εἰ καὶ κατὰ θάτερ' ἀστὸς ἦν, εἶναι πολίτην προσήκειν αὐτόν· γέγονε γὰρ πρὸ Εὐκλείδου. This condition would apply to Euxitheos' father and mother, but Euxitheos mentions it specifically with regard to his father, who was alleged to have been a *xenos*.

5 See further Chapter 3. On the rationale behind the year 403/2 in the context of the revision of the laws in the last decade of the fifth century see Todd (1993) 58.

6 Is. 6.47; law *ap*. Dem. 43.51: ἐκεῖ μὲν γὰρ ἔστι νόθῳ μηδὲ νόθῃ μὴ εἶναι ἀγχιστείαν μήθ' ἱερῶν μήθ' ὁσίων ἀπ' Εὐκλείδου ἄρχοντος. Dem. 43 (*Against Macartatus*) was long considered spurious, but its genuineness is defended by Usher (1999) 244, 266–7 with n. 78, and confirmed by MacDowell (2009) 87, who dates it to the late 340s.

7 Cf. Is. 11.11–12.

8 Ath. 13.577b: Ἀριστοφῶν δ' ὁ ῥήτωρ, ὁ τὸν νόμον εἰσενεγκὼν ἐπ' Εὐκλείδου ἄρχοντος ὃς ἂν μὴ ἐξ ἀστῆς γένηται νόθον εἶναι.

> parents were *astoi*, but that those before Eukleides were to be let off without problems.[9]

The fragments reflect legislation stating what counts as legitimate birth as an Athenian and making legitimacy a condition for the exercise of inheritance rights and for active participation in the *polis*. Together, these laws amount to citizenship laws so similar to Pericles' Citizenship Law of 451/0 that we may regard them as a re-institution of this law. Euxitheos' testimony confirms the implication of these three citations that these citizenship laws were not retroactive. All the citations are framed negatively, i.e. that someone with the status of *nothos/e* can *not* share. Passage b) specifies that birth from a citizen woman (*aste*) is crucial for citizen status, probably assuming an Athenian father as the default. What background made someone a *nothos* or *nothe*, and what this status meant for one's claims to membership of the family and the *polis*, are much disputed questions. I concur with Cynthia Patterson that a *nothos*/*nothe* was someone born from parents whose relationship was not the result of the solemn transfer of a bride by her father to a husband of equal status.[10]

In law, clearly legitimate birth from two Athenian parents and concurrent inheritance rights in the family (passages a and b) were fundamental for having a share and participation (*metechein*) in the *polis* (passage c), amounting to a conception of citizenship that was the core of Euxitheos' defence. What legitimately born citizens share in is indicated by the expression *hiera kai hosia* in passage a), whereas Demosthenes referred to citizens' *metechein* not in the *hiera kai hosia*, but in *hiera* and *koina* (common things).[11] *Koina* is a wider and less specific notion than *hosia*, and these passages suggest that *ta hosia* have a relationship to *koinonia* (community).

Hiera kai hosia feature also as the essence of the community in a defence Antiphon wrote for a citizen of Mytilene accused of being involved by an Athenian, Lykinos, in the murder of a certain Herodes, in ca. 420. It is uncertain whether this speech was composed for a real trial or as rhetorical

9 Schol. Aeschin. 1.39: Εὔμηλος ὁ Περιπατητικὸς ἐν τῷ τρίτῳ περὶ τῆς ἀρχαίας κωμῳδίας φησὶ Νικομένη τινὰ ψήφισμα θέσθαι μηδένα τῶν μετ' Εὐκλείδην ἄρχοντα μετέχειν τῆς πόλεως, ἂν μὴ ἄμφω τοὺς γονέας ἀστοὺς ἐπιδείξηται, τοὺς δὲ πρὸ Εὐκλείδου ἀνεξετάστως ἀφεῖσθαι.

10 Patterson (1990) 41: '*nothos* is properly contrasted with *gnesios* (legitimate, well-born) [but] not equivalent to the English terms "illegitimate" or "born out of wedlock". In general, a *nothos/e* is a child born of a mixed or unequal union – in the sense that the transfer of the woman (mother) to the husband (father) was not contracted by socially equal partners – who retains a recognized relationship with his or her father.' On the proper procedure and its effect on inheritance rights, see Chapter 3.

11 Dem. 57.3; see above, Chapter 1.1.

instruction, but in either case Antiphon had to make his arguments convincing, and to do so he had to engage ideas and values he expected his Athenian audience to share. The speaker claims that neither Lykinos nor he himself had any motive to desire the death of Herodes, let alone to run the risks involved in committing murder. When witnesses had testified that Lykinos had brought no legal action against Herodes, the speaker comments, not without irony:

> So this was supposed to mean that Lykinos let Herodes go, but instead decided to bring both himself and me into grave danger by killing the man, knowing that if he were found out, he would not only deprive me of my fatherland (*patris*) but also deprive himself of *hiera kai hosia* and of the other things that among mankind are valued the greatest and most highly.[12]

Exile – being excluded from the *polis* – is here tantamount to being excluded from *hiera kai hosia*, crucial elements without which a man has no social existence. As in the previous passages, *hiera kai hosia* seem to be the heart of what every Athenian shares both in the family and in the *polis*.

2.2 A Citizen-by-decree

In all these cases, sharing in *hiera kai hosia* was the key element in the status of citizens of legitimate birth from two Athenian parents. But the same expression occurs in the case of a man who was not an Athenian by birth, but made an Athenian by a decree of the *boule* and *demos*. Charidemos from Oreos on Euboea was a mercenary captain who had proved himself a valuable if wily helpmate of Athens in its struggles with Philip of Macedon and who had close ties to the kings of Thrace. The Athenians granted him citizenship probably in 357/6.[13] In 353, King Kersobleptes of Thrace sent an ambassador to persuade the Athenians that Charidemos could recapture Amphipolis for the Athenians if they appointed him their general. For the details of the case, we depend almost entirely on a speech written by Demosthenes for a certain Euthykles (Dem. 23).[14]

Following the debate in the *boule*, a certain Aristocrates proposed that Charidemos was to be inviolable. According to Demosthenes the proposed decree ran more or less as follows: 'if anyone kills Charidemos, he shall be

[12] Antiph. 5.62: ἀπεστέρει μὲν ἐμὲ τῆς πατρίδος, ἀπεστέρει δὲ αὑτὸν ἱερῶν καὶ ὁσίων καὶ τῶν ἄλλων ἅπερ μέγιστα καὶ περὶ πλείστου ἐστὶν ἀνθρώποις. Cf. Dem. 23.40; Lyc. *Leoc.* 5, 9: the *polis* represented by its *hiera koina*, and 77: the fatherland, with all things *hiera* and *hosia*.

[13] Demosthenes (23.203) adds 'because of Kersobleptes'. See Osborne T 51 (III, 56–8). Date: Lambert (2012a) 112 n. 33.

[14] For the identity of the speaker, given in Dion.Hal. *Amm.* 1.4, Martin (2009) 118–19.

liable to seizure everywhere and if any *polis* or private person rescues him, they shall be cut out from our pledges'.[15] Anyone who killed him, would be prosecuted for murder and any *polis* or individual who received the killer would be cut off from the sworn ties which bound them to Athens. Euthykles then brought a *graphe paranomon* against Aristocrates' proposal. He argued that it was against the laws of Athens but also against Athens's interests in a wider sense, and, above all, that Charidemos did not deserve all these honours (18).[16] Citizenship was given to Charidemos for pragmatic reasons: to encourage him to take Athenian interests more to heart than he probably otherwise would have done.[17] Against this instrumental view of honours for Charidemos, the speaker advances the need to respect the antiquity and value of Athens's institutions.[18] We should not take all the speaker's contentions at face value, but the speech is invaluable as an account of the political and religious values at Athens on which the speaker relied to make his case that the proposal was illegal,[19] and gives us an exceptional insight into the discourse in which *hiera kai hosia* and its meaning for citizenship were embedded.

After pointing out that the proposal grants to Charidemos a privilege even greater than is common for citizens by birth (24), the speaker embarks on an exegesis of Athens's laws on homicide. Being *hosios* (38, 54), respectful of the religious feelings (*eusebeia*) of the *polis* (25) and just (*dikaios*), these laws were absolutely precise concerning the when, why and how of the murder charge, defining various kinds of homicide and protecting from malice or unjust private vengeance what should be left to the archons and the courts to judge. By contrast, the proposed inviolability gives Charidemos licence to act as he sees fit, for no one would dare to take action against Charidemos or even defend himself, for fear of Athens's reprisal. Here, the proposal was 'manifestly against the laws – not

[15] Dem. 23.91: ἐάν τις ἀποκτείνῃ Χαρίδημον, ἀγώγιμος ἔστω, ἐὰν δέ τις ἀφέληται ἢ πόλις ἢ ἰδιώτης, ἔκσπονδος ἔστω; slight variations at 16–17: ἂν γὰρ ἀποκτείνῃ τις Χαρίδημον … ἀγώγιμον' ἐκ τῶν συμμάχων εἶναι. 27.35–36: πανταχόθεν, 'everywhere'.

[16] For the role of virtues and qualities in the assigment of honours to citizens and non-citizens, Chapters 5 and 6.

[17] For the importance of the 'hortatory intention' in Athenian honorific decrees, which became increasingly explicit at about this time, or shortly after, see Lambert (2011).

[18] MacDowell (2009) 196–206 argues that the legal arguments against Aristocrates' proposal are weak, but that Demosthenes' speech makes the most of its dangers by 'the effectiveness of its wording and rhetoric'.

[19] Martin (2009) 122–7 argues that Demosthenes presents the proposal as a potential source of *miasma*, because it would leave a future killer of Charidemos unpunished, and that Aristocrates, by defending such a law, is himself a source of impurity to the city.

only against the written law, but also against what is common (*koinos*) among the whole of mankind'.[20]

Now the speaker turns from the villainy of the man who made this unlawful proposal to the character of the man who is to be the recipient of this disastrous privilege. This man already had been granted the greatest gift the city could bestow, that of citizenship:

> It was we, men of Athens, who made Charidemos a citizen (*polites*), and by that gift bestowed upon him a share in our *hiera kai hosia*, in our traditions (*nomima*) and in everything in which it belongs to us (*meteinai*) to have a share.[21]

To evoke what this means, the speaker expounds extensively the fundamental institutions of Athens, beginning with the judicial functions of the Areopagus and the courts of the Palladion, the Delphinion and the Phreatto (65–81). The Areopagus stands out as the most venerable of all, instituted by the gods to sit in judgement on homicide, first on the killing of Halirrothios, son of Ares, by Poseidon, and next to adjucate between the Eumenides and Orestes (66).[22] When testifying at the Areopagus, the oath taker invokes destruction upon himself, his offspring and his goods, swearing on sacrificial animals slaughtered in the prescribed manner by *polis* officials (67–8). The laws defend both prosecutor and defendant, because these customs (*nomima*), instituted by heroes or gods, tried to make circumstances lighter in a humane way, in the best possible way they could.[23] The first clause of Aristocrates' proposal, 'if anyone kills Charidemos, he shall be liable to seizure everywhere', is an affront to these venerable institutions of Athens and the laws they uphold. The second clause, 'if any *polis* or private person rescues him, they shall be cut out from our pledges', violates 'the law that is common (*koinos*) among all mankind, that orders to receive a fugitive' (85).[24]

[20] Dem. 23.61: ... φανερῶς παράνομον, οὐ μόνον παρὰ τὸν γεγραμμένον νόμον, ἀλλὰ καὶ παρὰ τὸν κοινὸν ἁπάντων ἀνθρώπων.

[21] Dem. 23.65: Ἡμεῖς, ὦ ἄνδρες Ἀθηναῖοι, Χαρίδημον ἐποιησάμεθα πολίτην, καὶ διὰ τῆς δωρειᾶς ταύτης μετεδώκαμεν αὐτῷ καὶ ἱερῶν καὶ ὁσίων καὶ νομίμων καὶ πάντων ὅσων περ αὐτοῖς μέτεστιν ἡμῖν.

[22] Demosthenes deliberately portrays the origins of the Areopagus as ancient (τὰ παλαιὰ (66)); for the antiquity of the *polis* institutions founded by gods or heroes as a prominent feature of the conception of citizenship, see Chapters 3.5; 5.5. For a historical assessment of the origins of the Athenian courts, Carawan (1998) 114–18, 122, 133–5.

[23] Dem. 23.70.

[24] Dem. 23.85: τοὺς δὲ τὸν ἤδη πεφευγότα (θήσω γὰρ οὕτω) κατὰ τὸν κοινὸν ἁπάντων ἀνθρώπων νόμον, ὃς κεῖται τὸν φεύγοντα δέχεσθαι, ... εἶναι γράφει.

This section of the speech is framed by the gift of citizenship to Charidemos, opening with 'we gave him a share in our *hiera kai hosia*, in our traditions and in everything in which it belongs to us (*meteinai*) to have a share'. Demonstrating that Aristocrates' proposal in letter and in spirit violates the Athenian ancestral laws, values and traditions, the speaker evokes in the minds of the listeners the outstanding qualities of their institutions. Commitment to the laws on an equal basis is at the heart of being an Athenian citizen (86, 89). Not only is it unlawful to make laws that apply only to Charidemos but not to any other Athenian, but whoever is born an Athenian or is made into one has a share in all these laws, values and traditions that together make up the heart of the *polis* (126). Recurrent use of *eusebes*, *hosios* and references to the gods underscore the intimate connection between the piety of the *polis* and its laws, embodied in the *hiera kai hosia*. These, together with the *nomima* and *koina*, are, in Demosthenes' words, the core of the *polis* in its public domain, which Charidemos, who does not share in the *hiera kai hosia* of any Athenian family but, once made an Athenian, now shares. Gradually, the underlying question whether Charidemos was worth the exceptional honour of being made an Athenian citizen, and if his commitment to the *polis* can be trusted, is brought to the surface and answered negatively.

2.3 Sharing the City: Vocabulary

When Demosthenes (23 and 57) describes what citizenship entails, for born citizens as well as for citizens-by-decree, he uses *meta*-verbs combined with the expression *hiera kai hosia* or *hiera* and *koina*. This set of expressions was anchored in the laws on citizenship and legitimacy, and Demosthenes and Isaeus also use it in speeches on legitimacy and inheritance.[25] For Euxitheos, furthermore, Demosthenes calls being a citizen as 'to be a *polites*' or 'to be an Athenian'. When it concerns the grant of citizenship, he refers to this as 'to become a *polites*' (23.126), 'to make a *polites*' (65, 119, 141), 'asking for *politeia*' (127), 'to give *politeia*' (89, 151, 199, 200), but in inscribed citizenship decrees from the later fifth century onwards, what actually makes a citizen is not 'he will be a *polites*' but the speech act 'that *x* is an Athenian'.[26] In the decrees the phrase *hiera kai hosia* is absent,

[25] Dem. 39.35; Is. 6.47 (= Dem. 43.51).

[26] *Politeia* is used in citizenship decrees only in a non-formulaic, descriptive way; from the end of the fourth century on, εἰσαγαγεῖν τὴν δοκιμασίαν τῆς πολιτείας becomes a regular scrutiny clause. Osborne 1, 15–16. See below, Chapter 6.1.

as are *meta*-verbs used for citizenship. We thus find somewhat different strands of discourse on citizenship in law and oratory, and it is instructive to compare the vocabulary in these texts. What do all these terms mean and when are they employed?

Let us begin with the *meta*-verbs. The prefix, the preposition *meta*, indicates sharing, having something in common; *meteinai* and *metechein* are used very frequently in Greek discourse and normally their subject is a human being. In the vocabulary of citizenship the verbs with *meta* indicate that the subject is a part of the object (in the genitive).[27] From the fifth century onwards, the clearest expression for citizenship is *meteinai tes poleos*: it indicates not just accepted membership of the group, but also sharing in everything that belongs to that status, including a share in common property, actions etc.[28] An impersonal form of *meteinai*, for instance *metesti*, with something (in the genitive) and someone (in the dative) indicates that a share of the thing essentially belongs to that person.[29] A literal translation is 'it belongs to me intrinsically to have a share of this', and it is not easy to find an elegant equivalent in English that expresses the force of the construction. In both the personal and the impersonal forms, *meteinai* indicates that being a member and sharing are inherently connected and are an intrinsic element of one's existence. Euxitheos used all these forms of *meteinai* to indicate his claim to citizen status. Occasionally we find *prosekein* instead of *meteinai* in this construction, an expression Euxitheos also used.[30] Combined with the dative, *prosekein* means 'it belongs to me, it befits me to have this' and in this sense it is almost the same as *meteinai*. Yet *prosekein* puts the spotlight *on the person* to whom this belongs, whereas *meteinai* with genitive emphasises that one claims a share as a *part of a larger whole*, with others.[31]

While in citizenship contexts *meteinai* means *being* a citizen, *metechein* indicates *acting* as a citizen, because the verb with genitive means not just

27 LSJ *s.v.* μετά, I.

28 LSJ *s.v.* μετεῖναι. Likewise, for instance, a treaty in which all allies are equal shareholders (*meteinai*) in the command, when they decide on a common (genitive) military enterprise (Thuc. 5.47.7); cf. Hdt. 2.178 on the sanctuary called the Hellenion, founded in Egypt by nine cities from Asia Minor; other cities wishing to use this sanctuary (genitive) with (*meta*) the nine cannot claim to be equal participants (*meteinai*). But note that *meteinai* with a group of people in the *dative* indicates simply that one belongs to this group, without further claims; for instance, Zeus took beautiful Ganymede with him to Olympos to serve the wine, 'that he might be one of (*meteinai*) the immortals (dative)' (Hom. *Il.* 20.235).

29 LSJ *s.v.* μετεῖναι; μέτεστί μοί τινος.

30 Dem. 57.6: προσήκει μοι τῆς πόλεως; cf. Is. 10.16: a lawful claim.

31 LSJ *s.v.* μετά, I. Patterson (2005) points to *metechein* as the umbrella term for citizenship, with the rules of admittance to membership, which are the focus of citizenship law.

having a share, but active use of or participation in what one shares.[32] One could participate in 'everything', as shorthand for all activities the members of a Greek *polis* would do together.[33] *Metechein* often includes the property or other concrete things of the group, either shared ownership or using the property to some concerted end. Although the verbs *meteinai* and *metechein* occur frequently in Greek texts in multiple combinations with other lexemes, the expression *meteinai tes poleos* does not occur before the fifth century, *metechein tes poleos* not before the fourth.[34]

Polis and *politeia*, like *meteinai* and *metechein*, have some aspects in common while other aspects point in different directions. Historically, the notion of *polis* begins with the epic *p(t)olis*, referring to an acropolis (stronghold) where the community could find safety in times of danger and where the central cults and their sanctuaries were located; this meaning remained current unto the fifth century.[35] By extension, *polis* could mean the city with its surrounding countryside, a territory that included also many non-citizens, such as foreigners and slaves, who were nevertheless important for the *polis*'s social and economic life.[36] In the classical era the prevalent meaning of *polis* was 'community', a socio-political entity consisting of people with a common identity.[37] The *polis* included its landed property, partly common property and partly owned privately; as Aristotle put it, 'A *polis* is the total of the houses/families, the lands and the possessions enabling them to live well on their own.'[38] Since membership of the *polis* in this sense depended in the classical age on descent, not

[32] Examples of *metechein*: Theogn. 1.354: poverty shares the poet's life. Soph. *Phil.* 248; Eur. *Heracleid.* 8; *Ion* 1368; *Hel.* 1221; *Bacch.* 1184; Ar. *Eccl.* 590; *Plut.* 345; People are actively involved in a situation, be it prosperity or hardships, or join a group and share in its activities.

[33] Dem. 44.35.7: *koina* (common things); Andoc. 3.17: all share in all advantages of the peace; Is. 9.30.4: *koinonia* (community, here *thiasoi* of Heracles). Other forms of *metechein*: Thuc. 1 .27.1: founding a colony; Hyp. fr. 146: sharing *symmoria*; Hdt. 2.81: partaking in the Mysteries; Lys. 34.2: in rebellion in Piraeus; Pl. *Resp.* 465e2: burial.

[34] *Meteinai tes poleos* (fifth century): Soph. *OT* 630; (fourth century): Isoc. 16.46.8; Lys. 18.1; Dem. 57.1, 23, 55; Aeschin. 1.78.5, Arist. *Pol.* 1281a5. *Metechein tes poleos* (fourth century): Xen. *Hell.* 2.3.48; 4.4.6; [Lys.] 6.48.2; Dem. 57.51; Is. 3.37; Pl. *Leg.* 745c6; Arist. *Pol.* 1316b2; 1329a20; *Ath.Pol.* 26.3 etc. *Metechein* is used with respect to the law of 403/2 at Schol. Aeschin. 1.39 (above, n. 9), but this is a paraphrase, not a direct quotation.

[35] Hom. *Il.* 6.257; 11.181; 17.144; *Od.* 8.555; etc.

[36] Ober (1996) calls this the 'geo-*polis*'.

[37] I return to the meaning of *polis* below, Chapter 4.1–2. For an extensive discussion of the word and notion *polis*, developing from 'stronghold' to '(political) community', Sakellariou (1989) 27–211, summary on 208–11; Hansen (2000), Hansen (2007). *Polis* as the group of people sharing a habitat, Dem. 23.41; but sharing habitat insufficient to define a citizen, Arist. *Pol.* 1280b33–9; cf. 1275a7–8; 1278a15–35.

[38] Arist. *Oec.* 1343a10–11: Πόλις μὲν οὖν οἰκιῶν πλῆθός ἐστι καὶ χώρας καὶ κτημάτων αὔταρκες πρὸς τὸ εὖ ζῆν.

on actual habitation, an Athenian would be a member of the *polis* Athens whether s/he happened to be in Athens or elsewhere. In sum, a *polis* was in the first place a concrete entity (city, countryside, group of people), with a semantic range of on the one extreme the inclusion of people who were not citizens, on the other extreme the inclusion of citizens who lived elsewhere. *Polis* also acquired a more abstract meaning, like (political) community, state, but always with the concrete aspects of it implied. Although scholars rightly point out that a *polis* consists of its *politai*, the first cannot be equated with the latter; as Jacqueline Bordes aptly notes in her study of *politeia*:

> The word *polis* differs from *politeia* in that it expresses the tie between shared habitat and common past that assures the unity. *Politeia* inherits the values of *polis* and, without losing its concrete connotations, adds to them the notions of organisation and activity.[39]

The word *politeia* seems to emerge in the 430s and it soon became very common, widely attested in Thucydides, Antiphon, comedy, political philosophy and other writings of the late fifth and fourth centuries.[40] *Politeia* in all these texts refers to the body of rules which in the widest sense shape the *polis* as an organism: it includes unwritten rules and traditions, formal rules defining the political structure, and norms, values and customs moulding the way of life of the *polis*. The *politeia* comprises a part of the *polis* that deeply influences the whole, and it was generally felt that the convergence between the social climate of a *polis* and its *politeia* was strong and long-lasting. Their connection could be illustrated by the well-known organic metaphor in which the *polis* would be the body, the *politeia* its skeleton, but perhaps a better comparison would be its nerve system. In Isocrates' words, the *politeia* is 'the soul' (*psyche*) of the *polis*.[41]

We find, in sum, two different but obviously related words, *polis* coming into use much earlier than *politeia*. Their meanings overlap where they refer to the social and cultural aspects of community life, but in *politeia* the political structure of a society is more pronounced, especially when used in political philosophy.[42] In *Politics*, as we saw above, Aristotle moves from *polis* as socio-economic community to political community based on sharing, and for *politeia* slides from the order (*taxis*) of a *polis* to its system of political authority (*arche*). When Demosthenes used *politeia* in relation

[39] Bordes (1982) 128; transl. JB.
[40] The first occurrence in our record is Hdt. 9.33–4; see also Chapter 4.1.2.
[41] Isoc. *Areop.* 14. Cf. Dem. 21.63 for *politeia* as both the statutes and the spirit of the law.
[42] Bordes (1982) 91.

to grants of citizenship, however, he clearly meant that new citizens were to share (*metechein*) in the entire social, cultic and political system of Athens, not just in its political offices.[43]

2.4 Sharing in *Hiera kai Hosia*

Besides being combined with *polis*, the *meta*-verbs were also combined with *hiera kai hosia*, an expression that does not occur in inscribed Athenian decrees with grants of citizenship, but in a variety of other texts: historiography; forensic, civil and political oratory; political treatises; an inscribed oath; an honorific decree of a deme. With one exception, all of these occurrences originate in Athens and date to the fifth and fourth centuries.[44] Sometimes *hiera* and *hosia* as substantives appear with the articles, sometimes without.[45] As adjectives qualifying *chremata* (money, means), *hiera kai hosia* occur in fourth-century oratory on financial matters.[46]

Athenian literature also features many passages where *hieros* and *hosios*, either as adjectives or as substantives, occur separately but in close proximity, creating a resonance with each other. For instance, near the end of Aeschylus' *Seven against Thebes* of 467, the herald announces that Eteocles will be buried in the earth, because he shielded the gates of his city against the enemy and 'he died *hosios* towards the *hiera* of his fathers, beyond reproach where it is honourable for the young to die'.[47] *Hieros* and *hosios* also occur very frequently on their own as adjectives and substantives. Clearly *hiera kai hosia* played a crucial role in the conception of citizenship in Athens. To understand what this expression, which is not immediately obvious, meant, we need to clarify the components, the combination and its use in context.

[43] Dem. 23.89, 127, 151, 199, 200.

[44] Thuc. 2.52.3–4; Antiphon 5.62; Lys. 30.25; Dem. 23.65; Is. 6.47; Dem. 43.51; Aesch. 1.23; 1.39; Dem. 39.35; Dem. 23.40; Isoc. 7.66; Pl. *Leg.* 857b5; *Leg.* 878a7; Pl. *Resp.* 344a8; Xen. *Por.* 5.3–4; *Ath. Pol.* 46.3. [Dem.] 59.104, 111–12; Lyc. *Leoc.* 77; *SEG* 21.519; RO 88 ll. 8–9; *IG* II² 1215 (early third century). On many of these passages, Byzantine lexica offer commentaries, which I do not count among the primary sources here. The only non-Attic case is an honorific decree of the earlier third century, found in the sanctuary of Labraunda, in which a certain Diokles of Kos is granted *meteinai hieron kai hosion* with the Plataseis (*I.Labraunda* 48.13). Cf. Willamson (2013), on the possible connection of this decree with Athens.

[45] For instance, with articles: Isoc. 7.66; without articles: *Ath.Pol.* 43.6; RO 88 ll. 8–9.

[46] Dem. 24: τὰ χρήματα τά τε ἱερὰ καὶ τὰ ὅσια; 9, 11, 82, 96 (διοίκησις ἱερὰ καὶ ὁσία), 101, 111, 112, 120, 130, 137; Hyp. fr. 32. καὶ τὰ χρήματα τά τε ἱερὰ καὶ τὰ ὅσια.

[47] Aesch. *Sept.* 1010–11: ἱερῶν πατρώιων δ' ὅσιος ὢν μομφῆς ἄτερ / τέθνηκεν οὗπερ τοῖς νέοις θνήισκειν καλόν· Likewise Soph. *OC* 469–70 (the chorus asks the immigrant Oedipus to purify himself for the gods of the place he has entered): πρῶτον μὲν ἱερὰς ἐξ ἀειρύτου χοὰς / κρήνης ἐνεγκοῦ, δι' ὁσίων χειρῶν θιγών ('First bring *hieros* libations from an ever-flowing stream, touching them with *hosios* hands').

2.4.1 *What Are* Hiera?

Recent scholarship is more or less agreed on the essential features of *hiera* and on the 'embeddedness' of ancient Greek religion in social practices and values. I review here concisely the relevant elements.[48]

1) *Ta hiera* in the classical age was an umbrella term for things set aside for the gods.[49] Although the verb 'to give' is rarely used in combination with *ta hiera*, contextual evidence makes clear that normally *hieros* designated what belonged to the gods *as a gift from humans*.[50] *Ta hiera* captured a great variety of such gifts: primarily animal sacrifice (*thysia*), libations and other offerings, but also votives of many kinds, hymns and songs, dances, musical and athletic competitions, plots of land, buildings and money.[51] Once a thing was *hieros* it normally remained so indefinitely – there is no unambiguous evidence that *hieros* things were or could be desacralised.[52] For landed property in particular, 'ownership' in the sense of control of the property and its revenues was shared between the *polis* and the gods in a way which does not fit our modern notion of ownership as 'having

[48] Parker, *PS* describes most Athenian *hiera* in their social context of the fifth and fourth centuries in a way that mostly serves my purposes here very well.

[49] Older scholarship showed the etymology of *hieros* to indicate 'strength' (Jay-Robert (2009) 16–20) and occasionally (e.g. in lyric poetry) *hieros* indicates that a thing is dear to the gods or within their sphere of influence, but in classical Greek generally the meaning 'sacred, *of* the gods' is firmly entrenched; the adjective distinguished such items from things or persons that were innately pure or divine, called *hagnos*, *hagios*, *theios* or *semnos*, Parker (1983) 147–53, 323. LSJ *s.v.* ἱερός; Chadwick (1996) *s.v.* ἱερός; esp. 150–5. Cf. Rudhardt (1992) 29–30, for ἱερός meaning 'given to the god(s)'. Hesych. *s.v.* ἱερός notes σέμνος (holy), ἥμερος (cultivated), ἀγαθός (good); *s.v.* ἱερά· θυσία (sacrifices), κειμήλια (treasures); *s.v.* ἱερῶν: θείων. Ἀττικῶς ἐπὶ τῶν μελλόντων βουλὴ λέγεται, καὶ ἐκκλησία, 'of divine things; in Attic the things the council and assembly had to deal with'.

[50] Sacrifice is giving: Pl. *Euthyphro* 14c: Οὐκοῦν τὸ θύειν δωρεῖσθαί ἐστι τοῖς θεοῖς, τὸ δ' εὔχεσθαι αἰτεῖν τοὺς θεούς; Καὶ μάλα, ὦ Σώκρατες. 'Is it then the case that sacrificing is making a gift to the gods and praying is making a request to them?' 'Yes, certainly'. See Pl. *Pol.* 290c–d on the role of *hiereis* in the process of giving; the prefix *hier-* in the terms for and relating to cult personnel (*hiereus*, *hiereia*, *hieropoios* etc.) indicates those in charge of handling *hieros* things and the process of making them so; Connelly (2007) 8–10.

[51] Hdt. 2.40: how the Egyptians perform their *hiera* (sacrifice); 2.57 divination from sacrificial animals (*hiera*) originally an Egyptian skill, 7.21 reading *hiera* practised in Greece, 8.36 *hiera chremata*: all the valuables belonging to the goddess; 3.104.6: the Athenians and other Greeks send their choruses with *hiera* (sacrifices, gifts) to the festival on Delos; Demosthenes labels the robes worn at the Dionysia *hieros* (21.69) to imply that Meidias was also guilty of damaging the god's property. Dem. 21.114–15: the *hiera* (sacrifices) on behalf of the *boule* and *polis*; Dem. 20.126–7: *ta hiera* for the whole system of *polis* sacrifices etc. From the mid-third century (*IG* II^2 807.6–7) observations of the positive outcome of sacrifice are often inscribed (τὰ ἱερὰ καλά). For the terminology of gifts to the gods, Patera (2012) 17–51.

[52] Verbs like ἀφιερόω and καθιερεύω mean 'to consecrate, dedicate, fulfil what is due to the gods', never 'to bring property of the gods into human ownership'.

full title and full right of disposal'.[53] The *polis* did all the management, the nominal owner remained the god. This principle is particularly striking in the case of treasure belonging to the gods but borrowed by and circulating among humans, often for a very long time.[54] The singular substantive *hieron* usually referred to a sanctuary, a plot of land reserved 'to serve the gods'.[55] By extension *ta hiera* could encompass the entire process of honouring, consecration and gift-giving to the gods, making *ta hiera* the Greek word closest to 'religion'.[56]

2) Essential to *ta hiera* is what they mean and do. They are human gifts to the gods *in a chain of gratitude and obligation*, engendering *charis* in the divine recipients towards the human givers.[57] Humans toiled to achieve what they wanted, but they needed the divine powers (fertility, courage, justice, victory) to make their efforts effective.[58] For their contributions the gods expected fitting honours, gratitude and rewards, in the form of gifts and of the effort necessary to produce them, an aspect particularly tangible in the *hiera* that are a 'first share' of the produce.[59] The gods' engagement with a particular *polis*, in this case Athens, was captured in the expression that the gods 'held' the *polis* as its protectors and as the beneficiaries of its gifts.[60] Most scholars characterise the relationship between ancient Greeks and their gods as 'reciprocity', because the same sense of well-being, grace and gratitude (*charis*) that ideally

[53] Rousset (2013) esp. 125, *contra* Migeotte (2006) and Papazarkadas (2011). For the personnel of the *polis*'s administrative control of sacred property, see Chapter 5.

[54] E.g. Thuc. 2.13.3–5: when Pericles told the Athenians that they could use the treasure belonging to Athena for their self-preservation (ἐπι σωτηρίαι) provided they gave it back. This is what they did: the Golden Nikai melted down to strike coins in 407 were restored in the time of Lycurgus; [Plut.] *X orat.* 852b, Paus. 1.29.16. Cf. Samons (2000) 245–6 and n. 127. *Contra*: Patera (2012) 87 who, despite acknowledging that all borrowings from the gods had to be returned in one form or the other, nonetheless thinks that such loans were 'facts that contribute to nuancing the theory of the inalienability of gifts to gods' (transl. JB).

[55] Poll. *Onom.* 1.6–10. See Miles (2014) for the significance of temples as the focal points of religious commonality of Greek *poleis*.

[56] Rudhardt (1992) 26–9; Parker, *PS*, 61.

[57] Versnel (1981), Parker (1998), Jim (2014) 60–95 on the religious mentality involved in this reciprocity; Pulleyn (1997), Patera (2012) 57–73 on the connection between prayer, sacrifice and *charis*; Van Straten (1981), Van Straten (1995) 1–9 and 53–62, 159 for votives accompanying sacrifice; Keesling (2003) 3–10, Jim (2014) on *euche* (vow), *aparche* (first fruits) and *dekate* (tithe) as motives of votives. For scholarship on the gift, Wagner-Hasel (2003).

[58] For all the aspects of Athenian society for which the gods of Athens were essentially responsible, see Parker, *PS*, 387–415: 'Gods at work: protecting the city' and 416–44: 'Gods at work: the growth of plants and men'.

[59] *Aparchai* (the first produce) and *dekatai* (tithes), Jim (2014) 17–21.

[60] Dem. 19.257, 267; cf. Parker, *PS*, 2. When the Athenians evacuated Attica in 480, Pallas Athena also left the Acropolis, Hdt. 8.41. The gods holding 'Thebes' in Athenian tragedy, Aesch. *Sept.* 312, 822.

ensured human reciprocity as the outcome of gift exchange characterised the relations between humans and the gods.[61] Yet, not only were the gods immortal and humans mortal, but the gifts of the gods were inevitably much greater than humans could ever return; their relationship was thus infinitely more unequal than between any human parties. Given this insurmountable hierarchy between gods and humans, we find expressions of deep gratitude towards the gods as well as of a sense of debt.[62]

3) *Ta hiera* were both the instrument and the focus of *commonality*; and above all 'the *polis* anchored, legitimated, and mediated all religious actions'.[63] *Metechein* in *hiera* meant in the first place sharing in honouring the gods in cults, notably in the form of sacrifice. Sharing in sacrificial meat was the core religious action, creating simultaneously connections between humans and gods and among the humans involved.[64] But sharing in *hiera* also included partaking in the festivals, other cultic festivities and competitions of which sacrifice usually was a central event.[65] Not all Greek religion

[61] Reciprocity as fundamental attitude in Greek religion, Yunis (1988), Parker (1998), Jim (2014); in hymns Bremer (1998); in gifts Linders (1975), Lazzarini (1989–90). For the intimate connection between reciprocity and *charis*, Blundell (1989) 33, Goldhill (1998) 115, Jim (2014) 23–7. The qualification of a relationship as 'reciprocity' is typically made by an outside observer, not by the participants themselves, who usually apply culturally specific value terms and qualifications to their relationships. Different forms of reciprocity, Van Wees (1998); conceptions of reciprocity in classical Athens, Van Berkel (2012), esp. 40–8 on definitions and types.

[62] Gratitude: Jim (2014) 23–7; in the form of praise: Versnel (1981), Pulleyn (1997) 39–55; debt: Pl. *Resp.* 331b: τὸ γὰρ μηδὲ ἄκοντά τινα ἐξαπατῆσαι ἢ ψεύσασθαι, μηδ' αὖ ὀφείλοντα ἢ θεῷ θυσίας τινὰς ἢ ἀνθρώπῳ χρήματα ἔπειτα ἐκεῖσε ἀπιέναι δεδιότα, μέγα μέρος εἰς τοῦτο ἡ τῶν χρημάτων κτῆσις συμβάλλεται. For a just man the possession of substantial wealth is a benefit, if one does not cheat any other man even unintentionally and if 'one is not in debt to a god for any sacrifice (*thysia*) or to any human for money, so that one departs in fear to the other world'. The verb 'to owe' combined with 'in fear' belongs to the sphere of debt, rather than of reciprocity, a term most anthropologists reserve for dealings between persons who at least *could* be more or less equals, whereas debt by definition entails a hierarchical relationship. Cf. Jim (2014) 17, 68–86, 215, 278, capturing the religious attitude in the formula *do quia dedisti*, so absolving a debt, but Greek prayers holding an equivalent of *da quia dedisti* and *da quia dedi* (Pulleyn (1997) 26–38) remind the *god* of his or her previous gifts to the human in order that s/he will do so *again*, a logic of precedent typical of debt relations in pre-modern societies (Graeber (2011) 103–20).

[63] Sourvinou-Inwood (2000b) 15, Sourvinou-Inwood (2000a); cf. Burkert (1995), Polignac (1995a), Georgoudi (1998); piety as the basis of civic obligation, Liddel (2007) 133–6. Jones (1999), by contrast, does not treat cult as a constitutive factor of the *koinoniai* of Athens.

[64] The debate on the meaning of sacrifice and the ensuing commensality in ancient Greece is vast; see Parker (2011) 124–70, Versnel (2011) 354–76 (focusing on Hermes, with extensive refs.); views on sacrifice, Bremmer (2010); commensality, Schmitt-Pantel (1992); distribution of sacrificial meat, Ekroth (2008b), Ekroth (2008a).

[65] For the role of competitions in forging social coherence and alleviating the tension of political ambitions in a ritual context, Osborne (2010a); experience and diversity of festivals, Parker (2011) 171–223; for forms of participation, see Chapter 5.

took place in and sustained the *polis*,[66] but most of it did and that is the part of Athenian religion that is relevant here. The crucial points are that the commonality created by the *majority* of cultic actions concerned the *polis* and its subgroups, that for the *majority* of pan-Hellenic cults the *polis* was the indispensable mediator and that 'the city determined whether a particular religious conception, at least insofar as it affected actual practice, was to be granted right of residence within its walls'.[67] What this meant for citizens' participation will be discussed in Chapter 5.

Beside the common *hiera*, performative oaths were of special importance for the *polis*.[68] Oaths grounded social ties in *hiera* (animal sacrifice or libation), so breaking an oath crucially damaged one's relations with the humans and gods involved.[69] Usually, an oath was entrenched in a clause invoking destruction by the gods not only of the one who broke his oath, but also of his descendants and property – in sum, an individual's total annihilation. In this respect, a destructive oath was the reverse of honours such as citizenship conferred on someone together with his descendants. Some oaths were taken to create commitment of the *polis* in its entirety, either on a specific occasion or as a recurrent event.[70] All male citizens entering office in political and administrative bodies took oaths, often collectively, to guarantee performance of their duties according to the laws.[71]

66 For this critical supplement to *polis* religion, Kindt (2009) and other contributions to *Kernos* 2009; Kindt (2012) 16–25, and Kindt (2015); see also Versnel (2011) 119–42 for personal religiosity within a *polis* context.

67 Parker (2011) 58–9.

68 Performative oaths need to be distinguished from exclamatory oaths ('by Zeus!' 'By the gods!' etc.) which could be meant more or less stringently depending on context (Rydberg-Cox (2000)). For treaties as collective oaths with libations, Dem. 23.85: *ekspondos*, from *sponde*, libation. *IG* I³ 21.71 a treaty of Athens with Miletus, *IG* I³ 37.38, 40 with Kolophon, *IG* I³ 54 with Leontini, *IG* I³ 127 *sympoliteia* with the Samians, etc. Truce, Thuc. 4.118.1; treaty, Thuc. 5.18.1, 9; truces for religious purposes, Dillon (1997) 1–26; effectiveness of taking oaths in interstate relations, Low (2007) 118–26, Bolmarcich (2007). Significance of oaths to the *polis* generally: Berti (2006) and the contributions to Sommerstein (2007).

69 For the power of social cohesion within the *polis* created by oaths and the gods' guarding of them, Lys. 31.31; Lyc. *Leoc.* 79.

70 Specific occasions: the oath the Athenians swore to keep Solon's laws for ten years before he began his work (Plut. *Sol.* 25; Hdt. 1.29.2; Rhodes, *CAAP ad Ath.Pol.* 7.1, 135); the oath of Demophantos intended to prevent the establishment of a tyranny (Andoc. 1.96–8), conventionally dated 410/9 after the first oligarchic regime, Shear (2007b) but see Matthaiou (2011) 81, n. 18 for doubts about this date.

71 *Ath.Pol.* 22.2: the oath of the *bouleutai*; *Ath.Pol.* 55.5: oaths by the archons, the *diaitetai* and witnesses; Rhodes (2007b). For the force of oaths in Athenian jurisdiction, Martin (2009) 252–65; for the elaborate oath of the archons: *Ath.Pol.* 55.2–5, with Rhodes, *CAAP ad loc.* and below, Chapter 3.3. The bouleutic oath: *IG* I³ 40 (Chalcis decree); *IG* I³ 1453–4ter (Coinage decree), Lys. 26.8, 31.1–2, [Dem.] 59.4, Dem. 24.144, etc. with Rhodes (1972) 194–9, arguing for an origin shortly

Other public oaths required specific sacrificial victims or invoked specific gods.[72] Women at Athens took oaths in some religious bodies of the *polis* and when supplying witness statements in trials at the Delphinion.[73]

In sum, *ta hiera* were 'things of the gods' because they were gifts offered by humans in return for the gods' generative power and protection. *Ta hiera* simultaneously created and recreated the *koinonia* vertically, between gods and humans, and horizontally, among humans. In this bond, the composition of the parties – the gods on the one hand and the human group on the other – had come about over many years. In the classical period, the origins of this relationship lay in the (imagined) origins of the *polis*, but for the present it was for the *boule* and assembly to decide if more gods and new humans could join.[74] The long-lasting bond anchored in traditional *hiera* made these gods the *polis*'s own; the Athena of Athens was in some respects a different goddess from the Athena of Thebes, even if ultimately she could be taken to be the same.[75] Beside its bond with the pan-Hellenic gods, the *polis* maintained its cultic bond with the heroes and heroines of Attica, who enjoyed an exclusive relationship with Athens.[76] Among all the congruent levels of communal cultic relationships, ranging

after the reforms of Cleisthenes and extension over the years in response to historical conditions (ca. 446/5, 410/9, 403/2). The dikastic oath: Aeschin. 1.154, 1.170, 2.1, 3.6; Antiph. 5.7; Dem. 18.2, 20.118, 24.150, 45.50; Isoc. 15.21 etc. with Mirhady (2007), Harris (2007). Cf. Cole (1996) for oath-taking creating commonality among men. On oaths in archaic jurisdiction, Papakonstantinou (2008) 112–21.

72 In civic oaths, Ares and Athena Areia, who rarely figured in other contexts, were regularly invoked; e.g. in the ephebic oath (RO 88 ll. 17–18), also below; and see further Willamson (2013). For the oaths in a homicide trial before the court of the Areopagus sacrifice of 'a boar, a ram and a bull' was required, slaughtered by particular officials on prescribed days (Dem. 23.68). The sacrificial calendar of Thorikos listed the victims for the oaths taken when deme officials accounted for their year of office (*euthynai*) and the oath itself was included in the inscribed text; *SEG* 33.147 (with Lupu (2005) 115–70) ll. 12, 57–65. Van Straten (1995a) 170–86 argues that the main motive in the choice of animals was their price, but this is more convincing for private sacrifices than for public ones.

73 Religious bodies: the oath of the Gerarai, [Dem.] 59.73, with Parker, *PS*, 304. Women's oaths at the Delphinion: Dem. 40.11; Is. 12.9; they rarely appeared in court but their sworn witness statements were orally reproduced at the trial; cf. Foxhall (1996). Evidence from other *poleis* shows women participating in 'foundational' oaths, e.g. ML 5.45–6: women and children take the oath with men in the founding of the colony Cyrene; *SEG* 51.642, an oath of *sympoliteia* between Naupaktos and Messene, ca. 430–420, is sworn by men and women. Shear (2011) 208 assumes that the reconciliation oath in 403 (Andoc. 1.90) followed the same procedure as the oath of Demophantos, i.e. that it was sworn by the male citizens by tribes and demes. Though there is no evidence on the point, however, it would not be surprising if women were involved, because, considering their key role in the care and remembrance of the family's dead, it would have been appropriate for women to be involved in renouncing vengeance for the many deaths due to the regime.

74 For the imagined origins, see also Chapter 5; for the classical system, Connor (1988); Parker, *PS*, 89.

75 For the intricacies of 'same' and 'different', and of 'common' meaning 'identical' or 'shared' in the Greek pantheon, Polinskaya (2010) and extensively Versnel (2011) 88–119. For differences 'within' each divinity expressed in cult epithets, Parker (2003).

76 Pulleyn (1997) 118–20 for *agatha* not only from the gods but also from the dead, notably heroes.

from the widest (pan-Hellenic) to the smallest (*oikos*) in which every Athenian participated, it seems hardly contestable that the *polis* level was the most salient, the strongest and most durable.

2.4.2 *What Is* Hosios?

Whereas the meaning of *ta hiera* is hardly controversial, *ta hosia* ('*hosios* things'), the other component of the expression *hiera kai hosia*, has long been a topic of debate.[77] The meaning of the adjective *hosios* has posed difficulties, and so has *ta hosia* used on its own and in combination with *ta hiera*. Before looking into these difficulties, let us first try to determine the usual meaning of *hosios*.

From the early fifth century to the late fourth century, in texts ranging from historiography, oratory, tragedy and other poetry to inscribed laws, decrees and accounts, *hosios* and its cognates were used widely as a value term with regard to what people do or say. *Hosios* indicates the proper conduct and respect of humans towards the gods and towards other humans; together, all actions that are *hosios* set a norm that is indicated by the noun *hosie*.[78] The conduct and mentality evaluated as *hosios* (or not) clearly cluster around proper respect for the gods by showing them fitting honour, and by honouring relationships between humans by which the gods set great store. In Herodotus' *Histories*, for example, such conduct is indicated by the expression 'it is *hosie*' or 'it is *hosion*' to do something, often framed in the negative – it is not *hosie* or *hosios* to do a certain thing.[79]

[77] For the debate on *hosios* Van der Valk (1942), Jeanmaire (1945), Van der Valk (1951), Eatough (1971), Burkert (1985) 269–70, Maffi (1982), Parker (1983) 329–33, Connor (1988), Rudhardt (1992) 30–5, Jay-Robert (1999), Chadwick (1996) *s.v.* ὅσιος, Schmidt, Samons (2000) 325–9, Scullion (2005), Willi (2008), Jay-Robert (2009), Martin (2009) 5–7, Mikalson (2010) 140–52, Patera (2012) 40–7. I discussed the meaning of *hosios* and cognates also in Blok (2010), Blok (2011), Blok (2014a); for a full semantic study of *hosios*, Peels (2015).

[78] To avoid confusion between (*ta*) *hosia* and (*he*) *hosia* (Attic), I have retained Ionic *hosie* also in Attic contexts.

[79] Hdt.: (οὐκ) ὁσίη ἐστί: 2.45 sacrifice; 2.171 it is *hosie* not to mention holy things; (οὐκ) ὅσιον ἐστί: 2.61 to mention a holy thing; 2.170, 2.81.5 burial rites; 2.81.8 participation in rites; 6.81 not *hosion* for a stranger to participate in sacrifice; 8.37 not *hosion* to touch a holy thing. Actions: 2.119 to do *hosios* things; cf. to avoid doing not *hosios* things: 3.16 to act against religious rules; 3.19 to harm one's children; 3.120 to plan murder of someone who did not harm you; 4.154 to plan murder of one's child; 4.146 to claim *timai* unjustly; 6.86 not to return hostages; 9.79 to do and to say *hosios* things. Jay-Robert (2009) 53–74 takes *to hosion* to be a specific sphere of divinely sanctioned law, but I do not find this convincing. The usage of *to hosion* in this form, i.e. the substantive used as an abstract term for the sphere of *hosie*, is quite rare, occurring in philosophical discourse on human values and norms, see e.g. Thuc. 3.84.2: οὐ γὰρ ἂν τοῦ τε ὁσίου τὸ τιμωρεῖσθαι προυτίθεσαν τοῦ τε μὴ ἀδικεῖν τὸ κερδαίνειν, ἐν ᾧ μὴ βλάπτουσαν ἰσχὺν εἶχε τὸ φθονεῖν. 'For surely no one would have put revenge before *to hosion* and gain before wrong, if envy had

The same expressions feature in a few inscribed regulations on sanctuaries, stating it is not *hosie* for certain groups, notably strangers or women, to enter or to participate in the ritual.[80] Although these cases are rare, *hosie* refers here to a vital element in the rules of ritual exchange with the gods, namely who is to participate in the rite.[81]

All norms captured in *hosie* and actions or thoughts evaluated as *hosios* are predicated, as Saskia Peels convincingly argues, on human relations of 'long-term reciprocity' – first of all with the gods, and then with relatives, notably between parents and children, towards (guest) friends and suppliants, and in proper care of the dead. Typically *hosios* acts are sacrifice and other such ritual acts, care for (ageing) parents, burial of the dead and keeping oaths.[82] *Hosie* and *hosios* are first attested in the *Odyssey* and archaic poetry, but the values they represent and the actions they prescribe both predate this epic and continue far beyond the classical era.[83]

The meaning of *hosios* is further clarified by its antonym *anhosios*, which makes its first datable appearance in Aeschylus' *Septem* of 467.[84] When Eteocles and a scout describe how the enemies act contrary to the gods'

not got hold of him with blinding force.' In this sentence, Thucydides creates a series of abstracta (here translated as revenge, gain, wrong and envy) by adding the article *to* to the verbs meaning 'doing …' and to *hosios*. In Pl. *Euthyphro*, the discussants try to distil and define an essential, abstract quality *to hosion*.

80 *ID* 68 (Delos) fifth century: ξένωι οὐχ ὁσίη ἐσι[ένα̣ι] 'It is not *hosie* for a stranger to enter'; *IG* XII, 1 (Lindos II) 26 (ca. 400): γυναιξὶ ὀκ ὅσια. 'For a woman not *hosie*' (to enter? participate in sacrifice?); *IG* XII, 1, N. Suppl. Epig. Rodio 169, 20a (Rhodos; fourth century): γυναὶξι οὐχ ὁσία. Compare: *LSCG* 109 (*IG* XII, 5, 183; Paros) fifth century: ["Ο]ρος Ὑπάτο · ἀτ[ελ]έστοι οὐ θέμ[ι]ς, οὐδὲ γυναι[κ]ι. 'Boundary of (Zeus) Hypatos. (It is) not *themis* for an uninitiated (man) nor for a woman (to enter)'. Lupu (2005) 14–30 on entrance as not the same as participation in ritual; on rules forbidding entrance to foreigners, Butz (1996), Funke (2006), and to women, Cole (1992), who holds that such rules against women's participation were widespread, whereas Osborne (1993) convincingly argues that this was not the case, and Peels (2015) 168–206 shows that such regulations forbidding entrance are exceptions to an (implicit) convention of wide participation.

81 Comparable regulations pronounced 'it is not *themis*' instead of 'it is not *hosie*'; cf. Hesych. *s.v.* ὅσιη; Suda, η 152 Ἦ θέμις: ὡς νόμος, ὡς προσῆκον. *Themis* divine: Hes. *Th.*16, 135, 901 (mother of *Dike* with Zeus); *Themis* = justice: Suda θ 114 (Adler); foundation of *dikazein*, Stafford (1997); Gagarin (2008) 30; speaking *themis* = oracular response, Suda θ 118, 281. Themis and the Horai represent the cyclic aspects of time in the renewal of nature and recurrence of festivals (e.g. Pind. *Pae.* 1, 5–7); Rudhardt (1999); Pavlou (2011).

82 Care for parents also required of magistrates: Xen. *Mem.* 2.2.14; Aeschin. 1.28; Dem. 57.70; Dem. 19.311–12: Aeschines' besmirching the legacy of the dead ancestors deserves to be condemned by a *hosios* vote.

83 For the earliest cases of *hosios*/*hosie*, Hom. *Od.* 16.421–5; *Od.* 22. 411–15; *Hom. Hymn. Dem.* 207–11.

84 Doing *anhosios* things or being *anhosios*, Hdt. 1.59; 2.114–15; 8.106; 8.109; 9.78. Note especially the killing of the 'false Smerdis' by those nearest (οἰκηιοτάτοι) to him as an *anhosios* death (3.65). Two instances of *anhosios* occur in the fables attributed to Aesop: *Fab.* 57.6: one should not listen to a man who is *anhosios*; *Fab.* 304.1.3: a daughter reproaches her father, who has fallen in love with her, that he does *anhosia*.

will and defy divine supremacy, whereas the Thebans act with the gods on their side, the chorus of Theban girls exclaims how frightened they are,

> when I hear the loud boasts of these loud-mouthed
> *anhosios* men. If the gods are really gods,
> may they destroy them in this land![85]

Calling their enemies *anhosios*, the chorus denounces their deeds and attitude, testifying to their lack of respect for the gods. In the *Suppliants*, produced between 470 and 459, *anhosios* captures again the utter lack of respect for the gods displayed by the sons of Aegyptus, particularly their disregard of the conventions of supplication among humans protected by the gods.[86]

The strong values of *hosios* and *anhosios* made these adjectives and their cognates important ingredients of persuasive discourse. In Antiphon's speech *On the murder of Herodes*, the speaker tries to turn the values of *hosios* into proof of guilt or innocence:

> I hardly think I need to remind you that many a man who, without *katharos* (pure) hands or with some other form of pollution, has embarked on board a ship has destroyed, together with his own life, the people who are in a condition of being *hosios* towards the gods. Others, while they have escaped death, have had their lives imperiled owing to such polluted wretches. Many, too, have been proven to be *anhosios* as they stood beside a sacrifice (*ta hiera*), because they prevented the sacrifice to be as it should be. With me, the opposite has happened in every case. Not only have fellow passengers of mine enjoyed the calmest of voyages, but whenever I attended a sacrifice, the sacrifice has always been very successful.[87]

Pointing out that the gods are favourable towards him, and to the fellow men in his presence, the speaker draws here on shared notions of religious practice and norms to make his case. The gods accept sacrifice only from people who are *hosios*, of which purity is an indispensable condition. When everyone is *hosios*, the gods act favourably towards human society, keeping all safe and sound. Pollution (*miasma*) incurred by violent death, by contrast, affects first of all the killer, but with him the entire community, since the gods would be displeased towards a community harbouring

85 Aesch. *Sept.* 565–7; transl. A.H. Sommerstein (Loeb ed.).

86 Aesch. *Suppl.* 762–3; transl. A.H. Sommerstein (Loeb ed.). Peels (2015) 84–106 concludes that *anhosios* is not merely the antonym of *hosios*, but has a pragmatic use of its own: a strong rejection frequently used in emotionally highly charged contexts and usually due to multiple motives for disqualification.

87 Antiph. 5.82.

anhosios individuals.[88] Divine displeasure would be noticed immediately, as the community is hit by a misfortune such as drought or sickness – many tragedies staged at Athens depicted such calamities due to divine anger – nor would the gods accept the sacrifices offered to them, aggravating the perilous situation. Being *hosios* is therefore not only the virtue of a single person, but of great concern to the entire community.[89]

While the conditions for proper exchange with the gods create a partial affinity between *hosios* and *katharos*, proper exchange with other humans juxtapose *hosios* with *dikaios*.[90] When Socrates asks Euthyphro in the Platonic dialogue named after him what is *to hosion*, the essence of *hosios*, Euthyphro, although an acclaimed expert in *ta theia* (divine matters), is unable to give a satisfactory answer.[91] He first states:

> the part of the just (*to dikaion*) which has to do with service of the gods constitutes what is pious (*eusebes*) and *hosios*, and ... the remaining part of the just is that which has to do with the service of men.[92]

Euthyphro knows that *hosie* and *dike* have something in common but are not the same; the latter has more to do with the agreements between humans, whereas *to hosion* is primarily concerned with giving the gods what is their due. But when he proves unable to defend this definition more stringently, Euthyphro ventures that *hosios* is human conduct generally that pleases the gods, especially giving gifts to honour them and

[88] Athenian orators frequently refer to the threat of divine displeasure with the *polis* if murder were unpunished, causing *miasma*, or if *asebeia* were condoned, or oaths broken, Martin (2009) *passim*.

[89] Carawan (1998) 171–93 argues that Antiphon in *On the murder of Herodes* ascribes to *miasma* a more limited effect on society than in the *Tetralogies*, which claim that the risks of *miasma* may spread to the *dikastai* themselves and the entire *polis*. Carawan (171–93, 390–1) dates the *Tretralogies* shortly after 400 and *On the murder of Herodes* ca. 420.

[90] The earliest case of this juxtaposition is Theogn. 131–2: Οὐδὲν ἐν ἀνθρώποισι πατρὸς καὶ μητρὸς ἄμεινον/ἔπλετο, οἷσ' ὁσίη, Κύρνε, μέμηλε δίκη. 'Nothing, Kyrnos, among humans is better than a father and a mother who observe *hosios dike*.'

[91] Sluiter and Rosen (2008) argue that the interlocutors in Socratic dialogues are highly representative of everyday Attic language use; the attempts of Euthyphro to explain *to hosion* may accordingly be taken to render the common understanding of *hosios* in classical Athens.

[92] Pl. *Euthyphro* 12e: Τοῦτο τοίνυν ἔμοιγε δοκεῖ, ὦ Σώκρατες, τὸ μέρος τοῦ δικαίου εἶναι εὐσεβές τε καὶ ὅσιον, τὸ περὶ τὴν τῶν θεῶν θεραπείαν· τὸ δὲ περὶ τὴν τῶν ἀνθρώπων τὸ λοιπόν εἶναι τοῦ δικαίου μέρος. Socrates proposes the same description in Gorgias, 507a6–b3: Καὶ μὴν ὅ γε σώφρων τὰ προσήκοντα πράττοι ἂν καὶ περὶ θεοὺς καὶ περὶ ἀνθρώπους· οὐ γὰρ ἂν σωφρονοῖ τὰ μὴ προσήκοντα πράττων; – Ἀνάγκη ταῦτ' εἶναι οὕτω. – Καὶ μὴν περὶ μὲν ἀνθρώπους τὰ προσήκοντα πράττων δίκαι' ἂν πράττοι, περὶ δὲ θεοὺς ὅσια· τὸν δὲ τὰ δίκαια καὶ ὅσια πράττοντα ἀνάγκη δίκαιον καὶ ὅσιον εἶναι. Ἔστι ταῦτα. 'A wise man, I should say, acts towards gods and towards humans in a way that befits (*proseko*) them; and if he did not do so, he would not be wise.' 'Yes, that must be the case.' 'And doing what befits humans, that would be what is just (*dikaia*), and what befits gods, *hosia*; that means that doing *dikaia* and *hosia* is being *dikaios* and *hosios*.' 'Yes, indeed.'

feeling *charis* towards them.[93] Socrates finally objects that this definition is tautological, and the dialogue ends with the question unsolved.

Hosios typically captures humans' obligations towards the gods and not obligations of gods towards humans.[94] Discourse relating *hosios* with *dikaios* invokes an order in which everyone, human and divine, receives what is due and proper, *dikaios* referring to the relevant rules laid down in human laws, *hosios* to the obligation to please the gods by living up to these standards. It is the particular concern of Zeus that all of this will be observed. In classical Athens, litigants such as Euxitheos often referred to the oath the *dikastai* took to be just in accordance with the laws, reminding them that their votes should be *dikaios* (laws) and *hosios* (oath).[95]

If *dikaios* usually has to do with the laws of a particular *polis*, *dike* and *hosie* are norms that also go far beyond the boundaries of a single city: they are 'laws common to all mankind', to quote Demosthenes.[96] Supplication and its intended effect, protection offered to those who ritually ask for it, are crucial acts of *hosie* crossing the boundaries of *poleis* and other states, as the epigraph to this chapter illustrates. Persuasive use of *hosios* and *dikaios* between different *poleis* is well exemplified in Thucydides' account of the conflict between the Thebans and Plataians in 427, when the latter claim in their verbal contest before the Spartan adjucators:

> They [the Thebans] attempted to seize our city in time of truce and on a festival day; therefore we were right (*orthos*) in punishing them according to a law (*nomos*) which is valid among all, that it is *hosios* to repel him who comes to you as an enemy.[97]

93 Pl. *Euthyphro* 15b: E.: [the gods gain advantage from what they get from us. S.: What then would those gifts of ours to the gods be?] E: What else than τιμή τε καὶ γέρα καὶ ... χάρις;

94 A few cases of gods' conduct called *hosios* or following *hosie* (*Hom. Hymn Merc.* 130: ἔνθ' ὁσίης κρεάων ἠράσσατο κύδιμος Ἑρμῆς. 173: ἀμφὶ δὲ τιμῆς / κἀγὼ τῆς ὁσίης ἐπιβήσομαι ἧς περ Ἀπόλλων) demonstrably aim at a powerful effect by deliberately creating a reversal of the normal order, applying to the gods themselves the language of human obligations to the gods. These cases are precisely exceptions proving the rule that *hosie* and cognates designate human obligations to the gods. On these passages, Versnel (2011) 319–29, 367–76, with discussion of other readings. Expanding these cases with those in tragedies (e.g. Eur. *Or.* 595), Peels (2015) 149–67.

95 Antiph. 4.11: be very *hosios* and *dikaios*; 6.51: avoid being *anhosios*; cf. 5.141: be *eusebes* and *dikaios*. *Hosios*: Lys. 13.3, 4, 93, 97; Pl. *Leg.* 767c5–d5; Is. 6.65: ὑμεῖς τε τὴν ψῆφον ὁσίαν καὶ κατὰ τοὺς νόμους θήσεσθε, τοῖσδέ τε τὰ δίκαια γενήσεται. 'Cast your vote both with a *hosios* ballot and according to the laws, that to these people justice may come.' Is. 9.34–5: 'In accordance with the laws you made yourself, I claim my inheritance in a most *hosios* request'; Dem. 21 (Meidias) 148, 227: τὴν ὁσίαν καὶ δικαίαν ψῆφον, 'the *hosios* and *dikaios* ballot'; Martin (2009) 15–48.

96 Dem. 23.61: the right to defend one's home against intruders; Dem. 23.85: one must host suppliants; Thuc. 3.56.2: it is *hosios* to repel those who attack on a festival day, referring to *hosie* as proper conduct in honouring the gods.

97 Thuc. 3.56.2: πόλιν γὰρ αὐτοὺς τὴν ἡμετέραν καταλαμβάνοντας ἐν σπονδαῖς καὶ προσέτι ἱερομηνίᾳ ὀρθῶς τε ἐτιμωρησάμεθα κατὰ τὸν πᾶσι νόμον καθεστῶτα, τὸν ἐπιόντα πολέμιον ὅσιον εἶναι ἀμύνεσθαι.

Since all mankind knows that no one ought to attack in a time of truce guarded by the gods through the oaths taken, nor on a festival day in honour of the gods, it is *hosios* to punish those who do so, so the Plataians assert.[98] The Thebans, for their part, accuse the Plataians of treachery because they had broken their oaths before:

> We have discussed these matters ... that you [Spartans] may know that you will justly (*dikaios*) condemn them and we that we have still more *hosios* exacted vengeance.[99]

In this passage, Thucydides treats *hosioteros* more or less as a comparative of *dikaios*, cementing the link between both adjectives. In both cases, *hosios* positively evaluates human actions honouring the gods directly and conduct of humans towards each other as defined by rules supervised by the gods.

A particularly interesting instance of *hosios* as a central value in Athens occurs in the 'law against tyranny', made (allegedly after a Solonian precursor) after the oligarchic regime and confirmed by all Athenians in the 'oath of Demophantos'. The law stated that whoever tried to overthrow the democracy was an enemy of the Athenians and could be killed with impunity, and that 'whoever kills the man who has done any of these things (= established a tyranny) or plans to do so shall be *hosios* and *euages* (pure)'.[100] This meant that a man who destroyed the *politeia* was in a condition of war (*polemos*) with the *polis*; killing him was an act pleasing to the gods (*hosios*) and required no purification (*euages*). An earlier 'law against tyranny' did not say anything about homicide and declared anyone who attempted to set up a tyranny and his descendants *atimos*.[101] But now, in the late fifth century, recent experience made the fear of enemies of the democracy acute: in this law the *polis* effectively strengthened its bond

[98] Cf. Thuc. 5.104 (Melian dialogue): 'we trust that ... we shall through divine favour be at no disadvantage because we are *hosios* standing our ground against men who are unjust (*ou dikaious*)'. According to Eatough (1971), Thucydides is not indifferent towards the moral and religious appeal of *hosios*, but seeks to demonstrate that people act in their own interests, manipulating moral claims to justify them (cf. Thuc. 3.84.2). Badian (1993) 112–13, however, blames Thucydides' 'rationalism' for underestimating the value his fellow Greeks accorded to religion (notably here the Plataian festival day) and modern historians for following him in this.

[99] Thuc. 3.67.1–2: Καὶ ταῦτα, ὦ Λακεδαιμόνιοι, τούτου ἕνεκα ἐπεξήλθομεν καὶ ὑπὲρ ὑμῶν καὶ ἡμῶν, ἵνα ὑμεῖς μὲν εἰδῆτε δικαίως αὐτῶν καταγνωσόμενοι, ἡμεῖς δὲ ἔτι ὁσιώτερον τετιμωρημένοι. Breaking an oath not *hosios*: Dem. 19.70.

[100] Law *ap*. Andoc. 1.96–8. For the 'Solonian' origin of this law (F 94), LR 153.

[101] *Ath.Pol.* 16.10. The law is quoted beginning with θέσμια τάδε, 'these are the ordinances', an archaic formulation; for these (Solonian) laws on tyranny, LR F 37 a–c with comm. For *atimos*, see Chapter 5.

with the gods as stakeholders in the *polis* and its *politeia*. It did so again in a revision of the law passed by the *nomothetai* in 337/6, and directed against threats to the democracy from the Macedonians or members of the Areopagus in the aftermath of the battle of Chaeroneia.[102] Declaring anyone who killed the man who destroyed the democracy of Athens to be *hosios*, this law confirmed that the homicide to protect the *polis* of anyone who threatened its *politeia* would please the gods.[103]

Not only in the fifth century, when *hosios* and its antonym were frequently used, but also in the fourth *hosie* and *hosios* continued to hold a persuasive force with great religious–moral appeal.[104] From the fourth century onward, we find the designation of death as *ouk hosie* in grave inscriptions, especially in epigrams for the 'untimely dead'.[105] These epigrams seem to express the feeling that such a death upsets the natural order of things and represents an infringement of what humans might have expected from the gods in return for a pious life.[106]

In sum, transposed into concrete guidelines for human life *hosie* means rules of conduct relating to firstly, honouring the gods and fulfilling obligations towards them; in practice this usually means rules as to who, when, where and how to perform *ta hiera*;[107] and secondly, human relations conducted in ways valued particularly by the gods and overseen by them. *Hosie* includes conventions or regulations concerning guests, strangers and suppliants; keeping oaths, in particular in a juridical context; invoking the gods in laws, notably entrenchment clauses; care for the dead and burial; proper attitude towards relatives, especially respect for parents and care of them in old age. Between *poleis*, *hosie* entailed conventions regarding warfare and treaties, notably pious treatment of the dead, keeping oaths and respect for *hiera*, conduct associated with an

102 *IG* II³ 1, 320; RO 79; l. 11: ὅσιος ἔστω. The law was to be inscribed on two stelai, one set up 'by the entrance to the Areios Pagos where one goes into the *bouleuterion*, and the other in the *ekklesia*' (ll. 23–7). The Areopagus had grown in power since the 340s and was clearly regarded as a threat to democracy, RO comm., 390–1; for additional threats from Macedonians, AIO comm.

103 RO 79, l. 11; Parker (1983) 366–9 reads *hosios* as *katharos* in the ritual sense here. I do not think that here (or anywhere else) *hosios* is the exact equivalent of *katharos*; in the law *ap*. Andoc. purity is indicated by *euages*, not by *hosios*.

104 This is an important argument against the quite common view that Greek religion entailed no moral prescripts (e.g. Lanni (2006) 23).

105 E.g. *SEG* 30.291; *SEG* 28.354 (Attica 400–350), *SEG* 38.440 (fourth century, Thessaly) etc. This usage of course differs from the numerous grave inscriptions praising the deceased for having been *hosios* in his or her lifetime.

106 For the ceaseless human hope for divine justice, Versnel (1981), Yunis (1988) 38–58, Parker (1998).

107 Parker (1983) esp. 18–73. Scholars label all such regulations 'sacred laws', but the ancient Greeks saw no essential difference between these and other laws; for the usefulness of the modern notion 'sacred laws', Parker (2004), Lupu (2005) 8–112.

unwritten 'law' transcending the *nomoi* of individual *poleis* and even the cultural boundaries of the Greek world ('all mankind'). *Hosie* as rules of cult, by contrast, created ties between a group and a divinity and therefore applied to the conduct of the specific group involved, be it small or large. All these rules illuminate the range of issues involved in *hosie*, but in fact they were one set of values sustaining durable relations between humans and gods.[108]

2.4.3 Hosios *Things*

Things called *hosios* either metaphorically represent their human owners who act in a *hosios* way, or the things themselves are used for a purpose or in a way that complies with *hosie*, creating *charis* with the gods. A few examples taken from different text genres show this clearly. In the tragedy *Prometheus Vinctus*, the chorus evokes the benefits granted to humankind when living in accordance with the will of Zeus:

> May Zeus, the disposer of all things,
> never set his power in opposition to my will;
> nor may I be backward
> in approaching the gods with *hosios*
> feasts of slaughtered oxen
> beside the immortal stream of my father Okeanos . . .[109]

The sacrifice is to be offered in a *hosios* feast, pleasing to and honouring the gods. *Hosios* is also used recurrently in forensic oratory, for instance when, in a speech by Isaeus, the speaker asks the *dikastai* to 'cast your vote both with a *hosios* ballot and according to the laws, that to these people

[108] Cf. Hesych. *s.v.* ὅσιος· καθαρός. δίκαιος. εὐσεβής. εἰρηνικός. ἁγνός. From a comparative perspective, *hosios* has much in common with the Roman value term *pius*. As to nouns, the equivalent of *hosie* is probably *religio*, whereas the equivalent of *pietas* is not *hosie* but *hosiotes*, the virtue of observing *hosie* and a near equivalent of *eusebeia*, emerging in the late fifth to early fourth centuries (Plato, Isocrates) and widespread thereafter; Mikalson (2010). Cf. Cic. *Deor.Nat.* 1.2.4: *est enim pietas iustitia adversus deos*, going back to Posidonius (*Adv.Phys.* 1.124: ἔστιν ἡ ὁσιότης δικαιοσύνη τις πρὸς θεούς; Wagenvoort (1980) 10–11; Breij (2011)) and ultimately to Plato, *Euthyphro*.

[109] [Aesch.] *PV* 526–31: μηδάμ' ὁ πάντα νέμων / θεῖτ' ἐμᾶι γνώμαι κράτος ἀντίπαλον Ζεύς, /μηδ' ἐλινύσαιμι θεοὺς ὁσίαις / θοίναις ποτινισομένα / βουφόνοις παρ' Ὠκεανοῦ πατρὸς ἄσβεστον πόρον. Transl. A.H. Sommerstein (Loeb ed.), slightly modified. Cf. Emp. *DK* B 3.1–3: ἀλλὰ θεοὶ τῶν μὲν μανίην ἀποτρέψατε γλώσσης / ἐκ δ' ὁσίων στομάτων καθαρὴν ὀχετεύσατε πηγήν / καὶ σέ, πολυμνήστη λευκώλενε παρθένε Μοῦσα . . . 'But gods! turn aside their madness from my tongue / and channel a pure stream from *hosios* mouths. / And you, maiden Muse of the white arms, much-remembering, I beseech you . . .' (transl. B. Inwood, Toronto 2001). At Soph. *OC* 469–70 *hosios* is used of hands, pure for a libation honouring the gods. For the much-debated case of *hosios* in Ar. *Lys.* 743–4, Blok (2014a) 26–8, Peels (2015) 222–5.

justice may come'.[110] As we saw earlier, *hosios* (here perhaps best translated by 'righteous') can be juxtaposed with *dikaios* (just according to laws), covering different but complementary spheres of justice through the basic meaning of *hosios*. In these cases the adjective does not describe the way such things were obtained, but their purpose; the rewards the gods gave for human worship and conduct were usually called 'good things' (*agatha*).

Hosios was applied to concrete objects, but *hosia*, with or without the article *ta*, often seem to be abstract rather than concrete things. An instructive case occurs in Euripides' *Suppliants* (121–4), where Theseus questions Adrastos on the burial of the heroes slain in the siege of Thebes:

THES.: Did you rely on heralds of Hermes to bury the dead?
ADR.: Yes, and yet the slayers did not yield them to me.
THES.: But what did they say, then, when you asked of them *hosia*?

From the context it is clear that *hosia* here means in the first place taking care of the dead, who must be buried properly, also after a battle. The gods oversee observance of these rules (*hosie*) and if humans fail to do so, as was notoriously the case after the siege of Thebes by the Seven, the dreadful consequences will be immediately apparent, as portrayed in the opening scene of Sophocles' *Antigone*.

Conversely, doing *hosia* will make all the gods well disposed and grant prosperity to human society more widely. We saw this same train of thought in the passage of Antiphon: *hosios* men incur the favour of the gods not merely for themselves, but also for those in social contact with them. Other passages confirm this sense of *hosia*, supplying instances of conduct that meet with the approval of the gods, and showing that both the gods and their fellow human beings can be expected to react with benevolence to those who display such conduct.[111] A sanctuary

[110] Is. 6.65: ὑμεις τε τὴν ψῆφον ὁσίαν καὶ κατὰ τοὺς νόμους θήσεσθε, τοῖσδέ τε τὰ δίκαια γενήσεται. See also above, note 95. For *hosios* on the same side as but different from *dike*, cf. Aesch. *Ag*. 772–8: Δίκα δὲ λάμπει μὲν ἐν / δυσκάπνοις δώμασιν, τὸν δ' ἐναίσιμον τίει βίον. / τὰ χρυσόπαστα δ' ἕδεθλα σὺν πίνῳ χερῶν παλιντρόποις ὄμμασι λιποῦσ', ὅσια †προσέβα/ τοῦ† δύναμιν οὐ σέβουσα πλού /του παράσημον αἴνωι / πᾶν δ' ἐπὶ τέρμα νωμᾶι. 'But *Dike* shines out in smoky hovels / and honours the righteous man: / gold-spangled abodes where hands are not clean / she quits with eyes averted, and goes to *hosios* ones / not revering with praise the might of the wealth if it is counterfeit. She directs all things to their end' (transl. A.H. Sommerstein, Loeb ed.). In this passage, the wider meaning of *hosios* beyond *dikaios* is reinforced by the semantically related verb *sebein* (to revere).

[111] A list of rules how to live well: 'Stay away from *adika*. Witness *hosia*' (*IMTL Apollon/Milet* 2315.3–4: ἄδικα φεῦγε. μαρτύρει ὅσια; late fourth, early third century). The verb *martyro* situates the acts of witnessing in the judicial sphere. In curse tablets, all post-classical in date, (*ta*) *hosia* are used in the wider sense of a 'well-being' that one owes to the gods invoked but that is also effectuated by

at Mytilene required its visitors to 'enter the precinct *hagnos* (pure), thinking *hosia*'.[112]

2.4.4 Hiera kai Hosia*: a Bond between* Polis *and Gods*

We can now investigate the combination *hiera kai hosia* more fully: first I shall propose an interpretation of the expression based on some clear instances of its usage and then I shall consider a few cases where the expression poses more difficulties.

The first more or less datable passages in which *hiera kai hosia* occurs are in Antiphon's *On the murder of Herodes* of ca. 420 and in Thucydides' description of the plague that struck Athens in 430. Thucydides recounts the conditions at Athens when the city, overcrowded with people in the first year of the Peloponnesian War, fell victim to the plague:

> The temples (*ta hiera*), too, in which they had quartered themselves, were full of the corpses of those who had died in them; for the calamity which weighed upon them was so overpowering that men, not knowing what was to become of them, became careless of *hiera* and *hosia*. The customs (*nomoi*), which they had hitherto observed regarding burial, were all thrown into confusion and they buried their dead each one as he could. And many resorted to disrespectful modes of burial because so many members of their households had already died that they lacked the proper funeral materials.[113]

Due to the disastrous situation, people died in the temples where they should not have quartered anyway, causing pollution where no pollution was allowed. The Athenians breached *hosie* by the disrespect for the gods who owned the sanctuaries and of the rules of conduct valid there, and by the failure to bury the dead, falling short in observing ritual purity and in

one's fellow beings; the wish for being *hosios* is often combined with the wish to be *eleutheros*, free from destructive actions by enemies. See *Knidos* 256, b-2; *Knidos* 258.6–8; *Knidos* 262–9; *Knidos* 260, where Prosodion wishes for herself and her children ὅσια κατὰ πᾶν μέρος; *Knidos* 261 (= Gager (1992) no. 89, *DT* 4, who, however, translates *hosia* as 'permissible', drawing on the conventional view discussed below). Versnel (1990) argues that this particular group of *defixiones* comprises prayers for justice rather than curses. The opponent in the curse is to get *anhosia*, '(doing) everything terrible one can imagine', reaping all the adverse consequences.

112 *LSS* 82: ἁγνὸν πρὸς τέμενος στείχειν ὅσια φρονέοντα. Likewise above the entrance of the temple of Asclepius in Epidauros (*ap.* Porph. *Abst.* 2.19): Ἁγνὸν χρὴ ναοῖο θυώδεος ἐντὸς ἰόντα / ἔμμεναι· ἁγνεία δ' ἐστὶ προνεῖν ὅσια. 'One has to be pure (*hagnos*) on entering the temple; purity is thinking *hosia*.' Cf. Parker (1983) 322–3; although conventionally dated to the fourth century, Bremmer (2002) argues for a date around the beginning of the common era.

113 Thuc. 2.52.3–4; transl. C.F. Smith (Loeb ed.) modified; ἐς ὀλιγωρίαν ἐτράποντο καὶ ἱερῶν καὶ ὁσίων ὁμοίως.

obligations towards their fellow humans. Thucydides uses *hiera kai hosia* here in a general, abstract sense: *hiera* means proper worship of the gods ('religion') and *hosia* proper conduct towards gods and towards humans as approved by the gods, while the context evokes especially obligations towards the dead and ritual purity.

In Antiphon's speech, discussed above, a conviction of homicide would 'deprive me (speaker of Mytilene) of my fatherland (*patris*) but also deprive himself (Lykinos of Athens) of *hiera and hosia* and of the other things that among mankind are valued the greatest and most highly'. Demosthenes, using the same terminology and argument in his speech against Aristocrates, seems to flesh out what this means when he expounds the laws of Athens on homicide:

> [the lawgiver] debars the [killer] from everything in which the deceased used to have a share (*meteinai*) in his lifetime, first from his fatherland (*patris*) and all things therein, both *hiera* and *hosia*, assigning the frontier-market as the boundary from which he declares him excluded ... and from the *hiera* of the amphictyonic communities, in which he, if he was a Greek, had a share ... and from the Games pertaining to the whole of Greece, in which all have a share (*meteinai*) and hence also the victim.[114]

In this passage, Demosthenes partly quotes from an unnamed law that must be Draco's law on homicide, and partly gives a paraphrase with some later additions.[115] Membership of various communities (*meteinai*) is delineated by its reverse, i.e. exclusion from them; a killer was exiled from the communities to which his victim had belonged, and as long as he refrained from returning there, the law protected him from harm. These communities, at *polis* level and beyond it, are defined by the *hiera* they share. Of central importance is the *polis* of the victim ('fatherland') and all its *hiera* and *hosia*. Whether this expression was included in Draco's law cannot be ascertained, as the inscribed text of the decree is severely

[114] Dem. 23.40: ὅσων τῷ παθόντι ζῶντι μετῆν, τούτων εἴργει τὸν δεδρακότα, πρῶτον μὲν τῆς πατρίδος καὶ τῶν ἐν ταύτῃ πάντων καὶ ὁσίων καὶ ἱερῶν, τὴν ἐφορίαν ἀγορὰν ὅρον προσγράψας ἧς εἴργεσθαί φησιν, εἶτα τῶν ἱερῶν τῶν ἐν Ἀμφικτύοσιν: καὶ γὰρ τούτων, εἴπερ ἦν Ἕλλην ὁ παθών, μετῆν αὐτῷ. 'καὶ ἄθλων.' διὰ τί; ὅτι κοινοὶ πᾶσίν εἰσιν οἱ κατὰ τὴν Ἑλλάδ' ἀγῶνες, κατὰ δὲ τὴν πάντων μετουσίαν μετῆν καὶ τούτων τῷ πεπονθότι: καὶ τούτων οὖν ἀπεχέσθω. Transl. J.H. Vince (Loeb ed.), modified.

[115] The last lines of Dem. 23.40 are used to restore Draco's law on homicide in *IG* I³ 104 l. 27–9 (following Stroud (1968)): ὁ[ν ἀν]δρ̣[οφόνον κτένει ἒ αἴτιος ἒ͂ι φόνο, ἀπεχόμενον ἀγορᾶ]ς ἐφο- / ρί[α]ς κ̣[α]ὶ [ἄθλον καὶ *h*ιερο͂ν Ἀμφικτυονικο͂ν, *h*όσπερ τὸν Ἀθεν]αῖον κ̣ / [τένα]ν̣[τα, ἐν τοῖς αὐτοῖς ἐνέχεσθαι· For the relation between both texts, MacDowell (1963) 118–29, Carawan (1998), Phillips (2008). Cf. Antiph. 6.3–5 on homicide, laws, purification and exile. Besides the ritual purification, the pardon of the victim's family was required for the killer to be integrated into society again; Arnaoutoglou (1998) 72–4; Carawan (1998) 17–20, 69–83.

damaged, but the similarities with the passage from Antiphon are notable. From these two passages we may tentatively infer that in the late fifth century the law in its clause on exile after conviction for homicide referred at some point to the *polis* as the *patris* with its *hiera kai hosia*.

It seems that, by the last decades of the fifth century at the latest, sharing in *hiera kai hosia* had become a regular expression capturing what the Athenians thought belonging to the *polis* was about. This result sheds light on a text that purports to date to 427, though its authenticity is contested.[116] In Apollodorus' speech *Against Neaira* ([Dem. 59]) of ca. 340, the speaker refers to a decree granting Athenian citizenship *en masse* to the surviving Plataians in the early stage of the Peloponnesian War. The existence of the decree itself is not in doubt, but the passage in the speech that claims to be a literal quote from it has been questioned:

> Hippocrates proposed that the Plataians be Athenians (*einai Athenaious*) from this day, fully valued on the same footing (*epitimous*) as the other Athenians, and that they share (*meteinai*) in everything in which the Athenians share, both *hiera* and *hosia*, save any priesthood or ritual which belongs to a *genos*, nor one of the nine archons but to their descendants [it will be permitted]. The Plataians will be distributed among the demes and *phylai*; and when they have been distributed, it is not possible any longer for any Plataian to become an Athenian, unless he receives this [as a gift] from the *demos* of Athenians.[117]

The main arguments against authenticity are the differences between this passage and inscribed decrees.[118] For our present purposes, however, it is sufficient to note that the phrasing accords in relevant respects with citizenship discourse in these years: *Athenaious einai* is the stock formula of citizenship grants and sharing in the *polis* is captured in a *meta*-verb with *hiera kai hosia*, just as in Thucydides, Antiphon and the 'law on legitimacy'.

The combination *hiera kai hosia* occurs so frequently that it may be called a fixed expression. *Hiera* are the gifts given in gratitude to the gods

[116] Most strongly by Canevaro (2013) 196–208. Against his verdict of the decree to be a 'forgery', several arguments can be raised, here the fact that *hiera kai hosia* as the core of citizenship was common usage at the time of the decree; for more discussion, see Chapters 5.6, 6.1.

[117] [Dem.] 59.104: Ἱπποκράτης εἶπε, Πλαταιέας εἶναι Ἀθηναίους ἀπὸ τῆσδε τῆς ἡμέρας, ἐπιτίμους καθάπερ οἱ ἄλλοι Ἀθηναῖοι, καὶ μετεῖναι αὑτοῖς ὧνπερ Ἀθηναίοις μέτεστι πάντων, καὶ ἱερῶν καὶ ὁσίων, πλὴν εἴ τις ἱερωσύνη ἢ τελετή ἐστιν ἐκ γένους, μηδὲ τῶν ἐννέα ἀρχόντων, τοῖς δ᾽ ἐκ τούτων. κατανεῖμαι δὲ τοὺς Πλαταιέας εἰς τους δήμους καὶ τὰς φυλάς. ἐπειδὰν δὲ νεμηθῶσι, μὴ ἐξέστω ἔτι Ἀθηναίωι μηδενὶ γίγνεσθαι Πλαταιέων, μὴ εὑρομένωι παρὰ τοῦ δήμου τοῦ Ἀθηναίων. I use here Kapparis's text, Kapparis (1995) 361 and Kapparis (1999) with comm.

[118] See Chapter 6.1.

in the cycle of reciprocity, *hosia* are all human actions and property used to please the gods. Sharing in *hiera* was the quintessential means of forming communities in Greece at all levels, but sharing in *hiera kai hosia* appears to be an expression primarily used at Athens. We may conclude that *hiera kai hosia* synoptically represent the bond between humans and gods on which the well-being of the human community depended, and that they represent this bond specifically from the human perspective. At Athens, this bond was the heart of citizenship, anchored in the *polis*'s cults, customs, laws, obligations and social values.[119]

2.4.5 *Can* Hosios *Mean 'Secular'?*

The meaning of *hosios* established so far is entirely consistent. It is also uncontested: all scholars agree that the adjective refers to a condition aiming at and endorsed by divine approval. Nonetheless, a longstanding view holds that *hosios also* means 'secular' or 'profane'.[120] A genealogical search for the origins of this contention takes us to the lemma *hosios* in Henri Stephanus's *Thesaurus Linguae Graecae* of 1572, which translates *hosios* as 'sacred', but as 'profane or public' in passages where the adjective is juxtaposed with *hieros* in *hiera kai hosia*, and particularly when applied to money (*hiera kai hosia chremata*).[121] Is this view of the *Thesaurus* justified?

The *hiera kai hosia chremata* are central to the argument in Dem. 24 denouncing the proposal of a certain Timocrates on public money as illegal.[122] The speech concerned war booty, of which 10 per cent was intended for Athena and 2 per cent for the other gods, and the rest was to be public money: human property, belonging to the *demos*.[123] The first part, given to the gods, was *hieros*, the rest was called here *hosios*. Does that mean that *hosios* in this context *means demosios*, i.e. public property and secular, as the *Thesaurus* thought? This conclusion is unwarranted. In the earliest case

119 In Blok (2014a) I compare this conception of the bond between the *polis* and the gods with the Ancient Near Eastern notion of a covenant, which also underlies the Hebrew Bible idea of *b*e*rît*. This does not entail explicit codification in regulations, but 'any agreement or union among parties, that need not have any verbal expression at all [it is...] an action and a state, a relationship based on various symbolic rites enacting union', McCarthy (1978) 10–17.

120 LSJ *s.v.* ὅσιος, for 'sacred' and 'secular' as opposition to 'sacred' (see next note). Willi (2008) argues that *hosie* means 'religious favour' and nonetheless can mean 'the secular'.

121 *Hiera kai hosia* in these passages is translated *sacra & profana, seu publica*. Scott Scullion kindly brought this lemma to my attention (*per ep.*).

122 Dem. 24: 11, 82, 101, 111, 112, 120, 130, 137: τὰ χρήματα τά τε ἱερὰ καὶ τὰ ὅσια; 96: διοίκησις ἱερὰ καὶ ὁσία; Hyp. fr. 32: καὶ τὰ χρήματα τά τε ἱερὰ καὶ τὰ ὅσια.

123 Dem. 24.120.

of money being described as *hosios*, in the accounts of the deme Ikarion (*IG* I³ 253), *hosios* designates a particular fund. As I have argued elsewhere, this money was human property designated for a *hosios* purpose, namely the festivals of Dionysus and Ikarios. Generally, *hosia chremata* are human property, owned either collectively or privately, used for expenditures pleasing to the gods, fulfilling human obligations to them.[124] Inscribing such expenditures fits the *polis*'s epigraphical habits of the fifth century, when inscribed records differentiated between monies belonging to gods (*hieros*) and those belonging to the human community (*demosios*). Only those *demosios* monies were accounted for in stone that were to be used for *hiera*, for instance to pay for sacrifice or a votive or another obligation to the gods.[125] Income and expenditure through the year were recorded on perishable material, usually whitened boards.[126] But the money in the limelight, recorded on stone, was all due to the gods in some way. For this money, officials of the *demos* were accountable to the *demos* itself and the *demos* as a whole to the gods, while by the same token the gods were reminded of their part of the deal – to protect and advance the well-being of Athens. Below, we shall return to the effects of labelling certain *demosios* budgets, including that in Dem. 24, *hosios*.

Given that *hosios* in ancient Greek did not mean 'secular', also when used of money, we may now understand what may have happened in the lemma *hosios* in the *Thesaurus*. After duly registrating the normal meaning of *hosios* in other cases, the author abandoned this when turning to the juxtaposition of *hiera kai hosia*, notably when combined with *chremata*, and instead followed a different train of thought, reading in *hiera kai hosia* an analogy with the Christian conception of 'sacred and profane' as essentially separate spheres.[127] Once established, *hiera kai hosia* understood as

124 Blok (2010).

125 Samons (2000) 312–17; similarly Papazarkadas (2011) 71–2. Cf. Harp., Suda ο 687 s.v ὅσιον: Ὑπερίδης ἐν τῷ πρὸς Ἀριστογείτονά φησι: καὶ τὰ χρήματα, τά τε ἱερὰ καὶ τὰ ὅσια. καὶ Ἰσοκράτης: τοῖς ἱεροῖς καὶ τοῖς ὁσίοις. τὰ δημόσια ὅσια λέγοντες. καὶ Δημοσθένης δὲ ἐν τῷ κατὰ Τιμοκράτους σαφῶς διδάσκει τοῦτο. Δίδυμος δέ φησι διχῶς λέγεσθαι τὸ ὅσιον, τό τε ἱερὸν καὶ τὸ ἰδιωτικόν. '*Hosion*: Hypereides says in the *Against Aristogeiton*: and the money, both the *hiera* and the *hosia*. And Isokrates: with the *hiera* and the *hosia*. They call the *demosia hosia*. And Demosthenes explains this adequately in the *Against Timocrates*. And Didymos says that *to hosion* is used in two ways, both *to hieron* and *to idiotikon*.' Didymos' comment is incomprehensible when *hosios* (money) is translated as 'secular', but makes perfect sense when understood as *demosios* or *idios* money used for a *hosios* purpose, notably for *hiera*.

126 In the fourth century, this was still the case for many public transactions, see e.g. *Ath.Pol.* 47.2–3: the council is informed of the *tele* sold for a year written on whitened boards; 47.4: leases of land, of which the rents were due to the *polis*, listed on whitened boards.

127 Augustine had defended this Christian notion in his vision of the city of God and His grace as distinct from that of man. Money itself was considered a secular matter, 'belonging to Caesar'

'sacred and secular' became entrenched in classical scholarship and was incorporated in many translations of classical Greek texts in the Loeb and Budé series.[128] Furthermore, once *hosios* was understood to mean 'secular, profane' within the combination *hiera kai hosia*, it was also understood to have this meaning when used on its own. Given its meaning 'sacred', 'pleasing to the gods' established in other contexts, this notion presented a paradox that evolved into further interpretations of the adjective.[129] The most influential by far was that of van der Valk (1942), who tried to solve this problem by arguing that *hosios* was situated right in the middle between the sacred and the profane, meaning 'made free from the divine sphere for human use'.[130] Van der Valk's argument and especially

(Matt. 22:17–21) unless sanctified for a holy purpose by the Church. Emile Durkheim saw in the distinction between sacred and secular the basic ordering of society in his *Les formes élémentaires de la vie religieuse* (1912), a conception which became highly influential in the social study of religion in the first half of the twentieth century (Bremmer (1998)).

128 E.g. Isoc. 7.66: Καὶ μὲν δὴ καὶ τάδε τίς οὐ μνημονεύει τῶν ἡλικιωτῶν τῶν ἐμῶν, τὴν μὲν δημοκρατίαν οὕτω κοσμήσασαν τὴν πόλιν καὶ τοῖς ἱεροῖς καὶ τοῖς ὁσίοις ὥστ' ἔτι καὶ νῦν τοὺς ἀφικνουμένους νομίζειν αὐτὴν ἀξίαν εἶναι μὴ μόνον τῶν Ἑλλήνων ἄρχειν. 'And who of my own generation does not remember that the democracy arranged the city so well with the *hiera* and the *hosia* that all those who also now come to visit consider her worthy not only to rule over the Greeks but over the whole world?' G. Norlin (Loeb ed. (1929)) translates *hiera kai hosia* as 'temples and public buildings' (and so do G. Mathieu and E. Brémond in the Budé (1929)). There is no indication, however, that *hosia* here or anywhere else refers particularly to 'buildings'; the reading '*public* buildings' probably stems from reading *hiera* as 'temples' and *hosia* by analogy as 'secular buildings'.

129 Rousset (2013) 125–7 discusses inscriptions from outside Attica refering to land called both *hieros* and *demosios*: e.g. at Argos (only partly published), ἁ ἱερὰ καὶ δαμοσία χώρα; *IG* IX, 1 87 (Hyampolis?): [ἱε]ραν καὶ δαμοσίαν [χώραν *vel* γᾶν], and other cases; he argues that καὶ is conjunctive here, esp. when the article is absent in the second item, and that this land belongs *both* to the gods and to the *polis*, the proceeds benefiting both parties. This argument also clarifies a *horos* inscription from Corcyra (*IG* IX, 1 700): ὅρβος ἰαροῦ καὶ ὁσίου: the *horos* marks off from other territory a property that is both *hieros* and *hosios*, i.e. owned by gods and humans but the proceeds of which are all destined for the gods. On *horoi* in Attica, too, καὶ operates as conjunctive, joining and marking the items of property off from the rest in a group of clear cases (e.g. *IG* II² 2657 (+ 2655), 2679, 2724, *SEG* 44.82); other cases (*IG* I³ 1101, *SEG* 32.228) would seem more ambiguous, unless read as abbreviated versions of the first group. This evidence makes the reading of *IG* IX, 1 700 as 'boundary *between hieron* and *hosion*', meaning 'between sacred and profane' (Kurt Latte (*Heiliges Recht*, 55, n. 16, drawing on *CIL* I 2² 1486: *lapides profaneis, intus sacrum*) even more implausible.

130 Van der Valk (1942). Facing the paradox: 'because it [*hosios*] is used both as a synomym of *hieros* and in the meaning not-*hieros*, profane'; 113, transl. JB. The adjective would thus retain its relation with the two poles, moving more into the orbit of the one or the other by means of prepositions or verb forms or depending on context (119–20). The case on which Van der Valk based his interpretation of *hosios* as 'free from divine obligations' (with reference to Hdt. 1.199: when a woman in Babylon has served her turn in the sacred prostitution of the goddess Mylitta, ἀποσιωσαμένη τῃ θεῷ ἀπαλλάσσεται ἐς τὰ οἰκία) was in fact *not* borne out by the adjective *hosios* itself, but by *hosios* transposed into a verb and with a preposition, ἀφοσιοῦμαι, meaning 'to have fulfilled the *hosia*', cf. Suda α 4639 *s.v.* ἀφοσιούμεθα. For further discussion of Van der Valk's position and its sequence, Peels (2015) 10, 207–51.

its impact can only be understood when we take into account that virtually all scholars *accepted as a given* that *hosios* could mean 'profane', due to the tradition of the *Thesaurus*, and faced the resulting paradox, the solution of which they gratefully embraced.[131] Of Van der Valk's view also a 'light' version developed, holding that *hosios* normally indicates human conduct approved by the gods, but when used for money could mean 'secular' or 'free for human use'.[132] An even lighter version translates *hosios* also in other contexts as 'free from' religious claims in the widest sense.[133] Such renderings still carry traces of the 'made free from divine obligations' of Van der Valk, which is essentially wrong; *hosios* means the opposite. Since it is a highly positive value, I would argue, furthermore, that *hosios* preferably should be translated in positive terms.

In conclusion, the contention that *hosios* could mean 'secular' seems to derive from its being a part of the combination *hiera kai hosia*, which in older scholarship was understood as a reference to distinct divine and human spheres, i.e. 'sacred' and 'profane'. But in ancient Greece such a division into sacred and secular spheres does not apply.[134] The interaction between humans and gods could be more or less intense, but the conception of a 'secular' domain *per se* did not exist. Considering that *hosios* was

[131] Impact, especially since two prominent scholars followed Van der Valk: Burkert (1985) 269–70: *hosios* as 'free from obligation to the gods'; Parker (1983) 329–33. See also LSJ, *s.v.* ὅσιος, 2. Opp(osite) ἱερός, *permitted* or *not forbidden by divine law*.

[132] Dover (1974) 248 distinguishes *hosios* money, free from divine claims and to be spent on secular purposes, from the religious meanings of *hosios*; Papazarkadas (2011) 136, n. 174, Ismard (2010) 292–3, Martin (2009) 5–6, all following Burkert and Parker. Connor (1988) appreciates the significance of *hiera kai hosia* and the religious values of *hosios* for all aspects of the *polis* but contends that *hosios* applied to money meant 'secular', notably when it was labelled *demosios* (with reference to the Ikarion account; 165–6). Chadwick (1996) 225–6 argues that the religious meaning of *hosios* established in the other evidence also applies to money: *hosios* monies are 'due for religious reasons' and thus 'religious revenues', but in the case of the combination *hiera kai hosia chremata*, he supposed that *hiera*, of the gods, and *hosia*, of the *polis*, had the connotation 'sacred versus profane'. Samons (2000) 327–8, arguing that the terms 'sacred and secular' are not suitable for Athenian society nor for its financial organisation, but that no satisfactory translation of *hosios* is available in English, understands *hosia chremata* as 'non-sacral' and 'acceptable to the gods'. I think that the 'acceptable' is too weak for *hosios* and shows some residue of 'free for human use'. Cf. Rousset (2013) for the inadequacy of labelling *demosios* property by definition 'secular'.

[133] In the law on tyranny (*IG* II^3 1, 320; RO 79; l. 11; above, Chapter 2.5), *hosios* is translated by RO as 'undefiled', 'innocent' (Schwenk 6), 'blameless' (Meritt, see RO), 'without guilt' (AIO); Scullion (2005): *hosios* as 'secular' in the meaning 'religiously neutral'.

[134] Cf. Maffi (1982), expounding the inconsistencies in Van der Valk's argument and arguing that *hiera kai hosia* in no way meant 'sacred and secular' but referred to a religious–legal sphere that was central to the *polis*. Rudhardt (1992) 30–5, underlining the religious value of *hosios*, shows that the meaning 'made free from divine power for human use' makes no sense in the majority of the cases, and Chadwick (1996) *s.v.* ὅσιος demonstrates that there is no context in which a rendering of *hosios* as 'secular' is warranted.

applied to money that could be used for *hiera* and that the 'law on legitimacy' used *hosia kai hiera* with reference to inheritance, it appears that *ta hosia* could denote, beside words, deeds and thoughts in accordance with *hosie*, the concrete possessions (owned privately (*idios*) or collectively (*demosios*, *koinos*)) used for a *hosios* purpose.

In sum, we find that a) *hosios* refers to the human realm when and where it is oriented towards the divine world; if a 'religiously neutral' domain was conceivable for the Greeks at all, *hosios* was certainly not the adjective indicating this quality; b) *hosios* evaluates human conduct as pleasing to the gods; c) when used for concrete or abstract things, the meaning of *hosios* is the same, designating the use of the concrete objects or thoughts, actions or similar abstract matters to incur divine approval; d) *hiera kai hosia* are a *juxtaposition* incorporating the *distinction* between humans and gods, not conceived as an exhaustive opposition but as *complementary spheres* in a reciprocal relationship; e) within this complementary differentiation, the distinction between gods and humans *as owners*, notably of money, can be highlighted; and f) the binary opposition 'sacred versus secular' is not an adequate reading of *hiera kai hosia* and more generally is inadequate to understand the socio-religious values of ancient Athens.

2.5 *Hiera kai Hosia* and *Polis* Laws

Hiera kai hosia are central to three important texts that in various ways reflect the *polis*'s bond with the gods anchored in law. All laws embodied the *polis*'s responsibilities towards both the gods and the human community, a dual quality that was further marked by the placement of the *stelai* of inscribed decrees on the Acropolis and, after 410, on other places where they were relevant, notably in the Agora.[135] Proximity of inscribed decrees and treaties to the temples engaged the divine world in their authority and perpetuity, enhanced by the invocation *theoi* heading numerous decrees from the 430s onwards and reminding both humans and

[135] An average of 90 per cent of decrees on the Acropolis, see Liddel (2003). *Stelai* placed on the Acropolis akin to votive inscriptions, Lazzarini (1989–90), Keesling (2003) 1–16, Lambert (2011) and compare the votive quality of inscribed accounts mentioned above. Honorific decrees set up on the Acropolis to bring the commendable conduct of these people to the attention of gods and humans alike, Lambert (2004a), Lambert (2006), Lambert (2007), Lambert (2008b), Meyer (2013). Removal of *axones* of Solon and Draco to Stoa: *IG* I^3 104.6–8 (reinscribed Draco *axon*); Anaximenes *FGrH* 72 F 13, with Rhodes, *CAAP*, 131–5. For decrees on the Agora after the oligarchy of 411, Shear (2007a), Shear (2011) 96–134.

gods of their statutes and commendable conduct.[136] An orator – perhaps Demosthenes – in his speech *Against Aristogeiton* put it thus:

> It befits (*prosekei*) all to obey the law for many reasons, and most of all because every law is an invention and gift of the gods, a tenet of wise humans, a corrective of errors voluntary and involuntary, and a *koinos* agreement (*syntheke*) of the *polis*, in accordance with which it befits (*prosekei*) all in the *polis* to live.[137]

Of course, these words invoked an ideal state of affairs. In reality, regulations were often the object of dissent, and the ways in which the laws were actually applied depended on political and forensic discourse as well as on the choice of legal procedure.[138] Nonetheless, the gods' engagement in the *polis*'s laws was reinforced in day-to-day practice.[139] Every session of the assembly and *boule* was opened with a purification sacrifice, a curse against the enemies of the *polis* and a prayer, and we saw that the *bouleutai* and *dikastai* were bound by oath to maintain the laws.[140] Commitment of humans and gods was therefore essential to all laws, but in three key texts *hiera kai hosia* figure explicitly as the object of Athenian law. Why and how need some clarification.

[136] *Theoi* is added whether or not the subject matter of the decree was of a religious nature in the strict sense. The earliest cases in Athens are *IG* I³ 50 (ca. 435, on construction of a sanctuary), *IG* I³ 53 (433/2, an alliance with Rhegion), *IG* I³ 66 (427, goodwill towards Mytilene), *IG* I³ 34 (on tribute, now dated 425/4) etc. The invocation *theoi* on decrees is not only an Athenian (ca. 350 cases), but a general Greek phenomenon; scholarship on this phenomenon is surprisingly scarce (Pounder (1984), Meyer (2013) 471).

[137] Dem. 25.16 (*Against Aristogeiton* 1): οἱ δὲ νόμοι τὸ δίκαιον καὶ τὸ καλὸν καὶ τὸ συμφέρον βούλονται, καὶ τοῦτο ζητοῦσιν, καὶ ἐπειδὰν εὑρεθῇ, κοινὸν τοῦτο πρόσταγμ' ἀπεδείχθη, πᾶσιν ἴσον καὶ ὅμοιον, καὶ τοῦτ' ἔστι νόμος. ᾧ πάντας πείθεσθαι προσήκει διὰ πολλά, καὶ μάλισθ'ὅτι πᾶς ἐστι νόμος εὕρημα μὲν καὶ δῶρον θεῶν, δόγμα δ' ἀνθρώπων φρονίμων, ἐπανόρθωμα δὲ τῶν ἑκουσίων καὶ ἀκουσίων ἁμαρτημάτων, πόλεως δὲ συνθήκη κοινή, καθ' ἣν πᾶσι προσήκει ζῆν τοῖς ἐν τῇ πόλει. On the author, Martin (2009) 182–202, MacDowell (2009) 310–13. For similar ideas see Andoc. 1.113. Pl. *Crit.* 50c–d also contains the notion of an agreement (ταῦτα (= the laws) ὡμολόγητο ἡμῖν τε καὶ σοὶ) and pledge of loyalty between *polis* members and their laws, cf. 51a–b for the *patris* as of higher value among gods and men even than one's parents. Harris (2004) discusses the gods as source of (human) law. *Synthekai* (agreements between humans) were made legally binding by a law of Solon, according to Phillips (2009), who argues that the phrase 'Whatever one man agrees with another is binding' (ὅσα ἂν ἕτερος ἑτέρῳ ὁμολογήσῃ κύρια εἶναι; Hyp. 3.13; [Dem.] 47.77) represents a 'general law of contract'.

[138] Osborne (2010d).

[139] The result of observing the laws of one's city is *charis* (Xen. *Mem.* 4.3.16), assuming the laws support engagement with the gods and *hosie* conduct (Thphr. *On piety*, fr. 7); Mikalson (2010) 144–60.

[140] For the purification sacrifices and prayers before the assembly sessions see Ar. *Thesm.* 347–51; used in oratory: Aeschin. 1.23; curse: Din. 2.16, Lyc. *Leocr.* 31; prayer: Din. 2. 14. Liable to the curse were those who spoke against the interests of the *polis*, who betrayed the *polis*, who deceived the *boule* and *demos*, or who negotiated with the Persians; Rhodes (1972) 36–7.

2.5.1 *Nikomachos and the Law Code of Athens*

According to the speaker of Lysias 30, a certain Nikomachos had failed dramatically in his responsibility for the *hiera kai hosia*. Nikomachos was a member of the *anagrapheis ton nomon*, a committee instituted after the first oligarchic period to make a new edition of Athens's laws. The work took place in two stretches, from 410 to 404 and from 403 to 399.[141] Solon's laws and Draco's law on homicide formed its skeleton, but in fact the committee assessed all the laws valid in Athens and (re)inscribed many of them. Hence, the Athenians often referred to their laws as 'the *thesmoi* of Draco' or 'the *nomoi* of Solon', although many were demonstrably more recent.[142]

One of the central documents involved was the sacrificial calendar of Athens, listing the numerous provisions for sacrifices to the gods and heroes of Attica. The *polis* calendar included sacrifices belonging to the 'Solonian calendar' but also other more recent provisions. They were listed in their order throughout the year, differentiated as to frequency, such as annual or biennial sacrifices, and they contain rubrics indicating the legislative or religious authority for the sacrifice, and occasionally the particular authorities or groups that had to carry them out, such as members of the *gene* or the *phylobasileis*, the archons of the old Ionian *phylai*. The sacrificial calendar was erected in the Stoa Basileios because, like Draco's laws, it fell under the authority of the (archon) Basileus.[143]

When the project was finished, an Athenian citizen raised an objection at the *euthynai* of the officials responsible (Lysias 30). His main charge concerned the sacrificial calendar (17–24), but he began with other allegations intended to demonstrate that Nikomachos was not to be trusted with the *polis*'s laws.[144] His contention that the committee had

[141] For the revision of the laws, Andoc. 1.81–5, Lys. 30, Dem. 24.42; for the process and the main legal changes, Gallia (2004), Gagarin (2008) 182–8, both with furthers refs. Gallia argues that Draco's law had a unique position within the whole process due to the recent killings in 411/10; for the context, the restoration of democracy after the oligarchies, Shear (2011) 72–111. Fragments of the reinscribed laws: *IG* I³ 104 (Draco), *IG* I³ 105 (on the *boule*), *IG* I³ 236 = *SEG* 52. 48 fr. 3B (on the trierarchy), *IG* I³ 237 concerns other matters (taxes?); the sacrificial calendar *SEG* 52.48 (except fr. 3B). A list of all the fragments of the calendar, Shear (2011) table 6; of the other laws, table 7. For a detailed discussion of the fragments and the sources of the entries, Parker (1996) 43–8, Lambert (2002), Gawlinksi (2007).

[142] Rhodes (1991) 89–90, Shear (2011) 83–4. Solon's laws before and after the revision, Rhodes (2006).

[143] Shear (2011) 85–9 and table 9.

[144] According to the speaker, Nikomachos was the son of a slave who had obtained citizenship, hence a non-Athenian (30.1–2, 5); he had dodged a citizen's duties by taking far too long to finish the work, without properly accounting for it (30.1–6); his handling of the laws was just trickery,

not accounted for its duties was not exactly true, since it was officially discharged in 404 and later in 399; but the terms of office were certainly much longer than usual and than had been expected. Why Nikomachos was singled out becomes clear when the plaintiff seems to imply that Nikomachos was going to bring a charge of *asebeia* against him, for objecting to certain sacrifices.[145] They had been included by Nikomachos in the calendar, but according to the speaker they did not belong there (18–19). The speaker contrasts Nikomachos' calendar with 'ancestral *hiera*' (on the *kyrbeis* (17) identified with Solon's sacrificial calendar), *hiera* that 'will particularly benefit the *polis*' and 'those that the *demos* has decided and the costs of which we shall be able to pay from the incoming revenues' (19). Now these sacrifices had turned out to be far more costly than expected, causing a lack of funds to pay for them. This was disastrous for the city's well-being (20). Nikomachos had robbed the gods (*hierosylos*), although he claimed to have acted out of *eusebeia*, not for the sake of fiscal balance (*euteleia*) (21). In so doing he had raised the costs of sacrifice even if he knew of the city's financial problems, due to payments owed to the Spartans and Boeotians and to the need to repair the city walls (22). Citizens who had been put to death for robbing the *polis*'s treasury (*ta koina*) had only sinned for the moment, but 'these men who took bribes for their writing up of the laws (*nomoi*) and the *hiera* damage the *polis* for all time'.[146] In sum, 'he who was appointed to write down *ta hosia* and *ta hiera* has failed in both'.[147]

What do *ta hosia kai ta hiera* refer to in this passage? Among all the men engaged in 'writing up the laws and the *hiera*', Nikomachos is held

producing a law on demand for a trial (30.9–15), inserting some laws and erasing others as he saw fit (30.2, 5, 10–13). Accusations of partisanship during the oligarchic regimes (30.7–16; 26–30), in reaction to similar charges by Nikomachos, suggest that other scores were also being settled. Todd (1996) points to the suspicion of legal expertise in the case. Shear (2011) 83–5 shows that the *anagrapheis* had to collect laws from various places in the city and that, in the event, not all laws were inscribed on stone in one place. All of this could easily make the impression of 'inscribing some laws and erasing others' (30.2).

145 The speaker's remarks suggest a preemptive strike: Nikomachos, he says, *will try* to slander him (7: ἐμε διαβάλλειν πειράσεται) and is asking others to remember past wrongs (9: μνησικακεῖν, suggestive of the oligarchic period) unjustly, and Nikomachos was saying (λέγειν) that he was guilty of *asebeia* (17).

146 Lys. 30.25: καίτοι ἐκεῖνοι μὲν τοσοῦτον μόνον ὑμᾶς ἔβλαψαν ὅσον ἐν τῷ παρόντι, οὗτοι δ' ἐπὶ τῇ τῶν νόμων ἀναγραφῇ [καὶ τῶν ἱερῶν] δῶρα λαμβάνοντες εἰς ἅπαντα τὸν χρόνον τὴν πόλιν ζημιοῦσι. The words καὶ τῶν ἱερῶν, deleted by C.M. Francken in 1865, still appear in square brackets in most editions, but there is no ground to remove them; cf. Hansen (1990b) on 69–70 and note 27; Shear (2011) 83, n. 51.

147 Lys. 30.25: ὅς καὶ τῶν ὁσίων καί τῶν ἱερῶν ἀναγραφεὺς γενόμενος εἰς ἀμφότερα ταῦτα ἡμάρτηκεν.

particularly responsible for the *hiera* and the means to pay for them, i.e. for the sacrificial calendar. Listing the sacrifices Nikomachos has included in the final list, the speaker takes most issue with the costs. The snippets of information he weaves into this speech tie in with other evidence on the city's budgets.

The *hiera* (sacrifices and festivals) were paid partly from the gods' own monies (*hieros* funds) and partly from money owned by the *demos* (*demosios* funds). The proportion of *hieros* to *demosios* money going into each specific offering depended on many factors: when the offering had been instituted, by whom and on what conditions, and also if any changes had been made into the original set-up.[148] It was precisely this complicated system of numerous *hiera* and their costing into which the new calendar was to bring some order; the revision of the laws went hand in hand with a reconsiderations of the *polis*'s treasury (see below). We find the main distinction between *hiera* paid from both *hieros* and *demosios* funds, and *hiera* called *demoteles*, because the *demos* paid for them entirely and thus served its well-being more than anything else.[149] The *demosios* treasury (*ta koina*, 23) was filled by 'incoming revenue' (mentioned by the speaker) and next a part of it was to be used for the *hiera*, and a part for other expenditures. For the speaker, the bone of contention was that due to Nikomachos' calendar a larger sum from the common funds than before was spent on some *hiera* featuring on this list, causing the *polis* to run out of money for other *hiera* (some of which were also on the list) and for other important purposes, such as debts to the Spartans and the Boeotians, dilapidated ship houses and crumbling walls. The speaker pointed out that Nikomachos was responsible for writing up the *hiera* and the *demosios* money to be spent on the *hiera* – called the *hosia*, just like the *hosios* budget at Ikarion mentioned above.[150] His charge against

[148] To find some order in the budgets for public sacrifices, Rosivach (1994) 136–8 uses a model based on Isoc. *Areop.* 29, [Xen.] *Ath.Pol.* 11.9, to the effect that the *polis* distinguished between traditional cults (*patria thysia*), paid mainly from *hieros* money and with small numbers of animals sacrificed, and large-scale *heortai epithetoi*, paid by the *demos*. Although helpful, this model does not cover adequately the types of *hiera* nor the budgets involved; e.g. the festival of Artemis Agrotera was a *heorte epithetos* but does not appear in lists comprising the sale of the skins of other such *heortai* (the Dermatikon accounts; Rosivach (1994) 64), and the Panathenaea was a mixture of both systems; see Blok (2010), Papazarkadas (2011) 77–81.

[149] Thuc. 2.15.3, Hdt. 6.57, Pl. *Leg.* 935b6, Dem. 53.7 For *demoteles*, Pirenne-Delforge (2005). Prominent examples are the Theseia, the sacrifices for Artemis Agrotera and sacrifices for Athena Nike (Blok 2014b).

[150] Other laws, such as the law on trierachy inscribed on the back of one part of the calendar, did not belong to *hiera kai hosia*, nor does the text indicate that the speaker, when referring to *hiera kai hosia*, had such other laws in mind.

Nikomachos was not the last time that the *polis* was to face the unwelcome fact that the costs of its growing list of *hiera* were more than the public treasury could afford. For his decision to put the blame for this situation on the man in charge of its administation, the speaker had his own motives, but his charge brought centre stage that *hiera kai hosia* affected the entire *polis* economy.

2.5.2 *The Agenda of the* Boule *and Assembly*

Hiera and *hosia* also appear in texts relating to the agenda of the *boule* and assembly. Summarised, the *Ath.Pol.* 43.2–6, the best-known passage, reports that the assembly was to meet at least four times in each prytany, dealing with respectively:

In session 1, confirmation of the magistrates in office; food supply; defence; requests for *eisangeliai*, trials on charges of major offences against the *polis* by anyone who wishes (*ho boulomenos*); and issues regarding confiscated estates or heiresses;[151]

In session 2, petitions, namely anyone wishing to discuss a matter, either *idios* (private) or *demosios* (public), taking the form of a supplication;

In sessions 3 and 4, 'concerning other business (*ta alla*), in which the laws order there to be conducted three cases of *hiera*, three audiences of heralds and ambassadors, and three cases of *hosia*'.[152]

A comparable, though not identical, account of the agenda features in Aeschines' indictment of Timarchos in 346:

> How does [the lawgiver] tell the presiding board to conduct the business of the assembly? When the purification sacrifice has been carried around and the herald has made the ancestral prayers, he tells the board to conduct a vote to select matters for debate pertaining to the ancestral *hiera* and for heralds and embassies and matters pertaining to *hosia*, and after this the herald asks: 'Who of those over fifty years of age wants to address the assembly?' And when all these have spoken, he invites any

[151] In the sixth prytany, the desirability of an ostracism and several specific legal complaints were added to the agenda of the first session; *Ath.Pol.* 43.5.

[152] *Ath.Pol.* 43.6: αἱ δὲ δύο περὶ τῶν ἄλλων εἰσίν, ἐν αἷς κελεύουσιν οἱ νόμοι τρία μὲν ἱερῶν χρηματίζειν, τρία δὲ κήρυξιν καὶ πρεσβείαις, τρία δὲ ὁσίων. It is not entirely clear whether three cases of *hiera*, ambassadors and *hosia* are to feature in each session or in both combined, but most scholars agree that sessions 3 and 4 each contained the 3 × 3 items. For the place on the agenda of proposals documented in inscribed decrees, Hansen (1984), esp. 128–9 (translating *hosia* as 'secular' items).

> of the other Athenians who wants to (*ho boulomenos*), for whom it is permitted, to speak.[153]

Priority of the *hiera* on the agenda is well attested in Athens in inscribed decrees, as is the honour granted to important guests to speak immediately 'after the *hiera*'.[154] On the agenda, *ta hiera* included first of all the reports on the outcome of the sacrifices by *polis* priests and priestesses; and probably also all other matters regarding sacrifices, temples and other property of the gods.

But what were the *hosia*? *Ath.Pol.* does not explain what kind of issues this item included, but we may infer from the structure of the agenda that they were not 'secular' matters. The food supply and defence, probably the most common and pressing issues of this kind, and anything else of a 'secular' nature, were discussed in sessions 1 and 2 and could be raised again after *ta hosia*. Concerning *ta alla* (i.e. the agenda for sessions 3 and 4) the *Ath.Pol.* in no way suggests that 'three cases of *hiera*, three for heralds and ambassadors and three cases of *hosia*' *exhaust* this part of the agenda and that therefore all 'secular' matters belonged to *ta hosia*. On the contrary, the repetitive 'three' links all these topics together under one heading, as distinct from other issues. Heralds usually spoke under a *hieros* command, for instance when announcing a sacred truce, and as guests of the *polis* they, as well as ambassadors, were protected by Zeus Xenios. In sum, *ta hosia* on the agenda of *boule* and assembly are a category of human matters – that quality distinguished them from *ta hiera* – but *Ath.Pol.* does not imply that they covered *all* human affairs, notably 'secular' ones, nor is this assumption necessary to make sense of the agenda.

The earliest evidence of the agenda, however, does not refer to *hosia*, but rather to human affairs generally. In the constitution planned by the oligarchic regime of 411, according to *Ath.Pol.* (30.5), the agenda was to be: 'first *hiera*, second heralds, third embassies, and fourth the rest (*ta*

[153] Aeschin. 1.23: Καὶ πῶς κελεύει τοὺς προέδρους χρηματίζειν; ἐπειδὰν τὸ καθάρσιον περιενεχθῇ καὶ ὁ κῆρυξ τὰς πατρίους εὐχὰς εὔξηται, προχειροτονεῖν κελεύει τοὺς προέδρους περὶ ἱερῶν τῶν πατρίων καὶ κήρυξι καὶ πρεσβείαις καὶ ὁσίων, καὶ μετὰ ταῦτα ἐπερωτᾷ ὁ κῆρυξ· 'τίς ἀγορεύειν βούλεται τῶν ὑπὲρ πεντήκοντα ἔτη γεγονότων;' ἐπειδὰν δὲ οὗτοι πάντες εἴπωσι, τότ' ἤδη κελεύει λέγειν τῶν ἄλλων Ἀθηναίων τὸν βουλόμενον, οἷς ἔξεστιν. In this passage, Aeschines works towards the point where he will argue that Timarchos is not one for whom speaking in public is permitted; see Chapter 5.6.

[154] The first extant case at Athens is *IG* I³ 101.38 of 410/9; μετὰ τὰ ἱερά is restored here, based on the formulaic context; next, *IG* II² 1.73 (the grant of citizenship to the Samians) of 405/4 (also restored) and next about thirty cases in the fourth century. See also Rhodes, *CAAP*, 529 with further ref. and Lambert (2007) for the fourth-century honorific decrees.

alla)'. Something similar appears in a fragment of a law inscribed by the *anagrapheis* in ca. 409 on constitutional matters, notably the *boule* of Five Hundred, and other aspects of the democratic *politeia* after the oligarchic episode.[155] A few lines seem to set the agenda as '[first *hier*]*a*, second embassy, third *demosia*'.[156] Taking this evidence together with the passages in Aeschines and the *Ath.Pol.*, we may tentatively infer that in the last decades of the fifth century the agenda of the *boule* and assembly was fixed to begin with *hiera*, next heralds and embassies, and followed by *demosios* matters (called *ta alla* under the oligarchy), and that within that item *hosia* came to be distinguished from other *demosios* issues in the course of the fourth century. Owing to the patchy evidence we do not know what topics were listed under *hosia* and what under other rubrics. For instance, matters relating to public and private burial probably belonged under *ta hosia*. There is no extant evidence of these matters as items on the agenda of *boule* and assembly, but there is indirect evidence that they must have been discussed. Organisation of the public burial of the war dead and the selection of speakers of the *epitaphioi logoi* would have been a topic under '*ta hosia*', as would the management of cemeteries, including public burial of *proxenoi* and other prominent figures. Some aspects of citizens' conduct, if not brought under the heading of specific legal procedures or archons' authorities, might also have been discussed under *ta hosia*, notably if they had to do with conduct in sanctuaries and at festivals. Grants of citizenship, furthermore, would fit under *ta hosia*, because a new citizen was to be incorporated into the *polis*'s bond with the gods and all that came with it in the domain of participation; as we saw before, 'to share in *hiera kai hosia*' was a common notion in the discourse about citizenship. The suit against Nikomachos illuminates the financial side of *ta hosia* and their importance in the *polis*'s budget, and this may have contributed to the special place of *ta hosia* on the agenda. Asking if that was indeed the case takes us (again) to the *hiera kai hosia chremata* in the financial system of Athens.

155 *IG* I³ 105, with Shear (2011) 76–8, 100.

156 *IG* I³ 105 (ca. 409) l. 48–9: [... πρõτον hιερ]ά, δεύτερον πρεσβείαν, τρίτον δεμόσ[ια χρέματα ...]. Cf. Samons (2000) 169. The current restoration in *IG* of *chremata* after *demosia* is as yet unfounded: in decrees stating that the χρέματα of someone can become *demosios*, i.e. common property of the *demos* (*IG* I³ 14.32, 40.34, 46.28, 71.33, 89.54), the common phrase is 'his *chremata* will be *demosia*' (τὰ χρέματα αὐτô δεμόσια) but this is both in meaning and in structure quite different from *IG* I³ 105.

2.5.3 *Athens and* Hosios *Money*

In accounting for *hieros* and *demosios* resources, the *polis* observed distinct categories of ownership: there was no ambiguity as regards who particular budgets belonged to in terms of nominal ownership.[157] In terms of purposes, however, these resources were not kept separate. Public *hiera* (and other divine business) were paid for both from *hieros* money and from human property, either *demosios* funds or money or livestock contributed by individuals. This was both a matter of necessity – the *hieros* money of the gods was often insufficient, as the figures available for the fourth century demonstrate clearly – but also a matter of principle: the *demos* had to give from its own resources to the gods, if it were to be a gift at all. Conversely, *hieros* money was used for human business. Athens, like other *poleis*, borrowed heavily from its wealthy gods to finance the first stage of the Peloponnesian War. After the Archidamian War, Athens turned increasingly to other ways of funding, notably by raising the contributions of the allies, but loans from the gods remained in place until the end of the war.[158]

This financial give and take was a normal part of the reciprocity between the *polis* and its gods and posed no problems provided the *polis* paid back the *hieros* money it had borrowed. Athens's ambitions put great pressure on the city's finances and the *polis* reorganised the treasuries for its income and the channels for its expenditures several times. By the mid-fifth century, Athens had a *polis* treasury (*demosion*) for which the *apodektai* received the money and the *kolakretai* made the expenses; a treasury of the Delian League managed by the Hellenotamiai; the money of Athena managed by the Tamiai of Athena; and numerous smaller treasuries of *polis* gods and goddesses, often with their own *hieropoioi* or *epistatai*.[159] Around 433/2, the *polis* decided on Kallias' proposal to repay all the *polis*'s debts to the other gods plus the accumulated interest by creating a new treasury,

[157] For divine ownership, see Chapter 2.4.1 On income and expenditure of demes and *polis* from *hieros* and *demosios* resources, Whitehead (1986a) 152–8, Jameson (1988), Osborne (1988), Davies (1994), Jameson (1994), Rosivach (1994), Lambert (1997b), Jameson (1999), Samons (2000), Davies (2001), Horster (2004), Papazarkadas (2011), Pritchard (2015).

[158] The reasons for this change of policy are unclear; Samons (2000) 245–6 suggests that the *polis* perhaps felt uneasy about its huge debts to the gods, P.J. Rhodes (*per epist.*) that the *hieros* monies were simply insufficient to cover expenses.

[159] On the gradual formation of the *demosion* and the management of the League treasury, see Samons (2000), with full bibliography. Of the *hieros* treasuries of *polis* cults, some were located in demes; Linders (1975). For *polis* financial officials, Rhodes, *CAAP*, 391–2, esp. the *kolakretai* abolished ca. 418–415, certainly before 411/10; fourth century: Schuler (2005), with response by Rhodes (2007a).

with a new board of *tamiai* to 'supervise the money of the gods according to their powers and *hosion*'.[160] *Hosion* is an adverb here, indicating how the *tamiai* were to conduct their affairs, not an adjective describing the fund, which was not human property but *hieros* money, augmented with interest from the *demosion*.

In the last decade of the Peloponnesian War the control mechanisms for Athens's finances needed to be clarified and strengthened. The oligarchic regime of 411 entrusted both the *polis* treasury and that of the Delian League to an enlarged board of Hellenotamiai and intended to further reorganise the treasuries. In the 'future' constitution, the *boule*

> every year should consist of members over thirty years of age (who shall serve) without pay; from these shall come the *strategoi* and the Nine Archons and the *hieromnemon* and the taxiarchs and hipparchs and phylarchs and commanders for the guard posts and the ten Tamiai of the *hiera chremata* of the goddess (Athena) and of the Other Gods, and treasurers of the Greek fund (Hellenotamiai) and of all the other *hosios* monies, (numbering) twenty, and the *hieropoioi* and the *epimeletai*, (numbering) ten each; and all of these were to be elected from a list selected by the current *boule*.[161]

Although in other respects this plan did not materialise, the treasuries were in fact reorganised: by 406/5 all *hieros* treasuries were managed by the Tamiai of Athena and all monies belonging to the *polis* and her allies by the Hellenotamiai. This dual structure of the *polis*'s treasuries and their administration was more strictly aligned to the distinction between the gods and humans as owners of these monies and was kept in place for some time.[162] After the war, the Hellenotamiai were dissolved together

160 *IG* I³ 52 A; ML 58; (Kallias decree) l. 16: ℎόσα δυνατὸν καὶ ὅσιον. The intention of this phrase can be compared with the commendation for the *boule* to act 'as piously (ὡς εὐσεβέστατα) as possible' with regard to Demeter and Kore, *IG* II³ 1, 292 = RO 58 (the decree on the Sacred Orgas, 352/1) l. 15, 51. The date of the Kallias decrees A and B is contested; Wade-Gery (1931) and Rhodes (2009b) 5, n. 26: 434/3 for both decrees; persuasively Pritchett (1971): 432; Kallet-Marx (1989) different dates for Kallias A and B, cf. Samons (2000) 227–9: Kallias A decided in 432, 'Kallias' B decided in 422/1 and both B and A inscribed. Kennelly (2003): before 437 or after 431. For my purpose here, the exact date is not important.

161 *Ath.Pol.* 30.2: τούτων δ᾽ εἶναι τοὺς στρατηγοὺς καὶ τοὺς ἐννέα ἄρχοντας καὶ τὸν ἱερομνήμονα καὶ τοὺς ταξιάρχους καὶ ἱππάρχους καὶ φυλάρχους καὶ ἄρχοντας εἰς τὰ φρούρια καὶ ταμίας τῶν ἱερῶν χρημάτων τῇ θε[ῷ] καὶ τοῖς ἄλλοις θεοῖς δέκα καὶ ἑλληνοταμίας καὶ τῶν ἄλλων ὁσίων χρημάτων ἁπάντων εἴκοσιν οἳ διαχειριοῦσιν, καὶ ἱεροποιοὺς καὶ ἐπιμελητὰς δέκα ἑκατέρους· αἱρεῖσθαι δὲ πάντας τούτους ἐκ προκρίτων, ἐκ τῶν ἀεὶ βουλευόντων πλείους προκρίνοντας.

162 Samons (2000) 258–63; 'the reorganisation served a practical need to divide the *polis*' fiscal duties in a rational manner' (261). Papazarkadas (2011) 85 suggests that here perhaps are the earliest signs of the *merismos* that appears more clearly in the fourth century.

with the Athenian empire, and the treasury of Athens was reorganised once more.

If the adjective *hosios* as applied to a part of the money controlled by the Hellenotamiai appeared authentically in the text of *Ath.Pol.*,[163] it is the first time we hear of *hosios* money at *polis* level. What does it mean here? On analogy with the other cases we saw so far, this *demosios* money must have been labelled *hosios* because of its purpose to honour the gods. The Hellenotamiai feature here in a list of officials (*tamiai*, *hieropoioi*, *epimeletai*) who were all in charge of *hieros* monies. This applied to the Hellenotamiai in a different manner, as they converted human money into *hiera chremata* when they handed over the allies' *aparchai*, the sixtieth part of the tribute, to Athena. After 406/5 they also paid the interest due on *hieros* loans, together with such expenses on *hiera* as they funded, from the *polis* treasury in their care. In other words, it was appropriate to label some of the money in the charge of the Hellenotamiai *hosios*.

That all *polis* budgets could be termed *hosios* is implausible, for both administrative and financial reasons. After the Peloponnesian War, monies in the *dioikesis* (financial administration) were assigned to particular purposes by a process laid down in law, called *merismos*.[164] In Demosthenes' time, the *polis* distributed its *demosios* monies in two major categories, the *stratiotika* and the rest (consisting of several budgets). Military costs including those of the navy were in principle covered from the *stratiotika*, filled since 374/3 from various resources, including from the proceeds of sales of grain under the Grain Tax Law of that year, which were not included in the *merismos*.[165] The other treasury was filled by all kinds of revenues and divided into various budgets following the *merismos*, some of them with their own officials.[166]

Part of the *demosios* monies were used for *hosios* purposes: in a city famous for having more festivals than any other, paying for the *hiera* required a considerable amount of money. In 343/2 the annual *polis* revenue from sacred rentals was ca. 4–6 T., i.e. 1–2 per cent of the total *polis*

163 It is not certain that this adjective was used in the source of the *Ath.Pol.*, but the use of *hosios* for money in the account of Ikarion provides a contemporary parallel. Rhodes, *CAAP* , *ad loc.*, 391–2 and Samons (2000) 258–61 defend the present composition of the text, once suspected of being corrupt.

164 *Ath.Pol.* 48.2, Rhodes (2007a). The *merismos* is generally regarded as an invention of the early fourth century, but see n. 162.

165 *SEG* 47.96, RO 26.51–61, Stroud (1998), Rhodes (2007a) 355.

166 For some time, 'until the law of Hegemon', the officials who held the *theorika* were also responsible for many other public finances; Aeschin. 3.25, Harp. *s.v.* θεωρικόν, Hansen (1991) 261–4, Rhodes (2007a) 353.

revenue of approximately 400 T., and the first call on this was to fund building and maintenance of divine property. Only what was left over from these expenses could be used to fund sacrifices; the rest of the costs of sacrifices had to be paid by the *polis*.[167] Of particular importance in this context is the *theorika*, which subsidised citizens' participation in festivals and attendance at the Dionysian drama performances; the costs amounted from 15 to 100 T. a year.[168] Theatres used for dramatic festivals and other meetings needed to be built or refurbished from time to time.[169] Theatres were *hiera*, and were paid for mostly by *demosios*, hence *hosios* money. It would appear, then, that in the fourth century *hosios* money gained in prominence and size due to the flow of *demosios* money, through the *theorika* and otherwise, to the Dionysian festivals and theatres and to the growing number of Athenian *hiera* more widely. The Athenian *demos* benefited enormously from these events, in which the *polis* acted as its own *euergetes*, simultaneously pleasing the gods and themselves with spectacles and sacrifices and, for the *demos*, the enjoyment of meat. The funding of *hiera* did not comprise the majority of the city's expenses, but it was nevertheless substantial. Lycurgus is said to have raised the *polis*'s annual revenues from 600 to 1,200 T. to meet the costs of his extensive religious and cultural programme to revive the morale and status of Athens after the disaster of Chaeroneia.[170] Once the adjective *hosios* was applied to money, especially to the money the *polis* used for its *hiera*, it gradually seems to have changed from a describer of human conduct into a label firmly attached to this money (*hosia chremata*), but the meaning remained the same.

Towards the mid-fourth century, the frequent references in political and forensic oratory indicate that by then *hiera kai hosia chremata* were

[167] For the sacred rentals, *Ag.* 19.50, 6; calculations by Papazarkadas (2011) 93–8, with critical comments by Rousset (2013) 115. Even if the annual revenue from sacred rentals were entirely spent on sacrifice, it would pay for 360 oxen at 100 dr. apiece, half the number of oxen (724) slain between 334 and 331 according to the Dermatikon accounts (*IG* II² 1496) at only twelve *polis* festivals (for numbers and price of oxen, Rosivach (1994) 68–72). Beside the rentals, the gods received some income from *aparchai*, sacred fines and donations.

[168] *Ath.Pol.* 43.1; some ascribe creation of the *theorika* to Agyrrhios, who raised the attendance fee for the assembly (*Ath.Pol.* 41.3), but Rhodes (*CAAP*, *ad loc.* and Rhodes (2007a) 350) argues that the initiative probably belonged to Eubulus, who, shortly after 355, raised the share of the *demosios* money assigned to the *theorika*. For the costs of the Dionysia, Wilson (2008), Pritchard (2015) 48–51, 114.

[169] Wilson (2008). Wealthy individuals also contributed, especially in the demes, which honoured them for their *euergesia*; Wilson (2010).

[170] [Plut.] *X orat.* 842f, Humphreys (2004a) 84–5, Lambert (2010a). One case of such funding is the law and decree of ca. 335 on leasing the 'Nea' to enhance the 'Little' Panathenaea (*IG* II³ 1, 447 = RO 81). Sales of public lands enriched the *polis*'s treasuries, as well as those of the gods; see Lambert (1997b), Papazarkadas (2011) 242.

established and well-known categories of money. In Demosthenes' speech (24) against Timocrates of 353, as we saw above, they take centre stage. The trial itself concerned a *graphe paranomon* against a proposal by Timocrates that would, on provision of security, allow relief to anyone in debt to the *polis* treasury until the ninth prytany, when all money owed to the *polis* had to be paid. As the speaker's references to the system of public finance are both incidental and strongly rhetorical, the picture of public finance conveyed by this text is neither impartial nor exhaustive. It sheds, however, interesting light on the *hosios* money.

After a long passage denouncing the injustice of giving licence to debtors and other scoundrels who rob the gods and their fellow citizens, the speaker pictures the disastrous effects that this proposed law would have on the economy of the *polis* and hence on its political and military power (91–102):

> Moreover, men of Athens, he destroys the *dioikesis*, both the *hieros* and the *hosios*. I will tell you how. You have a law in force, one among many excellent laws enacted, that those who keep *hiera* and *hosia chremata* are to pay these in to the *bouleuterion*, and that if they don't, the *boule* is to recover the money by the laws applicable to tax (*telos*) farmers. On that law, the management of *ta koina* depends. It is this law that sees to it that the monies for the assembly, the sacrifices, the *boule*, the cavalry and the rest are provided. Because the revenues from the *telos* are insufficient for the *dioikesis* [to cover these expenses], the extra monies we call supplementary are paid in, under the force of this law. How would not all that is necessary for running the *polis* be shattered to ruin, when the income of the taxes (*tele*) would be insufficient for the *dioikesis*, but instead there would be a huge deficit, and when this deficit cannot be made up until the end of the year . . .?[171]

The speaker implies that the *polis* pays for *ta koina* from its income from taxes (*telos*) and from 'supplementary money', all of this being *hieros* and *hosios* monies. Individuals in charge of any such incomes must pay them

[171] Dem. 24.96–8. Ἔτι τοίνυν, ὦ ἄνδρες Ἀθηναῖοι, τὴν διοίκησιν ἀναιρεῖ, τήν θ' ἱερὰν καὶ τὴν ὁσίαν. ὡς δέ, ἐγὼ φράσω. ἔστιν ὑμῖν κύριος νόμος, καλῶς εἴπερ τις καὶ ἄλλος κείμενος, τοὺς ἔχοντας τά θ' ἱερὰ καὶ τὰ ὅσια χρήματα καταβάλλειν εἰς τὸ βουλευτήριον, εἰ δὲ μή, τὴν βουλὴν αὐτοὺς εἰσπράττειν χρωμένην τοῖς νόμοις τοῖς τελωνικοῖς. διὰ τοίνυν τοῦ νόμου τούτου διοικεῖται τὰ κοινά· τὰ γὰρ εἰς τὰς ἐκκλησίας καὶ τὰς θυσίας καὶ τὴν βουλὴν καὶ τοὺς ἱππέας καὶ τἄλλα χρήματ' ἀναλισκόμενα, οὗτός ἐσθ' ὁ νόμος ὁ ποιῶν προσευπορεῖσθαι. οὐ γὰρ ὄντων ἱκανῶν τῶν ἐκ τῶν τελῶν χρημάτων τῇ διοικήσει, τὰ προσκαταβλήματ' ὀνομαζόμενα διὰ τὸν τοῦ νόμου τούτου φόβον καταβάλλεται. πῶς οὖν οὐχ ἅπαντ' ἀνάγκη καταλυθῆναι τὰ τῆς πόλεως, ὅταν αἱ μὲν τῶν τελῶν καταβολαὶ μὴ ὦσ' ἱκαναὶ τῇ διοικήσει, ἀλλ' ἐνδέῃ πολλῶν, καὶ μηδὲ ταῦτ' ἀλλ' ἢ περὶ λήγοντα τὸν ἐνιαυτὸν ᾖ λαβεῖν ... For *telos*: Ostwald (1996) 166, Davies (1997) 33.

in as soon as possible; if they all waited until the ninth prytany because the penalties had been abolished, Athens's navy, 'the assembly, the sacrifices, the *boule*, the cavalry and the rest' would soon be undermined.[172] It seems that, by referring in the first sentence to the *hieros* and the *hosios dioikesis*, the speaker intends to cover the entirety of *ta koina* that he goes on to mention. Strictly speaking this cannot be correct, since only the budget for sacrifices and other *hiera* could be called *hosios*. This passage, therefore, is not straightforward.

Perhaps it was not meant to be. I would argue that the *hiera kai hosia chremata* here were what they normally are, i.e. money owned by the gods and that part of the *demosios* budget designated for *hosios* purposes, but that the speaker manipulates the expression the *hieros* and *hosios dioikesis* for his own ends. To incriminate Timocrates' proposal he states not only that the perpetrators were robbing the gods of their due and the *demos* of their *hosios* funds, but also that the illegal proposal will create havoc among *all* the expenditures of the *polis* due to the interdependence of the budgets in the *dioikesis* – just as the plaintiff did in his charge against Nikomachos. If money is spent on one purpose, it cannot be spent on another, and virtually all budgets were connected through the *merismos*. This was true enough. But by calling the whole *dioikesis hosios* Demosthenes brings all regular expenses under this umbrella, stretching the reference of *hosios* beyond its normal use. Demosthenes thus seems to bank on the adjective's positive value, evoking in one stroke the favour of the gods and the well-being of the people. About four years later, however, he ran up against the very same mentality of the *demos* he had used to bolster his policy against Timocrates. Trying to move the Athenians to help the Olynthians and spend more on the war effort, Demosthenes pressed the *demos* to redirect money from the *theorika* (*hosios*) to the *stratiotika* (not *hosios*).[173] He did not succeed.

If my view that *hosios* money to be used for the Athenian festivals became an increasingly important component of the budgets underlying *ta hosia*, and hence of the conception of *ta hosia* generally, is valid, it helps make sense of two rather opaque passages of Xenophon and Isocrates. In his treatise *Areopagiticus*, Isocrates pleaded for a *politeia* such as he envisioned Solon and Cleisthenes had created, in which the Areopagus embodied the virtues of the *polis* and all the citizens had been dutiful,

[172] Dem. 24.82, 111: debtors such as tax farmers who owed *hosios* monies had to pay double the amount as a fine, those owing *hieros* monies a tenfold fine if they failed to pay in time.

[173] Dem. *Olynth.* 1.20 (349); *Olynth.* 3.11 and *passim* (348), with Hansen (1976b).

frugal, just and courageous. To show that he does not object to democracy *per se*, but only to its extreme version practised in his own time, Isocrates praises the democracy of the later fifth century, rhetorically asking:

> And who of my own generation does not remember that the democracy arranged the city so well with respect to the *hiera* and the *hosia* that all those who also now come to visit consider her worthy not only to rule over the Greeks but over the whole world?[174]

He goes on to recall the misdeeds of the Thirty who had plundered the *hiera* and neglected the *hosia*.[175] *Hiera* that were plundered would mean especially the temples, but combined with *hosia* that were neglected this reference recalls the *hiera kai hosia* in the speech against Nikomachos, in other words the *polis*'s sacrificial and festival life laid down in the sacrificial calendar.

The phrase 'worth both seeing and hearing' recurs in relation to *hiera kai hosia* in Xenophon's *Poroi*. In the 350s, the *polis* faced recurrent financial difficulties, partly due to the rising costs of warfare. Xenophon argued that Athens could improve its financial situation by keeping peace:

> Then there will be those rich in corn and wine and oil and cattle; men possessed of brains and money to invest; artisans and professors and philosophers; poets and the people who make use of their works; those to whom *hiera* or *hosia* appeal that are worth seeing or hearing. Besides, where will those who want to buy or sell many things quickly meet with better success in their efforts than at Athens?[176]

The *hiera* and *hosia* intended here are patently the temples, the theatres and the processions, dramatic festivals and other competitions in sports and music in honour of the gods.[177] Xenophon argues here that the *hiera kai hosia* are not just a cause of expenditure but also a potential source of income in times of peace when visitors would flock to the city.

In sum, on the available evidence we may understand *hosia chremata* as the *demosios* money used for the *polis*'s *hiera*, in the fourth century

[174] Isoc. 7.66: Καὶ μὲν δὴ καὶ τάδε τίς οὐ μνημονεύει τῶν ἡλικιωτῶν τῶν ἐμῶν, τὴν μὲν δημοκρατίαν οὕτω κοσμήσασαν τὴν πόλιν καὶ τοῖς ἱεροῖς καὶ τοῖς ὁσίοις ὥστ᾽ ἔτι καὶ νῦν τοὺς ἀφικνουμένους νομίζειν αὐτὴν ἀξίαν εἶναι μὴ μόνον τῶν Ἑλλήνων ἄρχειν;

[175] Isoc. 7.66: τοὺς δὲ τριάκοντα τῶν μὲν ἀμελήσαντες, τὰ δὲ συλήσαντας. The construction seems to be chiastic: 'plundering' must refer to *hiera*, 'neglecting' to *hosia*.

[176] Xen. *Por.* 5.3–4: καὶ μὴν χειροτέχναι τε καὶ σοφισταὶ καὶ φιλόσοφοι, οἱ δὲ ποιηταί, οἱ δὲ τὰ τούτων μεταχειριζόμενοι, οἱ δὲ ἀξιοθεάτων ἢ ἀξιακούστων ἱερῶν ἢ ὁσίων ἐπιθυμοῦντες; ἀλλὰ μὴν καὶ οἱ δεόμενοι πολλὰ ταχὺ ἀποδίδοσθαι ἢ πρίασθαι ποῦ τούτων μᾶλλον ἂν τύχοιεν ἢ Ἀθήνησιν; transl. E.C. Marchant (Loeb ed.), slightly modified.

[177] Cf. Gauthier (1976) *ad loc.*

covering especially the costs of the flourishing festivals, including the dramatic festivals of Dionysus. Whether or not the costs of the *hiera kai hosia* were in reality high in comparison to other expenditures, the *hosios* money was in the first place of great ideological value for the benefits, social, cultural, religious and even nutritious, that it supplied for the *demos*. Enhanced by the inherent positive value of *hosios*, the *hosia chremata* must have carried much weight in any political argument, and once a purpose of public money was qualified as *hosios*, it was difficult to redirect such sums for other expenditures. While festival life grew in tandem with the expansion of the democracy, *hosios* money likewise became an increasingly important part of the *polis*'s budgets. This development probably played a prominent part in making *ta hosia*, a notion covering also many other matters such as public burials, a special item on the agenda of the *boule* and assembly.

2.5.4 *The Ephebic Oath*

Finally, *hiera kai hosia* also featured in the oath the ephebes swore on becoming an adult member of the *polis*. A text of the oath, together with the 'oath the Greeks swore when they were to fight the barbarians' – usually taken to be the oath of Plataia (479) but perhaps rather that of Marathon (490) – was dedicated in the deme Acharnai in the third quarter of the fourth century, together with a new altar by the priest of Ares and Athena Areia 'in order that the Athenians and the Acharnians may be pious (*eusebes*) towards the gods'.[178] The text of the inscription is as follows:

> Gods. The priest of Ares and Athena Areia, Dio son of Dio of Acharnai has dedicated this. (*v.*) The ancestral oath of the ephebes, which the ephebes must swear. (*v.*)
>
> 'I will not bring shame upon the sacred (*hieros*) weapons, nor shall I desert the man beside me (*parastates*), wherever I stand in the line. I shall fight in defence of *hiera kai hosia* and I shall not hand the fatherland (*patris*) on lessened, but greater and better both as far as I am able and in union with all. And I shall be obedient to whoever exercise power (*krainontes*) in a wise manner and to the laws (*thesmoi*) currently set up and to any set up in a wise manner in the future. If anyone destroys these, I shall not comply as far as I am able nor in union with all, and I shall honour the ancestral *hiera*. Witnesses: the gods Aglauros, Hestia, Enyo, Enyalios, Ares and Athena

[178] *SEG* 21.519; RO 88; ll. 9–10. Marathon rather than Plataia, Krentz (2007), Miles (2014).

> Areia, Zeus, Thallo, Auxo, Hegemone, Heracles, and the boundaries of my fatherland, wheat, barley, vines, olives, figs.'[179]

There are background issues here relating to the historical development of the *ephebeia* and the relationship to their originals (if any) of fourth-century texts that claim to be copies of much older ones – much debated questions that take us too far to discuss fully here.[180] *Ath.Pol.* 42 describes the programme of the *ephebeia* and its role in the *polis* institutions as set on a new footing on the initiative of Epikrates just before 334.[181] After a scrutiny (*dokimasia*) in the demes of the boys' citizen descent and age, the ephebes received two years of military training especially for defence of the frontiers. Before entering on their duties, the young men made a tour of the temples (*hiera*) of Attica, an experience intended, no doubt, to enhance the engagement with which they swore their oath in the sanctuary of Aglauros on the Acropolis. Some form of military training of young male citizens existed before the new set-up, and so did the oath. Aeschines quoted it when he urged the city to action against Philip of Macedon, and probably the priest in Acharnai inscribed the oaths for similar reasons, soliciting military alertness against the Macedonian threat, inspired by ancestral prowess.[182] For the purpose of this study we need to ask if *hiera kai hosia* in this text in any way complicates the understanding of the expression we have arrived at so far, and how the expression ties in with its context in the ephebic oath.

In the oath the ephebes swore not to bring shame upon the *hiera hopla* (l. 8), an expression attested only here.[183] It is not clear if *hieros* here means that the weapons had actually been dedicated to the gods at some point, or rather expresses the wish that they be placed 'under divine power and

179 Text and translation, RO 88; I have, however, changed their translation of *hiera kai hosia* in ll. 8–9: Οὐκ αἰσχυνῶ τὰ ἱερὰ ὅπλα, οὐδὲ λείψω τὸν παραστάτην ὅπου ἂν στοιχήσω· ἀμυνῶ δὲ καὶ ὑπὲρ ἱερῶν καὶ ὁσίων. For discussion of slightly different versions in Poll. *Onom.* 8.105–6, Stob. 4.1.48, see RO comm. 445–6.

180 Friend (2009) considers the *ephebeia* entirely a Lycourgan institution to defend the Attic borders, set up in 335 after Alexander's destruction of Thebes, whereas Reinmuth (1971) 124, Rhodes, *CAAP*, 494–5, Burckhardt (1996) 33 regard it as an older institution that was fundamentally reorganised after Chaeroneia. Chankowski (2010) 117–27 argues that ephebes pre-Epikrates were not a defined age class and that the *ephebeia* at this period was a voluntary (but socially expected) military service organised by law. *Ath.Pol.* 42.1–3 implies that all adolescent male citizens were included in the *ephebeia* programme, and so does Lyc. *Leoc.* 76, but that does not preclude a selective participation before Epikrates' law. For reinscribed 'old' documents, Davies (1996).

181 The programme is corroborated by numerous inscriptions honouring ephebes and their trainers: Reinmuth (1971), Friend (2009).

182 Aeschines quoting the oath: Dem. 19.303 (of 348); *ephebeia*: Aeschin. 1.49, 2.167; Xen. *Por.* 4.51–2. Motive: RO comm. 447–8.

183 RO 88, l. 8; Lyc. *Leoc.* 76.

protection'. Defence of *hiera kai hosia* then leads directly to commitment to the *patris* (fatherland, ll. 9–10), a sequence recalling (Draco's) homicide law. The use of the archaic term *thesmoi* for written laws, and *krainontes* (perhaps referring to *archontes*) instead of the *demos* as the legitimate authority, both suggest a original date for this text before Cleisthenes.[184] Finally, the promise to honour the ancestral religion (*hiera ta patria*) picks up again the earlier *hiera* and *patris*.

Fittingly, the witnesses are divinities associated with warfare (Enyo, Enyalios, Ares and Athena Areia), growth (Thallo, Auxo, Hegemone?) and young men (Heracles), Zeus as the god of social order, including keeping oaths, and Hestia, the goddess of the *polis*'s hearth. Ares and Athena Areia were common deities in civic oaths.[185] The prime figure is the heroine Aglauros: in her *hieron*, on the east slope of the Acropolis, the ephebes swore their oath. She was, in one version of the myth, a daughter of Cecrops who, following an oracle of Apollo, sacrificed herself for the city by throwing herself off the Acropolis, when Athens was threatened by King Eumolpos.[186] Aglauros was *kourotrophos*, taking care of the young and giving an example by her courage and patriotism.[187] Her cult, combining fertility and maturation – the precious crops mentioned in the ephebic oath are both Athens's youth and its agricultural produce – with genealogical–cultic myths on the origins of the *polis* goes back to the archaic age.[188]

184 RO comm. 445–6. For the development of (archaic) *thesmos* into (classical) *nomos* referring to written law, Ostwald (1969), Hölkeskamp (2002a), Gagarin (2008) 33–4. Linguistic evidence of early date: Chankowski (2010) 128, RO comm. 440–8.

185 For the gods in the oath, Parker, *PS*, 397–8, 434–7.

186 According to Philochoros (*FGrH* 328 F 105–6 = *Schol.* Dem. 19.303) Aglauros was the first priestess of Athena; the name of the heroine is rendered here as Agraulos. The Agraulos theme was recast in the daughters of Erechtheus, the Hyakinthidai who sacrificed themselves for the city in the war against Eumolpos in Eur. *Erechth.* fr. 65; in his version, Praxithea was the first priestess of Athena Polias.

187 Her sister Pandrosos was *koretrophos* of young girls, especially the *arrhephoroi*, girls between seven and eleven years of age entrusted with a various duties in the cult of Athena, among them helping with weaving the *peplos*. The two heroines protected the maturation of both sexes symmetrically; see Sourvinou-Inwood (2011) 28–111, who argues that Aglauros' role as nurse of the infant Erichthonios was an elaboration of her original cultic–mythical complex. Their cults were embedded in the Plynteria and Kallynteria, festivals of Athena Polias, in which young men (ephebes) and young girls (*plynterides* or *loutrides*) washed and dressed the old wooden statue of the goddess; Parker, *PS*, 478–9.

188 Her cult was also observed locally, e.g. at Thorikos and Erchia in the context of the Plynteria; the fact that, in Thorikos, the festival was celebrated at a date other than that of the *polis* suggests an independent tradition; Thorikos: *NGSL* no. 1, ll. 52–4; Erchia: *LSCG* 18.57–8; archaic elements and kourotrophic features in cult: Kron (1981), Kearns (1989) 23–7, 57–63, Larson (1995) 39–41, Parker, *PS*, 434. Date of Thorikos Plynteria: Parker, *PS*, 76–7. Cult of Aglauros by the Salaminioi, a *genos* that originated in the sixth century at the latest: RO 37.45.

Whatever the particular adaptations made in the Lycurgan age, parts of the ephebic oath certainly preceded the fourth century and probably the fifth. Aeschines' speech and Lycurgus' *Against Leocrates* show that in the fourth century public speakers could draw on the oath to impress or persuade their audience: all or most adult men had once sworn these very words and they heard the same words sworn by others every year. P. Siewert points to fifth-century texts that seem to echo words or phrases typical of the oath: Aeschylus' *Persians* of 472, where the chorus bewails (l. 957) 'those who stood beside you (*parastatai*)', Sophocles *Antigone*, where Creon pronounces (ll. 664–71) that one must obey those who are in power (*kratunousin*) and that one can trust a man who holds his post and remains a loyal fighter next to his comrade (*parastates*), and, more generally, Pericles' speeches in Thucydides (1.144; 2.37).[189]

If, then, the oath seems to have existed in the fifth century more or less as inscribed in Acharnai, it is worth asking whether we find, in earlier literature, allusions to the clause 'I shall fight in defence of *hiera kai hosia*'. I would tentatively suggest there might be such an allusion in a famous episode in Xenophon's *Hellenika* when the democrats had won a victory against forces of the Thirty, and Kleokritos, one of the Kerykes, addressed Athenians of both parties on the battlefield:

> Fellow citizens, why do you drive us out of the city? Why do you want to kill us? As you know, we never did you any harm, but we have shared with you (*metechein*) the most solemn *hiera* and sacrifices (*thysia*) and the most beautiful festivals (*heortai*), we have been companions in the *choros* and schoolmates and comrades in arms, and we have been through many dangers with you both by land and by sea on behalf of the safety and freedom of us both. In the name of the gods of our fathers and our mothers, of our relations as relatives and in-laws and of our comradeship – for many of us share all these things with one another – cease out of respect for both gods and men to do wrong to your fatherland, and do not obey the most *anhosios* Thirty, who for the sake of their private gain have killed in eight months more Athenians, almost, than all the Peloponnesians in ten years of war. And when we might live in peace, these men bring upon us a war that is most shameful and terrible, utterly *anhosios* and hated among gods and men, a war with one another. Nonetheless, you should know that for some of those now slain by us not only you, but also we grieve deeply.[190]

Allusions to the 'ephebic oath' in this speech may be charted (Table 2.1).

[189] Siewert (1977).
[190] Xen. *Hell.* 2.4.20–2; transl. C.L. Brownson (Loeb ed.), slightly modified.

Table 2.1. *Possible allusions to the ephebic oath in Xen.* Hell. *2.4.20–2*

I shall not shame the *hieros* weapons οὐκ αἰσχυνῶ τὰ ἱερὰ ὅπλα I shall defend *hiera kai hosia*	Oppose the most *anhosios* Thirty . . . who bring a most shameful, damaging, *anhosios* and hateful war among ourselves
ἀμυνῶ δὲ καὶ ὑπὲρ ἱερῶν καὶ ὁσίων	μὴ πείθεσθε τοῖς ἀνοσιωτάτοις τριάκοντα . . . οὗτοι τὸν πάντων αἴσχιστόν τε καὶ χαλεπώτατον καὶ ἀνοσιώτατον καὶ ἔχθιστον καὶ θεοῖς καὶ ἀνθρώποις πόλεμον ἡμῖν πρὸς ἀλλήλους παρέχουσιν.
	We *metechein* with you in all the most solemn *hiera* and *thysia* and most beautiful festivals
	μετεσχήκαμεν δὲ ὑμῖν καὶ ἱερῶν τῶν σεμνοτάτων καὶ θυσιῶν καὶ ἑορτῶν τῶν καλλίστων
Stay with *parastatês*	we faced many dangers together with you both by land and by sea on behalf of the safety and freedom of us both.
οὐδὲ λείψω τὸν παραστάτην	πολλὰ μεθ' ὑμῶν κεκινδυνεύκαμεν κατὰ γῆν καὶ κατὰ θάλατταν ὑπὲρ τῆς κοινῆς ἀμφοτέρων ἡμῶν σωτηρίας τε καὶ ἐλευθερίας.
with all (2 ×)	the same upbringing (*syn-*) in a *choros* together (*syn-*) comrades in arms (*syn-*)
μετὰ ἁπάντων . . . μετὰ πάντων	συγχορευταὶ καὶ συμφοιτηταὶ γεγενήμεθα καὶ συστρατιῶται,
hand on the fatherland not lessened, but greater and better	cease out of respect for both gods and men to do wrong to your fatherland
ὀκ ἐλάττω παραδώσω τὴν πατρίδα, πλείω δὲ καὶ ἀρείω	αἰδούμενοι καὶ θεοὺς καὶ ἀνθρώπους παύσασθε ἁμαρτάνοντες εἰς τὴν πατρίδα
I shall honour the *hiera* of the fathers	by the gods of our fathers and mothers
τιμήσω ἱερὰ τὰ πάτρια	πρὸς θεῶν πατρῴων καὶ μητρῴων

It is difficult to tell how close Xenophon's text comes to Kleokritos' actual speech: either the gist of it was remembered quite well because of its allusions to the oath, or Xenophon may have highlighted such allusions; we know from the *Poroi* that he was interested in the *ephebeia* as an institution that could enhance the *polis*'s discipline and effectiveness in war.[191] At all events, the meaning of *hiera kai hosia* in the oath accords with the connotations of the phrase we have observed earlier in terms of the intimate connection between the *polis* and its gods.

2.6 The Core of the *Polis*

Key texts of the fifth and fourth centuries allow us to conclude that *hiera kai hosia* was an expression representing the bond between the *polis* and the gods perceived from the human perspective, a long-term reciprocity that was pleasing to the gods and essential to the well-being and continuity of the *polis*. *Hiera kai hosia* does not mean 'matters sacred and profane', but refers to human obligations to the gods in two distinct but related ways, namely the human gifts to the gods (*hiera*) and conduct towards gods and humans showing proper respect for the gods (*hosia*). Being part of this bond was essential simultaneously at the level of the *polis* and in the private life of the family, and *hiera kai hosia* played a pivotal role in discourse about citizenship since in this bond the *polis* had entrenched its values, laws and institutions.

Over time, the adjective *hosios*, which normally denoted proper reverence for the gods and when used of objects metaphorically signalled the *hosios* conduct of their owners, came to be applied more and more frequently to human property, notably money, used for a *hosios* purpose. Especially for money owned by the *demos* to be used for *hiera* this expression came to be used on such a scale that these monies were regularly labelled *hosia chremata*, parallel to *hiera chremata*. By the mid-fourth century, these funds were highlighted as part of the *dioikesis*, earmarked for festivals and other *hiera*, notably the Dionysia. The *hosia* became a fixed item on the agenda of the *boule* and assembly, after the *hiera* and heralds. Though this agenda item will have included other *hosios* matters such as those relating to public funerals and oaths, the *hosia chremata* funding sacrifices and festivals were presumably a major component. This development reveals, beside the increasing sophistication of the *polis*'s budgeting systems, the successful efforts of the *demos* in making the *polis*'s institutions serve simultaneously divine interests and their own.

191 Xen. *Por.* 4.51–2.

3

The Value of Descent

> We have also other evidence to give … that we are the children of Kiron's daughter. For as was fitting because we are the children of his own daughter, he never offered any sacrifice without us … and not only were we invited to such sacrifices, but he always took us into the country to the Dionysia … and when he sacrificed to Zeus Ktesios … we participated with him in the sacrifice and laid our hands with him on the *hiera* and shared with him all the rites, and he prayed for us to have health and good wealth … Our father, when we were born, introduced us to the phrateres and swearing an oath according to the established laws that he introduced children from an *aste* woman married by *engye* …
>
> Isaeus, *On the estate of Kiron*, 15–16, 19[1]

Being a citizen of classical Athens, I argued in the previous chapter, meant sharing in the *polis*, and the core of the *polis* was its bond with the gods, embodied in the gifts due to them (*hiera*) and in proper conduct towards the human and the divine world by which the gods set great store (*hosia*). In this chapter we turn to the fundamental question of membership. *Who* were the citizens? On what grounds was someone considered a citizen of the Athenian *polis* and why? An initial answer to these questions has been clear from the first lines of this study: in classical Athenian law, someone was a citizen because his or her parents were Athenian citizens. *Descent* was the defining criterion, more precisely legitimate descent from Athenian parents; it justified all claims to participation, as we saw Euxitheos going

[1] Is. 8.15–16: Ἡμεῖς τοίνυν καὶ ἄλλα τεκμήρια πρὸς τούτοις ἔχομεν εἰπεῖν … ὅτι ἐκ θυγατρὸς ἡμεῖς Κίρωνός ἐσμεν. Οἷα γὰρ εἰκὸς παίδων [ὑέων] <ὄντων> ἐξ ἑαυτοῦ θυγατρός, οὐδεπώποτε θυσίαν ἄνευ ἡμῶν οὐδεμίαν ἐποίησεν, ἀλλ' … πανταχοῦ παρῆμεν ἡμεῖς καὶ συνεθύομεν. Καὶ οὐ μόνον εἰς τὰ τοιαῦτα παρεκαλούμεθα, ἀλλὰ καὶ εἰς Διονύσια εἰς ἀγρὸν ἦγεν ἀεὶ ἡμᾶς … τῷ Διί τε θύων τῷ Κτησίῳ, … ταύτης ἡμεῖς ἐκοινωνοῦμεν καὶ τὰ ἱερὰ συνεχειρουργοῦμεν καὶ συνεπετίθεμεν καὶ τἄλλα συνεποιοῦμεν, καὶ ηὔχετο ἡμῖν ὑγίειαν διδόναι καὶ κτῆσιν ἀγαθήν. 19: Ὅ τε πατὴρ ἡμῶν, ἐπειδὴ ἐγενόμεθα, εἰς τοὺς φράτερας ἡμᾶς εἰσήγαγεν, ὀμόσας κατὰ τοὺς νόμους τοὺς κειμένους ἦ μὴν ἐξ ἀστῆς καὶ ἐγγυητῆς γυναικὸς εἰσάγειν.

to great lengths to demonstrate. Now we may note that transmission of citizen status by descent was the regular practice throughout the Greek world, as it has been and still is virtually universally: once someone is a citizen, his (or her, depending on the relevant laws) children are citizens too.[2] Given the ubiquity of this practice, the fact that at Athens the same principle obtained would hardly need explaining. Nonetheless, descent had not always been the primary criterion, so we want to know *when* and *why* it became the preferred way of organising the *polis*, and once this was the case, we should ask what *particular* meaning the Athenians assigned to descent and its function for transmitting citizenship.[3] What did it mean to be 'from' two Athenian parents? To answer these questions, I need to unpack them into smaller segments.

First of all, what do we mean by the modern word 'descent' that we use to encapsulate Athenian citizenship? Conceptions of descent give social meaning to the biological ties between parents and a child, connecting it to a wider network of family ties (kinship).[4] From the subjective perspective of an individual, descent ties you to the parents who gave you life, to your first social network (the family) and to the place where you came to know the world and the world came to know you. Beyond these origins in the immediate sense lie the origins of one's family and of the groups to which they belong, over generations back in time, up to the first remembered or imagined ancestors. Besides referring to an ancestral past, descent points to the future by rules for the transmission of kinship and, depending on the society in question, this includes transmission of property to

[2] Given descent as the criterion of citizen status, other questions present themselves: for the citizens, if additional criteria applied for specific roles within the community, and for outsiders, how one could enter the citizen body. These questions are addressed below, Chapters 5 and 6.

[3] Surprisingly few scholars have asked this question. Davies, who does so in the article discussed in Chapter 1, concludes (Davies (1977)) 121: 'the descent-group criterion ... lasted so long, I think, not because it was natural and logical, or because it was uncontentious, but because it represented the least troublesome compromise among violently opposing forces'. In brief, in Davies's view Athens chose 'descent' because it was the most practical and unambiguous criterion compared to many others. Lape (2010) takes a radically opposite view, arguing that the descent criterion was a sign of and supported an all-encompassing conception of race in Athens. However, as I argue here, descent was not typical only or mainly of Athens and the phenomena that Lape sees as signs of 'race' can be better explained differently.

[4] For a current anthropological definition of descent, see www.anthrobase.com/Dic/eng/index.html, *s.v.* descent: 'Kinship figured "downwards" from grandparents to parents to children to grandchildren etc. In many societies, descent is an important principle for distribution of inheritance and definition of group membership.' *S.v.* descent group: 'A group defined on the basis of descent from a common ancestor or ancestress. The group can consist of children of the same father/mother, of grandchildren of the same grandmother/father, great-grandchildren of the same great-grandparent etc., or of the descendants of these persons.'

new generations. The rights of a child to inherit require that it is recognised as heir, first by its parents and next by the group to which the family belongs. In other words, if the child is to take possession of inherited property without too much strife, a conception of legitimacy, i.e. authoritative societal rules concerning claims to descent and inheritance, is necessary. Rules of inheritance also include regulations on how the property is to be distributed amongst the legitimate heirs. As will become clear for the case of Athens, an inheritance consisted not only of material property but also of immaterial goods and obligations. In sum, descent is an arrangement to organise biological kinship into a social network and to ensure an optimal transmission of inheritance from one generation to the next, fitting the rules and expectations of society at large.

Starting from these general characteristics, can we tease out why and how the Athenians applied the idea and practices of descent to citizenship, that is how did they create and understand the connection between family and *polis*? How did the transmission of membership actually work, and did any significant changes in the system take place over time?

3.1 Claiming an Inheritance

The transmission of citizenship was laid down in Pericles' law mentioned in *Ath.Pol.* 26.3, to the effect that 'no one who was not born from both *astos* parents would participate (*metechein*) in the *polis*'. The law was confirmed in the laws of 403/2, to which Euxitheos referred when he asserted his citizen status as being born from two citizen parents.[5] In Chapter 2, we saw the relevant part of these laws, stating that 'no male or female *nothos* (bastard) has any claim, based on kinship on either side (*anchisteia*), to *hiera kai hosia*, as of the archonship of Eukleides'. It was quoted in two forensic speeches in which the right of inheritance to a family estate is at stake, one by Isaeus (6) on the inheritance of a certain Philoktemon, one in a speech by Demosthenes (43) on the much-disputed wealth of a certain Hagnias. In both speeches, the orators confirm that only those may lay claim to (a part of) the inheritance who are legitimate offspring, i.e. born from an Athenian father and an Athenian mother solemnly pledged; a *nothos* or *nothe* cannot inherit a share, on the male or the female side of the family.[6] Isaeus calls the disputed inheritance the *oikos* of Philoktemon, but in other speeches he also uses *oikos* in the sense of 'family' and uses the

[5] See Chapter 1.1; Chapter 2.1.

[6] For the rights of succession, see Chapter 3.4.

term *kleros* to designate the estate.[7] Demosthenes, referring to Hagnias' *oikos* which by the time of this lawsuit had been split into several *oikoi*, means by *oikos* 'family' and uses the term *kleros* to refer to the estate.[8] What do these terms mean?

An *oikos* in the sense of 'family' was not a defined entity in Athenian law, as D. MacDowell rightly pointed out, but the inference he draws, that Athenian law recognised not rights of families but only of individuals, does not follow.[9] The *oikos* as 'household' was a shell holding, at a certain point in time, the people who lived in the house (*oikia*), the family lines they represented and all its real estate and moveable goods, protected by the household gods.[10] The court cases about inheritances express the interests of families not only in the estate in the material sense, but also in the continuity of the family line and its ancestral cults; when orators refer to the *oikos* in inheritance cases, they are generally using the term in this comprehensive sense. In these respects, the *oikos* is analogous to the *polis*, likewise a shell including the people who belonged to it, its collective properties and its cults, each of which were the object of law, without the *polis* itself being a defined entity in law. For our present purposes, there can be no doubt that the court cases of Isaeus and Demosthenes just mentioned deal with claims to an inherited part of private property and interests, called *hiera kai hosia* in the laws.

The same expression, *hiera kai hosia*, is used in yet another speech by Demosthenes, which he wrote probably in 348/7 for a certain Mantitheos in a trial against his half-brother Boiotos (Dem. 39). In this lawsuit, one in a series about complicated claims to an inheritance, more was at stake than the property itself. Boiotos had successfully claimed legitimate birth from the same father, Mantias, as Mantitheos, but with a different mother; now no longer a *nothos* but a legitimate son, Boiotos had acquired his part of the patrimonial estate.[11] But he also asserted that his

7 *Oikos* meaning 'estate': Is. 6.47, 3.30, etc. *Oikos* meaning 'family': Is. 7.44, 10.4, 7 etc. The law inserted in Dem. 43.51 refers to the inheritance as *chremata* (all useful goods).

8 Dem. 43 (fifty-six passages).

9 MacDowell (1989). *Contra* MacDowell, Todd (1993) 205–6 points out that there was generally no way in which words became legally defined in Athens and that 'the absence of a word from legal statutes does not necessarily imply the absence of the corresponding idea from the legal system'. On a review of the evidence he concludes: 'Athenian law does deal with the interests not merely of individuals but of families as corporate groups.'

10 Foxhall (1989), Todd (1993) 204–10, Cox (1998) 130–5. Household gods: Parker, *PS*, 10–14. Difference between *oikia* and *oikos*, Xen. *Oec.* 1.5. For Aristotle (*Pol.* 1252b13–15) the *oikos* formed the smallest *koinonia* of the *polis*.

11 For the course of events, in which Plangon, Boiotos' mother, had made Mantias acknowledge the children as his, Dem. 39.3–4, *APF*, 364–8, Cox (1998) 86–7.

name was actually not Boiotos, but Mantitheos, the family name already carried by his half-brother, and he insisted on using it; by this name, he underscored his claim that he was in fact the elder brother, named after the paternal grandfather. To the first Mantitheos, this action represented an affront to his social *persona*, one that he tried to oppose in every way. Defending his exclusive claim to his name, Mantitheos conveyed to the *dikastai* his full willingness to grant Boiotos his legitimate birth and all the claims to property that came with it, but he also created a vivid picture of the immense difficulties the existence of a second Mantitheos would cause to himself and to the *polis*.[12] Turning to his half-brother, he implored him:

> (34) But, Boiotos, you terrible mischief maker, stop with what you are doing now, and if you don't want to, at least, by Zeus, listen to my advice: stop making trouble for yourself, stop filing baseless lawsuits against me, but enjoy that now you have a *polis*, property and a father. No one tries to rob you of those, and certainly not I.[13]

Boiotos was harming his own cause, Mantitheos continued, because by pestering his brother and claiming what was not his, everybody would think that he had intruded himself into a position that did not befit him (*proseko*). It was not his, Mantitheos', fault that for a long time their father had failed to recognise Boiotos as his son, nor was it his duty to find and recognise his father's children.

> (35) All the time that he [Mantias] did not do so, I also did not consider you as one who belonged (*proseko*), but since he has done so, I also regard you as such. What is the proof of this? You possess your portion (*meros*) of the ancestral estate (*ta patroia*) after my father's death. You share (*metechein*) in *hiera and hosia*. No one takes that away from you. [turning to the *dikastai*:] What does he want?[14]

In the first passage (34), Mantitheos pictures a chain of relations that together constitute the legitimate birth of Boiotos and its ensuing claims. Because legitimate birth is a condition of participating (*metechein*) in the *polis*, we would expect Mantitheos to present this chain as leading

[12] See Van 't Wout (2010b) for the necessity for both brothers to settle the issue in public, with both the (material) property and the (immaterial) claim to social *persona* equally at stake.

[13] Dem. 39.34: Ἀλλ', ὦ χαλεπώτατε Βοιωτέ, μάλιστα μὲν ὧν πράττεις πάντων παῦσαι, εἰ δ' ἄρα μὴ βούλει, ἐκεῖνό γε πρὸς Διὸς πείθου· παῦσαι μὲν σαυτῷ παρέχων πράγματα, παῦσαι δ' ἐμὲ συκοφαντῶν, ἀγάπα δ' ὅτι σοι πόλις, οὐσία, πατὴρ γέγονεν. οὐδεὶς ἀπελαύνει σ' ἀπὸ τούτων, οὔκουν ἔγωγε.

[14] Dem. 39.35: ὅν μὲν τοίνυν οὐκ ἐποιεῖτό σε χρόνον, οὐδ' ἐγὼ προσήκονθ' ἡγούμην, ἐπειδὴ δ' ἐποιήσατο, κἀγὼ νομίζω. τί τούτου σημεῖον; τῶν πατρῴων ἔχεις τὸ μέρος μετὰ τὴν τοῦ πατρὸς τελευτήν· ἱερῶν, ὁσίων μετέχεις· ἀπάγει σ' οὐδεὶς ἀπὸ τούτων. τί βούλει;

from the father acknowledging his son to membership in the *polis*. But Mantitheos presents the chain as running in the opposite direction, leading from the *polis* to private property and to the father, perhaps suggesting that the acknowledgement of Boiotos' relationship with his father was a result of the acceptance of his claims by the *dikastai*, i.e. the *polis*, in previous trials.

In (35), he begins the 'chain of legitimacy' with the paternal estate and next mentions the ensuing claim to share in *hiera* and *hosia*. Whether with this expression Mantitheos refers to the family or to the *polis* or to both is not clear. In fact, even the expression *ta patroia* is ambiguous in this respect: it means 'the things of the fathers' or 'ancestral things'. In this case, the term refers first of all to the private, paternal estate of their father, Mantias. But the term also evokes the 'ancestral' heritage of *all* the Athenians, as we saw in Chapter 2 and is exemplified in the quote from Demosthenes' *On the crown* (141) heading that chapter. There appears to be a congruence between the *hiera kai hosia* and sharing (*metechein*) in them in the private and in the public domains, anchored in the laws 'on legitimacy' and transposed to the public domain by the law 'on citizenship'. Each speech clarifies the focus of the relevant laws: in Isaeus' lawsuits on inheritances, the focus is a claim in the family, in Mantitheos' case the focus is primarily the family but with it also the *polis*. From this analysis we can conclude that the legal criteria for sharing in the inheritance of a family were identical to the criteria for justifiable claims to sharing in the *polis*, namely legitimate birth from Athenian parents.[15]

However, the passage of the *Ath.Pol.* 42 describing the practice of citizenship puts it slightly differently from the phrasing in the laws: 'Those who are born from *astos* parents on both sides share in the *politeia*, and they are enrolled in the demes when they are eighteen years of age'.[16] Using the term *politeia* and mentioning in the same breath enrolment in the demes, a procedure that underpinned the political and military participation of men and did not apply, therefore, to women citizens, this passage of *Ath.Pol.* has played a prominent role in the conception of citizenship as political role restricted to males that I discussed in Chapter 1. But the

[15] Legal scholars, beginning with A. Ledl (*Das attische Bürgerrecht und die Frauen*, 1907), but most systematically Wolff (1944) and Patterson (1990), have long recognised the connection between claims to inheritance and claims to citizenship based on legitimate birth in classical Athens, but it seems that this insight has had little impact on the debate about citizenship; see further below, Chapter 3.4.

[16] *Ath.Pol.* 42.1.2–3: μετέχουσιν μὲν τῆς πολιτείας οἱ ἐξ ἀμφοτέρων γεγονότες ἀστῶν, ἐγγράφονται δ᾽ εἰς τοὺς δημότας ὀκτωκαίδεκα ἔτη γεγονότες.

passage deviates from the Athenian laws we just saw in some respects. *Ath.Pol.* in the first lines refers to *politeia*, not to *polis* as used in the laws on citizenship. Furthermore, *Ath.Pol.* omits an explicit clause on legitimacy: is just having two *astos* parents enough, or must the *astos* mother have been betrothed by *engye* to the *astos* father for the boy to be acceptable? The answer to this much-debated question begins a few lines further down in the same passage, where *Ath.Pol.* explains that the demesmen check the age of the boy, and next whether he is of free status and 'born in accordance with the laws'.[17] The last phrase implies that more than one law was meant, not only that each parent should be *astos* but also the legal requirement of *engye*. These considerations strongly suggest that the first lines of *Ath.Pol.* 42 are neither a comprehensive description of citizenship at Athens nor a full quotation from the relevant laws.

Returning to the congruence in criteria for inheritance in the family and for sharing in the *polis*, in the laws on legitimacy (Is. 6.47; law *ap*. Dem. 43.51) and in Dem. 39 the goods one received a share of were the *hiera kai hosia*; the fact that the same expression was used for sharing in the *polis* (see Chapter 2) confirms the analogy between the family and the *polis*. Within inheritance, furthermore, we must distinguish between material and immaterial goods.[18] Mantitheos had conceded to Boiotos his share of the family's material goods, but he tried to refuse him the name that tied him to his paternal grandfather Mantitheos.[19] *Hiera kai hosia*, too, consist of material and immaterial elements, as I argued in the previous chapter: *hiera* are concrete gifts to the gods but also in a wider sense the cultic relations with the gods, *hosia* are god-pleasing thoughts and actions, which often imply the use of concrete property, notably to pay for gifts of honour to the gods and to the dead.[20] On these observations, I propose that the

[17] *Ath.Pol.* 42.1.7: γεγονέναι τὴν ἡλικίαν τὴν ἐκ τοῦ νόμου. 42.1.9: γέγονε κατὰ τοὺς νόμους.

[18] Cf. Harrison 1, 123: 'we must be constantly on our guard against the anachronism of regarding succession in classical Athens as a purely economic matter, concerned merely with the transmission of material goods ... a man's heir was still looked upon as owing to him a primary duty to preserve the *sacra* of the "house". Among material goods, the Athenians distinguished various categories, including visible and invisible, productive and unproductive, ancestral and acquired, terms most of which are far from clear in meaning' (for these categories, see Harrison 1, 228–35). Below, I will briefly refer to the categories ancestral and acquired, but the other categories are not relevant to my argument.

[19] Mantitheos' defence had implicitly drawn on the contention that a name is something one cannot share, but this was difficult to maintain in Athens, where descendants in various branches of a family often had the same names (personal, patronymic and demotic). The same now applied when Mantitheos failed to win his case: *IG* II^2 1622.435–43 (ca. 342/1) records settlement of a debt of Mantias of Thorikos by Pamphilos of Thorikos, Mantitheos of Thorikos and Mantitheos (of Thorikos).

[20] Here I disagree with Harrison 1, 130, who supposes that of the private inheritance the *hiera* are the religious obligations and household cults, and *hosia* are therefore the material property.

laws at Athens construed citizenship, that is membership of the *polis* with the right to participate, as a quality that an individual *inherits*. More precisely, what is inherited is a claim to a share, whether of the family's goods or of the *polis*, in both cases consisting of material and immaterial goods. Effectuating these claims depended on additional conditions: for inheritance proper the death of one's parents, for citizenship reaching a particular age and other qualifications that we shall investigate later.[21]

To test the validity of this interpretation, we need to investigate what inheritance consisted of and how it was transmitted. Among the 'immaterial goods', 'membership' itself needs to be considered first, that is belonging to the group (family, *polis*) and being treated in a fitting way (*time*), in accordance with law and custom. Membership of the group also meant having a part in the relationship of the group with others, both gods and humans, with concomitant benefits and obligations. Other immaterial goods could also be involved, such as specific claims to status.[22] The other part of the inheritance is the material goods; they are relevant as wealth in its own right, but also in their capacity to sustain social relations. Although material and immaterial goods were tightly connected, the distinction between them needs to be made because within the family sons and daughters did not have equal claims to inheritance of material property, but they inherited immaterial property equally. Within the classical *polis* the claims of individuals and families to material and to some immaterial property were unequal, while their claims to other immaterial benefits were equal.

3.2 Before and after Solon

Looking for what can feasibly be identified as the origins of Athenian citizenship in the sphere of descent and inheritance, it is clear enough that Solon in 594 transformed existing practices into a shape that maintained its essential outlines until the classical era and beyond, even if the texts of Solon's laws can only be tentatively and partially reconstructed from fragmentary evidence of later date.[23] Solon brought together and established in law those elements that jointly made up the essential features of

[21] See Chapter 5.
[22] See for instance the *gene*, see Chapters 3.5 and 5.5.
[23] Cf. Lape (2002/3). The fragments of Solon's laws collected in the edition of Leão and Rhodes (a revised edition of Ruschenbusch (1966), Ruschenbusch (2010) and Martina (1968)) amount to more text than is feasible to reproduce here; with a few exceptions, I refer to LR by fragment number.

classical citizenship: the bond between the human community and the gods, particularly as codified in a sacrificial calendar; the rules of membership and its transmission down the generations; and the rules of participation in the *polis*.[24] Pericles' Citizenship Law and the subsequent laws on legitimacy did no more and no less than change the requirement for legitimate status from one to two citizen parents. It is therefore justifiable to designate Solon's laws as a watershed, for in effect they were the formal beginning of the classical system of citizenship. I shall describe the classical rules of kinship and inheritance in more detail below; here, a summary of Solon's laws, with Leão/Rhodes's fragment numbers, reveals the essentials of legitimate birth and inheritance rights in Athens:[25]

1) F 47b: prohibition of marriage between descendants of the same mother.
2) F 48a, b: definition of legitimate (*gnesios*) children as those born from a woman who has been pledged by ritual (*engye*) by her male kin to her husband, with special rules for a woman without male relatives, i.e. an heiress (*epikleros*).[26]
3) F 49a–h: the inheritance passes to legitimate male children, but if there are none nor adopted ones, the legatee may bequeath his inheritance to someone else.[27]

[24] Solon's reform: *Ath.Pol.* 6–9; Plut. *Sol.* 15.2–16.4. Manville (1990) 93–6 notes that no formal conception of citizenship before Solon can be detected, even in land 'ownership', a notion which itself only developed over time (see below). Ober (1993) points to a basic notion of citizenship created by Solon's law barring debt slavery of Athenians. Although some scholars, for instance Hansen (1990), dispute that Solon's laws were still extant and visible in the fourth century, I agree with Stroud (1979), Sickinger (1999) 24–9, Rhodes (2006), Ruschenbusch (2010) 83–118 (on the authenticity of the relevant fragments of family law) that they were. Scafuro (2006a) offers criteria for identifying elements of Solonian laws in later evidence.

[25] Solon's measures in this area include inheritance rights (LR 47a, 49a–h; 50a–c), epiklerate (LR 47a, 51a–d, 51/1–3, 52a–c, 53, 54), marriage and legitimacy (LR 47b, 48a–b), adoption of children (LR 58a–b, 58/c), obligations of children towards parents (LR 55a–c, 56/a–c, 57/a–b), adultery and other matters concerning women and concerning sexuality (LR 26, 27, 28a–c, 29a–b, 30a–b, 30/c–d, 30/1a, 31a–b).

[26] Dem. 46.18; cf. 44.49; Hyp. 5.17: Ἣν ἂν ἐγγυήσῃ ἐπὶ δικαίοις δάμαρτα εἶναι ἢ πατὴρ ἢ ἀδελφὸς ὁμοπάτωρ ἢ πάππος ὁ πρὸς πατρός, ἐκ ταύτης εἶναι παῖδας γνησίους. ἐὰν δὲ μηδεὶς ᾖ τούτων, ἐὰν μὲν ἐπίκληρός τις ᾖ, τὸν κύριον ἔχειν, ἐὰν δὲ μὴ ᾖ, ὅτῳ ἂν ἐπιτρέψῃ, τοῦτον κύριον εἶναι. 'If a woman is pledged for lawful marriage by her father or by a brother of the same father or by her grandfather on her father's side, her children shall be legitimate. In case there are none of these (relatives), if she is an *epikleros* (heiress), her guardian shall take her to wife, and if she is not, that man shall be her guardian to whom she may entrust herself.' The archaic wording (e.g. *damar* for wife) is one of the reasons why this law, referred to and inserted into the text of Dem. 46, is attributed to Solon, Harrison 1, 5.

[27] If he had no sons, a father could make a will and leave his property to whomever he liked, but he had to provide for a daughter, giving her a dowry (her inheritance part) and marrying her off, before he could will the rest of his property away. In practice, men were inclined to make a will

4) F 47a, 50a–c: if there are no legitimate sons and the legatee has not willed his inheritance away, the inheritance falls to legitimate daughters (*epikleroi*); if there are none, the inheritance passes to kin to a certain degree first on the father's, then on the mother's side, a group together labelled the *anchisteia*.

All of this concerns what in modern terms is family law. Only a single law of Solon is known on citizenship in the sense of membership of the *polis* beyond the family. Plutarch recounts that Solon permitted citizenship to be granted only to those who came to Athens in permanent exile due to a blood feud and to those who came with their family to work in a craft.[28] If, as most scholars agree, this account has a kernel of historical truth, Solon referred in this measure to citizenship at *polis* level. What precisely did this mean? How was 'being a citizen' established or consolidated? The written evidence on early Attica being too patchy to allow firm conclusions, for over a decade the scholarly debate on these questions has been in flux.[29] Paulin Ismard and Alain Duplouy argue that in the archaic age the community in effect consisted of a variety of associations, some of which identified by their shared professional lives (as farmers, seamen, grand landowners, craftsmen etc.), others by their shared cults (*orgeones*), common burials (*homotaphoi*) or prominence in performing the cults of others (*gene*) or other characteristics.[30] The *polis* gradually developed from the clustering of these groups, reinforced by integrative laws, among which Solon's 'law on associations' that made agreements between members of these groups binding.[31] This approach is attractive in that it clarifies a stage

only if they had no children at all, or did not want to adopt one either when still alive or by will. Wills were often contested in the courts. Plut. (*Sol.* 21.3) says that before Solon every inheritance was to remain within the family group (*genos*) without any freedom allowed to a legatee; while according to Ruschenbusch (2010) 96–102 this testimony is perhaps not authentic, LR 49b and comm. 82–3 point out that it is based on authentic fragments.

[28] Plut. *Sol.* 24.4; LR 75: Παρέχει δ' ἀπορίαν καὶ ὁ τῶν δημοποιήτων νόμος, ὅτι γενέσθαι πολίτας (Loeb ed.: πολίταις) οὐ δίδωσι πλὴν τοῖς φεύγουσιν ἀειφυγίᾳ τὴν ἑαυτῶν ἢ πανεστίοις Ἀθήναζε μετοικιζομένοις ἐπὶ τέχνῃ. The vocabulary used here, like the μέθεξις τῆς πολιτείας later on in this passage, is typical of a much later time than Solon's. For the possible genuineness of this law, Davies (1977), Lambert (1998) 381, Ismard (2010) 72–4.

[29] Recent discussions of Solon's laws have been characterised by an attempt to disengage from a teleological analysis of them as leading to democracy in Athens, and to find a new perspective on archaic Greece more broadly, within which to reassess the laws of Solon and the ancient historiography on them; see esp. Foxhall (1997), Raaflaub (2006), Van Wees (2006) who are all interested in the 'Solonian' property classes for their effect on political office in the first place, unlike the literature in the following note.

[30] Duplouy (2006), Ismard (2010) 44–83, Duplouy (2014).

[31] The so-called 'law of Solon on associations' (*Dig.* 47.22.4; LR 76a and b) declares agreements between members of a 'deme, phratry, *hiera orgia*, and sailors, *syssitoi*, *homotaphioi*, *thiasotai*' and individuals binding when not conflicting with the law; for discussion of the authenticity of

in the development of Athenian citizenship that is difficult to reconstruct, but it necessarily handles the concept 'citizenship' in a very loose fashion. It shows how belonging to the *polis* came out of belonging to constituent subgroups, but leaves in the dark how before Cleisthenes coherence among these groups came about, how political office was distributed across them and how descent operated as a factor in this constellation.

A quick glance at what went on before Solon sheds some light on this issue. In Attica, as throughout the Greek world, historical traces can be found of phratries, clusters of families who among themselves were not related, in so far as we can ascertain.[32] The families belonging to a phratry assisted each other in matters of birth and death, and the men could be assembled to form military units; not belonging to a phratry meant not belonging to society.[33] On the antiquity of the phratries, the evidence is thin: linguistic evidence and variety in the particulars of the phratry festival Apatouria suggest that the phratries predated the Ionian migration of the late Bronze and Dark Ages.[34] In Attica, phratries clearly had ties with specific locations, notably where their sanctuaries and altars were situated, and together more or less covered the whole of Attica. This unmistakable relation of the phratries with these geographical centres points to a function of the phratries in the emerging *polis*, if by this we mean the notion of a collective roughly encompassing 'Athens' and incorporating local

this law, Ismard (2010) 45–57, and, more sceptical, Lambert (1998) 249–51; for a sixth-century, Solonian law on binding agreements, Phillips (2009) (above, Chapter 2, n. 137). Two fragments of early Athenian laws possibly offer evidence that being a (male) citizen meant being in a phratry. Philochoros, *FGrH* 328 F 35a (Phot. ο 443/Suda ο 510 *s.v.* ὀργεῶνες): τοὺς δὲ φράτορας ἐπάναγκες δέχεσθαι καὶ τοὺς ὀργεῶνας, καὶ τοὺς ὁμογάλακτας, οὓς γεννήτας καλοῦμεν, 'and the phratry members had to accept the *orgeones* and the *homogalaktes*, whom we call *gennetai*'. Krateros, *FGrH* 342 F 4 (Harp./Suda *ν* 86 *s.v.* ναυτοδίκαι): ἐὰν δέ τις ἐξ ἀμφοῖν ξένοιν γεγονὼς φρατρίζῃ, διώκειν εἶναι τῷ βουλομένῳ Ἀθηναίων, οἷς δίκαι εἰσί· 'if someone born from both foreign parents acts as if he were a phratry member, he may be prosecuted by anyone of the Athenians who so wishes who may take legal action'. But to which law these fragments belong is disputed: either Solon's laws or Pericles' law, see Andrewes (1961), Lambert (1998) 45–9, 261–6, 381–3, Theodoridis (2002), Blok (2009b). For the connection with other associations, Ismard (2010) 44–57.

32 For the Attic phratries, I follow here mainly the essential work by Lambert (1998).

33 Military units: Hom. *Il.* 2.362–3; society: Nestor denounces any man who makes strife among his own as ἀφρήτωρ, ἀθέμιστος, ἀνέστιός (*Il.* 9.63–4: without a phratry, without *themis*, without a hearth).

34 Lambert (1998) 268–73 on the antiquity of the phratries, with discussion of previous scholarship and linguistic evidence: whereas in all Indo-European languages *phrater vel sim.* means (blood) brother, in all Greek dialects it means phratry member, showing that the Indo-European meaning was entirely displaced at an early stage. Festival: nearly all Ionian *poleis* shared the phratry festival Apatouria; in Athens, it may have been derived in some way from the Ionians since in the Athenian calendar no month was called after the festival, unlike in Miletus and on Delos – the Athenian Apatouria took place in Pyanepsion, called after the festival for Apollo Pyanopsia (Hall (2007) 54; cf. Bickerman (1980) 20, Hannah (2005) 71–82).

groups and associations, in the (early) archaic age.[35] The first extant evidence of Attic phratries shows their role in matters of death. Draco's law on homicide of ca. 620 assigned to the phratries a decisive role in seeking retribution for the death of a member or deciding to pardon the killer, in case no relatives of the victim were alive.[36]

In the classical age, the main role of the phratries was oversight of the legitimate birth of the children of their members, as Stephen Lambert has shown convincingly.[37] They established the social and ritual context of legitimate marriage by the *gamelia*, the festive presentation and acceptance of a wife in her husband's phratry, and next supervised the legitimacy of citizen children in a series of rituals at intervals in the children's lives. Acceptance of a child as a member of the family and the *polis* in accordance with the law remained a matter of social acknowledgement, witnessed by people rather than reified in writing, and few rules were committed to writing in an unequivocal way.[38] Some rituals belonged to the family only, beginning with the acceptance of the child by the father in the *amphidromia*, a ritual by which the child was accepted at the hearth of the home, identified with the goddess Hestia, and within the father's family. The ritual created the child's connection with the family of the father, while that with the mother was considered proven by nature.[39] On the tenth day after birth a sacrifice was made on behalf on the child, and after this the new family member participated in the *hiera* of the family.[40]

[35] Hedrick (1991) 266–8, who connects his findings on the phratries to the arguments of D. Roussel (see below). However, Hedrick's view that the archaic, 'non-tribal' origins would mean that 'the issue of kinship is a red herring. The phratry was in origin a political entity, an institution of the *polis*' (267), by which he characterises the *polis* as an exclusively political entity, essentially distinct from kinship groups, is unconvincing in the light of the evidence on phratries and undermines the very significance of the phratries to the *polis* that Hedrick sets out to demonstrate.

[36] *IG* I³ 104 (ML 86) 16–23; date, Stroud (1968) 66–70; Lambert (1998) 25, 248–9. Likewise, the Labyadai at Delphi, presumably a phratry, were in charge of proper burial rites in the late sixth century (see RO 1; Blok (2006) with further refs).

[37] Lambert (1998) 279–370. In the classical era, eleven phratries are named, six more are possible, and on a few fragments of evidence the name is not attested. On estimated population size, we may tentatively assume at least thirty and at most 140 phratries in the fourth century; in the archaic age, their number might have been smaller. Lambert shows that phratries split and fused over time, so we cannot assume a fixed number, nor fixed associations. With an estimated male citizen population of 30,000, the average would be 1,000 men in the case of 30 phratries, but in fact the phratries clearly differed in size. The number 140 is derived from the number of Cleisthenic demes (18–20).

[38] Witnessing the essential testimony: Humphreys (1986), Humphreys (2007 (orig. 1985)), Scafuro (1997), Scafuro (1994). Ambiguity of some terms of legitimacy and inheritance rights, *Ath.Pol.* 9.2; Harrison 1, 1–80; Patterson (1998) 85–101.

[39] Rudhardt (1962), Gherchanoc (1998); Parker, *PS*, 13–14 notes that it is not clear what act the *amphidromia* exactly was or who carried it out.

[40] Participation in *hiera*: Is. 6.48–9 (in deme Thesmophoria); 7.1; 8.16, 19; 9.21; Dem. 57.54.

This included, finally, observance of the family's tomb cult, consisting of rituals on the third, ninth and thirtieth day after burial (the latter marking the termination of formal mourning and death pollution), and next annual rituals on the Genesia.

For the role of the phratries, the evidence suggests a common pattern for the main procedures and rituals, with some differences in the details. Extant evidence pertains almost entirely to boys, but daughters, too, belonged to the phratries in some way and evidence shows some phratries introducing daughters to members, at least the *epikleroi*.[41] The essential moments were the presentation of the child to the paternal phratry at the Apatouria with a sacrifice, on which an introducer, often but not always the father, swore the child by oath to be legitimate, i.e. born to the Athenian man from an *aste* who had been pledged to him as stated in the law.[42] If a phrater objected to the introduction of the child, the procedure was to lead the sacrificial victim from the altar. The first ritual of this kind took place in infancy (*meion*), the second one at adolescence (*koureion*), at which the boy's hair was cut and sacrificed, followed by acceptance (or rejection) by the phratry, a ritual which *ipso facto* determined his acceptance (or rejection) as a member of the *polis* before his presentation to the deme.[43] Crucial in the procedure was the common sacrifice by the phratry, the father taking his oath and the partitioning of the sacrificial meat among the phrateres after acceptance of the child (see also below). There could be no clearer manifestation of the centrality of religious ritual to citizenship – partaking in sacrifice means one belongs to the group, if one does not share the sacrifice, one does not belong.

In all of this, each phratry acted as a group with its own traditions and cults, but also as a representative of the overarching unity of all the phratries. This unity was embodied in the common ancestral cults of kinship and family, notably the cults of Zeus Phratrios and Athena Phratria (particularly associated with the phratries), of Apollo Patroios (particularly

[41] Lambert (1998) 36, 178–89, 347, Wilgaux (2000) and Wilgaux (2009) show the necessity of daughters being introduced, if the legitimate connection between bride-giving and bride-taking families was to be effective. After Pericles' law, introduction of daughters became particularly important, while *epikleroi* must certainly have been known to the phratry (e.g. Is. 3.73); another way of confirming the legitimacy of daughters was assembling phratry members as guests/witnesses at her marriage feast: Is. 3.18–20; 8.8–9, 18–20; Dem. 57.43; Lambert (1998) 178–88.

[42] Sacrifice and oath: Andoc. 1.126; Is. 8.19–20; Dem. 43.11–15; on the Apatouria, Lambert (1998) 143–78; Parker, *PS*, 458–61.

[43] Schol. Ar. *Ach.* 146: 'the third day (of the Apatouria) is called *koureotis*, after the registration of the *kouroi* and *korai* in the phratries'. The name *koureotis*, however, derives presumably from *keirein*, to cut (the hair); Lambert (1998) 162–3.

associated with the patrilinear family) and of Zeus Herkeios (of the enclosure, particularly associated with the household).[44] Zeus Ktesios, attested widely in Greece as generating and protecting material possessions, was worshipped primarily in the *oikos*: since the wealth of a *polis* consisted in the first place of the collective wealth of its *oikoi*, this cult was anchored in the *koinonia* where this wealth was produced.[45] At Athens, among the ancestral cults connecting the household with the *polis*, the cult of Zeus Herkeios was enshrined in the *oikos*, next incorporated in the cults of the phratries and finally at *polis* level in the cult of Zeus Herkeios at the sanctuary of Pandrosos on the Acropolis.[46] The cult of Hestia was located in the centre of the house and in the *prytaneion* (the city hall, notional home of the prytany, the executive committee of the *boule*), in the Agora, and the cults of Athena Phratria, Zeus Phratrios and Apollo Patroios, guarding the connection between family and *polis* as descent groups, were situated at the various phratry sanctuaries and in the Agora. Sharing in the cults of Zeus Phratrios and Athena Phratria, Apollo Patroios and Zeus Herkeios, which connected family, *oikos* and *polis*, generally marked a person as a citizen.[47]

By establishing the legitimacy of a child, a phratry thus confirmed a child's membership of the family as well as of the overarching group, the *polis*, of which the phratry was the intermediate aggregate, and validated the child's right to his inheritance in the *polis*. This evidence now seems to confirm that in the classical age membership of the *polis* was not only *analogous* to membership of the family, in being based on legitimate descent, but that a legitimate child indeed *inherited with* its position in the family *both a share* in the *hiera* of its *oikos and a share of* the *hiera* of the *polis*. This fact, that every family and household contained a small part of the *polis*'s *hiera* and that every Athenian thus inherited a part of private and common *polis* cults, also explains the widely attested Athenian concern that no *oikos* should become empty by lack of heirs – with an end to a family's line, a tiny share of the *polis*'s bond with the gods was lost.[48]

[44] Parker, *PS*, 16–36; for the cults of Zeus Phratrios and Athena Phratria, Lambert (1998) 207–16, for Apollo Patroios, Hedrick (1988a).

[45] Brulé (2005) 41–5; evidence on his cult beyond the house is very thin.

[46] Zeus Herkeios in *oikos*: Hom.*Od*. 22.334–5, Hdt. 5.68, Suda ε 3015 *s.v.* Ἑρκεῖος Ζεύς; phratries: Din. fr. 32, Hyp. fr. 94, Demetrius of Phaleron, *FGrH* 228 F 6; Acropolis: Philochoros, *FGrH* 328 F 67.

[47] Dem. 57.54, 67; *Ath.Pol*. 55.3–5; Lambert (1998) 213–14; Parker, *PS*, 9–36; Brulé (2005) imaginatively compared these structures with a Russian doll: the largest *babouchka* is the *polis*, and inside one finds ever smaller *babouchkas* all similar to the outer model.

[48] Parker, *PS*, 16–36.

What the organisation of legitimacy and citizenship was like in the (early) archaic age is impossible to state with confidence, but it is plausible that it took a long time to develop into what we know of the classical system. Once Solon's laws were in place, only legitimate children, born from a mother pledged by her kin to her husband, could be accepted as members and heirs by a father, the phratry and the *polis*. A *nothos* or *nothe*, a child born to a father from a woman other than the pledged wife and whom he accepted as his, could be part of family life in some way but did not count as heir and legitimate offspring in either the family or the *polis*.[49] Arguing backwards, we may speculate that before Solon's archonship, any child that a phratry accepted on the testimony of the father as his offspring and heir was accepted as such both at the level of the family and the *polis*, and that perhaps elite men were able to enforce acceptance of their *nothos* children as heirs.[50] Whether or not this speculation is correct, with Solon's laws the rules of legitimacy applied in principle to all Athenians equally. Until Pericles' law, the wife did not have to be an Athenian; what mattered was that she was pledged by her family by the appropriate rituals; in effect, this applied to all free women.

Beside phratries, other subgroups are relevant here, membership of which was likewise based on descent. In Athens these are the *gene*, groups of families who provided the priests and priestesses for the common cults of the phratries, the *phylai* and the *polis*, in other words the *hiera* that sustained the Athenian *polis* as a community. *Gene* are best known from inscriptions and disparate pieces of evidence in lexicographers, making a complete picture difficult to attain. About the origins of the *gene* there is no consensus, nor about their number: in 1996 Robert Parker listed forty-seven 'certain and probable' and thirty-three 'uncertain and spurious' *gene*, and since then at least one more *genos* has come to light.[51] As with the phratries, the extent to which there were real kinship relations between families belonging to a *genos* is questionable. Because of their functions and of the claims to pure descent on which their privileges were based, their role in Athenian citizenship will receive special attention below, in Chapter 5.5.

49 For a *nothos*, Patterson (1990), and see above, Chapter 31.1.

50 Lape (2002/3) 119–20.

51 Parker (1996) app. 2 for an overview of nearly all *gene*; for the Eunoridai, a newly identified *genos*, Lambert (2008a); on the origins of the *gene*, Ferguson (1938), Bourriot (1976) who defends different types of *gene* with different origins, effectively refuted by Lambert (1998) 59–74; Lambert (1999); for territorial aspects and semi-independent subgroups, Ismard (2007).

Phylai are also attested in Attica, as elsewhere in Greece. In Attica in the archaic age, there were four (Ionian) *phylai*, the Geleontes, Hopletes, Argades and Aigikores, headed by *phylobasileis*, and each *phyle* was subdivided into *trittyes*. As a social unity that could be marshalled in warfare,[52] together with the naucraries (navy units) the *phylai* may have provided a platform for political participation, but the evidence is very thin.[53] Besides the *phylai* had some judicial functions and, as *koinoniai*, of course their own cults. This can be inferred from evidence of the classical era, showing that the *phylobasileis* still had responsibilities in the judicial sphere in cases of homicide, and from the new edition of the sacrificial calendar, which drew among others on lists of sacrifices under authority of the *phylobasileis*.[54] Clearly, Cleisthenes did not abolish the Ionian *phylai* when he created ten new *phylai* in 508/7, just as he left the phratries and traditional priesthoods unchanged,[55] even if the weight of the political, military and religious organisation of Athenian men shifted entirely to the new *phylai*. The continuity of the Ionian *phylai* in some form is corroborated by the finale of Euripides' *Ion* of ca. 410, when Athena creates citizen identities by mythological descent: Ion, as a descendant of hero-king Erechtheus through his mother Creousa, is to be the legitimate king of Athens and will have four sons, who will give their names to the four *phylai* who inhabit Athena's land.[56] The passage would make little sense if the four pre-Cleisthenic *phylai* had entirely ceased to exist at the time of the performance.

To summarise, before and after Solon citizenship entailed an individual's membership of the *polis* through ritual acceptance in phratries, based on ritual acceptance in a family, as born from an Athenian parent (father) and, after Solon, from a pledged wife. Membership of phratries was perhaps conditional for, but at least closely connected to, membership of other associations in the *polis*. That this conception of citizenship applied to wealthy and poor Athenians alike and already existed before Solon may tentatively be inferred from Solon's decision to redeem those Athenians

[52] Hom. *Il.* 2.362–3.

[53] Lambert (1998) 251–61. For the naucraries as fiscal, beside military, institutions, Van Wees (2013) 44–61.

[54] *Phylobasileis*: judicial function in cases of homicide, *IG* I³ 104 l. 12, on which Carawan (1998) 33–4, 49–51, 69–71, summary 133–7. The Ionian *phylobasileis* and the trittys Leukotainai of the *phyle* Geleontes in the sacrificial calendar of Athens, *SEG* 52.48: face A, fr. 1, col. III, ll. 6–8, and Lambert (1998) 256–8.

[55] Phratries and priesthoods unchanged, *Ath.Pol.* 21.6, with Lambert (1998) 245–8; Lambert (2010b).

[56] Eur. *Ion*, 1575–81.

who had been reduced to slavery and even been sold abroad.[57] For arguably this measure could only conceivably be acceptable to (wealthy) Athenians if all those belonging to Athenian families and to phratries were really regarded as members of the community and their release from slavery an obligation of the *polis* at large. We may therefore conclude that, whether or not an Athenian actually had material property to bequeath, membership of the family and the *polis* embodied in the common cults was an immaterial good that an Athenian received as his or her share in the ancestral inheritance.[58]

3.3 The Cleisthenic Moment and Beyond

The main features of Cleisthenes' reform of 508/7 are well known.[59] In the regime change following the expulsion of the tyrants, he won popular support by proposing to reorganise the *polis*.[60] Creating a new subdivision of the *demos* into demes and ten new *phylai*, and a new *boule* of 500 based on them, Cleisthenes set up the framework of the political system that developed into the full democracy, due to deliberate innovations and to historical contingencies of the next century and a half. For our present concerns, we need to understand what, on balance, Cleisthenes did and did not change in the *polis*'s structure with regard to the criterion of descent for citizenship.

According to the *Ath.Pol.* (21.4) Cleisthenes included people in the new system as citizens of Athens who formerly had not been so:

57 Solon F 36 W, 9–12; Plut. *Sol.* 15.5. Although Lardinois (2006) rightly warns us that traditional Solonian elegiac poetry may not be the lawgiver's own words, the poetry concerning the *seisachtheia* is associated too specifically with Solon to be easily transferred to other individuals (Blok and Krul, in press).

58 Werlings (2010) 256–63 argues that Solonian poetry likewise reflects a view of the Athenian population as a coherent group, a *demos* in the sense of a body that may act as a unitary political entity.

59 On Cleisthenes' reform see Hdt. 5.66–7, 69–70; 6.131; *Ath.Pol.* 20–22.1, with Rhodes, *CAAP ad loc.* Osborne (2009) 279–88 situates the Cleisthenic reform in the context of late archaic change, showing contrasts between the Athenian and Spartan systems. Information on the implementation of Cleisthenes' system needs to be pieced together from other evidence, most of it epigraphical; fundamental are Whitehead (1986a) on the Attic demes, on Cleisthenes esp. 16–30, and for kinship structures Lambert (1998) 25–57, 245–75. For continuity and change in the social and geographical organisation of Attica before and after Cleisthenes, Lewis (1963), Kienast (2005), in cults Kearns (1985), Parker (1996) 102–21; for the resulting *polis* set-up, Traill (1986); for a fresh approach to the nature of the Cleisthenic policies, Anderson (2003).

60 Ober (1993) draws an attractive picture of the *demos* reinventing itself as a sovereign body in the revolution of 508/7, but nonetheless it was Cleisthenes who mapped the new political system. I agree with Raaflaub (1998) and Anderson (2003) 76–83 that full democracy did not come about with Cleisthenes; however, whereas they see Ephialtes' changes of 462 as the most radical step, I argue below why Pericles' Citizenship Law may rather be regarded as inaugurating the definitive stage.

> And he made those living in each of the demes fellow demesmen of each other, in order that they would not draw attention to those who were new citizens (*neopolitai*) by addressing them by their patriliny (*patrothen*), but calling them after their demes; as a result, the Athenians also call themselves after their demes.[61]

As it stands, however, this passage cannot be entirely accurate. The demotic existed before, and was scarcely used in the first half century after Cleisthenes; in the first decade, demotics appeared only on some votives and then in larger numbers on ostraka.[62] The normal way of naming a person was and remained the personal name and the patronymic (father's name), referring to the patriliny; only in the last decades of the fifth century do demotics appear in somewhat higher numbers.[63] It is therefore highly unlikely that Cleisthenes introduced the obligatory use of the demotic, as *Ath.Pol.* believes and as was common by the time *Ath.Pol* was written. That Cleisthenes included new citizens who were not of Athenian descent cannot be ascertained, let alone whether he used any criteria in doing so and whether this change added a significant number of people to the group of citizens. Yet circumstantial evidence shows why some reorganisation of the citizen body was not only a sensible thing to do, but also a necessary one.

In the course of the sixth century, the population of Attica had seen some considerable changes. We just saw that according to the tradition non-Athenians had come to live in Attica, either for economic reasons or due to exile or otherwise; the extent to which these newcomers had integrated into the citizen community and had become phratry members is hard to tell, but we may suppose this varied considerably. Moreover, of the citizens by birth who owing to Solon were no longer slaves, probably many had lost much or all of their lands and with it their roots in their villages of origin. Besides such changes among the population, Attica had acquired new border regions. The island of Salamis, a long-time object of strife between Megara and Athens, had been won by the latter in the sixth century, perhaps also on Solon's initiative. Now the island had to be incorporated into the *polis*; perhaps the creation of a *genos* effecting the cultic inclusion of Salamis in

[61] *Ath.Pol.* 21.4: καὶ δημότας ἐποίησεν ἀλλήλων τοὺς οἰκοῦντας ἐν ἑκάστῳ τῶν δήμων, ἵνα μὴ πατρόθεν προσαγορεύοντες ἐξελέγχωσιν τοὺς νεοπολίτας, ἀλλὰ τῶν δήμων ἀναγορεύωσιν. ὅθεν καὶ καλοῦσιν Ἀθηναῖοι σφᾶς αὐτοὺς τῶν δήμων.

[62] Winters (1993); Lambert (1998) 264; Rhodes, *CAAP ad loc.*, 254–6; Whitehead (1986a) 69–75 for an increase in individual cases on dedications, the totals remaining very low. For the ostraka, Siewert (2002).

[63] Meyer (1993).

the *polis* was a step in this direction.[64] Around the turn of the fifth century, Athens decided to allow *klerouchoi* to settle there.[65] In the new structure, Cleisthenes did not make the population of Salamis into an Attic deme like the others, but he did include the traditional hero of Salamis, Ajax, into the group of heroes who were to represent the Athenian *demos*.[66] Another region to be incorporated was Eleutherai, on the border with Boeotia; it did not become a deme location, but it marked Dionysus' entrance into the city since the old wooden statue of the god was carried from there to Athens.[67] Finally, after the fall of the tyrants, everyone was measuring up everyone else's allegiance to the people of Athens, a process probably later remembered as a *diapsephismos* of the citizen body when citizens wished to decry others as of less pure Athenian descent than themselves.[68]

Besides adjusting the composition of the citizen body to accommodate both uprooted citizens and newcomers, the main point of the new structure was famously to reorganise the citizens into new clusters to increase citizens' engagement with the *polis*. The 140 demes of varying size into which Cleisthenes partitioned the *demos* were also called *demoi*, the use of the same word reinforcing the parallels between the subgroup and the whole.[69] Each deme was based in an existing village (*kome* or deme) or a part of the city Athens, and this was the location where most of the

[64] For this strife and further history of Salamis, Taylor (1997). About the origins of the *genos* Salaminioi, attested in two extensive inscriptions of 363/2 (RO 37) and ca. 265/4 as consisting of two branches, opinions diverge, except that they obviously had something to do with Salamis; for their cults, Parker (1996) 308–16. In a discussion with a new rendition of the texts, Lambert (1997a) argues for a link between the *genos* and the first Athenian settlers on Salamis in the sixth century; for the connection between the Salaminioi and the spatial formation of Attica, but arguing for an earlier date, Osborne (1994).

[65] *IG* I³ 1, 'the decree for Salamis'. Taylor (1997) 12–16 summarises the discussion on its date, rightly warning that the evidence is insufficient to decide whether the decree dates before or after Cleisthenes. The *klerouchoi* in l. 1 are the most likely restoration (cf. *SEG* 41.2).

[66] For Ajax as hero of Salamis, Hdt. 5.66; for Ajax's special role in the Cleisthenic organisation of Attica, de Polignac (2007); on the special position of Salamis in the deme system, Taylor (1997) 74–82, 105–95. See also below, n. 157.

[67] Eleutherai: Paus. 1.38.8. The procession with the festive entrance of the god into the city from Eleutherai recreated the connection between the border community and the centre. Parker (1996) 93–5 points out that there is no necessary connection between Dionysus Eleuthereus ('liberating') and the inclusion into the *polis* of the village Eleutherai.

[68] *Ath.Pol.* 13.5, with Rhodes, *CAAP ad loc.*; Lambert (1998) 261–6 argues that the new system gave access to larger numbers of male citizens to be actively involved in running the *polis* but that the phratries, as descent groups, probably had nothing to do with the Cleisthenic revisions; *contra*: Welwei (1967) and Manville (1990) 173–85 who take it to have been a real scrutiny as to Athenian descent.

[69] According to *Ath.Pol.* 21.5, the demes entirely replaced the old naucraries, subgroups of the *phylai* probably forming navy units; Lambert (1998) 251–7, 385–8; van Wees (2004) 204 and 305, n. 8. See Osborne (2010c) 40–2 for the intentional parallels between deme and *polis* in the noun *demos*. For

demotai lived in 508/7, with its own meeting place and sanctuaries, and with property that can be identified as deme territory.[70] Nonetheless, the Cleisthenic deme was primarily a social unit, as can be inferred from the fact that membership was hereditary. Citizens usually had property in their deme location, but if they had none or moved house they remained members of their original deme.[71] In this respect, too, the deme was a microcosm of the *polis*, which in the classical age had its territory with sanctuaries but was primarily a social entity – an Athenian remained an Athenian, even if s/he lived somewhere else.

The deme as a 'constitutional' entity became an essential unit of citizen activity. In the first place, the deme (re)created its identity as a *koinonia* in its cultic life, in which male and female citizens participated.[72] Some of these cults already existed before Cleisthenes, but now became part of the deme's cultic programme and the deme acquired responsibility for them, including their financial aspects, often listed in cultic calendars and inscribed in deme accounts. Here the principle that the group celebrating the cult was also the one to run it, and to decide on its rules and participation, applied at the basic level of the *polis*. Instances of this widely attested process are Ikarion's old Dionysus festival, which became the leading cult of the deme Ikarieis; and the cult of Nemesis, which had existed in Rhamnous at least since the early sixth century and now came under the supervision of the demarch of the Rhamnousians.[73] For the ancient festival of the Thesmophoria, celebrated by female citizens all over Attica, the deme now became the primary organisational unit, representing celebration as a *polis* festival.[74] New cults of the demes also sprang up. The

a long time, the number of Cleisthenic demes was taken to be 139, but if Acharnai is treated as a split deme, their number is 140; Traill (1986) 123. Hdt. (5.69) supposed that originally there were 100 demes, whence Lohmann (1993) 122, 270 suggested that newer communities such as Atene, dating to the post-Cleisthenic classical period, were added at a later revision of the system.

[70] Papazarkadas (2011) 156–62 for a clear discussion of the debate on the territoriality of the demes, showing that evidence including *horoi*, sales of deme lands, the metic formula οἰκῶν ἐν + deme name and a series of third-century honorific decrees from Rhamnous on the protection of the chora of the deme (e.g. *I.Rhamnous* 3, ll. 8–12) indicate that demes could be conceived of as having a territory at least in the fourth century and possibly earlier.

[71] Property in the deme location, Osborne (1985) 47–63; Cox (1998) 38–67 for geographical mobility of citizens.

[72] For the cultic life in the classical demes, see Mikalson (1977), Whitehead (1986a) Chapter 7, Parker (1987a), Humphreys (2004b). For the role of the demarch, primarily concerned with cultic activities and their finance, Georgoudi (2007).

[73] For cultic continuity in the demes before and after Cleisthenes, Kearns (1985).

[74] Is. 3.80; 6.49–50 (demes unknown); 8.19–20 (Pithos); *IG* II² 1184 (Cholargos); *IG* II² 1177 (Peiraeus); Schol. Arist. *Thesm.* 80 (Halimous); Whitehead (1986a) 79–81. On the Thesmophoria as a *polis* festival, Versnel (1993) 229–88.

Plotheians provided in a decree for cultic obligations at the level of their old *trittys* Epakreis, at the level of the *polis* and among themselves, i.e. as the new deme.[75] Euxitheos mentioned among his dealings with his fellow demesmen his role as demarch with its financial responsibilities and his standing as candidate for the priesthood of Heracles, a cult of the hero run by the deme Halimous.

For male citizens, as mentioned above, the deme was also the basis of political and military participation, beginning with a scrutiny of legitimate citizen birth at the age of eighteen, followed by acceptance and enrolment in the deme.[76] By clustering the demes in thirty new *trittyes*, ten each from the city, coastal and inland regions, Cleisthenes created the ten new *phylai* by combining a *trittys* from each of the three regional groups. Depending on its size, each deme sent representatives to the new *boule* of 500 members, not directly but by *phyle*.[77] Moreover, the *phylai* were the basic units of military operations, and some scholars regard this military set-up as the original rationale behind the system.[78] Although the importance of the *phylai* as military units is beyond any doubt, such a single, focused purpose seems unlikely, considering the roles of the ancient *phylai* for judicial and religious matters.[79] The new *phylai* likewise became key organisational units for men's participation in the political, social and religious life of the *polis*.[80]

These ten newly mixed *phylai*, comprising the males of the changed and expanded citizen body, needed to be anchored in the *polis*'s bond with the gods. To that end, ten Attic heroes were selected as the eponymous heroes, whose cults were foundational for the *phylai* and who had to be

75 *IG* I^3 258, with Blok (2010).

76 *Ath.Pol.* 42.1.

77 For the *phylai* as representative bodies, Jones (1995).

78 Siewert (1982); for the role of year classes within the *phylai*, Van Wees (2004) 103.

79 Interestingly, *Ath.Pol.* begins (21.2) its discussion of the system with the division into ten *phylai*, whereas the principle of mixing is better understood when approached 'bottom-up', that is from the demes upwards. Next (21.3), *Ath.Pol.* mentions the council of 500, the composition of which depended on the *phylai*. This suggests that *Ath.Pol.* regards the *phylai* system as not primarily a military, but as a much broader administrative framework. That said, it should be kept in mind that *Ath.Pol.* describes a system created nearly 200 years before, and evaluates it with standards of the late fourth century.

80 Papazarkadas (2011) 106–11 shows that the *phylai* developed into fully fledged associations, with some landed property from which to pay for their sacrifices, but that these rents were insufficient to cover all (cultic) costs, hence they had to incur loans to pay for their tribal activities. Priesthoods allotted *ex hapanton* (from all) were in the fourth century distributed by rotation through *phylai*, the priesthood of Asclepius being the best-known case; see Lambert (2010b). Our sources are silent on whether this system also applied to women's priesthoods *ex hapanton*, such as the priestess of Athena Nike; if this silence is significant, it confirms the character of the *phylai* as subgroups of male citizens alone, also indicated by the choice of only male heroes as representative eponyms.

accepted as their representatives by the gods. Which method Cleisthenes employed for this selection is not entirely certain. According to *Ath.Pol.* 21.6, he drew up a list of one hundred Attic heroes and asked the Pythia at Delphi to select ten.[81] In this account, the method was similar to *klerosis ek prokriton* (sortition from a pre-selected group), the method Solon had introduced to select the archons from the newly constituted upper census class and that Cleisthenes also used for the selection of the members of the *boule*.[82] On the other hand, it was highly desirable for Erechtheus to be included in the list if this prominent hero–king, who figured as protector of Athens in the *Iliad*, was to continue in such a role for the *demos*, and also for Ajax to be included, if the incorporation of Salamis were to be solidified. It is therefore not impossible that Cleisthenes did not ask the Pythia to select from a long list, but rather to approve the ten he had chosen himself.[83] Either way, according to the tradition Cleisthenes founded the ten new *phylai* on cults for their ten eponymous heroes approved by the gods, and he did so by asking support from Apollo's oracle at Delphi, with which he had long-standing connections.[84]

In this brief overview I identified the main changes Cleisthenes made to the composition and organisation of the citizen body; in other respects, I would argue, he left the *polis* the way it was. There is no sign that he changed Solon's rules of legitimacy. Citizenship was still a hereditary status, passed from fathers to sons and daughters conceived within a pledged union with a woman and acknowledged by the phratries. Pericles' law further required that the mother had to be an *aste*. On this evidence, there is no reason to doubt that by the time of *Ath. Pol.* legitimacy in this sense, i.e. birth from a Athenian woman pledged by *engye*, was implied in every notion of citizenship, and consequently that the statement in *Ath.Pol.* 42.1 we discussed above, that 'those who are born from *astos* parents on both sides share in the *politeia*', should be interpreted in this way. Furthermore, *Ath.Pol.* 21.6 states that Cleisthenes left the *gene* and the phratries and the priesthoods *kata ta patria*, and the evidence, scarce though it is, confirms this statement.[85] In other words,

[81] *Ath.Pol.* 21.6; cf. Hdt.5.66.2, pointing out that all the heroes were Attic, except Ajax, who was a neighbour and a foreigner. Paus.1.5.2–4 discusses the eponymous heroes and their statues on the Agora; for these heroes and their cults: Kron (1976), Kearns (1989), Parker (1996) 117–21.

[82] For the selection of archons and Solon's methods, see Chapter 5.

[83] As Kron (1976) 29–31 argues; Erechtheus: Hom. *Il.* 2.546–8, and below, Chapter 3.5.

[84] *Ath.Pol.* 19.4; Plut. *Sol.* 11.2.

[85] *Ath.Pol.* 21.6: τὰ δὲ γένη καὶ τὰς φρατρίας καὶ τὰς ἱερωσύνας εἴασεν ἔχειν ἑκάστους κατὰ τὰ πάτρια. If ἑκάστους is taken to refer to the demes mentioned in the previous sentence, as H. Rackham in the Loeb ed., the demes were to keep their *gene*, phratries and priesthoods *kata ta*

Cleisthenes did not define citizenship,[86] but he added the new participatory superstructure of demes, trittyes and *phylai*, using conventional terminology for new elements, to the existing foundations. In the deme, citizen status based on legitimate descent was checked *again*, formally in the case of male citizens on reaching adulthood by a procedure among the demesmen,[87] and informally by the conventions of (religious) participation in the case of female citizens.[88] In sum, under Cleisthenes citizenship in terms of membership of the *polis* (*who* shares?) was expanded to include 'new citizens' but not altered in essence; the *polis*'s bond with the gods (in *what* do they share?) and the ways in which this bond was maintained remained as they had been before. The changes concerned new associations through which participation in political and other contexts was organised (*how* do they share?), and as we shall see in the following chapters, these Cleisthenic beginnings were to have a major impact in the longer run.

A few examples may further illuminate my argument that the Cleisthenic system, which was intended to engage citizens more intensively in running the city's politics, administration and cults, did not replace an 'archaic' concept of citizenship based on birth and religious arrangements, but was based on, grew out of and expanded this very concept.

The first example concerns the evidence of citizenship used in court. In the course of time, demes came to draw up lists of their members.[89] This

patria. Alternatively, and better, as P.J. Rhodes translates in Penguin Classics, ἑκάστους should be taken to refer to the *gene*, phratries and priesthoods themselves, who were left to remain as before. The main point is that the system of descent and legitimacy and the assignment of priesthoods did not change. The continuity of the *gene*, phratries and priesthoods is contrasted in *Ath.Pol.* 21.5 with the naucraries, the only type of unit that Cleisthenes abolished and replaced by the demes (see above). Arist. *Pol.*1319b19–27 mentions that Cleisthenes created more *phylai* and *phratries* than there used to be; for the *phylai*, this is certain, and for the *phratries* not impossible, considering the expansion of the citizen body (but note the doubts of Lambert, above n. 68).

86 See also Lambert (1998) 261–7; his and my view differs from that of, for instance, Whitehead (1986a), Manville (1990) 185–209 and the 'Paris school', that Cleisthenes' system disrupted and redefined citizenship and/or was the first definition of citizenship.

87 *Ath.Pol.* 42.1. I am not convinced by Osborne (1985) 146–51 in regarding citizen descent on both sides and acceptance by the deme as two different, *conflicting* criteria of citizenship in Dem. 57; as I argue in Chapter 1, if Euxitheos succeeded in showing his Athenian descent, he could by due right expect to be accepted as a citizen also in the deme. Cf. Lambert (1998) 28–9, n. 13.

88 For instance Is. 6.49–50, where the citizen status of a woman is denied and her participation in the Thesmophoria held against her; in Is. 3.80 the fact that a man did not support financially the participation of a woman in the deme's Thesmophoria is adduced as evidence that she was not his wife. On the level of the *polis*, Phano's role as Basilinna in the Anthesteria was denounced since she was allegedly not of citizen status ([Dem.] 59).

89 *Ath.Pol.* 42.1; on the uncertain origins of the *lexiarchikon grammateion*, indisputably attested for the first time in 434 (*IG* I^3 138, l. 6), in a military context, see Whitehead (1986a) 35, n. 130; on the possible archaic origins of such lists, Lambert (1998) 261–2. No undisputable deme list inscribed

list was called the *lexiarchikon grammateion*, literally 'written list of claims to offices', from the noun *lexis*, meaning a claim to an inheritance and hence any claim that might be brought in a lawsuit.[90] But such deme lists played virtually no role in establishing a citizen's identity when his or her status really mattered, notably in court. This was still the case in the fourth century, when the use of documents was gradually becoming more widespread and accepted than in the fifth century. In trials where a citizen's status was contested, oral testimony prevailed: witnesses to the relevant rituals would typically give their evidence in person and orally.[91] Yet it is not merely due to the weight accorded in general to oral testimony over written documents that the first was decisive in court, but rather what this oral testimony was about. As we saw above, the father or representative kinsman was required to swear in the phratry as to the legitimacy of the child by putting his hand on the slaughtered animal provided by the father and lying on the altar. When considered necessary, the *phrateres* might cast votes near the altar and a majority of votes would prevail. Such a case would be an adoption, as in the speech *Against Makartatos* (Dem. 43) on the inheritance of Hagnias. The speaker, Sositheos, is the father of a boy, Euboulides (III), whom he introduced as his legitimate son in the phratry of his father-in-law Euboulides (II), who had adopted the boy, a son of his only heir, his daughter Phylomache, and Sositheos:

> I introduced this boy to the *phrateres* of Hagnias and Euboulides, to which group Theopompos, the father of Makartatos here, belonged during his lifetime, and to which Makartatos now belongs. And the fellow *phrateres* of Makartatos here, who knew better than any others the pedigree of the family, seeing that he [Theopompos, the father of Makartatos] himself did not choose to risk a contest and did not remove the victim from the altar, as he should have done had the introduction of this boy not been legitimate, but demanded that they commit perjury, took the ballot while the victims were still burning, and carried it from the altar of Zeus Phratrios in the presence of the defendant Makartatos, and gave a just verdict, men of the jury – that this boy was duly and rightfully introduced as the adopted son of Euboulides into the family of Hagnias.[92]

The acceptance of legitimate children in the phratry, as this passage illustrates, involved 'heavy' rituals, unlike the voting in the demes, even if the

on stone is extant (compare *IG* II² 2344, a phratry list, and *IG* II² 2342, a descent list of a *genos* (Kerykes?)), whereas numerous other lists are extant that seem to have a honorific rather than an administrative function. Presumably, deme lists were made on perishable material.

90 Harrison II, 88; LSJ *s.v.* λῆξις.

91 Scafuro (1994); cf. Todd (1993) 173; Thomas (1989) 38–55: distrust of written documents.

92 Dem. 43.14; transl. A.T. Murray (Loeb ed.), slightly modified.

latter could have serious legal consequences. In cases of citizen status and legitimacy speakers expected to persuade the *dikastai* with evidence on phratry rituals because of their more significant and enduring weight. The epigraph heading this chapter is one among many examples of such ritual events brought as decisive facts into court. Recurrent remarks in the literary evidence indicate that acceptance by demes was widely considered to be liable to corruption, whereas disputed phratry testimony was not only rare, but taken to be a break of the fundamental trust in the oath.[93] In other words, deme membership did not replace the overseeing of legitimacy by the *phrateres* and participation in their *hiera* as the vital evidence of legitimate birth and citizenship in court.

The second example illustrating how the Cleisthenic system was built on but did not replace the existing model of citizenship concerns the archonship. The nine archons were beyond a doubt the most significant magistrates of Athens, even if in the course of the fifth century the *strategoi* gradually overtook them in actual political leadership.[94] *Ath.Pol.*'s report on the *dokimasia* (scrutiny) of the archons before entering office contains exemplary evidence of the fundamental role of descent anchored in cult as the persistent criterion of citizenship. As *Ath.Pol.* 55.3–5 reports, the candidates had to answer the following questions:

> 'Who is your father, and from which deme, and who is the father of your father, and who is your mother, and who is the father of your mother and from which deme?' And [they ask] if he has an Apollo Patroios and Zeus Herkeios, and where these shrines are. And next if he has family tombs and where these are. Next, if he treats his parents well, and if he pays his *telos*, and if he has done his military service. And when he has answered all these [questions], the official says 'call the witnesses to these statements'.

The interrogation in this passage consists of two parts. The first question concerns membership of the deme and therefore must be post-Cleisthenic. Moreover, legitimate descent of both father and mother are to be testified, indicating a date after Pericles' Citizenship Law. In the second part, the candidate is questioned about his hereditary share in the *hiera patroia*, the gods honoured in his family who are the ancestral gods of the *polis*, and about his *oikos* where these cults were located – the chain of cults

93 Cf. Rubinstein (1993) 44; Whitehead (1986a) 291–301, 327–45. Corruption in demes: Aischin. 1.114; Is. 6.22–5; [Dem.] 44.37–42; Dem. 57.8–17; Din. fr. 7; Hyp. 4.3; see also Chapters 5 and 6.2. Demes selling offices: *Ath.Pol.* 62.1. Andoc. 1.126–7: denounces testimony on perjury in phratry and *genos* of the Kerykes; [Dem.] 59.59–60: Phrastor tries to present his (allegedly) non-*astos* son to the phratry and the *genos* of the Brytidai, but shirks from committing perjury to achieve this.

94 See further below, Chapter 5.

belonging to the domain of the phratries. The family tombs likewise are evidence of hereditary membership of the *polis* and sustain the connection with the ancestors; tomb cult sustained one's own inherited part of the *polis*'s bond with the gods.[95] Moreover, taking care of the dead typically was *hosios* conduct, as was treating one's parents well; at Athens, it was both a moral imperative and laid down in Solon's laws.[96] Paying *telos* and doing military service were primarily obligations to the human community, but as we saw in the previous chapter, the ephebic oath engaged military loyalty in the domain of *hiera kai hosia*, and *telos* was used for many purposes, among which *hiera* (i.e. *hosios* money). In other words, it seems that in their *dokimasia* the prospective archons, having been scrutinised as members by descent entitled to their inherited share in the bond of the *polis* with the gods, were asked about their *active* sharing in *hiera kai hosia*. On this questioning and a verdict by the *boule* and if necessary a *dikasterion*, the approved candidates took the oath on sacrificial victims on the special stone on the Agora, swearing they would exercise their office (*archein*) in conformity with *dike* and with the laws, and not accept bribes. Finally, they went up to the Acropolis and there took the oath again, and next entered their office.

So far we have seen that citizenship in Athens was based on birth from a citizen parent (father) and entailed membership of and inheritance rights in the family and in the *polis*. Although from a wider historical perspective transmission of citizenship by descent is far from unusual, as I mentioned before, nonetheless the foundational role of descent in citizenship raises some further questions.

Older scholarship generally regarded political structures based on personal ties, notably those of kinship, as a primitive form of association, to be replaced by a more developed conception of the state, based on impersonal, legally defined rights and duties, upheld by formal institutions. In the study of archaic Athens, historians used to see the *phylai*, phratries, *gene* and the somewhat elusive elite group the Eupatridai as social entities whose claims to power were based on (high) birth and therefore were typical of a tribal or aristocratic past *preceding* the *polis* as a state with formal institutions and more equal rights.[97] This point of view was

[95] Continuity of legitimate kinship emphasised by taking care of the tombs of one's ancestors: Dem. 57.54; Is. 6.51; 8.25–7.

[96] Moral imperative: see Chapter 2; laws: Solon: LR 55a–c; 56/a–c; 57/a–b; *Ath.Pol.* 56: the archon eponymous was in charge of the *graphai* and *dikai* for ill-uses of parents and of orphans.

[97] This view, which originated in the eighteenth century, was elaborated in historical and anthropological scholarship in the nineteenth century, and continued to influence studies of the archaic *polis*

gradually abandoned after 1976, when F. Bourriot and D. Roussel showed independently, firstly, that *phylai* and *gene* were not based on real but on fictive descent and therefore could not have been the instruments of an aristocracy of birth that the older scholarship had taken them to be, a revision that particularly affected the view of *gene* as providers of priesthoods; secondly, that *phylai* and *gene* had developed *together with* the emerging *polis*; instead of a primitive *Vorstufe*, they were themselves *polis* institutions of a sort.[98] Lambert, as we just saw, similarly demonstrated that the phratries played a key role in citizenship, exercising controls on legitimacy by descent, both before and after Cleisthenes. The results of Bourriot, Roussel and Lambert are corroborated by our findings here: Solon's laws tightened the rules of legitimacy, Cleisthenes consolidated this citizenship system by adding a layer of *polis* organisation based on the same descent principle, and Pericles tightened the rules of legitimacy further by requiring Athenian descent on both sides (the effects of which are to be discussed later). In other words, the criterion of descent *increased* in stringency and force, rather than giving way to more impersonal *polis* structures, as the older scholarship, wrongly but not unreasonably, had assumed.

How can we explain this development, which is even more remarkable when compared with, for instance, the turn citizen status took in Roman law at an early stage towards an abstract, formal, quality? On the evidence discussed above, I would tentatively argue that the conception of citizenship as sharing in the *inheritance* of the family and the *polis*, notably of the bond with the gods, represented in *hiera kai hosia*, played a formative role in this. Continuity of this bond required on the human side not only keeping up the performance of *hiera kai hosia* in the correct ways, but also ensuring the transmission of the ancestral bond with the gods to the true heirs of those who had first entered this reciprocal relationship with the divine; on the side of the immortals, obviously no measures for perpetuity were necessary. Once incorporated in the very foundations of the *polis*, this conception became effective in every ramification of its organisation. To flesh out this argument, we need, firstly, to chart how transmission actually worked, i.e. the nuts and bolts of kinship and inheritance at Athens, and, next, to clarify the role of inheritance for the organisation of the *polis*.

until recently; see e.g. Maurizio (1998) who ascribes the inclusion of women in the Panathenaic procession to 'archaic' notions of citizenship based on descent and cult, whereas the participation of men reflected the contemporary principle of political participation.

[98] Bourriot (1976), Roussel (1976); for the reception of both in the first decade after publication, Schneider (1991/2); comparative study of the *genos* and the Roman *gens*, Smith (2006).

3.4 Descent and Inheritance Rights

With this agenda in mind, I should like to sketch concisely how the kinship structure and transmission of inheritance worked in classical Athens and their significance for citizenship. I shall pay particular attention to the differences between material and immaterial goods, and to women's inheritance and property rights, which, to judge by the work of, among others, Davies and Manville, discussed above, seem commonly to be only partly understood. Once we have obtained an accurate picture of all of this, it will also be easier to gauge the implications for women's roles as citizens and for Pericles' law. Although in the course of time the Athenian laws concerning inheritance were revised in various respects, notably as to wills and to adoption, not all of these issues are relevant here, and I will trace only the main lines.[99]

The structure of Athenian kinship was bilateral – kinship was not only biologically but also socially recognised both on the father's and on the mother's side – but with a patrilinear emphasis: in all matters of kinship and inheritance, male had precedence over female, and children were aligned primarily to the father's family line and only secondarily to the maternal side.[100] I use the word 'family' for a patrilinear kingroup and *oikos* for the product of a union made between two such families by marriage. A legitimate marriage was arranged between the father of a woman and her future husband (or his father) and required a pledge (*engye*), a speech act by which the daughter of the bride-giving family was 'lent' to the bride-receiving family for the procreation of legitimate children. The *engye* played a crucial role as testimony in court, notably in cases of legitimacy and inheritance, where a woman was typically claimed to be 'a citizen by birth (*aste*) pledged according to the laws', with all due consequences for the transmission of claims to membership and property.[101]

[99] This section is based on the court cases of Lysias, Demosthenes and Isaeus concerning legitimacy, inheritances and other issues of family law, with Wyse (1904), Wolff (1944), Wolff (1952), Harrison I, Humphreys (1986), Patterson (1990), Hunter (1993), Rubinstein (1993), Todd (1993), Hunter (1994), Leduc (1994–5), Cox (1998), Gherchanoc (1998), Lambert (1998), Patterson (1998), Vérilhac and Vial (1998), Wilgaux (2000), Wilgaux (2009).

[100] Scholarship for a long time failed to recognise the bilateral character of descent and inheritance in ancient Athens, due to the patrinilear emphasis in the inheritance system, the *kyrieia* of male Athenians over their female relatives, influence of Roman law on the study of Athenian law (cf. Todd (1993) 14–17) and a selective use of sources (cf. Wilgaux (2009) 225–9). This misunderstanding is disappearing only slowly; for instance, Ogden (1996) 47–58, 117 erroneously assumes, on the authority of H. Wade-Gery (Wade-Gery (1958a, orig. 1931); Wade-Gery (1958b)) that Athenian patrilinearity meant legitimacy and inclusion in kin groups only through the male line, and consequently takes the legitimacy policies of phratries and *gene* to be the opposite of what was the case in reality.

[101] Is. 3.5, 39, without *engye* no legitimacy for inheritance; 6.26; 8.20; Dem. 57.41. etc. For *aste*, see below, Chapter 4.4.

Once married by *engye* and given away by *ekdosis*, a daughter's original family 'parted' with the children she would bear: they were to belong to the paternal family in the first place, following the rules just mentioned. But this was indeed only the case in the first place; depending on circumstances, different scenarios applied, as we shall see below. Usually a bride also literally moved into her husband's house or created a new household with him (*ekdosis*), but occasionally the couple came to live in her original home; the *oikos* by definition combined persons from at least two families.[102] The choice of actual home made no difference to the essence of the union, because it was not place of residence but the family of the father (his or her father respectively) that defined the household as a social unit, notably in the deme.[103] When the bride festively changed her paternal into her marital home, the *gamelia* ritual in the phratry also took place, confirming the original pledge into a union acknowledged by the phratry, to guarantee the legitimacy of children born from it.[104] The wife brought the cultic relations her family had maintained with the gods with her, and she was integrated into the cults of her husband's family, the ritual marking acceptance of her as the mother of the future heirs in her husband's family. Sharing the family cults made the *oikos* into a *koinonia*.[105] Within the *oikos*, an adult, married man was the *kyrios*, in a hierarchal relationship as a father over his minor sons and his daughters and as a husband over his wife. A woman passed from her father's *kyrieia* into that of her husband, or in case of the latter's death, of another adult male relative (often an adult son). Yet a husband's authority over a woman was much weaker than her father's had been and a wife usually found further support in her family of birth, notably her brothers.

[102] A couple could take residence either with his original *oikos* (virilocal) or her original *oikos* (uxorilocal; to be expected in the case of an *epikleros*) or they could form a new *oikos*; women were often buried with their husband, but also alone or with their family of birth; the pattern is varied. An interesting example is the family group in which Archippe, daughter of Meixiades of Aegilia, was buried not only with her husband, fellow demesman Prokleides, with Prokles their son, and with Prokleides' parents Praxagora and Sostratos, but also with Archippe's brother Pamphilos and his son Prokleides II (*IG* II^2 5374, 5376, 5378, 5379; with Humphreys (1983b) 114–15, 129; Cox (1998) 51). These people had probably formed an *oikos* in life and were buried together.

[103] Todd (1993) 209, Wilgaux (2009) 230–1. For the ideal of the unequal but companionable relation between husband and wife, cooperating for the good of the *oikos*, Arist. *Eth.Eud.* 1238b26; *Pol.* 1253b9–10, with Versnel (1987).

[104] Lambert (1998) 36, 181–5.

[105] For the cultic heritage of the family, Parker, *PS*, 9. Household slaves also belonged to the *oikos* and were ritually integrated into this *koinonia*; they did not become family members with inheritance rights, however, and therefore are not further discussed here.

The aim of inheritance rules was to continue the legacy of the paternal family line.[106] This legacy, embodied in the material and immaterial goods passed down over generations, was captured in the term *ta patroia*.[107] Heirs were obliged to maintain their *kleros* (part of the inheritance) with the utmost care, and alienation was not regarded as a normal or common practice. Solon's laws, as we saw, laid down that only legitimate (*gnesios*) children could inherit and they were the sons and daughters accepted by the father and by the phratry. They were legally members of his family line and both sons and daughters carried their father's patronymic.[108] Although on marriage a daughter separated from her father's household, her ties with her family of origin remained strong. She continued to belong to her father's family in terms of kinship, just like her brothers, and often continued to cooperate with her brothers to preserve the paternal estate.[109] A family leaving no heirs at all was considered a dramatic event, not only for the family itself, but also for the *polis*, as we saw above.[110] For the family continuation of the family line was essential, and there was a strong feeling that only descendants, the prime heirs, could be safely entrusted with the tomb cult: in the Athenian perception, care of the burial rites was intimately linked both with inheritance rights and with the duty to care for one's parents in recompense for one's upbringing as an Athenian

106 For the main principles concerning legitimacy and inheritance at Athens, Harrison I, 61–2, 122–62; Patterson (1990); Lambert (1998) 25–58; Patterson (1998) 85–100; Carawan (2008). Whether *nothoi* born from two Athenian parents who had not been married with *engye* or *epidikasia* (assignment by *dike* to a spouse, usually of an heiress to a husband) were legitimate and citizens has been disputed (see Harrison 1, 61–8; Todd (1993) 178–9), but I argue here that they were not, in agreement with amongst others Wolff (1944); Wolff (1952); Rhodes (1978); Patterson (1990); Lambert (1998); Vérilhac and Vial (1998) 55 against Harrison 1, 65–8 and MacDowell (1976).

107 Harrison 1, 125 notes a difference made in some texts between πατρῷια, the ancestral heritage, and ἐπικτητά, property acquired during someone's lifetime, but the two categories were not clearly distinguished when it came to leaving and dividing the inheritance. Cf. Todd (1993) 225–6, 242.

108 In the course of the fifth century, sons came to use their father's demotic themselves, while women were referred to by the demotic of their father or their husband. Pomeroy (1995) and Vestergaard (2000) 89 paradoxically perceive the patronymic in the case of women as a sign of a 'passive' non-identity defined by her male relatives, whereas in the case of men they see the same nomenclature based on the same principles as a sign of a man's 'active' identity as representative of the patrilinear *oikos*.

109 Cox (1998) concludes her analysis of the practical operation of the inheritance system (129): 'Ironically, a legal system that emphasized the male actually promoted the role of the woman in the preservation of the paternal and/or fraternal estate: a sister and her brother worked together to protect her dotal property, or, in order to protect her brother's estate, she could ally with him against another brother.'

110 Preventing the *oikos* from becoming empty (ἔρημος) is a common concern (e.g. Is. 7.30ff., Dem. 43.77ff.), closely connected with concern about tombs, since in both the continuity of the cults of household gods and *polis* gods is at stake: Is. 1.10; 2.36ff., 45ff.; 4.19, 26; 6.39ff.; 8.21–7, 38ff.; 9.4, 32; Dem. 43.11ff., 78ff.; [Dem.] 44.32; [Dem.] 48.12.

citizen.[111] Included in the private inheritance was a share of the *patroia* of the *polis*; with the extinction of a family, its part of the original bond of the *polis* would be lost. Preventing such a loss was a prime responsibility of the *polis*, supervised by the archons and often invoked in court speeches as a sentiment shared by all citizens.[112] One of the ways the *polis* fulfilled this responsibility was by regulating – but not prescribing – adoption, as we shall see below.

A daughter inherited her part of the parental heritage of *hiera kai hosia* just as her brother did; the 'law on legitimacy' clearly implies this in barring a *nothos* and *nothe* from a share in the inheritance.[113] When she, in her turn, left this share of her parental property and immaterial goods to her own sons and daughters, this share was occasionally called *metroia*.[114] In Isaeus 7.25, the speaker, who was adopted into another family, tries to make the most of his claim to an inheritance through his mother, proclaiming that 'the act of adoption into another family does not separate a child from his mother, but she remains his mother all the same, whether he stays in his father's *oikos* or in his adoptive one'.[115] The speaker clearly tapped into the common awareness that patrilinear links with concomitant property, duties and obligations devolved equally to daughters and sons, and later to the heirs of those sons and daughters.

In the division of the inheritance, the distinction between the material and immaterial goods of the family is relevant. Daughters and sons inherited equally the immaterial goods, i.e. membership of the family, participation in the *hiera kai hosia* of the family and the *polis*, and any other claims flowing from this membership. Examples of such immaterial goods, duties and obligations are the family's cults, the right to share tombs, the care of the dead, eligibility for priesthood (male and female) in the *gene*, but they included also undesirable 'goods', such as the infamous curse of the Alcmaeonidai, which devolved on Pericles through his mother.[116]

111 Care for parents as recompense for upbringing as citizens: Lyk. *Leoc.* 94; Aeschin. 1.28. *Dokimasia* of archons as to care for parents: *Ath.Pol.* 55.3, Dem. 57.70. Cf. Rubinstein (1993) 66–8, 72–6.

112 Is. 7.30–2; cf. Parker, *PS*, 32–6.

113 Is. 3.62: the legitimate daughter inherits *ta patroia* from her father; adoption: Dem. 44.32.

114 *Ta metroia*: Hdt. 3.53 (here including allegiances); Dem. 36.38. Xen. *Hell.* 2.4.21: *patroios* and *metroios* gods.

115 Is. 7.25: Μητρὸς δ' οὐδείς ἐστιν ἐκποίητος, ἀλλ' ὁμοίως ὑπάρχει τὴν αὐτὴν εἶναι μητέρα, κἂν ἐν τῷ πατρῴῳ μένῃ τις οἴκῳ κἂν ἐκποιηθῇ.

116 Tombs and cult of the dead, Is. 9.7; Is. 9.13, 21, 30–3; Dem. 57.28, 70; in Dem. 57.40 Euxitheos calls as witnesses for his kin relations the relatives of his mother and 'those who share (burial in) the same tombs' on his mother's side; and 70: the right to bury his mother 'in her *patroios* tomb'. For literary and archaeological evidence, Humphreys (1983b), Houby-Nielsen (1995), Blok

For material goods, different rules applied. Daughters received a dowry that was not an equal share, but a fair and proportionate part of the estate, making her a valuable bride for a husband fitting her status.[117] The dowry was in concept and effect a woman's part of the material inheritance and it remained hers.[118] The usufruct went into the *oikos* of her marriage and if the dowry was substantial, it gave her serious economic power there.[119] Whether she could actually use her money is a much-disputed question. In one passage, the single reference in the classical record, Isaeus mentions a law stating that a woman could not dispose of property more than one *medimnos* of barley in value.[120] In the classical age a *medimnos* of unworked

(2006) with further refs. Transmission of eligibility in *gene*, Blok and Lambert (2009). Curse of the Alcmaeonidai: Hdt. 6.131; Thuc. 1.126–7. The chorus in Soph. *El.* 156–63 describe Electra, her two sisters and brother Orestes as: πρὸς ὅ τι σὺ τῶν ἔνδον εἶ περισσά, οἷς ὁμόθεν εἶ καὶ γονᾷ ξύναιμος; '[those] with whom you share your lineage and your blood'.

117 According to Dem. 43.54, a law prescribed an amount for the dowry according to property class (500, 300 and 150 dr. for the highest three classes; Harrison 1, 135–6), but the extant evidence shows great variety, suggesting that these amounts were perhaps minimum sums enforceable in court. The dowry was supposed to suit the status of the family to which the daughter belonged, creating pressure towards substantial dowries among the wealthy, but the desire to keep the property as much as possible within the patrilinear family created counter-pressure to keep the dowry modest and have daughters marry within their own status group and even their own kin group. Schaps (1979) 99, app. 1 shows variety in size according to type of evidence (*horoi*, orators, literary sources) and Cox (1998) 116–20 lists dowries ranging from 4.4 to 27.7 per cent of total estate value attested in fourth-century court cases. On the value of a dowry as equivalent (but often not of equal value) to what her brothers received, Foxhall (1989) 32.

118 Goody (in Goody and Tambiah (1973) 17): '[D]owry is part of a familial or conjugal fund, which passes down from holder to heir, and usually from the parents to the daughter. It is thus part and parcel of the transfer of familial property, but a process of transfer that includes women as well as men; that is, male property is transmitted to women as full heirs, semi-heirs or residual heirs. Consequently, dowry belongs to a type of transmission that I have called "diverging devolution" (or "the woman's property complex").' For the dowry as a daughter's part of the parental inheritance in ancient Athens, Wilgaux (2009) 230, and Cox (1998) 105, 117, 134, who argues (128) that due to the dowry a daughter was not a rival for the rest of the paternal estate. Hunter (1994) 19–29 documents women's property consisting of real estate, slaves, movable goods and money, often invested in land.

119 Dowries were important in sealing family connections; Vérilhac and Vial (1998) 86–9 argue that 87 per cent of attested marriages concerned couples from different patrilinear families, ca. 10 per cent endogamous marriages with paternal kin, notably marriages of cousins; allowing for a similar number of endogamous marriages of maternal kin (see for such cases Cox (1998) 31–3, 63–4), ca. 20 per cent of all marriages were endogamous. Vérilhac and Vial ascribe endogamy to special circumstances such as sudden poverty or political problems, but I am more convinced by Wilgaux (2009), who shows the structural pressures towards endogamy, and by Cox (1998) 38–67, who observes a greater variety of marriage strategies and property policies, and regional differences, familial heterogamy being stronger in the city than in the rural demes, where endogamy was rather frequent.

120 Is. 10.10: ὁ γὰρ νόμος διαρρήδην κωλύει παιδὶ μὴ ἐξεῖναι συμβάλλειν μηδὲ γυναικὶ πέρα μεδίμνου κριθῶν. LSJ *s.v.* συμβάλλω interpret the verb to mean 'to advance, lend', but the context in Isaeus, making a will, rather emphasises (entering) a contract. The value measured not in drachmae, but *medimnos* points to an archaic origin.

barley cost on average three drachmae and of hulled barley meal four drachmae, providing a family of four for two weeks with the barley (but not with other foodstuffs) they needed. A skilled labourer earned, again on average, one drachma a day in the fifth and two drachmae a day in the fourth century.[121] For a poor family the value of a *medimnos* of barley was therefore substantial, for a family of median or great wealth it was a very small sum – not exactly what one would expect to matter very much for Isaeus' clients. Whatever its meaning in Isaeus' text, the (disparate) evidence strongly suggests that in the classical age this law on the *medimnos* of barley was in effect a dead letter, in that women did hold substantial property and women with a substantial dowry used it as their own.[122]

A fine example is Xenokrateia, who in the last decade of the fifth century dedicated a sanctuary to Kephisos and commemorated her gift with a beautifully carved relief showing herself, her son and eleven divinities, with the following inscription:

> Xenokrateia founded the sanctuary (*hieron*) of Kephisos and dedicated this gift to the gods who share his altar because of their instruction, daughter and mother of Xeniades of Cholleidai, for whoever wishes to sacrifice for fulfilment of good gifts (*agatha*).[123]

While many aspects of this relief and inscription are topics of debate (whose instruction is meant here? Who are all these gods and goddesses?), several points seem clear. Xenokrateia presents herself as an Athenian citizen, referring to her own father and her son with their demotic, but without mentioning her husband, unlike, for instance, Kekropia, who dedicated a statue made by Kephisodotos to Demeter and Kore at Eleusis in her own name, also

[121] Markle (2004) 110–11, with further refs.

[122] De Ste. Croix (1970) accepted this law to be fully effective, while Schaps (1979) 52–8 concurs but on 74–88 seems to disagree. Acting as a *kyria* of her own wealth seems to be implied in (costly) votives dedicated by women in their own name, such as Smikythe (*IG* I³ 794; *DAA* 380) and Xenokrateia (see main text); Kron (1996). Hunter (1994) 19–29 presents further evidence (Dem. 20.53–4: a citizen woman *kyria* of four talents; Dem. 41.8–11: a citizen woman making and sealing financial transactions well over 1,800 drachmae; the woman in Is. 10.23, who is *kyria* of her inheritance) that this law was a dead letter, observing: 'What is curious about the method of both de Ste. Croix and Schaps is their refusal to deal seriously with evidence that contradicts this view [that women could not own and dispose of property].' Cf. Harrison 1, 236: whether or not women could own property in the law is largely 'a matter of definition'; Harris (2006) 345: 'even though the money in a household legally belonged to the husband, the wife might still administer the household's finances and make important decisions about how to manage larger sums of money'. For Archippe, widow of the banker Pasion, see below, Chapter 6.2.

[123] *IG* I³ 987 (II² 4548): Ξενοκράτεια Κηφισο˜ ἱερ/ὸν ἱδρύσατο καὶ ἀνέθηκεν/ ξυμβώμοις τε θεοῖς διδασκαλ/ίας τόδε δῶρον, Ξενιάδο θυγάτ/ηρ καὶ μήτηρ ἐκ Χολλειδῶν/ θύεν τῶι βουλομένωι ἐπὶ/τελεστῶν ἀγαθῶν. On this relief Gaifman (2015); Parker, *PS*, 430 and n. 49; Dillon (2002) 24–5 with further refs.

mentioning her father and her husband.[124] Xenokrateia's self-presentation can be explained in several ways: she may have been a (war) widow or an *epikleros* or both. Whether her father was still alive when she made her dedication and had anything to do with it cannot be deduced from the monument; its central message is Xenokrateia's own gift to the gods. Her citizenship of Athens is further expressed in the choice of two identifiable gods on the relief, Apollo Pythios (*patroios* god of Athens) and Kephisos, river god of Athens. And her citizenship is expressed in the remarkable invitation to other worshippers: the altar may be used by whoever wishes (*ho boulomenos*), an expression intimately tied to the public discourse of assembly and jurisdiction at Athens and here uniquely used in the context of sharing in the bond with the gods.[125] Dedication and inscription testify to Xenokrateia's share as a citizen in *hiera kai hosia*, and to her agency, financially and socially, in doing so – making the relief a fitting image for the cover of this book. Just how much the *hieron* and the monument cost is difficult to say, but we can be confident it was vastly more than three or four drachmae.[126]

In the case of divorce, a woman took her dowry, which her former husband was obliged to return, with her, usually to engage in a new marriage. In other words, her connections to her paternal family were in a sense suspended or subdued upon her marriage, but activated again in case of divorce. If on her death she was still married to her husband or his widow, her dowry fell entirely to the husband's *oikos* and became a part of the inheritance of the children. A woman could not herself bequeath her dowry or any other part of the inheritance, unlike a man, who could do so when he had no living (natural or adopted) legitimate children.[127] But it is

[124] *IG* II² 4552: τοῖν θεοῖν ἀν[έθηκεν] / Κεκροπία Καλ[λιστρά]/το, Ἱππ.../Αὐτοκλ[έος γυνή]. *vac.* Κηφισό[δοτος ἐποίησεν]. Of Xeniades of Cholleidai nothing else is known. For a similar phrasing of the family relationship, see below: Hegelochos, father and son of Ekphantos.

[125] The expression ὁ βουλομένος is most common in legal and political texts; epigraphical instances are *IG* I³ 14.8; *IG* I³ 34.34; *IG* I³ 41.61; *IG* I³ 63.13; *IG* I³ 84.26; *IG* I³ II, 337.23.

[126] No archaeological traces of the *hieron* were found, but other dedications (a relief by Kephisodotos with a stele dedicated to several gods and heroes, *IG* II² 4547) were found nearby the findspot of Xenokrateia's monument at Neo Phaliro, in an area that must have been inside the Long Walls. For the figures carved for the Erechtheion frieze from 60 to 240 drachmae were paid (*IG* I³ 476); this may have included the price of the stone itself and of polishing it. High costs were involved in the transport of stone, which for the Erechtheion was included in the building project but which for Xenokrateia's dedication of relief, base and altar probably had to be independently organised (as Helle Hochscheid informs me *per epist.*). All in all the costs of Xenokrateia's gift may be estimated at several hundred drachmae.

[127] See e.g. Is. 3.42–50, where the existence of a legitimate daughter is adduced as evidence against a will. A distinction is sometimes made (e.g. Schaps (1979) 9–13, with ref.) between a woman's own valuables (jewels, clothing) and other property she would bring as a dowry, but the many grave stelai of late fifth- and fourth-century Athens showing women holding a box and a (painted) necklace do not so much point to her private trinkets but to the entire dowry she brought into her

important to note that men, too, were not absolute owners of their property. They were expected in the first place to take care of their *patroia* and pass it to descendants; the estate was regarded as ancestral goods rather than as wealth possessed absolutely by an individual. An Athenian who squandered his *patroia* could lose his position as an active citizen. As the term indicated and was mentioned earlier, the *patroia* (and *metroia*) of an individual family were considered to be a part of the common *patroia* of the *polis*. For classical Athens, modern notions of 'ownership' do not, or only partially, apply, either for men or for women.[128]

When a woman had no (surviving) brothers and she was the only one to inherit from her father, the rights of the daughter (or daughters) as descendant from her father's family became preeminent and she became an *epikleros*, i.e. guardian/owner 'holding' the paternal *kleros* (inheritance).[129] This situation must have been quite frequent and therefore something families commonly had to reckon with.[130] Ideally, her father had, when still alive, sought a husband for her himself and adopted her son as his own, or adopted a son and had him marry the daughter. If the father had failed to do this, the *epikleros* would marry a male kinsman, and the law laid down the order in which the right to marry her (or arrange a marriage for her) fell among the *anchisteia*. The same order obtained in the devolution of inheritances, and with these rights came duties and obligations to the relatives, care for elderly parents and for burial and death

family of marriage. It makes more sense to regard a woman's dowry as part of her *patroia*, held in trust by her, just as a man's inheritance was held in trust by him.

128 Foxhall (1989) 28 argues (with Hes. *Op.* 376–8; Lys. 19.32; Pl. *Leg.* 776b against Arist. *Rhet.* 1361a14–28) that the paternal inheritance in the *oikos* was held 'in trust' by the male head of the household, not in absolute private ownership. Cf. Todd (1993) 210; see also above for discussion of the notion of 'ownership' in ancient Greece.

129 On the epiklerate: Harrison 1, 132–8; Todd (1993) 228–31; Cox (1998) 94–9; Patterson (1998) 91–103; Vérilhac and Vial (1998) 101–7.

130 Epiklerate is often treated in scholarship as an exceptional case, but it must have been fairly common: statistically, one in five families has only girls. Ingalls (2002) argues, *contra* Pomeroy (1997) 116–21, Pomeroy et al. (1999) 234, that in ancient Greece, like for instance in modern India, girls were not deprived of life chances or exposed at birth by their fathers to avoid providing a dowry; on the contrary, the high mortality rate in ancient Greece due to war, poverty and disease (an estimated 50 per cent of all children did not reach adulthood) must have had disastrous effects on survival of offspring, and daughters were as essential to the survival of families as sons. For instance, Euktemon (in Is. 6) had three sons, who all predeceased him without issue, and two daughters, only one of whom had only one daughter. Marrying women of somewhat higher status (hypergamy), furthermore, was considered attractive among Athenian men (Wilgaux (2009) 230), giving additional value to daughters. All of this, however, applies to well-to-do citizens; 'differential parent-investment' (read: relative neglect of girls compared to boys) may have been not uncommon among poor sections of Greek populations, to go by the evidence on immigrants to Miletus; Günther (2014) 298–9.

rituals – in other words, *hosia*.[131] In either case the *kleros* went with the *epikleros:* it did not disappear, but continued to exist as part of the material and immaterial assets, and under the legal protection, of another family.[132] Since the right to inherit lay squarely with an *epikleros*, her children became her regular heirs, and did not need to be adopted into her family of origin to be so.[133]

In all these arrangements concerning legitimate birth, death and inheritance, the patriliny was essentially anchored in the *anchisteia*, the patrilinear families on both sides of a married couple taken together.[134] We have seen this group already present in the laws on legitimacy and citizenship in the clause 'according to the law no male or female *nothos* has any claim, based on kinship on either side (*anchisteia*), to *hiera kai hosia*, as of the archonship of Eukleides'. Within the bilateral *anchisteia*, the masculine emphasis arranged precedence of the father's family over that of the mother, of males over females and of descendants over collaterals.[135] In practice, this meant that an inheritance first devolved within the father's family on sons and their descendants – with daughters' portions in the shape of dowries – and in the absence of sons, on daughters and their descendants. Normally, therefore, children would inherit, ultimately from their paternal grandfather, the share their father

[131] Harrison 1, 9–12. If there was no relative to take responsibility, the heiress was allocated to a suitable husband by a court (*epidikasia*).

[132] The conventional view, that an *epi-kleros* was a woman who 'came with' the inheritance (to be married to) the next male in line in the *anchisteia*, is unconvincing. Of course the *epikleros* embodied the interests of the family line, but construing her as merely instrumental of that interest (e.g. Todd (1993) 230–1) underestimates the *epikleros* as heiress and as *kyria* of her inheritance; see Vérilhac and Vial (1998) 102, Hunter (1994) 23, who argues that in Is. 10, where the target is a mother's substantial inheritance, the speaker, her son, deliberately describes it as hers (10.15, 17, 23 etc.) and would not have stood a chance with the *dikastai* if they could plausibly have thought this idea absurd. Schaps (1979) 32–42 argues that the function of the epiklerate cannot have been merely to continue the *oikos* but that the law protected the marital prospects of the *epikleros*.

[133] Rubinstein (1993) 89–91; Is. 3.50, 8.31, 10.12, fr. 26; [Dem.] 46.20, Hyp. Fr. 63 Teubn. A son of an *epikleros* could be adopted by his maternal grandfather, and the scarcity of court cases about them (e.g. Dem. 43) suggests such adoptions were rarely contested.

[134] Patterson (1998) 88–91 sees the *anchisteia* as a kin construction around an Athenian male, ceasing to exist at his death, because it operated to regulate his responsibilities and obligations; she emphasises, however, the web structure of the *anchisteia* and its bilateral foundations. However, exactly the same laws and rules apply to a female, as for instance Is. 5 and 8 show. Wilgaux (2009) sees the *anchisteia* coming about through marriage (union of man and woman) and remaining in place after death, burial and inheritance (cf. Patterson (1998) 89), and this indeed applies to both men and women. However, Wilgaux's model on 232 shows only one (the paternal?) side of the *anchisteia*, whereas Patterson (1998) 83, fig. 1 shows the whole *anchisteia*.

[135] Todd (1993) 218–21. Is. 7.20 and 8.33 feature disagreements about who in the *anchisteia* is closer to the deceased: a sibling, because both are descendants of the same father, or his children, because they are his own descendants.

had inherited and ultimately from their maternal grandfather the share their mother had received as a dowry.[136] If no representative of the family of the deceased's father was still alive, the inheritance would pass to the mother's side. An eloquent recognition of the priority of the paternal line and the significance of the mother's family as both sides of the *anchisteia* is found in naming practice: in the classical age, sons were usually named after their grandfathers, the eldest son after his paternal grandfather and the second son after his maternal grandfather.[137] For the same reason, as we saw, an Athenian inherited his or her relations with the gods from both their father's and their mother's families.

Jerome Wilgaux observes that a married woman, who combined membership of two families, was the key figure connecting the two kin groups into one *anchisteia*.[138] However, the double allegiance of the wife could also create a feeling that she remained to some extent an outsider in her husband's household, not entirely to be trusted with the interests of her in-laws. This ambiguity could fuel suspicion about her conduct, notably in sexual terms, and stimulate a perception of women as in some respect 'other' than the men whose patriliny prevailed in the conjugal household to which she belonged.[139]

Finally, the inheritance could be left to an adopted heir, a solution frequently sought in Athens, as is hardly surprising considering the high mortality rates among both children (of all ages) and adults (due to war, shipwreck, childbirth).[140] All features of adoption in classical Athens fit the pattern we saw so far, and the framework of the system seems to have

136 For example, in Is. 5, the estate of Dikaiogenes I, a wealthy Athenian, had been left to a son, who had four daughters and a son, Dikaiogenes II. On the death of the latter, the son of one of the daughters filed a claim to his mother's share of the estate. In Is. 8.15, the claims of grandchildren to the estate of their maternal grandfather are defended.

137 A good example is the sons of the orator Lycurgus, the eldest named Lycophron after Lycurgus' father, the second Habron, after the father of Lycurgus' wife, Kalliste. [Plut.] *X Or.* 843a–c; Lambert (2004b); Blok and Lambert (2009) 109–10.

138 Wilgaux (2009) 226, 235.

139 Whereas the conjugal family and household were primarily defined by the man's patriliny, the woman's family of origin would often come in to take responsibility if circumstances required, for instance in cases of guardianship of minor heirs; a favourite person in such circumstances was the mother's brother (maternal uncle), who was only second in line to inherit the estate. For this pattern, Bremmer (1983), Cox (1998) 116, 124, 127. Just (1989) 76–125 sees in the ambiguous integration of women into the new household the cause of the suspicion of women's sexuality (fear of adultery) and of the ideological (dis)qualification of women as 'other' in Greece.

140 Rubinstein (1993) 13, 45, 62–9: benefits adopter, guarantees heir, responsibility of archons; 22–3: adoptees from *anchisteia*; 17, 25–8: *epikleros* cannot be superseded; 84, 116: continuity from Solon to Hellenistic age.

been in place from Solon to the Hellenistic age, with changes over time in the laws of legitimacy. Adoption was meant to benefit the adopter, not the adoptee, i.e. to provide an heir who would continue the adopter's family line, observe his tomb cult and, when still alive, tend him in old age. Adoption was legally possible when there was no male heir, but when there was a daughter her rights as *epikleros* could not be superseded; in that case, the adoptee was married to her or, if she already had a son, it was he who was adopted. Most adoptees were male, but adopted females are known; in these cases, their children were not adopted but became the regular heirs after their mother.[141] An adoptee had to be an Athenian citizen according to the law; since the legitimacy of adoptees could be disputed and allegations raised that he or she was actually *nothos/e*, most adoptees were chosen from among the *anchisteia*, the group who had inheritance rights anyway. How exactly an adoptee would take possession of the estate depended on the conditions of his/her adoption.[142] In all adoptions, the adoptee cut the social ties with his paternal family line, losing his claims to inheritance there, but not with his mother's family; s/he could still inherit from her. With the change towards a different patrilinear family came concomitant new social ties: typically, adoptees had to be presented to and accepted by the new phratry and, in the case of males, to the new deme, to confirm their position: acknowledgement as legitimate heir of a family was ultimately a *polis* affair.[143]

Of special importance here are the ways in which inheritances were allocated. The part left to the sons consisted mainly of the immovable property, the part divided among the daughters as dowries usually were moveable possessions or an equivalent in money. Each of these parts was divided equally among the heirs; partible inheritance was typical of Greek inheritance rights generally.[144] The equal shares were assigned to the heirs by lot. When the inheritance of the paternal *oikos* was called *patroia*, this

[141] Adoptions of females are attested in Is. 7.9 (uterine half-sister of Apollodoros), Is. 11.8 (niece of Hagnias), Is. 11.41, 45 (daughter of Theophrastos' sister). No law prescribed the children of an *epikleros* to be adopted by their maternal grandfather: Rubinstein (1993) 113.

[142] Rubinstein (1993) 45–6: *inter vivos*, by will (after the adopter's death), or posthumously (on the initiative of others).

[143] Rubinstein (1993) 2, 43, 52–3; note the same vocabulary of adoption (ποιέομαι) in the family as with the creation of new citizens by decree in the *polis* (e.g. [Dem.] 46.15); also below, Chapter 6.1.

[144] Is. 6.25, Lane Fox (1985), Todd (1993) 219, Berman (2007) 128–33. Primogeniture is not attested as an effective principle of inheritance in archaic and classical Athens, nor in Greece generally, except in the case of the Spartan monarchies, and in Athens for *sitesis* (the privilege of receiving meals in the *prytaneion*) granted, for example, to the (eldest son of the?) descendants of the tyrannicides Harmodios and Aristogeiton (*IG* I[3] 131; Is. 5.47) and to the eldest son of the orator Lycurgus, Lycophron ([Plut.] *X Or.* 843c, 851f). On these exceptions, Blok and Van 't Wout (in press).

term was strongly imbued with the values of ancestral tradition. But when it came to actual assignment, the inheritance was called *kleros*, and so was each share of it, which was also called *meros*: *kleros*, indicating the lot by which the shares were distributed among the heirs, came to denote the shares thus distributed.[145] We shall return to the allocation by lot among equal heirs when we look at the modes of participation in the *polis* in Chapter 5.

3.5 Citizenship: the Value of Descent

Descent played a key role not only at the level of families and their strategies of inheritance, but also in a much wider sense in the structure of the *polis*. We saw that the Athenian *polis* as a *social* organisation seems to have developed out of the phratries and *phylai* that gradually made their practices compatible and consistent. They were descent groups, in the sense that membership was passed down by descent, but since the families belonging to these groups were not related among themselves, scholars usually label these groups *fictive* descent groups.[146] Terminology and imagery of descent employed to form the network and identity of social groups that are not biological relatives, and therefore in fact create fictive kin, are well known in anthropological literature and hardly need explanation.[147] What is important here are the *kinds* of ideological connection the Athenian descent groups envisaged as embodied in their commonality. Many of these groups carried names ending in *-idai* or *-adai* (e.g. the phratries Demotionidai and Medontidai; the *gene* Eteoboutadai and Eumolpidai) suggesting common ancestry, others had names indicating them as a collective (e.g. the phratry Dyaleis, the *phyle* Geleontes, the *genos* Bouzygai) that in some way claimed a relationship to an original founder. In all cases, this relationship took the form of a genealogical narrative, usually only a minimal account with hardly more than the name of the founder and some indication of how offspring had come about. Before I turn to some examples, a few words about their context are in place.

The genealogical accounts of the Athenian descent groups exemplify a genre of genealogical myth that plays a conspicuous role in ancient Greece

145 LSJ *s.v.* κλῆρος.

146 E.g. Patterson (1998) 48–50, 87.

147 In many pre-modern societies, descent terminology and concepts are employed to shape social networks in which biological (kin) connections are very thin or even non-existent. How descent operates as a classificatory notion in specific societies is strongly debated, see e.g., Parkin and Stone (2004), Dumont (2006).

generally. An abundance of archaic and classical texts and images testify to stories by which prominent families and entire *poleis* proclaimed their descent from an extraordinary ancestor. Emerging at some point in the deep past and the first one to do something or to be somewhere, this *archegetes* infused the place or the action with his or her presence, making it his/her own to be transmitted to his/her descendants. *Poleis* and *ethne* created their identities by aligning their heroic forebears to particular landscapes, often with foundational royalty.[148] A comparable strategy produced the 'aristocracy' of archaic and early classical Greece.[149] Successfully competing for economic and military power, such families employed various means to cast themselves as an elite of honour with fitting prerogatives. One was to claim descent from a god or hero or another exceptional ancestor. Drawing up genealogical lines, few of which were more than three generations long but proudly projected venerable descent in the suffix *-idai* or *-adai*, the claims of powerful families to fictive descent *increased* in the course of the archaic age, as Alain Duplouy convincingly shows.[150] The analogy between these invented traditions in elite families and the results of Bourriot and Roussel on *polis* subgroups is striking: descent as organising factor did not precede but developed *pari passu* with the formation of the *polis*.

Such genealogical myths may be considered a branch of the wider genre of cultural memory, in so far as they subsume memories of imagined and real events into a shared, effective narrative, the purpose of which ultimately lies in the present.[151] I would argue that one of the most important aims of Greek genealogical myths is to cast the *archegetes* as the first to have particular assets and their descendants – the present narrators – as their heirs. The effects of this model are twofold: firstly, the heirs lay a legitimate claim to the *assets* left by the ancestor, and secondly, the heirs

[148] On the construction of ethnic identities in Greece, usually on mythological foundations, Hall (1997), Hall (2002), Cifani and Stoddart (2012); Athens: Parker (1987b) (for autochthony, see below); Boeotia: Kühr (2006), Larson (2007); Arcadia: Nielsen (2002); Phokis: McInerney (1999) esp. 120–53; colonies: Dougherty (1993), Blok (1996), Malkin (2003).

[149] See on 'fictive descent' in genealogies Patterson (1998) 48–50, 87; family memories merging with genealogical myths provided an important framework of historical remembrance, see Thomas (1989) 155–72 on the Philaidai, and 144–82 on the Alcmaeonidai; West (1985) 11–30 and Irwin (2005) on the Hesiodic *Catalogue of Women* as a repository of such descent claims.

[150] Duplouy (2006) 37–78, Duplouy (2010). See also Thomas (1989) 95–131, and Assmann (1999) on 'communicative memory' through a few (often three) generations.

[151] For genealogy as a form of cultural memory, especially as a means to cover a fractured past, Löwisch (2015). 'Cultural memory' is a wider notion than 'collective memory', as it entails a self-reflexive perception of the past drawing on such memories and shaping them in turn, Assmann (1999).

share the assets *equally*. We need to be aware that all fictive descent structures ultimately converged in the present, in real descent of existing families and inheritance rights as laid down in law. The assets that the *archegetes* had made his or her own were first of all the (original) bond with the gods and would further include material property, especially land, and immaterial qualities, such as type of being (divine, semi-divine or human), character, skills, fame, knowledge and other privileges. These assets formed the traditional inheritance (*ta patroia*). The heirs, the present claimants, enhanced the legitimacy of their claim to *ta patroia* by asserting that they handled it *kata ta patria*, i.e. in exactly the same way as the ancestors (supposedly) had done.

Furthermore, I think it is helpful to distinguish within these genealogical accounts two modes of fictive descent, namely mythical and metaphorical descent. By mythical descent I mean descent from an ancestor who belonged to primordial or epic times and was of a mythical nature; the genealogical line to the narrator's present was usually very vague, but nonetheless believed to exist in some way. Mythical descent by itself carried high prestige. The mythical ancestor by definition belonged to the deep past when gods regularly walked the earth and consorted with humans. Usually, s/he was herself immortal or semi-divine, but even if s/he was mortal, the mythical ancestor belonged to the domain of the mythical past or, even better, had been one of those who had created the original bonds between humans and gods. The value attached to the mythical and cultic origins of the *polis* was reflected in the high social value accorded to an ancient lineage (*eugeneia*). Families who successfully claimed to be the heirs of the 'first creators of the *polis*' constituted an aristocracy of birth in terms of citizenship within the *polis*.[152]

'Metaphorical descent' is in many respects similar to 'mythical descent', but in metaphorical descent the predecessor–founder, from whom the group of 'heirs' claimed material or immaterial assets as their inheritance, was *not* considered a 'real', 'physical' ancestor. A good example are the Homeridai, the singers of epic stories who collectively perpetuated Homer's poetic legacy; they named themselves after him, with the suffix *-idai* indicating descent, but they did not all claim to be his 'real' descendants. What mattered was their claim to Homer's 'inheritance'.[153] The successful use of metaphorical descent to create and sustain status leads us to conclude that descent-and-inheritance was a

[152] For 'aristocracy of birth', notably of the *gene*, Lambert (2015).

[153] For the Homeridai and their particular claims, cf. West (1999).

social model of such compelling authority that it was effective also in metaphorical shape. The Greek word for a descent group, *genos* and its cognates, includes a wide range of meanings, all of which indicate belonging to a group and claims to inheritance as the significant element defining the group's identity, but in which physical descent is an essentially ambiguous factor.[154]

An example of such metaphorical descent is the relation between the Athenians of the classical era and their mythical king, Erechtheus. In Athenian genealogical myths he played a prominent role, but neither his 'earthborn' beginnings nor his relations with human society are clear or consistent.[155] The Catalogue in *Iliad* 2.546–8 mentions

> the men who held Athens, the strong-founded citadel, the *demos* of great-hearted Erechtheus, whom once Athena tended after the grain-giving fields had born him, and established him to be in Athens in her own rich temple.[156]

The passage testifies to the strong bond between Erechtheus, here as an earth-born creature, Athena and the people of Athens. Herodotus, too, knew Erechtheus to be *gegenes* (born from the earth), perhaps echoing the *Iliad*, which also mentions his cult on the Acropolis and an annual sacrifice of bulls and rams.[157] The *Odyssey* (7.81) portrays Athena going to Athens and entering the house of Erechtheus, a scene evoking Erechtheus in his role of king–hero, who became popular in Athenian drama and visual arts of the fifth century.[158] Erechtheus is represented perhaps for the first time ca. 510–500 in black-figure scenes, as the founder of the chariot races in the Panathenaea.[159] The foundation of the festival itself was later attributed to Erichthonios, who at some point emerged as Erechtheus'

[154] See clearly and concisely Patterson (1998) 48–50, 87, who labels 'fictive kin groups' what I call here 'metaphorical descent'.

[155] Kron (1976) 32–9, Miller (1983), Parker (1987b), Rosivach (1987), Kearns (1989) 110–33, 160; for this section, see also Blok (2009a).

[156] Transl. R. Lattimore (Chicago 1951), slightly modified; a sixth-century interpolation of the lines into the Homeric text is possible, but Kron (1976) 32–7, Kearns (1989) 110–15 consider this less plausible due to the antiquity of his cult on the Acropolis. Although this argument cannot be decisive, the lines reflect the sharing of Athena and Erechtheus of the same temple, which was still the case in the classical period.

[157] Hdt. 8.55; Hom. *Il.* 2.550–1; in the classical age, according to the Sacrificial Calendar of Athens (*SEG* 52.48, face A, col. 3 l. 5), Erechtheus received a three-year-old lamb in the month Boedromion; see also Kron (1976) 40–55.

[158] For the prominence of Erechtheus in fifth-century Athens, Connelly (2014) esp. 131–48, who argues that the Parthenon frieze commemorated the legendary battle between Erechtheus and Eumolpos, king of Eleusis.

[159] Kron (1976) 74–7; Kron (1988) nos 49–50.

earth-born *alter ego*.[160] This evidence exemplifies how strongly 'historical' myths were connected to the cultic traditions of Athens. In the fifth century, the Athenians were called (or called themselves) occasionally Erechtheidai, a name suggesting descent by the suffix *-idai*, but no descent from Erechtheus as an ancestor seems to be intended. Pindar in *Isth.* 2 (ca. 470) calls the Athenians by this name without implying any 'physical' descent,[161] and such an implication is also absent in *Pyth.* 7.10 (486), where the '*astoi* of Erechtheus' refers to the Alcmaeonidai. 'Erechtheidai' thus seems to indicate the Athenians as 'the people of Erechtheus', the metaphorical heirs of the hero taking care of his cult or following his rule as a king, reminiscent of the Homeric passages, rather than as 'real' descendants.[162] The ambiguity of descent vocabulary prevails in most cases where the Athenians are addressed or described as Erechtheidai, whether in a serious way or mockingly.[163]

In Athens, metaphorical descent is also prominently represented in the *polis* subgroups. The eponyms of some phratries are known, but on the whole they 'tend to lack distinction'.[164] For instance, the Thymaitadai had one shrine in the city and one in the deme Thymaitadai, with which it was apparently connected via their common eponym Thymaites, a descendant of Theseus who played a central role in the Athenian Apatouria myth. But Thymaites is an obscure figure with at best an unpleasant reputation, and Lambert concludes that he must have played hardly any role in the phratry. Their name Thymaitadai was probably formed when the Cleisthenic deme of the same name was created.[165] In this and other phratries, so far as we can see, the line of 'descent' from the eponym was vague or simply

160 Founding of Panathenaea: Kearns (1989) 161; earliest attested stories about Erichthonios as son of Hephaistos and Earth in Pindar and an epic *Danaïs*: Hellanicus *FGrH* 323a F 27 = Harp. *s.v.* αὐτόχθονες. Hephaistos' pursuit of Athena is attested ca. 460 on a red-figure amphora: Shapiro (1998) 138, fig. 7, n. 53.

161 Pind. *Isth.* 2.19: καὶ τόθι κλειναῖς <τ'> Ἐρεχθειδᾶν χαρίτεσσιν ἀραρώς ταῖς λιπαραῖς ἐν Ἀθάναις, 'and when he [Xenokrates of Akragas] gained the glorious favor of the Erechtheidai in shining Athens, he had no cause to blame the chariot-preserving hand' (transl. W.H. Race, Loeb ed.); the reference seems to be to Erechtheus as *archegetes* of the Panathenaic chariot races.

162 Soph. *Ajax*, like the *Iliad* (2.557–8), portrays Ajax and his men as Salaminians (cf. Kearns (1989) 141), but also (201–2): ναὸς ἀρωγοὶ τῆς Αἴαντος, γενεᾶς χθονίων ἀπ' Ἐρεχθειδᾶν, 'Crew of the ship of Ajax, descendants of the underworld Erechtheidai'. If thus not originally Athenians, the (metaphorical) descent of Ajax's men from Erechtheus seals the sixth-century incorporation of Salamis in Attica by projecting this connection, institutionally confirmed in the Athenian *phyle* Aiantis and encapsulated in the genealogical myths of the Philaidai (Thomas (1989) 161–5) into the past.

163 Serious: Eur. *Med.* 824; *Hipp.* 151; *Suppl.* 387, 681, 702; *Herc.* 1166; *Ion* 24, 1056, 1060; *Phoen.* 852; mockingly: Ar. *Eq.* 1015, 1030.

164 Lambert (1998) 328, cf. 220–2.

165 Hedrick (1988b), Hedrick (1991) 244–5, Lambert (1998) 328.

irrelevant. Phratries owned sanctuaries and other property, but ownership was clearly not their *raison d'être*, even if managing their property was a serious task.[166] These cases thus exemplify the overall question of this chapter: why precisely was descent a good principle of organisation and what was the use of being 'heirs' if there was neither a conspicuous founder nor a conspicuous inheritance?

Before attempting to answer this, we first turn to the *gene*. Here, we find stronger constructions of descent than in the phratries, presumably because in their case the inheritance was beyond doubt a conspicuous one, namely their exclusive claim (until the mid-fifth century) to holding *polis* priesthoods, which was squarely based on their constructed descent. The Eteoboutadai advocated their descent from Boutes, the first priest of Poseidon Erechtheus, whose shrine they kept on no less a place than the Acropolis. A passage from [Plut.] *X Orat.* 843a–c on Lycurgus, who belonged to the Eteoboutadai, is illuminating:

> The *genos* was descended ultimately from Boutes and Erechtheus the son of Ge and Hephaistos and immediately from Lykomedes [I, great-grandfather of the orator] and Lycurgus [III, grandfather of the orator], whom the *demos* honoured by public burial [cf. 852a]; and this succession in the *genos* of those who have been priests of Poseidon is on a complete tablet (*pinax*), set up in the Erechtheion, painted by Ismenias of Chalkis [ca. 307–304].[167]

Boutes and Erechtheus together are marshalled here as the *archetegai* of the *genos*, with Boutes as the ancestor of the lineage and founder of the priesthood, with an (unidentifiable) link to the real ancestors in the present, Lykomedes and the elder Lycurgus.[168] As the name Eteo-boutadai professed to show, Boutes was the *archegetes* of this *genos* and since he left his priestly office to his heirs, this may be called a clear case of mythical descent. But the priesthoods the *genos* held could not all be traced back to him. The priestesshood of Athena Polias, the other priesthood held by the *genos*, was arguably even more prominent than the priesthood of Poseidon Erechtheus, but it did not derive from Boutes.[169] The entitlement to the

[166] Many phratries are known through inscribed *horos* stones and similar documents marking their property, for which Lambert (1998) appendix 1.

[167] [Plut.] 843a: κατῆγον δὲ τὸ γένος ἀπὸ Βούτου καὶ Ἐρεχθέως τοῦ Γῆς καὶ Ἡφαίστου, τὰ δ'ἐγγυτάτω ἀπὸ Λυκομήδους καὶ Λυκούργου, οὓς ὁ δῆμος ταφαῖς ἐτίμησε δημοσίᾳ· καὶ ἔστιν αὕτη ἡ καταγωγὴ τοῦ γένους τῶν ἱερασαμένων τοῦ Ποσειδῶνος ἐν πίνακι τελείῳ, ὃς ἀνάκειται ἐν Ἐρεχθείῳ, γεγραμμένος ὑπ' Ἰσμηνίου θοῦ Χαλκιδέως·

[168] For the full genealogy of the Eteoboutadai, Blok and Lambert (2009).

[169] In Eur. *Erechtheus*, the goddess Athena makes Praxithea, daughter of the river god Kephisos and married to Erechtheus, the first priestess of her cult as Polias on the Acropolis.

priestesshood devolved on a different branch of the *genos*, whose relationship to the Poseidon branch is obscure.

In some cases, mythical descent was a transformation of what had begun as metaphorical descent. Among the cultic duties of the *genos* Bouzygai was performing the sacred ploughing each year below the Acropolis. Their name 'oxen-yokers' clearly referred to their function, and initially their (metaphorical) origins were no more than that. All families belonging to the *genos* were eligible for their cultic role and they bequeathed this privilege to their descendants. At some point, however, their name was taken to indicate descent from a certain Bouzyges, who had been the first to yoke the oxen to use for agriculture; no worship of him is known but his plough was dedicated on the Acropolis.[170] Bouzyges supplied the group with a more identifiable *archegetes* in the mythical past of the *polis*, and a concomitant legacy, than just the act of ploughing could do. The same process may have been at play in the case of the Kerykes, a prominent *genos* supplying the herald (*keryx*) of the pan-Hellenic sacred truce and the *dadouchos* at the Eleusinian Mysteries. Their name, too, was clearly derived from their function, but later was taken to mean descent from Keryx, a son of Hermes and a daughter of Cecrops, or a son of Eumolpos, the acclaimed forebear of the *genos* Eumolpidai.[171] The cases of the Bouzygai and Kerykes illustrate that metaphorical descent as conception of entitlement to inheritance was not essentially different from mythical descent but that the latter perhaps provided a more visible anchorage in the past, resembled real descent more closely and was more easily linked to it in the present.

Returning to the question,why descent was such a highly privileged mode of social organisation in ancient Athens, we find that genealogical stories with mythical and metaphorical modes of descent all created a common status among the narrators as 'heirs'. In elite families, the heirs usually acquired with their illustrious pedigree a substantial material property. In the *polis* subgroups, this was only rarely the case, although we should not disparage the property owned by the phratries nor the remunerations coming with some *polis* priesthoods. Yet, at the level of *polis* subgroups and next of the *polis* itself, I would argue, a different aim prevailed – material goods were not the primary 'inheritance'

170 Schol. Aeschin. 2.78; Kearns (1989) 152.

171 Keryx: son of Pandrosos, daughter of Cecrops, and Hermes (Androtion *FGrH* 324 F 1); or Aglauros and Hermes (according to the Kerykes) or descendant of Eumolpos (Andron *FGrH* 10 F 13; Paus. 1.38.3).

here.[172] What was transmitted were in the first place immaterial goods, namely, firstly, *membership* of the group with a shared identity and common interests, notably in the bond with the gods; secondly, entitlement to share in the inheritance on the normal conditions of a real inheritance, that is *equality* among the heirs.

All of this suggests that claiming a right to (share) an inheritance was the socially most authoritative model available in ancient Greece for expressing a legitimate claim to material and immaterial goods, and that this fact caused descent, of which inheritance was the desired result, to become a central mode of organisation in society at large.[173] In other words, descent in the 'real' sense was anchored in *polis* laws on kinship, inheritance and citizenship, but also operated beyond this sphere, transposed into a metaphorical notion about just transmission of claims to material and immaterial goods and their distribution in the *polis* as a whole. This multiple function of the notion 'descent' may be clarified by the concept of 'institution' as defined by the economic historian Douglass North within the wider debate on institutions as keys to understanding societies. For North, institutions are not in the first place the established organisations themselves, but rather the rules, customs and relationships underlying such organisations. In other words, the key to understanding societal organisations is to be found in the rules that produced them.[174] These rules are conceived in a wide sense, both as customs as and as informal rules with concomitant networks and as formal rules with concomitant organisations, which over time cluster into more stringent organisations each with their specific rules, influencing and directing people's conduct and interaction. I would submit that in ancient Greece, and in classical Athens in particular, 'descent' was such an institution in the Northian sense: a 'rule' validating transmission over generations of claims to immaterial goods, notably to belonging to the *polis* and its subgroups and sharing

[172] It is even clear that some *gene* were not wealthy at all. Phrastor, the first husband of Phano, was a poor man although a *gennetes* of the Brytidai, and apparently won over with a dowry of 30 mnae ([Dem.] 59.50). Lambert (2015) shows convincingly that wealth was not the primary criterion of the prominence of the *gene*, but their (proclaimed) descent.

[173] Concerning inheritance rights it is arguably appropriate to speak of rights (conceived in general terms, clearly applicable to individual cases, enforceable in court) at Athens, rather than merely of claims, even if these rights were complicated and allowed for different interpretations.

[174] 'Institutions are the rules of the game in a society, or, more formally, are the humanly devised constraints that shape human interaction. In consequence, they structure incentives in human exchange, whether political, social or economic' (North (1990) 3); see also below, Chapter 5. North's conception of institutions belongs to a debate about the possible (co-)existence of markets with other kinds of economic structures in pre-modern societies, but this purpose does not invalidate the usefulness of his definition in other contexts.

its bond with the gods, and to one's fair share of the benefits, including material goods (property). This primary rule was elaborated and consolidated into the legal and social structures of the *polis*, in ever more intricate 'sub'-rules, applied with increasing stringency, detail and control in every particular *polis* organisation in the course of the sixth to the fourth centuries.

Looking at citizenship from the perspective of a political centre, the proliferation of descent claims throughout the *polis* and the tightening of legitimacy rules seem hard to understand – why not replace all of these by an independent institution providing an abstract criterion of citizenship in terms of participation? But looking at the *polis* centre from the perspective of the family, as actual laws, notably the citizenship laws of 403/2, in fact did, descent and inheritance provided their own logic, consolidating the *polis* by the laws that sustained kinship and with it citizenship. Understanding descent and its inherent inheritance rights as institutions in the sense just mentioned will be instrumental in our analysis of the dynamics of participation in the *polis* and, emphatically, to understanding the roles of female citizens. Since daughters and sons inherited immaterial goods equally, male and female Athenians inherited their share of the *polis* equally in terms of its immaterial goods – membership of the group, membership of relevant subgroups and crucially one's share in the bond with the gods.

4

Citizens, Male and Female: Vocabulary

> Athens … in Attica, of which Charax relates that when Theseus brought the eleven *poleis* in Attica together into one community, he founded the festival of the *synoikia* at Athens. The *polites* is *Athenaios* and the feminine *Athenaia*.
>
> Stephanus Byzantinus, *Ethnica*[1]

Who were the citizens? In the preceding pages we saw that in the law of classical Athens 'citizens' were those who claimed membership of the *polis* on the criterion of birth and with that status could lay claim to participation in the *polis* in some way. As I have argued, this citizen status entailed that citizens saw themselves as the heirs of the original bond between the *polis* and the gods, represented, in fifth- and fourth-century terminology, in the *hiera* and *hosia*. In this discussion, I used the English word 'citizen', but, as we saw in Chapter 1, in modern usage 'citizen' refers in the first place to an individual with legal rights to equality in law and political participation. Rather than using this modern vocabulary, the meaning of which is not necessarily identical with the ancient conception, we want to know what citizens of Athens called themselves and why. Which words were used to refer to 'citizens' and to what qualities or capacities did these words refer?[2]

Previous inquiries into the Greek vocabulary of 'citizenship' have concentrated on the issue of political qualifications, following either modern usage or Aristotle's view that a 'citizen' is someone entitled to *arche* and *krisis*.[3] This approach is not very helpful, for two reasons. As we saw briefly

1 Steph. Byz. *Ethnica s.v.* Ἀθῆναι …ἐν Ἀττικῇ, περὶ ἧς φησι Χάραξ ὅτι ὁ Θησεὺς τὰς ἕνδεκα πόλεις τὰς ἐν τῇ Ἀττικῇ συνοικίσας εἰς Ἀθήνας συνοίκια ἑορτὴν κατεστήσατο. ὁ πολίτης Ἀθηναῖος καὶ θηλυκὸν Ἀθηναία.

2 This chapter revises and expands arguments published as Blok (2005).

3 Reinau (1981) finds that *polites* does not imply political office, but nonetheless he assumes that women were not citizens. Patterson (1986) points to the symmetrical terminology for male and female citizens, but retaining the political meaning of *polites* she cannot clarify *politis*. Sealey (1983) sees the pair *epitimos* and *atimos*, which he translates as 'with and without citizen rights', as operational in the change from 'inhabitant' to 'citizen' in the political sense. However, *atimos* means that

before and will be further explored here, Greek citizenship vocabulary was symmetrical for men and women, although the first could and the latter could not hold political office; a satisfactory analysis should be able to account for this gender symmetry in normal language use without resorting to solutions of exceptionality.[4] Furthermore, many male citizens did not have access to political office either, as was the case in Athens before Cleisthenes and during the oligarchic episodes, but nonetheless were free members of the *polis*, for whom the same vocabulary obtained as for those citizens who did have such access. It was partly due to the variety of usages of *polites* in this respect that Aristotle felt the need to coin his own definition in *Politics*, book 3. Which words were used for the people who belonged to the *polis*? And did Greek language use indicate specific capacities or qualities of citizens, and if so, which ones?

In answering these questions we must take into account the variety of texts offering words for 'citizen' *vel sim.* in their discursive context. Put very generally, for the archaic age the extant texts are mainly poetry, a few early laws and votive and funerary inscriptions, most of which are difficult to date. For Athens the archaic evidence is very scarce, so in tracing developments from the archaic to the classical age we cannot limit ourselves to linguistic evidence from Athens, but must begin with Greece more widely. In the classical age, the amount of documents rises substantially, especially in Athens, most significantly from the mid-fifth century onwards. Beside drama and other poetry, a wide array of prose genres take the floor and an increasing range of inscriptions, notably laws and decrees,

someone is not accepted by the *polis* as would befit his or her normal social value (see Chapter 5); it did not involve losing a clear-cut set of citizenship 'rights' (Van 't Wout (2010b); Van 't Wout (2011a)). Moreover, *atimos* occurs frequently, but *epitimos* rarely in classical Athenian evidence; these terms therefore cannot have been common terminology to distinguish between citizens with and without political rights. Cohen (2000) 49–78 interprets *politai* and *astoi* as respectively citizens with political rights in the Aristotelian sense and 'locals'. In the main text, I clarify why I arrive at a different reading, although I agree with him that the boundaries of the classical Athenian *polis* as a group were more open and flexible than is commonly supposed. Osborne (2011) 85–105 uses a substantial part of the material I also discussed in Blok (2005); we agree on *politai* and *polites* (first appearing mainly as a plural; generic meaning 'citizen of the *polis*' without political overtones), but I have difficulties agreeing with his view of *astos* (see below).

4 E.g. Todd (1993) classifies the *polis* population by distinctions in status and gender into male citizens, slaves (m/f) and metics (m/f) and 'Athenian citizen women as a fourth and separate group' (171; see above Chapter 1, n. 83), stating (178): 'an *astos* then is a (male) citizen, though whether it is right to translate *aste* as "citizen woman" depends largely on what precise rights we regard as defining characteristics of citizenship'. Todd reflects here on the symmetrical pair *astos* and *aste*, which he proposes to deal with *linguistically* in a way different from the precisely symmetrical pair *doulos* and *doule* by adducing *the difference in social status* of citizens and slaves, arriving at a circular argument on the allegedly distinct meanings of *astos* and *aste*.

gain enormously in number and prominence. Handled with due care, we may infer from these texts some clear developments in citizenship vocabulary over time.

4.1 *Polites* and Cognates

To go by Aristotle's *Politics*, it would seem the Greek word for citizen *par excellence* was *polites*. Whether that was true for the fourth century remains to be seen, but tracing its appearance back in time we are in for a surprise: before the 430s, the lexeme *polites* does not occur in the singular in our records: with very few exceptions, we find only the plural *politai*.[5]

4.1.1 Politai *in the Archaic and Classical Evidence*

In extant epic poetry, as in other archaic texts, *politai* (Ionic *polietai*) appear as a collective, attested only in the plural.[6] It does not occur frequently, because, as we shall see below, *astoi* was preferred, beside *laos*, referring to the collective of the people under the authority of a ruler, and *demos*, designating those inhabiting the same territory.[7] Meaning roughly 'those who belong to the *polis*', *politai* is a generic term, first of all in gender: *politai* may refer to men only or to men and women, as all masculine plurals referring to a group of people may do, and depending on context the audience would envisage either the one or the other or no gender specifically. No distinctions in social status among the *politai* are indicated either; they may belong to every step on the social scale. Slaves were included in the *polis* in so far as they belonged to the *oikos*

[5] Occasional cases of the singular seemingly belonging to a date before the mid-fifth century turn out to be later on closer inspection, e.g. *FGrH* 1 T 11a (Hecataeus of Miletus being the *polites* of Anaximander) is in fact a passage in Strabo (1.1.1). For the exceptions, see below.

[6] In epic: Hom. *Il.* 15.557–8: πρίν γ' ἠὲ κατακτάμεν ἠὲ κατ' ἄκρης / Ἴλιον αἰπεινὴν ἑλέειν κτάσθαι τε πολίτας, 'till either we kill them or the citadel of steep Ilion will be taken and its *politai* killed'; the word recalls all those who live inside the walls of the city, but usually the men were killed and the women taken captive and sold into slavery. *Il.* 22.429–30: Ὣς ἔφατο κλαίων, ἐπὶ δὲ στενάχοντο πολῖται·/ Τρῳῇσιν δ' Ἑκάβη ἁδινοῦ ἐξῆρχε γόοιο, 'Thus he spoke, weeping; and the *politai* mourned with him. And with the Trojan women Hecabe began her lament.' *Il.* 2.803–6: πολλοὶ γὰρ κατὰ ἄστυ μέγα Πριάμου ἐπίκουροι, / ἄλλη δ' ἄλλων γλῶσσα πολυσπερέων ἀνθρώπων· / τοῖσιν ἕκαστος ἀνὴρ σημαινέτω οἷσί περ ἄρχει, /τῶν δ' ἐξηγείσθω κοσμησάμενος πολιήτας, 'There are many allies all over the great city of Priam, and they all have different tongues among mankind scattered everywhere; let each man instruct those of whom he is the leader and lead them forward, when he has marshalled his *polietai*.' *Od.* 7.131; *Od.* 17.206; *Hom. H. Dem.* 99: ὅθεν ὑδρεύοντο πολῖται, 'from where the *politai* fetch water'; the gender reference is neutral, referring to the inhabitants of the city, but the narrative context evokes the presence of women.

[7] Werlings (2010) 47–87.

of a master, but the strong connection between *politai* and freedom even before Solon plausibly restricts *politai* to the free inhabitants. Considering again Aristotle's choice of *polites* for the '*political* citizen', we note that the archaic evidence does not portray the *politai* as enjoying any political prerogatives, but instead as doing things in the *polis* collectively: convening in the Agora, cheering victors of the games, fetching water, gossiping about each other, mourning the dead, in other words sharing in the life of a Greek community.[8] This use of *politai* remains unchanged.

The *polis* to which *politai* linguistically and historically belonged was originally the *acropolis*, the stronghold on a hilltop or other high location offering a refuge in times of danger and holding the central cults and sanctuaries of the community. For the formation of the *polis* Athens in the wider sense, archaeological and epigraphical evidence show, albeit in broad outlines, a process of gradual dispersion of communities across Attica from the early Iron Age onwards, with networks developing between the various social groups and local communities growing in number and size.[9] Signs of this commonality evolving across Attica were cults of gods and heroes whose worship clearly encompassed the whole *polis* territory, with a central focus on the cult of Athena and other gods on the Acropolis – written with capital A, to distinguish this site at Athens from the local *acropoleis*.[10] Richly attested around 750, Athena's cult declined strongly after 680 when more wealth was dedicated at sanctuaries in the Attic countryside, but it revived by the end of the seventh century and continued to be embellished hereafter.[11] A further sign of commonality is demonstrated in shared laws on common interests, whose construction seems to coincide with the gradual incorporation of the inhabitants into a collective descent group,

[8] Cheering victors: Pind. *Nem.* 2.24; gossip: Pind. *Pyth.* 11.28; and see the epic passages in n. 6. Osborne (2011) 93 ('it is the plural form that is most commonly found'; 'this continues to be the pattern of usage into the fifth century'), 103 ('I have noted that *polites* is a term found first in the plural, to refer to a group doing things together') and overall on the absence of the 'political' meaning in the generic use of *polites*, apparently agrees with my findings as published in Blok (2005).

[9] Osborne (2009) 37–46.

[10] Van den Eijnde (2010) shows that beside cults also other forms of ritual, notably ritual feasting connected to (imagined) dead ancestors, lay at the foundation of communities in Attica. See de Polignac (1995a), de Polignac (1995b) for the connection between *polis* formation and cults at the central and border sanctuaries in Greece generally, and de Polignac (2007) for Attica. Thuc. 2.15–16 points to the cults of Athena and the other gods on the Acropolis and those of Zeus Olympios, Apollo Pythios, Ge and Dionysus in Limnai near the city centre as signs of the unification of Attica by Theseus, in line with Attic tradition. Across Attica, archaeological evidence shows the formation of *polis* territory by marking the boundaries clockwise in the sanctuaries of Eleusis, Mt Parnes, Marathon, Brauron, Sounion and Mounichia.

[11] Van den Eijnde (2010) 91–100.

supported by the phratries and their cults; Draco's law on homicide is an important testimony to this.[12]

With group formation and commonality, both at a local and at *polis* level, anchored in shared *hiera* as discussed in Chapter 2, the connection between (*acro*)*polis*, *polis* as descent group, *politai* as the members of this group and cults was an essential one, at least from the early sixth century. Although after the early Iron Age the Acropolis retained its fortified character, it served no longer as a place of normal human habitation or of regular political meetings, but became and remained the cultic heart of the *polis*.[13] In the classical era, its status as the place *par excellence* where *polis* decrees were set up reflects the convergence of the political with the cultic domain.[14] In the extant epigraphical record of the fifth century, *polis* meaning 'acropolis' is by far the most prominent and numerous usage, with approximately one hundred decrees preserving a clause requiring them to be set up *em polei*, on the Acropolis.[15]

In Attica's countryside we see a similar shift from *acropolis* as high, focal location to *polis* as cultic centre, reflected in the usage of the word *polis*. In the deme Erchia, for instance, the sacrificial calendar inscribed in ca. 375 listed a sacrifice to Zeus Polieus to be made *em polei en astei*, on the Acropolis of the *asty* (city) Athens, as distinguished from the (*acro*)*polis* of Erchia itself.[16] The use of *polis* underscores the congruence between Erchia as a deme of the *polis* Athens and the *polis* in its entirety. An interesting case of community formation centered on cults are the four demes in the north-eastern part of Attica, which since the early Iron Age identified themselves as the Tetrapolis, in fact a sub-*polis* of the *polis* Athens consisting again of four sub-*poleis*, Marathon, Oinoe, Probalinthos and

[12] Beside Draco's law, reinscribed in 409/8 (*IG* I³ 104), for pre-Solonian laws only indirect evidence exists; such regulations must have been in place for the archonships (*Ath.Pol.* 3, the specifics of which are unreliable), for various forms of taxation and military organisation (van Wees (2013) 17–30, 39–82, 107–23) and for groups such as phratries (see Chapter 3).

[13] The only Athenians who lived 'symbolically' on the Acropolis were the *arrhephoroi*, two (or four) young girls in the service of Athena Polias (Paus. 1.27.3; Parker, *PS*, 220–1). The supposition that the tyrant Pisistratus lived in a palace on the Acropolis is both unfounded (no evidence) and implausible, Hurwit (1999) 118–20; Blok (2000).

[14] Liddel (2003): in the classical era, an average of 90 per cent of all decrees were set up on the Acropolis; cf. Meyer (2013).

[15] In *IG* I³ 4 A.12 and B.1 reference is made to constructions *em polei*, on B 13, 14 to priestesses and cult personnel *em polei*; extant decrees set up *em polei*: *IG* I³ 11, 17, 23, etc. Beside this fixed formula, a few other phrases refer to 'the *polis*' or 'this *polis*' meaning the Acropolis: *IG* I³ 45, 52.4, 127, 718, 1179.11, using either the nominative or the accusative. In the fourth century, writing *acropolis* in full became common.

[16] *SEG* 21.541, col. C, 17–18.

Trikorinthos. Their unity consisted of a shared cult practice, laid down in a sacrificial calendar inscribed around 375. Nearly all common sacrifices took place within the territory of one of the four member demes, the unity arising from the fact that all four participated in every cult, in effect thus creating a Tetrapolis territory in terms of cult.[17]

Down to the classical period, *polis* and *politai* retained their flexible and generic meaning, which depended on context for specification. Aristotle used *polis* to mean either a community comprising all those necessary for its economic existence or a core group among these inhabitants identified by descent, or a social unity sharing a *politeia*. In decrees of the classical period, *politai* occurs only rarely, extant only in two honorific decrees.[18] After the fourth century, *politai* occurs a dozen times in honorific decrees as the 'people of the *polis*' – a generic group for whose benefit the honorand had exerted himself.[19] In their capacity as politically autonomous group, the Athenians usually referred to themselves not as *politai*, but as the *demos*.

4.1.2 Polites

Before the mid-fifth century, words for 'citizen' in the singular are very rare.[20] Long before the noun *polites* we find Polites as a personal name, in the *Iliad* of one of Priam's many sons and of one of Odysseus' companions in the *Odyssey*.[21] In Athens, the personal name is attested in the second half of the fifth century, but it remains rare and seems to disappear

[17] For the text of the calendar and the name Tetrapolis: Lambert (2000) A, col. 240; for the territorial and social function of the cults, Lambert AIO paper 1.

[18] *Ag*. 16.20 [1] fr. E l. 20 (restored); *IG* II³ 1, 396, l. 11.

[19] E.g. *IG* II² 374.8, 493.21, 500.15 etc.

[20] *Astos* occurs twice before the mid-fifth century, Pind. *Pyth*. 2.82 (of unknown date) and 4.78 (of 462), in both of which *astos* is in a contrasting pair with *xeinos* (see below). Another singular attested before the mid-fifth century is *etes* in Aesch. *Supp*. 247 (ca. 465) and fragments; the plural is found in a treaty between the Lakedaemonians and Argives, quoted by Thuc. 5.79.4. Occurring as *wetas* in a treaty of Elis (*IvO* 9.8; *Nomima* 1, 52; ca. 500) in a contrasting series with *telesta* (magistrate?) and *damos* (the whole community), *etes* was highlighted by Ehrenberg (1937) 151–2 as an early term for a private member of the *polis* and picked up again for that reason by Davies (1997), see also Davies (2004). *Etai* are predominantly attested in Homeric epic in the plural only, once paired with *hetairoi* (*Il*. 7.295), four times with 'relatives' (*Il*. 9.464; 16.456 = 16.674; 6.239; *Od*. 15.273), once with 'neighbours' (*Od*. 4.16) and twice on its own (*Il*. 6.262; *Od*. 4.3). The Elis decree and the passages in Aeschylus and Thucydides suggest that in the fifth century *etas* was used on the Peloponnese, but not in Attica; in Aeschylus, its use was presumably meant to evoke an ancient, 'Argive' atmosphere. The general sense seems to be 'those who belong to the group, or community', as confirmed by Hesych. *s.v.* ἐταί: ἑταῖροι. συνήθεις. πολῖται. δημόται. φίλοι. ἐπίκουροι; 'comrades; those living together; *politai*, demesmen, friends, supporters'.

[21] Hom. *Il*. 2. 791–5; 13.533–6; etc. *Od*. 10.224.

by the end of the classical age.[22] The feminine *politis* is first attested in the plural *politides* around the 420s before appearing, regularly though not frequently, in fourth-century literary documents. As a personal name, Politis is attested much later than the noun and just once.[23] In Athens generally, personal names with *asty-* are far more numerous than those with *poli-*.[24]

From the 430s onward, the increasing use of *polites* and *politis* in literary texts seems to mark a shift in citizenship vocabulary: while the collective *politai* could refer to men and women, for individuals a gendered singular was necessary. At first, *polites* appears not very frequently. Herodotus uses the term in only two passages (see below), preferring *aner ton aston* or comparable expressions for 'a man belonging to the *polis*'.[25] *Aner ton aston* emphasises the individual citizen's membership of a community, thus retaining a focus on the collective. Thucydides, likewise, uses *polites* rarely; he employs both *aner ton aston* and *mesos polites* (a middling *polites*) to describe the tyrannicide Aristogeiton. In three other passages he uses the singular *polites* in a speech commending action of a 'good citizen'.[26] In Sophocles' extant works, *polites* does not occur, but Euripides uses the word seven times.[27] In Aristophanes' comedies, *polites* occurs nine times, with a peak in *Knights* (424).[28] Once the singular *polites* had become current in the later fifth century, it was used regularly in the fourth century.

Herodotus exemplifies this new usage in an interesting way. He either designates peoples and persons with their ethnics or indicates the people belonging to a city as *astoi* or *poli(e)tai*.[29] The singular *polietes* occurs in two episodes. In the first, Xerxes explains to his council his preference for the Persian Achaimenes' advice to that of the Greek, Demaratos, but

22 Polites: on casualty lists *IG* I³ 1162.23 (447); 1186.66 (ca. 441); 1032.469 (ca. 410?). Cf. Lambert (2001) 62, n. 10: 'the last Athenian citizen called "citizen" is attested in the very last decade of the classical democracy' (*IG* II² 1566.24 (330–320)).

23 Politis: *SEG* 32.318, third century; the Athenian background of this woman is not certain.

24 Personal names with prefix *asty-* compared to those with *poli-*: in Attica 7:1, in the eastern Aegean 3:1 (*LGPN* vol. I and II).

25 Hdt. 9.33–4.

26 Thuc. 6.54.2–3; cf. Thuc. a 'good citizen': 3.42.5 in a speech about Mytilene (427); 6.9.2; 6.14.1: in speeches about the Sicily campaign (415).

27 Eur. *Iph.Taur.* (413) 495; *Phoen.* (409) 887; *Bacch.* (408) 271; Frs 50.13, 360.13, 512.1, 886.1; cf. [Eur.] *Rhes.* 946.

28 Ar. *Ach.* (425) 595; *Eq.* (424) 335, 773, 944, 1304; *Pax* (421) 910–11; *Ran.* (405) 1041, 1427; *Eccl.* (392) 574.

29 In a proportion of 2.5 (*astoi*) to 1 (*politai*): masculine *astoi* 42 occurrences, feminine *astai* once, *polietai* 17 times.

defends the latter against charges of ill will. Demaratos, so Xerxes, has given the best advice he can, and one sees

> in reality that a *polietes* is jealous of a *polietes* who prospers, and keeps silent in his hatred, and when an *astos* asks for advice, not a single *polietes* will tell him what he thinks is best, unless he is truly excellent, but such people are rare. But a *xeinos* is towards a *xeinos* who prospers the best-disposed of all men, and will give, when so asked, the best advice he has. Therefore I ask you not to speak any more evil of Demaratos, since he is a *xeinos* to me.[30]

In this simile, evoking a scene in the Agora of a Greek *polis*, *polietes* means 'someone who is a fellow member of that city community'. The generic meaning is intensified through the contrast with *xeinos*, i.e. anyone who does not belong to one's own community, a stranger who can also be a guest or, even more closely, a guest friend; the latter is clearly what Xerxes has in mind. *Astos*, a more common contrast term with *xeinos* than *polietes*, figures here as an equivalent of the latter. In this passage, then, *astos* and *polietes* seem to be basically the same: a fellow inhabitant of one's city, as distinct from an outsider.

In the second passage (Hdt. 9.33–4), the Spartans asked Tisamenos, an Elean diviner whom they hoped to enlist as their leader in war, what he wanted as a reward (*misthos*). Tisamenos asked that 'they make him their *polietes*, giving him a share (*metadidomi*) in everything'. At first, the Spartans refused, but when the need rose, they asked Tisamenos again, who now raised his price: not only he, but also his brother Hagias 'was to be a Spartiate on the same conditions'.[31] Herodotus compares Tisamenos' successful negotiations with the clever moves of Melampos, a seer who became king in Argos. When the Argives turned to him for help to restore the mental health of the women, Melampos first asked for half of the *basileia*, and when the Argives after hesitation returned to him, he asked them also to give a third share (*metadidomi*) of the *basileia* to his brother. So in return for the great benefits they had bestowed on their host *polis*, both seers managed to receive similar rewards, namely citizenship and kingship respectively, and here Herodotus adds 'in so far as one

30 Hdt. 7.237: καὶ τῷ ἐόντι, ὅτι πολιήτης μὲν πολιήτῃ εὖ πρήσσοντι φθονέει καὶ ἔστι δυσμενὴς τῇ σιγῇ οὐδ᾽ ἂν συμβουλευομένου τοῦ ἀστοῦ πολιήτης ἀνὴρ τὰ ἄριστά οἱ δοκέοντα εἶναι ὑποθέοιτο, εἰ μὴ πρόσω ἀρετῆς ἀνήκοι· σπάνιοι δέ εἰσι οἱ τοιοῦτοι· ξεῖνος δὲ ξείνῳ εὖ πρήσσοντί ἐστι εὐμενέστατον πάντων, συμβουλευομένου τε ἂν συμβουλεύσειε τὰ ἄριστα. Οὕτω ὦν κακολογίης [πέρι] τῆς ἐς Δημάρητον, ἐόντος ἐμοὶ ξείνου, ἔχεσθαί τινα τοῦ λοιποῦ κελεύω.

31 Hdt. 9.33: ἤν μιν πολιήτην σφέτερον ποιήσωνται τῶν πάντων μεταδιδόντες … Ὁ δὲ γνοὺς τετραμμένους σφέας οὐδ᾽ οὕτω ἔτι ἔφη ἀρκέεσθαι τούτοισι μούνοισι, ἀλλὰ δεῖν ἔτι <καὶ> τὸν ἀδελφεὸν ἑωυτοῦ Ἡγίην γίνεσθαι Σπαρτιήτην.

can compare asking for *politeia* and for *basileia*'.[32] In the Tisamenos story, *polietes* means 'fellow citizen' in a strong sense, articulated by 'a share in everything'. With the prefix *meta* referring to part of a larger whole, joined to *didomi* (to give) and *ton panton* (everything), this phrase resembles the citizenship decree for the Plataians inserted in [Dem.] 59.104, 'that they share in everything', and may point to a contemporary common expression of citizenship. Moreover, Tisamenos and his brother are not only to be *polietai*, but more poignantly Spartiatai, the ethnic referring to the *polis* as a descent group. That as fellow Spartiates they are to share in 'everything', including political participation, is enhanced by the Melampos episode that compares *politeia* (here meaning being a *polites* and rule by *politai*, together making up the notion 'citizenship') with a different form of political power, *basileia* (kingship). This occurrence of *politeia* here offers the first instance in our record of the contemporaneous debates about political systems that famously recur in the constitutional debates of book 3.[33]

In sum, *polites* can be used in two ways: either to articulate the difference between one's own community (all *politai*) and outsiders; or to designate, among all those living in the *polis*, a member of the descent group, who participates in 'everything', including political office. The semantics of the singular *polites* appear here to be analogous to those of *polis* and *politai*: starting with a basic meaning referring to the entirety of a city community, the term could also be used to refer more narrowly to the an inner group of members of the *polis* by descent and their participation in everything in which such members were entitled to share (*meteinai*).

In the first extant appearances of the Attic *polites*, beginning with Aristophanes' *Acharnians* of 425, the singular *polites* is accompanied by a qualification.[34] The citizen is singled out from the collective *politai* for being a good citizen (*agathos polites*) or a citizen who makes himself useful to society (*chrestos* or *chresimos polites*) or, conversely, a citizen who spoils the life of his fellows (*polites oxines*).[35] In either case, the citizen is conceptualised as an individual with obligations defined by and directed

[32] Hdt. 9.34: Ταῦτα δὲ λέγων οὗτος ἐμιμέετο Μελάμποδα, ὡς εἰκάσαι βασιληίην τε καὶ πολιτηίην αἰτεομένους.

[33] Hdt. 3.189, situating Greek political theories among Persian discussants; he discusses constitutions here, but does not employ the word *politeia*. For Herodotus' involvement in current debates, Thomas (2000) and in those about politics especially Raaflaub (2002).

[34] Ar. *Ach.* 595: *chrestos polites*, in contrast to citizens only keen on their own profit.

[35] *Polites agathos*: Thuc. 3.42.5, 6.9.2, 6.14.1; Ar. *Eq.* 944; Ar. *Pax* 911: 'a *chrestos* fellow for all *politai*'; cf. Phryn. fr. 59; Eup. fr. 118. A *polites oxines*: Ar. *Eq.* 1304. Cf. Lys. 24.3: τούτου βελτίων εἰμὶ πολίτης, 'I am a better citizen than he'; Eup. fr. 101.1, Ar. *Ran.* 1041: ἀνὴρ πολίτης.

towards the community. All these instances occur in speeches with persuasive intent, suggestive of a debate to which the contemporary author of the *Constitution of the Athenians* also seems to refer when he contends that

> the *demos* in Athens recognise who among the *politai* are useful to society and who are worthless; but although they recognise this, they like those who are nice to them and back their interests, even if they are good for nothing, whereas they rather hate those who are useful to society. For they (the *demos*) do not think that the qualities of such citizens are by nature inclined to do them well, but to damage them.[36]

Apparently, this discourse signifies expectations that citizens participate actively in the *polis*, fitting the change in citizenship discourse visible in the 430s with the appearance of *politeia* discussed above.

In the fourth century *polites* continued to be used in the generic way, but also in the more emphatic meaning highlighting the citizens' claims upon and obligations to the *polis*.[37] Some decrees use *polites* in this sense for men who had received citizenship in the past. Interestingly, at the time of these decrees the formula actually bestowing this grant was 'that X is an Athenian',[38] but in looking back at this event the decree referred to it as 'X had been made a *polites*' – here clearly in the stronger sense of being a member of the descent group with everything that belongs to that status.[39] Apart from these few decrees, the singular *polites* occurs very rarely in the epigraphic record of classical Athens, in line with the scarce occurrence of the plural *politai* in decrees.[40] In sum, in Athenian decrees the lexeme *polites* is rare; it means in the first place a member of the *polis* by descent or by decree who shares in everything, political office being surely implied, but not highlighted.

36 [Xen.] *Ath.Pol.* 2.19: φημὶ οὖν ἔγωγε τὸν δῆμον τὸν Ἀθήνησι γιγνώσκειν οἵτινες χρηστοί εἰσι τῶν πολιτῶν καὶ οἵτινες πονηροί· γιγνώσκοντες δὲ τοὺς μὲν σφίσιν αὐτοῖς ἐπιτηδείους καὶ συμφόρους φιλοῦσι, κἂν πονηροὶ ὦσι, τοὺς δὲ χρηστοὺς μισοῦσι μᾶλλον· οὐ γὰρ νομίζουσι τὴν ἀρετὴν αὐτοῖς πρὸς τῷ σφετέρῳ ἀγαθῷ πεφυκέναι, ἀλλ' ἐπὶ τῷ κακῷ.

37 See for instance the generic use of *politai* in Lys. 34.3: it would be unjust to exclude *politai* (who are all Athenians) from *meteinai* in the *politeia* due to a criterion of owning landed property; and the emphatic use in Dem. 57 (above): Euxitheos shows by his birth from *astos* parents that he is a *polites* (46); he distinguishes between those who try to *metechein* by stealth although being *xenoi*, and those who can show that they are *politai*.

38 See below, and Chapter 6.1.

39 *IG* II^2 17, for Storys of Thasos (394/3): ll. 1–12 look back to the proxeny of his ancestors and that Storys had been made a *polites* (l. 8), while ll. 13–15 contain the formula of the original decree. *IG* II^2 492, for a certain Apollonides (303/2): l. 17: because the *demos* had already made him a *polites*, so now they are praising him (etc.). A decree (*IG* II^2 46) on *xenodikai* between Athens and Troizen poses a different case, where in l. 37 a *polit*... is probably the subject of a legal provision as member of his *polis*, but the text is too fragmentary to make sense of.

40 *IG* I^3 94; all other occurrences postdate the classical era.

4.1.3 Politis

The first feminine form of the lexeme *polites* to appear in our record is plural *politides*, in two tragedies, Sophocles' *Electra* and Euripides' *Electra*, predating other attestations in literary texts by a few decades.[41] *Politis*/*-ides* does not occur in inscriptions in classical Athens at all, although it does later and also outside Attica.[42] This picture is hardly surprising, considering the historical fact that occasions when female citizens only were a topic of decrees must have been extremely rare, and even more so considering the linguistic fact that the (masculine) *polites* and *politai*, who *were* such a topic frequently, were scarce in epigraphic evidence, too.

Since scholars have on the whole overlooked or underestimated the remarkable innovation in citizenship vocabulary that use of *politides* entails, at the same juncture as citizenship discourse in Athens was taking a different direction, the case deserves a more detailed analysis.[43] The emergence of this new feminine form is notable because the generic *politai* could refer to female citizens in cases where the gender could be made clear from the context, and a tragic chorus of citizen women is certainly such a case. The two *Electras* are not unique in presenting such a chorus.[44] By choosing the feminine plural *politides*, in passages they could have

[41] Until 300: Isoc. 14.51; Pl. *Leg.* 814c; Arist. *Pol.* 1275b32, 1278a28; Is. 8.43; [Dem.] 59.107; Dem. 57.31, 57.43; Dem. 23.213; Men. *Sic.* 197.

[42] In Athens attested only in ethnics with *-polis*, e.g. Ἀμφιπολῖτις (e.g. *IG* II² 8077, 8079 etc.) and in the common sense 'female citizen' only late (and restored:) *IG* II² 1136.4, honorific decree for the priestess Chrysis. Outside Athens ca. twenty-five cases, e.g. Miletus (McCabe 41.8; 205/4): all male and female citizens who volunteer to give 3,600 drachmae to the city (τοὺς μὲν βουλομένους τῶμ πολιτῶν ἢ πολιτίδων δοῦνα[ι] τῆι πόλει δραχμὰς τρισχιλίας ἑξακοσίας) and many other cases, see Günther (2014); *SEG* 50.589 (Macedonia, Hellenism): list of names, including five χῆραι πολίτιδες; *SEG* 3:666 (= *IG* XI, 4 1054; Delos, ca. 230–220) l. 5 πολίτιδας; Lindos II 252 (ca. 115) l. 36, 159 where a distinction seems to be made between a πολῖτις and other women; likewise in Cos (Paton-Hicks 10; 202/1) where the names will be announced τῶν τε πολιτᾶν καὶ πολιτίδων καὶ νόθων καὶ πα[ρ]οίκων καὶ ξένων; *Insc. di Cos*, ED 178 (ca. 196/5), ll. 16–17, where the πολίτιδες, νόθαι and πάροικοι all are to present themselves before Aphrodite on their marriage; and in *Insc. di Cos*, ED 180 (first century): on the sale of the priesthood of Heracles, sacrifice is to be made on behalf of the πολίται, πολίτιδες and κατοικευντες in the city. A different way of indicating male and female citizens, Sicily, Entella A3.11–12, an *isopoliteia* decree of late fourth century: ἁλόν των ἁμῖν τῶμ πολιτᾶν πολλῶν καὶ ἀνδρῶν καὶ γυναικῶν ἐβοαθόησαν αὐτοῖς καθὰ ἐδύναντο.

[43] The appearance of *politides* has, however, been discussed by Finglass (2005), who shows the importance of the *polis* behind the 'private' setting of Soph. *Electra* (204–5). Roisman (2004) argues that women, individually or collectively as a chorus, can speak in an unconstrained fashion (with *parrhesia*) in Greek drama 'to affirm the supremacy of the fulfilment of family and religious duties over obedience to arbitrary authority, and (*parrhesia*) is identified with the values of Athenian democracy'.

[44] Choruses of female citizens appear among others in Aesch. *Choeph.*; Soph. *Trach.*; Eur. *Bacch.*, *Troades*, *Suppl.*; Ar. *Lys.*, *Thesm.*, *Eccl.*

phrased differently, it seems both playwrights wanted to highlight the role of these women as *polis* members at this point in their plays.

Scholars generally assume that the two *Electra*s are a dialogue of sorts between the two playwrights, and the occurrence of *politides* in both plays confirms this idea: the use of an uncommon word at comparable positions in the plots can hardly be a coincidence. The dates of the plays, however, are uncertain.[45] On metrical grounds, Euripides' *Electra* has been dated between 422 and 416.[46] Sophocles' *Electra* is generally taken to be a late work and is now dated by several scholars to ca. 410.[47] On these views, Euripides' would be prior to Sophocles' rendering, but without unequivocal criteria to establish the order of appearance of the *Electra*s the question of who responded to whom in this dialogue must remain unanswered. More relevant here is to ask what particular light the tragic context sheds on the use and meaning of *politides*.

Electra is one of the most conspicuous female characters of Athenian drama. As the daughter of Clytaemnestra, who has killed Agamemnon, her husband, in revenge for sacrificing their daughter Iphigeneia for the sake of war, and the sister of Orestes, who is to avenge their father's death, her life revolves around vengeance. On Apollo's command, Orestes is to kill his mother and her lover Aegisthus in retaliation for his father's murder, while Electra, who has long awaited this moment, is to help him. Sophocles and Euripides both present the problems inherent in Orestes' duty to avenge his father as conflicts between ritual purity and justice, and between obligations to gods and to humans – in other words, of *hosie*, *dike* and *eusebeia*. These conflicts are prominently voiced in the dialogues between Clytaemnestra, who killed the husband who mortally wronged her, and Electra, who identifies passionately with the duty to avenge her father.[48] Since both choruses, too, consist of women, the major points of view in both plays are represented by women. The results created in each play, however, are dramatically different.

Against Apollo's feeble argument in Aeschylus' *Eumenides* (657–67) that Orestes is to be absolved from matricide because a mother is not a blood

[45] Older scholarship saw a connection between a reference to ships near Sicily in Euripides' *Electra* (1347) and the Sicilian expedition of 415–413, e.g. Arnott (1993 [1981]) 413, but this view is now abandoned; for concise discussion of the date, Kovacs (1998) 142–3.

[46] I.e. after *Hecuba* (ca. 427) and *Supplices* (424) and before *Hercules Furens*; see also Cropp (1988) l–li: before 415, near 420s; Diggle (1981) 58: between 422 and 416; Kovacs (1998): ca. 420.

[47] Konstan (2008), elaborating views of other scholars, argues that the play fits the political situation after the fall of the oligarchic regime of 411.

[48] Soph. *El.* 516–659; Eur. *El.* 998–1146.

relative of her children, Euripides portrays the matricide in its unspeakable horror, for which Apollo, fulfilling what is preordained, is effectively responsible (1264–9; 1301–8).[49] Euripides presents a Clytaemnestra who is tyrannical as a queen and has done *anhosia* (1170) as a wife, but who is nevertheless still the mother of her children. Electra herself is a social and ritual anomaly.[50] Living with a farmer who has refrained from consummating his marriage with a princess, she is a *parthenos* who in the course of the play first presents herself as a *nymphe* (a married woman but not yet a mother) and next as a *gyne* (the mother of a child). When the chorus, which seems to consist of *nymphai* and *parthenoi* from the Argolid countryside (174, 179, 761), invites Electra to join their festival of Hera, she refuses to share in the *hiera* because of her ambivalent marital status.[51] When she tells Orestes to be the man (*aner*) and kill Aegisthus, she summons the chorus to be a witness and addresses them as *gynaikes* (694), thus emphasising the opposition male–female, expressed by the pair *aner–gyne*. But her own life as an adult, married woman (*gyne*) is in fact non-existent. She belongs only to her family of birth: her brother as well as her mother.

Euripides makes it unequivocally clear that in the killing of Clytaemnestra any claim to *dike* as the revenge for murder is outweighed by the ritual pollution and human abhorrence of killing one's mother.[52] After their atrocious act, Electra and Orestes realise that they cannot belong to the community any longer.[53] For Electra, this means exclusion from a normal married life that would have given her a fitting role in the *polis* as a cultic community and its family structure (1198–1205). Then the Dioskouroi appear to resolve their predicament and make them follow the path of *themis*. Although sharing equally in the guilt of their mother's death, atonement observes gender distinction: Orestes is to be tried for his deed in the *hosios* city of Athens, Electra is to marry Pylades and go with him to Phocis. At this turning point, Electra says:

> Farewell, my *polis*; and fare you truly well, *politides*.[54]

49 Kovacs (1998) 144–9: Euripides responded to Aeschylus' representation in a deliberately different manner.
50 Zeitlin (1970).
51 In the final scene, the Dioskouroi again call Electra both a *kore* (maiden) and a *damar* (wife) (1284).
52 Eur. *El.* 1244: Castor: 'the treatment she received was just (*dikaia*), but the act that you (Orestes) did was not'. At the end of the play, the Dioskouroi attribute the guilt of Clytaemnestra's death squarely to Apollo. In *Orestes*, Euripides portrays the man who killed his mother as mad with agony, haunted by the Erinyes.
53 Eur. *El.* 1190–1200.
54 Eur. *El.* 1337: ὦ χαῖρε, πόλις·/ χαίρετε δ' ὑμεῖς πολλά, πολίτιδες.

With these words Electra acknowledges that she must leave because she is forever barred from the women of the *polis*, their participation in its *hiera* (Hera's festival) and their *hosios* life.[55] As a result of her terrible deed, her children will belong not to the *polis* of Argos, but that of Phocis.

How the outcome of Sophocles' play is to be evaluated is a topic of intensive debate, because Sophocles does not overtly condemn the matricide.[56] In the *agon* in the middle of the play, the positions of Clytaemnestra and Electra in terms of *dike* seem balanced in more and less justifiable claims.[57] When on Orestes' feigned death Electra plans to do the killing herself, she is warned by her sister Chrysothemis that shedding human blood is not a woman's job (992–1014). The tension increases when Orestes reveals his identity and assumes the manly duty to do the killing, retaliating for the pollution of Agamemnon's unrevenged death. At this turning point, Electra addresses the chorus of women:

> Dearest women friends (*gynaikes*), my *politides*, see Orestes here, who by a device seemed to be dead, but by a device is now alive and safe.[58]

With these words, Electra's intended action changes from desperate, private revenge into proper justice to be carried out by a man (1398–9). Involving the chorus in her joy, she addresses them first as *gynaikes* (adult women) and next as *politides*. The chorus of Argive women had just praised her because, in her duty to her father, Electra 'wins the highest prize in the observance of the greatest laws, by her piety towards Zeus' (1095–7), while for her part Electra assured Orestes that these women were loyal and to be trusted (1203–4). Calling them *politides*, Electra now seems to appeal to them as those who, like herself, carry a major responsibility for the *polis*'s cultic obligations and acts of *hosie* towards the family and the dead. Piety is foremost on their minds: at the climax of the play Electra implores Apollo and all the gods to help Orestes punish impiety (1376–83).

55 Throughout the play, acts are evaluated as being *hosios* or not: for instance Clytaemnestra's *anhosia* (1170) and 1198–1205: El.: 'Ah me, ah me! Where shall I go, to what dance / or to what marriage? What husband will receive me / into a bridal bed?' Chorus: 'Again, again your mind / veers round with the changing breeze. / Your mind now thinks *hosia*, though before it did not so, and you have done a terrible thing, / my friend, to your reluctant brother' (transl. D. Kovacs, Loeb ed.).

56 Konstan (2008) summarises the extensive scholarship on the 'amoral view', holding that Sophocles primarily wanted to present a good piece of drama with vocal space for all sides, the 'justificatory' view, that Sophocles ultimately agreed with the necessity to carry out Apollo's command, and the 'ironic' view, holding that Sophocles cast fundamental doubts on the justification of matricide, but did so implicitly.

57 Soph. *El.* 516–659.

58 Soph. *El.* 1227–9: ὦ φίλταται γυναῖκες, ὦ πολίτιδες, / ὁρᾶτ' Ὀρέστην τόνδε, μηχαναῖσι μὲν / θανόντα, νῦν δὲ μηχαναῖς σεσωμένον.

We find that Sophocles and Euripides used *politides* to opposite effects: in Sophocles' *Electra*, the heroine identifies herself with the *politides* because they share her commitment to piety and justice, whereas Euripides highlights the distance Electra has created between herself and the *polis* as a community sharing *hiera kai hosia* and tied by its family relationships. But both playwrights used *politides* at the crucial moment in a plot highlighting piety and familial duties towards the dead (*hiera kai hosia*) as focal values of the *polis*.[59] Even if they did not share in political office, in other respects these female citizens are pictured here as 'sharing in everything'.

From other texts we can infer that *politis*/*-ides* were members of the *polis* by descent. Isocrates in his *Plataicus* refers to the intermarriage between Plataians and Athenians following on the citizenship grant, in the words of the Plataian speaker:

> For we are not at all strangers to you, but all of us are close to you in our good-will and the majority even in actual kinship; for we are born from your *politides* owing to the right of intermarriage given to us.[60]

Aristotle, too, uses the word in this manner in *Politics*, in a passage dealing with descent as a criterion of citizenship:

> But in many constitutions the law admits some people (to citizenship) even from foreigners (*xenoi*); for in some democracies someone who is born from a *politis* is a *polites*, and the same rule is valid in many places also for *nothoi*. Nevertheless, since they make such people into citizens because of a lack of *gnesios* citizens (from two citizen parents) – because they make such use of the laws due to under-population – as soon as they are doing well in the mass of their population, then they gradually rid themselves first of those born of a male or female slave, and next of those from women (*gynaikes*) [only]; in the end, they only make those citizens (who are) born from both citizen (*astos*) parents.[61]

Polites and *politis* in this passage are citizens of legitimate birth, and legitimacy can be conferred by one or two parents, either the mother or the

[59] For these values and concomitant obligations to the *polis*, Liddel (2007) 133–6, 211–27.

[60] Isoc. 14.51: Καὶ γὰρ οὐδ᾽ ἀλλότριοι τυγχάνομεν ὑμῖν ὄντες, ἀλλὰ ταῖς μὲν εὐνοίαις ἅπαντες οἰκεῖοι, τῇ δὲ συγγενείᾳ τὸ πλῆθος ἡμῶν· διὰ γὰρ τὰς ἐπιγαμίας τὰς δοθείσας ἐκ πολιτίδων ὑμετέρων γεγόναμεν. See also below, Chapter 6.1.

[61] Arist. *Pol.* 1278a26–33: ἐν πολλαῖς δὲ πολιτείαις προσεφέλκει τινὰς καὶ τῶν ξένων ὁ νόμος· ὁ γὰρ ἐκ πολίτιδος ἔν τισι δημοκρατίαις πολίτης ἐστίν, τὸν αὐτὸν δὲ τρόπον ἔχει καὶ τὰ περὶ τοὺς νόθους παρὰ πολλοῖς. οὐ μὴν ἀλλ᾽ ἐπεὶ δι᾽ ἔνδειαν τῶν γνησίων πολιτῶν ποιοῦνται πολίτας τοὺς τοιούτους (διὰ γὰρ ὀλιγανθρωπίαν οὕτω χρῶνται τοῖς νόμοις), εὐποροῦντες δὴ ὄχλου κατὰ μικρὸν παραιροῦνται τοὺς ἐκ δούλου πρῶτον ἢ δούλης, εἶτα τοὺς ἀπὸ γυναικῶν, τέλος δὲ μόνον τοὺς ἐξ ἀμφοῖν ἀστῶν πολίτας ποιοῦσιν. Compare *Ath.Pol.* 26.3: μὴ μετέχειν τῆς πόλεως ὃς ἂν μὴ ἐξ ἀμφοῖν ἀστοῖν ᾖ γεγονώς.

father, depending on the *politeia*, but preferably both. To consider a citizen mother only sufficient for citizen status is typical of some democracies, so Aristotle, and is due to a lack of citizens, but when the population is large enough only those from two *astos* parents are accepted as a *polites*, a phrasing reminiscent of Pericles' Citizenship Law. Contrary to Aristotle's argument here, this law was enacted when the number of citizens at Athens was dramatically low, but it stimulated the development of the democracy as Aristotle knew it in the later fourth century.[62] What might *astos* parents be?

4.2 *Astoi, Astos, Aste, Astai*

Despite the prevailing interest of modern scholarship in the word *polites*, until the fifth century the most common word for citizens was not *politai* but *astoi*.[63] Solon, for instance, employed *astoi* and *Athenaioi* twice in the poems ascribed to him, but never *poli(e)tai*; his laws, so far as they can be reconstructed, contain neither.[64] The lexeme *astos* is derived from *asty* (city, with its walls) in a similar way that *polites* is from *polis* (acropolis of the city). Unlike *polis*, which was also used of cultic centres of demes and for the whole territory of the city state, *asty* in Attica always refers to Athens as city centre. *Astoi* in the masculine plural designates all those who live in the same city or belong to the community.[65] Like *politai*, *astoi* occurs almost exclusively in the plural until the second half of the fifth century: again, the inhabitants are pictured as a collective.

The slow change from *astoi* to *politai* as the common term for 'those belonging to the *polis*' can be traced by an overview of how *astos*, *polites* and the ethnic *Athenaios*, mainly in the plural, appear in a sample from sixth- to fourth-century authors. For the sake of clarity, occurrence of these terms in per cent of total words per author is included in Table 4.1. However, what matters is the ratio (roughly) within each author, which indicates, independently from the increasing number of texts over time and the size of the works in each case, the gradual shift from *astos* to *polites*.

[62] For this paradox, cf. Hannick (1976), Davies (1977).

[63] In archaic texts, which are nearly all poetic, the more frequent occurrence of *astoi* than of *politai* could be accounted for by metre, but considering the variety of metres employed in different types of poetry, this is not the most persuasive explanation. Cf. Lévy (1985).

[64] Solon (W.) *astos*: F 4.6, F 10.1; *Athenaios*: F 4.30, F 2.2.

[65] E.g. Hom. *Od.* 13.193–4: 'so that his wife and *astoi* and friends would not know him, until he had made the suitors pay for their shameless oppression'.

Table 4.1. *Ratio of occurrences and percentages of* astos-polites-Athenaios *in authors from the sixth to the fourth centuries.*[66]

	Astos/astoi	*Polites/politai*	*Athenaios/ Athenaioi*	*Ratio astos: polites: Athenaios*
Solon	0.11	–	0.11	1:1*
Theognis	0.00.083	0.02	–	4:1**
Pindar	0.087	0.017	0.021	4:1:1
Aeschylus	0.025	0.039	0.001	2:3:> 1
Sophocles	0.022	0.011	0.001	2:1:> 1
Euripides	0.019	0.026	0.010	2:2:1
Aristophanes	0.007	0.027	0.038	1:4:5
Thucydides	0.005	0.019	1.009	1:4:20
Lysias	0.003	0.159	0.149	1:50:50
Isocrates (pol. speeches)	–	0.144	0.012	12:1***

* Solon: no use of *polites*, so omitted from ratio.
** Theognis: no use of *Athenaios*, so omitted from ratio.
*** Isocrates: no use of *astos*, so omitted from ratio.

In the second half of the fifth century, *Athenaioi* became ever more current, as the playwrights chose dramatic themes increasingly focusing on Athens, prompting more frequent use of the ethnic. The *Athenaioi* were also the chief protagonists of Thucydides' historiography on the Peloponnesian War, so obviously they figure abundantly in his work, whereas *politai* and *astoi* may be the citizens of any *polis*. Thucydides uses *polites* four times in the singular, but *astoi* (still) only in the plural. Beginning with Lysias, the speeches of the fourth century use *politai* and *Athenaioi* normally to designate the citizens (see below), the comparison with Isocrates' political treatises showing that orators were inclined to address their audience as *Athenaioi* when actually speaking in the assembly or the courts. We shall return to *Athenaios* below.

In the earliest records, *politai* and *astoi* seem to differ little or not at all in meaning, as we saw above. Beside this, we find *astoi* used as a contrast term. Sporadically, *astoi* classifies humans as opposed to gods.[67] The usual construction, however, is the contrast between *astoi* and *xenoi*, designating the *polis*'s own members as insiders versus outsiders. As a part of

[66] All texts were sampled from the *TLG*, including fragments; final check in March 2015.
[67] Solon, F 4.1–6 (W.).

this contrasting pair with *xenos*, *astos* appears occasionally in the singular before the mid-fifth century.[68] In these cases, the singulars do not refer to individual citizens or strangers, but to a single representative of a group, reinforcing its conception as a collective.[69] In decrees, the pair '*astos* and *xenos*' seems to be a fixed expression indicating that the decision applies to *everybody*, of whatever (free) status.[70] The combination remained in use, although scarce, even when *astoi* was no longer common as a generic word for 'citizen'.[71]

The relationship between *astos* and *polites* clearly interested later lexicographers. The Hellenistic grammarian Aristophanes saw no difference between the two words, giving *polites* as equivalent to *astos*.[72] Hesychius in the early Byzantine era described *polites* as 'he who belongs to and lives in the same *polis* as somebody else', emphasising the membership of a community, not political status, and thus again getting very close to *astos*.[73] The difference would become clear in *astos* as contrast term, exemplified in a Byzantine scholion to Hesiod's *Works and Days* line 225, where the poet uses the pair *xeinos* and *endemos*: 'the *astos* is the opposite of the *xenos*, and the one who is away from his country (*apodemos*) is the opposite of the one who is in his own country (*endemos*)'.[74] Although *polites* and *astos* were (almost) synonyms, clearly *astos* was the regular word when used in the stronger meaning 'belonging to us' in a contrast. Likewise, *asty* could be used as a synonym for *polis*, but it could also indicate with emphasis the urban centre in contrast to the countryside or a smaller town nearby, for instance Athens as *asty* in contrast to Eleusis.[75] Both terms in all meanings could include men or men and women, depending on the context.

[68] Pind. *Pyth.* 4.78; 3.70–1. *Pyth.* 2.82–3 creates a contrast between a deceitful *astos* and good men, underlined by a contrast in the following lines between friends and enemies. *IG* I³ 1194bis, 'Tetichos epigram', ca. 575–550, l. 1: [εἴτε ἀστό]ς τις ἀνὲρ εἴτε χσένος. An early case of the adjective *astos* occurs in laws at Gortyn: ϝαστίαν δίκαν, the *dike* of the *asty* (*Nomima* I, no. 1, l. 2, g–h; *IC* IV, 13; seventh century; *Nomima* I, no. 8, *IC* IV, 64, l. 4; early fifth century): the context suggests *astos* is used here as as a contrasting term to *xenos*. For a similar case of *etas* in the singular as an example of a group, see above, n. 20.

[69] *Astos* as insider versus outsider: Hdt. 1.173, 2.160, 3.8; Soph. *OT* 222; Eur. *Ion* 290, 674; *Med.* 223.

[70] *IG* I³ 138.3 (plural; restored), date in *IG*: before 434; *IG* I³ 1453 (Coinage decree; shortly before 414) B, l. 10: plural, contrast with χσένοι is legible, but the pair could be either ἀστοι or πολίται. *IG* II² 125.3 (357/6) regulates behaviour of any *xenos* or *astos* (singular).

[71] Pl. *Ap.* 30a4; *Prot.* 309c5; *Resp.* 563a1; *Leg.* 869d3; Arist. *Pol.* 1300b32; [Dem.] 46.22.2 etc.

[72] Ar.Byz. *Nom. aet. fragmenta, s.v.* ἀστός (*Lex.Gr.Min.* ed. Miller, 278.23).

[73] Hesych. *s.v.* πολίτης· ὁ συμπολιτευόμενός τινι καὶ συνών.

[74] Schol. Hes. *Op.* 225 ter.

[75] *Asty* = Athens: *IG* I³ 1023: *asty* on a herm of Hippparchos (?) ca. 520; *IG* I³ 503/4 (monument for Marathon battle) l. 4; contrast Athens and Eleusis: *IG* I³ 32 ll. 23–5 (432 or later; Cavanaugh (1996) 19–27; 93); *IG* I³ 79.5–6 (422). Unmarked *asty* = *polis*, Hesych. *s.v.* ἄστυ.

In the second half of the fifth century, the morphological developments undergone by the *asto-* terms appear comparable to those of *polites* terms. Where relevant, *astoi* is distinguished into *astoi* and *astai*, and the singular feminine *aste* appears beside the already attested *astos*. Important evidence of the use of *astos* is the *Ath.Pol.*'s rendering of Pericles' Citizenship Law of 451/0 with the phrase (26.3): 'no one who was not born from both *astos* parents shall participate in the *polis*'.[76] Once this law was in force, it made being an *astos* a quality of individual members of the *polis* on different conditions than had been the case before. As we just saw, the singular *astos* was used occasionally before the mid-fifth century, notably when the speaker made a contrast between insiders and outsiders. In Athenian texts after that date, some passages use *astos* in the same manner but with a strong emphasis on descent from citizens playing an unmistakable role. A subtle irony about being a stranger and belonging to the citizens is at play in Sophocles' *Oedipus Tyrannus* of probably the 430s, when Oedipus enters the stage:

> I shall speak these words as a stranger (*xenos*) to the story and a stranger (*xenos*) to the deed; no, I could not get far on the track, unless I had some link with you. But as things are, since I have become a citizen with the rest (*astos* with the *astoi*), though late, I utter to all Kadmeians this proclamation![77]

As the audience knows well, Oedipus is not at all a *xenos*, but the son of the murdered king. His own ignorance of that fact, combined with his declared insistence that now he belongs to the *astoi* owing to his marriage with the queen, evoke a strong awareness among the listeners that Oedipus belonged to the Kadmeians as an *astos* by descent from the beginning. In Aristophanes' *Birds* of 414, the speaker denounces someone who is allegedly a Scythian pretending to be an Athenian:

> he's a non-citizen (*ouk astos*) trying to force his way in, while we, being of good standing (*time*) in *phyle* and *genos*, solid citizens (*astoi* among *astoi*), with no one trying to shoo us away, have up and left our country with both feet flying.[78]

[76] For the text of the law and the probability that the phrase with *astos* belonged to it, see Blok (2009b).

[77] Soph. *OT* 219–23 (transl. H. Lloyd-Jones, Loeb ed.): ἁγω ξένος μὲν τοῦ λόγου τοῦδ᾽ ἐξερῶ, / ξένος δὲ τοῦ πραχθέντος· οὐ γὰρ ἂν μακρὰν / ἴχνευον αὐτό, μὴ οὐκ ἔχων τι σύμβολον. / νῦν δ᾽, ὕστερος γὰρ ἀστὸς εἰς ἀστοὺς τελῶ, / ὑμῖν προφωνῶ πᾶσι Καδμείοις τάδε.

[78] Ar. *Av.* 32–5 (transl. J. Henderson, Loeb ed.; slightly changed): ὁ μὲν γὰρ ὢν οὐκ ἀστὸς εἰσβιάζεται, / ἡμεῖς δὲ φυλῇ καὶ γένει τιμώμενοι / ἀστοὶ μετ᾽ ἀστῶν, οὐ σοβοῦντος οὐδενὸς / ἀνεπτόμεθ᾽ ἐκ τῆς πατρίδος αμφοῖν τοῖν ποδοῖν.

Being a member of the *phyle* and *genos*, as we saw in Chapter 3, was normally only possible for those who could claim to be Athenian by descent, and by the time of *Birds* to be so on both sides; *astos* here distinguishes between those who are acknowledged as such and those who are not.

In Euripides' *Ion* of ca. 410, being an *astos* among the Athenians is a major theme. When Ion thinks that his father is Xouthos, a Dorian, he expresses his hope that his still unknown mother might be an Athenian:

> If it is right to do so, I pray that she who bore me may be a woman from Athens, so that I may have free speech (*parrhesia*) from my mother's side. For when a *xenos* lands in a pure city, though he may be an *astos* in name, yet he's got a slave's tongue, and has no freedom of speech.[79]

There is an intricate play here on the word *astos*. When Ion contends that he may be considered a fellow citizen by virtue of living in the same city, he uses *astos* as contrast to *xenos*. But he thinks that he may not be a true *astos*; only when he is born from an Athenian woman can he enjoy the freedom of speech that is typical of true citizens. This value of citizen status recurs in Aristophanes' *Thesmophoriazusae* of 411, which portrays the citizen women of Athens giving judgement on Euripides during their major festival, the Thesmophoria. A kinsman of Euripides, disguised as a woman to insinuate himself into the event, tries to defend the latter, exclaiming:

> There *is* freedom of speech here, and all of us who are citizens (*astai*) *are* entitled to speak . . .[80]

In both passages, the *astoi* and *astai* are no longer just the inhabitants of the *asty* but emphatically insiders in contrast to outsiders of the city; because they are *astoi* in legal status (due to their descent from citizen parents) they enjoy the freedom of speech typical of citizens. It is notable that in *Ion* having an Athenian *mother* is decisive for being a true *astos*; that Ion's father is not, does not seem to be an impediment for this status. This presentation seems at odds with the laws of Athens before Pericles' law, when one of the parents had to be an Athenian; usually this was the father, but in the exceptional case that only the mother was an Athenian and the couple remained in Athens, her child from a lawful union with a non-Athenian

[79] Eur. *Ion*, 670–5: εἰ δ' ἐπεύξασθαι χρεών, / ἐκ τῶν Ἀθηνῶν μ' ἡ τεκοῦσ' εἴη γυνή, / ὥς μοι γένηται μητρόθεν παρρησία. / καθαρὰν γὰρ ἢν τις ἐς πόλιν πέσηι ξένος, / κἂν τοῖς λόγοισιν ἀστὸς ἦι, τό γε στόμα / δοῦλον πέπαται κοὐκ ἔχει παρρησίαν. On *parrhesia* as an attitude rather than as a 'right', Carter (2004).

[80] Ar. *Thesm.* 540–1 (transl. J. Henderson, Loeb ed.): εἰ γὰρ οὔσης παρρησίας κἀξὸν λέγειν ὅσαι πάρεσμεν ἀσταί.

had to be adopted by her father into his family and accepted by his phratry and deme if the child was to be an Athenian too.[81] After Pericles' law, Athenian descent required legitimate birth from an *aste* mother as well as from an *astos* father.[82] Compared to this legal situation, Ion's option in this passage is impossible. Yet, even if we should perhaps not expect a tragic plot, the story of which is taking place 'long ago', to be strictly in accordance with the laws, anachronism is not the most satisfactory explanation of this passage. Firstly, the audience knows that Ion's father is not Xouthos, but Apollo, who as *patroos* protected the Athenian phratries, and Creusa, daughter of Erechtheus; Hermes has reminded the audience of these facts at the beginning of the play.[83] In terms of the phratries, Ion's pedigree is therefore beyond reproach. Secondly, some evidence suggests that Pericles' law, by raising the value of citizen descent, increased that of citizen women in particular.[84] If before Pericles' law the existence of the term *metroxenos* suggests that having a foreign mother was not unheard of but equally a cause of social discomfort, after Pericles' law charges made in comedy or the courts of being not of true citizen descent are predominantly directed towards persons for allegedly having non-Athenian *fathers*, although the word *patroxenos* did not come into existence.[85] In other words, being born from an Athenian woman, a social value that before Pericles' law was more or less latent, after the law became not only legal condition for citizen

[81] Very few cases of Athenian women married to non-Athenians are known, one being a daughter of Themistocles, who married a man from Chios, whence the poet Ion of Chios, who lived at Athens at the time (Plut. *Cim.* 5.3, 9.1) called her an *Athenaia xene* ('Athenian foreigner'; *FGrH* 392 F 11); the phrase is an oxymoron in Athens but not in Chios. Themistocles' daughter would be of marriageable age in ca. 470–460; cf. Vérilhac and Vial (1998) on *polis* endogamy as a common pattern in classical Greece, esp. 46 for the value commonly expressed in Athenian drama that women should marry within their *polis* of origin.

[82] Pollux, *Onom.* 3.21: καὶ γνήσιος μὲν ὁ ἐκ γυναικὸς ἀστῆς καὶ γαμετῆς – ὁ δ' αὐτὸς καὶ ἰθαγενής – νόθος δ' ὁ ἐκ ξένης ἢ παλλακίδος· ὑπ' ἐνίων δὲ καλεῖται μητρόξενος. 'Legitimate (offspring) is from a woman who is *aste* and truly wed – and this is also *ithagenes* – but *nothos* ("bastard" offspring) is from a *xene* (woman from elsewhere) or a concubine; and this is called by some *metroxenos*.' Cf. Ar. Byz., *Nom. aet.* (*fragmenta*) 277, 14–17: Ὅμηρος τοὺς γνησίους υἱοὺς καὶ ἠθαγενεῖς (l. ἰθαγενεῖς) ὀνομάζει· τοὺς νόθους Ῥόδιοι, μακροξένους (l. ματροξένους) ὠνόμαζον· σκότιοι δέ, οἱ λάθρα γεγονότες. 'Homer calls the sons *gnesios* (legitimate) and *ithagenes*; the Rhodians call those with a foreign mother (*matroxenos*) *nothoi*, but those born secretly (outside wedlock) *skotioi* (gloomy).' Legitimacy through the mother, with a latent role for the father Apollo, is in fact what happens to Ion in Euripides' play.

[83] Eur. *Ion* 8–27; for Apollo, Hedrick (1988a); Lambert (1998) 208–17, a role he shared with Zeus Phratrios and Athena Phratria.

[84] Osborne (1997) argues that the effect of Pericles' law is visible in the representation of women on grave stelai from the later fifth century onward, emphasising the foundation of citizen status in the family, at the heart of which are citizen women.

[85] Cf. Vérilhac and Vial (1998) 43–6.

status but normative for every Athenian. It is this sense of essentially 'true' Athenian descent that is effective in Euripides' *Ion*, in which Ion's birth from Creusa goes back to 'earthborn' Erechtheus.

A similar emphatic meaning of *astai* and *aste* is employed by Herodotus, when in book IV he tells how the Minyans integrated into the Lakedaemonian *polis*.[86] The Minyans, expelled from their own lands, claimed that they were of the same descent as the Lakedaemonians and ought to share in their lands and their *timai* and to exchange marriage partners. The Lakedaemonians allowed them in as they had asked, but after a while the Minyans became troublesome: they wanted to share in the kingship and did other not-*hosios* things. Hence the Lakedaemonians captured and planned to kill them:

> As they (the Lakedaemonians) were about to kill them, the wives of the Minyans, who were *astai* as well as daughters of the most prominent Spartans, asked permission to go into the prison and each talk with her own husband. The men allowed them inside, because they did not expect a ruse from them (their own daughters).[87]

But the women, once inside, disguised their husbands in women's clothes and smuggled them to safety. In his description of these women as *astai* Herodotus switches from 'Lakedaemonians' to 'Spartans' as a core group among them, known to be of Spartan descent on both sides, and indicates their status as members of this group. By giving their *astai* daughters in marriage, the Spartans had shown that they considered the Minyans truly as their own and they trusted their daughters to be loyal to their high families of birth. The women, however, by virtue of the same qualities, knew how to act and protect their interests, which now lay, they thought, with their husbands. In another passage featuring *aste* and *astos*, Herodotus describes the unique *nomos* of the Lycians: they call themselves after their mothers, not their fathers.

> And indeed, when an *aste* woman is married to a slave, their children are legitimate (*gennaios*); but if an *astos* man, even if he is the most prominent among them, has a *xenos* wife or a concubine, the children are not acknowledged as full members of the community (*atimos*).[88]

[86] Hdt. 4.145–6.

[87] Hdt. 4.146: Ἐπεὶ ὦν ἔμελλόν σφεας καταχρήσεσθαι, παραιτήσαντο αἱ γυναῖκες τῶν Μινυέων, ἐοῦσαι ἀσταί τε καὶ τῶν πρώτων Σπαρτιητέων θυγατέρες, ἐσελθεῖν τε ἐς τὴν ἑρκτὴν καὶ ἐς λόγους ἐλθεῖν ἑκάστη τῷ ἑωυτῆς ἀνδρί. Οἱ δέ σφεας παρῆκαν, οὐδένα δόλον δοκέοντες ἐξ αὐτέων ἔσεσθαι. Αἱ δὲ ἐπείτε ἐσῆλθον, ποιεῦσι τοιάδε.

[88] Hdt. 1.173: Καὶ ἢν μέν γε γυνὴ ἀστὴ δούλῳ συνοικήσῃ, γενναῖα τὰ τέκνα νενόμισται· ἢν δὲ ἀνὴρ ἀστός, καὶ ὁ πρῶτος αὐτῶν, γυναῖκα ξείνην ἢ παλλακὴν ἔχῃ, ἄτιμα τὰ τέκνα γίνεται.

In both passages, Herodotus employs *aste* and *astos* for a legitimate member of the descent group with all the ensuing claims, which in Greece would include capacity to lawful marriage and transmission of inheritance rights.

The plural *astai* occurs only rarely in the classical era, for occasions where adult citizen women were active as a collective were relatively few, and occasions when such collectives were mentioned in writing even fewer.[89] But the singular *aste* occurs more frequently, because of its part in the legal formula, laid down in 403/2 and probably reiterating the wording of Pericles' Citizenship Law, for the Athenian conception of legitimacy and citizenship: a child was legitimate when it was born from (*sc.* an *astos* man and) 'an *aste* woman solemnly pledged'.[90] To understand the meaning of *astos* in fourth-century sources, we should first consider its legal use. Isaeus uses the masculine *astos* twice; in Is. 4, the estate of Nikostratos is at issue:

> These were the men who at the very beginning swooped down upon the estate of Nikostratos. Chariades at that time made no claim, but came forward later, foisting in not only himself but also his child by his mistress. It was all the same to him whether he was going to inherit the estate or have his son made an *astos*. He, too, perceiving that he would be defeated on the question of the child's birth, jettisoned the child's claim and paid a deposit to bring an action asserting his own right under a will.[91]

According to the speaker, Chariades brings both himself and his son forward as heirs to the estate of Nikostratos, allegedly trying to have his *nothos* son accepted as an *astos*, that is to say a legitimate son of an *aste* woman with all incumbent claims and rights. The primary aim of this move on behalf of the son is an inheritance, but the boy would of course also be entitled to other status claims as an *astos*. The second case concerns the disputed citizen status of Euphiletos. *Astos* (masc.) figures in an emendation of the text in the clause on legitimate birth:

> [The only way to prove that one is an Athenian is] that his mother was an *aste* and <married to> a father <who was an *astos*> as well, and that he can produce his kinsmen to witness that what he says is the truth.[92]

[89] Beside Hdt. 4.146, Ar. *Thesm.* 541; Ion of Chios (*FGrH* 392 F11), Dem. 57.35, 45.

[90] See above, Chapters 2 and 3: Is. 8.19: ἐξ ἀστῆς καὶ ἐγγυητῆς γυναικός; Is. 7.16: ἐξ ἀστῆς καὶ γαμετῆς γυναικός. Cf. Hdt. 4.78.11; Is. 7.5, 26; Dem. 57.35, 54 etc. See also Leduc (1994–5) 59 on the emergence of the individual *aste*.

[91] Is. 4.10 (transl. E.S. Foster, Loeb ed., slightly modified): ταὐτὸ δ' ἦν αὐτωι ὡς ἢ τῶν χρημάτων κληρονομήσοντι ἢ τὸ παιδίον ἀστὸν ποιήσοντι.

[92] Is. 12.7.

In the following paragraphs (12.9–10) birth from an *aste* woman is stressed again three times. Here, *astos* and *aste* indicate Athenian status, which devolves from the *astos* parents to the legitimate son, with all incumbent claims and rights, here to be acknowledged as an Athenian citizen.

Isaeus' vocabulary can be compared with that of Demosthenes in his private speeches dealing with matters of legitimacy and inheritance, with the speech of Apollodoros against Neaira ([Dem.] 59) focusing on legitimate descent as the basis of *polis* membership and participation, and a sample of political speeches of Demosthenes.[93] The vocabulary in these forensic and political speeches is also compared with the political treatises of Plato and Aristotle. The relevant terms are *astos* and *polites*, each split into masculine and feminine forms as well as taken together, and *Athenaios*, which in the singular is mostly used in these texts as an emphatic ethnic (stipulating that someone is an Athenian), but in the plural as a generic ethnic, either as a form of address to the audience of the speech or as the subject of the *polis*'s laws (Plato, *Leg.*). In Table 4.2, both absolute numbers and percentages of occurrences in each selected corpus are listed for the sake of clarity, but it is again the ratio that is significant to assess the actual usage.

In the speeches, *astos* and *aste* occur primarily in private speeches on issues of citizen status, where legitimate descent is at stake. In these lawsuits, either concerned with inheritance or with citizen status more broadly, the status of the mother was vital for legitimacy; the feminine *aste* is as frequent in these speeches or more so than its masculine counterpart. Women's legal status was more easily contestable than that of men, who were more often scrutinised in their lifetime on their citizen status than women. As these texts exemplify, *astos* features in the fourth century as the adjective qualifying a citizen in the context of (legitimate) birth within the descent group with all ensuing rights and claims. By contrast, *astoi* in the generic sense of 'citizens', as common in archaic usage, disappears; the two passages where Demosthenes uses *astoi* in this sense in his political speeches are quotes from Sophocles' *Antigone* and Solon fr. 4 respectively.[94] The singulars *polites* and *politis* are used next to *astos* in private speeches. Generally, the masculine *polites* and *politai* occur far more frequently than

[93] I have tried to include various topics in both sections, but the distinction between political and private speeches is not always watertight. Isaeus: all twelve private speeches and fragments; Demosthenes: eleven political speeches, both long and short ones: 1–8, 15, 18, 19; twelve private speeches: 30, 34, 39, 41–43, 45, 52–55, 57.

[94] Dem. 19.247.22, 19.255.14.

Table 4.2. *Ratio of occurrences based on absolute numbers (and in per cent of total number of words) of* astos, polites *and* Athenaios *in fourth-century political and forensic prose.*

	astos/astoi	*aste*	*polites/politai*	*politis/politides*	*Athenaioi*	*Athenaios*	Ratio *astos/i*: *aste*: *polites/politai*: *Athenaios*	Ratio *astos* + cogn.: *polites* + cogn.
Isaeus private speeches	2 (0.006)	6 (0.018)	17 (0.051)	1 (0.003)	3 (0.009)	2 (0.006)	1:3:8:1	1:2
Demosthenes pol. speeches	2 (0.002)	–	54 (0.064)	–	426 (0.5121)	2 (0.002)	1:27:1*	1:27
Demosthenes priv. speeches	7 (0.018)	7 (0.018)	27 (0.069)	2 (0.005)	92 (0.237)	8 (0.020)	1:1:4:1	1:2
Apollodoros, *Neaira* ([Dem.] 59)	5 (0.054)	20 (0.216)	12 (0.130)	2 (0.021)	30 (0.325)	13 (0.140)	1:4:2:2	2:1
Plato, *Resp.*	3 (0.0033)	–	38 (0.043)	– *gyne/gynaikes* 83 = (0.094)	–	1 (0.001)	1:13 **	1:13
Plato, *Leg.*	11 (0.010)	–	82 (0.078)	1 *gyne/ gynaikes* 98 = (0.093)	9 (0.008)	1 (not including the speaker)	1:8 ***	1:8
Aristotle, *Pol.*	2 (0.003)	–	161 (0.245)	2 (0.003)	6 (0.009)	–	1:80	1:80

* Both occurrences of *astos* are in quotes from earlier texts, so Demosthenes' own use is nil.

** and *** Plato prefers *gyne/gynaikes* to *aste/ai* or *politidis/es*, so his usage of the latter two cannot be established and is omitted from the ratio.

the feminine *politis* and *politides*. This is hardly surprising: female citizens rarely figured in political speeches, and private speeches concerned their status as citizens usually rendered as *aste*, less commonly as *politis*, so generally in Athens *politis*/*politides* remained quite rare.

Comparing the sample of rhetorical texts with political philosophy and other political treatises, we find the same picture. Isocrates (see Table 4.1) does not use *astos* at all in his political work: his eulogies revolve around civic virtue, not Athenian citizenship as a legal status. *Astos*/*astoi* occur in three passages in Plato's *Republic* and in eleven passages of the *Laws*.[95] In nearly all of these, *astos*/*astoi* operates as a contrast term, setting off those who enjoy the legal status of free citizens against *xenoi*, *metoikoi* and *douloi*. Plato uses *polites* /*politai* for the (male) citizens of the *polis* when it comes to their share in the *politeia*. In both texts, he discusses extensively (though in quite different ways) the roles of female citizens in the city, but uses here *gyne*/*gynaikes* rather than *politis*/*-ides*.[96] In Aristotle's *Politics*, the same pattern obtains, with *politai* used for those sharing in the *politeia* and *astos* typically used where legitimate descent or the contrast with *xenoi* are at issue.[97] But the contrast is not absolute: as we just saw, in his discussion of descent as a criterion of citizenship, Aristotle calls female citizens *politides*.

In other words, growing out of the traditional usage of *astos* as a contrast term with *xenos*, a stronger meaning developed indicating citizen status in law due to legitimate birth from Athenian parents, with all claims to participation and rights of inheritance attached to that status. The difference between the two words remained a subtle one because they are functionally connected in the fourth century: one can only be a fully fledged *polites*/*politis* if one is an *astos*/*aste*. What these claims to participation entailed – sharing in cults for both men and women, sharing in politics for men – will be discussed in Chapter 5.[98]

95 E.g. Pl. *Resp.* 563a1: disappearance of distinctions between *astoi* and *metoikoi* undesirable; but see 613e1: the unjust will be made to suffer by *astoi* and *xenoi* alike; *Leg.* 849b3: legal regulations of sales by *astoi* to *xenoi*; 866c3: laws of homicide concerning *metoikoi* and *xenoi*, compared to *astoi* etc. Cf. 917c5: anyone of the *astoi* over thirty who is present must punish a seller of goods who swears falsely about the price of his wares.

96 *Leg.* 814c4: all *politai* and *politides* must equally observe the laws on the importance of military service and up to a reasonable point fulfil the necessary athletic training.

97 Arist. *Pol.* 1278a34: descent from two *astos* parents; 1300b32–3: distinction *astos* – *xenos*.

98 Osborne (2011) 100 quite rightly notes that Plato consistently uses *astos* for a citizen's *legal* status, contrasted to the status of *xenos*, *metoikos* and *doulos*. However, his contention that 'Plato's use of *astos* offers straightforward confirmation of the way in which that term became the term of choice for *political* status' (my emphasis) is odd, if by 'political' he means the conventional meaning of that adjective. On 99–100, Osborne supports his view by claiming that '*astos* is used by Isaios six

4.3 *Athenaios*

Whereas *astos* and *polites* were generic terms for 'a member of the *polis*', it was the ethnic referring to a region, a city, a common god or shared ancestor, with the verb 'to be', that expressed belonging to a *particular polis*: 'I am a Theban, a Megarian, etc.' In this function, the ethnic was comparable to a name. A male or female citizen's names indicated his or her links to the groups to which s/he belonged: the personal name usually referred to the paternal or maternal family, the patronymic indicated one's patrilinear descent, and the ethnic the *polis* as overarching group. Designating the collective identity of all *polis* members, the ethnic applied to both men and women.[99] As we saw in Tables 4.1 and 4.2, the use of the ethnic *Athenaios* increased in the course of the classical age. In the fourth century its high frequency is due, among other reasons, to the custom for speakers to address their audience in the assembly and courts as *Athenaioi*.

M.H. Hansen takes *polis* ethnics to be 'political flags', which indicated a citizen with his political rights in a particular *polis*.[100] This meaning of

times, and always with possession of political rights at issue, either directly (as when he talks of "making a child an *astos*") or indirectly, as when he stresses the *astos* status of parents in order to stress the consequent status of the child'. Of the six passages in Isaeus to which he refers, however, only two (4.10, 12.7), discussed above in the main text, feature *astos* in the masculine, while the others (6.25, 7.19, 8.19, 12.9) all refer to legitimacy due to birth from an *aste* (fem.) and all except one are concerned with legitimacy for the sake of inheritances. Only in Is. 12 is a man's legitimacy at issue not for an inheritance but for his political rights, as in the case of Euxitheos (Dem. 57), who advances having received his *kleros* as a sign of his legitimacy. Conversely, an *astos* man who lost his right to political participation, being made *atimos*, remained an Athenian citizen in every other legal respect, such as transmitting his citizen status to his children if married to an *aste*. Collapsing all these aspects of legal status (*astos*) into the single notion 'political' status, as Osborne does, is confusing, and unconvincing in the light both of frequency of occurrence and of close reading of specific passages.

99 The symmetry in ethnics for men and women, differentiated by morphological gender, is abundantly attested in the lemmata in Steph. Byz. *Ethnica*.

100 Hansen (1996) assigns a political meaning to the ethnic but observes that if city ethnics were purely political we would expect that, like sub-ethnics (as, for example in Athens, the demotic), they were attested in the masculine but hardly ever in the feminine. 183: 'This squares with the evidence of public documents in which … women are conspicuous by their absence, but private inscriptions present a different picture.… feminine city-ethnics are far more common than feminine sub-ethnics … sub-ethnics are almost invariably used within the polis, whereas city-ethnics are mostly found outside the polis.… Their use of the ethnic in sepulchral inscriptions [by people living as foreigners in another *polis*] would no longer be felt as an indication of their status as citizens; and under such status it would only be natural to apply the ethnic to women as well as to men.' 194–5: 'Sub-ethnics are strictly political and always mark the bearer as the citizen of a polis. City-ethnics are primarily political and usually mark the bearer as a citizen of a polis.… A citizen would only be called by his sub-ethnic when he was at home; whenever he was abroad, or if in his own *polis*, he had to be recorded side by side with citizens from other *poleis*, the sub-ethnic was commonly replaced by the city-ethnic …' But even sub-ethnics were not 'strictly political', if we must understand the latter to be a quality distinct from membership by descent (see Chapter 3).

the ethnic causes difficulties when we note the equally numerous ethnics of women, who had no access to political office. Hansen explains this apparent contradiction by arguing that the strong political meaning of the *polis* ethnic weakened somewhat due to the fact that such ethnics were used in their grave inscriptions by male and female emigrants buried in *polis* territories other than their own. Such emigrants had gradually abandoned their political rights in their home towns, thus facilitating the use of ethnics in a non-political way by women; hence, *polis* ethnics became a name by which citizens more generally distinguished themselves from others, according to Hansen. However, the evidence does not support his views. Whatever the use of ethnics on grave inscriptions outside the *polis* of origin, no reverse effect on the usage within the *polis* is plausible. Ethnics were used abundantly within the *polis* and not only when the point was to distinguish the carrier of the ethnic from others. At Athens the ethnic *Athenaios* was used in the classical era for all *polis* members by descent, both male and female, the overwhelming majority of whom lived in Attica, and they were called or called themselves *Athenaioi* also when no others were around. The conclusion must be that Hansen's point of departure that the *polis* ethnic had a 'primarily political' meaning does not hold.

4.3.1 Athenaios, Attikos

Trying to envisage how in the archaic age the ethnic *Athenaios* came into being, we must assume two interactive processes, for which very little evidence is available: a growing coherence of Attica as a social entity and a gradual inclusion of all the inhabitants of Attica within the scope of the ethnic *Athenaioi*. The adjective *Attikos*, meaning belonging to Attica as a geographical entity, also appears as the ethnic *Attikoi* in the sixth century, with *Attikos* and, in the fifth century, *Attike* as gendered singulars or adjectives.[101] The earliest instances of the ethnic *Athenaioi* feature in Homeric epic, in passages the dating of which is problematic because of the possibility of sixth-century interpolation into the Homeric text. The name

[101] *Attikos* as adjective in Aesch. *Eum.* 681–2: 'Now hear my ordinance, people of Attica (Ἀττικὸς λεώς) who give judgement at the first trial on bloodshed.' Feminine *Attike*: Ar. *Lys.* 56–7: 'you'll find that they are women of the true Attic stuff (σφόδρ' αὐτὰς Ἀττικάς), who always do everything later than it should be done.' *Attikoi/-os* is not very frequent, however, and *Attikai* even less. With the article, *Attike* usually referred to Attica (Hdt. 5.76: 'this was the fourth time that the Dorians invaded Attica (τὴν Ἀττικὴν)'. From the (scarce) use of *Attikai* for Athenian women, Patterson (1986) deduced, unnecessarily, that women's civic status was expressed in this ethnic rather than in *politis/politides* or *Athenaia*.

referred to the goddess Athena, whose cult the *demos* observed on the Acropolis, together with that of Erechtheus.[102] In the *Iliad*, the *Athenaioi* appear as bands of (elite) warriors, while in the *Odyssey* Athena's name, identifying the place of her worship, extended both to the city and to a wider territory called 'Athens'.[103] This evidence leads us to assume that the *Athenaioi* were probably so called because they were aligned to her cult in some way.

In Athens itself, in the texts attributed to Solon the ethnic comes hardly better into focus than in epic. His laws, in so far as they can be reconstructed, never indicate whom exactly they are addressing; no *polis* name is extant in the fragments. Apparently, the people for whom these laws were valid could identify themselves as belonging to that group, presumably due to the coalescing descent structures discussed in the previous chapter. That such may have been the case and that by now they called themselves *Athenaioi* may be inferred from the first attestation of the ethnic in Athens, in (the re-inscription of) Draco's law on homicide of probably ca. 620. In absence of near male kin of the deceased, the law gave responsibility to his phratry to decide on the reconciliation with the killer, and in lines 26–9 stated:

> If anybody / kills a killer, or is responsible for his being killed, when he is keeping away from a frontier / market and Amphictyonic contests and rites, he shall be liable to the same things as for / killing an Athenian (*Athenaios*).[104]

When this text was drafted, it was apparently sufficiently clear who was an *Athenaios* falling within the jurisdiction of this law.

In the fourth century, a corpus of poems was firmly attributed to Solon, but we cannot be sure he was their author, nor of the poems in the shape known today, and not even that they were by one and the same author. The main body of the poems date to the sixth century, being the only Athenian texts of some length from the archaic period, but changes in the texts were made at a later date. There are good reasons, however, to accept Solon as the author of the 'Eunomia' elegy (F 4), and here the speaker describes himself as the one who is to instruct the *Athenaioi* about a just

[102] Hom. *Il.* 2.546–8; *Od.* 7.81. Kron (1976) 32–7, Kearns (1989) 110–15.

[103] Place of worship Ἀθηναί, Hom. *Od.* 3.287: '*hieros* Sounion, the cape of Athenai'; 3.307: Orestes came back 'from Athenai'; 11.323: Theseus wanted to bring Ariadne to the 'hill of *hieros* Athenai'. Hom. *Il.* 4.328; 2.551: κοῦροι Ἀθηναίων; 2.558: Ἀθηναίων φάλαγγες; 13.196: ἀρχοὶ Ἀθηναίων; 13.689; 15.337; *LfgrE*, *s.v.* Ἀθηναῖοι.

[104] *IG* I³ 104, 26–9, transl. P.J. Rhodes (AIO).

social order.[105] In a fragment of another poem, the speaking 'I', expressing his shame over the loss of Salamis, calls himself both *Athenaios* and *Attikos*:

> In that case I would rather be a man of Pholegandros or Sikinos, instead of an Athenian, changing my fatherland; for this word would quickly go all over the world: 'this man is an Attikos, of the Salamis-yielders'.[106]

In this fragment, the speaker calls himself an Athenian, whose fatherland makes him an *Attikos*, the first attested case of this singular. Both *Athenaios* and *Attikos* indicate a social identity based on the heritage of the ancestors, *Athenaios* probably with its cultic connotation, *Attikos* designating the land of Attica. It is not inconceivable that the name *Athenaioi* carried some prestige, connoted by the heroic fighters in the *Iliad* and the cult of Athena at the heart of the city where the archons met, whereas *Attikoi* indicated the people who lived in Attica, reflecting their habitat and existence drawn from the very Attic land. Yet, besides the Solonian poem other evidence also suggests that in the sixth century *Athenaios* and *Attikos* had more or less the same meaning, without apparent social distinction.[107]

In the middle of the sixth century a votive inscription from Eleusis mentions the *demos Athenaion*, the people of the Athenians.[108] Next to Draco's law, the text provides early epigraphical evidence of the ethnic *Athenaioi*, as the people for whom a certain Alkiphron erected a stele and laid out a stadion (?) at Eleusis to incur the *charis* of Demeter. The word *demos* ensures that the ethnic here included the whole *polis*, including the lower classes. It is impossible to tell whether *demos* carried here any connotation of a decision-making body, as it did in a contemporary law from Chios and as it would do in the Athenian decrees of the fifth and fourth centuries.[109] But the text of the dedication itself and the political situation

[105] F 4.30 (W.). For Solon's authorship, Lardinois (2006), Stehle (2006), and see Chapter 3, n. 57.

[106] Solon, F 2.2 (W.): εἴην δὴ τότ' ἐγὼ Φολεγάνδριος ἢ Σικινήτης / ἀντί γ' Ἀθηναίου πατρίδ' ἀμειψάμενος· / αἶψα γὰρ ἂν φάτις ἥδε μετ' ἀνθρώποισι γένοιτο· / 'Ἀττικὸς οὗτος ἀνήρ, τῶν Σαλαμιναφετέων'. Pholegandros and Sikinos are tiny islands in the southern Cyclades.

[107] Hecataeus *FGrH* 1 F 21, 93, 136 all use *Attikoi/os*; only F 127 uses *Athenaioi*, but this is in fact Herodotus' wording (6.137) of an account by Hecataeus of Athenian power expanding from the area around the Acropolis into the area occupied by the 'early inhabitants, the Pelasgians' at the foot of the Hymettus. Simonides: F 1 (W.), *Anth.Gr.* 7.254; 16.232: *Athenaioi*. Hellanicus of Lesbos (*FGrHist* 4) in the fifth century refers to *Athenaioi* frequently and to Attica only as a region. See also de Ste. Croix (1972) 396–7 for the equivalence of *Athenaios* and *Attikos*, and Patterson (1986) for the feminine *Attike* as the equivalent of *Athenaia*.

[108] *IG* I^3 991; Hansen (1983) no. 301; ca. 550; *PAA* no. 122365. First two lines in *boustrophedon*; δέμοι Ἀθεναίον ἄ[ρχον] / στέλ̣α̣ς καδέθεκεν / Ἀλκίφρον / καὶ τόνδε δρόμον ποίεσεν / ἐραστὸν / Δέμετρός τε χάριν / [καὶ Φερσεφόνες τ]ανυπ̣έπλ̣ο. The restoration ἄ[ρχον] in l. 1 is highly uncertain.

[109] Chios: ML 8, ll. 1–2: δήμο ῥήτρας.

at Athens at the time make this unlikely. Rather, the text seems to reflect the increasing cultic integration of Attica and the involvement of the *Athenaioi* with Eleusis.

The next epigraphical instance dates about forty years later, when the *Athenaioi* commemorated their victory over the Boeotians and Chalcidians in 506 in a dedication to Athena.[110] The monumental text records that the *paides Athenaion* (children of the Athenians) defeated the *ethne* of the Boeotians and Chalcidians. The statue of a four-horse chariot group used the imagery of an athletic victory for a military one, suggesting divine selection for the victory.[111] Dedicating this group on the Acropolis, the Athenians showed their gratitude to the gods and to Athena in particular, with whom they had a special relationship reflected in their own name, here prominently displayed in deliberate distinction to the defeated *ethne*.

The next cases of *Athenaioi* are on the dedication of the statue of the tyrannicides of 477/6, i.e. the new copy made by Kritios and Nesiotes after the Persians had carried off the original statue made by Antenor, where *Athenaioi* is restored;[112] and on a portico of ca. 500–470 which the Athenians dedicated at Delphi from war booty.[113] It is notable that, in all these early cases, it is in the context of their reciprocal relationship with the gods that the *Athenaioi* identify themselves as a collective.

The first extant decree mentioning the *demos* as decision-making body, implying '*Athenaion*' in the enactment clause, concerns the settlement of clerouchs on Salamis of ca. 510–500; *Athenaioi* is restored in the lines stating that the settlers are to pay taxes and serve in the army like the Athenians.[114] From the 470s onwards the *Athenaioi* appear in the decrees of the *polis*, initially rarely, but after 450 with increasing frequency with the rising number of extant decrees.[115] In these texts, the *Athenaioi* appear as the members of the *polis* in whose interests the decrees are made by the men voting in the council or assembly. The ethnic itself does not indicate political participation, but it evokes the community of the Athenians with all the claims and obligations of belonging to that group.

[110] ML 15; *DAA* 168; *IG* I^3 501: [δεσμôι ἐν ἀχνύεντι(?) σιδερέοι ἔσβεσαν hύβ]ριν / παῖδε[ς Ἀθεναίον ἔργμασιν ἐμ πολέμο] / [ἔθνεα Βοιοτôν καὶ Χαλκιδέον δαμάσαντες] / τôν hίππος δ̣[εκάτεν Παλλάδι τάσδ' ἔθεσαν].

[111] Keesling (2003) 170–5.

[112] *IG* I^3 502.

[113] ML 25.

[114] ML 14; *IG* I^3 1.2–3; Taylor (1997) 11–21. The Salamis decree is perhaps not the first inscribed Athenian decree; the Hecatompedon inscription (*IG* I^3 4) may be a re-inscription in 485/4 (archon Philocrates) of an earlier decree pre-dating the Salamis decree; Jordan (1979), Butz (2010) ix.

[115] After the above-mentioned texts, *Athenaioi* figures in dated decrees in *IG* I^3 6 (ca. 460), 10 (450s), 14 (ca. 453), 15, 18, 19 (ca. 450s?) and frequently thereafter.

Since Solon's laws, being an *Athenaios* depended on birth, a status reinforced by Cleisthenes, as we saw in the previous chapter. Pericles' Citizenship Law of 451/0 in all likelihood used the expression *Athenaion einai* (to be an Athenian) to indicate Athenian citizenship on the condition of birth from two *astos* parents.[116] *Athenaion einai*, showing the centrality of the ethnic to the concept of citizenship, also became a part of the formula by which a non-Athenian was made an *Athenaios* by decree, in other words, in a grant of citizenship. We return to the conditions and effects of citizenship grants in Chapter 6, but here we should ask when the formula *Athenaion einai* came into use. The first extant citizenship decree with the formula 'to be an Athenian' and enrolment into a *phyle* and a phratry was for Thrasyboulos of Kalydon, of 410/9.[117] But this cannot have been the first such decree ever and considering the gradual development of the formulas of inscribed decrees, as seen for example in the development of prescripts, it is not implausible that for naturalisation decrees also it took some time for the formal procedure and its vocabulary to take shape.

This use of *Athenaios* in the regular, legal formulas of citizenship demonstrates, I would argue, that by the fifth century the ethnic was the preferred mode of describing the core group of citizens by descent, rather than, for instance, use of *politai*/*polites*. Simultaneously, the practice and law of naturalisation and the use of *Athenaios* in this context also demonstrates that the birth criterion was flexible in that it could accommodate others *as if* they were born Athenians. In the later fifth and especially the fourth century, *Athenaioi* became the regular way to indicate the citizens of Athens.

4.3.2 Athenaia

In its feminine form, however, the use of the ethnic was not so straightforward. Just like the collectives *astoi* and *politai*, the plural *Athenaioi* could refer to Athenian men or to Athenian men and women, and like most ethnics the singular distinguished between masculine and feminine. *Athenaia*, the feminine counterpart of *Athenaios*, is attested in the singular in the fifth and fourth centuries, first in Ion of Chios' characterisation (460s?), as we saw above, of Themistocles' daughter as an *Athenaian xenen* – an oxymoron playing on the contrast between ethnic insiders and outsiders.[118]

[116] Blok (2009b).

[117] *IG* I³ 102.15–17. Cf. Osborne I, D2 and II, 21.

[118] See above, Chapter 1, n. 101 for the evidence. Ion of Chios (*FGrH* 392 F 11) ca. 480–420 (if the conventional dating of this fragment is reliable).

A striking case of *Athenaia* might be implied, on the most plausible restoration, in the decree on the construction of the temple of Athena Nike and the procedure for the appointment of the priestess, to be dated between the 440s and 423. The decree prescribed that a priestess was to be appointed by lot from all *Athenaion*, a genitive plural derived almost certainly from *Athenaiai*.[119]

Nonetheless, although normal vocabulary in these respects, *Athenaia* does not appear to have been frequently used. Unlike the cases of *astai* and *politides*, this scarcity is not only due to the fact that there were simply very few occasions when only female citizens were mentioned, and still fewer occasions when these words were also recorded and the records preserved.[120] Ancient commentators, foremost among them lexicographers and other scholars interested in language, already noticed the relative rarity of *Athenaia*, in contrast to *Athenaios* on the one hand and *aste* on the other, and adduced various explanations.[121] One story, for which Varro (first century BC) is our earliest source preserved in Augustine's *City of God*, drew on the myth about the competition between Athena and Poseidon to be the protector of Athens in the dawn of its existence.[122] The women were loyal to Athena and helped her gain the victory, but when Poseidon in his anger sent a flood, the men punished the women by prohibiting matrilinearity, excluding women from political decision making and prohibiting them from being called *Athenaia*. This story has gained pride of place in scholarship of recent decades on women's status at Athens, following Loraux's view that the alleged exclusion of women from the ethnic *Athenaios* meant that women were excluded from Athenian citizenship, and that such a being as an *Athenaia* did not even exist.[123] I would argue, however, that the reasons for the relative scarcity of *Athenaia* are of an entirely different nature and in fact arise from Athenian women's active share in the *hiera kai hosia* of the *polis* Athens.

Varro's story belongs to a group of lexicographic and other learned accounts about the naming of Athenian women. Divergent though these

[119] *IG* I³ 35 (ML 44; OR 137; AIO), see Blok (2014b) for text and date; ll. 5–6 for the relevant words ([....12....] ἐχς Ἀθεναίον *h*απα[σõν]). The alternative – hardly plausible given the available space – would be ἐχς Ἀθεναίον *h*απά[ντον], in which case the masculine *Athenaioi* would include women.

[120] On the impact on the presence of women in extant evidence of unwritten rules governing public and private discourse and its recording in writing, Blok (2001).

[121] Other grammarians contrast *Athenaia* with *Attike* (*gyne*) meaning Attic/Athenian woman, but this word too occurs very rarely (e.g. Ar. *Lys.* 56). For the aims and means of ancient etymological explanations, Sluiter (2015).

[122] Varro *ap.* Aug. *CD* 18.9.

[123] See Chapter 1.5.

accounts are, they all reflect on the relationship between the feminine ethnic *Athenaia* and the proximity of the mortal women of Athens to the goddess Athena. The crucial factor here is the homonymy between *Athenaia*, meaning an Athenian woman, and *Athenaia*, the name of the goddess Athena. Indeed, there is no visible or audible difference between *Athenaia* (= Athena) or *Athenaiai* (= dative singular, to Athena), inscribed on the numerous votives dedicated to Athena on the Acropolis in the sixth to fourth centuries, and *Athenaia* (= Athenian woman) or *Athenaiai* (= nominative plural, Athenian women).[124] A pun based on this homonymy seems to be at work in Aristophanes' *Birds*, where two Athenian citizens are creating an entirely new city with new gods. When asked who will be the god holding the citadel in the new *polis*, the protagonist Peisetairos answers: 'Why shouldn't we let *Athenaia* be the *polias*?'[125] His words could be taken to be 'let an Athenian woman (*Athenaia*) . . .' instead of Athena. A scholion explained the issue:

> 'Why not *Athenaia*?' Because they called the goddess *Athenaia*. That is why they did not call a citizen woman (*politis*) *Athenaia*, avoiding homonymy, but *aste*. Nonetheless they appear to call a *politis Athenaia* in many places.[126]

One might suppose that the context in which these words appeared usually resolved any ambiguity about the identity of mortal and immortal. In the decree for Athena Nike, for instance, the genitive plural *Athenaion* unequivocally suppressed the homonymy with Athena, simultaneously putting the *Athenaiai* as a collective on a par with the *Athenaioi*.[127] But in the singular there might indeed be some tension between reference to a mortal woman and to the goddess. We know from the onomastic evidence that in the classical age homonymy between citizens and gods was absolutely avoided. No mortal citizen woman, for example, was

[124] In votive inscriptions the dative *Athenaiai*, 'to Athena', is common. Moreover, as Keesling (2003) shows, among the *korai* dedicated on the Acropolis in the sixth and early fifth centuries no visible difference can be identified between representations of female dedicators and representations of the goddess herself; it is only due to context and inscriptions that viewers could figure out whom these *korai* might represent.

[125] Ar. *Av.* 828: τί δ' οὐκ Ἀθηναίαν ἐῶμεν πολιάδα;

[126] Schol.vet. in Ar. *Aves* 828: τί οὐκ Ἀθηναίαν: Ὅτι τὴν θεὸν οὕτως ἔλεγον Ἀθηναίαν. διὸ καὶ τὴν πολῖτιν οὐκ Ἀθηναίαν, φεύγοντες τὴν ὁμωνυμίαν, ἀλλ' ἀστήν. φαίνονται μέντοι καὶ τὴν πολῖτιν Ἀθηναίαν λέγοντες πανταχοῦ.

[127] In the epigram for the first priestess of Athena Nike, Myrrhine (*IG* I³ 1330; OR 179; AIO), ll. 14–16, she is called a priestess ἐκ πάντων κλήρωι 'by lot from all', *sc.* male and female Athenians, in other words, the entire citizen body. Jacquemin (2005) 345 argues further that in the phrase ὁ δῆμος τῶν Ἀθηναίων one cannot see or hear whether male *Athenaioi* or female *Athenaiai* are meant, whence the invoking of the good fortune for both the *demos* of the *Athenaioi* and the *demos* of the *gynaikes* when the women meet for the Thesmophoria (Ar. *Thesm.* 304–9).

called Demeter or Aphrodite, no citizen male carried the name Apollo or Poseidon.[128]

Apart from Varro, there are interesting accounts in Photius and Eustathius.[129] Both ancient scholars record debates among linguists as to whether *Athenaia* is proper Attic, some denying this to be so, even if they know that Attic writers did use it. All these learned commentators point to the avoidance of homonymy, but their accounts of this phenomenon vary considerably. According to some, respect for the goddess was initially a reason to call the women precisely *Athenaiai* (*sc.* to be as close to her as possible), but eventually the same respect made them avoid this seeming identity between humans and divinity. Eusthatius reports that when the women began to call themselves *Athenaiai*, the citizens decided to contract the name of the goddess from *Athenaia* to *Athena* – the homonymy was thus terminated not by changing the name of Athenian women but of the goddess herself.

One story, recorded by both Photius and Eustathius and derived from a little-known author, Megakleides, tells us that Athenian men were called *Athenaioi* and women *Attikai*, because married women did not want to offend the unmarried woman (= Athena) when addressing her.[130] What lies behind this story is not immediately obvious, but possibly it draws on the custom that women and men became *Athenaiai* and *Athenaioi* respectively on reaching civic adulthood. Women did so when they got married and had their first child, men when they had fulfilled their *ephebeia* (at least in the fourth century) and passed their *dokimasia*. This transition was ritually marked in the Apatouria, the festival celebrating admission of male citizens as adult members into the phratries and women citizens who had had their first child, providing as mothers of citizens the indispensable guarantee of citizenship through descent, following on the phratry offering at the *gamelia* upon marriage.[131] The goddess Athena, however, was

[128] Theophoric names, which were popular in ancient Greece, were derived from divine names, but never identical to them when used for free citizens in the classical era: e.g. Dionysios, not Dionysus. Lucian (*Pr.Im.* 4) claims that some people called themselves Zeus, Leto or Hermes, but his comment clearly refers to his own time and place; evidence of such naming practices all date to the post-classical era. On this see Parker (2000), who also observes (64) that theophoric names were more frequent among men than among women in Attica. It is not (yet) clear why this was the case.

[129] Phot. *Lex.* α 466; Eust. *ad Iliad.* α 197, vol. 1, p.133. These passages also include the account of Megakleides (*FHG* 4, 443), see below.

[130] Megakleides, *FHG* 4, 443.

[131] For the Apatouria as a festival of male citizens and of female citizens after giving birth to their first child, see above and Schmitt-Pantel (1977); for a relief showing a married couple presenting their children to Athena, perhaps at the Apatouria, see Palagia (1995); Keesling (2003) 120–1.

proud of her virgin status, and addressing her as if she were married like any mortal female would have been an insult. According to Megakleides, the women of Athens, out of respect for the patron divinity of their city, let go of her name.

In all these stories, authors from Hellenistic and later times tried to clarify a linguistic phenomenon they observed in classical texts, namely a discrepancy in use between the masculine ethnic *Athenaios* and the feminine *Athenaia*, by situating it in an explanatory context. In some respects, these stories shed more light on the time and place of their authors than on the fifth and fourth centuries. The explanatory power of the Varro/Augustine account, for instance, is obviously crippled by the fact that its point of departure, that classical Athenian women were not any longer called *Athenaia*, is simply not true. Augustine, moreover, uses the story to reveal the fickleness of pagan demons like Poseidon and Athena: Athena abandons the women of Athens to the vengeance of their husbands, not even taking care that the women, who had been so loyal to her, could keep her name. Varro's own version, which anyway may have been somewhat different from Augustine's text, presumably had a quite different context. Furthermore, although avoidance of homonymy in theophoric names was less prominent when these authors were writing than in the classical age, this language use was well known, to the point of being a commonplace, in linguistic scholarship.

Yet I would argue that this was the correct explanation. *Athenaia*, as the ethnic name of a mortal woman, was indeed exactly the same as the name of the goddess. The evidence on *Athenaia* suggests that homonymy was avoided *absolutely* in the case of personal names for individuals and *strongly* in the case of the feminine ethnic of individuals. The evidence confirms that the religious problem was not merely an aetiology adduced to explain the linguistic problem, but reflected the Athenian *mentalité* in the classical age. In sum, the normal avoidance of *Athenaia* for mortal citizen women in the language use of the classical period was an act not of social dismissal of women as citizens at Athens, but of the Athenians' piety towards the gods.

4.4 Citizenship Vocabulary and Citizen Status

When we survey the usage of the regular terms designating 'citizen', i.e. *polites*, *astos* and the ethnics *Athenaios* and *Attikos*, some developments can be distinguished.

In texts from epic to the mid-fifth century, *politai* and *astoi* appear overwhelmingly in the plural: citizens are conceived primarily as a collective. The

(Acro)*polis*, the place of safety where the central sanctuaries were situated, signified the essential connection between the community, their common cults of gods and heroes and the territory they inhabited; by the fifth century the Acropolis was the place where laws and decrees were set up. This sense of *politai* and *astoi* as all those sharing the same habitat, social life and cults, for short 'the members or inhabitants of the *polis*', we might label the generic meaning of the lexemes *polites* and *astos*. In the course of time, a gradual and partial shift in meaning is visible from *politai* in this generic sense towards *politai* as those sharing a common descent. Underlying this development we saw that the *polis* (community) became the overarching aggregate of the subgroups to which *politai*/*astoi* belonged, and of which descent increasingly became the defining criterion. *Politai* and *astoi* are very close in meaning, but *astoi* has somewhat stronger overtones of 'belonging to us' than *politai*, a difference articulated in the contrast between *astoi* and others, usually outsiders; in this contrastive context, the singular *astos* denotes a single representative of the citizens.

Athenaioi occurs several times in epic and occasionally in other archaic poetry, where *Athenaioi* and *Attikoi* seem to be more or less identical. In the late seventh century, *Athenaios* is used in Draco's law on homicide, and in the mid-sixth century *Athenaioi* is used for the first time with explicit reference to the whole *demos*. Although the inscription concerned marks especially Athens's interest in the cults of Eleusis, it is attractive to assign a wider significance to this use of *demos Athenaion*: the inclusion of *all* free inhabitants of Attica, brought about by a growing social coherence after Solon's social, religious and political reorganisation and subsequently the reorganisation of the Panathenaea in 566/5. Bringing the population of Attica together in Athens for the cult of Athena every year, *Athenaioi* by then could be all those who participated in the Panathenaea.[132] After 550, the ethnic is used occasionally in literary and epigraphical sources. In the 460s, *Athenaios*/*a* had become the regular word for a member of the *polis* Athens, which by then was based on descent. The widespread use of ethnics for women demonstrates that the ethnic itself does not imply active political participation, but may evoke that sharing in the *polis* which was normal for citizen men and women. *Attikos*, a common word for the inhabitants of Attica in the sixth century, vanishes in the fifth century in the case of men, being replaced by *Athenaios*; for women, *Attikai* is used exceptionally in the fifth century and then disappears.

[132] Shear (2001) 124: 'the focus of the parade [in the early decades of the festival] was on the Athenians who demonstrated their status by publicly taking part in the proceedings'.

In the masculine plurals, *politai*, *astoi* and *Athenaioi* are neutral in gender reference; they may include men and women or, depending on context, specify the citizens as men. None of the generic references reveals a manifest relation between the words used for 'citizen' and political entitlement in the narrow sense; we know from other sources, or from other places in the same sources, that among the *politai* a few or, depending on the city and time in question, many men were engaged in active politics, and most men and women in cultic activities. Specific references to women citizens occur rarely in our evidence. Considering the large proportion of the extant evidence dealing with the political aspects of public life in ancient Greece, this scarcity is to be expected.

At Athens from the mid-fifth to the end of the fourth century we find some clear changes in citizenship vocabulary, some of which seem primarily due to different types of texts with their concomitant different usages, but on the whole we discern a wider shift in citizenship discourse.

Firstly, an increase in the use of *politai* in proportion to *astoi* is notable. Moreover, *politai* may mean not just 'members of the *polis*' but more emphatically 'the core group of the *polis* participating in *polis* life'. Often such an emphasis is implicit in the context rather than explicitly stated; for instance, speeches to the citizens or texts about civic matters may picture the *politai* as having obligations to the community in a way that must have been clear enough for the contemporary listeners. The modern reader, furthermore, may infer such an emphasis by taking account of the wider historical context. After the reforms of Ephialtes in 462/1 and in the heyday of the Delian League, the male *politai* of Athens were well aware of their potential power, both within and outside Athens, an awareness that naturally bolstered their self-consciousness as citizens. The self-confident atmosphere in the political domain was reflected in the splendour of large-scale festivals such as the Panathenaea and City Dionysia, while the number of cults comprehended within the framework of the *polis* religion increased.[133] As we shall see in Chapters 5 and 6, in these cultic festivities the participants were distinguished as between citizens and others, and according to gender and age; for the citizens, participation was both proof of their membership and a way of putting that membership into practice. Finally, a new sense of citizenship seems to have emerged following the onset of the Peloponnesian War, when the Athenians had to leave their local, ancestral *polis* (i.e. deme) for the first time after countless generations and to live packed with their fellow Athenians within the walls of

[133] Parker (1996) 122–98.

the city, in proximity to the Acropolis of Athens.[134] Due to these developments, being *politai* of Athens might have acquired a stronger sense than would otherwise have been the case. We must note, however, that this emphatic sense never entirely replaced the generic meaning, but, depending on context, could add a qualification or specification to it.

Secondly, beside these shifts in meaning of long-standing vocabulary, around 430 a new discourse seems to emerge in our texts articulating the role of citizens as active members of their community. The new noun *politeia*, indicating the organisational structure and concomitant social climate of a *polis*, reflects awareness of a *polis* as a society run by its citizens. Simultaneously, the singular *polites* and the singulars *astos* and *aste* become more numerous and reveal growing interest in male and female citizens *individually*. The first attestations highlight the individual *polites* for his attitude towards the community and likewise, in the *Electra*s by Euripides and Sophocles, *politides* designates female citizens characterised by their active share in the *polis*; the singular *politis* is first attested in the fourth century.

Also in the late fifth century, the connotations of the words *astoi* and *politai*, which hitherto had been close, drifted apart. *Astos/aste* figure especially in contexts concerned with the legal status of citizens with concomitant claims to fitting roles in the *polis*. Changing from meaning 'belonging to us' in a generic sense into 'belonging to us *by legitimate descent*', *astos/aste* feature in fourth-century court cases dealing with legitimate birth of male and female citizens from citizen parents, with the inherent rights of inheritance and other ensuing claims in society. The terms also feature in political philosophy articulating distinctions between citizens and other inhabitants of a *polis* in terms of their legal status, effective in cults, politics and jurisdiction. The focus on the individual citizen, male and female, due to his/her legal status depending on legitimate descent, captured in *astos/aste*, points to Pericles' Citizenship Law as the major event in bringing an additional stringency to a legal conception of citizenship that had been developing since Solon.

The most significant word for citizens *of Athens* was now the ethnic *Athenaios*, identifying the members by descent of this particular *polis*, with all the claims and obligations between individuals and the community that this entailed. From the mid-fifth century, the evidence shows abundantly the *Athenaioi* as the protagonists of historiography and drama, as

[134] Thuc. 2.16; cf. the single *polites* (Ar. *Eq.* 1304) as victim of the war. Meyer (1993) ascribes the increased use of demotics in these decades to this situation.

the addressees of oratory and as the collective of citizens setting up their decrees to regulate their interests among themselves and with others. Depending on genre of text and on context, the *Athenaioi* are either the male citizens or all Athenian citizens, male and female, collectively.

Over time, citizenship vocabulary thus shows a gradual shift from a generic collective of inhabitants into a citizen group whose legal status becomes increasingly stringently defined by descent and increasingly the carrier of claims, obligations and, in some areas, rights, laid down in law as distinct from others who do not belong to this citizen community. For male and female citizens, a symmetrical vocabulary is used: in terms of legal status with its inherent claims (*astos*/*aste*; *Athenaios*/*Athenaia*) and of membership of the *polis* (*polites*/*politis*) no essential difference between men and women is articulated, despite a difference in the frequency with which men or women are the topic of discourse and in the types of evidence referring to either or both, differences depending in turn on different spheres of action. This symmetrical vocabulary, I would argue, reflects a fundamental layer of citizenship in which men and women shared equally and which is essential to the *polis* as a whole, whereas the features of difference indicate domains where gender distinctions prevailed. To see how this citizenship vocabulary mapped onto shared or differentiated participation in the *polis* in reality, we now turn to the organisation of public roles in Athens.

5

Participation: Public Roles and Institutions

> [T]he *demos* should receive the *agatha* which the priest and the *hieropoioi* report took place in the sacrifices which they made to Dionysus and the other gods for the health and safety of the *boule* and the *demos* of the Athenians ...[1]
>
> From an honorific decree for a priest and *hieropoioi*, *IG* II³ 1, 416 (ca. 340–330)

> At this point the most virtuous of citizen women will be angry at you that you have considered this woman worthy to participate equally with themselves in the *polis* and the *hiera* ... and to participate in the rituals (*teletai*) and *hiera* and *timai* belonging to the *polis*.[2]
>
> Apollodoros, *Against Neaira* [Dem.] 59, 111–13

The capacity to perform defined roles in the public domain is generally regarded as an important, if not the most important, component of citizenship.[3] At Athens, active participation (*metechein*) was the touchstone of being a citizen, both in law and in practice, for which citizen status (*meteinai*) was the basic qualification. To understand Athenian citizenship we therefore want to identify what kinds of public roles in the *polis* citizens were expected to fulfil, how access to these functions was organised and why it was organised in this way. By public roles I mean roles and functions that the *polis* formally recognised or legally established to support its life as a community. Whereas the *polis* awarded various kinds of public honours to outsiders, public offices were the only *timai* that normally only citizens had access to.[4] My discussion aims in particular to clarify how at

[1] *IG* II³ 1, 416 ll. 11–15: τὰ μὲν ἀγαθὰ δέχεσθαι τὸν δῆμο/ν, ἃ ἀπαγγέλλουσι ὁ ἱερεὺς καὶ οἱ ἱεροποιοὶ γεγονέναι ἐ/ν τοῖς ἱεροῖς, οἷς ἔθυον τῶι Διονύσωι καὶ τοῖς ἀλλοῖς θε/οῖς ἐφ ὑγιείαι καὶ σωτηρίαι τῆς βουλῆς καὶ τοῦ δήμου τõ / Ἀθηναίων etc.

[2] [Dem.] 59.111: οὐκοῦν ἤδη αἱ μὲν σωφρονέσταται τῶν γυναικῶν ὀργισθήσονται ὑμῖν, διότι ὁμοίως αὑταῖς ταύτην κατηξιοῦτε μετέχειν τῶν τῆς πόλεως καὶ τῶν ἱερῶν; 113: καὶ τελετῶν καὶ ἱερῶν καὶ τιμῶν μετέχειν τῶν ἐν τῇ πόλει.

[3] See Chapter 1.7.

[4] The only exceptions seem to be mercenary captains appointed *strategoi* in the fourth century, for example Charidemos of Oreos, introduced in Chapter 2, who later also received citizenship. These functions were perhaps not in all respects the same as citizen *strategoi*.

Athens public roles were meant to support the *polis*'s *hiera kai hosia* and what qualifications, especially with regard to gender, were required for performing such roles.

5.1 *Timai* and *Archai*

All public offices collectively were called *timai* ('honours'), a subgroup of which were also called *archai*.[5] Scholars have tended to discuss the *archai* as a category quite separate from other *timai*, especially priesthoods, dividing the *polis* into two domains of action, the political and the cultic, each with its distinct institutions and offices.[6] *Arche*, as an abstract conception meaning (*inter alia*) 'the leading principle', is usually rendered in the context of the *polis* as 'political rule', but in the present-day notion of the political, religion is not an inherent part, whereas *arche* meant authority over and responsibility for all the interests of the *polis* that in ancient Greece definitely included religion. The *archai* were the multiple concrete functions effectuating this *arche*, which can be translated by 'magistracies' provided that in this notion the essential connection with religion is maintained. For understanding the public functions both in their responsibility for *hiera kai hosia* and in their distribution over gender, it is essential to delineate how the *polis* conceptualised the *archai* and cultic *timai*, notably priesthoods that are usually considered the most typical case of *polis* offices that were not *archai*, both in terms of their duties and in the requirements for office holding. Furthermore, in scholarship *archai* are usually

[5] Hdt. 1.59: Ἔνθα δὴ ὁ Πεισίστρατος ἦρχε Ἀθηναίων, οὔτε τιμὰς τὰς ἐούσας συνταράξας οὔτε θέσμια μεταλλάξας, ἐπί τε τοῖσι κατεστεῶσι ἔνεμε τὴν πόλιν κοσμέων καλῶς τε καὶ εὖ. 'From then on Pisistratos ruled the Athenians; he did not destroy the existing *timai* nor change the laws, but keeping the established laws he reigned the *polis* in a proper and well-ordered way.' Eur. *IA* 19: 'the men ἐν τιμαῖς': the men in office. Arist. *Pol.* 1281a31: τιμὰς γὰρ λέγομεν εἶναι τὰς ἀρχάς, ἀρχόντων δ'αἰεὶ τῶν αὐτῶν ἀναγκαῖον εἶναι τοὺς ἄλλους ἀτίμους. 'For we call the offices (*archai*) honours (*timai*), and if the same persons always hold the offices, the others are inevitably *atimos*.' Pl. *Ap.* 35b: ὅτι οἱ διαφέροντες Ἀθηναίων εἰς ἀρετήν, οὓς αὐτοὶ ἑαυτῶν ἔν τε ταῖς ἀρχαῖς καὶ ταῖς ἄλλαις τιμαῖς προκρίνουσιν, οὗτοι γυναικῶν οὐδὲν διαφέρουσιν. '[Anyone might say] that those Athenians who are distinguished in excellence, whom they themselves choose to endow with *archai* and with the other *timai*, would be no different than women [in their fear of the death penalty].'

[6] On the background of this view, see Chapters 1.5 and 1.6. For this distinction, see for instance Hansen (1989) who defines 'institutions' only as political in the strict sense; Develin (1989) 1 provides a list of officials 'who were subject to election, by whatever means, to positions in the service of the state or sections thereof where there is some connexion with the operation of state functions', in which he includes the Tamiai of Athena but no priest(esse)s. Ober (2008) casts his net of *polis* institutions much wider than Hansen to demonstrate the pervading influence of knowledge in the Athenian democracy but nowhere refers to religion. Conversely, studies such as Clinton (1974) and recently Dignas and Trampedach (2008) approach cultic personnel as active in a world of religion only marginally connected to the *polis* as a social–political entity.

distinguished from other kinds of honours (*timai*) granted to citizens and to non-citizens, and from the issues of (civic) status or individual honour entailed in the singular *time*. Before proposing a different approach, I will first look into the arguments for making such distinctions.

Regarding the offices open to citizens, scholars distinguishing between *archai* and other *timai*, notably priesthoods and other cultic personnel, usually follow Aristotle's *Politics*, with further support of the list of Athenian *archai* in *Ath.Pol.* 42–62.[7] In this approach, *archai* appear as the really important offices for running the *polis*, whereas other *timai* such as priesthoods were of a distinct nature and without effective authority. M.H. Hansen, who has investigated the Athenian *archai* systematically, summarises:

> the term *archai* does not include all those with public duties chosen by election or lot: for example, neither priests nor *choregoi* nor criers nor envoys count as *archai* in the proper sense. The *archai* were a well-defined group of state officials, and they were defined in various laws, paraphrased by Aeschines in his speech *Against Ktesiphon*.[8]

In this speech, Aeschines wants to show that a superintendent of the walls (*teichopoios*) – the office held by his opponent Demosthenes – is an *arche* and that for this official, as for other *archai*, public honours, in this case a crown, could only be awarded after the *euthynai* and in the Pnyx and nowhere else. The typical features of *archai* that Hansen collects from Aeschines and from additional evidence are: 1) an age limit of thirty years of age; 2) selected by election or lot; 3) undergoing preliminary scrutiny by the council or court (*dokimasia*) as to citizen descent, age and any conduct leading to *atimia*; 4) holding office for at least thirty days; 5) rendering account (*euthynai*) on terminating office. Their rights included: a) presiding over the courts on cases relevant to their sphere of office; b) imposing minor fines; c) controlling public funds and supervising public workers.[9]

I agree with Hansen that there must have been differences between *archai* and other *timai*, as the existence of two words with quite distinct roots suggests, and that probably some of the features just mentioned were relevant for this distinction, but I would contest that *archai* were

[7] Arist. *Pol.* 1298a22, 1299a14–20, 1318b21–2; Aeschin. 3.13–15, 28–30. For the basic distinctions between priesthoods and *archai*, see below. For the debate on the public roles of priests, Garland (1984), Garland (1990), Chaniotis (2008), Henrichs (2008); of priestesses, Connelly (2007).

[8] Hansen (1991) 226.

[9] Hansen (1980) 153; Hansen (1991) 226.

'well-defined', notably that the 'Athenians had a special law delimiting the offices, probably a *nomos* about *dokimasia* defining *arche* in the technical sense'.[10] The criteria distinguishing *archai* from other *timai* seem to be more equivocal than Hansen contends. Let me explain this in more detail.

Priesthoods were not *archai*, so Hansen, because priests and priestesses did not undergo *dokimasia* and priestesses, being women, could not hold an *arche* anyway.[11] However, some evidence points to *dokimasiai* for priests and priestesses. By law they had to be of sound body,[12] and of citizen descent on both sides: men who were made Athenians by decree were by law not allowed to hold an archonship or a priesthood, but their descendants from a union with an *aste* could do so.[13] This evidence suggests that before entering a priesthood a *dokimasia* as to citizen descent as well as to being of sound body took place.[14] The latter requirement also applied to the nine archons,[15] suggesting a kinship between these two functions to which we return below. For some offices, such as the archons and the *bouleutai*, the *dokimasia* in the fourth century held a question as to the oligarchic leanings of the selected candidate; if this also applied to priests, we do not know.

The right to impose small fines on citizens would seem a somewhat firmer criterion to distinguish (some) *archai* from priesthoods, as the only explicit evidence we have of a priest doing so concerns a priest imposing a fine on other citizens together with the demarch.[16] However, again the picture is more complicated. In the decree of the case just mentioned,

[10] Hansen (1980) 153; but Scafuro (2006b) shows that Hansen underestimates the rhetorical drive behind Aeschines' depiction of *archai*.

[11] Priests and especially priestesses not *archai*: Hansen (1980) 170. In n. 45 Hansen adduces Dem. 57.46 as evidence: *dokimasia* is mentioned with an *arche* (namely *demarchos*) but passed over in silence with reference to the priesthood of Heracles. This argument is not valid, however, because 1) *dokimasia* always took place not before selection but when a person was selected, before entering office; Euxitheos was selected as demarch, but did not get the priesthood of Heracles, so never entered this office; 2) Euxitheos was expected to qualify for the priesthood anyway because of his *eugeneia* (as a *gennetes*; see also below), in other words, to be able to pass his *dokimasia*.

[12] Anaxandrid. Fr. 39 (Kock) 9–10: τοὺς ἱερέας ἐνθάδε μὲν ὁλοκλήρους νόμος / εἶναι, παρ' ὑμῖν δ', ὡς ἔοικ', ἀπηργμένου.

[13] [Dem.] 59.92, 105. See also Chapter 6.1.

[14] Pl. *Leg.* 759c1–7 requires such a scrutiny for *polis* priesthoods after selection by lot, followed by a check of descent from families without any blemish with regard to homicide or offences against *ta theia* on the maternal and paternal sides. Since Plato's *Laws* respond to existing Athenian practices but always in a critical manner, we may speculate that the *dokimasia* he proposes in this passage is stricter than the one applied at Athens.

[15] Lys. 24.13.

[16] *IG* II[2] 1362, late fourth century, obliging the priest of Apollo Erithaseos to punish a slave caught chopping wood in the sanctuary with fifty lashes and reporting his name and that of his master to the *basileus* and the *boule*, and if a free man is caught with this offence, the priest with the demarch is to impose a fine of fifty drachmae and to report his name.

the priest proclaims the penalties for chopping wood in the sanctuary 'on behalf of himself, of the demesmen and of the *demos* of the Athenians'.[17] If in the latter two capacities he acts on a par with an *arche*, what is the role of the demarch? Is fifty drachmae above the level of a fine the priest could impose alone? Hansen adduces, furthermore, that priests did not handle public money. This cannot be correct. For instance, a decree of ca. 460 for the cult of Eleusis rules that the *hieropoioi* will receive a half-obol from each *mystes*, that the priestess of Demeter and Kore receives one obol for the Lesser and one for the Greater Mysteries from each *mystes*, that all this money is for the goddesses, except 1,600 drachmae from which the priestess is to pay the necessary expenses, as she did previously.[18] Priests and priestesses, like citizens holding *archai*, had to render account of their office (*euthynai*), in which accounting for the public money used in their office was a central concern.[19] Edward Harris situates this evidence within the wider responsibility the *polis* devolved on priests and priestesses for their sanctuaries, keeping them pure and well ordered, a duty for which the *polis* invested the priests and priestesses with powers and, where necessary, with personnel to carry it out and for which it held them accountable in return.[20] The evidence shows a steady growth in the number of *hieropoioi*, *epimeletai*, *epistatai* and *tamiai* in the course of the fifth and fourth centuries, documented especially in epigraphical evidence, and Hansen adds a useful list of these and other offices that *Ath.Pol.* and *Politics* omitted.[21] Below, more personnel is added to these lists, including female cult personnel. There were multiple reasons for adding such offices to sanctuaries; for instance, some of the cults concerned were new and needed new personnel, e.g. the cult of Asclepius, inaugurated in 420 and run in the fourth century by a priest allotted by tribe and three to ten *epistatai*.[22] New officials were added to existing cults as well, for instance the *hieropoioi* we just saw in the cults at Eleusis. Since handling public money for these cults and festivals was prominent among the tasks of

[17] *IG* II^2 1362, ll. 2–4: ὁ ἱερεὺς τοῦ Ἀπόλλωνος τοῦ Ἐριθασέου π[ρ]/οαγορεύει καὶ ἀπαγορεύει ὑπέρ τε ἑαυτ[οῦ] καὶ τῶν δημ[ο]τῶν καὶ τοῦ δήμου τοῦ Ἀθηνα[ί]/ων.

[18] *IG* I^3 6, C, ll. 5–20.

[19] *Euthynai* of priests: Aeschin. 3.18: all priests and priestesses, both individually and collectively, for instance the *gene* of the Eumolpidai, the Kerykes 'and all the rest'. *IG* II^3 1, 359.21–2: priest of Asclepius; 416.16–22: the priests of Dionysus, Poseidon Pelagios, Zeus Soter and Ammon.

[20] Harris (2013) 32–4. The earliest extensive document of this kind is *IG* I^3 4, the Hekatompedon decree, (re-)inscribed in 485/4. See also Lambert (2010b) for the control of priesthoods by the *polis*.

[21] Hansen (1980) 156–66. It is noteworthy that *Ath.Pol.* discusses many of these *hieropoioi et al.*, but, just like Aristotle in the *Politics*, is hardly interested in priests, whereas Plato especially in *Laws* pays much attention to priests, their selection and duties.

[22] Hansen (1980) 163.

these *hieropoioi*, *epistatai et al.*, it is attractive to see a connection between the rising number of officials and the growing amount of public money involved, as discussed in previous chapters, and through these *polis* (or deme) officials the *polis* exercised a more centralised, direct control over these cults and sanctuaries than before. Yet they did not fully replace the financial and cultic duties of the priests and priestesses themselves. Fourth-century accounts of the sanctuary of Asclepius, for instance, show that the priest was responsible for the money of his cult, despite the presence of the *epistatai*; in other cults, priests and officials acted together but were separately accountable.[23] The fine imposed by a priest and a demarch together mentioned above seems an instance in this pattern of shared authority.

The right to preside over a court for charges concerning its authority seems a plausible criterion for an *arche*. But whether this was a right of *every arche*, as Hansen claims, is questionable, as is the contention that *only archai* held this right. The main evidence is again Aeschines' *Against Ktesiphon*. In par. 13, he refers to *archai* as 1) those whom the Thesmothetai select by lot in the Theseum, 2) those selected by popular voting (*cheirotonia*), notably 'the *strategoi*, *hipparchoi* and similar *archai*', and in par. 14 adds 3) all who do some service for the *polis* for more than thirty days; 4) all to whom presidency of a court is given. In par. 27 he states about Demosthenes' *arche*: 'he handled public money, as well as imposed fines, like the other *archontes*, and held the right to preside over courts'.[24] In par. 29 he reiterates: *archai* are 1) those selected by election or lot; 2) those doing a service for the *polis* for more than thirty days; 3) all others who hold a presidency of a court. From these passages it is not unambiguously clear whether Aeschines means that this latter privilege is a right of every *arche*, or that it is a right of some *archai*, among which that held by Demosthenes, which are to be added to the list. Adele Scafuro argues convincingly that the latter is the case, and, while it was Aeschines' intention to 'squash the defense', not to be precise on points of law, that precisely here he suggested that Demosthenes as *teichopoios* had the right to preside over a court while in fact that was not the case. She demonstrates, adducing epigraphical evidence, that the right to preside over a court was a fixed

[23] *IG* II² 1532, 1539 shows the priests of Asclepius accounting for the property dedicated in their sanctuary. In *IG* II³ 1, 416 the priests of Dionysus, Poseidon Pelagios, Zeus Soter and Ammon and the *hieropoioi* with whom they sacrificed and performed other *hiera* are honoured with a crown of 500 drachmae, but they seem to give their *euthynai* separately, in two groups.

[24] Aeschin. 3.27: καὶ τὰ δημόσια χρήματα διεχείριζε, καὶ ἐπιβολὰς ἐπέβαλλε, καθάπερ οἱ ἄλλοι ἄρχοντες, καὶ δικαστηρίων ἡγεμονίας ἐλάμβανε.

right of a group of 'traditional' *archai* who all had to undergo scrutiny and to submit *euthynai*, and that it could be granted by special decree to the many *ad hoc* 'magistrates' or boards of such officials (*epimeletai*, *epistatai*, various *-poioi* etc.) when the *nomothetai* considered holding this right necessary for their duties. Normally these functions did not have this right, but when it was given and such an office was continued and had become 'traditional', this right was normally continued as well.[25]

While thus the right to preside over a court was demonstrably not a typical feature of every *arche*, some priests did have the right to preside over a court, as Hansen himself concedes; the *genos* Eumolpidai had jurisdiction over matters concerning *asebeia* including the right to preside over courts on these matters.[26] And if this was the case for the Eumolpidai, then probably the same would apply to other prominent priests in cases concerning their province. So for this criterion, too, the boundaries between *archai* and priesthoods are not absolute.

Conversely, regarding a criterion that for Hansen applies to priesthoods and not to *archai*, namely that 'they receive *geras* only (= for offering sacrifice) and pray for you to the gods' (Aeschin. 3.18), we find that also many *archai* included sacrificing, caring for *hiera* and saying prayers, although indeed they did not receive *geras* for doing so, but (in the fourth century) rather *misthos* for the sessions of their office.[27] Of the numerous *hieropoioi*, *epistatai* and other offices attached to cults, responsibility for *hiera* was obviously part of their job, but performing sacrifice, praying and organising festivals were crucial duties of many other prominent *archai* too, notably the nine archons, the *boule* and the military *archai*, as I show in more detail below. Of some *archai*, it is difficult to tell whether performing *hiera* or taking care of them in some way was a substantial part of their duties, and if so, what and how exactly. For instance, the superintendent of the wells (*Ath.Pol.* 43.1) was in charge of the city's water supplies, a task that included keeping the wells clean and that certainly meant taking care of *hiera*, since many rivers and springs at Athens were considered divine, such as the river Kephisos to whom Xenokrateia dedicated a sanctuary, as we saw previously. But what exactly were his duties? For example, the spring of (the nymph) Halykos was *hieros* and drinking from its water

[25] Scafuro (2006b) esp. 30, 41. She also notes (33, n. 9) that 'the numerous *epistatai*, *epimeletai* and *hieropoioi* who appear in our sources as attached to sanctuaries would only belong to the first group [holding the right to preside over a court] if they all underwent scrutiny and submitted accounts' and that Hansen 'cites little evidence to show that these are "technical magistrates"'.

[26] Dem. 22.27: *dikai*; Hansen (1980) 170, n. 42.

[27] Blok (2015) for the evidence and the debate on *misthos* for *archai*, with further refs.

required paying an obol every year to the Nymphs; the decree of ca. 440–430 regulating this states that if anyone breaks this rule and drinks without paying, he must pay five drachmae; if anyone takes some of the water away without paying the obol, he must pay fifty drachmae for every amphora.[28] Who was in charge of the payments of the obol or the fines? Was there a priest(ess) around to keep an eye on the spring, or was this the province of the superintendent of the wells, or both? No evidence tells us. A full, systematic list of all *archai* and their duties for *hiera* is therefore impossible, but the available evidence indicates that cultic duties belonged to a large number of *archai*.

On the other hand, although the *polis* could regulate many aspects of its cults, the laws – or perhaps rather customs? – fenced off the province of (traditional) priesthoods from at least some interventions by the people, notably concerning their religious rules. For example, according to an account by Plutarch the priestess of Demeter and Kore Theano famously refused to obey the decree of the people to curse Alcibiades when he was found guilty of profaning the Eleusinian Mysteries, on the grounds that she was made a priestess to pray, not to curse.[29] She was not charged in court for this refusal and she could apparently claim sufficient authority over her actions as a priestess to withstand this wish of the *demos*. The *genos* Salaminioi was in charge, not only of cults of their own, but of an impressive array of *polis* cults, sacrifices and priesthoods. In a decree of 363/2 settling a dispute about which cultic duties and properties fell to either of their two branches, the *genos* apparently could arrange these matters on their own, with five arbitrators who do not seem to represent the authority of the *polis*, although the Salaminioi served the cultic interests of the *polis* also involving public money.[30] The *polis* did not impose the cultic and financial arrangements on the Salaminioi, but in effect it worked the other way round: given that the *polis* had entrusted these cults to the *genos*, they arranged the specific tasks and perquisites among themselves and the *polis* had to accept the results.

[28] *IG* I^3 256.

[29] Plut. *Alc.* 22, 33. According to the accuser Thessalos, son of Kimon, Alcibiades and his friends had acted 'against the laws and institutions of the Eumolpidai and Kerykes and of the priestesses of Eleusis' (παρὰ τὰ νόμιμα καὶ τὰ καθεστηκότα ὑπό τ' Εὐμολπιδῶν καὶ Κηρύκων καὶ τῶν ἱερέων τῶν ἐξ Ἐλευσῖνος). For reading here ἱερέων as ἱερείων, 'priestesses', Clinton (1974) 70, n. 12. Clearly, the priestly personnel of Eleusis held ultimate authority over the religious rules of their cult. For Theano as a hieronymic name for priestesses and other female religious personnel widespread in Greece, Connelly (2007) 11.

[30] For the arbitration decree and the cults of the *genos*, Lambert (1997a), RO 37, Parker (1996) 308–16.

Finally, Hansen states as a matter of course that a firm criterion between *archai* and other *timai* is that the first were not held by women. At first sight this seems to be clear-cut: a diversity of evidence suggests that it was considered improper if a woman wielded authority over an adult man; in this sense the *archai* of the *polis* can be considered an extension of the gender hierarchy of the *oikos*.[31] There can be no doubt that women had no access to a large section of the *polis*'s offices. But at closer scrutiny even this picture is more varied.

Firstly, in the contexts of *hiera* there are clear connections between women and *archai*. Some were very prominent. During the Anthesteria, after a procession led by the Basileus, his wife the Basilinna engaged in the *hieros gamos* with Dionysus, presumably in the temple of Dionysus in Limnai. Apollodoros made the holiness and antiquity of the ritual and the *time* involved in performing it the core issue in his suit against the former *hetaira* Neaira, capturing the significance of the Basilinna as follows:

> she [Neaira's daughter Phano] performed on behalf of the *polis* the ancestral rituals (*ta patria*) for the service of the gods, rituals that are many and holy (*hagios*) and not to be named.[32]

Whatever Apollodoros' specific aims in this trial, he was right in emphasising that in this ritual the Basilinna acted as the female counterpart of the Basileus: although she did not wield power over men in an *arche*, like her husband, she conducted essential, traditional rituals on behalf of the whole *polis*, and with the same necessary qualifications of purity of descent to perform these rituals as the male archons and as priests and priestesses. This duality in the elevated *timai* of the Basileus and the Basilinna has a counterpart in the more modest masculine *archontes* of *polis* subgroups and the feminine *archousai* who were in charge of the Thesmophoria, the festival of adult citizen women, which made the celebrants for a limited time the dominant presence in the public domain of city.[33] That the ritual

31 Cf. Sourvinou-Inwood (1995). One of the few theoretical texts explaining this phenomenon is Arist. *Pol.* 1259a38–1260a20, where Aristotle compares the relationship between husband and wife in the household with that between ruler and ruled who, unlike their namesakes in a *polis*, do not take turns in *arche*. The reason is that women have the deliberative capacity, just like men, but without authority; in children this capacity is not yet developed, whereas slaves do not have it at all (ὁ μὲν γὰρ δοῦλος ὅλως οὐκ ἔχει τὸ βουλευτικόν, τὸ δὲ θῆλυ ἔχει μέν, ἀλλ' ἄκυρον, ὁ δὲ παῖς ἔχει μέν, ἀλλ' ἀτελές). This argument is strikingly circular: women have no *arche* because they have no power (κύρια, a near equivalent of ἀρχή). Here, as in other cases (see for instance the debate on slavery, Chapter 1, n. 51), we cannot tell whether Aristotle is voicing a generally shared view or is giving an argument of his own to clarify what he sees is actually happening.

32 [Dem.] 59.73.

33 The *archousai*: Is. 8.19–20. For the parallelism between masculine and feminine *archai* in Ar. *Thesm.*, Jacquemin (2005) 344–5.

'society of women', although in the first place a festival of human and agricultural fertility, also had a political nature – the meeting place of the celebrants in the *asty* was next to the Pnyx, and the assembly did not meet there on the festival days – has long been recognised.[34] In this and other respects, the Thesmophoria were a festival of reversal.[35] But in its organisation, the festival drew on an underlying pattern of *polis* conventions that for the Thesmophoria did not need to be reversed: in preserving the bond with the gods, the cultic duties of men and women were partly symmetrical, partly the same. Priestesses had authority in their functions over (adult) men, most conspicuously prominent priestesses such as the priestess of Athena Polias during the annual Panathenaea and the priestess of Demeter and Kore in the cults at Eleusis.[36]

Secondly, various texts envisioned the involvement of women in the political domain, either for fun, as in Aristophanes' *Lysistrata* and *Ecclesiazusae*, or as thought experiment, as in Plato's *Republic* and *Laws*, or as a topic for reflection on the relationship between obligations to family and gods (*hosia*) and the authority of law and lawgivers, as in Sophocles' *Antigone* and Euripides' *Suppliant women*. These well-known texts need no elaboration here, but they signify awareness in classical Athens that women's share in the *polis* involved the political domain in multiple ways and justified their acting on these interests as *politides* for the well-being of the *polis*.[37]

In sum, I would submit that at Athens all public offices were known as *timai*, that a subgroup of these were known as *archai* but that the laws did not define clearly what *archai* were, nor what distinguished them from the other *timai*, but rather described the criteria for all *timai* in terms of eligibility and the procedures for entering and terminating office and for

34 One meeting of the assembly on the first day of the Thesmophoria *in the theatre* is recorded (*IG* II^2 106, ll. 50–1; 122/1); no meetings are recorded on the second, most holy day of the Thesmophoria; Mikalson (1975) 71–3, 189.

35 Versnel (1993) 235–41.

36 For this equivalence of men and women in the cultic domain, Sourvinou-Inwood (1995).

37 Van Bremen (1996) has studied the widespread participation of women in public roles in the Greek cities of the Hellenistic East, and their use of wealth, their family's as well as their own, for fulfilling these roles, which were not limited to cultic offices, although their civic roles did not include 'political' office. She points to euergetism as the context of this phenomenon, by which wealthy families extended their sphere of influence over the whole city, thus widening the scope for women to do so, too. Although her view is in many respects convincing, I would argue that the change from classical to Hellenistic is not at all an abrupt one and that euergetism was not the only driving force behind women's public involvement, but that the latter was already a structural ingredient in Athens in the classical era, even if on a more limited scale and put on display in honorific inscriptions and statues far less than in later centuries, a restriction prevailing generally in the classical city and specifically in terms of gender representation.

extra honours such as a crown. Athenian discourse, too, highlights the eligibility for and the prestige of holding *timai*, what the *demos* might expect from those in such a position of prominence and their accountability towards the people who had granted them this honour, with little interest in defining *archai* and other *timai* in a substantive manner. A fine example is Demosthenes' charge against Meidias, where he argues that the Athenians granted such *timai* to a man who did not deserve it:

> Your votes, men of Athens, made him a treasurer of the *Paralos* (a man like that!), and also a hipparch (though he wasn't capable of riding through the Agora in processions), an *epimeletes* of the Mysteries, and some kind of *hieropoios*, and a purchaser of cattle for sacrifice, and so on. Well then, by the gods, do you consider it a small reward and favour (*charis*) that his natural baseness and unmanliness and wickedness is set right by the *archai* and *timai* and votes (*cheirotonia*) which you give him?[38]

All the offices Meidias had held were *archai*, according to the list in *Ath. Pol.*, but Demosthenes is interested not in their formal features, but in the wealth necessary for being a treasurer or a hipparch, to set off the wealthy Meidias' conceit against the honour the people had granted him by electing him for these offices. Collecting *archai*, *timai* and voting in one breath, Demosthenes captures the system of public evaluation and acclaim for public office. That in these respects he (successfully) persuades his audience to regard the *archai* as the same as other *timai* is borne out in an earlier passage of the same speech where he argues that a chorus leader (like himself) is a figure endowed with honour by the people, like a Thesmothetes or the Archon, not a private person:

> If one strikes or slanders him [someone holding such a position of honour] when he's wearing his crown, one becomes *atimos*; if as a private individual, one is liable to private prosecution. And this applies not only to them, but to all on whom the city confers any crown or any *time*.[39]

Considering that on the evidence just reviewed *archai* and cultic *timai* seem to have been valued collectively for the *time* they conferred and to

[38] Dem. 21.171–2: ὑμεῖς γάρ, ὦ ἄνδρες Ἀθηναῖοι, ἐχειροτονήσατε τοῦτον τῆς Παράλου ταμίαν, ὄντα τοιοῦτον οἷός ἐστι, καὶ πάλιν ἵππαρχον, ὀχεῖσθαι διὰ τῆς ἀγορᾶς ταῖς πομπαῖς οὐ δυνάμενον, καὶ μυστηρίων ἐπιμελητὴν καὶ ἱεροποιόν ποτε καὶ βοώνην, καὶ τὰ τοιαῦτα δή. εἶτα πρὸς τῶν θεῶν τὸ τὴν τῆς φύσεως κακίαν καὶ ἀνανδρίαν καὶ πονηρίαν ταῖς παρ᾽ ὑμῶν ἀρχαῖς καὶ τιμαῖς καὶ χειροτονίαις ἐπανορθοῦσθαι μικρὰν ὑπολαμβάνετ᾽ εἶναι δωρειὰν καὶ χάριν; Transl. D.M. MacDowell (1990), slightly modified.

[39] Dem. 21.33: καὶ πάλιν γε τὸν ἄρχοντα, ταὐτὸ τοῦτο, ἐὰν μὲν ἐστεφανωμένον πατάξῃ τις ἢ κακῶς εἴπῃ, ἄτιμος, ἐὰν δ᾽ ἰδιώτην, ἰδίᾳ ὑπόδικος. καὶ οὐ μόνον περὶ τούτων οὕτω ταῦτ᾽ ἔχει, ἀλλὰ καὶ περὶ πάντων οἷς ἂν ἡ πόλις τιν᾽ ἄδειαν ἢ στεφανηφορίαν ἤ τινα τιμὴν δῷ. Transl. D.M. MacDowell (1990), slightly modified.

have been organised on quite similar procedural rules, I will leave the distinctions between them aside for now and first consider more precisely why and how *timai* signified the *time* of those on whom they were conferred.

5.2 *Timai* and *Time*

Timai meaning 'honour(s)', referring to all kinds of public honours and offices that the *polis* conferred on citizens and non-citizens, is the plural of *time*, which in the singular indicates the standing of a person in a community.[40] Every use of *time* builds upon its fundamental meaning of 'value'; the stem *tim-* implies evaluation that needs exchange and agreement between two parties to be effectuated. Used for material goods and property, *time* means 'price', 'worth (in monetary terms)' and (negatively) 'fine'; in social terms, it means 'recognition', 'honour', 'office', 'reward', 'compensation', 'satisfaction' and (negatively) 'penalty'.[41] Generally, the notion of 'value' rests on the economic worth a particular society grants to objects, but for 'value' in the abstract sense this valuation is transposed to the level of human relations, from which in turn objects may derive a symbolic value. David Graeber, summarising the extensive anthropological work on this topic, describes 'value' as 'the way people represent the importance of their own actions to themselves … [that] can only happen through that importance being recognized by someone else'.[42] For Graeber, 'actions' include both the production of goods and the maintenance of social relations, with 'value' indicating the relative distribution

[40] The frequency of *tim-* vocabulary in the *TLG* throughout antiquity reflects the centrality of this notion in Greek societies: the verb τιμάω (giving someone his or her due *time*) shows nearly 25,000 occurrences, the noun τίμη itself 27,000. All *tim-* vocabulary relies on recognition of value by others, both within the legal sphere and beyond it. The meanings revolving around evaluation and negotiation are also present in the cognate verbs. Analysis of *time* and its meanings deserves a study of at least the size of the present one. Scholarship so far has focused mainly on *time* in Homer and Homeric society, e.g. Van Wees (1992), Cairns (1993), Finkelberg (1998), Scodel (2008) and *philotimia* as a virtue and incentive for Athenian citizens, e.g. Whitehead (1983), Luraghi (2010), Osborne (2010a), Lambert (2011). For recent discussions, notably on understanding *time* not only as 'honour' but more widely as 'value', Cairns (2011); Van 't Wout (2010b), Van 't Wout (2011a) shows that the translation of *time* by 'honour' is inadequate to understand its usage in many social contexts.

[41] LSJ *s.v.* τιμή. Most examples in LSJ concerning *time* derive from literary texts. In fifth- and fourth-century inscriptions *time* is normally used for price or value/costs (of objects) (*IG* I³ 64 B 28, 30; 182.12; 370.65 etc.); evaluation of persons is normally expressed by the specific honours given (e.g. praise, privileges) or their reverse (penalties, fines). For the immediate connection between the 'positive' and 'negative' sides of the same social values, Graeber (2001) 83–4. For reciprocity underlying Athenian notions of crime, transgression and punishment, Allen (2000) 50–72.

[42] Graeber (2001) 23–47 for critical discussion of several anthropological theories of value; quoted 45.

of all these 'actions' and the recognition of their importance to and by the society concerned. *Time* fits this conception of 'value' well, as it indicates such an evaluation both as a process and as its outcome pertaining to all 'actions' (goods, social relations).

In a social context, *time* entailed recognition of one's social *persona*, shown by receiving what one might expect to be one's due. Between two individuals, such behaviour expressed in *tim-* vocabulary entailed being treated with due respect, for instance seeing one's request 'honoured'. At the level of the *polis*, *time* was the outcome of what the individual offered to the community and what the community would give in return. Underlying this process we recognise the workings of reciprocity, with concomitant management of expectations on both sides of the relationship. To understand *timai* as the outcome of a wider system of *time*, i.e. a shared notion of 'value' setting the rules for the assignment of *timai*, I return to Douglass North's conception of 'institutions' introduced in Chapter 3, now quoting him at some length:

> A crucial distinction in this study is made between institutions and organizations. Like institutions, organizations provide a structure to human interaction.... Conceptually, what must be clearly differentiated are the rules from the players. The purpose of the rules is to define the way the game is played. But the objective of the team within that set of rules is to win the game.... Organizations include political bodies, economic bodies, social bodies, and educational bodies. They are groups of individuals bound by some common purpose to achieve objectives ... they influence how the institutional framework evolves... [I]nstitutions are the underlying rules of the game, ... the focus on organizations (and their entrepreneurs) is primarily on their role as agents of institutional change.... Separating the analysis of the underlying rules from the strategy of the players is a necessary prerequisite to building a theory of institutions.[43]

With North's conceptions we can characterise *time* as a fundamental institution of the *polis* for the distribution of *timai*. *Time*, as we just saw, is a particular form of recognition of reciprocity; the necessary negotiation of and recurrent disagreements over *time* are widely attested in our sources. Combined with 'positive' evidence on the procedures and the discourse of such evaluation, we can delineate the main rules of the process: 1) the assessment of one's value to the community, based on valuation of one's material (wealth) and non-material ('good' birth, prowess, knowledge etc.) assets, with additional rules for the significance of gender and age; 2) the display of conduct appropriate to one's value; 3) the bestowal of *visible*

[43] North (1990) 4–5.

recognition of the valuation thus attained (*time*) by the community; with 4) the possibility to achieve particular honours (*timai*), among which public offices.[44]

For understanding how *time* fed into the organisation of the *polis* and vice versa, we need to appreciate a second aspect of North's conception: institutions, as the rules of the game, shape people's attitudes, aims and expectations underlying their actual doings in organisations and society at large. The difference between such informal constraints and formal ones (qualifications, procedures) is one of degree, not essence.[45] On this view, we may identify various norms concurrent with and supportive of *time* in the *polis* as informal constraints and the numerous procedures (wealth assessment, means of selection, *dokimasia*, *euthynai et al.* mentioned above) as the formal ones on the effectuation of *time*. This approach helps to explain why it proves so difficult to identify features that clearly distinguish *archai* from other *timai*: they all belonged to the same institution of social evaluation in which they followed in major respects the same rules for their assignment as public office and honour. Once we understand this underlying pattern, we may better appreciate the differences between them.

Historical changes in the assignment of *archai* have been studied intensively. I do not intend to reproduce that work here, but building on it I discuss how both *archai* and other *timai* were distributed on the four main rules of assignment outlined above. Beginning with the basic notion of *time*, I move on to the assignment of *timai* with special attention for the connection between 'politics' and 'religion' in the *archai* and other *timai*, and for gender as a criterion for access. Beside formal procedures, evaluation of conduct was a partly formal, partly informal constraint on the assignment of *time*. Of specific importance, especially in the eyes of the Athenians, in the assignment of *timai* were the means of selection – election, allotment or a combination of both. In the conclusion of this chapter I return to differences between *archai* and priesthoods and to the meaning of gender in their distribution.

5.3 Assessment of *Time*: the Baseline

To assign *time* to individuals, the *polis* classified all with whom it entertained a relationship into *groups*, by estimating what they might contribute

[44] For the importance of visibility in granting *time*, Van 't Wout (2010b).
[45] North (1990) 3–4, 36–46.

to the community and of what was due to them in return in terms of recognition by or claims in the *polis*. Based on this general reciprocity, the *polis* granted fitting value (*time*) to these groups and to the individuals belonging to them. From time to time the *polis* revised and established its estimation of the qualifications of groups and their access to *timai* in law. Vital questions are who represented 'the *polis*' and what was considered 'fitting'. In the classical age, the answer to the first question was firmly the assembly, and in case of conflict the courts. The answers to the second question changed over time and were influenced by contingent factors as well. No two groups were expected to contribute the same kinds of assets or value to the community, so the system differentiated between groups in terms of quantity and quality of their (expected) values and consequently tended to prioritise or even fix a hierarchy between them. As each citizen belonged to several groups (for instance, being a female citizen of marriageable age or a male citizen over thirty), everyone knew what her/his basic *time* in the *polis* normally would be. The evidence from Athens suggests that the many variables making up the *time* of groups and individuals constituted an intricate web of values and expectations that every Athenian was familiar with. Negotiation and hence strife were inherent in this system, and our sources tend to highlight conflicts at least as much as social consensus. Each individual might expect to receive *time* at different levels, or to different degrees; individuals could surpass or fall short of the others in the same group.[46]

The first and major group with whom the *polis* had established its reciprocal relationship were the gods, and the *time* the *polis* gave them (and the *time* the gods granted humans, both individually and collectively) was also a key value in the relationships at human level.[47]

On the human side of the *polis*, *time* as primary recognition and *timai* – in the general meaning of 'honours' – were granted both to citizens and to outsiders; to articulate the value of these individuals to the *polis*, a vocabulary developed of what David Whitehead has aptly called 'cardinal

[46] For such contests and the importance of settling them publicly in 'a situation of critical reference', Van 't Wout (2010b), Van 't Wout (2011a). An individual's *time* could be affected by contingent factors in one's life, either positively, for instance by victory in the Olympic Games or winning a battle, or negatively, for instance by family disasters like debts to the *polis*. See also below, Chapter 5.6, for citizens' conduct.

[47] E.g. Pl. *Euthyphro* 15a9: 'Well, what would those gifts of ours to the gods be?' 'What else than *time* and *geras* and, what I mentioned before, *charis*?' Eur. *Hipp.* 55–6: Hippolytos offers *time* to Artemis in hymns; 1402: Artemis explains to Hippolytos the reason for Aphrodite's anger that ultimately made Theseus discard him and that caused his death: 'she complained about her [neglected] *time* and hated your chastity'. [Lys.] 6.3: 'the two goddesses take recompense (*timoreo*) of those who act against *dike*'.

virtues' that in law and discourse were the motive for awarding *timai*.[48] Implementing the notion of *metechein* both at an elementary level and in more prominent *timai*, the *polis* developed a great diversity of participatory roles for the various groups making up the community of citizens.[49] In the archaic age, so Duplouy and Ismard, these groups were probably identified by their professional or economic functions and their contributions to cult.[50] The criterion of descent gradually intervened into this social fabric and became the predominant criterion of being 'citizens', as we saw in Chapter 3. In the classical age the *polis* distinguished, firstly, between free and slave, although the rituals of inclusion of domestic slaves in the *oikos* show that they were valued differently from other slaves. Among the free the crucial distinction between 'citizens' and 'non-citizens', drawn by citizens' descent from citizen parents, became more stringently defined over time, especially in Pericles' law.

A citizen's primary *time* entailed his or her recognition as a member by the *polis* for being of legitimate birth (*astos*, *aste*; *Athenaios*, *Athenaia*) and that recognition created particular expectations and enabled performance of particular roles. Being an acknowledged citizen meant that one was accepted in the relevant groups, i.e. that one was justified in expecting to be heard when one raised one's voice, to participate in activities of these groups and to fulfil fitting roles in them following formal rules or conventions, gender and age usually being important criteria. Refusing a citizen any of these if there was no reason to question his or her being a legitimate Athenian meant refusing due *time*, and an affront. The *polis* could justly do so only in case of a citizen's conflict with or damage to the community (see section 5.6 below).This elementary recognition of citizen status with concomitant participation I call the baseline of *time*.

The first domain in which all citizens who met the criteria of legitimate birth were expected to participate was that of *polis* cult in the widest sense. That for one's status as a citizen and hence one's *time* participation in cult

[48] Whitehead (1993); see further below, Chapter 5.6. General honours: Lys. 2 (*Or.*) 79: 'the memories of them will be timeless, their *timai* will be striven after by all mankind'. The so-called *megalai timai*, i.e. privileges and other honorific gifts that the *polis* could confer on citizens and non-citizens, usually with public praise immortalised on a stele, were *inter alia* a meal at public cost in the *prytaneion* (*sitesis*); sitting in the front row of the theatre (*prohedria*); a valuable golden crown to be dedicated to the gods; a statue, and many others.

[49] This chapter is concerned with the *timai* of citizens, but the valuation of outsiders (non-citizens) followed the same rules, for which see Chapter 6.

[50] See also above, Chapter 3, n. 30; Duplouy (2014) 653, also drawing on Ismard (2010) 13–39, 44–57, identifies 'functional groups who defined themselves and based their identity on their daily life in certain practices of archaic Athenian society, after the example of the groups in the law on associations (LR F 76a–b) ascribed to Solon' (transl. JB).

was of prime importance is borne out by the court cases on legitimate descent, where to prove their citizen status the defendants point to their sharing, without anyone objecting, in *hiera* of the *polis* and its subgroups, in the case of men especially of the phratries, never to their presence in the assembly or *dikasterion*.[51] The reasons for this focus on cult participation, I would argue, are both practical and principal: practical in that the scrutiny of legitimate descent took place in the phratries, groups of a relatively small size where all members knew each other, and where one's membership was grounded in 'deep' ritual; principal in that citizens were expected to share actively in the cult of the gods of the *polis* in the conventional manner whether or not they partook in political office, as the trial for *asebeia* of Socrates, who had served on the *boule*, exemplifies.

In some respects, the institution of *time* also applied to children: once accepted as of legitimate birth, they participated in various festivals and rituals, preparing them for *polis* life from an early age.[52] Such cultic activities for citizen children ranged from the rituals of the phratry to the Choes feast, a day of drinking wine, of the Anthesteria (a feast perhaps mainly for male citizens but the vases show girls, too, so the sources are ambiguous here) and in the cult of Artemis Brauronia (mainly girls, but also votives for boys are attested).[53] Others were open only to boys, such as participating in boys' contests at the Dionysia, or only to girls, such as the procession of young girls in the Delphinia, the roles of little bears in the cult of Artemis Brauronia and the prominent public role of an *arrhephoros* in the cult of Athena (the latter two probably elite girls only).[54] The Basileus also selected a so-called 'child of the hearth', a girl or a boy who played a ritual role in the Mysteries.[55] Children fulfilling such prominent roles also conferred honour on their parents. However, as holding a formal function in

[51] Dem. 57.54; Humphreys (2007 (orig. 1985)) for the social character of evidence in such witnesses.

[52] Arist. *Pol.* 1275a14–18 describes children as citizens 'in potential', on their way to the full citizenship as he defines it, and compares them with elderly men who are active citizens no longer; apparently, Aristotle had in mind the capacity for military service as a criterion for active citizenship. Citizen children were also by law especially protected against what might be labelled sexual harrassment, notably by slaves, which was surely felt as an infringement of their and their parents' *time*.

[53] Parker, *PS*, 232–48, 290–316. Boys: statue of a little boy, museum at Brauron, room 2; Themelis (1971) 70 and photo opposite.

[54] *Arrhephoroi*: Parker, *PS*, 219–23; Goff (2004) 180–1. On the *arktoi* and whether or not only a select group of girls participated, Parker, *PS*, 232–48; Goff (2004) 181–3; Hamilton (1989).

[55] For the child of the hearth, first attested ca. 460 (*IG* I^{3} 6, C. 24–6), the means of selection are unclear. In the fourth century the child was selected by the Basileus by lot from all who were registered (*Ag.* 16.56 [3] (367–348?), ll. 41–2; Harp. / Suda α 4590 *s.v.* ἀφ ἑστιάς μυηθῆναι (referring to Isaeus); Clinton (1974) 98–100). In the second century AD, the child sacrificed and prayed for the *polis*; evidence for its actual role in the classical age is lacking. Between the second century BC and the first century AD, thirteen individual boys and girls 'of the hearth' are known.

public affairs is central to the notion of citizenship, only adults normally count as citizens and, in what follows, we focus on them.

The variety in terms of gender and age in the groups sharing cults and festivals was immense, but never random: the rules of their composition were well established by law or custom and so were the ways in which each group was to participate.[56] In some cults and festivals distinction as to gender, further specified by age, was the leading principle. These gender-separated festivals tended to be concerned with the ritual stages of maturation from child to adult for each sex, for adult men with the *phylai* as political and military communities and for adult women with fertility and sexuality for the procreation of the *polis*. An Athenian boy, on acceptance in the phratry, participated in the festivities of the Apatouria together with the adult *phrateres*. Girls were presented to phratries, too, and women (wives) were presented to the phratries during the *gamelia*, but in the main sacrifices and the oaths on legitimacy only men were involved.[57] In ritual competitions, for instance in the choruses for Dionysus, adult men and boys participated, but now separated into distinct groups with their own cultic programmes. For the adult men, the *phylai* were the major organisational units for which admission, through the demes, was fixed at age eighteen, to be followed by the *ephebeia* (at least in the later fourth century); within such units, men could compete in a variety of roles (chorus member, chorus leader, a range of athletics etc.). The major festival of adult citizen women was the Thesmophoria in honour of Demeter, celebrated all over Attica and organised by the women.

Other festivals and cults were celebrated by men and women together, usually with distinct roles according to gender. In the Oschophoria, commemorating the mythical tribute to Minos and Theseus' successful struggle against it, young men played a prominent role, but so did married

[56] For festivals and their dates, Mikalson (1975) and Parker, *PS*, 155–77 and App. 1. For many festivals the evidence for participation is uneven or inconclusive, but certainly or probably for women only (some for *astai* only, others for all free women) were the Thesmophoria, Thesmophoria in Halimous, Stenia, Haloa, Theogamia, Adonia, Tauropolia, Brauronia and *pannychides* (all-night revels) in several other festivals (Bendidea, Epidauria, Asklepieia); see also Dillon (2002) 109–38. Predominantly for women with a few men in specific roles: Skira. Certainly or probably for men only: Artemis Agrotera, Theseia, Dipolieia, Olympieia, Demokratia, Pandia. Certainly or probably mixed with different roles for and numbers of men and women: Anthesteria, Chalkeia, Kronia, Panathenaea, Genesia, Plynteria, City Dionysia, rural Dionysia, Lenaia, Proerosia, Oschophoria. In the Eleusinian Mysteries, no gender differences seemed to apply. See also Blok (2001) 112–15; representation in Athenian vase painting of groups in religious actions according to gender, Borgers (2008).

[57] The exact age of boys at this ritual is not known and may have varied from phratry to phratry; Lambert (1998) 161–8. Girls and women, see above, Chapter 3.

women representing the mothers of the youths sent off with Theseus.[58] Before the Great Mysteries at Eleusis, ephebes held a procession from Athens to Eleusis and back again, carrying *hiera*; next, the whole *polis* participated in the festival.[59] In the procession of the Panathenaea, representatives of various groups in terms of gender and age of citizens (and metics) had roles of prominence: the citizens were represented among others by *kanephoroi*, elderly men, and hoplites, the metics by girls carrying parasols, women carrying *hydriai* and men clad in crimson mantles. A long line of Athenian demesmen followed, many others belonging to the *polis* watched the procession and the whole was supervised by the priestess of Athena Polias. Similarly, the City Dionysia opened with a *pompe* in which the whole *polis* participated, citizens and metics, women and men, with distinct clothing and attributes.[60] The Anthesteria, celebrating Dionysus, included, beside Choes, a day of offering to Hermes Chthonios (Chytroi) in which the whole household was involved.

Normally, at the baseline citizens' participation in the cults of the *polis* meant receiving a citizen's portion of meat at a common sacrifice, walking in a procession, being initiated into the Eleusinian Mysteries (non-Athenians needed an introduction), joining a *pannychis* (nightly feast) and all other forms of sharing a cult or festival, roles that even if they were obscure were essential in the performance of citizenship.[61] The other side of this coin was that participating in a cult as if one were a citizen when one in fact was not was a severe transgression. Doing so was already offensive in an obscure role, but could be made out to be unforgivable in one of the more prominent *timai* of the ritual. A client of Dinarchus accused a certain Agasikles of being a metic who had bribed his way into citizen status, presenting his sons in the Panathenaic procession as Athenian ephebes instead of *skaphephoroi* as had befitted them as metics.[62] The passage from Apollodoros heading this chapter concerns the high-profile case against the former *hetaira* and non-Athenian Neaira, which is discussed in more detail below.

Beside the domain of cult, the domain of *arche* was central to participation in the *polis*. In *arche*, gender distinction predominated: in this

58 Parker, *PS*, 214–15.

59 For the representative character of the Panathenaea, see Chapter 4, n. 32; Chapter 5, n. 87; for metics, Chapter 5.2.

60 Sourvinou-Inwood (1994) 270–2.

61 For such obscure roles, Jameson (1999). In Chapter 3, I argued that Solon's measures to redeem Athenians in debt bondage presupposed that it was more or less clear who were Athenians, a notion that probably was based, beside on descent, on presence at cults and festivals.

62 Din. fr. 7; cf. Hyp. 4.3.

domain men prevailed overwhelmingly, although we must keep the reservations made above in mind, avoiding the circular argument that an *arche* was *defined* by being fulfilled by a male citizen. Whether before Solon this baseline participation in *arche* required ownership of some land or a prolonged claim to tenure cannot be ascertained, but free status was surely conditional.[63] In the classical age, at the baseline all men over eighteen accepted as legitimate citizens in their demes could participate in deme meetings and in the *polis* assembly; from the age of thirty, all citizen men could present themselves for serving in the *dikasteria*. For practical as well as principal reasons, it makes sense to distinguish these two roles from access to the majority of *archai*, which in the fifth century required further distinctions.[64] As mentioned before, *archai* and their distribution have been studied intensively; in what follows I highlight some specific features to clarify their role in the larger fabric of *timai*.

5.4 Beyond the Baseline

Beyond the baseline the *polis* could grant specific *time* in recompense for higher qualifications, larger contributions or services rendered, in the form of privileges and honours, among which the formal, more prominent roles or offices of the *polis*. For access to such *timai*, formal and informal distinctions were made between citizens due to wealth or birth. Assessment of wealth (*timema*) for offices shows in the *tim-* vocabulary the transformation of the value of property into recognition for positions of social prominence. Some *archai*, notably the Tamiai of Athena, probably instituted by Solon, were selected by lot from among the group defined by law as the wealthiest (the Pentakosiomedimnoi) still in the fourth century.[65] For

63 Since in the classical age only citizens could own land, except when the *demos* granted an outsider the same right, some scholars (e.g. Manville (1990) 93–6, Boegehold (1994)) assume that citizenship depended on ownership of land, but they do not explain what they mean by citizenship, in particular whether this means baseline participation or access to (elevated) *archai*. Foxhall (1997) 117–19 criticises both studies for using unsuitable ethnographic comparisons on landholding. If we accept as historical the account that Solon allowed capable outsiders settling in Attica to become *politai*, these men probably attended the assembly without owning land.

64 Aristotle (*Pol.* 1275a24–30) regards the fact that jury service and participation in the assembly are not restricted in time, an argument against classifying them as *archai*, but the political role of the courts in their control of magistrates, their oversight of fellow citizens and the importance of justice for a well-ordered *polis* as arguments in favour of such a qualification. For the *dikastai* as *archai*: Ar. *Vesp.* 578–87; cf. Blanshard (2004) 34–5. For the assembly in the Agora as the elementary form of political participation from Homer onwards, Hölkeskamp (1997), Hölkeskamp (1999) 271, Hölkeskamp (2002b).

65 Tamiai of Athena selected by lot from the Pentakosiomedimnoi: *Ath.Pol.* 8.1; *IG* I^3 52A, 13–15; Suda τ 58 *s.v.* Ταμίαι: ἄρχοντές εἰσιν Ἀθήνησι κληρωτοὶ ἀπὸ τῶν πεντακοσιομεδίμνων, οἳ τὰ ἐν τῷ ἱερῷ τῆς Ἀθηνᾶς ἐν ἀκροπόλει χρήματα ἱερά τε καὶ δημόσια φυλάττουσιν, ἀλλὰ καὶ αὐτὸ

performing liturgies such as the *choregia* and the trierarchy, financial contributions that bestowed honour on the giver (unlike taxes such as the *eisphora* that did not ostensibly did so), individuals were elected from among those citizens (and depending on the occasion, metics) estimated wealthy enough to be able to perform them; no legal criteria for this wealth seem to have been set.[66] For other *timai*, birth in a particular family was required; this pertained notably to priesthoods held by the *gene*, to be discussed below. For other honorific roles, the impression is that only 'elite' citizens had access to them, but we do not always know exactly which criteria, formal or informal, were used.

Traditionally, wealth and birth in a prominent family were thought to engender merit, but democratic values counteracted such conventions. Democracy meant increasing emphasis on equality among citizens, enacted in lowering or abandonment of the criteria for specific *timai*, so that ultimately (nearly) all citizens could share in the majority of them; the fact that their basic *time* made them in principle equally eligible for these offices was precisely what constituted the core value of the fully developed democracy. Democracy also meant an expanding ideology to participate in the *polis*, with strong obligations of every citizen to contribute to the city's welfare,[67] and a political discourse aiming at control by the *polis*, represented in the *boule* and assembly, over its own affairs.

As a result of these tendencies, the number of *timai* and *archai* increased over time, many of which as multiple boards and filled by rotation.[68] This was not a steady increase, as the growth of the Athenian empire and its loss in the fifth century first added and subsequently reduced the

τὸ ἄγαλμα τῆς Ἀθηνᾶς. According to *Ath.Pol.* 4.1, the Tamiai were elected in the 'constitution of Draco', generally held to be of a later date than claimed by the *Ath.Pol.*, an impression now convincingly grounded by Van Wees (2011).

66 Davies, *APF*, xx–xxi draws on attested figures for various liturgies and for the capital owned by families (usually inheritances), on the individual members of which he collected the evidence, to conclude that property below three talents was 'free from liturgical obligations, while men whose property was worth over 4 tal. were very unlikely to escape such obligations in the long run' (xxiv). Although Davies often uses the term 'census class', apparently no clear-cut capital criterion was laid down in law: very wealthy families clearly were obliged to pay liturgies, those not well-off clearly were not, leaving a grey area in the middle liable to negotiation, contestation or the effects of *philotimia*. For *eisphora*, see also below, Chapter 6.2.

67 See for these obligations esp. Liddel (2007), and for avoidance of them Christ (2006).

68 In the fourth century, there were about 1,200 *archai*, according to Hansen (1991) 230–1, of which 500 *bouleutai* and 600 other *archai* were selected by lot and ca. 100 *archai* were filled by election; for a description of the selection and their political functions, Hansen (1991) 225–65. To this number, the *dikastai* drawn for each session from a pool of 6,000 must be added. Allen (2000) 310–16 arrives at the same numbers, all based on the lists in *Ath.Pol.*, without additional epigraphic evidence. For rotation, lot and the function of multiple bodies of office in Athens's democratic system, Manin (1997) 8–41, Headlam (1933).

number of *archai*, but the list of offices in the late fourth-century *Ath.Pol.* 42–69 is very likely much longer than a similar list would have been in the early fifth century. Not only the number of *archai* increased. The festival calendar at Athens grew in the course of the fifth and fourth centuries into a densely packed schedule of cultic festivities for which the *polis* became famous. For all of these activities, cult personnel and (financial) supervision were necessary, providing new roles (*timai*) for citizens. The evidence offers far more information on male positions than on female ones, partly due to the overall bias of our sources towards the parts of the public domain in the male sphere of interest, and partly because the number of offices for men increased far more than those for women and consequently left more traces.[69] I discuss a few instances of this process, first very briefly the gradual lowering of criteria for *archai*, next the role of gender in the distribution of *timai* in the sphere of cult and its finances, and finally the responsibility of the archons, the *boule* and other *archai* for *hiera kai hosia*.

The most elevated *archai* of the *polis* were the nine archons, even if in the course of the fifth century the *strategoi* overtook them in influence in the assembly. Archons, *bouleutai* and *dikastai* had to be at least thirty years of age.[70] Before Solon, the archonships apparently circulated among an elite whose *time* due to wealth or military power was bolstered by accounts of impressive descent from gods or heroes; strife must have been recurrent in this system.[71] On the *Ath.Pol.*'s account, some division into property classes existed before Solon regulated access to the archonships and the Tamiai by quantifying the contributions in agricultural produce of households, called either *tele*, referring to the agricultural *telos* (result) or *timemata*, the evaluations of a household's contribution to the *polis*'s economy and military capacity, and restricting the most prestigious *timai* to the wealthiest group.[72] How such *timemata* were carried out, is unclear;

[69] *Ath.Pol.* 43–53 lists several male cultic offices but no female one, such as we know from other, literary and epigraphical, evidence; the male offices mentioned by *Ath.Pol.* were selected by the assembly, but we do not know the means of selection of many of the women's.

[70] Xen. *Mem.* 1.2.35; Dem. 22.1.1.

[71] For the composition of the archaic elite, Duplouy (2006), and especially Duplouy (2010) and Duplouy (2014) for a refutation of the so-called Eupatridai as a true 'aristocracy of birth' before Solon, and Węcowski (2014) 19–83 (both building on work of Benedetto Bravo).

[72] *Ath.Pol.* 7.3–4 with Rhodes, *CAAP ad loc.*; *Ath.Pol.* 8.1; Isoc. 12.131; Diod.S. 18.18.4; Poll. *Onom.* 8.129. Among scholars who basically accept the account of *Ath.Pol.* there is no consensus if Solon restricted the archonship to the top one or top two classes. In the debate over the Solonian property classes, both on the structure of the evidence and on the meaning of the classes themselves, I agree with Foxhall (1997) and Van Wees (2006) that the *tele* were based on landed wealth, rather than military recruitment, as defended by Raaflaub (2006).

W.R. Connor suggested that wealthy households presented themselves showing agricultural produce, a mode akin to the offering of first fruits in agricultural festivals and thus drawing on existing religious practices.[73] Solon's four property classes and the concomitant distribution of political office are currently fundamentally questioned, among others by Duplouy, who doubts Solon's institution of census classes but does not address the question how the archonships were distributed among claimants from the groups constituting the *polis*. That such property divisions existed and regulated access to *archai* in the fifth century is certain, but if Solon was not the man who introduced the census classes, was it Cleisthenes, or rather Ephialtes, as K.A. Raaflaub supposes?[74] If Solon introduced some system for assigning the archonships, which in itself is not improbable, it functioned only partially in the sixth century.[75] Cleisthenes reintroduced a more open selection of archons, and in 457 candidates from the class of the *zeugitai* could present themselves.[76] Membership of the Cleisthenic *boule* of 500 was an *arche* filled perhaps not in principle but in practice by the more wealthy, at least in the fifth century, until payment of *misthos* opened offices also to citizens of the poorer classes; *misthos* for the *bouleutai* is attested from the 420s onwards.[77] The 'Solonian' criteria gradually lost their meaning for the selection of most *archai*, although officially they were never abolished.[78] For some *timai* such as liturgies and the most important financial offices, however, substantial wealth remained a practical or a formal requirement.

For the *polis*'s *hiera*, the *polis* appointed first of all priests and priestesses. Their primary duty was offering sacrifice on behalf of the *polis* or a subgroup, to say prayers and to carry out other rituals prescribed by tradition;[79] furthermore, they were responsible for their sanctuaries, their purity and their finances. The gender required for the priesthoods often corresponded to that of the deity, i.e. a male priest served a male god and a priestess a goddess, but the exceptions to this rule are numerous: just as

[73] Rhodes, *CAAP* 141–2; Connor (1987) 47–9.

[74] Raaflaub (2006).

[75] *Ath.Pol.* 13; Hdt. 1.59; Thuc. 6.54.5–7. For the methods of selecting archons in the long sixth century, Develin (1979).

[76] Cleisthenes: *Ath.Pol.* 22.1, 5; *zeugitai*: *Ath.Pol.* 26.2.

[77] For clear discussion of the ambiguous evidence, Rhodes (1972) 4–6. Payment of *bouleutai* is indicated in *IG* I³ 82, a decree on the festival of Hephaistos of 421/0; in l. 20, βολευταί is restored, but given the context very plausible. Thuc. 8.69: when in 412 the Four Hundred sent the *bouleutai* of the abolished democracy home, they gave them their *misthos* till the end of their office year.

[78] *Ath.Pol.* 47.1.

[79] Many prayers were orally transmitted within the restricted circle of the office, professional knowledge that gave special authority to the priests and priestesses; Hitch (2011).

in participation at the baseline, in the *timai* serving cults gender separation was far from absolute. For instance, the goddesses Demeter and Kore at Eleusis were served by priestesses of the *genos* Philleidai as well as by the male hierophants of the *genos* Eumolpidai and dadouchs of the *genos* Kerykes. The procession and sacrifices of the Oschophoria for Theseus were led by the priestess of Athena Skiras of the *genos* Salaminioi. Fourteen Geraiai (or Gerarai), who probably belonged to the *genos* Theoinai, celebrated rites for Dionysus at the Anthesteria.[80] All of these were priesthoods and cultic roles belonging to the *gene*, to whose qualifications based on birth I return below.

Of the other personnel carrying out rituals, assisting with the sacrifice or administering the property of a god(dess), some were modest, others very prominent, but the status of offices is not always borne out by the evidence, nor are the details of selection and time of office. I select a few examples.

At the age of around sixteen, girls were selected to be a *kanephoros*, to carry the *kanoun* (sacrificial basket) in front of a procession, as the chorus famously sings in Aristophanes' *Lysistrata* (640–6). In this scene the *koryphaia* (leader of the women's chorus) recounts this series of feminine *timai* as her upbringing by the city, in recompense for which she now offers her advice to the *polis*. She does so in terms of her *meteinai* of the community, over and against the men who have squandered their *patroia* in the war and hence their right to *meteinai*.[81] Young men, too, served as *kanephoroi*; to go by the representations in vase paintings, they held this role less frequently than female *kanephoroi*.[82] Also the way they did so differs in these scenes: the girls carry only the *kanoun*, on their heads, walking in an upright position that suggests a demarcated, ritual role; the young men carry the *kanoun* more loosely, often together with other things such as sprigs, *oinochoai*, a horn and a spit, in a way suggestive of a more practical, less ritualised role. Presumably being a *kanephoros* was initially a role restricted to the elite, but it may have become more widely accessible in the course of the time.[83] Considering the frequency of cultic

[80] Geraiai: Parker, *PS* 163, 304; individual Geraiai in the classical age: Chairestrate (*IG* II² 6288, fourth century).

[81] Ar. *Lys*. 638–57. The evidence shows many such rituals and roles for *parthenoi*, some of which carried the character of initiation rites; Parker, *PS*, 218–52.

[82] I owe these observations to Renée Dircks (Dircks (2012) 49–53). On vases depicting processions dating 570–420, Dircks found seventeen female and seven male *kanephoroi*.

[83] *Kanephoroi*: Parker, *PS*, 223–6, 258–66; Shear (2001) 130–2. Elite: Philochoros *FGrH* 328 F 8. Girls close to marriageable age, wearing a special type of 'back mantle', represented on around sixty grave and votive reliefs found at Athens, may well be *kanephoroi*; see Roccos (2000) 261.

actions requiring sacrifice of an animal to be taken to the altar in a festive procession, be it large or small, the number of *kanephoroi* every year must have been pretty large and in fact increasing over time. In the classical age, nearly fifty substantial sacrificial processions of the *polis* took place every year, usually in the context of a festival, some of which consisting of more than one day with several sacrifices.[84] Some of the most prominent seem to have been headed by more than one *kanephoros*, such as the Panathenaea, which was preceded by a large number of these basket bearers.[85] To this number the sacrificial processions of *polis* subgroups (phratries, *gene*, *phylai*, demes) and perhaps of the semi-private cult societies (*thiasoi*, *orgeones*) should be added, which were also probably headed by a *kanephoros*.[86]

Other examples of cultic roles for women were the *trapezophoroi* (who carried *trapezai* for sacrifices) and the *diakonos* of Athena Polias, who assisted the priestess.[87] The function of *zakoros* (serving in a temple) was held both by women and by men: female *zakoroi* were active in the sanctuaries of Athena Polias and of the Mother of the Gods; male *zakoroi* are attested for Demeter and Kore and for Asclepius.[88]

In the domain of *hiera* the *polis* set up specific offices, filled by male citizens, to manage parts of the cults, the sanctuaries and especially the finances, posts that were either added to the existing cult personnel or

84 Based on Mikalson (1975): *Hekatombaion*: Hekatombaia, Kronia, Synoikia with a pre-sacrifice (biannual), Panathenaea; *Metageitnion*: sacrifice of the Salaminioi; Metageitnia, Eleusinia (biannual); *Boedromion*: Niketeria; festival for Athena to celebrate the battle of Plataia; Genesia; Artemis Agrotera (battle of Marathon); Boedromia; festival for the 'heroes of Phylai' (= Demokratia?); sacrifice for Demeter and Kore (pre-Mysteries); Epidauria; *Pyanopsion*: Proerosia (?); Oschophoria; Pyanopsia; sacrifice for Konnidas; Theseia (sacrifices to Theseus and the Amazones); Stenia; Thesmophoria in Halimous; Thesmophoria; Chalkeia; Apatouria; *Maimakterion*: Pompaia; *Posideon*: Posideia; Haloa; rural Dionysia; *Gamelion*: Theogamia; Gamelia; Lenaia; *Anthesterion*: Anthesteria; Diasia; Mysteries at Agrai; *Elaphebolion*: sacrifice to Asclepius; City Dionysia; Pandia; *Mounichion*: festival for Artemis Mounichia; Olympieia; *Thargelion*: Thargelia; Bendideia; Plynteria; Kallynteria; *Skirophorion*: Arrhephoria; Skira; Dipolieia; sacrifice to Zeus Soter. Date unknown: procession and sacrifice to the Semnai Theai.

85 The law and decree on the Little Panathenaea (RO 81; ca. 335) in B l. 15 arranges meat portions to be given to the [κανηφόροι]ς. Lycurgus is credited ([Plut.] 852b) with providing 'gold ornaments for a hundred *kanephoroi*' for the Panathenaea, but this large number was perhaps not active on every single occasion (see Parker, *PS*, 224 with refs).

86 The presence neither of *kanephoroi* nor of any other such attribute provides a clear distinction into 'public' or 'private' processions, Blok (2009c).

87 *Trapezophoros*: *IG* II² 1534.337 (ca. 275); the *diakonos* Syeris, assisting the priestess of Athena Polias, Lysimache, *IG* II² 3464 (third century) with Keesling (2012). For female cult personnel, Georgoudi (2005), for the public representations of all cult personnel Von den Hoff (2008).

88 Female *zakoroi*: Athena: *IG* I³ 4, B l. 14 (Hekatompedon inscription) inscribed 485/4, see Chapter 4, n. 114. Mother of the Gods: *IG* II² 1328 (183/2). Male *zakoroi*: [Lys.] 6.54: Zakoros, hierophant of Demeter and Kore (probably a case of hieronymy). *Zakoroi* of Asclepius: *IG* II² 4466, 4481, 4514 (Roman times); the opinion of Weiss (2004) 152 that in Roman times the *zakoros* 'was often a slave' (transl. JB) is not supported by the Athenian evidence.

taking over their financial responsibilities, as we saw above. Sacrifices were paid for, in kind or in money, partly by the gods themselves, partly by humans; in the course of time more human money, public as well as private, came into the picture.[89] The *polis* and its subgroups arranged to pay for these sacrifices, some of which are listed with the necessary costs in inscribed sacrificial calendars.[90] The Tamiai of Athena were the first and most prominent offices of this kind, whose financial authority extended beyond the cult of Athena proper and at some point included responsibility of the *polis*'s treasuries.[91] After the Tamiai, the *polis* set up such offices for increasing numbers of cults. The athletic competitions for the Panathenaia were initially organised by *hieropoioi*, who carried out other duties for the festival when they were replaced by *athlotetai* in the fifth century.[92] *Hieropoioi* appear in many cults and festivals in the fifth and fourth centuries, as do *epistatai*, for instance of the Eleusinian Mysteries, and *epimeletai*, among whom those organising the Dionysia, and many others we saw listed in the *Ath.Pol.* as *archai*.

Given their combined duties for the *hiera* and their finances on behalf of the *demos*, it makes no sense to try to separate 'cult' from 'politics' in these *archai*. That responsibility for *hiera kai hosia* was central to *arche* more widely is exemplified first of all in the three most prominent archonships described in *Ath.Pol.* (56–8): in many cults and festivals, they oversaw the proper performance of the sacrifices or other rituals carried out by or under the authority of the priests and priestesses, and the Polemarchos also carried out sacrifices himself.[93] *Hosie*/ *hosia* were involved in three ways: (1) *hosie* in the sense of rules about *hiera*, including the composition of the (sacrificial) group, in this case the *polis* of the Athenians; (2) *hosie* in

89 On public and *hieros* property funding *hiera*, see Chapter 2.5.3; for increasing private next to public funding in the sixth to fourth centuries, Whitehead (1986a) 174.

90 The first calendar for the *polis* in its entirety that we know of was drawn up by Solon (LR F 83–6), edited and republished by Nikomachos and his colleagues (see Chapter 2.5.1). Demes: Thorikos, *NGSL* no. 1; Erchia (*LSCG* 18) with Lambert (2000b), Eleusis (*LSCG* 7), Teithras (*LSS* 132); for the arrangements of private funding for deme sacrifices in the Marathonian Tetrapolis (Lambert, in press); groups: the *genos* Salaminioi, Lambert (1997a).

91 See above, n. 66. The earliest epigraphical evidence for the office of the Tamiai is *IG* I³ 510 (mid-sixth century); on the Tamiai see now Bubelis (2016) which appeared after I finished this study.

92 *Hieropoioi* in the mid-sixth century: *IG* I³ 507, 508, 509; running the Panathenaic procession in the fourth century, RO 81 B. ll. 6, 17–18, 31.

93 *Ath.Pol.* 56–8 begins with the Archon Eponymous, the last to have been instituted according to the tradition, when archonship became an annual office (*Ath.Pol.* 3.4; 684/3?; Develin (1989) 27–8). Although most scholars agree that in archaic Athens responsibilities must have been distributed between the archons, Foxhall (1997) 120 observes that as offices the archaic archonships were not clearly defined. *Ath.Pol.* 56–8 probably reflects the fourth-century organisation of their duties, many of which dated back to the early archaic age.

the sense of *hosios* human conduct towards gods and humans in observing obligations, including proper burial; and (3) *hosia* in the sense of human property to be used for *hiera* or other god-pleasing purposes, both public and private.

The role or duties of the Archon (Eponymous) as listed in *Ath.Pol.* 56 included:

His name fixed the Athenian year in time (1);[94]
He announced that all would keep and control their property until the end of his office (3);
He appointed three *choregoi* for tragedies from among the wealthiest (1, 3);
He authorised *choregoi* appointed by *phyle* for men's and boys' competitions, for the comedies at the Dionysia, and for men's and boys' choruses at the Thargelia (1, 3);
He dealt with *antidosis* for these choruses and claims of exemption of liturgies (1, 3);
He appointed *choregoi* for Delos and a procession leader for the ship (1, 3);
He supervised the processions of Asclepius, of the City Dionysia (together with *epimeletai*, formerly: ten wealthy men elected, now ten allotted from the *demos* with ten mnae state funding), of the Thargelia, and of Zeus Soter (1, 3);
He was in charge of the competitions at the Dionysia and the Thargelia (1, 2);
He was in charge of the *graphai* and *dikai* for ill-uses of parents, of heiresses, of orphans (2), and of all to do with *epikleroi*, orphans and widows (2, 3).[95]

The (Archon) Basileus (*Ath.Pol.* 57) was in charge of

the Eleusinian mysteries (with four *epimeletai*: two elected from all Athenians, one from the Eumolpidai, one from the Kerykes) (1);
of the Dionysia Lenaia (of the procession the Basileus plus the *epimeletai*, of the competition the Basileus),
of the torch races and the ancestral sacrifices (1);
of the *graphai* for *asebeia* (2);
of *dikai* about priesthoods and perquisites in the *gene* (1, 2, 3);

[94] Perhaps this 'calendrical' role of the Archon represented his responsibility for *themis*; for its equivalent with *hosie*, see above, Chapter 2.4.1.

[95] On the Solonian origin of the 'archon's law on conduct towards parents, heiresses and orphans', Scafuro (2006a). Cf. Xen. *Mem.* 2.2.14: respect for one's parents also a duty towards the gods (= *hosie*).

of cases for homicide, with various courts at various locations depending on the charge (2);
and he announced exclusion from *hiera* (1, 2).[96]

The Polemarchos (*Ath.Pol.* 58), finally,

sacrificed to Artemis Agrotera and Enyalios (1, 3);
he was in charge of the funeral games of the war dead (1, 2);
he sacrificed *enagismata* for Harmodios and Aristogeiton (1, 2);
he was in charge of *dikai* concerning foreigners (*metoikoi* and *proxenoi*), and distributed such cases by lot to *phylai* and assigned the *dikastai* (2).

The list in *Ath.Pol.* is far from exhaustive; for the cults at Eleusis, for instance, it does not mention that the Basileus also selected the 'child of the hearth', but the general picture is clear. Fittingly, the archons wore the same crowns as priests and like them had to be 'pure'.[97]

For the *strategoi*, the bond with the gods was as vital a part of their duties as it was for the Polemarchos, whom they soon superseded in effective authority. At war, officers sacrificed when they crossed the boundary of the *polis* to the gods of both territories, and before and after battle to consult the gods' inclination and thank them for support.[98] These rituals are less abundantly attested for Athenians in literary evidence than for some others. The Spartans were famous for their piety, sacrificing at every crossing of the border and before battle (*sphage*), for instance at Plataia in 479 on behalf of all the Greeks. Thucydides let the commander of the Boeotians base his expectations on their sacrifices before the battle of Delion (4.92.7) but not so the Athenian commander Hippocrates, who in fact had made a bastion of the precinct of Apollo there, amounting to sacrilege. Xenophon, clearly a pious man, mentions the frequent sacrifices he made both on his own behalf and of the men under his command.[99] The Athenian evidence is primarily epigraphic, notably on votives from war booty and often as a result of vows.[100] Proper treatment of the bodies of

96 The Archon Basileus in his cultic role as representative of the entire *polis*, cf. [Lys.] 6.4–7.

97 Parker, *PS*, 97 and below.

98 For Athens, Parker, *PS*, 103–4. Spartan piety at crossing of the border (Thuc. 5.54.2; Xen. *Hell.* 4.4.3); *sphage*: Van Wees (2004) 121; Parker (2011) 155–65. Sacrifice before Plataia: Thuc. 2.71.2; Hdt. 9.33, 36. Delion: Thuc. 4.92.7.

99 Xenophon: *Anab.* 3.1.6: to ask advice about his enterprise; sacrifices every morning, 5.4.22, 7.8.20; before battle 6.4.12; gratitude for safety 3.2.9; recommends a *hipparchos* to begin his duty with sacrifice, *Hipp.* 1.1.

100 *IG* I^3 1464, the Athenians in Delphi after Plataia; *IG* I^3 511 and 512, the *hippeis* and their hipparchs, ca. 450–430; *IG* I^3 515, the *prytaneis* of Erichtheis, 408/7; *IG* II^2 2789, the Athenians and their allies to Apollo, ca. 365/4; *IG* II^2 2795 and 2795a, the *demos* to Demeter and Kore, ca. 330–310 (war?).

the war dead after battle belonged to the rules comprised in *hosie* observed (ideally) by all mankind.[101] In peace time, the *strategoi* assisted *hieropoioi* at festivals, for instance with the processions during the Panathenaea.[102]

Responsibility for the *polis*'s *hiera kai hosia* combined with 'ruling' their fellow citizens were also the duties of the (Cleisthenic) *boule*. The *boule* had corrective and punitive powers: it held the *dokimasia* of the archons, subjected higher officials to judicial control and checked the credentials of orphans and invalids entitled to an obol subsistence from the *polis*.[103] Some trials were held before the *boule*, especially those following on the procedure of *eisangelia*.[104] The *boule* was directly involved in *hiera kai hosia* in various ways, beginning with sacrifice and prayer on behalf of the *polis* at the altar of Zeus Boulaios and Athena Boulaia in the *bouleuterion*.[105] The *boule*'s prime function was to prepare the agenda of and give advice to the assembly, and in Chapter 2 we saw how the *hiera kai hosia* of the *polis* became a fixed item on this agenda. Furthermore, the *boule* was primarily responsible for the management of divine property, notably *hieros* money.[106] In this task, the *boule* carried through what we can retrospectively see to have been the steady policy of the *demos* in the course of the fifth century to extend its control, financially and otherwise, of the cults in Athens and beyond.[107] Intervening in the Eleusinian cults, the *polis* installed *hieropoioi* in charge of the treasury which was (largely) removed to Athens.[108] In 432, the *polis* added new *epistatai* to the sanctuary of the Two Goddesses to oversee the finances and other matters of the cult.[109] In 454, the treasury of the Delian League was brought to Athens, where the *aparchai* that Athena received from the league's tributes were collected on the Acropolis. In (probably) 432/1 a new fund was created – later called the treasury of the Other Gods – with new boards of officials for the treasuries.[110] Every step in these and similar financial

[101] As claimed by both parties after Delion (Thuc. 4.107–8), with Krentz (2002).
[102] Dem. 4 (*First Philippic*) 25–6.
[103] Blok (2015) with further refs.
[104] *Ath.Pol.* 45.1–4; Rhodes (1972) 179–207.
[105] Antiph. 6.45: ὑπὲρ τῆς πόλεως.
[106] Financial and religious duties of the *boule*, *Ath.Pol.* 47–9; Rhodes (1972) 88–100, 127–34.
[107] For this process within Attica, Linders (1975); connection with democracy and empire, Parker (1996) 122–51.
[108] *IG* I³ 6, Eleusis, before ca. 460?, date based on letter forms; ll. 37–8 [ἐμ] πόλει: on the Acropolis; for transfer of *aparche* from Eleusis to the Acropolis in the first quarter of the fifth century, Cavanaugh (1996) 73–4, and *hieropoioi* initially of Eleusis, later of the *polis*, and institution of *epistatai*, 92–3; cf. Samons (2000) 135; *IG* I³ 259–72 accounts of the tribute *aparchai*, beginning 454/3, Samons (2000) 35–41.
[109] *IG* I³ 32 with Cavanaugh (1996) 1–27.
[110] Kallias decree *IG* I³ 52A (ML 58A), *boule* in charge of the process, ll. 9–10, Samons (2000) 114; date, see Chapter 2, n. 160; centralisation of cult budgets into treasury of the Other Gods: Linders (1975).

operations was supervised by the *boule*, either a small group selected from the *bouleutai*, or the *epistates* and secretary cooperating with the *epimeletai* of the sanctuary, or by the *boule* as a whole.[111] In the fourth century, the role of the *boule* to prepare decisions pertaining to the *hiera* of the *polis* is paramount, exemplified conspicuously in 352/1 in arranging the consultation of the Delphic oracle on the Sacred Orgas and in the law and decree on the Little Panathenaea of ca. 335.[112] Like the archons, the *bouleutai* wore 'priestly' crowns and derived their religious authority from the hearth, the Hestia in the *prytaneion*.[113] If the *bouleutai* were holding *archai* that perhaps initially were less conspicuous than those of the archons, their large numbers must have ensured a steadily growing experience among the male citizens in carrying responsibility for the *polis* and its bond with the gods, adding to the political significance of the *boule* itself.

With the gradual democratisation of the *polis*, the high qualifications set for access to elevated *timai* in the archaic age had almost all disappeared by the fourth century, when equality of access had become the leading principle for most *polis timai* and virtually all citizens were eligible for virtually all prominent functions fitting their gender and age. With a religious element at the heart of almost all *timai*, the *polis* was responsible both towards the human community and towards the gods for the quality of *all* its citizens, and misconduct in this domain could be made out to be disastrous for the *polis*'s well-being. A highly conspicuous case was the trial of ca. 342 on the citizen status of the former *hetaira* Neaira and of Phano, whom the plaintiff Apollodoros claimed was her daughter. Phano had been pledged in marriage first to a certain Phrastor, who had repudiated her, and next she was married to a certain Theogenes. When the latter was selected by lot to be Basileus, Phano became the Basilinna, a prominent *time* which included performing the *hieros gamos* (sacred union) with Dionysus during the festival Anthesteria, as mentioned before. Ritual convention inscribed in a law near the sanctuary prescribed that

111 *Boule*: supervision of contracts of Kallikrates for Athena Nike temple, *IG* I³ 35.15–18; in charge of collecting tributes for Apollo, *IG* I³ 138.9–12; supervision of *paradosis* of the Tamiai of Athena (cf. *Ath.Pol.* 47.1), dated to archon and secretary of the *boule*: *IG* I³ 370 (418–414), 375.1–2 etc. (410/9); Parthenon accounts, *IG* I³ 446.313, 449.370–4, 450.412–15, dated to archon and secretary of the *boule*; accounts of Athena Parthenos statue, *IG* I³ 455.4–6, 457.5–8, idem; Propylaia accounts, *IG* I³ 463.61–2, 465.115 (434/3), idem; statues of Athena and Hephaistos, *IG* I³ 472.5, idem; *boule* controlling *epistatai* in Eleusis (*IG* I³ 32.4, 13–15); in charge of (sacrifices for?) Bendis, *IG* I³ 37 (ca. 413/12); supervision of melting down votives and cleaning sanctuary of Asclepius (*IG* II² 1534 B; ca. 275; *IG* II² 1539; 215/14) and Heros Iatros (*IG* II³ 1154; 220/19); cf. Linders (1975) 29–30.

112 Decree on the Sacred Orgas (*IG* II³, 1 292 = RO 58) ll. 51–4. Little Panathenaea (RO 81, B ll. 7–8): the decisions on the sacrifices (and the money involved) prepared by the *boule*.

113 Parker, *PS*, 97, 404–5.

the Basilinna had to be an *aste* (of Athenian descent on both sides) and the Basileus her first husband.[114] Since according to the plaintiff Neaira was not an *aste*, Phano was not one either and she also failed on the latter qualification for her role. Apollodoros' aim in contesting Phano's citizen's status was to have Neaira, the companion of Stephanos, his adversary in this and previous court cases, convicted for posing as a citizen woman instead of acting as the *xene* she was in reality. After expounding the enormities of Phano's sacrilege as the culmination of Neaira's disgraceful life, Apollodoros reminded the *dikastai*:

> At this point the most virtuous of citizen women will be angry at you that you have considered this woman worthy to participate equally with themselves in the *polis* and the *hiera* [... if you acquit this woman, the laws of Athens will no longer protect citizen women, but you give full licence to prostitutes to bear children to whomever they want] and the worth of free women will be lowered to that of *hetairai*, if they are given licence to bear children to whoever they like and yet to participate (*metechein*) in the rituals (*teletai*) and *hiera* and *timai* of the *polis*.[115]

Here, as elsewhere in this speech, Apollodoros drew strongly on the awareness of the *dikastai* that sharing in the *polis*'s cults was an essential part of their wives' *time* as full citizens and as mothers of legitimate children.[116] To be worthy of the *time* that the *polis* granted its citizens, every citizen had to meet the conditions of Athenian birth and proper conduct, now that *any* woman who was an *aste* and married in first marriage to her husband became Basilinna if her husband happened to be selected Basileus, who likewise now could be *any* man who passed his *dokimasia* as to being an *astos* eligible for the archonship and took his oaths.

5.5 The Case of the *Gene*

The *gene* deserve special attention here, since they illuminate with exceptional clarity the nuts and bolts of citizenship in classical Athens: their *time* was based on their (allegedly) impeccable Athenian descent, entitling them to prominent *timai* in the *polis*. I introduced the *gene* in Chapter 3

114 [Dem.] 59.73–7; Parker, *PS*, 303–4. A parallel case of first marriage required of women holding cultic *timai* concerned the women responsible for the cult of Athena Pallenis (Ath. 6.235a, with Schlaifer (1943)).

115 [Dem.] 59.111–13: ὁμοίως αὐταῖς ... μετέχειν τῶν τῆς πόλεως καὶ τῶν ἱερῶν; 113 ... τὸ δὲ τῶν ἐλευθέρων γυναικῶν ἀξίωμα εἰς τὰς ἑταίρας, ἂν ἄδειαν λάβωσι τοῦ ἐξεῖναι αὐταῖς παιδοποιεῖσθαι ὡς ἂν βούλωνται καὶ τελετῶν καὶ ἱερῶν καὶ τιμῶν μετέχειν τῶν ἐν τῇ πόλει. See also the epigraph to this chapter.

116 [Dem.] 59.114–15, 122.

to exemplify how privileges and prominence might be derived from mythological or metaphorical descent.[117] Until the mid-fifth century, the *gene* had exclusive access to the priesthoods, the highest cultic *timai* of the *polis*, as well as to numerous supporting cultic roles, all of which they retained after the introduction of the so-called 'democratic priesthoods'.[118] Like all *timai*, *genos* priesthood was both an honour and an obligation. From the 330s at least, if a young male *gennetes* was selected for priesthood while still in his ephebic training but got involved in a suit about his priestly office, he was excused to break off his *ephebeia*.[119]

How in historical reality the *gene* came to acquire their privileged position with respect to *polis* cults is unclear. The variety among the *gene* in the range and prominence of their cults, in the number of families each *genos* consisted of, in wealth, in geographical dispersion and in many other respects, indicates that each *genos* must have found its own ways to ensure their exclusive performance of the ritual or cult.[120] The Salaminioi, for instance, consisted in the classical era of two subgroups of at least five and seven different families from different parts of Attica respectively. Together they provided the priesthoods of Athena Skiras, of Heracles at Porthmos, of the hero Eurysakes and of Aglauros, Pandrosos and Kourothrophos, and performed another twenty-three *hiera* for various divinities. To go by their name, the *genos* must have had something to do with Salamis and perhaps more particularly with the partial inclusion of the island into the *polis* by the later the sixth century, but it is unknown what this motive was.[121] In the classical age the social standing of the *gene* in terms of wealth varied considerably. Very few *gennetai* can with confidence be identified as belonging to the liturgical class. One family belonging to

[117] Above, Chapter 3.5. I use the noun *genos* here in the specific meaning of a group of families at Athens holding exclusive access to *timai* for *polis* cults. Beside the *polis* cults, the *gene* had cults of their own. Arguments supporting this section were published as Blok (2009a), Blok (2009b, Blok (2009c) and Blok and Lambert (2009).

[118] See Feaver (1957) 124 for the distinction of priesthoods into 'gentile' (filled from a *genos*) and 'democratic' (filled from all Athenians). Examples of supporting cultic roles: a young man who carried the sacred laurel branch (*eiresione*) at the Pyanopsia and Thargelia, provided by the Erysichthonidai who probably also provided several priests of Apollo; a group of female Hesychidai made wine-less cake offerings to the Semnai Theai, beside the role of the *genos* in the prominent procession; either the Praxiergidai, who also put the peplos on the statue of Athena Polias, or the Bouzygai accompanied the ephebes in the procession to the sea and back at the Plynteria; for these and other examples, Parker (1996) 284–327.

[119] *Ath.Pol.* 42.5.

[120] Since Roussel (1976) and Bourriot (1976) showed convincingly that the *gene* were not a survival of a proto-historical aristocracy but had developed as groups in charge of cults *pari passu* with the *polis*, the question of their origins is open again, on which Parker (1996) ch. 5, Lambert (1999).

[121] For their possible connections with Salamis, Osborne (1994), Lambert (1997a), Taylor (1997) 47–63.

the Eleusinian Kerykes were among the richest in Attica, but Apollodoros depicted Phrastor, a member of the *genos* Brytidai, as a working man sufficiently poor to be persuaded by a dowry of thirty mnae to accept a bride of doubtful repute.[122] While thus the early history of the *gene* may be dim and the differences between them and even between the families belonging to one *genos* unmistakable, a few features are typical of all of them.

First, all *gene* claimed great antiquity for themselves and their cultic privileges. According to their legends their cultic offices were created for or by an *archegetes* in the deep past, when the gods, who walked the earth at that time, had given the service of the cult to the founding figure, and because this time roughly coincided with the origins of the *polis*. Among the cults the *gene* served, quite a number were devoted to divinities fostering the growth of crops, cattle or children and to the ancient heroes and heroines of Attica.[123] Since the *gene* could also point to ancient tombs and sanctuaries of their *archegetai* and performed sacred duties that were ancestral (*patroia*) by definition and publicly recognised as family privileges, they could sustain their claims to their *time* more compellingly than other Athenians. On the tomb of Phytalos, the acclaimed *archegetes* of the Phytalidai, for instance, a Hellenistic epigram proclaimed:

> Here, king hero Phytalos once received revered Demeter, when she first created fruit of the harvest, that the *genos* of mortals have given the name of sacred fig; whence the *genos* of Phytalos got *timai* for ever.[124]

The word play on *genos* catches the eye: the whole *genos* of mankind knows the sacred fig, but Demeter's gift to Phytalos in return were the privileges passed down as inheritance in the *genos* Phytalidai, whose name reminded not just the *genos* but the whole *polis* of the growth in the goddess's care and who held among their *timai* a priesthood of Demeter. On such old claims new *timai* could be grafted: when Kimon inaugurated new sacrifices for Theseus in the 470s, he gave the honour of performing the ritual to the Phytalidai, since Phytalos had purified Theseus when he had killed Sinis and his tomb was in the deme Lakiadai to which Kimon belonged.[125]

[122] [Dem.] 59.50, 59, see above, Chapter 3, n. 167.

[123] Amynandridai: priest of Cecrops (Parker (1996) 285–6); Bouzygai: sacred ploughing of Attica; Charidai: priest of Cranaos (Paus. 1.31.3); Euenoridai: cultic role for Aglauros; Eumolpidai: descent from Eumolpos, ancient king (*Hom.Hymn.Dem.* 154, 476) or son of Poseidon; Coneidai: descent from Coneides, *paidagogos* of Theseus (Plut. *Thes.* 4); Pyrrakidai: descent from Pyrrhakos, descendant of Erysichthon (Hesych.); Salaminioi: priestesses of Athena Skiras, Aglauros, Pandrosos and Kourotrophos; etc.

[124] Paus. 1.37.2, l. 4: ἐξ οὗ δὴ τιμὰς Φυτάλου γένος ἔσχεν ἀγήρως. On the Phytalidai, Parker (1996) 169, 318.

[125] Plut. *Thes.* 12.1, 23.5; *Cim.* 8.5–7.

Members of the Bouzygai spoke a curse against anyone who denied his or her fellow men the basic necessities of life, such as fire, food and water, reminiscent of the time the *polis* was founded.[126] The Eteoboutadai consisted of two branches of apparently a single family each, and provided some of the highest priesthoods of the *polis*, in the one branch the priestess of Athena Polias, in the other the priest of Poseidon Erechtheus. More than any other *genos* the Eteoboutadai boasted high and ancient lineage through descent from Ge and Erechtheus, which forged a close relationship with the mythical kings of Athens and located the *genos* at the heart of Athenian *polis* religion from the earliest days of Athenian existence. Presumably, their original name was Boutadai but was changed into Eteo- ('real, true') Boutadai to distinguish the *gennetai* with a superior move from the Cleisthenic deme Boutadai.[127]

Second, whatever the surrounding 'ancient' story, each *genos* derived their *time* from the *archegetes* because they cast themselves as his or her *legitimate heirs*, whose inheritance consisted of the offices of *polis* cults (the *timai*) 'belonging to' the *genos* and of the *eligibility* for holding these offices. This inheritance was passed down to the legitimate descendants in the *genos* families in the same way as other inherited goods, as brought out clearly in fourth-century court cases among *gennetai*, many of which revolved around disputes about legitimacy and the rights of inheritance of *genos* status.[128] Such *dikai* were the special province of the (Archon) Basileus, as we just saw, because the outcome immediately concerned the correct performance of the traditional *polis* cults, i.e. by the proper priest or priestess of the *genos*.

The construction of gennetic *time* as inherited good had important consequences, first of all for its distribution among *genos* members. Eligibility

[126] Hesych. *s.v.* Βουζύγης; Plut. *Mor.* 144b; Parker (1996) 286–7; for their curse, Pulleyn (1997) 77.

[127] Harp. *s.v.* Βούτης· οὗτος ἔσχε τὴν ἱερωσύνην· καὶ οἱ ἀπὸ τούτου Βουτάδαι· καὶ Ἐτεοβουτάδαι οἱ ἀπόγονοι τοῦ Βούτου· τὸ γὰρ ἐτεὸν ἀληθές. Ὅμηρος 'εἰ ἐτεὸν σός εἰμί.' 'Boutes: he received the priesthood; and those after him Boutadai. And the Eteoboutadai are the descendants of Boutes, because "*eteos*" is "true". Homer says: "if I am truly yours".' *Lex.Patm.* (*Lexica Graeca Minora*, ed. K. Latte/H. Erbse) *s.v.* Ἐτεοβουτάδαι· γένος Ἀθήνησιν ἱερόν, καὶ ὄντως Ἀττικὸν καὶ γνήσιον, ἐξ οὑ ἐγίνοντο τῆς Ἀθηνᾶς αἱ ἱέρειαι. 'Eteoboutadai: sacred *genos* in Athens, and really Attic and legitimate, from which came the priestesses of Athena'. From the mid-fifth century onward, the branch of the Athena Polias priestess was represented in a family from Bate, not Boutadai like the Poseidon branch. The centre of the deme Boutadai, to which the *genos* name referred, was quite close to the *asty*; on the Eteoboutadai, Parker (1996) 290–3, Lambert (2015).

[128] For instance Is. 7.15–17 (legitimacy established both in *genos* and phratry), see Feaver (1957) 114–17; Lambert (1998) 66–8, 171–7. For the dispute between the Krokonidai and the Koironidai, two minor Eleusinian *gene*, which hinged on alleged illegitimacy and the concomitant claims to *timai*, Parker (1996) 302–4. The dispute among the Salaminioi (RO 37) did not involve problems of legitimacy, but claims to priesthoods of the branches of the *genos*.

for priesthood followed the same trajectory as all other inheritance (see Chapter 3): sons and daughters were all heirs, while descendants in the male line had precedence over those in the female line. The difference between material goods, divided equally among sons with a fitting portion in the form of a dowry for daughters, and immaterial goods, of which all sons and daughters were equal heirs, was highly relevant in the *gene*: eligibility, an immaterial good, devolved to all descendants equally for the priesthoods the *genos* held in common and which were open to descendants of the relevant sex and age. The fact that for a particular cult either a man or a woman was required made the *effective* heirs of eligibility scarcer in number and distributed differently from other inherited property. For instance, in a *genos* with a priestesshood, eligibility passed as inheritance through sons and daughters, but only daughters could actually take up the priestesshood. The number of candidates depended on the number of suitable descendants from the families making up the *genos*; within large *gene*, such as the Kerykes, the number was larger than in small ones such as the Eteoboutadai. Among all the candidates of the right sex and age of the *genos*, the office was assigned, as all inheritance, by allotment.[129] This method reinforced the projected nature of *genos* privilege as an inherited good, prevented strife within the families and underscored the equality of the candidates. In section 5.7, I return to the allotment in the *gene*.

Furthermore, due to the construction of their *time* as inherited good, the *gene* could assert they were of immaculate Athenian descent on both sides. Like other goods, eligibility for the *genos* priesthoods devolved to female heirs who brought their *kleros* into the *oikos* into which they married, and in absence of relatives on the paternal side, the *kleros* would go to heirs on the maternal side. This scenario was not merely theoretical, but happened in reality. In the Poseidon branch of the Eteoboutadai, the heritage of the *genos* was passed on several times through *epikleroi*, since all male kinsmen had died, and in the Athena Polias branch it switched

[129] Selection by lot among the *gene* in the classical age is well attested; see for instance *Ath.Pol.* on the earliest history of Athens (F3 (Kenyon) = F2 (Chambers) = *Lex. Patm. s.v.* γεννῆται): καὶ γένος ἕκαστον ἄνδρας εἶχε τριάκοντα τοὺς εἰς τὰ γένη τεταγμένους, οἵτινες γεννῆται ἐκαλοῦντο, <ἐξ> ὧν αἱ ἱερωσύναι <αἱ> ἑκάστοις προσήκουσαι ἐκληροῦντο, οἷον Εὐμολπίδαι καὶ Κήρυκες καὶ Ἐτεοβουτάδαι; 'each *genos* had thirty men marshalled in the *gene* who were called *gennetai*, from whom the priesthoods that belonged to each of them were appointed by lot, such as the Eumolpidai, Kerykes and Eteoboutadai' (cf. Harp. *s.v.* γεννῆται) and further Blok and Lambert (2009). There is scholarly consensus (see Lambert (1998) app. 2, 371–80; Smith (2006) 121–3) that the division into four *phylai*, each again in three *trittyes* called *phratriai* and those again into thirty *gene* each, attributed to ancient Attica in *Ath.Pol.*, is a fiction, but clearly in the fourth century allotment was seen as the traditional means of selection in *gene*, considered to be among the oldest groups of Attica.

twice to (descendants of) in-law families (from Amphitrope and Phlye) when the original family holding the priestesshood (from Bate) had died without issue.[130] Consequently, for the transmission of *polis* priesthoods to suitable heirs not only *genos* descent in the normal patrilinear way was essential, but also the choice of marriage partners: in-laws of *genos* families should be persons entitled to a share in the *polis*'s cults, since the *genos* heritage could pass into the *anchisteia* on the maternal side. In sum, because eligibility for priest(ess)hood was passed down following the normal patterns of inheritance in Athens, but was also a special good in that it embodied the (potential) service of the gods on behalf of the *polis*, *genos* members appear to have been effectively obliged to marry only born Athenians, who were legal descendants (heirs) of the same ancestors who had entered the bond of the *polis* with the gods, even before Pericles' Citizenship Law.[131] Among the well-known Athenians who married non-Athenians before the law, there are no indisputable *gennetai* and definitely no *genos* priests and priestesses.[132]

From this evidence we may infer that eligibility for priesthood required birth from two Athenian parents, also before Pericles' law, and that the *gene* successfully claimed such a pedigree.[133] This inference is corroborated by other evidence. In court cases over citizen status and legitimacy,

[130] For the evidence, Blok and Lambert (2009) priestesses no. 5, Theodote, and no. 6, Penteteris; in the Poseidon branch no. 5, Aristonymos, no. 6, Kallias, no. 7, Medeios.

[131] For the full documentation on the transmission of eligibility and selection by lot among the *gene*, Blok and Lambert (2009). There is no indication that there had ever been a change in methods of appointment to *genos* priesthoods; in fact, *Ath.Pol.* 21.6 says explicitly that Cleisthenes, the obvious candidate to have made such a change, left the *gene* unchanged.

[132] A *gennetes* who married a non-Athenian probably gave up his/her eligibility for the *genos* priesthood, but there is no evidence on this matter. The only exception to the endogamy rule would seem to be Themistocles, who was a *metroxenos* but in late Hellenistic times was said to have been a member of the *genos* Lykomidai. Plut. *Them.* 1.1, 2.1 mentions his obscure birth as son of Neokles of Phrearrioi, but says in 1.4 that he belonged to the Lykomidai because after its destruction by the Persians he rebuilt the *telesterion* of the Mysteries of Phlye, of which the Lykomidai were in charge. The Lykomidai were wealthy and all carried the demotic Phlyeus, so Davies accepts the existence of two branches, a prominent one of Phlye and a modest one of Phrearrioi (*APF* no. 6669; 212, 216–17; no. 9238, 346–7). However, after the war Themistocles also built the sanctuary of Artemis Aristoboule in Melite (Plut. *Them.* 22.2–3; *Mor.* 869c–d), which had nothing to do with the Lykomidai. His membership of the *genos* is not supported by classical sources, whereas Themistocles became a popular figure for archaising emulation in late Hellenistic times, illustrated in Themistocles, son of Theophrastos of Hagnous, of 20/19, who as *dadouchos* belonged to the *genos* Kerykes (Clinton (1974) no. 14); on the archaism of the *gene* at this time, Aleshire and Lambert (2011). In sum, I share the doubt of Parker (1996) 305 about Themistocles' status as *gennetes*; he certainly was not a priest. A similar case is Andocides, wrongly said to be one of the Kerykes in [Plut.] *X Or.* 834c because Andocides recounts (1.132) that he introduced friends into the Mysteries (cf. *APF* no. 828, 27).

[133] For the requirement of two born Athenian parents for priesthood, and after Pericles' law also for archons, see below, Chapter 6.1.

gennetai – whether holding cultic functions or not – were citizens *hors concours*, whose antecedents were considered secured by the traditions of their *genos*.[134] In his defence before the Athenian court, Euxitheos supported his assertion that he was of Athenian descent on both sides by his *eugeneia* – his birth as a *gennetes*, i.e. from two Athenian parents one of which a *gennetes*. His *eugeneia* made him also eligible for a priesthood, in this case not a *genos* priesthood but the deme's priesthood of Heracles.[135]

The necessity of producing legitimate offspring of the right gender for the priesthood and their claims to pure ancestry seem to have made the *gene* more cognizant of their genealogy, not merely in terms of mythical ancestry but also in the 'real' descent of the family, more than other Athenians, for whom ultimately an heir of either sex would do. In the most complicated of Isaeus' inheritance cases, claims were traced back through four (Is. 5, Dikaiogenes) and five (Is. 11, Hagnias) generations, but usually through no more than three. Among the Eteoboutadai, however, at the crucial junction in the continuity of the 'Athena branch' mentioned above, eligibility for office of priestess of Athena Polias of Penteteris, daughter of Hierokles of Phlye, and Theodote, daughter of Polyoktos of Amphitrope (both late third century), was based on descent from a common ancestor, Drakontides of Bate (mid-fifth century), who preceded these women by five to seven generations. And likewise at a moment of complicated transfer of office, in the late fourth century, the 'Poseidon branch' of the Eteoboutadai presented a genealogical list, which later, when a witness saw it, covered at least four centuries.[136]

Whether or not such genealogies were grounded in fact mattered less than that they could convince fellow Athenians of their veracity and hence of the legitimate transmission of *genos* status. While many prominent families boasted an ancient, famous founder such as an Homeric hero, but had to leave the connection between this ancestor and recent generations in the dark,[137] the *gene* could substantiate continuity in their families over many generations, despite the founders of *gene* being rather dim figures, because of the uninterrupted transfer of their *timai*. The antiquity and purity of their Athenian descent thus distinguished the *gene* not only from

134 Dem. 57.23–7; Andoc. 1.125–7; Isae. 7.15–17; [Dem.] 59.59–61. Cf. Philochoros *FGrH* 328 F 35 with Lambert (1998) 46–9 on *genos* membership providing automatic acceptance in a phratry.

135 Dem. 57.23–4, 46–7.

136 The list of Eteoboutadai priests for Poseidon Erechtheus, see above, Chapter 3.5; [Plut.] *X Or.* 843f: 'the *pinax* was dedicated by Habron, his son, having been allotted the priesthood from the *genos* and having yielded it to his brother Lycophron; and for this reason Habron is portrayed passing the trident to him'.

137 For aristocratic (non-*genos*) genealogies, Thomas (1989) 155–61.

the *demos* but also from many other prominent families.[138] In this sense, the *gene* constituted an elite conceived in terms of birth only, regardless of wealth or political power.[139] Yet probably they were hardly ever asked to trace the line of metaphorical descent from the present *gennetai* back to the *archegetes* from generation to generation: the projected image of this descent, bolstered by tombs, altars and other visual proofs, combined with the more solid genealogies of the recent past, probably sufficed for the *gene* to create a convincing idea of continuous, pure Athenian descent owing to their endogamy. Their success in all of this presumably accounts for the epithet *ithagenes* that the *gene* acquired at some point. Hesychius added this epithet to many *gene* in his lexicon as a quality specific for the Athenian *gene*.[140] The epithet itself was well known from the passage in Homer where Odysseus pretends to be the illegitimate son of a Cretan nobleman beside the *ithageneis* sons of his father.[141] *Ithagenes* means 'of true, straight descent', indicating legitimate birth in the case of individuals and autochthony when used for peoples – apparently congruent meanings.[142] Whereas in Athens before Pericles' law one of the parents, usually the father, had to be an Athenian while the mother could be a non-Athenian, 'true descent' required and emphasised legitimate descent through a woman born in the same citizen group (*aste*).[143] This condition fits the endogamy rules of the Athenian *gene* inferred from the evidence. When precisely the *gene* received or adopted the epithet we cannot say, but on comparison with the name of the Eteoboutadai, conceivably *ithagenes* highlighted the claims to uninterrupted, purely Athenian descent of the *gene* vis-à-vis the other Athenians, who could pretend to be 'pure' after

[138] Beside their marriages with non-Athenians in historical times, e.g. the Alcmaeonidai (Paus. 2.18.8–9) and the Pisistratidai (Hdt. 5.65.3) traced their origins to Pylos, as did Melanthos, one of the early Athenian kings (Rhodes (1981) 79, 186–7); on the origins of the Philaidai on Salamis, see Chapter 3, n. 158.

[139] Cf. Lambert (2015) on 'an aristocracy of birth'. The Gephyraioi, who with allegedly non-Attic origins (Hdt. 5.57–61) seem the exception proving the rule, were probably excluded from certain priesthoods and had a position of their own in the network of Attic cults, Brulé (1987) 303–5, Lambert (1998) 53, n. 120, Parker (1996) 288–9; Ismard (2007) 25–8, Lambert (2010b) 10–11.

[140] Parker (1996) 284–5.

[141] Hom. *Od.* 14.203.

[142] Legitimate birth: ἰθαγενής versus born from a concubine: Hom. *Od.* 14.203; Hesych., Phot. ι 72, ἰθαγενής· αὐτόχθων. γνήσιος; ἰθαγενέεσσι· γνησίοις τέκνοις καὶ καθαροῖς, οὐκ ἐκ παλλακίδος. ἰθαγενής versus ἐπήλυδες: Hdt. 6.54; Hellanicus *FGrH* 4 F 79a; Strabo 7.7.8: DL *Vit.* 1.22; Hesych. αὐθιγενής· αὐτόχθων γνήσιος. αὐθιγενές· ἐγγενές, ἐπίγονον. ἐπήλυδας· νεωστὶ ἐλθόντας ἐξ ἑτέρας γῆς. ἐπιλεκτούς. ἢ οὐκ ἰθαγενεῖς. 'Springing straight from': Hdt. 2.17.24; Arist. *Metereol.* 364a16; Plut. *Mor.* 991e. Relevance to *gene*: (*Lex.Patm.*) *s.v.* Ἐτεοβουτάδαι· γένος Ἀθήνησιν ἱερόν, καὶ ὄντως Ἀττικὸν καὶ γνήσιον (cf. above, n. 127).

[143] See above, Chapter 4.2.

Pericles' law but could never vouchsafe being of 'true' Athenian descent right from the beginning.

In sum, in the classical age the *gene* conceived of themselves and were conceived by their fellow citizens as the quintessential Athenian citizens: of pure Athenian descent on both sides, allegedly since the beginning of the *polis*, the sons and daughters of the *genos* families were equal heirs of the privilege of performing the major *timai* in *polis* cults, notably the priesthoods. Since these cults represented the ancestral heritage of the *polis*'s bond with the gods, the *genos* priesthoods thus embodied this bond more conspicuously and effectively than other Athenians. The *time* of the *gene* was based on their special birth qualifications, giving them exclusive access to these prominent *timai*. Within this framework, the equality of the male and female *gennetai* was part and parcel of the regular Athenian inheritance system, which in the case of the *gene* was particularly effective in bringing out the role of a daughter as heir to the assets of her ancestors in cases where she was not literally an *epikleros* (she might have brothers) but technically was the sole heir of the female priesthood (or other cultic role) of her *genos*. Among the candidates of the right gender and age of the *genos* families, the lot decided who was to fulfil the priesthood for life.

5.6 *Time* and Citizens' Conduct

Time was not just a matter of being valued among the citizens because one met certain criteria, but also required conduct fitting a citizen that complied with the values that were believed to underlie the well-being of the *polis*. For conduct, just as for participatory roles, it is useful to distinguish between a baseline, i.e. proper conduct followed by fitting *time* for any citizen of the same gender and age; situations below that baseline, i.e. bad conduct and its consequences; and excellent conduct, outdoing the baseline, leading to more *time* than for an average citizen. Honorific decrees became the documents *par excellence* by which the *polis* publicly conveyed its appreciation of a citizen's special value for the *polis* and commended his or her conduct to be followed in the future. Opening with public praise, the *demos* could grant other signs of public honour such as a crown, the right to sit in the front row in the theatre, dining at public expense in the *prytaneion*, or erection of a statue, and some such honours were bestowed also on the honorand's descendants.[144] An individual thus

[144] Formulas of public praise and honours: Henry (1983). For the vocabulary of citizens' 'cardinal virtues', in particular *philotimia* and *andragathia*, leading to special *time*, Whitehead (1993), Veligianni-Terzi (1997), Whitehead (2009). Inscribing praise to commend such conduct for the

could enjoy more or less *time* than the others of the same group, a matter ultimately for the *polis* to decide. In this area, citizens knew what to expect and anticipated the reactions of others and of the *polis* as a whole (assembly, courts), while much could go wrong due to friction, distrust or other collisions between the parties involved.[145]

When a citizen met the criteria for citizenship and did not behave in unacceptable ways, s/he might expect the *polis* (represented in its subgroup or another body) to reciprocate with fitting valuation; this was the baseline. For access to a public *time* or *arche*, formal criteria were set for any citizen to be selected and to carry out her or his duties in the correct manner. Some offices remained only accessible by election, a rule highlighting differences among citizens, while the majority of offices were distributed by allotment (see below). An individual who felt unjustly slighted in what s/he might expect to be his/her due (in words, actions, roles or whatever was at stake) could complain that s/he had been rendered *atimos*, a situation that the other party, if they accepted the rebuke, had to redress.[146] This general social rule in ancient Greece applied with great persuasive force to the relation between a citizen and the community of the *polis*.

The opposite adjective *epitimos*, i.e. enjoying the social recognition (*time*) with ensuing claims due to him or her as a member of the group, occurs less frequently. It first appears in the law of Solon on 'amnesty' (LR F 22/1) of which the exact social and legal context is obscure.[147] In classical texts and documents, *epitimos* appears much later than *atimos*, the first recorded case being in Thucydides' account of the Spartans taken on Sphakteria:

future, Luraghi (2010), Lambert (2011). For *sitesis* restricted to the eldest male descendants, see Blok and Van 't Wout (in press). For honours to non-Athenians and their descendants, notably *proxenia* and citizenship, see Chapter 6.

145 Conflicts in the sphere of *time* appear from the earliest evidence onwards in Greek society and literature, beginning with Agamemnon's slighting of Achilles in the *Iliad* (1.94). Measured throughout antiquity, the verb ἀτιμάω occurs 445 times, ἀτιμάζω 3,400 times and the adjective ἄτιμος 3,500 times in the *TLG*.

146 *Atimos* retained a strong connection with the wider spectrum of *tim-* vocabulary beyond its specific use in the context of the *polis* and its laws, notably with the verbs ἀτιμάω and ἀτιμάζω, i.e. not giving someone the due s/he might have expected to receive in any social relation. For instance Eur. *Med.* 1208: a god has killed the princess *atimos* (her father might have expected differently); Soph. *OT* 787–90: Apollo did not give him the answer he hoped for (sent him away *atimon*); Soph. *El.* 1214–15: Electra is robbed of the capacity to bury her dead brother – an affront that makes her *atimos*. Van 't Wout (2010b) shows that in the court scene at Athens in Aesch. *Eum.* 788–92, when the Erinyes complain that the outcome of the Areopagus' trial to acquit Orestes leaves them *atimos*, Athena is obliged to make amends for this situation.

147 LR F 22/1 (Rusch. Fr. 70; Plut. *Sol.*19.3).

> As to those of them who had been taken captive on the island and handed over their arms, the Spartans made them *atimos*, although some of them held *archai* just now, fearing that they might think that due to what had happened they would be slighted and might attempt a revolution if they remained *epitimos*. This *atimia* entailed that they could neither hold an *arche* nor have the legal capacity to buy or sell anything. After some time, however, they were made *epitimos* again.[148]

Epitimos, unlike *atimos* typically used of citizens and of no other groups,[149] seems to emerge in reaction to a specific use of *atimos* in sixth- and fifth-century decrees. Some *polis* laws deliberately declared citizens *atimos* who had damaged the *polis* in some way or, in a pre-emptive strike, those who threatened to do so.[150] Usually the threat was to make *atimos* both the offender and his descendants, and to confiscate his property, giving a part (normally a tithe) to the gods.[151] The passage in Thucydides shows the same intentions: the men whose potential subversions of the *polis* are feared are made *atimos deliberately*, barring them from access to prominent political roles that would normally have been open to them, but also barring them from making valid sales or purchases, i.e. depriving them from being recognised as fellow citizens in exchanges. *Epitimos* indicates their restitution to their former status, either in practice or by a formal decree.

[148] Thuc. 5.34: τοὺς δ᾽ ἐκ τῆς νήσου ληφθέντας σφῶν καὶ τὰ ὅπλα παραδόντας, δείσαντες μή τι διὰ τὴν ξυμφορὰν νομίσαντες ἐλασσωθήσεσθαι καὶ ὄντες ἐπίτιμοι νεωτερίσωσιν, ἤδη καὶ ἀρχάς τινας ἔχοντας ἀτίμους ἐποίησαν, ἀτιμίαν δὲ τοιάνδε ὥστε μήτε ἄρχειν μήτε πριαμένους τι ἢ πωλοῦντας κυρίους εἶναι. ὕστερον δὲ αὖθις χρόνῳ ἐπίτιμοι ἐγένοντο. From Homer to the late fourth century, the lexeme ἄτιμος occurs over 300 times, the lexeme ἐπίτιμος from Thuc. to the late fourth century occurs 42 times. The latest classical passage is Din. 2.2, where the speaker contrasts the state debtor Aristogeiton (who is implicitly *atimos* since debts to the *polis* were a common cause of becoming *atimos*) with the *epitimos* citizens whom he harasses. After this passage, there is a gap of more than a century until the next occurrences of *epitimos* (in the Septuagint, Dion.Hal. etc.). No reliable cases of *epitimos* in inscribed decrees are extant; it is used for the Plataians in the decree of disputed authenticity [Dem.] 59.104, see above, Chapter 2.4.4. For *epitimos* typically used of citizens, Canevaro (2013) 203–4; comparison with other terms for 'citizens', see above, Chapter 4, n. 3.

[149] Being or feeling *atimos* by definition occurs between people who have a more or less established relationship and therefore usually within a specific community; Demosthenes, for instance, sees the necessity to explain the (paradoxical) fact that the Athenians made Arthios of Zelea *atimos* (Dem. 9 (*Third Philippic*) 42). This community can also consist of gods, for instance the Erinyes who make the Olympian gods *atimos* (Aesch. *Eum.* 213–15), whereas later in the play the reverse happens (809–47); see n. 146.

[150] Some decrees made anyone who would act against its statutes *atimos*, others declared *atimos* who tried to change or disrupt the (text of the) decree itself; for the entrenchment clause ἄτιμος ἔστω/εἶναι in laws of Solon see LR F 22 (= Dem. 23.62), 37a, and in fifth-century decrees see *IG* I^3 21.27–8; 40.33–4; 46.27 etc. Van 't Wout (2011a) argues that the clause meant to prevent negotiations to be reopened if someone felt slighted by the decisions. Hansen (1976a) 55–89 for conditions of *atimia* as a legal penalty, but see the critical notes of Van 't Wout (2011a) and Van 't Wout (2011b).

[151] Actions leading to *atimia* and enforcement of it for the most part depended on citizens' initiative; Allen (2000) 201–2; Jim (2014) 264–6 for evidence and discussion of such tithes.

The latest extant case in the classical age of the clause 'he shall be *atimos*' is in the Athenian law of 336 against tyranny.[152] Any Areopagite, it states, will be made *atimos* who, when the democracy is overthrown, continues to perform his office on the Areopagus; his right and that of his descendants to participate normally in the *polis* will be terminated. This threat contrasts with the statement a few lines earlier that the man who kills anyone who tries to harm the democracy will be *hosios* (pleasing to the gods).[153]

These cases illustrate that a citizen could be excluded from participation, not because of doubts that he or she met the criteria, but due to his or her conduct. The baseline of citizens' participation comes into sharper focus when we look at its reverse, the situation in which offenders could be excluded from basic *time* or from particular *timai* due to bad conduct. One such measure was exclusion from the *polis*'s *hiera*, announced by the Basileus, effectively casting the culprit out from sharing in the *polis*'s bond with the gods.[154] This penalty, which must have been socially and psychologically devastating, could be imposed upon a variety of offenders.

A law attested in the fourth century excluded a citizen woman found guilty of adultery from the *demoteles hiera*.[155] What exactly motivated this penalty is not made explicit in our evidence, but implicitly can hardly be mistaken.[156] Violating the social integrity of the *oikos*, the smallest unit, her misconduct could be taken to damage the integrity of the entire *polis*: by jeopardising the legitimacy of her children, she undermined their

152 RO 79 (*Ag.* 16.73; *IG* II³ 1, 320) l. 20.

153 See also above, Chapter 2.4.2, for this law.

154 Basileus announcing exclusion from *hiera* (*Ath.Pol.* 57), see also above.

155 [Dem.] 59.85–6; the law at 87: Ἐπειδὰν δὲ ἕλῃ τὸν μοιχόν, μὴ ἐξέστω τῷ ἑλόντι συνοικεῖν τῇ γυναικί· ἐὰν δὲ συνοικῇ, ἄτιμος ἔστω. μηδὲ τῇ γυναικὶ ἐξέστω εἰσιέναι εἰς τὰ ἱερὰ τὰ δημοτελῆ, ἐφ' ᾗ ἂν μοιχὸς ἁλῷ· ἐὰν δ' εἰσίῃ, νηποινεὶ πασχέτω ὅ τι ἂν πάσχῃ, πλὴν θανάτου. 'After he has caught the seducer, the man who caught him shall not be permitted to continue living with the woman. If he continues living with her in marriage, he is to be *atimos*. And the woman with whom a seducer has been caught shall not be permitted to attend the public cult ceremonies. If she enters, she is to suffer whatever she suffers, except death.' Transl. Kapparis (1999) 141, slightly modified.

156 The same law on *moicheia* is discussed in Aeschin. 1.183. Canevaro (2013) 190–6 argues, *contra* Kapparis (1999) 356–7 and Carey (1992) 129, that the document quoted in [Dem.] 59.87 is not authentic but that the clause about the woman is derived from an authentic law; since he found no evidence supporting the clause about the case of a husband who refused to divorce the woman, Canevaro doubts the authenticity of this clause because the law should also apply to a woman without a husband. However, although the absence of corroborative evidence must be taken into account, the clause about the husband is a logical consequence of the pollution of the *oikos*'s *hiera kai hosia* caused by the adultery and the condoning of that condition by the husband were he to remain with his wrongdoing (*anhosios*) wife. For adultery as damage to the *oikos* as social unit, Cohen (1991) 98–132.

rightful share to the *hiera kai hosia* of the *oikos* and the *polis*, and forfeited her own position in the chain of citizenship. Her conduct made herself impure, depriving her forever of the *hosios* condition necessary to share in the cults of the household gods and of the gods of the *polis*. The latter effect made her case comparable to that of a male citizen who could find himself barred from *timai* and political prominence when convicted of having lived disgracefully. In his speech against Timarchos in 346/5, Aeschines listed four grounds for a citizen's conviction for disgraceful conduct: maltreating parents, desertion or cowardice, prostituting himself and squandering his ancestral inheritance (*patroia*).[157] Aeschines expounds that the reason why the male citizen who has prostituted himself cannot hold an archonship, any priesthood and any other *time* or *arche* on behalf of the *polis* is because such functions required wearing the priestly crown; in other words, one had to be *hosios* to fulfil such *timai* and clearly his physical abuse of himself made a man impure.[158] The *atimia* involved in this case also prevented a man from addressing his fellow citizens in the assembly and excluded him from sharing the life – the gymnasium, loving honourable youths – that the law allowed to free male citizens but typically not to slaves.[159] In sum, the law robbed a citizen convicted of disgraceful living of his or her basic *time*.[160]

Since from the mid-fifth century onward gradually all citizens had become eligible for the majority of *timai*, the *polis* had become responsible for the quality of all its citizens, as we saw above in the case against Phano and Neaira. Speakers in court could insist on proper conduct of citizens not just for the practical damage they caused, but because misconduct of one could damage the whole community. Such concerns were voiced, for instance, by the speaker in Lysias 6 who supported a complaint against Andocides. If the *dikastai* allowed Andocides, who had returned to the city after his exile for his role in the profanation of the Mysteries, to be restored to normal *time* despite his offences against the goddesses of Eleusis, so he contended, the man would immediately be qualified to

[157] Aeschin. 1.28–32; disgraceful: αἰσχρῶς. For the date and background of the trial, Fisher (2001) 2–8; moral judgement on specific kinds of sexual behaviour, 36–51; laws against disgraceful behaviour and trials following the *dokimasia* of men intent on prominent political functions, 39–40, 51–3. Aeschin. 1.15–17 is crucial evidence for the much-debated law on *hybris*; the laws inserted at 1.16 and 21 are not authentic.

[158] Aeschin. 1.19–20. For the significance of this fact, also Parker, *PS*, 97.

[159] Aeschin. 1.138.

[160] Aeschin. 1.160: τὸν πράξαντα κελεύει μὴ μετέχειν τῶν τῆς πόλεως κοινῶν, '[the law is not interested in how the disgrace was committed, but] rules that the man who did so can no longer participate in the *koina* of the *polis*'.

stand for allotment to become (Archon) Basileus and thus to sacrifice and pray for all Athenians and preside over the Mysteries as if he were pure – an affront to the goddesses and to all the Greeks who would come to celebrate in this major Athenian cult. Now, the speaker concluded, the *dikastai* had to do what was *dikaios*: this man should not be accepted as a full citizen under ancestral law.[161] Of course, statistically the chances were very small that Andocides would be selected by lot to be Basileus, but that did not matter for the speaker. He pointed out that the Athenians collectively were responsible for the (religious) quality of those who performed their *hiera* for them at one of their major cults, in this case also for all their guests at a pan-Hellenic cult. With *all* Athenians enjoying equal *time* in eligibility for the archonships, *all* Athenians had to have the same impeccable credentials in terms of descent and conduct.

For bad conduct highlights what was normally expected: the correct conduct and also what went beyond the average: citizens who behaved better than others. From the mid-fourth century onwards we find the *polis* inscribing honours for Athenians who had held *polis* offices and had done their duties excellently, granting them a golden crown of 500 or 1,000 drachmae, a sum for sacrifice and a stele proclaiming this particular honour as the commendable result of *philotimia*.[162] Certainly the *polis* had honoured citizens before, notably successful generals, and the *phylai*, too, had honoured successful members, but *inscribing* such honours had been quite unusual.[163] Stephen Lambert points out that these mid-fourth-century inscribed honorific decrees at *polis* level entail an innovation he explains by the increasing bureaucracy of the *polis* that invited an expanding epigraphical practice and which needed the excellent secretaries who are prominent among those honoured in these decrees.[164] One of these decrees, furthermore, is for Pytheas of Alopeke, for a quadrennial elective office, a superintendent of the water supply, a decree which hints heavily

161 [Lys.] 6.3–7.

162 For the epigraphical evidence and discussion of this development, Lambert (2012a) 3–47, with further refs. He collects nine decrees honouring councillors and secretaries of the *boule* (*inter alia* *IG* II³ 1, 306; 323; 327 a–c; 469); five decrees for cultic personnel and priests (e.g. *IG* II³ 1, 416; 359), three decrees for office holders connected with the Amphiareion; nine decrees for other office holders, among which two (no. 25 and 26) for allotted offices; and four decrees for other officials, who were certainly or presumably not allotted.

163 Whitehead (1993) 64–9; Lambert (2012a) 3–47. Honouring citizens and inscribing these honours in *polis* decrees seems to have begun in the early fourth century with *ateleia* and a statue granted to Konon (Dem. 20.69), but these highly exceptional honours were for *strategoi* after successful battles. The novelty after 346/5 concerns inscribed decrees honouring citizens holding various kinds of administrative *polis* offices.

164 Lambert (2012a) 5–6.

at financial contribution from the honorand.[165] It seems noteworthy that a number of these honorific decrees concern *allotted* offices, not only the secretaries mentioned but also councillors, annual priests and *hieropoioi*.[166] Whereas elected officials, many of whom military *archai* such as generals, enjoyed possibilities for attaining more *time* than open to average citizens,[167] with these honorific decrees the *polis* conveyed particular honours to citizens who had been selected by virtue of their baseline *time* by lot. They were were thus publicly praised for their *philotimia* in the performance of their offices, while the *polis* did not need to change the system of selection to encourage their *philotimia*.

5.7 Distribution of *Timai*: Means of Selection

In the classical era, all citizens could participate in the *polis*'s public life at the base level but only a limited number could get one of the prominent *timai*. For the stability of the *polis* it was essential that the system was felt to be just and working in the correct manner: that the offices were properly distributed to the right persons, and that the right persons were selected in the proper way. Distribution to the right persons depended on the criteria of access: a particular office was open only to the qualified groups. *Within* each group all were in principle more or less equal, unless other factors came into play; just distribution of *time* therefore depended equally on proper means of selection.

There were basically two methods. In election *differences* in qualities between citizens within the same group were recognised and rewarded with *timai*. Allotment (*klerosis*), by contrast, was (and still is) justly considered a means essentially tied to *equality*, not only by drawing on the 'more or less' equality of the candidates from among the same group but

[165] *IG* II³ 1, 338; Lambert *per ep.*

[166] The *grammateus* for the prytany was until the 360s elected by show of hands, but by the time of *Ath.Pol.* (54.3) selected by lot; Lambert (2012a) no. 2 (337/6?), no. 3 (336/5 and 335/4) and no. 4 (340–525) are such *grammateis* selected by lot; this perhaps also applies to the *anagrapheus* (Lambert no. 5). The priests (Lambert nos 10 and 11; *IG* II³ 1, 416 and 359) were allotted, but the *hieropoioi* in no. 10 (l. 23) are οἱ αἱρεθέντες ὑπὸ τῆς βουλῆς, i.e. 'selected by the *boule*', here probably 'elected', although αἵρεσις and αἱρέσθαι do not always mean 'election', but rather 'selection', according to Abel (1983) 18–19, Rhodes, *CAAP*, 41. The *hieropoioi* of Lambert no. 13 were allotted (*Ath.Pol.* 53.6–7). For the change in the method of selection of the *grammateus* of the *boule*, Taylor (2007) 337 with further refs.

[167] Taylor (2007) argues that the absence of evidence that elections for the *strategia* were manipulated would suggest that 'elected positions were not highly sought' (338). This argument would seem to conflict, however, with her observation that *strategoi* could wield great influence, that the office allowed the *demos* to vote for expertise after its own preferences and that elections allowed the elite a forum of controlled competition.

also enforcing absolute equality because the decision made by the lot puts an end to evaluation of their differences.[168] In this respect, allotment is the opposite of election.[169] A third way, known as *klerosis ek prokriton*, applied *prokrisis*, selection based on differences (wealth, birth, merit) to create a group among whom the lot was to select.[170]

According to *Ath.Pol.* (43.1), in contemporaneous Athens all *archai* were selected by lot, except the *tamias* of the *stratiotika*, the *tamias* of the *theorika*, the *epimeletes* of the wells and all military offices. The *Ath.Pol.* mentions that the means of selection of quite a number of offices had changed over the years, in most cases from election to allotment, but the recent institution of new financial offices filled by election shows that change towards allotment was not a linear development applied to all *archai*, but applied selectively. Scholars following the lead of the Old Oligarch take these exceptions to indicate that in the classical democracy the Athenians preferred election for offices that required special capacities or expertise, and the lot for all other offices.[171] Most allotted *archai* were corporate offices, often based on the ten Cleisthenic tribes, and increasingly drawn from virtually all male citizens (the Tamiai of Athena being a prominent exception in being selected from those of great wealth). Combining allotment and rotation in these bodies, the system maximised citizen participation, with the result that the distance between those being administered and those doing the administering was exceptionally small.[172] In contrast to these corporate offices, the new priesthoods allotted from among all male or female citizens by lot in the years after the mid-fifth century were individual offices and in the case of the priestess of Athena Nike, at least, the office was probably not limited to a single year.[173] The remarkable fact of the Athenian democracy is not so much the use of the lot itself, which is attested in many ancient societies as a means of selection and distribution,

[168] Stone (2011) 29–41 for use of the lot as 'decision making without reasons' and 42–4 for sortition as divination, 'a decision based on someone else's reasons'.

[169] I intend to discuss the use of the lot at Athens more extensively elsewhere, and limit my discussion here to a few points relevant to this study.

[170] *Ath.Pol.* 8.1; Arist. *Pol.* 1298b8–11: *klerosis* with *prokrisis* leans towards aristocracy; for the function of *prokrisis* in the process of allotment, Demont (2001). LSJ *s.v.* προκρίνω and cognates show that *prokrisis* always entails a form of explicit preference, e.g. by election, judgement or other predefined qualifications; cf. Abel (1983) 7–13, 68.

[171] [Xen.] *Ath.Pol.* 1.2–3.

[172] On democracy and rotation, Arist. *Pol.* 1298a10–35; above, n. 68. Rotation by the use of the lot was applied to the turns of the prytanies and the appointment of secretaries in the *boule*, according to Arist. *Pol.* 1298a15–17, and is confirmed in Athens by epigraphical evidence of decrees; above, n. 166.

[173] Blok (2014b) with further refs.

but its use for assigning *timai* on an exceptionally large scale in a domain that historically and as a system was more geared to rewarding difference than to equality.

Why should this be so? Few explicit arguments in Athens *pro* or *contra* allotment can be found that go beyond the (dis)advantages of the effects of the lot, such as Isocrates' contention that Athens's 'ancient constitution' had elected the best to run the *polis*, instead of selecting them all by lot as current in his own time.[174] An obvious reason, that the use of the lot is an effective means to prevent strife – no one is to blame for the result – was not articulated; instead, the absence of judgement on qualities in allotment was a point of dissent for critics of the democracy.[175]

In the classical age, the lot was strongly associated with democracy, equality being the crucial link between the two.[176] Yet the same means of selection was used in aristocracies and oligarchies, where it likewise (re-) enforced equality among the candidates.[177] It is not just the lot itself, but the *size* of the group involved that determines the political nature of the equality to which the lot gives effect: in a democracy that group comprises all citizens, in an oligarchy just a few.[178] But if the size of the group is important, would *election* by all from all have had the same effect? Aristotle classified such as system as a democracy,[179] although throughout the *Politics*, he characterises election as typical of an aristocracy or

[174] Isoc. 7 (*Areop.*) 22: οὐκ ἐξ ἁπάντων τὰς ἀρχὰς κληροῦντες, ἀλλὰ τοὺς βελτίστους καὶ τοὺς ἱκανωτάτους ἐφ' ἕκαστον τῶν ἔργων προκρίνοντες. 'They did not select by lot from all for the offices, but chose those who were the best and most able to do each of the tasks.' De Ste. Croix (2004) 101–3 argues that Isocrates uses προκρίνειν here in the more common sense, 'prefer, select', rather than the technical sense, 'elect prior to allotment'.

[175] See esp. Plato, *Leg.* 757b–e for a sophisticated discussion of the difference between human and divine justice in equality effectuated by the lot.

[176] Lot as typical of democracy: Hdt. 3.80.27; [Xen.] *Ath.Pol.* 1.2–3; Xen. *Mem.* 1.2.9; Pl. *Resp.* 561b3–5; Isoc. *Areop.* 7.21–2; Arist. *Pol.* 1300a32; 1317b20–2; 1365b30–1; for the nucleus freedom, equality, democracy, Arist. *Pol.* 1287a7–25; 1317b10–1318a10.

[177] Arist. *Pol.* 1300b1–4: τὸ δὲ τὰς μὲν ἐκ πάντων τὰς δ' ἐκ τινῶν πολιτικὸν ἀριστοκρατικῶς, ἢ τὰς μὲν αἱρέσει τὰς δὲ κληρῷ, τὸ δὲ τινὰς ἐκ τινῶν <αἱρέσει> ὀλιγαρχικὸν καὶ τὸ τινὰς ἐκ τινῶν κλήρῳ (μὴ γινομένου δ'ὁμοίως), καὶ τὸ τινὰς ἐκ τινῶν ἀμφοῖν. τὸ δὲ τινὰς ἐξ ἁπάντων τό τε ἐκ τινῶν αἱρέσει πάντας ἀριστοκρατικόν. 'To appoint some offices from all and the others from a certain class is constitutional with an aristocratic bias; or to appoint some by vote and others by lot. And for a certain class to appoint from a certain class (by vote) is oligarchical, and so it is for a certain class from a certain class by lot (although not working out in the same way) and for a certain class to appoint from a certain class by both methods. And for a certain class to make a preliminary selection from the whole body and then for all to appoint from among certain persons (thus selected) is aristocratic.' Transl. H. Rackham (Loeb ed.).

[178] Cf. Demont (2001).

[179] Arist. *Pol.* 1300a33–6: τούτων δ' αἱ μὲν τρεῖς καταστάσεις δημοτικαί, τὸ πάντας ἐκ πάντων αἱρέσει ἢ κλήρῳ [γίνεσθαι] ἢ ἀμφοῖν, τὰς μὲν κλήρῳ τὰς δ' αἱρέσει τῶν ἀρχῶν, 'three ways of appointment are democratic: that all are appointed from all by election or by lot or by both – some offices by lot and others by election'.

an oligarchy (terms he does not always use consistently) because in both selection is made depending on differences in *time*, good birth and wealth respectively.[180] His argument seems to be that election is oligarchic or aristocratic if a *politeia* uses this method intentionally to limit the number of voters and especially the number of candidates. But in the historical reality of Athens, election even when applied by all from all was associated with recognising citizens' differences in individual *time* of whatever kind. Signs of this perception are suggestions in oratory, such as Demosthenes' portrayal of Meidias above, elected to various *timai* by show of hands due to his wealth, and the factual results of election and allotment at Athens, the first resulting in a predominance of wealthy citizens living in demes in or close by the *asty*, the latter in a representation of 'average' citizens far more evenly spread over Attica, as Claire Taylor has shown.[181] It seems the Athenians knew themselves well enough to counter the effects of election by those of the lot in order to keep the desired level of equality among the citizens.

Nonetheless, if these arguments explain to some extent the implementation of equality by use of the lot in the fourth century, they only partly explain why equality could be or become such a powerful political value in the first place and why the lot was considered the preferred means to effectuate it, whereas in the first half of the fifth century the democracy was still prevailingly based on formal distinctions in wealth and birth among citizens. In other words, we need to ask more fundamental questions as to the social foundations of the value of equality and the successful application of the lot as a means of selection to implement this, in the face of the tradition to assign *timai* due to differences in *time*. Using the framework developed by North, we need to look for underlying institutions for distributing goods by means of the lot with concomitant valuation for equality in this distribution and for the lot as a means of decision making, institutions that could have been instrumental in making this method acceptable and even attractive in the sphere of *timai*. Three institutions with features relevant to our issue seem to converge here: the division and assigning of inheritances by use of the lot, with the inherent idea of equality; decision making by the lot as a sign of divine decision and justice; and descent as the institution underlying citizenship. I begin with the institutional connection between lot and inheritance.

[180] E.g. Arist. *Pol.* 1283a16–18: διόπερ εὐλόγως ἀντιποιοῦνται τῆς τιμῆς οἱ εὐγενεῖς καὶ ἐλεύθεροι καὶ πλούσιοι. '[In the context of a state] it is reasonable that the well-born, the free and the wealthy lay claim to *time*.'

[181] Taylor (2007).

Kleros (lot, part, part assigned by lot), the root of *klerosis* (distribution by lot) and the verb *kleroo* (to distribute by lot), indicates something that belongs to one as a part of a larger whole, just like *moira* and *meros*, all three nouns which etymologically refer to partition and which in the archaic age could be used interchangeably. Dividing and apportioning such parts was indicated by the verb *nemein*;*isonomia* meant, besides equality in law, distribution of equal parts. Receiving one's fitting part by lot was indicated by the verb *lanchanein*. Such parts could be one's share of an inheritance, notably of land, or of sacrificial meat, and metaphorically could mean one's share in life; in the classical age the latter became the prevailing meaning of *moira*, while *kleros* remained the normal word for (one's part of) the inheritance. Ancient Greece generally and also Athens, as I discussed in Chapter 3, applied partible inheritance, and *kleros*, unlike *moira* / *meros*, therefore normally implied an *equal* share.[182]

Using lots to make a decision was regarded as making Zeus's will known; in the *Iliad*, this is vividly portrayed in the selection among the *basileis* for the honour of championship in a duel.[183] The selection by lot is seen here as a sign of divine justice, a notion that was also effective in the distribution of the equal parts of the inheritance among the heirs, for which two scenes from Homeric epic offer 'canonical' pictures. In *Iliad* book 15, Iris takes a message from Zeus to Poseidon forbidding him to influence the course of the war. Poseidon retorts that he need not accept any command from his brother, who, although the elder, is his equal. As the legitimate sons of Kronos and Rhea, the three of them – Zeus, Hades

[182] For the use of the lot in assigning parts to heirs, Berman (2007) 120–32. Despite some evidence that indivisibility of land is desirable (e.g. Pl. *Leg.* 740b6–8), in practice the system of equal division prevailed everywhere; Lane Fox (1985). For the terminology of *kleros* and *moira*, especially with reference to sacrificial portion, Borecky (1963). *Pace* the latter, *moira* / *meros* is not by definition an *equal* share nor especially tied to sacrifice. The earliest reference to *isomoiria*, Solon fr. 34: 'With the help of the gods, I have accomplished what I said I would, and other fruitless measures I did not take; it gives me no pleasure to act (?) with the violence of tyranny or to share the country's rich land equally (*isomoirie*) between the lower and the upper classes' refers to land, not to sacrifice and needs to indicate the equality of shares explicitly – it is not inherent in the notion *moira*.

[183] Hom. *Il.* 3.264–339: the duel between Menelaos and Paris is to take place under the supervision of Zeus as god of justice. The lot (*kleros*) is cast to determine which of the two champions is to throw his spear first, and the army prays that Zeus will see to it that he, who is guilty of the war, will die. In *Il.* 7.161–80, in the drawing of lots (*kleroi*) for the championship against Hector, nine volunteers enter the competition and put their lot into a helmet. The army prays to Zeus: 'Father Zeus, grant that the lot fall on Ajax or the son of Tydeus or else on the king himself of Mycene rich in gold.' The Greek sources are not consistent on Zeus as the *auctor* of the world order dispensing one's just *moira* to each, or as himself also subject to this order; Sarischoulis (2008). In Athens, connection between *moira* and Zeus is visible in a preparatory sacrifice to the Moirai and to Zeus Moiragetes (and other gods, presumably Ge) offered by the *genos* Praxiergidai, *IG* I^3 7.12.

and himself – partitioned the world into three equal parts; each acquired his portion by lot (*lanchano*) and they are *homotimos* (of the same *time*), *isomoros* and of *isos aise* (with equal *moira* and *aise* = share).[184] Poseidon's insistence in this episode on equality between the three sons of Kronos and Rhea has a counterpart among mortals in the scene in the *Odyssey* mentioned above, where Odysseus pretends to be a son of a Cretan noble with a concubine (*pallakis*). When still alive, his father treated him with the same *time* as his many legitimate (*ithageneis*) sons, but after his death they distributed the inheritance in *kleroi* amongst themselves, giving only a small part to the bastard brother.[185] Again, the distribution takes place among the equal heirs/legitimate descendants and among them the portions are assigned by lot. In the classical era, this conception of *kleros* as inheritance is attested massively, whether or not the distribution of the parts of the inheritance actually took place by lot.[186]

The lot as a sign of divine decision was not only used for assigning portions of the inheritance, but also the method *par excellence* for the selection of priests and priestesses.[187] In classical Athens, on the current evidence, all priests and priestesses were selected by lot, in the *gene* among the *gennetai* holding this priesthood and in the democratic priesthoods among all the citizens. Plato observed on this procedure in his philosophical–critical commentary on the *politeia* of Athens, the *Laws*:

> As to the priests, we shall entrust it to the god himself to ensure his good pleasure, committing their selection to the divine *tyche* of the lot, but each person who gains the lot (*lanchano*) we shall scrutinise, first, as to whether he is of sound body and legitimate descent, and, second, if he comes from families (households) which are as pure as possible, being himself clean

[184] Hom. *Il.* 15.185–221; λαγχάνω: 190–2; ὁομότιμος: 186; τιμή of each: 189; μοῖρα of each: 195, 206; ἰσόμορον καὶ ὁμῇ πεπρωμένον αἴσῃ: 209. Note that the equality needs to be expressed explicitly when the shares are called μοῖρα and αἴση. Burkert (1992) 90–1, West (1997) 109–10 and Gysembergh (2013) point to similarities with the division of the world and assignment by lot between the gods in Mesopotamia, but in the Homeric setting the division concerns an *inheritance* and *equal* parts, unlike the division of land among the Mesopotamian gods.

[185] Hom. *Od.* 14.200–9: πολλοὶ δὲ καὶ ἄλλοι / υἷες ἐνὶ μεγάρῳ ἠμὲν τράφον ἠδ' ἐγένοντο / γνήσιοι ἐξ ἀλόχου· ἐμὲ δ' ὠνητὴ τέκε μήτηρ / παλλακίς, ἀλλά με ἶσον ἰθαιγενέεσσιν ἐτίμα Κάστωρ; … τοὶ δὲ ζωὴν ἐδάσαντο / παῖδες ὑπέρθυμοι καὶ ἐπὶ κλήρους ἐβάλοντο.

[186] To take possession of one's inheritance was usually rendered as κλῆρον λαχεῖν; e.g. in Is. 3.2, 3.30 etc. it concerns the inheritance of an only daughter, so there was no need of division; in Is. 4.24 and 11.9, 13, 15 the expression concerns again a single claimant of an inheritance; in Is. 5.16.6, however, it concerns a share (*meros*) of an inheritance, and in Is. 8.1 likewise the inheritance of more than one claimant.

[187] Feaver (1957) 128, who supposed, however, that before allotment *prokrisis* was used; the *gene*, see above; democratic priests: Lambert (2010b).

> from murder and all such offences against divine order, and with a father and mother who have lived by the same rule.[188]

Clearly, the idea was that in the selection of his/her priest(ess) the godd(ess) had a choice of her/his own. Humans had a say in the procedure before this moment, by defining the group of candidates, and after this moment, that is in the *dokimasia* of the selected person, which in Athens always took place after, not before, selection. In these respects Plato's description reflects the actual practices of his time.

In the *gene*, the two usages of the lot converged: it was a divine sign selecting the right candidate to serve the gods, and, by this very choice, it assigned the *kleros* (part of the inheritance) to the right person. Since both institutions using decision by lot were deeply embedded in Greek traditions attested in the archaic age, it reasonable to assume that in the *gene* allotment for office already existed in the early sixth century. If this supposition is valid, the selection for *polis* priesthood among the *gene* would offer a commendable model for selection by lot in other *polis* offices, especially those highly profiled in religious duties.[189] I would argue on a brief analysis of the evidence that this could be a possible scenario.

In what the Athenians regarded as their 'ancestral *politeia*' allotment for offices was instituted by Solon, as a new method for the, formerly elected, archonships and for the probably new office of the Tamiai of Athena. According to the *Ath.Pol.*,

> Solon had the officials appointed by allotment from a shortlist of men elected by each of the tribes. For the nine archons each tribe elected ten candidates, and lots were drawn among those: because of this it is still the practice of each of the tribes to pick ten men by lot, and then for an allotment to be made among them. That Solon stipulated appointment by lot from the property classes is confirmed by the law on the Tamiai [of Athena], which remains in use even today: it orders the appointment of the treasurers by lot from the Pentakosiomedimnoi.[190]

188 Plato, *Leg.* 759c: τὰ μὲν οὖν τῶν ἱερέων τῷ θεῷ ἐπιτρέποντα αὐτῷ τὸ κεχαρισμένον γίγνεσθαι, κληροῦν οὕτω τῇ θείᾳ τύχῃ ἀποδιδόντα, δοκιμάζειν δὲ τὸν ἀεὶ λαγχάνοντα πρῶτον μὲν ὁλόκληρον καὶ γνήσιον, ἔπειτα ὡς ὅτι μάλιστα ἐκ καθαρευουσῶν οἰκήσεων, φόνου δὲ ἁγνὸν καὶ πάντων τῶν περὶ τὰ τοιαῦτα εἰς τὰ θεῖα ἁμαρτανομένων αὐτὸν καὶ πατέρα καὶ μητέρα κατὰ ταὐτὰ βεβιωκότας. transl. R.G. Bury (Loeb ed.); slightly modified. Note that the phrase 'being clean of murder ... lived by the same rule' could be captured in 'living *hosiôs*'. Plato's insistence that in his ideal *polis* priests must be allotted carries particular weight, because for all the other *archai* he preferred election due to merit; Morrow (1960); Abel (1983) 49–53.

189 For the conventional, opposite view that methods for selection of priesthoods were always secondary and subsequent to those of the *archai*, notably the archons, e.g. Aleshire (1994) 334.

190 *Ath.Pol.* 8.1: Τὰς δ'ἀρχὰς ἐποίησε κληρωτὰς ἐκ προκρίτων οὓς ἑκαστη προκρίνειε τῶν φυλῶν. προὔκρινεν δ᾽ εἰς τοὺς ἐννέα ἀρχοντας ἑκάστη δέκα, καὶ τούτων ἐκλήρουν· ὅθεν ἔτι διαμένει

Scholars have often argued that, by having the lot decide the final selection, Solon prevented strife, creating equality among the candidates of the newly established property classes of fixed thresholds of wealth but mixed social background. Other scholars, notably M.H. Hansen, do not believe *Ath.Pol.*'s account of Solon's introduction of the lot, due to a passage in *Politics* that Solon 'did not abolish elements that existed before, concerning both the council [Areopagus] and the selection (*hairesis*) of *archai*', but added the people's court to control the magistrates.[191] Hansen further calls the *Ath.Pol.* into question because he takes the lot to be a democratic method that in the sixth century would have been unacceptable to select the archons, especially the Polemarchos who was to lead the army.[192] I do not find these objections convincing.

The allotment of the archaic offices was not made 'from all' but from the few, a vital difference that Hansen neglects. *Ath.Pol.* and *Politics* do not contradict each other because the procedure they ascribe to Solon, *klerosis ek prokriton*, retained election before, or as a component of, allotment. In the *gene*, the purity of Athenian descent and their inherited privileges provided the relevant *prokrisis*; among them, the lot selected for priesthood. For the archonships, the *demos* elected from among elite men, who claimed to be qualified for their *timai* by their wealth, their military lifestyle and their proclaimed descent from Homeric heroes with divine ancestry, a group of candidates among whom the lot would decide.[193] We saw above that among groups with such 'aristocratic' values the lot was

ταῖς φυλαῖς τὸ δέκα κληροῦν ἑκάστην, εἶτ᾽ ἐκ τούτων κυαμεύειν. σημεῖον δ᾽ ὅτι κληρωτὰς ἐποίησεν ἐκ τῶν τιμημάτων ὁ περὶ τῶν ταμιῶν νόμος ᾧ χρώμενοι διατελοῦσιν ἔτι καὶ νῦν· κελεύει γὰρ κληροῦν τοὺς ταμίας ἐκ πεντακοσιομεδίμνων. Transl. P.J. Rhodes, slightly modified; a law of Solon on this matter repeated in *Ath.Pol.* 47.1. On the use of the lot for appointment of archons see also Staveley (1972) 34; Rhodes, *CAAP ad.* 8.1, 146–8; Develin (1979).

191 Arist. *Pol.* 1273b36–1274a4: ἔοικε δὲ Σόλων ἐκεῖνα μὲν ὑπαρχοντα πρότερον οὐ καταλῦσαι, τήν τε βουλὴν καὶ τὴν τῶν ἀρχῶν αἵρεσιν, τὸν δὲ... The topic of discussion is the ultimate democratic effect of the people's courts.

192 Hansen (1990) and de Ste.Croix (2004) 94–6 deny any significance of the early use of allotment in religious contexts for the classical *polis*. Hansen further contends that the original *axones* no longer existed, hence *Ath.Pol.* could not really know what Solon had done, but merely reflects fourth-century ideas about Solon. That *Ath.Pol.* shows some fourth-century views of Solon is certainly true, and the state of the *axones* in the fourth century is much disputed, but that does not preclude knowledge of archaic Athens and its laws from other sources; for this controversy, see Stroud (1979), Sickinger (1999) 24–33, Rhodes (2006).

193 Wade–Gery (1958b) 113 observed some of this effect, although he followed the then current viewpoint distinguishing between the pre- and post-Solon elites: 'When an aristocratic office (such as the archon held in Solon's day ...) was filled by a hereditary noble, his birth gave him a clear divine sanction: his fitness was divinely ordered, he was *diotrephes* [fostered by Zeus]. But if you break with heredity, as Solon did ... you must replace it with something. By ... the *klerosis ek prokriton* ascribed to Solon, the responsibility is shared between man and God, God having the last word; and, from the point of view of the man chosen, his sanction is partly at least divine.'

regarded as selection by divine will and hence an appropriate method to attain more *time*, on the example of the heroes of the *Iliad*. This notion of divine selection could be made out to be particularly relevant for the archonships and the Tamiai, *polis* offices whose duties lay for a large part in the sphere of *hiera* and in this respect shared essential features with priesthoods. That the archons used to be selected by *klerosis ek prokriton* must have been known in the late fourth century, when *prokrisis* for these offices was no longer practised, but transformed (reduced) into a double allotment; it would be rather pointless to attribute an obsolete procedure to the past if that was not generally known to have existed. For the Tamiai, *prokrisis* based on wealth took place before selection by lot, in the sixth century and still in the fourth.

This possible origin of allotment for *archai* in archaic Athens, transferred from the *gene* to the archons and the Tamiai, cannot be more than a hypothesis. It seems certain, however, that once it was used for the archons and the Tamiai, the lot was employed for other offices as well. For such a step to be feasible, we would expect certain institutional conditions had to be met: a conception of a community with an inherent tendency towards equality to make the radical equality of the lot acceptable, but simultaneously modified by procedures accommodating the deeply entrenched values on differences in *time* between citizens, such as *prokrisis*. I would argue that Cleisthenes' system created both.

The new structure of citizenship included all free inhabitants of Attica into a notion of common metaphorical descent as Athenians, anchored on the traditions of the phratries, making them all heirs to *ta patroia* of the *polis*. On this condition, all citizens became equals among whom the lot could distribute parts, in this case public office, if such a distribution could be persuasively made out to be appropriate. In the first half of the fifth century, as far as we know, this only applied to the role of *dikastes*. For the other *archai* and *timai*, *prokrisis* still prevailed in the form of wealth criteria, birth criteria or election before allotment, notably in selection of the archons and *bouleutai*. The first case that we know of assignment by lot 'from all' (*ek (ha)panton*), that is without any further qualification except basic *time*, to a single, prominent *time*, was the priestesshood of Athena Nike, at some point between the 440s and 420s.[194] Given the scarcity of the evidence it is impossible to say with certainty that this was the very first case of such a selection from all, but in the available sources

[194] The epigram for her proudly mentioned selection 'from all' (*IG* I³ 1330.11–17): πρώτε Ἀθηναίας Νίκες ἕδος ἀμφεπόλευσεν / ἐκ πάντων κλήρωι, Μυρρίνη εὐτυχίαι. 'Myrrhine was the first to serve the sanctuary of Athena Nike to good fortune by lot from all.'

no earlier case is mentioned or seems to be implied, neither for an *arche*, nor for a priesthood. The latter could only become feasible with Pericles' Citizenship Law: once legitimate Athenian citizens had to be born from two Athenian parents, they were raised to the same birth qualifications as the *gene* and hence eligible for priesthood – which were necessarily new priesthoods, now to be filled by one from among all the Athenians. In this radical step, all three institutional frameworks of allotment converged, providing a foundation for selection for a priestesshood, for which a well-known precedent existed in the Pythia at Delphi.[195]

5.8 Evaluating Equals

Pericles' Citizenship Law had several incisive effects. Making marriage with non-Athenians highly unattractive for Athenians, the law in effect closed the ranks of the Athenian *demos*.[196] Among this group, the law removed a formidable distinction between *gene* and others in terms of birth, as we just saw, by raising all citizens, male and female, to the same level. Following on the gradual lowering of property requirements for the archonships, the law thus made the final step towards equality among all citizens, stimulating this principle to be effectuated in public office and other areas of participation.[197] Furthermore, adopting and adapting the traditional, metaphorical descent stories of the *gene*, the whole *demos* now rapidly developed an image of themselves as of ancient and immaculate Athenian lineage, projecting their origin as a collective into the very earth of Attica and boasting to be autochthonous.[198] In descent and participation, every individual Athenian was now a citizen equal to others, a quality reflected in the vocabulary discussed in Chapter 4.

This multifaceted idea of equality of all citizens did not sit easily with the institution of *time*. One way of dealing with this tension, as Robin Osborne persuasively argued, was the outlet provided in the competitive festivals, where citizens could realise their ambitions either by excelling in

[195] Plut. *Mor.* 405c–d; Eur. *Ion* 1322–3: Φοίβου προφῆτις, τρίποδος ἀρχαῖον νόμον / σῴζουσα, πασῶν Δελφίδων ἐξαίρετος. 'Prophetess of Phoebus, preserving the ancient law of the tripod, selected from all Delphic women'. For αἵρεω / αἵρεσθαι meaning 'to select' regardless of the means used, see above, n. 166; Plut. 405c–d implies that selection was unpredictable, i.e. by lot. She was appointed for life: Aesch. *Eum.* 38; *FD* III 1: 553, Roman era; Diod.S. 16.26.6; see also Blok (2014b).

[196] See further Chapter 6.

[197] One means to put this principle into practice was to provide *misthos* for *polis* offices; for the evidence and historical development, Blok (2015).

[198] Blok (2009a).

performance or in paying for them.[199] Another way directed this tension between equality and *time* inward, into the citizen community. Valuing others was a structural ingredient of the Athenian *politeia*: citizens scrutinised each other's qualifications (*dokimasia*), assessed each other after performance of office (*euthynai*), and resolved each other's disputes in large courts filled by allotted *dikastai* and even more numerous onlookers. As a result, an individual citizen could be found wanting and be punished with loss of *time*, for instance in the shape of a fine, or the reverse, he could be valued for higher achievements than others and praised with a vocabulary capturing new, democratic virtues. Whitehead argues persuasively that in praising fellow citizens 'for what they had done, rather than who they were', the Athenians changed the elitist-sounding notion *arete* (excellence) into *andragathia*, the abstract noun of 'being an *agathos* man', a virtue of the excellent fitting the ideology of the equals.[200] *Philotimia* was (striving for) *time* directed towards the community, leading to special *timai*.

This continuous and intensive valuation by Athenian citizens of themselves and their peers created a specific attitude, I would argue, which is illuminated by the use of the adjective *axios* and its cognates. *Axios* reflects the image of a set of scales, denoting weight, value and judgement; used in a social context, it elicits balancing contributions – in words, deeds, property, character or any other means – in a relationship between two parties.[201] The cognate verb *axioo* means 'to think worthy of' and 'to ask', but clearly with the connotation of asking recognition of what is one's due.[202] *Axios* and *time* thus both evaluate what each party contributes to a reciprocal relationship, but whereas *time* is directed towards recognition of difference, *axios* evaluates one's performance in a framework that aims at equality, represented by the balance of the scales. *Axios* and cognates, not surprisingly, appear more frequently in political and forensic discourse than, for instance, in historiography.[203] Some passages exemplify its use.

Thucydides famously offers an ideal version of citizenship and its vocabulary in his account of Pericles' funeral speech in the winter of 431/0:

199 Osborne (2010a).

200 Whitehead (1993) 43–7, 60–2; Whitehead (2009).

201 LSJ, *s.v.* ἄξιος. *Ta axia* not 'rights' but one's 'deserts', based on claims and expectations, Allen (2000) 149–50.

202 LSJ, *s.v.* ἀξιόω; its meaning of 'to ask' differs from ἐροτάω, 'to ask a question', with connotations of investigation or dispute.

203 The verb ἀξιόω is used more frequently than the adjective ἄξιος; both lexemes combined appear in Antiphon, Isocrates and Isaeus at an average of 3 per 1,000 words, in Lysias 4.5 per 1,000; in Thucydides and Xenophon's *Hellenika* (generally, not distinguished into narrative and speeches) at an average of 0.5 per 1,000.

> We live in a *politeia* that does not strive for the laws adopted by our neighbours, but instead we are more a model for others than that we imitate them. To be sure, our *politeia*, because we involve not few but many, has the name democracy; but, while in accordance with our laws there is, in the face of their individual (*idios*) differences, equality for all (*metesti*), in accordance with the esteem (*axiosis*) that comes with distinction in whatever field, an individual enjoys higher standing (*time*) in relation to matters of common concern (*koinos*) on the basis not so much of belonging to a group (*meros*) as of personal merit; while at the same time, with regard to poverty, someone who is capable of benefiting the city is not prevented from doing so by obscurity of status (*axioma*).[204]

Pericles' speech propagates here a conception of citizenship, in which the equality of the citizens as shareholders (*meteinai*) in the *politeia* willingly accommodates recognition of the special value (*time*) of individual citizens *if and when* their merits serve the benefit of the *polis* (*axios*). In Aristophanes' *Knights* of 424, the protagonists – a prominent group among the citizens – try to put this principle into practice. Rejecting the conspicuous public *timai* that other citizens individually claim for their war efforts, they 'ask for themselves (*axioomai*) to defend the *polis* and its native gods freely just like the ancestors'.[205] The knights ask for the privilege to live up to their sense of *noblesse oblige* by valorously fighting for the city, a privilege they ground in their defence of what *they share with all the Athenians*; as a reward for their efforts, they ask only to be allowed to be different – in their posh lifestyle.[206] In court, however, benefits and obligations were to be dispensed on strict equality, as Isocrates underlined in a private lawsuit on behalf of a poor citizen against a wealthy defendant:

> it would be a most shocking state of affairs if in a democratic *polis* we should not be in exactly the same position; and if, while judging ourselves worthy (*axioo*) of *metechein* in the *archai*, yet we should deprive ourselves of what is just (*ta dikaia*) in the laws; and if, though willing to die in battle for our *politeia*, we would assign more value to the wealthy when casting our votes [as *dikastai*].[207]

[204] Thuc. 2.37.1: Χρώμεθα γὰρ πολιτείᾳ οὐ ζηλούσῃ τοὺς τῶν πέλας νόμους, παράδειγμα δὲ μᾶλλον αὐτοὶ ὄντες τισὶν ἢ μιμούμενοι ἑτέρους. καὶ ὄνομα μὲν διὰ τὸ μὴ ἐς ὀλίγους ἀλλ᾽ ἐς πλείονας οἰκεῖν δημοκρατία κέκληται· μέτεστι δὲ κατὰ μὲν τοὺς νόμους πρὸς τὰ ἴδια διάφορα πᾶσι τὸ ἴσον, κατὰ δὲ τὴν ἀξίωσιν, ὡς ἕκαστος ἔν τῳ εὐδοκιμεῖ, οὐκ ἀπὸ μέρους τὸ πλέον ἐς τὰ κοινὰ ἢ ἀπ᾽ ἀρετῆς προτιμᾶται, οὐδ᾽ αὖ κατὰ πενίαν, ἔχων γέ τι ἀγαθὸν δρᾶσαι τὴν πόλιν, ἀξιώματος ἀφανείᾳ κεκώλυται. Transl. Winton (2004), modified.

[205] Ar. *Eq.* 575–6: ἡμεῖς δ᾽ ἀξιοῦμεν τῇ πόλει προῖκα γενναίως ἀμύνειν καὶ θεοῖς ἐγχωρίοις.

[206] Their (old-fashioned) long hair and 'the use of luxurious bathing utensils' (Ar. *Eq.* 580: μὴ φθονεῖσθ᾽ ἡμῖν κομῶσι μηδ᾽ ἀπεστλεγγισμένοις).Transl. J. Henderson (Loeb ed.).

[207] Isoc. 20.20: Ἔτι δὲ καὶ πάντων ἂν εἴη δεινότατον, εἰ δημοκρατουμένης τῆς πόλεως μὴ τῶν αὐτῶν ἅπαντες τυγχάνοιμεν, ἀλλὰ τῶν μὲν ἀρχῶν μετέχειν ἀξιοῖμεν, τῶν δ᾽ ἐν τοῖς νόμοις

With the same vocabulary, Demosthenes forcefully defined democratic equality in law in his speech against Timocrates, as part of an agreement between all citizens:

> [The law] does not allow introducing a law that is not valid for all citizens, a rule in the best democratic spirit. As to every man belongs an equal (*ison*) share (*metesti*) in the *politeia* generally, so this statute appraises (*axioo*) each to participate (*metechein*) equally in the laws as well.[208]

This stringent prescription of equality in the law (*isonomia*) and in active commitment to the *polis* was meant to override any tension among the citizens due to differences in position, wealth or other capacities.

Citizens' commitment was crucially tested during the dramatic events in the last years of the Peloponnesian War and especially during the regime of the Thirty Tyrants. Although Pericles' law was reinstituted immediately after the war, it could be made out that *meteinai* in the *polis* due to birth was not a sufficient condition of citizenship: only by what they actually did one could recognise what every citizen stood for. In speeches dealing with these trying years, Lysias and Isocrates created a telling contrast between those who had demonstrated their faith in the city, sharing danger, slavery and misfortune, and those who had not, with the verb *metechein*.[209] The oligarchs and their supporters were called 'those who *metechein* in the *politeia* at the time' or 'those who *metechein* in the oligarchy'.[210] In this discourse, the *politeia* (political system and social habitus) of the Thirty was sharply distinguished from the *politeia* (traditional way of life based on norms and laws) of democratic Athens. This conventional ideal of citizenship was complicated by the knowledge that numerous metics and slaves had taken up the democratic Athenian cause, some more so than many citizens and often to the peril of their lives. In the words of Lysias, some might be a citizen by birth (*physei*), but only those were really citizens who also set their mind on being so and who shared in (*metechein*) the city's hardships as well as in her

δικαίων ἀποστεροῖμεν ἡμᾶς αὐτούς, καὶ μαχόμενοι μὲν ἐθέλοιμεν ἀποθνῄσκειν ὑπὲρ τῆς πολιτείας, ἐν δὲ τῇ ψήφῳ πλέον νέμοιμεν τοῖς τὰς οὐσίας ἔχουσιν. Transl. L. Van Hook (Loeb ed.), modified.

208 Dem. 24.59: ὥσπερ γὰρ τῆς ἄλλης πολιτείας ἴσον μέτεστιν ἑκάστῳ, οὕτω καὶ τούτων ἴσον μετέχειν ἕκαστον ἀξιοῖ. Cf. the obligations of *dikastai* to give judgements *axios* of the laws; Dem. 58.25, 39.31.

209 Lys. 16.3, 16.5, 18.19, 31.6, 12.65, 12.76; Isoc. 16.39–40.

210 Lys. 12.77, 16.3, 18.4, 26.21; Isoc. 21.2, 18.49; compare [Arist]. *Rhet. ad Alex.* II, 1424a39–1424b14: in an oligarchy a few participate in the *politeia*, but all citizens (*politai*) are entitled to fair treatment and need to be protected by law against misdemeanour by the oligarchs.

prosperity.[211] A proposal to grant citizenship to all non-Athenians who had fought for the restoration of the democracy was rejected, however.[212] Despite the amnesty confirmed by oath on conduct in the oligarchic years proper, in 400/399 and subsequent years many lawsuits took place against citizens accused of having damaged the *polis* in some way. Most notorious were charges against Socrates, Andocides and Nikomachos for damaging the relationship between the *polis* and the gods (*asebeia*); clearly the *polis* considered these men to be partly the cause of Athens's misfortunes and tried to purge the city from misdemeanour with these trials. In one of the first occurrences of the expression *metechein tes poleos*, the author denounces Andocides, who had not suffered anything for the safety of the city, but who now claimed to be worth (*axios*) to *metechein* in the *polis* where he had committed his impiety.[213] All these events may explain the appearance of *metechein tes poleos* next to *meteinai* in the first decades of the fourth century, and hereafter becoming a frequent expression for citizenship throughout the century.

Finally, we saw that in the very same year 346/5 the *polis* held the *diapsephismos* causing many alleged non-citizens to be dispelled from their demes, that Aeschines charged Timarchos for indecent conduct, but also that the *polis* began inscribing public honours for citizens holding office at *polis* level. The fragmentarily known man (-doros son of Kalli-), honoured for his previous year of office,[214] and Euxitheos son of Thoukritos thus represent both ends of the scale of the values accorded by the *demos* to its own members. In sum, in this year the institutional drive of the *polis* to evaluate its citizens reached a sudden intensity, probably due to the tensions caused by the relations with Macedon.[215] In the persecution of citizens like Euxitheos and Timarchos this came down to a purge which on the one hand recalled the first years of the fourth century and on the other hand prefigured the expulsion of the 'traitor' Leocrates that Lycurgus tried to bring about some years after Chaeroneia. The inscribed honours for citizens, by contrast, marked growing public acknowledgement of individual citizens, some of whom were prominent and wealthy; the *polis*'s

[211] Lys. 31.5–6: ὅσοι δὲ φύσει μὲν πολῖται εἰσι … τοὺς πρὸς τῶι εἶναι πολίτας καὶ ἐπιθυμοῦντας τούτου … μετέχειν το μέρος τῶν δεινῶν, ὥσπρ καὶ τῶν ἀγαθῶν μετεχουσι. Cf. Bakewell (1999).

[212] See below, Chapter 6.1.

[213] [Lys.] 6.48: Ἀνδοκίδης δὲ ἀπαθὴς τούτων τῶν κακῶν γενόμενος … εἰς τὴν σωτηρίαν τῇ πατρίδι, ἀξιοῖ νυνὶ μετέχειν τῆς πόλεως, ἀσεβῶν ἐν αὐτῇ.

[214] *IG* II^3 1, 301; Lambert (2012a) 42–5, no. 18.

[215] Fisher (2001) 62–5.

gratitude for their contributions would gradually develop into structural euergetism.

5.9 Citizenship and *Polis* Institutions

For Athenian citizens, participation in the *polis* meant taking an active part by holding public offices, *timai*. Drawing on Douglass North's conception of institutions, I have argued that all public offices were allocated following basically the same rules recognising and conferring *time*, an individual's value to the community. This evaluation differentiated first between groups, usually with distinctions as to gender and age, and next between individuals. Granting *time* not only gave shape to the relationship between the *polis* as a community and individual citizens, but also between the *polis* and outsiders, and *timai* could take forms other than public offices, such as privileges and honours. For citizens, *timai* were primarily the public offices that normally were open only to them.

At the baseline, citizens' equal *time* allowed them participation in elementary roles. For more elevated *timai*, most traditional formal distinctions due to wealth were gradually abandoned, but they never disappeared entirely. The distinction due to birth of the *gene* was not abolished either, but evened out by the elevation of the *demos* to the same qualification and fitting *timai*. Informally, prominent social standing remained influential for elected offices. Holding public office was open to citizens whose conduct was above reproach. The procedures for selection to *timai* and *archai* articulated two different views on the roles of citizens: election for office drew on and enhanced differences between citizens in terms of their *time*, allotment underscored their equality. It is conceivable that the increasing use of *klerosis* for *polis* office was facilitated by the traditional use of this method and its terminology in another fundamental institution of the *polis*, the distribution of equal parts of an inheritance to equal heirs, in which, furthermore, divine justice was taken to be effective. With the increasing emphasis on descent as the foundation of citizenship, the practice of *klerosis* forged the double meaning of the inheritance of the *polis* of which every citizen had a share (*kleros*) and that of equal *time* for all citizens effectuated in the developing democracy.

Most of the criteria scholars have used to define the differences between the *archai* and other *timai*, notably priesthoods, are difficult to maintain in view of the evidence. In terms of procedures, all offices required setting criteria for access, selection by the *polis*, *dokimasia* after selection and final accountability (*euthynai*) to the *polis*. They all served the *polis* for more than thirty days, and the right of jurisdiction for their province, held by some or perhaps all *archai*, was held by at least some male priests for their cults as well. Concerning their duties, serving the gods on behalf of the *polis* was either an integral part or the primary duty of virtually all public offices, as was responsibility for the finances involved, whether belonging to the gods or to the *polis*. In other words, distribution of responsibility for *hiera kai hosia* over *archai* and priesthoods seems to have been one of degree, rather than of essence.

That the Athenians recognised a substantial correspondence between *archai* and priestly *timai* can be inferred from several institutions in the political heart of the *polis*. First, archons, priests and *bouleutai* all wore the crown of leaves (*stephane*) as symbol of their office that required purity of body. Second, in the honorific decrees for both kinds of officials, inscribed from the mid-fourth century onwards, the *polis* honoured both groups of *timai* for the ways in which they had served the well-being (*agatha tyche*) of the *polis* in exactly the same terms, as Stephen Lambert has shown.[216] Third, in the *boule* and assembly, after the purification sacrifice, the agenda began with the *hiera*, the results of the *polis* sacrifices performed by the priests and priestesses and reported to the *demos*; the *boule* and assembly needed to ascertain that the *agatha* for the *polis* were assured for any deliberation to go forward. Some such *hiera* were called *eisite(te)ria* and *eisa gogeia*, meaning sacrifice at the beginning of office. The evidence is ambiguous whether the beginning of priesthoods or *archai* is meant, but the fact that the *polis* issued honorific decrees for performing these *hiera* suggests that such *hiera* inaugurated *archai*. If this is correct, the ritual further confirmed the correspondence between *polis* priesthoods and *polis archai*. Finally, Aristotle, too, noticed this correspondence in his *Politics*, where he lists the essential offices of a *polis*, and in the domain of cults observes:

> Connected with this is the *arche* that sees to all the common sacrifices (*thysia*) that the law does not assign to the priests but to those who receive their *time* from the common sacred hearth; in some *poleis* these are called archons, in others *basileis* and in others *prytaneis*.[217]

This correspondence between *archai* and priestly *timai* fits the ways in which cults were organised in Athens.

[216] For the evidence and arguments on this structural correspondence between priests and holders of *archai* in honorific decrees, Lambert (2012b); inaugurating *hiera* are attested for Zeus Soter, Aglauros and Asclepius.

[217] Arist. *Pol.* 1322b26–30. See also Parker, *PS*, 97.

Polis cults enacted not only reciprocity but also collaboration between humans and gods. Basically, the *polis* decided which gods were included in this bond and set up the institutional context (access to, finance of) the cults guaranteeing the proper *time* for the gods, while the religious contents (beliefs, rules) of most cults were believed to be determined by the gods themselves and thus for a considerable part outside the sphere of influence of the *polis* (*boule*, assembly). On the human side, the organisation of cults changed visibly over time. At Athens, we see the *polis* taking more and more initiatives in this domain; in case of uncertainty the gods were consulted, usually by the oracle at Delphi. One such element in which we see this cooperation was the choice of a priest(ess): the *polis* decided on the group from which priests or priestesses were to be selected and in the final selection the god(dess) made a choice by the lot that the *polis* respected, confirmed and implemented. In the case of the *gene*, their privileges over cults were construed in genealogical narratives that foregrounded the wishes of the gods and took the historical facts of the *polis*'s acceptance and implementation of the divine preferences for granted. I would argue that the major distinction between priesthoods and *archai* consisted in the idea that priests and priestesses were selected by and bound to the gods in a strong way not equalled by other offices, because they served those parts of the cults that the gods themselves had laid down and thus lay beyond the authority (and even beyond the room for negotiation) of the *polis*.

At the human level, the correspondence between cultic *timai*, notably the priesthoods, and the *archai* allows a better understanding of gender as a criterion in access to public offices. In the domain of cult we find a structural symmetry in the public roles open to men and women in institutional terms of selection, accountability and contents of their duties. This is most strikingly the case for priesthoods: those filled by women and those filled by men were the same in their principal duties, preparing the animal for sacrifice and overseeing the proper performance of the slaughter, cutting and division of the meat, reciting the customary prayers and finally reporting on the outcome of the sacrifice, and taking care of the sanctuary.[218] Priests and priestesses accounted to the *polis* for their cultic duties and its finances, but whether priestesses reported themselves on the *hiera* to the male audience of the assembly, or were represented for this aspect of their duties by male kinsmen, is disputed; the latter option would seem more likely and, if so, would reflect the gender

[218] Cf. Georgoudi (2005).

difference prevailing in the political bodies of the *polis*.[219] That nonetheless the *polis* saw a basic parallel between male and female priesthoods is corroborated by the honorific decrees studied by Lambert: priests and priestesses were praised in the same ways and in the same terms for the same duties, namely taking care of the sacrifices in the proper way. Whereas on *private* monuments such as graves, votive reliefs and statues priests were depicted with a sacrificial knife and priestesses with the key to the temple doors, thus dividing the two major duties of priesthood between the two sexes, in its *public* monuments the *polis* honoured priestesses primarily in the 'masculine' role of sacrificer.[220]

Since both at the baseline of participation and in the prominent *timai* in cults the symmetry between men and women was paramount, while simultaneously the significance of the domain of cult for the *polis* was not limited to 'religion' but in fact encompassed the self-conception of the *polis* in the widest sense, it seems reasonable to conclude that in this fundamental respect the status of male and female citizens was symmetrical, a notion reflected in the symmetrical terminology for male and female citizens discussed in Chapter 4.

The one great divide in terms of gender was between other *timai* and *archai* in that the latter were, with some minor reservations, exclusively open to men. Again, differentiation in roles according to gender and age structured the whole system of participation, but in the *archai* gender distinction fenced off a large and prominent domain of participation from women. In archaic and early classical Athens effectively only elite men held *archai*, while lower-class men at best attended the assembly; in these conditions, a priestess presumably enjoyed more public presence and status than a baseline male citizen. But when after Cleisthenes' reorganisation more *archai* were created and access to offices was gradually extended to in principle almost all men, sharing in *archai* became a prominent feature of men's identity as citizens. This very prominent asymmetry transposed the gender hierarchy of the *oikos* into the public sphere, poised over and against the symmetry of the *polis*'s cultic life.

[219] In *SEG* 33.115, an honorific decree for Timokrite, the priestess of Aglauros, ca. 250/49 (Lambert (2012c) no. 8): she reports on *eisite(te)ria*, on the good things for the well-being etc., and she is praised for her piety; her son does the actual reporting to the *boule* (ll. 9–10). In *IG* II³ 1, 1026, an honorific decree for the priestess of Athena Polias (ca. 236/5?); the restored beginning suggests that the priestess reports herself, but it is an inference based on square brackets, see Lambert (2012b) no. 10 and p. 79, and his comment to this decree, esp. l. 6, on AIO. For the representation of priestesses by the *kyrioi* and kinsmen, Georgoudi (2005) 79–80.

[220] Lambert (2012b) 78; iconography of priestesshood, Connelly (2007) 85–104: clothes and temple key, and 222–57 especially on grave reliefs.

6

Outlook: Athenians and Others

> And in return for the good which they have done for the Athenians,
> and because they now attach importance to the Athenians
> and propose good things for them, be it resolved
> by the council and the people that the Samians shall be Athenians,
> living under whatever constitution they wish.
>
> Athenian grant of citizenship to the Samians, 405/4[1]

In this book, I have argued that citizenship at Athens entailed a conception of the *polis* as a community shaped by its bond with the gods. As a member of this community, an individual citizen had a share in the benefits and obligations included in that bond, a share that came to be conceived of as an inheritance. Legitimate birth from Athenian parents, a precondition for inheritance both in the private sphere and in the *polis*, was the foundation of membership of the *polis*. It allowed every male and female Athenian to participate actively in the *polis* in roles which corresponded to their value for the community. The notion that legitimate descent was a condition of citizenship became more and more influential over time, increasingly translated into legal requirements, and supervised by the phratries, progressing from basic legal rules on legitimacy in *oikos* and *polis* in Solon's time to further anchorage in the demes, especially for male citizens, after Cleisthenes. This process culminated in Pericles' law of 451/0, which required two Athenian parents for citizen status, making all citizens in birth on the same level as the *gene*.[2]

[1] *IG* II[2] 1; *Syll.*[3] 116; ML 94; *IG* I[3] 127; OR 191; transl. OR. ll. 11–13: καὶ ἀντὶ ὧν εὖ πεποιήκασιν Ἀθηναίοις καὶ νῦν περὶ πολλõ ποιõνται καὶ ἐσηγõνται ἀγαθά, δεδόχθαι τῆι βολῆι καὶ τῶι δήμωι Σαμίος Ἀθηναίος ἔναι, πολιτευομένος ὅπως ἂν αὐτοὶ βόλωνται. The decrees indicate *sympoliteia* and a citizenship grant. For the complex relations between the text of the decree (republished in 403/2) and the relief heading the stele, showing a *dexiosis* (giving right hands) of Athena with a figure (Hera?) representing Samos, Elsner (2015) with further refs.

[2] In Blok (2009b) I argue that Pericles' law is likely to have been motivated not by the 'large number of citizens', as *Ath.Pol.* 26.3 claims, but rather to boost citizen morale by further democratisation.

In this final chapter, we shall look briefly into some questions raised by this conception of citizenship. First of all, what did it mean for the two groups whose position came nearest to that of born citizens, namely those made into Athenian citizens by a *polis* decree and free foreigners living at Athens as metics (*metoikoi*)? Until Pericles' law, non-Athenians acquired access to citizen status for their children by marriage with an Athenian citizen, but Pericles' law made a mixed marriage highly unattractive to an Athenian partner, and in the early fourth century such unions were made illegal. In the classical period there was a general tendency towards endogamy in many Greek *poleis*, whether or not the laws required double citizen parentage for citizen status.[3] We do not need therefore to assume that most metics, many of whom were citizens of other Greek *poleis*, were keen to marry Athenians, or that many Athenians had been eager to marry metics until the law made them think twice about it.[4] Before 451/0, occasionally Athenians married women from abroad. Well-known cases are marriages of some high-profile Athenian men, such as Pisistratus marrying an Argive woman and Miltiades marrying into a Thracian family, to which also Thucydides' father Oloros belonged, while ordinary Athenians may have found wives when abroad in the context of the Athenian empire, but there is no evidence to gauge the size of this group.[5] Yet it is undeniable that Pericles' law and the conception of citizenship it stood for drew a clear line between citizens and other groups in legal terms, which may in turn have affected their social exchange.

The second question we shall consider is whether the conception of citizenship outlined in this book was typical of Athens alone, or whether a similar conception applied in other Greek *poleis*. In other words, was the Athenian way a specific case of a wider Greek pattern, or did Athens take a singular route?

6.1 Citizens-by-decree

Could outsiders become Athenians? How did this work, and what were the results?

[3] For *polis* endogamy as the prevailing model in ancient Greece, Vérilhac and Vial (1998) 42–81. Evidence for citizen descent being *required* on both sides exists for Miletus, Sparta, Rhodes, Delos, Cos, Tenos, Byzantium; other cities are known to have entered an *epigamia* treaty with one another, effectively implying a system of dual affiliation, See also Wilgaux (2000) for a sophisticated model of practices of endogamy and exogamy within a *polis*.

[4] Blok (2009b) 156–7 with further refs.

[5] For the political effects of marriages of elite Athenians with foreign women, Humphreys (1974); for possible effects of the Athenian empire on marriage patterns Osborne (1997).

According to their own traditions, the Athenians had always welcomed new people in their midst. One such group were refugees, of whom Athenian drama provided many mythological examples. An interesting case is reported by Herodotus (5.57, 61–2). The *genos* Gephyraioi, to which the tyrannicides Harmodios and Aristogeiton belonged, were immigrants from Eretria, according to their own tradition, but Herodotus believed that originally they had come from Phoenicia with Kadmos and received a *moira* of land in Tanagra. When due to various troubles the Gephyraioi were forced to leave Boeotia, they had turned to Athens. The Athenians, receiving them, made them citizens (*polietai*) on fixed terms, 'laying upon them to be excluded from a few, but insignificant matters'.[6] The Gephyraioi instituted *hiera* of their own in Athens in which the other Athenians did not participate, and this applied in particular, claims Herodotus, to their sanctuary and rites of Demeter Achaia. The arrival of the Gephyraioi would have taken place in the very distant past, quite close to 'mythical' time. But whatever its historicity, this (orally transmitted) account illuminates some important principles of naturalisation as it is known in fifth-century Athens. That the terms set for the Gephyraioi marked an exception implies that normally newly made citizens shared in everything like other Athenians. Since the peculiarity of the Gephyraioi was defined by the exclusion of the other Athenians from (some of) their *hiera*, we may suppose that the 'few but insignificant matters' from which the Gephyraioi were excluded likewise belonged to the sphere of *hiera*.[7] That the Gephyraioi excluded other Athenians from their *hiera* is particularly remarkable since Herodotus calls them a *genos*; typically, *a genos* would have served a cult for *all* Athenians. It seems that for this exceptional state of affairs Herodotus' story supplies a historical *aition*.[8]

Most historical cases of naturalisation of individuals concerned people who had something to offer the *polis*. Plutarch (*Sol.* 24.4) ascribed to Solon

[6] Hdt. 5.57: Ἀθηναῖοι δέ σφεας ἐπὶ ῥητοῖσι ἐδέξαντο σφέων αὐτῶν εἶναι πολιήτας, ὀλιγῶν τεων καὶ οὐκ ἀξιαπηγήτων ἐπιτάξαντες ἔργεσθαι (*OCT* ed. N.G. Wilson).

[7] Thuc. 6.56.1 says that the tyrant Hipparchos, refused by Harmodios, retaliated by rejecting Harmodios' sister as a *kanephoros* at a procession (the Panathenaea?), because 'she was unworthy' (*axios*). Lambert (2015) 184–5 attractively suggests that this role in the procession was one of the 'insignificant matters' from which the girl, as a Gephyraia, was allegedly excluded.

[8] Lambert (2010b) 152–3 sees the Gephyraioi's exclusivity of cult as the exception that proves the rule of the *gene*; Parker (1996) 288–9 mentions other possibilities, among which that Herodotus is wrong in that the Gephyraioi excluded Athenians from all their cults, since the deme of Marathon sacrificed to [Demeter] Achaia in the early fourth century (*SEG* 50.168). It is also conceivable that Herodotus was mistaken in that other Athenians were excluded from the *private* cults of the Gephyraioi (compare the private cults of the Salaminioi), which Herodotus took to be *polis* cults served by the *genos*.

a law that limited acceptance into citizenship to foreigners who came to Athens as exiles (such as the Gephyraioi perhaps) or settled there with their whole family as craftsmen. This law was intended, claims Plutarch, to give full citizenship (*methexein tes politeias*) to deserving newcomers.[9] Although we cannot be sure that Plutarch is describing accurately a genuine sixth-century law, we can, I think, be confident about the authenticity of the underlying principle: in establishing enduring ties with others, the *polis* followed the conventional rules of *time*, i.e. it assessed the value of the individual for the *polis* and reciprocated with acknowledgement and fitting *timai*.

More often than not, a grant of citizenship was the culmination of a cycle of honours bestowed by the *polis* in return for a long series of benefits that the honorand had bestowed on Athens. A number of citizens-by-decree are known to have formerly been *proxenoi*, men who in their own city looked after the public and private interests of Athens and its citizens. In return Athens would offer refuge in case of emergency, and various privileges, which might include *enktesis* (the right to own land and/or a house in Attica) and *ateleia* (tax freedom).[10] Although the institution of *proxenia* was older, at Athens the first inscribed *proxenos* decrees appear around the mid-fifth century, when generally decrees begin being inscribed in larger numbers, and they show the main features typical of the genre throughout the classical period; clearly, by then the institution was well established, including its condensed, formalised vocabulary in *polis* decrees.[11] The virtues for which the *polis* praised the recipient on granting citizenship converged in *andragathia* towards the Athenian people, i.e. employing military assistance or great wealth to the benefit of the *polis*; accordingly, only men qualified for this award.[12] Although in [Dem.] 59.89 Apollodoros stated that the law allowed citizenship only to be given

[9] Osborne (IV, 141–9) sees this law as stimulating immigration rather than mass naturalisation. Plutarch's vocabulary in this passage does not reflect sixth-century usage.

[10] Herakleides of Klazomenai, who was a *proxenos* and benefactor of the city from 424 (*IG* I³ 227), received citizenship in ca. 390 (Osborne T 27); a Rhodian (*IG* II² 19, of 394/3); Sthorys of Thasos, whose ancestors had long been *proxenoi* of Athens (*IG* II² 17, also of 394/3). On *enktesis* see Peçirka (1966); Rubinstein (2009) makes a useful distinction between *ateleia* as privilege for honorands and as an incentive for new craftsmen and other skilled labour. For the exchange of benefits between city and outsiders see also Domingo Gygax (2006), Mack (2015) 38–43.

[11] *IG* I³ 18, 19, 23, 27, 74 etc. The recipient is called *proxenos* and *euergetes* of the Athenians and the status of *proxenos* is conferred on him and his issue. For the pattern of *proxenia* expressed in the formulaic vocabulary of the decrees see Mack (2015) 22–43; on proxeny in the fifth century, Walbank (1978), in the fourth century, Culasso-Gastaldi (2004).

[12] At *polis* level, *andragathia* is used only for outsiders until the 330s; for citizens it is used at first only at tribal level (e.g. *IG* II² 1138, 1139), Whitehead (1993) 55–7.

to people who had demonstrated *andragathia*, inscribed decrees rarely use this expression.[13] More common is the statement that the honorand 'is an *agathos* man for the Athenians', which, by comparison with the use of *agathos* in decrees more widely can be seen to mean a man 'who is beneficial' to the people.[14] Whitehead persuasively argues that *andragathia* as an abstract noun replaced its aristocratic sounding corollary *arete*, being largely synonymous with the adjective *agathos*, used in inscriptions.[15]

With citizenship a status due to birth, making a non-Athenian into an Athenian entailed *adopting* the prospective citizen into the *polis*. Although the lexeme *demopoietos* became current only in the later fourth century,[16] 'made (a citizen) by the *demos*' is an apt description of this status throughout the classical age: in the Cleisthenic constitution it was the *demos* which conferred this status upon someone, and *poieisthai* is the legal term for 'to adopt'.[17] Michael Osborne and Whitehead regard Cleisthenes' institution of the demes as the first legal definition of citizenship and hence the introduction of a legal process of 'naturalisation' as a consequence of this event. I argued in Chapter 3 that Solon's laws on legitimacy preceded Cleisthenes' reorganisation as legal framework for citizenship, but that it is unclear what 'making someone a citizen' entailed before 508/7. In the fifth century a clearly structured procedure developed, of which enrolment into a deme was an indispensable part if the new Athenian was to implement his new status. So in effect the Cleisthenic organisation became the legal and social framework in which naturalisation took shape.

The decision to grant citizenship, prepared by the *boule*, had to be voted in the assembly, and from ca. 385/4 until the end of the fourth century a second assembly vote was needed.[18] This decision by the assembly might affect the female citizens specifically, for a citizen-by-decree could enter into marriage exchange among the Athenians. In practice, however, many

[13] [Dem.] 59.89: πρῶτον μὲν γὰρ νόμος ἐστὶ τῷ δήμῳ κείμενος μὴ ἐξεῖναι ποιήσασθαι Ἀθηναῖον, ὃν ἂν μὴ δι' ἀνδραγαθίαν εἰς τὸν δῆμον τὸν Ἀθηναίων ἄξιον ᾖ γενέσθαι πολίτην. Osborne IV, 141–5 regards Pericles' Citizenship Law as the possible origin of this law on *andragathia*, due to the similarities in negative formulation (no one will be … who is not …), but such negative formulations are a very common feature of ancient laws and cannot be regarded as distinctive.

[14] *IG* II^{2} 1 l. 70 awards citizenship to the Samians, and *IG* II^{2} 25 ll. 2–3 (Osborne D 9) to Hipparchos and Archippos of Thasos ἀνδραγαθίας ἕνεκα; but *IG* I^{3} 102 (Osborne D2) ll. 6–7 for Thrasyboulos of Kalydon, *IG* II^{2} 103 (Osborne D 10) ll. 21–2 for Dionysios of Syracuse and his sons, *IG* II^{2} 19 (Osborne D 7) l. 6 restored, *IG* II^{3} 1, 295 (Osborne D 12) l. 5 for Orontes, because they are *agathos* men. For *agathos* as 'beneficial', *IG* I^{3} 48 fr. C, l. 14; 101, fr. E-g, l. 34; 106, fr. A-c, l. 19 etc.

[15] Whitehead (1993) 57–62; cf. Whitehead (2009). For *agathos*, *andragathia* and other virtues motivating honours for citizens, see above, Chapter 5.6. and 5.8.

[16] [Aeschin.] *Ep.* 12.13.4; Hyp. *Fr.* 94.1–2; 146.1.

[17] Osborne IV, 139–40; Whitehead (1977) 16, 143–7.

[18] Osborne I, 15–20.

citizens-by-decree did not take up actual residence in Athens, and some were already married and their wives were not normally made explicitly into Athenians, an issue to which we return below. Around sixty-six such citizenship grants made in the classical democracy of the fifth and fourth centuries are known, amounting to an average of one grant in every three years (though we cannot know what proportion of actual grants our evidence represents). Five concern groups, sixty-one individuals. The evidence on these cases, collected by Osborne, consists of accounts of such grants in various literary texts on the one hand and actual inscribed decrees recording the grants on the other.[19] The decrees allow us insight above all into the formal aspects of the grant, criteria for eligibility, the formulas used, its implementation in practice and succinctly the motivation for it, notably in the choice of the value terms employed, whereas the literary accounts tend to illuminate the historical context and the discourse around the decision-making process.

The formula conferring citizenship in the decrees stated the recipient *to be an Athenian* (*Athenaion einai*).[20] In the course of the fourth century, 'to give *politeia*' or 'to make a *polites*' figure occasionally in political and forensic discourse and in decrees where such grants made in the past are referred to, but these expressions were not adopted into the formula of the decrees for individuals.[21] This language use suggests that in the decrees *Athenaion einai* operated as a speech act effectuating the status of Athenian. Furthermore, normally the decree invited the new Athenian to choose a deme, *phyle* and phratry to be enrolled in. The earliest extant inscribed citizenship grants contain the main formulaic elements, though not always consistently. The order of decisions in the earliest extant grant, for Thrasyboulos of Kalydon (410/9) who had killed the oligarch Phrynichos, is quite typical: the gift of citizenship follows in a rider (ll. 15–17) to a decree which had praised the honorand ('a good man towards the Athenian people and intent on doing whatever good he could') and

[19] Osborne I: decrees (D); II: commentary; III: other written testimonia (T); IV: commentary.

[20] This was the formula until ca. 229. See Osborne I, 15–22 for the form of citizenship decrees, including the formula εἶναι αὐτὸν Ἀθηναῖον bestowing citizen status, clauses on the enrolment of the new citizen in *phyle*, deme and phratry, after 385/4 a clause on the second vote, and a clause requiring scrutiny (*dokimasia*) of the new citizen.

[21] These expressions are used to refer to a grant to an ancestor in the past, now reaffirmed for the beneficiary: *IG* II³ I, 411, for Arybbas of Molossia, in ll. 1–2 [ἡ πολιτ]εια ἡ δοθε[εῖ]σα (the grant given to his (grand)father) and *IG* II³ I, 333, for Archippos of Thasos (333/2) ll. 18–19 (grant to his father); *IG* II² 17 (394/3), two related decrees for Sthorys of Thasos, mention that his father had been made a *polites* (ll. 7–8), but declare that he himself *Athenaion einai* (l. 30). *Ag.* 16.101 (Osborne, D 29) for Ainetos of Rhodes (319/8) is headed θεοί. Πολιτεία Αἰνήτωι Ῥοδιωι, whereas the formula (ll. 34ff.) is again *Athenaion einai*. For *politeia* and *polites*, see also above, Chapter 2.3.

awarded him the honour of a gold crown to be bestowed at the Dionysia; the grant itself included the formulas *Athenaion einai* and the choice of *phyle* and phratry (much restored).[22]

Literary evidence tells us that several others received citizen grants before him.[23] The earliest case mentioned in our sources was Menon of Pharsalos in ca. 476, who had helped the Athenians in the siege of Eion in 477; he seems to have been archon in 473/2 and a candidate for ostracism in 471.[24] Menon's office is interesting here because after Pericles' law citizens-by-decree were explicitly debarred from the archonship, a provision whose significance we shall discuss further below. No decree is extant relating to Menon's grant, nor to what might be another early case, not included in Osborne's catalogue. In the mid-470s, a certain Hegelochos dedicated a statue made by the sculptors Kritios and Nesiotes to Athena,[25] with an epigram on its base:

> The father and son of Ekphantos dedicated me to the Parthenos Athena as a memory of the labours of Ares.
>
> Hegelochos, having a share (*moira*) of great friendship towards strangers (*philoxenia*) and all excellence (*arete*), received a share (*nemomai*) in this *polis*.
>
> Kritios and Nesiotes made it.[26]

By this dedication, Hegelochos commemorated the efforts of his father and himself on behalf of Athens in the Persian War of 480–479, but also marked the fact that now he held a share in the *polis*. Hegelochos is

22 *IG* I³ 102 (Osborne D 2); praise ll. 6–9: ὁς ὄντα ἄνδρα ἀγαθο[ν περὶ τὸν δεμ]ον τον Ἀθεναίον και πρόθυμον π[οιεν *h*ό τι δύνα]ται ἀγαθον. Of the next one, for King Euagoras of Salamis (ca. 407; Osborne D 3), only fragments of the honorific decree are extant (*IG* I³ 113; cf. [Dem.] 12.10; Isoc. *Euag.* 9.54).

23 Earlier grants: Osborne T2: Polygnotos of Thasos, ca. 460; T3 Carystion of Samos, ca. 439; T4 Sadokos, son of king Sitalces, of Thrace, 431; T6 Tharyps of Molossia, ca. 428–424.

24 Osborne T1 (= Dem. 23.199) 20–3. The majority of the ostraka of a find dated to 471 (Lewis (1974)) naming a Menon (Siewert (2002); Kerameikos III (Peek) B, 67–145) add patronymic and/or demotic Menekleidou Gargettios; on Kerameikos O 6092, he is called an *archon* (Siewert (2002) 63). Lewis (4) identifies this man with the Menon who was archon in 473/2.

25 According to Keesling (2003) 186–92, the votive statue might well have been a portrait of Hegelochos' father Ekphantos: the few extant portrait statues of the fifth century are dedicated by sons in honour of their fathers and represent the latter.

26 *IG* I³ 850, *CEG* 272; [Πα]ρθένοι Ἐκφάντο με πατὲρ ἀνέθε/κε καὶ *h*υιὸς ἐνθάδ' Ἀθεναίει μν*h*μα / πόνον Ἄρεος Ἑγέλοχος μεγάλες τε φι / λοχσενίες ἀρετε͂ς τε πάσες μοῖραν / ἔχον τένδε πόλιν νέμεται / Κριτίος καὶ Νεσιότες ἐποιεσάτεν. Pouilloux (1951) 96–7 suggested an origin of this family in Thasos, for in ca. 385 Athens asked a certain N… and Ekpha[ntos] to record the names of a group of exiles from Thasos to be received in the city (*IG* II² 33, l. 9), but Ekphantos was a common name, supplying insufficient grounds for establishing a connection in this case. *Pace* Raubitschek (*DAA* 121) and Pouilloux, Hegelochos must be the single dedicant, referring to himself as father of a son and as son of a father both called Ekphantos.

considered by some scholars to have been a metic,[27] but text and object also invite a stronger interpretation. The primary meaning of the verb in line 5 in the active form (*nemein*) is to distribute shares among a group, but in the middle voice, used here, it refers to receiving a portion befitting one's status within the group and enjoying the fruits of that portion. Such a portion can be one's inherited share in ancestral goods, while in the context of sacrifice *nemomai* normally indicates acquiring a share of sacrificial meat.[28] The juxtaposition of Hegelochos' 'share' (*moira*, his 'portion' in life) of friendship for foreigners (*sc.* towards the Athenians) and his excellence (*arete*; *sc.* in the war) with the 'share' he received of the *polis* suggests a direct connection between the two: for the one he received the other. Since Hegelochos' votive stood on the Acropolis addressing the viewer, and since in inscriptions of these years *polis* usually indicates the Acropolis, *this polis* would seem to refer in the first place to the cultic centre of the *polis*.[29] Written on an impressive statue dedicated to Athena on the Acropolis, a rare gift by a non-Athenian,[30] the epigram suggests commemoration of a more profound event, namely that Hegelochos had become an Athenian citizen in return for his support of the city.[31]

Hegelochos' role in Athens is expressed in a way similar to that of born Athenians, namely as 'having a share' in the city, notably in its cults. His son, if my reading is correct, would now also be an Athenian, since

[27] On my reading of *nemomai*, the epigram shows that *metoikia* entailed sharing in some *polis* cults; see further below. Shear (2007c) 236–7 doubts that Hegelochos was made an Athenian citizen, and translates τένδε πόλιν νέμεται as 'he lives in this city'. This translation is too weak a rendering of νέμωμαι, which, when used for living in a place, means 'holding and using as one's property' rather than simply 'living in', according to LSJ *s.v.* νέμω, A. II, Med.; and it fails to take account of the fact that τένδε πόλιν must connote, on a dedication in this location, the Acropolis.

[28] LSJ *s.v.* νέμω, A. II, Med., e.g.: *Od.* 20.336: πατρώια πάντα νέμεσθαι: share all ancestral goods among them. Sacrificial meat: *IG* I³ 244 A3, 20, C12; RO 37 (Salaminioi) ll. 23, 39, 42, 47; *IG* II² 47.35, 1183.34, 1204.12, 1231.10; Ekroth (2008b), Ekroth (2008a) 99–100.

[29] Compare *IG* I³ 718 (early fifth century): Σμίκρο καὶ παίδον μνε͂μ' ἔχοι*h*έδε πόλις, 'may this (acro) polis hold the monument (of the labours) of Smikros and his sons', a votive to 'mighty Athena who holds this *polis*'. *IG* I³ 1179.11, on a monument for warriors fallen at Potidaia, 432, found in the Agora: ἄνδρας μὲμ πολις *h*έδε ποθεῖ και δέ[μος 'Ερεξθο͂ς]: 'this *polis* pines for its men and (so does) the *demos* of Erechtheus'. In this passage, since the *demos* is subject of the verb, it is unlikely it would be duplicated in *polis* meaning 'community'; rather, *this* polis refers to the (acro)polis, visible from the Agora, which together with the *demos* of Erechtheus constitutes the *polis* Athens.

[30] Keesling (2003) 188.

[31] Raubitschek (*DAA*) 128 was the first to suggest that Hegelochos was made a citizen; Osborne, I–IV, did not follow him, but *LGPN* did, listing Ἔκφαντος 1) the father and 2) the son, together with others of this name including 4) who was archon in 235/4. Neither *LGPN* nor *FRA* lists the Ekphantos mentioned in *IG* II² 33. Siewert (2002) 54 thinks that an ostrakon with the name 'Hegelochos Erikiathen', found in the Kerameikos, dated tentatively to 471 (*LGPN* no. 7), concerns our Hegelochos, but given that his demotic is unknown, this seems overly speculative.

citizenship was by definition hereditary. Public knowledge of his grant, achieved via an inscribed decree or social knowledge or both, was indispensable if he was to actively use his new status and if his children and their descendants were also to be accepted as Athenians.[32] Furthermore, in order to implement his citizenship, the citizen-by-decree must be enrolled in a deme, tribe and phratry.[33] The extant decrees, therefore, normally provide for both conditions, pronouncing the new status and inviting the new citizen to enrol in the *polis* subgroups of his choice.

For group grants, however, this last element caused difficulties. Grants to groups were anyway not seen as exactly the same as those to individuals, if we take the vocabulary of the decrees as a guideline. Two inscribed decrees are extant, for the Samians and for a varied group defenders of the democracy in Phyle; in both the enactment formula is unfortunately missing.[34] In the latter, preserved text suggests a restoration, 'there will be *politeia* (*sc.* for them)'.[35] *Politeia*, as we just saw, does not occur elsewhere in grant formulas at this period and these restorations must either be taken as exceptional for these exceptional collective grants or considered dubious. In favour of the first option is the fact that the follow-up, the enrolment of the new Athenians of these grants in the subgroups of the *polis*, also did not work in the same way as in individual cases. A closer look is necessary here.

In 427, those Plataians who had survived the destruction of their city, which had been a staunch ally of Athens for many years, received citizenship *en masse*.[36] Far from being a mythological story, the influx of

[32] Several decrees concern persons receiving citizenship reaffirming former grants to their father or grandfather, e.g. *IG* II³ 1, 411, D 14, for Arybbas of Molossia, ca. 342; *IG* II³ 1, 316, D 16, for Phormion and Karphinas of Akarnania, 338/7; although legally they were already Athenians, the family had not previously taken up residency in Athens and the new decree now implemented their status.

[33] For membership of deme, *phyle* and phratry as crucial for recognition and practical enactment of citizen status, see above, Chapter 3.

[34] Beside the decrees for groups discussed here, an obscurely worded honorific decree for the Elaiousians (*IG* II³ 1, 309; D 15; 341/0) might be a grant of citizenship, and there is literary evidence for a grant, compared to that for the Plataians, to the slaves who joined the crews in the Arginousae battle (Osborne T 10; Ar. *Ran.*, 31–4, 693; and Hell. *FGrH* 4 F 171); cf. Xen. *Hell.* 1.5.24; Diod.S. 13.97.1.

[35] For the Samians, *IG* I³ 127 = *OR* 191 l. 33 is restored: [ε῏ναι δὲ τὴν δωρειὰν Σαμίων τοῖς ἤ]κοσιν, but *IG* II² 1 l. 33: [ἔναι δὲ πολιτείαν]; *IG* II² 10 ll. 5–6 for the 'heroes of Phyle': ε῏ναι αὐτοῖς καὶ ἐκγόν[οις πολιτεία/ν].

[36] For the background, Thuc. 3.55.3, 3.63.2. Thucydides makes the Plataians claim in a speech that they already had Athenian citizenship (3.55.3) and adds that they had been allies of the Athenians since 519 (3.68.5); he does not refer to the grant by decree at issue in [Dem.] 59.104. MacDowell (1985) 319, assuming that Thucydides must be right and that the Plataians had been Athenian citizens since 519, suggested that once the Plataians were to live in Athens in 427, the Plataia decree

these very real fugitives may still have been in the Athenians' mind when Euripides' *Suppliant women* was produced in the late 420s. The authenticity of the decree about the Plataians inserted in [Dem.] 59.104 is heavily disputed, but not the fact of this grant, which was the first of its kind as far as we know.[37] Although the grant was probably meant for the men in the first place, the group included women.[38] The enactment clause in [Dem.] 59.104 is *Athenaious einai,* conforming to the grants to individuals, whereas its provision that the Plataians were to be distributed over demes and *phylai,* but not phratries, is comparable to the (later) inscribed decrees for groups; finally, they were excluded from access to priesthoods and archonships, limitations that will be discussed below. As Stephen Lambert argues, since the Plataians were actually living at Athens and implemented their citizenship, they were not to choose their deme and *phyle* themselves, as was normally the case for individuals, and were not to be distributed into phratries at all, because their numbers would upset the existing distribution and numbers of these *polis* subgroups, but instead may have formed a phratry-of-sorts of their own.[39] After a *dokimasia* to ensure that each of them really was a Plataian, their names were listed on a stele on the Acropolis to support any claims they might have

was necessary to arrange this. Osborne (II, 11) supposed that the Plataians claimed long-standing citizenship because they wanted to render their connections with Athens as closer than they were; in reality, the Plataia decree was the first grant. Kapparis (1999) 375–88 points out that on the events around the fall of Plataia Apollodoros stays close to Thucydides (2.22–7, 71–8; 3.20–4, 52–69), but that the latter apparently did not investigate the decree, presumably because its contents were not relevant to his account of the war, but instead erroneously inferred from the decree the Plataian claim of their Athenian citizenship, sustained by the long-standing alliance between the two *poleis.* In my view, whatever form the alliance between Plataia and Athens took in 519, it cannot have had the same legal form and the same implications in terms of descent, enrolment and other factors implied in grants of citizenship in 427; by then, for the Plataians to be 'Athenians' in the legal sense, a decree was necessary.

[37] Osborne (I) included the text in his volume of inscribed decrees (D 1) because of the enactment formula, but this is a tricky issue since it is not really an inscribed decree but a literary reference to one. Comparison of such 'decrees' preserved in literary sources with inscribed ones, as carried out by Canevaro (2013), is important, but one must also take into account that the Plataian decree was the first of its kind and that the vocabulary and formulation of such decrees may not yet have been fixed in 427; cf. Kapparis (2015) 43. I advance further evidence on features of this decree that fit contemporaneous vocabulary and regulations, and hence would support the possibility of authenticity, in Chapters 2.4.4 and 5.6.

[38] When the siege of Plataia by Spartans and Thebans began in 429, a large group of women, elderly people and children were sent off to safety in Athens; ca. 400 Plataian men, 110 Plataian women and 80 Athenians remained in the city (Thuc. 2.78). During a break-out after more than a year, 212 Plataian men escaped to Athens (Thuc. 3.24); after the surrender of the city, the remaining 200 Plataian men and 25 Athenians were killed, the women sold into slavery (Thuc. 3.68). In 386, they returned to their city but the tragedy of a sack, again generating refugees, occurred again in ca. 373 (Xen. *Hell.* 6.3.1).

[39] Lambert (1998) 51–3.

in Athens and prevent those not entitled to the grant from exploiting it improperly.[40]

The Samians received a mass grant in 405/4 (reinforced in 403/2) in gratitude for their loyalty to Athens in the years of adversity, as quoted in the heading to this chapter, in a decree stating that they *Athenaious einai*, but also that they could arrange their *polis* in whatever way they liked and use their own laws.[41] Clearly, they were not necessarily all expected to take up residence at Athens. A group of Samians who *were* in Athens at the time, however, were assigned to *phylai*, but not to demes or phratries; apparently they were not expected to participate in Athenian life to the same extent as the (other) Athenians.[42] Thrasyboulos proposed a citizenship grant for all the non-Athenian men who had joined him fighting for the democracy in 404/3, but his proposal was rejected because some of the proposed honorands were manifestly slaves (*Ath.Pol.* 40.2). Eventually a group of around seventy to ninety non-Athenians (metics and *xenoi*) of hoplite status who had sided with him from the beginning received citizenship; all others received *isoteleia*.[43] The extant decree of 401/0 honouring them is much damaged, but it is clear that the beneficiaries were distributed across the *phylai*, with the decree including a list of the beneficiaries by *phyle*. In sum, for all these groups of citizens-by-decree we see comparable arrangements: they were not enrolled in phratries, while some were so in demes and/or *phylai*, limitations that would influence the ways they shared in the *polis*, at least in the first generation. The names of the beneficiaries were publicly registered, both as an honour and to be used for later reference.

While citizens-by-decree were regarded as almost the same as born Athenians, the decrees do not inform their readers what *Athenaion einai* in fact entailed, other than the procedural steps necessary to become an

[40] [Dem.] 59.105–6. Whether the Plataian women also received citizenship and, if so, whether their names were included in the list, is unknown. Miletus, which in the late classical and Hellenistic age required citizen descent on both sides for citizen status, like Athens, did give citizen status to immigrant women by decree and, as Athens did for the (male?) Plataians, listed their names; Günther (2014) 263–302.

[41] *IG* II² 1; RO 2 (only parts ii and iii); i l. 13; πολιτευομένος ὅπως ἂν αὐτοὶ βόλωνται. Osborne (II, 25) therefore classifies the decree not as a true grant of citizenship, but rather an act of *isopoliteia* (a term not used at Athens at this period).

[42] *IG* I³ 127/*IG* II² 1, i ll. 33–4: [ε῀ναι δὲ δὲ τὴν δωρειὰν /πολιτείαν Σαμίων τοῖς ἥ]κοσιν, καθάπερ αὐτοὶ αἰτο῀νται, καὶ νε῀μαι / [αὐτὸς αὐτίκα μάλα τὸς ἄρχοντας ἐς τὰ]ς φυλὰς δέκαχα·

[43] *IG* II² 10; Osborne D 6 and comm. II, 26–43; RO 4 with comm.; Shear (2011) 232–4. *Isoteleia* probably applied only to the free *xenoi* and metics. The essential clauses in the citizenship grant (ll. 5–6) are restored in *IG*: ε῀ναι αὐτοῖς καὶ ἐκγόν[οις πολιτεία/ν καὶ φυλῆς καὶ δήμο καὶ φρατρίας ἧς ἂν βόλωνται] but on the parallels with the other group grants I prefer RO: ἐναι αὐτοῖς καὶ ἐκγόν[οις πολιτείαν· καὶ νε̃μαι αὐτος αὐτίκα μάλα ἐς τὰς φυλὰς δέκαχα].

Athenian – everyone was expected to know. For all beneficiaries presumably the general rules of membership and participation customary for Athenians applied.[44] The decree for the Plataians included in [Dem.] 59.104 states so explicitly ('they will be *epitimos* like the other Athenians') and in Lys. 23, a speech delivered in 400/399 against Pankleon, a man allegedly pretending to be a Plataian with the rights of an Athenian while he was not, the speaker clearly assumes that these rights overlapped to a considerable extent. Nonetheless, the decree also excluded the Plataians explicitly from priesthoods and archonships in the first generation. Individuals made into Athenians often enjoyed specific honours, such as *ateleia* or *prohedria*, which had been granted them at an earlier stage, or in the citizenship decree itself.

Given that a man who received citizenship was in a position to demonstrate *andragathia*, he normally was of an age to be married and a father at the time of the grant. What was now the status of his wife? There is only circumstantial evidence to attempt to answer this question. Osborne argues that she probably did not receive citizenship because the status of Athenian women, who were not entered in the deme lists and were always in the charge of a *kyrios*, made 'enfranchising' a woman inconceivable and perhaps impracticable.[45] By 'citizenship', Osborne apparently is thinking of men's (political) roles in the *polis*, whereas what matters here is membership in terms of descent. As we saw in Chapter 3, not being enrolled in demes did not affect women's status as *astai*, and as to the *kyrios*, one could also suppose a woman's status to depend on his. So I do not think that Osborne's argument is conclusive, but the fact that the evidence on the matter is so scarce is perhaps telling. A much-disputed case is Archippe, the wife first of Pasion, an ex-slave turned into metic and made a citizen-by-decree because of his contributions to the *polis* as a banker, and after his death, on terms of his will, the wife of his successor, Phormion, who followed the same social route from slave to citizen status. Had Archippe, who originally was a metic, become a citizen, too? Her children with Pasion were demonstrably citizens, but when she married Phormion in

[44] Isoc. *Plataicus* makes the (fictitious) Plataian speaker plead for help from Athens, appealing to their common descent due to prolonged intermarriage between the two groups, and referring to intermarriage between Plataian men and Athenian women (14.51): Καὶ γὰρ οὐδ' ἀλλότριοι τυγχάνομεν ὑμῖν ὄντες, ἀλλὰ ταῖς μὲν εὐνοίαις ἅπαντες οἰκεῖοι, τῇ δὲ συγγενείᾳ τὸ πλῆθος ἡμῶν· διὰ γὰρ τὰς ἐπιγαμίας τὰς δοθείσας ἐκ πολιτίδων ὑμετέρων γεγόναμεν. 'For we are not at all strangers to you, but all of us are close to you in our good-will and the majority even in actual kinship; for we are born from your *politides* owing to the right of intermarriage given to us.'

[45] Osborne IV, 150.

or shortly after 370, he was still a metic; by then, marriage between a citizen and a metic was illegal, as Apollodoros, one of Pasion and Archippe's sons, pointed out at great length in his case against Neaira. And how to assess the fact that Archippe held vast wealth in her own name, including landed property, such as only possible for citizens and metics with the right of *enktesis*?[46] After reviewing all aspects of the case, Whitehead and Carey arrive at partly the same and partly different results: the first concludes that Archippe's status was ambiguous between citizen and metic (Athenian law had no permanent, clear-cut solution here), the latter holds that she was and remained a metic.[47]

An important factor is the status of the children of citizens-by-decree when Pericles' law was in full force, that is from 433/2 (eighteen years after the law of 451/0) to (approximately) the last decade of the fifth century and from 385/4 (eighteen years after the reinstitution of 403/2) to the end of the third century. Some other *poleis* with the same rules for citizen status did make women into citizens, thus 'providing' two citizen parents to their offspring.[48] It seems, however, that the Athenians chose another solution: citizenship grants were made retroactive for the descendants of the beneficiaries, such as for the sons of Pasion born before the latter received his grant.[49] Extant decrees from the years Pericles' law was in force, the first case that for Dionysios of Syracuse dating to 369/8, explicitly stated that their children were now Athenians too.[50] This 'positive' measure, combined with the

[46] By will, she received a large dowry of three talents, including a house and many valuables, beside inheriting slaves, jewellery and moveable property (Dem. 36; 45.28) of which she was the *kyria* (Dem. 45.74; 50.60), giving each of her children 2,000 drachmae.

[47] Whitehead (1986b) underlines Archippe's ownership of landed property for her status as a citizen. However, his contention that she could have become an *aste* is misleading; she might have been made an *Athenaia*, but no *aste*; see below. Carey (1991) argues that, if she were made a citizen like Pasion, the latter would certainly have married her off (in his will) to another citizen, instead of to Phormion. However, in that scenario the bank would have come, ultimately, into the hands of Archippe's future citizen husband, instead of his former slave and collaborator Phormion. Cohen (1992) 102–10 situates Archippe as either a citizen or a metic woman, and her wealth in the context of banking families. Kapparis (1999) 17–19 for metic women handling large sums of money and holding property.

[48] For late classical and early Hellenistic Miletus, see n. 40; Osborne IV, 150–1, n. 58 mentions cases in Dodona, among which *SEG* 15.384 (ca. 370). On the latter case, Meyer (2012) argues persuasively that the grant of *politeia* to a woman was made to secure double citizen descent for the religious personnel of the sanctuary at Dodona.

[49] For the relevant evidence and arguments, Davies, *APF*, 427–42.

[50] Osborne IV, 151–4, 171–6; Dionysios of Syracuse: *IG* II² 103, l. 20: sons; D 10, with [Dem.] 12.10. Carey (1991) argues that men, on becoming Athenian citizens, would easily repudiate their first wives and marry an Athenian, as sentiment played no substantial role in ancient Greek marriages. Regardless of whether the latter point is entirely true, the Athenian system made such a separation unnecessary, as the children of the *demopoietos* were made citizens anyway. The argument from silence that in Athens conventionally women (wives) were not made into Athenians is confirmed

'negative' silence in our sources, suggests that wives of men made Athenians by decree normally were not made Athenians like them.[51] Consequently, there were now two differences in law between born Athenians and Athenians-by-decree: the decree conferring citizen status worked retroactively, whereas normally Athenian laws did not do so; and the descendants of Athenians-by-decree were Athenians with a citizen father and, depending on circumstances, a non-Athenian mother, also when for other Athenians both parents had to be Athenians for citizen status.

These tentative conclusions are confirmed by the fact that some significant restrictions applied to citizens-by-decree.[52] As Apollodoros explained in his suit against Neaira, comparing (his view of) her case to that of the Plataians:

> With much prudence the *demos* has acted on behalf of itself and of the gods, to ensure that the sacrifices on behalf of the *polis* are performed with piety (*eusebeia*). This can be inferred from the fact that the law explicitly does not permit those whom the *demos* of Athenians makes *politai*, to become one of the nine archons or to hold (*meteschein*) any priesthood. But to their offspring, the people have granted a share (*metadidomi*) in everything and added 'if they are from a formally pledged union with an *aste* according to the law'.[53]

This passage shows several important principles. Only someone actually *born* from two Athenian parents was allowed to perform sacrifices on behalf of the *polis*; more precisely, only someone born from an *aste* might do so, and only an Athenian was allowed to marry an *aste*. Therefore, anyone who was *made* an Athenian was not permitted to do so, but if he married an Athenian *aste*, who was herself the bearer of rights to inherit the *polis*'s bond with the gods, their *children* met the necessary condition. This implies that for an Athenian-by-decree his status as was recognised as a legal fiction, *as if* he were a born Athenian, which was *not* the equivalent of real Athenian birth, whereas the actual birth from an *aste* was decisive for transmitting real Athenian-ness.[54] In other words, being an Athenian

by Niku (2007) 18–19, who shows that after 229/8 the regulations for citizens-by-decree changed and offspring of mixed marriages also were accepted as Athenians; in all known cases the woman is the foreign spouse.

51 For scarce evidence on Plataian men and women living at Athens, Blok (2009b) 167, n. 109, among which we may tentatively identify a couple of a Plataian husband with a Plataian or Athenian wife, but not an Athenian husband with a Plataian wife.

52 Cf. Kamen (2013) 79–86.

53 [Dem.] 59.92–3; repeated 106.

54 Cf. Osborne IV, 173–6: 'The aim clearly was to keep priesthoods and offices closely involved with state religion from pollution by foreign blood, and Apollodoros twice insists upon the religious nature of these disabilities.'

was not the same as being an *astos*; one could be made an Athenian, but never be made an *astos*; for the latter condition, one had to be born from a plegded *aste*. This is exactly what Pericles' law and its reinstitution laid down as the condition for citizenship. A parallel for this partially fictive aspect of 'adoption by the *polis*' is the fact that private adoptions changed the formal (legal and cultic) paternal kinship of an adoptee, but not his or her ties, legal as well as otherwise, with maternal kin, i.e. through the *aste* mother.[55] All this evidence once again underlines the crucial importance for Athenian citizenship of not just being an Athenian, but of being born from an Athenian mother who was a pledged *aste*.

The principle that only someone actually *born* from two *astos* parents was allowed to perform sacrifices on behalf of the *polis* applied in the first place to priesthoods; we saw in Chapter 5 that this rule determined the privilege of the *gene* of holding cultic *timai*, also before Pericles' law. Interestingly, the law for the Plataians inserted in [Dem.] 59.104 includes an explicit prohibition for the newly made Athenians on holding, not just any priesthood as Apollodoros states in his speech, but any priesthood or rite belonging to a *genos*. At first sight, this clause would seem redundant, since no one had access to *timai* of the *gene* who was not of *genos* descent, but clearly the intention here was to emphasise not the ineligibility for these *timai* of first-generation recipients of the citizenship grant, but the eligibility of descendants of a Plataian married to a member of a *genos*. In practice, considering that the grant of citizenship probably was made for the male Plataians in the first place, the clause would apply to a male Plataian marrying a female *gennetes*; through her, their children could inherit eligibility for the priesthoods of the *genos*.[56] The difference between the wording of the decree and of the speech may be due to the fact that the *gene* were not relevant to Apollodoros' argument, or may be a sign of the inauthenticity of the decree, but other explanations are worth considering.[57] The provision concerning *genos* priesthoods fits the situation in 427, when, on present evidence, there either did not yet exist

[55] See above, Chapter 3.4.

[56] On the capacity for *genos* membership to be inherited in the female line, see above, Chapters 3.4, 5.5; also Blok (2009b) 166–8 and Blok and Lambert (2009) 104, where we argue that the alternative explanation by Kapparis (1995) 369, that this clause provided for the case of an adoption by a *genos* of a naturalised Plataian, is theoretically possible but implausible, given the conventions of adoption in Athens.

[57] Canevaro (2013) 196–208 argues against the authenticity of this law inserted in [Dem.] 59.104 because the text differs from extant decrees, whereas conversely Osborne, IV, 174 argues that, since Apollodoros' reference to the clause 'if they are from a formally pledged union with an *aste* according to the law' is the only attested instance of this provision, this is 'if anything, an indication that Apollodoros does have access to an authentic decree'.

any priesthood for which all Athenians, not just the *gennetai*, were eligible, or, if the priesthood of Athena Nike had been founded before this, only a priesthood of this kind for women.[58] In short, in 427 access to a priesthood for male citizens-by-decree was not yet a potential issue to be addressed. In the 340s, at the time of the case against Neaira, by contrast, there were quite a number of democratic priesthoods, both for men and for women;[59] Apollodoros' repeated phrase, 'they are not allowed to hold any priesthood', thus turned the clause of the decree concerning *gene* into a restriction that applied to the situation of *timai* of his own time. From this perspective, the discrepancy between inserted decree and speech would be an argument in favour of the authenticity of the decree.

However, as Apollodoros stipulated, the principle that only those born of an Athenian male and an *aste* could sacrifice for the *polis* also applied to archons in the decree. This was a new feature compared to the situation before Pericles' law: Themistocles, the son of an Athenian father and a non-Athenian mother, and of Menon of Pharsalos, the citizen-by-decree we met above, both held archonships.[60] Since citizens-by-decree had access to all other *archai*, the crucial element distinguishing the archonships were apparently the traditional sacrifices and other *hiera patroia* which were part of their duties. Apollodoros made the most of the antiquity of the *hiera* and of the purity of descent and conduct required by law of the archons performing them, since it was precisely the role of Basilinna, the wife and female counterpart of the Basileus, that Neaira's daughter had allegedly performed illegally.

In the light of these considerations I agree with Osborne that apparently a law existed which regulated the status of the children of a naturalised Athenian; the law was drawn up probably either as a part of or in the wake of Pericles' Citizenship Law, since it was the requirement of two Athenian parents for citizen status that made such a law necessary.[61] At some point in this legislative process, so it seems, the archonships were formally distinguished from the other *archai* and aligned closely with the priesthoods by bringing them into the same category with the same rules

58 Dates proposed for the foundation of the priestesshood of Athena Nike range from 448/7 to 425; see Blok (2014b).

59 See above, Chapter 5.4; Lambert (2010b).

60 Plut. *Them.* 1–3, who takes Themistocles to have been a *nothos*, erroneously since his parents had been properly married; cf. Patterson (1990) 63–5. The common use of the adjective *metroxenos* (having a foreign mother), with reference to Themistocles and others, suggests that before Pericles' law descent from a non-Athenian mother occurred regularly, but that, with the term's negative connotations, this was not viewed favourably.

61 Osborne II, 21; IV, 142–5, 155–61.

of access.[62] To this law Apollodoros apparently refers in the quote above. Pericles' law and its associated legislation thus highlighted the fundamental connection between citizen status by descent, not just on the male but emphatically also on the female side, and the *hiera* of the *polis*.

6.2 *Metoikoi* (Metics)

In Athens, as in many other Greek *poleis*, people from elsewhere took up residence; a large number of them were free persons who came voluntarily to the city. Prominent among them were skilled workers, for instance sculptors whose names are preserved on votive statues on the Acropolis from the sixth century onwards, and the workmen at the Erechtheion, whose names are included on the works' accounts.[63] Scholars agree that the number of immigrants grew rapidly in the course of the fifth century, notably after 483 when Athens began building its fleet. The Athenian empire drew large numbers to Athens to help build, man and maintain the navy, and after 479 the reconstruction of the walls of the Acropolis and other building projects attracted more foreign skilled labour.[64] As metics, they also served in the infantry as hoplites, as light-armed auxiliaries and on the fleet.

The question when the status of *metoikia*, which changed generic 'immigrants' into 'metics', was instituted, is greatly debated, partly because the evidence is disparate and ambiguous. Tied in with the question as to when, is the assessment of the reasons why and the manner in which this status was created. Scholars follow basically three lines of approach: linguistics and philology, i.e. the meaning of the word *metoikos* and its uses in context; demography, i.e. the numbers of citizens and non-Athenians; and analysis of social functions, i.e. the forms of and motivations for the duties and privileges of metics in the *polis*. Whereas most scholars agree that the economic and military contribution of metics to Athens was substantial, that their numbers, although somewhat fluctuating, attained the level of perhaps (very roughly) one to five citizens, and that their status was gradually filled out with legal, fiscal and cultic arrangements, there is no consensus as to the exact origins of metic status or as to how it

[62] For the closeness of archonships to priesthoods, see also above, Chapter 5.

[63] Keesling (2003) 208–9: among thirty-two inscribed sculptors' names of the archaic and classical periods, nine are non-Athenians, two are Athenians, and the ethnics of the others are not stated. In the Erechtheion accounts (*IG* I^3 474; *IG* II^2 1654; with Lambert (2000a), Randall (1953)) nearly 40 per cent of the workers are metics.

[64] Miles (2014) 123–6 for the reconstruction of much of the destructed temples and other buildings in Athens, Attica and beyond, beginning immediately after 479.

should be evaluated.[65] In his meticulous study of *metoikia* (1977), David Whitehead noted the remarkable inclusion of metics in some Athenian cults, but ultimately judged metics to be outsiders to Athenian society, measured by the yardstick of the politically active citizen defined by Aristotle.[66] Elizabeth Meyer, in her study of the so-called *phialai* inscriptions of the 330s, stresses that in the fourth century metics were seen primarily as people who owed the *metoikion* tax to the city and were strongly pressed to pay.[67] I will attempt here to contribute a few arguments to this debate from the perspective of this study.

The question how many metics, also in comparison to the number of citizens, lived in Attica is difficult to resolve. Estimates of the population on the eve of the Peloponnesian War are based on Thucydides' reports on the Athenian armed forces in 431: 14,000 citizen hoplite and cavalry and 3,000 metics. One among several problems here is the estimation of the size of relevant age classes of those in active service, those serving for the defence and others; the results of these calculations vary considerably.[68] Hans van Wees, for instance, argues that in 431 there was approximately one male metic to every five male Athenian citizens in the status-and-age group of the hoplites, leading to estimated figures in Attica of ca. 12,000 male metics to 60,000 male citizens, and that these figures were approximately one to six in the later fourth century (ca. 5,000 to ca. 30,000), but others arrive at 40,000 male citizens in 431.[69] To these figures should be added an unknown number of female metics, both wives of male metics and independent female metics.

Cynthia Patterson argued in her groundbreaking study (1981) that the rise in numbers of citizens from 480/79, which she calculated at ca. 25,000–30,000 male citizens (on Hdt. 8.44, 46; manpower at the battle of Salamis), to double that number in 431 cannot have been the result of

65 On the rights and status of metics, see Peçirka (1966); Whitehead (1977); Hansen (1991) 116–20; Todd (1993) 194–9; Hunter (2000); Meyer (2010); Kamen (2013) 43–61; Wijma (2014) 13–36.

66 Whitehead (1977), pointing out that metics could not own land and could not fulfil a *polis* office.

67 Meyer (2010) proposes to identify the *phialai*, usually thought to have been dedicated by manumitted slaves, as dedications arising from failed lawsuits filed by citizens against metics for evading the *metoikion*.

68 Thuc. 2.13.6–7, 2.31.2, resulting in either 60,000 male citizens (Hansen (1982); Hansen (1986); Hansen (1988) 28) or 40,00–50,000 (Gomme (1933) 26; Patterson (1981) 68–71; Strauss (1986) 70–81; Giovannini (2002)). Garland (2001) 61 holds that the number of metics who did not qualify for hoplite service was probably larger than the number who did. Figures for the fourth century are based on various kinds of evidence, among which rosters of ephebes and the report by Ctesikles (*FGrH* 245 F 1) on the census conducted by Demetrius of Phaleron, each with strengths and weaknesses, for which Van Wees (2011). Hansen (1988) 11 arrives at an estimated ratio metics to citizens of 1:3 for the fourth century.

69 Van Wees (2004) 241–3; Van Wees (2011), figures on 104, 110–11; for other figures, see previous note.

natural growth; apparently, many outsiders were admitted to become citizens until Pericles' Citizenship Law imposed a strict criterion valid for the whole *polis*. To account for this influx of outsiders, she pointed out that the demes were notoriously flexible in admitting to citizenship many who were not legally entitled to it, a contention we also saw Euxitheos making in contrast to his own claim grounded in membership of the phratry and *genos*.[70] Recently, James Watson, elaborating Patterson's conclusions, has argued that consequently Pericles' law must have resulted in the creation of *metoikia* to accommodate henceforth the non-citizens.[71] Although flexibility of admittance in demes and influx of immigrants into the citizen body seem plausible to some degree, the strong version defended by Patterson and Watson lacks conviction in my eyes. Firstly, the numbers we are working with are very shaky and it is hazardous to base further hypotheses on them; with a high estimation of citizens in 480 (30,000) and a low one in 431 (40,000), the demographic problem looks quite different. Secondly, on accepting the high estimations, between 480 and 451/0 ten to fifteen thousand immigrants would have acquired citizenship surreptitiously in the demes, bypassing the phratries and their rituals of legitimacy, so up to around a quarter of the citizen population.[72] In these figures, the numerous citizen war dead of the 450s on the one hand, and the numerous immigrants who remained *xenoi* (or metics) on the other, are not even taken into account. It is a scenario I find very hard to believe, indeed so much so that it rather serves as a warning, again, how precarious the estimated figures are.[73]

Not only immigrants but other free persons in Attica who were not citizens were enrolled as metics, as mainly attested in the fourth century. Among them were manumitted slaves, although this group is hardly visible in our evidence,[74] but a perhaps more sizeable group were illegitimate children of Athenians, including those deemed to be so after the

[70] Patterson (1981). On all too flexible admissions in the demes, Dem. 57.59, and above, Chapter 1, n. 12; Chapter 3, n. 94.

[71] Watson (2010) argues that Pericles' law 'specified to the demes and phratries that only certain men – immigrants not amongst them – could become citizens' (272), thereby creating metic status. Beside the problems with his figures that I discuss in the main text, his argument is further marred by the absence of a definition of 'citizenship' (participation? *quasi* birth?) and by neglect of the differences between demes and phratries in access to citizenship.

[72] For these figures, Watson (2010) 268.

[73] Cf. Whitehead (1977) 97–8, who observes prudently that arriving at reliable figures for numbers of metics is all but impossible.

[74] Dem. 22.61; Harp. *s.v.* μετοίκιον (below); Harrison 1, 187–8; for the *phialai eleutherikai*, usually taken to be dedicated by manumitted slaves, see below. For the social composition of the *metoikoi*, Kamen (2013) 43–61.

diapsephismos of 346/5.[75] Since for *nothoi* originally other social and ritual arrangements existed in the *polis*,[76] it would seem that these categories of people, who did not fit the traditional status groups of citizens on the one hand and slaves on the other, were also brought under the umbrella of *metoikoi* once this status was more fully established. Considering the widely different backgrounds of the people brought under this heading, we may wonder how the metics organised themselves when they were asked to send 'representatives' to *polis* activities (see below). At all events, that *metoikia* began as a status for immigrants – already a varied group – can hardly be doubted, and I discuss the *metoikoi* here from this perspective.

As to terminology, the earliest instance of vocabulary relating to *metoikia* is on a grave monument set up in the Kerameikos in ca. 500 for a certain Anaxilas from Naxos. The epigram states that the Athenians esteemed Anaxilas for his prudence (*sophrosyne*) and his excellence (*arete*), calling him a *metaoikos*, a description which seems intended to suggest that this Naxian had a more intimate relationship with the *polis* than a passing stranger would enjoy, as one 'who lived among us'.[77] The preposition *meta* (with accusative) refers to movement; in this sense, a *meta-oikos* has moved his house and is therefore, in modern terms, a migrant.[78] But *meta* (with genitive or dative) means 'among, with, having a part', so prominently used in *meteinai* and *metechein*. Two entries in the lexica offer both these conceptions of *metoikos*. According to Aristophanes of Byzantium,

> a *metoikos* is, whenever a man comes from abroad and resides in (*oikein en*) the city, paying tax (*telos*) for some fixed needs of the city; up to a certain number of days he is called a visitor (*prepidemos*) and is free from taxation (*ateles*), but if he exceeds the limited period, he then becomes a *metoikos* and subject to taxation.[79]

[75] Van Wees (2011) 101–4.

[76] For such arrangements for *nothoi*, Humphreys (1974); Patterson (1990).

[77] *SEG* 12.388; *IG* I³ 1357: δακρυόεν πολυπενθὲς Ἀναχσίλα ἐδ' ὀλοφυδνὸν / λάϊνον ἕστεκα μνε̃μα καταφθιμένο / Ναχσίο ὃν τίεσκον Ἀθεναῖοι μετάοικον / ἔχσοχα σοφροσύνες ἕνεκεν ἐδ' ἀρετε̃ς / το̂ι μ' ἐπὶ Τιμόμαχος γεραρὸν κτέρας οἷα θανόντι / θε̃κεν Ἀρίστονος παιδὶ χαριζόμενος. The text can only be dated by letter forms. Baba (1984) shows that the spelling *metaoikos* was not a mistake, but deliberate, and concludes that at the time of this epigram the contracted word *metoikos* was not yet in use. However, we must bear in mind that the metre required a word of the length of the uncontracted version. Baba further suggests that Anaxilas' *arete* consisted in his military valour and speculates that he received this honorific monument because he assisted the Athenians in the battle with Boeotians and Chalcidians in 506. This, however, does not perhaps account adequately for the *sophrosyne* for which Anaxilas is also praised.

[78] LSJ *s.v.* μετά (C. I).

[79] Ar.Byz. fr. 38 (Nauck): Μέτοικος δέ ἐστιν ὁπόταν τις ἀπὸ ξένης ἐλθὼν ἐνοικῇ τῇ πόλει, τέλος τελῶν εἰς ἀποτεταγμένας τινὰς χρείας τῆς πόλεως· ἕως μὲν οὖν ποσῶν ἡμερῶν παρεπίδημος

This description does not refer specifically to Athens, but the lemma on the *metoikion* by Harpokration does:

> Hypereides in the speech *Against Aristagora*. A *metoikos* is anyone from one city who *meta-oikein* in another city, not visiting briefly like a *xenos*, but having established residence (*oikesis*) there. Twelve drachmae were given by them each year, which was called the *metoikion*, as Eubulus [the comic poet] makes clear in his *Plangon*.... a man pays twelve drachmae and a woman six, and if the son pays, the woman need not, but if he does not, then she must. Slaves freed by their masters also paid the *metoikion* ... If however *metoikoi* did not pay the *metoikion*, they were taken to the *poletai*, and when they found them guilty, they were sold, as Demosthenes says in *Against Aristogeiton*.... The comic poets called the metics 'tray-carriers' since they carried trays (*skaphai*) in the procession.[80]

Arrangements for immigrants were put into place in many *poleis*, but Athens was the first, so far as we know, to create a special status for such people with quite detailed privileges and obligations.[81] In the later fifth century, when the use of demotics for citizens increased, inscribed decrees and other documents referred to metics by their name followed by *oikein en* + deme name – i.e. as living in their deme of residence.[82] This administrative description removes any doubt that *metoikos* meant someone of metic status here, and with the rise of *meta-* vocabulary in discourse about sharing in the *polis*, in the noun *metoikos* the meaning 'someone who has made his house among us' may gradually have superseded the former notion of migration. For earlier references to *metoikos* and cognates, however, we cannot be so sure what exactly is meant by *metoikos*. A decree of the deme Skambonidai of uncertain date but possibly before the mid-fifth century, dealing with the apportioning of sacrificial meat among the deme members and the *metoikoi*, offers the earliest extant reference to a *group*

καλεῖται καὶ ἀτελής ἐστιν, ἐὰν δὲ ὑπερβῇ τὸν ὡρισμένον χρόνον, μέτοικος ἤδη γίνεται καὶ ὑποτελής· παραπλησίως δὲ τούτῳ καὶ ὁ ἰσοτελής. Trans. Meyer (2010) 29, after Whitehead (1977) 7.

80 Harp. *s.v.* μετοίκιον: Ὑπερείδης ἐν τῷ κατ' Ἀρισταγόρας. μέτοικος μέν ἐστιν ὁ ἐξ ἑτέρας πόλεως μετοικῶν ἐν ἑτέρᾳ καὶ μὴ πρὸς ὀλίγον ὡς ξένος ἐπιδημῶν, ἀλλὰ τὴν οἴκησιν αὐτόθι καταστησάμενος. ἐδίδοντο δὲ ὑπ' αὐτῶν καθ' ἕκαστον ἔτος δραχμαὶ ιβ', ὅπερ ὠνόμαστο μετοίκιον, ὡς δηλοῖ Εὔβουλος ἐν τῇ Πλαγγόνι.... ὁ μὲν ἀνὴρ ιβ' δραχμὰς ἐτέλει μετοίκιον, ἡ δὲ γυνὴ ϛ', καὶ ὅτι τοῦ υἱοῦ τελοῦντος ἡ μήτηρ οὐκ ἐτέλει· μὴ τελοῦντος δ' ἐκείνου αὐτὴ τελεῖ. ὅτι δὲ καὶ οἱ δοῦλοι ἀφεθέντες ὑπὸ τῶν δεσποτῶν ἐτέλουν τὸ μετοίκιον ... οἱ μέντοι μὴ τιθέντες τὸ μετοίκιον μέτοικοι ἀπήγοντο πρὸς τοὺς πωλητὰς, καὶ εἰ ἑάλωσαν ἐπιπράσκοντο, ὥς φησι Δημοσθένης ἐν τῷ κατ' Ἀριστογείτονος.... ἐκάλουν δὲ οἱ κωμικοὶ σκαφέας τοὺς μετοίκους, ἐπεὶ ἐν ταῖς πομπαῖς. Cf. Poll. *Onom.* 3.55: 'the metic is the one who pays the *metoikion*'.

81 Whitehead (1977) 75–7: the institution of the *metoikion* spread from Athens to Oropos, Aegina and Megara; cf. Meyer (2010) 29–30.

82 The first occurrence is *IG* I³ 421 b. l. 33, of 414; it may have come to be used for military or fiscal purposes, see Whitehead (1977) 152, and further below.

of immigrants; probably metics are meant here, but their status cannot be ascertained.[83] Occurrence of the verb *metoikein* in Aeschylus' *Suppliants* of ca. 463 is perhaps not very significant, but in *Eumenides* of 458 Athena welcomes the Erinyes to live among the Athenians and to be honoured with crimson cloaks in a procession.[84] This role has such striking similarities to the role typical of *metoikoi* in the Panathenaic and other *pompai*, as attested in the lexica, that we may infer the audience was expected to recognise a practice that by then was familiar.[85] On this evidence, in the 460s *metoikos* and its cognates could convey specific reference to metics, beyond the generic meaning 'immigrant'.

Lexicographers describe the metics as represented in the Panathenaic and Dionysian processions by four groups: *skaphephoroi* (tray-bearers, male), *hydriaphoroi* (hydria-carriers, male and female), *skiadephoroi* (parasol-bearers, female) and *diphrophoroi* (stool-bearers, female).[86] In her study of metics' religious participation in classical Athens, Sara Wijma discusses several vase paintings, beginning in the 470s, showing (young) men as *skaphephoroi*, and a *skiadephoros* holding her parasol over a *kanephoros*.[87] Since only metics are known to have performed these roles, she argues that these vases show metics and that in these years the *polis* must have instituted their participation in the Panathenaic *pompe*. Wijma considers this assignment of specific new roles in the Panathenaic procession, one of the major religious events at Athens with a carefully selected representation of the *polis*, to be the initial step towards *metoikia* as a status close to but distinct from Athenian citizens and distinct from non-Athenian strangers (*xenoi*) generally.[88] Wijma attractively situates this as a step in Athens's developing policy of assigning distinct roles to citizens and metics of various ages and gender and, occasionally, to others (for instance its

[83] *IG* I^3 244, C l. 8; its conventional dating to the 460s in *IG* seems to be based on letter forms and on the passage in Aeschylus' *Eumenides*.

[84] Aesch. *Suppl.* 609–14: ἡμᾶς μετοικεῖν τῆσδε γῆς ἐλευθέρους; *Eum.* 1028–31.

[85] Bakewell (1997); Wijma (2014) 53.

[86] Hesych., Harp. Suda, *s.v.* σκαφηφόροι; ὑδριαφόροι; διφροφόροι; Poll. *Onom.* 7.174. For further evidence and the question whether these roles were an 'honour or humiliation', Wijma (2014) 44–64.

[87] *Skaphephoroi*: Attic red-figure kylix by the Pan Painter (Ashmolean 1911.617; *CVA*, *Oxford*, 1.6 pls 2.9, 7.3–4; *ARV*^{2} 559, 152); Attic red-figure amphora, Metropolitan Mus. New York (no. 20.244); *skiadephoros*: Attic red-figure lekythos by the Brygos Painter, ca. 480–470, Paestum, Museo Archeologico Nazionale, *ARV*^{2} 384.212. Wijma (2014) app. 1, 165–6, listing in total seven cases of possible representations of metics in various cultic roles.

[88] For the Panathenaic procession as a selective (re)presentation of the *polis*, Parker, *PS*, 253–69; Shear (2001) 120–230; Maurizio (1998); Brulé (1996); Parker (1996) 91. For a long time, scholars saw in the Parthenon frieze a representation of the Panathenaic procession, including the metics in their special roles (e.g. Neils (2001) 146–50; Shear (2001) 742–61), but this interpretation has been called into question by Connelly (2014).

allies in the empire) in its festivals to articulate their roles in the *polis*. Like the citizens, the metics were represented in the Panathenaic procession grouped as to gender and age, among which young men and women on the brink of contributing fully to the *polis*; their crimson cloaks, which distinguished them from the citizens, were an unmistakable sign of the wealth metics were known and expected to bring to Athens. After the Panathenaic procession, metics were also included in other festivals, at both *polis* and at deme level.[89] Particularly in the festivals for Dionysus the *polis* was on display, to itself and to the world. In the Lenaia, as well as in the Dionysus festival at Ikarion, metics participated in every way also open to citizens, namely in the procession, as member of the chorus, as *choregos* with concomitant honours and as audience, in both cases probably since the 440–430s.[90] By contrast, during the City Dionysia, the Athenians presented themselves in the theatre as the 'core *polis*' to all others, among whom were now also the metics. Discussing a range of Athenian cults and festivals, Wijma shows that metics did not participate in all festivals, but in those in which they did, their role usually was different from the Athenians'. In this way metics were included in the *polis* more intimately than before, but simultaneously the distinctions between them and Athenians were marked and displayed.

An essential difference between Athenians and all others was and remained sharing in sacrificial meat at *polis* festivals: sharing in the *hiera* defined the composition of the group (see Chapter 2.4.1) and normally strangers could participate in such sacrifices only by invitation and on an individual basis. Occasionally, however, metics received sacrificial meat *as a group* – and this, I would argue, marked a significant difference between them and other non-Athenians. The deme Skambonidai, as discussed above, was such a case, where meat was distributed to *metoikoi* as a *group*, whether or not this group were metics in the legal sense. In 421/0, young metic men were included in the Hephaisteia, a festival especially of young men and artisans, on which occasion the *polis* gave them three bovines for sacrifice *as metics* – recognising them as a group entitled to a sacrificial share in a *polis* festival, but, again, in a different manner from Athenian citizens.[91] This sacrificial share perhaps recognised metics' characteristic roles in artisanal trades of which Hephaistos was patron.

89 Deme level: on Skambonidai (above) Wijma (2014) 103–9; in the Dionysia at Ikarion, *IG* I³ 254, esp. l. 3, with Wijma (2014) 109–16, Wilson (2015).

90 Wijma (2014), on the Lenaia, 66–75, date 68–9; on the Dionysia, 75–85.

91 *IG* I³ 82, esp. ll. 23–4; Wijma (2014) 88–94, underlining that the metics got their meat raw, that they got less meat than citizens and that they had a limited part in the organisation of the festival;

Just as metics were included in Athenian society through some cults, so gods from elsewhere were invited to share in the Athenians' bond. New gods had come to Greece before the fifth century, notably Dionysus who by nature was an 'incoming' god. But in the second half of the fifth century the new gods included in the cultic system at Athens are conspicuous in number and origin.[92] These were not only familiar gods from Greece, such as Asclepius (420) from Epidaurus, who soon became one of the most popular deities in Athens and elsewhere, but also Bendis, the hunting goddess from Thrace, with whom the Athenians set up a formal relationship that also accommodated the numerous Thracians who lived at Athens, probably in around 434.[93] Ammon, the oracular god from Egypt, and Kybele, the mother goddess from Phrygia, likewise were integrated with cults encompassing sanctuaries, cult personnel and festivals in the *polis* calendar.

Participation by metics in cults and festivals and in the *choregia* for the Lenaia are attested before the first references to the *metoikion* in ca. 409.[94] When the *metoikion* was instituted is unknown, but Whitehead persuasively connects the introduction of the registration of metics in demes ('the *oikon en*-system', appearing in the 410s) with the introduction of the *metoikion*.[95] Unlike liturgies, the *metoikion* was a poll tax, a fixed amount for every metic, not, aside from the different rates for different genders, a reflection of a person's individual value to society, but applied specifically to this particular social group. Some scholars therefore regard the *metoikion* as by definition dishonourable. Whitehead, for instance, proposes that the repeated payment of a small amount (a drachma each month for a man, half a drachma for a woman) emphasised the distinction between metics and citizens 'for all to see'.[96] Certainly, living as a

cf. Parker, *PS*, 471–2. It is unfortunately unclear if this provision was for a single occasion or was an innovation to be continued on a regular basis.

92 For this process, Parker (1996) 152–98; Garland (1992).

93 The founding text of the Asclepius cult at Athens, in which a certain Telemachos advertised the role he had played on the authority of the *demos*, is *SEG* 47.232; on Bendis, see Lambert (2010b) 162; for her cults accommodating the integration of Thracians in Athens, Wijma (2014) 126–55.

94 The earliest references to the *metoikion* may date to c. 409 (*IG* I^3 106, l. 7; *IG* I^3 107, l. 3, both restored). This provides only a *terminus ante* for the introduction of the *metoikion*; whether, for instance, *ateleia* for *proxenoi* before that date implied freedom from the *metoikion* or from other taxes is not explained in our sources; see for instance the proxeny grant to Herakleides of Klazomenai of 423 or later (OR 157; *IG* II^2 8; ML 70) with comm. in OR. According to Diod.S. 11.43.3, Themistocles tried to entice *xenoi* to come and settle in Piraeus, offering them freedom from taxes as metics, but no evidence corroborates this report. Literary references all date to the fourth century and later.

95 Whitehead (1977) 31–2, 76, 152–3.

96 Whitehead (1977) 76; also 152–3: *metoikion* the opposite of citizen *misthos*; Todd (1993) 197–8; Niku (2007) 41; Meyer (2010) 30.

xenos or a metic in a *polis* by definition entailed having fewer privileges and responsibilities – in that sense a lower status – than full citizens and paying the *metoikion* was a sign of that. But I think the view that the *metoikion* was deliberately humiliating needs modification when understood in the wider system of taxes.

Since the sixth century, citizens had paid taxes of various kinds.[97] In the earliest extant decree, the first rule Athens laid down for the settlers on Salamis was that they had to pay taxes (*telein*) and serve in the army like the Athenians.[98] To judge what part of his wealth (*telos*) a citizen owed the *polis*, the value of citizens' estates was assessed, probably partly on the basis of self-assessment, landed property being central to the assessment.[99] In the classical age, *eisphorai* were levied on all free residents whose property was valued at more than a certain amount; wealthy metics fell under this tax regime, just like citizens, but since they normally did not own land, their wealth was measured in a different way.[100] Wealthy metics were also expected to provide liturgies. Besides such *tele* based on the valuation of every household, a tax of 1 per cent was levied on property sales, which normally concerned only citizens. Non-Athenians, including metics, honoured with the right of *enktesis*, i.e. the right to own land and/or a house, presumably had to pay this sale tax when they had in fact bought such property and sold it again.[101] Demes could levy a tax (*enktetikon*) on property in their community held by non-demesmen, whether citizens or metics-with-*enktesis*. Furthermore, metics normally also payed the *xenika tele*, a market tax paid by non-Athenians, and the *pentekoste*, a 2 per cent tax on all commercial goods passing the harbour at Piraeus, paid by metics, citizens and others alike.[102]

It seems, therefore, that normally wealthy metics fell under the same tax regime as wealthy citizens (*eisphorai*, liturgies), that all metics paid the *metoikion*, that metics working in the market (probably not wealthy people) paid the *xenika tele*, that all involved in trade paid the *pentekoste*,

97 Van Wees (2013) 83–106 argues that direct forms of taxation of wealthy citizens were continuous since the times of the tyrants and probably since Solon.

98 *IG* I³ 1 ll. 2–3; cf. *IG* II² 287, stipulating twice that the honoured *proxenos* is to be subject to the same tax regime as the Athenians.

99 Isoc. 17.49; Dem. 27.7, 42.18; Cf. Ostwald (1996) 166; Davies (1997) 33; Fawcett (2006) 141–70.

100 Lys. 12.20; Isoc. 17.41, but it is not clear how this worked.

101 *Enktesis* in the fourth century of 'land and house': *IG* II³ 1, 352a–b l. 29; 367, ll. 19–20; 324b ll. 44–5; 473 ll. 11–12; *IG* II² 505 l. 53; 786 b. l. 8; of a house: *IG* II² 554 ll. 29–30; for the metic status of these recipients, Whitehead (1977) 28–31. The lists of *hekatostai* of the sale of public lands, dating to the second half of the fourth century, the proceeds of which went into the treasury of Athena and the Other Gods, show only citizen buyers; Lambert (1997b) 278–91.

102 *Xenika tele*: Whitehead (1977) 11–12; *pentekoste*: Garland (2001) 88.

whereas citizens, rich and poor alike, paid sales tax on property. On balance, this does not seem unreasonable, nor does the *metoikion* stand out as a deliberate humiliation. The application to metics of a tax regime different from citizens may have been due largely to practical factors. Some metics lived in Athens for a lifetime, others just a few years; they normally did not own property, their wealth consisted of changing and varying amounts of cash, saleable goods, tools, their physical strength, intellectual capacities or whatever earning their living required. In the absence of any systematic registration of income, a tax of a fixed amount per capita was a practical solution.

Taken together, this evidence suggests that the creation of *metoikia* as a status was a gradual one, remaining under construction, just like the status of citizens, throughout the classical age. Although there is evidence of a variety of ways in which metics participated at deme level, the institution of *metoikia* as a status was essentially a *polis* matter. Offering what can be no more than a very tentative interpretation, I would argue that the features of *metoikia* invite us to identify it as a framework set up by the Athenians in which the contributions of the numerous immigrants to the *polis* in the form of work, money and military service were reciprocated in the form of certain *timai*, namely specific roles in some *polis* festivals and thus a share in the *polis*'s bond with the gods, and certain rights. Such a framework, in which both parties knew what they might expect from each other in terms of money and work, legal and cultic rights and financial and military duties, may have worked as an incentive both for outsiders to settle at Athens and for the *polis* to live up to the rules of reciprocity.

If this view carries some plausibility, it helps to make sense of the evidence, in which the *timai* granted to metics and obligations imposed on them appear unevenly and haphazardly, by understanding the one as structurally tied to the other. Formal reciprocal relations between the *polis* and groups or individuals usually began on the level of the wealthy and prominent. Once the cycle of reciprocity was formally and ritually established, further elements were added over time in the spheres of honours, rights and duties. For metics, this would mean that after a stage in which the most wealthy were involved, further steps for all social classes were put into place, in the sphere of rights access to the courts by a representative and protection against various kinds of malice, and in that of duties the *metoikion*, other taxes and more forms of military service. On these considerations, we might expect that the roles for (prominent) metics in the Panathenaic procession, appearing on vases and in literary sources since the 470s, were the counterpoise for *eisphora* or other financial contributions, although the latter are not attested. For the participation of metics in the Lenaia, attested from the 440s–430s onwards, to be possible, it would seem that *metoikia* had acquired a more solid administrative shape. Some such organisation must have existed for (wealthy) immigrants to be able to present themselves with a chorus for the dramatic festival on behalf of this very varied group. The same applies, *mutatis mutandis*, for the share of metic young men in the Hephaisteia of 421/0. It is therefore attractive to suppose that in these years the *oikon-en* system and the *metoikion*, i.e. local registration and payment of poll tax, were largely in place, although the evidence for both appears only in the last decade of the fifth century.

In this hypothesis, the model for participation of this new status group in the *polis* was the same as the one for citizens: reciprocating the value of the group for the community, the *polis* granted basic *timai* for the whole group and specific *timai* for exceptionally valuable individuals (or the reverse in case of failure). Just as among citizens, gender, age and differences in wealth or other forms of success determined which *timai* could thus be attained. Equality, in the sense of having *the same* rights and duties as citizens, however, did not apply in Athenian society, in which status distinctions between citizens and non-citizens preceded the assignment of rights. The differences in status between citizens and metics thus led to different outcomes of the same institutional process. Because they were not of citizen birth, metics could not partake fully in the *hiera kai hosia*; they shared in some of the *polis*'s honours for the gods on specific conditions and only exceptionally in the *polis*'s sacrifices. From an Athenian perspective, the establishment of the *metoikia* in this way must have seemed logical, with an institutional rationale comparable to that applicable to citizens, giving a fair share in return for their value but keeping the difference between born citizens and others intact. After Pericles' law, involving the metics in the religious, social, legal and economic structure of the *polis* in this manner may have strengthened the ties with metics, to compensate for the formidable distance between citizens and non-citizens that the law had brought about. Since granting *time* in return for contributions was not restricted to Athens but was an institution of ancient Greece more widely, for those metics at Athens who were citizens from other Greek *poleis* it cannot have been too difficult to come to terms with the rules of the game. This takes me to the final considerations.

6.3 Outside Athens

This study is concerned with citizenship at Athens, in the first place for the practical reasons of available evidence. But we face at once the legitimate question whether citizenship was conceived and shaped in other *poleis* in ways similar to Athens. Again for practical reasons an extensive answer lies beyond the scope of this study, but I would like to offer here some brief remarks.

This question engages us in the debate on the unity of Greek law; whether, in other words, the conspicuous variety amongst and similarities between the laws of different Greek *poleis* indicate so many variations on common legal themes or rather quite different legal frameworks that developed some common features. As I emphasised in Chapter 5, the proliferation in the number and kinds of *polis* offices in classical Athens was a result of the democracy – because they were the very means to implement it – as well as of the exceptional size of Athens as a *polis*. Other *poleis* had similar offices, cultic and otherwise, but rarely exactly the same and certainly not as many.

A telling example is access to priesthood. In some parts of the Greek world, for instance on the isle of Cos, priesthoods were assigned by being sold. I have argued that at Athens arrangements for access to priesthood were a sign of the high value (*time*) enjoyed by the priest/ess, but the material sense of value shown in the sales at Cos for this purpose would have been utterly alien to an Athenian. The successful bidders on Cos, however, had to be of Coan descent; indeed, some laws stated that the priest/ess had to be a third-generation citizen of Cos at least, going beyond the rules at Athens in this respect.[103] In sum, at Athens and in Cos the rules for access to priesthoods were on the one hand quite different, on the other quite comparable, and one could argue that both systems fitted the rules of *time* for the distribution of honours. Similarly, the rules of legitimate descent also embodied in rules of succession to inheritance show quite important differences in detail between *poleis*, but also some fundamental features in common: partible inheritance, bilateral inheritance with priority of male over female and of descendants over collaterals, and considerable emphasis placed on rules for *epikleroi*. Although many *poleis* required double citizen parentage for citizen status, the *gene* at Athens

[103] Parker and Obbink (2000) esp. 424. Numerous *leges sacrae* at Cos require priests and priestesses to be ὁλόκλαρος, compare at Athens, above, Chapter 5.

were, to the best of my knowledge, quite unique in Greece in successfully forging their identity as a descent group with exclusive access to priesthoods on such a scale, as must their effect have been on the idea of citizenship, descent, the antiquity of the *polis*'s cults and ultimately on the idea of Athenian autochthony. The *genos* of the Branchidai, for instance, who held the cultic offices of the oracular shrine of Apollo at Didyma until the Persians captured Miletus, boasted a similar metaphorical descent from a very ancient *archegetes* of their office, but unlike the Athenian *gene* had no demonstrable effect on the city's internal policies, being a single *genos* and accused of betraying the sanctuary in the Persian assault at that.[104]

Perhaps even more significant is whether the larger institutional and conceptual frameworks which I proposed shaped Athenian citizenship were also effective elsewhere. These are first of all the idea that citizenship was intimately woven into the fabric of *polis* religion, especially into the notion of *hiera kai hosia* (albeit expressed differently, since *hiera kai hosia* is typically Athenian) and secondly the rules of *time* (value) in shaping the rights, claims, duties and obligations of citizens, of which the bond with the gods was an essential element. There can be no doubt that *polis* religion, including the religious feelings involved in it, was a Greek phenomenon, not just an Athenian one, even if Athens is the place where we can see it most vividly, in most detail and on a broad canvass. It is clear that the underlying notion of the reciprocity between *polis* and gods guided the self-conception of all Greek cities and the ways in which they were organised. Let me give just two examples.

At Athens, so I argued in Chapter 2, the conception of *hiera kai hosia* implied a dual responsibility of the *polis* towards the divine and the human worlds: responsibility towards the gods for the *polis*'s obligations to them and for the proper conduct of relations among themselves as human beings, and responsibility towards the human community for ensuring that fair rules were in place governing its mutual obligations. This notion was found to underlie the laws at Athens, but it can be traced from the seventh century onwards, when writing was first used for decrees, in the laws of many *poleis*. It appears explicitly in some early Cretan laws, which address the affairs of the *polis* as *ta damosia ta theia kai t' anthropina*.[105] In this way the *polis* distinguished the obligations of

[104] For the Branchidai, descendants of Branchos and their ancient cult (Hdt. 1.157.3; Paus. 7.2.6; Strab. 9.9), see further Hammond (1998).

[105] E.g. Arcades (Crete), *SEG* 27.631, 'Spensithios'- decree (*Nomima* 1, no. 22), ca. 550–500, 1–10: '[to grant] to Spensithios and his descendants freedom from all taxes as long as he records and

the *demos* (*ta damosia*) towards the gods (*ta theia*) from those towards humans (*t'anthropina*), but underlined their complementary nature by proclaiming its responsibility for both in one breath. The same expression *ta theia kai t' anthropina* was used for the dual obligations of private individuals.[106] This expression is clearly akin to *ta hiera kai ta hosia*, likewise used for both public and private matters, but with *ta hosia* the divine norms to be observed in human affairs are made explicit, whereas this is not the case with *ta anthropina*.

A second example is a decree dating to the early fifth century regulating the relations between the colonists of Naupaktos, a colony settled from East Locris, and their mother *polis*:

> The *apoikia* (goes) to Naupaktos on these terms. A Locrian of the Hypoknemidians, when he has become a Naupaktian, being a Naupaktian, is permitted to receive his due portion by lot (*lanchanein*) and to sacrifice (*thyein*) where it is *hosie* for a stranger when he is present [*sc.* in Locris] if he so wishes. If he so wishes, he may sacrifice and receive his due portion by lot of the *demos* and of the subgroups, he himself and his descendants, for ever.[107]

What is significant here is that both the new *polis* and the old one are defined by *hosie*, rules as to who is to share in sacrifice. Once a citizen of the new *polis*, the former Locrian who finds himself in Locris again may choose whether he participates as a stranger (because now a Naupaktian) in the rites of his *polis* of origin (if *hosie* allows participation by strangers) or as a Locrian in the sacrifices of the *polis* and its subgroups. In other words, the *polis* and its colony both conceive of themselves as communities in the first place on the terms of their bonds with the gods. This foundational part of the decree is followed by a statute on the payment of *telos* and next nine numbered sets of rules on the political organisation, taxation, jurisdiction, inheritance rights to the *kleroi* in the colony and many other human concerns.

remembers public matters, both divine and human (τὰ δαμόσια τά τε θιήια καὶ τἀνθρώπινα) for the city. And no one else beside Spensithios and his descendants is to record and remember for the *polis* public matters either divine or human, unless Spensithios and his family give permission.' On the complementary nature of these spheres in these decrees, cf. Gagarin (2011).

106 The Gortyn Code (*IC* IV.72.10.42–3) states that an adopted son inherits from his adopted father if 'he fulfils the adopter's obligations, divine and human (θήια καὶ ἀνθρώπινα)'.

107 *IG* IX, 1^2 3: 718; *Syll.* 47; ML 20; Körner no. 49; *Nomima* I, 43; for the object, www.britishmuseum.org/research/collection_online. I discussed this document more extensively in Blok (2011) 240–1; see also Peels (2015) 191–2.

Documents as specific and explicit on these matters as the foundation decree of Naupaktos are rare, but numerous decrees of the ancient Greek world attest to similar conceptions and societal structures in a less direct but also eloquent way. In-depth investigation of these documents and concomitant written and material evidence would sharpen or modify what I have proposed here for Athens, and help us to arrive at a model offering a better understanding of citizenship in ancient Greece.

Bibliography

Abel, V.L.S. (1983). *Prokrisis*. Königstein.

Aleshire, S.B. (1994). 'The demos and the priests: The selection of sacred officials at Athens from Cleisthenes to Augustus', in Osborne and Hornblower, 325–37.

Aleshire, S.B., S.D. Lambert (2011). 'The Attic *gene* and the Athenian religious reform of 21 BC', in *Priests and state in the Roman world*. J.J. Richardson, F. Santangelo (eds). Stuttgart, 553–75.

Allen, D.S. (2000). *The world of Prometheus: The politics of punishing in democratic Athens*. Princeton.

Anderson, G. (2003). *The Athenian experiment: Building an imagined political community in ancient Attica, 508–490*. Ann Arbor.

(2009). 'The personality of the Greek state', *JHS* 129, 1–22.

Andrewes, A. (1961). 'Philochoros on phratries', *JHS* 81, 1–15.

Arnaoutoglou, I. (1998). *Ancient Greek laws: A sourcebook*. London/New York.

Arnott, W.G. (1993 [1981]). 'Double vision: A reading of Euripides' Elektra', in *Greek tragedy*. I. McAuslan, P. Walcot (eds). Oxford, 204–17.

Assmann, A. (1999). *Erinnerungsräume: Formen und Wandlungen des kulturellen Gedächtnisses*. Munich.

Baba, K. (1984). 'On Kerameikos inv. I 388 (*SEG* XXII, 79): A note on the formation of the Athenian metic-status', *ABSA* 79, 1–5.

Badian, E. (1993). *From Plataea to Potidaea: Studies in the history and historiography of the Pentecontaetia*. Baltimore/London.

Bakewell, G.W. (1997). '*Metoikia* in the *Supplices* of Aeschylus', *ClAnt* 16, 209–28.

(1999). 'Lysias 12 and Lysias 31: Metics and Athenian citizenship in the aftermath of the Thirty', *GRBS* 40, 5–22.

Berent, M. (2004). 'In search of the Greek state: A rejoinder to M.H. Hansen', *Polis* 21, 107–46.

Berkel, T. van (2012). *The economics of friendship: Changing conceptions of reciprocity in classical Athens*. Diss. Leiden.

Berman, D.W. (2007). *Myth and culture in Aeschylus Seven against Thebes*. Rome.

Berti, I. (2006). '"Now let Earth be my witness and the broad heaven above, and the down flowing water of the Styx …" (Homer, *Iliad* XV, 36–37): Greek oath-rituals', in *Ritual and communication in the Graeco-Roman world*. E. Stavrianopoulou (ed.). Kernos Suppl. 16, Liège, 181–209.

Bickerman, E.J. (1980). *Chronology of the ancient world* (rev. ed.). London.

Blanshard, A.J.L. (2004). 'What counts as the *demos*? Some notes on the relationship between the jury and "the people" in classical Athens', *Phoenix* 58, 28–48.

Bleicken, J. (1994). *Die Athenische Demokratie (2nd ed.)*. Paderborn/Zürich etc.

Blok, J.H. (1996). 'A tale of many cities: Amazons in the mythical past of Greek cities in Asia Minor', in *Proof and persuasion: Essays on authority, objectivity and evidence*. S. Marchand, E. Lunbeck (eds). Turnhout, 81–99.

(2000). 'Phye's procession: Culture, politics and Peisistratid rule', in *Peisistratos and the tyranny: A reappraisal of the evidence*. H. Sancisi-Weerdenburg (ed.). Publications of the Netherlands Institute at Athens, Amsterdam, 17–48.

(2001). 'Virtual voices: Towards a choreography of women's speech in classical Athens', in *Making silence speak: Women's voices in Greek literature and society*. A. Lardinois, L. McClure (eds). Princeton, 95–116.

(2004). 'Recht und Ritus der Polis', *HZ* 278, 1–26.

(2005). 'Becoming citizens: Some notes on the semantics of "citizen" in archaic Greece and classical Athens', *Klio* 87, 7–40.

(2006). 'Solon's funerary laws: Questions of authenticity and function', in Blok and Lardinois, 197–247.

(2009a). 'Gentrifying genealogy: On the genesis of the Athenian autochthony myth', in *Antike Mythen: Medien, Transformationen, Konstruktionen. Fritz Graf zum 65. Geburtstag*. C. Walde, U. Dill (eds). Berlin, 251–75.

(2009b). 'Perikles' citizenship law: A new perspective', *Historia* 58, 141–70.

(2009c). 'Citizenship in action: "Reading" sacrifice in classical Athens', in *Rollenbilder in der athenischen Demokratie: Medien, Gruppen, Räume im politischen und sozialen System*. C. Mann, M. Haake, R. von den Hoff (eds). Wiesbaden, 89–111.

(2010). 'Deme accounts and the meaning of *hosios* money', *Mnemosyne* 63, 61–93.

(2011). '*Hosiê* and Athenian law from Solon to Lykourgos', in *Clisthène et Lycurgue d'Athènes: Autour du politique dans la cité classique*. V. Azoulay, P. Ismard (eds). Paris, 233–54.

(2013). 'Citizenship, the citizen body and its assemblies', in *A Companion to ancient Greek government*. H. Beck (ed.). Malden/Oxford, 161–75.

(2014a). 'A 'covenant' between gods and men: *Hiera kai hosia* and the Greek *polis*', in *The city in the classical and post-classical world: Changing contexts of power and identity*. C. Rapp, H.A. Drake (eds). Cambridge/New York, 14–37.

(2014b). 'The priestess of Athena Nikê: A new reading of *IG* I³ 35 and 36', *Kernos* 27, 99–126.

(2015). 'The diôbelia: On the political economy of an Athenian state fund', *ZPE* 193, 87–102.

Blok, J.H., J.H.E. Krul (in press in *Hesperia*). 'Debt and its aftermath: The Near Eastern background to Solon's *seisachtheia*'.

Blok, J.H., S.D. Lambert (2009). 'The appointment of priests in Attic *gene*', *ZPE* 169, 95–121.

Blok, J.H., A.P.M.H. Lardinois (eds) (2006). *Solon of Athens: New historical and philological approaches.* Mnemosyne Suppl. 272, Leiden/Boston.

Blok, J.H., P.E. van 't Wout (in press). 'Table arrangements: Sitêsis as a polis institution (*IG* I³ 131)', in *Feasting and polis institutions.* F.v.d. Eijnde, J. Blok, R. Strootman (eds).

Blundell, M.W. (1989). *Helping friends and harming enemies: A study in Sophocles and Greek ethics.* Cambridge.

Boegehold, A.L. (1994). 'Perikles' citizenship law of 451/0 B.C.', in *Athenian identity and civic ideology.* A.L. Boegehold, A.C. Scafuro (eds). Baltimore, 57–66.

Bolmarcich, S. (2007). 'Oaths in Greek international relations', in Sommerstein and Fletcher, 26–38.

Bordes, J. (1980). 'La place d'Aristote dans l'évolution de la notion de *politeia*', *Ktèma* 5, 249–56.

(1982). *POLITEIA dans la pensée grecque jusqu' à Aristote.* Paris.

Borecky, B. (1963). 'The primitive origin of the Greek conception of equality', in *Geras: Studies presented to George Thomson on the occasion of his 60th birthday.* L. Varcl, R.F. Willets et al. (eds). Prague, 41–60.

Borgers, O. (2008). 'Religious citizenship in classical Athens: Men and women in religious representations on Athenian vase-painting', *BABesch* 83, 73–97.

Bourriot, F. (1976). *Recherches sur la nature du génos: Étude d'histoire sociale athénienne – periodes archaique et classique.* Lille.

Breij, B. (2011). 'Dilemmas of pietas in Roman declamation', in Lardinois, Blok, van der Poel, 329–48.

Bremen, R. van (1996). *The limits of participation: Women and civic life in the Greek east in the Hellenistic and Roman periods.* Amsterdam.

Bremer, J.-M. (1998). 'The reciprocity of giving and thanksgiving in Greek worship', in *Reciprocity in ancient Greece.* C. Gill, N. Postlethwaite, R. Seaford (eds). Oxford, 127–38.

Bremmer, J.N. (1983). 'The importance of the maternal uncle and grandfather in archaic and classical Greece and early Byzantium', *ZPE* 50, 173–86.

(1998). '"Religion", "ritual" and the opposition "sacred vs. profane"', in *Ansichten griechischer Rituale: Geburtstags-Symposium für Walter Burkert (1996).* F. Graf (ed.). Stuttgart/Leipzig, 9–32.

(2002). 'How old is the ideal of holiness (of mind) in the Epidaurian temple inscription and in the Hippocratic oath?', *ZPE* 141, 106–8.

(2010). 'Greek normative animal sacrifice', in *A companion to Greek religion.* D. Ogden (ed.). Malden/Oxford, 132–44.

Brulé, P. (1987). *La fille d'Athènes: La religion des filles à Athènes à l'époque classique, mythes, cultes et société.* Paris.

(1996). 'La cité en ses composantes: Remarques sur les sacrifices et la procession des Panathénées', *Kernos* 6, 37–63.

(2005). '"La cité est la somme des maisons": Un commentaire religieux', in *Idiai kai demosiai: Les cadres 'privés' et 'publics' de la religion grecque antique.* V. Dasen, M. Piérart (eds). Liège, 27–54.

Bubelis, W.S. (2016). *Hallowed stewards: Solon and the sacred treasurers of ancient Athens.* Ann Arbor.

Burckhardt, L.A. (1996). *Bürger und Soldaten: Aspekte der politischen und militärischen Rolle athenischer Bürger im Kriegswesen des 4. Jht. v. Chr.* Stuttgart.
Burkert, W. (1985). *Greek religion.* Cambridge, MA (transl. J. Raffan; orig. 1977).
(1992). *The orientalizing revolution: Near Eastern influence on Greek culture in the early archaic age.* Cambridge, MA.
(1995). 'Greek poleis and civic cults: Some further thoughts', in *Studies in the ancient Greek polis.* M.H. Hansen, K.A. Raaflaub (eds). Stuttgart, 201–10.
Busse, D., F. Hermanns, W. Teubert (eds) (1994). *Begriffsgeschichte und Diskursg eschichte: Methodenfragen und Forschungsergebnisse der historischen Semantik.* Opladen.
Butz, P.A. (1996). 'Prohibitionary inscriptions, *ξένοι*, and the influence of the early Greek polis', in *The role of religion in the early Greek polis.* R. Hägg (ed.). Stockholm, 75–95.
(2010). *The art of the Hekatompedon inscription and the birth of the stoichedon style.* Leiden/Boston.
Cairns, D. (1993). *Aidôs: The psychology and ethics of honour and shame in Greek literature.* Oxford.
(2011). 'Honour and shame: Modern controversies and ancient values'. *Critical Quarterly* 53, 23–41.
Canevaro, M. (2013). *The documents in the Attic orators: Laws and decrees in the public speeches of the Demosthenic corpus.* Oxford.
Carawan, E. (1998). *Rhetoric and the law of Draco.* Oxford.
(2008). 'Pericles the Younger and the citizenship law', *CJ* 103, 383–406.
Carey, C. (1991). 'Apollodorus' mother: The wives of enfranchised aliens in Athens', *CQ* 41, 84–9.
(1992). *Apollodoros against Neaira.* Warminster.
Carter, D.M. (2004). 'Citizen attribute, negative right: A conceptual difference between ancient and modern ideas of freedom of speech', in *Free speech in classical antiquity.* I. Sluiter, R.M. Rosen (eds). Mnemosyne Suppl. 254, Leiden/Boston, 197–220.
(2007). 'Could a Greek oath guarantee a claim right? Oaths, contracts and the structure of obligation in classical Athens', in Sommerstein and Fletcher, 60–72.
Cartledge, P. (2000). 'Greek political thought: The historical context', in *The Cambridge history of Greek and Roman political thought.* C. Rowe, M. Schofield (eds) Cambridge, 11–22.
Cavanaugh, M.B. (1996). *Eleusis and Athens: Documents in finance, religion and politics in the fifth century* B.C. Atlanta.
Chadwick, J. (1996). *Lexicographica Graeca: Contributions to the lexicography of ancient Greek.* Oxford.
Chaniotis, A. (2008). 'Priests as ritual experts in the Greek world', in Dignas and Trampedach, 17–34.
Chankowski, A.S. (2010). *L'éphébie hellénistique: Étude d'une institution civique dans les cités grecques des îles de la Mer Égée et de l'Asie Mineure.* Paris.
Christ, M. (2006). *The bad citizen in classical Athens.* Cambridge.

Cifani, G., S. Stoddart (eds) (2012). *Landscape, ethnicity and identity in the archaic Mediterranean area*. Oxford.

Clinton, K. (1974). *The sacred officials of the Eleusinian mysteries*. *TAPhA* n.s. 64, Philadelphia.

Cohen, D. (1991). *Law, sexuality, and society: The enforcement of morals in classical Athens*. Cambridge/New York.

Cohen, E.E. (1992). *Athenian economy and society: A banking perspective*. Princeton.

(2000). *The Athenian nation*. Princeton.

Cohen, H.F. (2010). *How modern science came into the world: Four civilizations, one 17th century breakthrough*. Amsterdam.

Cole, S.G. (1992). '*Gynaiki ou themis*: Gender difference in the Greek *leges sacrae*', *Helios* 19, 105–22.

(1996). 'Oath ritual and male community at Athens', in *Demokratia: A conversation on democracies, ancient and modern*. J. Ober, C. Hedrick (eds). Princeton, 227–48.

Connelly, J.B. (2007). *Portrait of a priestess: Women and ritual in ancient Greece*. Princeton/Oxford.

(2014). *The Parthenon enigma: A journey into legend*. New York/London.

Connor, W.R. (1987). 'Tribes, festivals, processions: Civic ceremonial and political manipulation in archaic Greece', *JHS* 101, 40–50.

(1988). '"Sacred" and "secular": *Hiera kai hosia* and the classical Athenian concept of the State', *AncSoc* 19, 161–88.

Coşkun, A. (2014). 'Perikles und die Definition des Bürgerrechts im klassischen Athen: Neue Vorschläge zu Inhalt, Hintergrund und Auswirkung seines Bürgerrechtsgesetzes', *HZ* 299, 1–35.

Cox, C.A. (1998). *Household interests: Property, marriage strategies, and family dynamics in ancient Athens*. Princeton.

Cropp, M.J. (1988). *Euripides Electra*. Warminster.

Culasso-Gastaldi, E. (2004). *Le prossenie ateniesi del IV secolo a.C.: Gli onorati asiatici*. Alexandria.

Davies, J.K. (1977). 'Athenian citizenship: The descent group and the alternatives', *CJ* 73, 105–21; repr. (2004) in *Athenian democracy*. P.J. Rhodes (ed.). Oxford, 18–39.

(1994). 'Accounts and accountability in classical Athens', in Osborne and Hornblower, 201–12.

(1996). 'Documents and "documents" in fourth century historiography', in *Le IVe siècle av. J.-C.: Approches historiographiques*. P. Carlier (ed.). Nancy, 29–39.

(1997). 'The "origins of the Greek polis": Where should we be looking?', in *The development of the polis in archaic Greece*. L.G. Mitchell, P.J. Rhodes (eds). London/New York, 24–38.

(2001). 'Temples, credit, and the circulation of money', in *Money and its uses in the ancient Greek world*. A. Meadows, K. Shipton (eds). Oxford, 117–28.

(2004). 'The concept of the citizen', in *Poleis e politeiai: Atti del Convegno Internazionale di Storia Greca, Torino 2002*. S. Cataldi (ed.). Alessandria, 19–30.
Demont, P. (2001). 'Le tirage au sort des magistrats à Athènes: Un problème historique et historiographique', in *Sorteggio pubblico e cleromanzia dall'antichità all' età moderna*. F. Cordano, C. Grottanelli (eds). Milan, 63–82.
Detienne, M. (1989). 'The violence of wellborn ladies: Women at the Thesmophoria', in *The cuisine of sacrifice among the Greeks*. M. Detienne, J.-P. Vernant (eds). Chicago/London, 129–47 (transl. P. Wissing; orig. Paris 1979).
Develin, R. (1979). 'The election of Archons from Solon to Telesinos', *AC* 48, 455–68.
(1989). *Athenian officials 684–321* BC. Cambridge/New York.
Diggle, J. (1981). *Euripidis fabulae*, vol. II. Oxford.
Dignas, B., K. Trampedach (eds) (2008). *Practitioners of the divine: Greek priests and religious officials from Homer to Heliodorus*. Cambridge, MA.
Dillon, M. (1997). *Pilgrims and pilgrimage in ancient Greece*. London/New York.
(2002). *Girls and women in classical Greek religion*. London/New York.
Dircks, R. (2012). Fibers and functions: The participation and representation of men and women in sacrificial processions on Attic vases dating from the sixth and fifth century B.C. RMA thesis, Utrecht.
Domingo Gygax, M. (2006). 'Contradictions et asymétrie dans l'évergétisme grec: Bienfaiteurs étrangers et citoyens entre image et réalité', *DHA* 32, 9–23.
Dougherty, C. (1993). *The poetics of colonization: From city to text in archaic Greece*. New York/Oxford.
Dover, K.J. (1974). *Greek popular morality in the time of Plato and Aristotle*. Oxford.
Dumont, L. (2006). *An introduction to two theories of social anthropology: Descent groups and marriage alliance*. New York/Oxford (transl. R. Parkin; orig. Paris 1971).
Duplouy, A. (2006). *Le prestige des élites: Recherches sur les modes de reconnaissance sociale en Grèce entre les Xe et Ve siècles avant J.-C.* Paris.
(2010). 'Observations sur les noms en -idês et en -adês aux époques archaïque et classique', in *La cité et ses élites: Pratique et représentation des formes de domination et de controle social dans les cités grecques. Actes du colloque de Poitiers, 19–20 Octobre 2006*. L. Capdetrey, Y. Lafond (eds). Bordeaux, 307–44.
(2014). 'Les prétendues classes censitaires soloniennes: À propos de la citoyenneté athénienne archaïque', *Annales HSS* 69, 629–58.
Eatough, G. (1971). 'The use of *hosios* and kindred words in Thucydides', *AJPh* 92, 238–51.
Ehrenberg, V. (1937). 'When did the polis rise?', *JHS* 57, 147–59.
Eijnde, F.v.d. (2010). *Cult and society in early Athens, 1000–600* BCE*: Archaeological and anthropological approaches to state formation and group participation in Attica*. Diss. Utrecht.

Ekroth, G. (2008a). 'Burnt, cooked or raw? Divine and human culinary desires at Greek animal sacrifice', in *Transformations in sacrificial practices: From antiquity to modern times*. E. Stavrianopoulou, A. Michaels, Cl. Ambos (eds). Berlin, 87–111.

(2008b). 'Meat, man and god: On the division of the animal victim at Greek sacrifices', in *Mikros hieromnemon: Meletis eis mnemen Michael H. Jameson*. A.P. Matthaiou, I. Polinskaya, (eds). Athens, 259–90.

Elsner, J. (2015). 'Visual culture and ancient history: Issues of empiricism and ideology in the Samos stele at Athens', *ClAnt* 34, 33–73.

Fahrmeier, A. (2007). *Citizenship: The rise and fall of a modern concept*. New Haven/London.

Faulks, K. (2000). *Citizenship*. London.

Fawcett, P.W. (2006). *Athenian taxation from the Pisistratids to Lycurgus, 550–325 BC*. Diss. Durham University (http://etheses.dur.ac.uk/2632).

Feaver, D.D. (1957). 'Historical development in the priesthoods of Athens', *YClS* 15, 123–58.

Ferguson, W.S. (1938). 'The Salaminioi of Heptaphyloi and Sounion', *Hesperia* 7, 1–71.

Finglass, P.J. (2005). 'Is there a *polis* in Sophocles' Electra?', *Phoenix* 60, 133–42.

Finkelberg, M. (1998). 'Timē and Aretē in Homer', *CQ* 48, 14–28.

Finley, M.I. (1981). 'Introduction', in *The legacy of Greece: A new appraisal*. M.I. Finley (ed.). Oxford, 1–21.

Fisher, N.R.E. (2001). *Aeschines: Against Timarchos. Translated with introduction and commentary*. Oxford.

Foxhall, L. (1989). 'Household, gender and property in classical Athens', *CQ, n.s.* 39, 22–44.

(1996). 'The law and the lady: Women and legal proceedings in classical Athens', in *Greek law in its political setting: Justifications not justice*. L. Foxhall, A.D.E. Lewis (eds). Oxford, 133–52.

(1997). 'A view from the top: Evaluating the Solonian property classes', in *The development of the polis in archaic Greece*. L.G. Mitchell, P.J. Rhodes (eds). London/New York, 113–36.

Friend, J.L. (2009). *The Athenian ephebeia in the Lycurgan period, 334/3–322/1 B.C.* Diss. University of Texas, Austin (http://repositories.lib.utexas.edu/handle/2152/6635).

Funke, P. (1998). 'Die Bedeutung der griechischen Bundesstaaten in der politischen Theorie und Praxis des 5. und 4. Jh. v. Chr. (Auch eine Anmerkung zu Aristotl. pol. 1261a 22–29)', in *Politische Theorie und Praxis im Altertum*. W. Schuller, W. Hoepfner, E.L. Schwandner (eds). Darmstadt, 59–71.

(2002). 'Europäische *lieux de mémoire* oder *lieux de mémoire* für Europa im antiken Griechenland?', *Jahrbuch für Europäische Geschichte* 3, 3–16.

(2006). 'Fremde und Nicht-Bürger in den griechischen Heiligtümern der antiken Mittelmeerwelt: Eine historische Einführung', in *Stranieri e non cittadini nei santuari Greci: Atti del convegno*. A. Naso (ed.). Florence, 1–11.

Gagarin, M. (2008). *Writing Greek law*. Cambridge.

(2011). 'Writing sacred laws in archaic and classical Crete', in Lardinois, Blok, van der Poel, 101–12.

Gager, J.G. (1992). *Curse tablets and binding spells from the ancient world.* New York/Oxford.

Gaifman, M. (2015). 'Visual evidence', in *The Oxford handbook of ancient Greek religion.* E. Eidinow, J. Kindt (eds). Oxford, 51–66.

Gallia, A.B. (2004). 'The republication of Draco's law on homicide', *CQ* 54, 451–60.

Garland, R.S.J. (1990). 'Priests and power in classical Athens', in *Pagan priests: Religion and power in the ancient world.* M. Beard, J. North (eds). London, 73–91.

(1992). *Introducing new gods: The politics of Athenian religion.* Ithaca, NY.

(2001). *The Piraeus* (2nd ed.). Bristol.

(1984). 'Religious authority in archaic and classical Athens', *ABSA* 79, 75–124.

Gauthier, P. (1976). *Un commentaire historique des Poroi de Xénophon.* Geneva/ Paris.

Gawlinski, L. (2007). 'The Athenian calendar of sacrifices: A new fragment from the Athenian Agora', *Hesperia* 76, 37–55.

Georgoudi, S. (1998). 'Sacrifices dans le monde grec: De la cité aux particuliers: quelques remarques', *Ktèma* 23, 325–34.

(2005). 'Athanatous therapeuein: Réflexions sur des femmes au service des dieux', in *Idia kai demosia: Les cadres "privés" et "publics" de la religion grecque antique. Actes colloque CIERGA, Fribourg Sept. 2003.* V. Dasen, M. Piérart (eds). Liège, 69–82.

(2007). 'Les magistrats au service des dieux: Le cas des démarques en Attique', in *Athènes et le politique dans le sillage de Claude Mossé.* P. Schmitt-Pantel, F. de Polignac (eds). Paris, 83–109.

Gherchanoc, F. (1998). 'Le lien filial dans l'Athènes classique: Pratiques et acteurs de sa reconnaissance', *Metis* 13, 313–44.

Giovannini, A. (2002). 'Xenophon, der Arginusenprozess und die athenische Demokratie', *Chiron* 32, 15–50.

Goff, B. (2004). *Citizen Bacchae: Women's ritual practice in ancient Greece.* Berkeley/Los Angeles/London.

Goldhill, S. (1994). 'Representing democracy: Women at the Great Dionysia', in Osborne and Hornblower, 347–69.

(1998). 'The seductions of the gaze: Socrates and his girlfriends', in *Kosmos: Essays in order, conflict and community in classical Athens.* P.A. Cartledge, P.C. Millett, S. von Reden (eds). Cambridge, 105–24.

Gomme, A.W. (1933). *The population of Athens in the fifth and fourth centuries* BC. Oxford.

Goody, J., S.J. Tambiah (1973). *Bridewealth and dowry.* Cambridge.

Graeber, D. (2001). *Toward an anthropological theory of value: The false coin of our dreams.* New York.

(2011). *Debt: The first 5,000 years.* New York.

Günther, L.-M. (2014). *Bürgerinnen und ihre Familien im hellenistischen Milet: Untersuchungen zur Rolle von Frauen und Mädchen in der Polis-Öffentlichkeit: Mit einem Beitrag von Lara S. Köcke*. Wiesbaden.

Gysembergh, V. (2013). 'Le tirage au sort des provinces divines chez Homère (Iliade 15, 185–199) et ses antécedents Mésopotamiens: Un état de la question', *REG* 126, 49–64.

Hall, J. (1997). *Ethnic identity in Greek antiquity*. Cambridge.

(2002). *Hellenicity: Between ethnicity and culture*. Chicago/London.

(2007). 'Polis, community, and ethnic identity', in *The Cambridge companion to archaic Greece*. H.A. Shapiro (ed.). Cambridge, 40–60.

Hamilton, R. (1989). 'Alkman and the Athenian Arkteia', *Hesperia* 58, 449–72.

Hammer, D. (2009). 'What is politics in the ancient world?', in *A Companion to Greek and Roman political thought*. R.K. Balot (ed.). Malden/Oxford, 20–36.

Hammond, N.G.L. (1998). 'The Branchidae in Didyma and in Sogdiana', *CQ* 48, 339–44.

Hampshire-Monk, I., K. Tilmans, F. van Vree (eds) (1998). *History of concepts: Comparative perspectives*. Amsterdam.

Hannah, R. (2005). *Greek and Roman calendars: Constructions of time in the classical world*. Oxford.

Hannick, J.-M. (1976). 'Droit de cité et mariages mixtes dans la Grèce classique: À propos de quelques textes d'Aristote', *AC* 45, 135–48.

Hansen, M.H. (1976a). *Apagoge, endeixis and ephegesis against kakourgoi, atimoi and pheugontes*. Odense.

(1976b). 'The Theoric fund and the *graphê paranomon* against Apollodoros', *GRBS* 17, 235–46.

(1980). 'Seven hundred *archai* in classical Athens', *GRBS* 21, 151–73.

(1982). 'Demographic reflections on the number of Athenian citizens 451–309 BC', *AJAH* 7, 172–89.

(1984). 'The number of *rhetores* in the Athenian *ekklesia*, 355–322', *GRBS* 25, 123–55.

(1986). *Demography and democracy: The number of Athenian citizens in the fourth century* BC. Herning.

(1988). *Three studies in Athenian demography*. Copenhagen.

(1989). 'On the importance of institutions in the analysis of Athenian democracy', *C&M* 40, 107–13.

(1990). 'When was selection by lot of magistrates introduced in Athens?' *C&M* 41, 55–61.

(1990b). 'Diokles' law (Dem. 24. 42) and the revision of the Athenian corpus of laws in the archonship of Eukleides', *C&M* 41, 63–71.

(1991). *The Athenian democracy in the age of Demosthenes: Structure, principles, and ideology*. Oxford (repr. ed. Norman 1999).

(1993). 'Introduction: The polis as a citizen-state', in *The ancient Greek city-state: Acts of the Copenhagen Polis Centre Vol. 1*. M.H. Hansen (ed.). Copenhagen, 7–29.

(1996). 'City-ethnics as evidence for polis-identity', in *More studies in the ancient Greek polis*. M.H. Hansen, K.A. Raaflaub (eds). HE 108, Stuttgart, 169–96.

(1998). *Polis and city-state: An ancient concept and its modern equivalent*. Copenhagen.

(2000). 'A survey of the use of the word *polis* in archaic and classical sources', in *Further studies in the ancient Greek polis*. P. Flensted-Jensen (ed.). HE 138. Stuttgart, 173–215.

(2006). *Polis: An introduction to the ancient Greek city-state*. Oxford.

(ed.) (2007). *The return of the polis: The use and meanings of the word polis in archaic and classical sources*. HE 198. Stuttgart.

Hansen, P.A. (1983). *Carmina epigraphica graeca, Texte und Kommentare*, vol. I. Berlin/New York.

Harris, E.M. (2004). 'Antigone the lawyer, or the ambiguities of *nomos*', in *The law and the courts in ancient Greece*. E.M. Harris, L. Rubinstein (eds). London, 19–56.

(2006). 'Women and lending in Athenian society: A *horos* re-examined', in *Democracy and the rule of law in classical Athens*. Cambridge, 333–46 (orig. 1992).

(2007). 'The rule of law in Athenian democracy: Reflections on the judicial oath', *Etica & Politica/Ethics & Politics* 9, 55–74.

(2013). *The rule of law in action in democratic Athens*. Oxford.

(2015). 'The family, the community and murder: The role of pollution in Athenian homicide law', in *Public and private in ancient Mediterranean law and religion*. C. Ando, J. Rüpke (ed.). Berlin, 11–37.

Headlam, J.W. (1933). *Election by lot at Athens* (2nd ed.; orig. 1890). Cambridge.

Hedrick, C.W. (1988a). 'The temple and cult of Apollo Patroos in Athens', *AJA* 92, 185–210.

(1988b). 'The Thymaitian phratry', *Hesperia* 57, 81–5.

(1991). 'Phratry shrines of Attica and Athens', *Hesperia* 60, 241–68.

Henrichs, A. (2008). 'What is a Greek priest?', in Dignas and Trampedach, 1–14.

Henry, A.S. (1983). *Honours and privileges in Athenian decrees*. Hildesheim.

Hitch, S. (2011). 'Embedded speech in the Attic *leges sacrae*', in Lardinois, Blok, van der Poel, 113–41.

Hoff, R. von den (2008). 'Images and prestige of cult personnel in Athens between the sixth and the first century BCE', in Dignas and Trampedach, 107–41.

Hölkeskamp, K.-J. (1997). '*Agorai* bei Homer', in *Volk und Verfassung im vorhellenistischen Griechenland: Beiträge auf dem Symposium zu Ehren von Karl-Wilhelm Welwei in Bochum, 1.2. März 1996*. W. Eder, K.-J. Hölkeskamp (eds). Stuttgart, 1–19.

(1999). *Schiedsrichter, Gesetzgeber und Gesetzgebung im archaischen Griechenland*. HE 131. Stuttgart.

(2002a). 'Nomos, Thesmos und Verwandtes: Vergleichende Überlegungen zur Konzeptualisierung geschriebenen Rechts im klassischen Griechenland', in

Demokratie, Recht und soziale Kontrolle im klassischen Athen. D. Cohen (ed.). Munich, 115–46.

(2002b). 'Ptolis and Agore: Homer and the archaeology of the city-state', in *Omero tremilia anni dopo*. F. Montanari, P. Ascheri (eds). Rome, 297–342.

Horster, M. (2004). *Landbesitz griechischer Heiligtümer in archaischer und klassischer Zeit*. Berlin/New York.

Houby-Nielsen, S. (1995). '"Burial language" in archaic and classical Kerameikos', *Proceedings of the Danish Institute* 1, 129–91.

Humphreys, S.C. (1974). 'The *nothoi* of Kynosarges', *JHS* 94, 88–95.

(1983a). 'The evolution of legal process in ancient Attica', in *Tria corda: Scritti in onore di A. Momigliano*. E. Gabba (ed.). Como, 229–56.

(1983b). 'Family tombs and tomb cult in classical Athens: Tradition or traditionalism?', in *The family, women and death: Comparative studies*. London/Boston, 79–130 (orig. 1980).

(1985). 'Law as discourse', *History and Anthropology* 1, 241–64.

(1986). 'Kinship patterns in Athenian courts', *GRBS* 27, 57–91.

(2004a). 'Lycurgus of Boutadai: An Athenian aristocrat', in Humphreys (2004c) 77–129.

(2004b). 'A sense of agency: Religion in the Attic demes', in Humphreys (2004c) 130–96.

(2004c) *The strangeness of the gods: Historical perspectives on the interpretation of Athenian religion*. Oxford.

(2007). 'Social relations on stage: Witnesses in classical Athens', in *The Attic orators* (Oxford readings in classical studies). E. Carawan (ed.). Oxford, 140–213 (orig. 1985).

Hunter, V.J. (1993). 'Agnatic kinship in Athenian law and Athenian family practice: Its implication for women', in *Law, politics, and society in the ancient mediterranean world*. B. Halpern, D. Hobson (eds). Sheffield, 100–21.

(1994). *Policing Athens: Social control in the Attic lawsuits, 420–320* BC. Princeton.

(2000). 'Introduction: Status distinctions in Athenian law', in *Law and social status in classical Athens*. V.J. Hunter, J.C. Edmonson (eds). Oxford, 1–29.

Hurwit, J.M. (1999). *The Athenian Acropolis: History, mythology, and archaeology from the Neolithic era to the present*. Cambridge.

Ingalls, W. (2002). 'Demography and dowries: Perspectives on female infanticide in classical Greece', *Phoenix* 56, 246–54.

Irwin, E. (2005). 'Gods among men? The social and political dynamics of the Hesiodic *Catalogue of Women*', in *The Hesiodic Catalogue of Women: Constructions and reconstructions*. R. Hunter (ed.). Cambridge, 35–84.

Isin, E.F. (2002). *Being political: Genealogies of citizenship*. Minneapolis/London.

Ismard, P. (2007). 'Les associations en Attique de Solon à Clisthène', in *Individus, groupes et politique à Athènes de Solon à Mithridate: Actes du colloque international Tours, 7–8 Mrs 2005*. J.-C. Couvenhes, S. Milanezi (eds). Tours, 17–33.

(2010). *La cité des réseaux: Athènes et ses associations* VIe–Ier *siècle av. J.-C.* Paris.

Jacquemin, A. (2005). 'Un autre conte de deux cités, ou Athéniennes et fières de l'être', *Ktèma* 30, 337–47.

Jameson, M.H. (1988). 'Sacrifice and animal husbandry in classical Greece', in *Pastoral economics in classical antiquity*. C.R. Whittaker (ed.). Cambridge, 87–119.

(1994). 'Theoxenia', in *Ancient Greek cult practice from the epigraphical evidence*. R. Hägg (ed.). Copenhagen, 35–57.

(1999). 'The spectacular and the obscure in Athenian religion', in *Performance culture and Athenian democracy*. S. Goldhill, R. Osborne (eds). Cambridge, 321–40.

Jay-Robert, G. (1999). 'Essai d'interpretation du sens du substantif *hosiê* dans l'Odyssée et dans les Hymnes Homériques', *REA* 101, 5–20.

(2009). *Le sacré et la loi: Essai sur la notion d'hosion d'Homère à Aristote*. Paris.

Jeanmaire, H. (1945). 'Le substantif HOSIA et sa signification comme terme technique dans le vocabulaire religieux (1)', *REG* 58, 66–89.

Jim, T.S.F. (2014). *Sharing with the gods: Aparchai and dekatai in ancient Greece*. Oxford.

Johnson, C. (1984). 'Who is Aristotle's citizen?', *Phronesis* 29, 73–90.

Jones, N.F. (1995). 'The Athenian *phylai* as associations: Disposition, function, and purpose', *Hesperia* 64, 503–42.

(1999). *The associations of classical Athens: The response to democracy*. New York/ Oxford.

Jordan, B. (1979). *Servants of the gods: A study in the religion, history and literature of fifth-century Athens*. Göttingen.

Just, R. (1989). *Women in Athenian law and life*. London/New York.

Kallet-Marx, L. (1989). 'The Kallias decree, Thucydides, and the outbreak of the Peloponnesian War', *CQ* 39, 94–113.

Kamen, D. (2013). *Status in classical Athens*. Princeton.

Kapparis, K.A. (1995). 'The Athenian decree for the naturalisation of the Plataeans', *GRBS* 36, 359–81.

(1999). *Apollodoros "Against Neaira" [D. 59]: Edited with introduction, translation and commentary*. Berlin/New York.

(2015). 'Review of Canevaro (2013)', *Gnomon* 87, 40–3.

Kearns, E. (1985). 'Change and continuity in religious structures after Cleisthenes', in *Crux: Essays presented to G.E.M. de Ste. Croix on his 75th birthday*. P. Cartledge, F.D. Harvey (eds). Exeter/London, 189–207.

(1989). *The heroes of Attica*. London.

Keesling, C.M. (2003). *The votive statues of the Athenian Acropolis*. Cambridge.

(2012). 'Syeris, diakonos of the priestess Lysimache on the Athenian Acropolis (*IG* II^2 3464)', *Hesperia* 81, 467–505.

Kennelly, J.J. (2003). 'Kallias A (*IG* I^3 52A) and Thucydides 2.13.3', in *Gestures: Essays in ancient history, literature, and philosophy presented to Alan L. Boegehold*. G.W. Bakewell, J.P. Sickinger (eds). Oxford, 284–6.

Keyt, D. (1991). 'Three basic theorems in Aristotle's *Politics*', in *A companion to Aristotle's Politics*. F.D.J. Miller (ed.). Cambridge, 118–41.

Kienast, D. (2005). 'Die Funktion der attischen Demen von Solon bis Kleisthenes', *Chiron* 35, 69–100.
Kindt, J. (2009). 'Polis-religion: Critical appreciation', *Kernos* 22, 9–34.
(2012). *Rethinking Greek religion*. Cambridge.
(2015). 'Personal religion: A productive category for the study of ancient Greek religion?', *JHS* 135, 35–50.
Körner, R. (1993). *Inschriftliche Gesetzestexte der frühen griechischen Polis. Aus dem Nachlass von Reinhard Koerner hg. von K. Hallof.* Akten der Gesellschaft für Griechische und Hellenistische Rechtsgeschichte, Bd. 9. Cologne/Weimar/Vienna.
Konstan, D. (2008). 'Sophocles' *Electra* as political allegory: A suggestion', *CPh* 103, 77–80.
Koselleck, R. (1979). *Vergangene Zukunft: Zur Semantik geschichtlicher Zeiten*. Frankfurt a.M.
Kovacs, D. (1998). 'Introduction', in *Euripides: Suppliant women, Electra, Heracles*. D. Kovacs (ed. and transl.) (Loeb Classical Library). Cambridge, MA/London, 142–50.
Krentz, P. (2002). 'Fighting by the rules: The invention of the hoplite *agôn*', *Hesperia* 71, 23–39.
(2007). 'The oath of Marathon, not Plataia?', *Hesperia* 76, 731–42.
Kron, U. (1976). *Die zehn attischen Phylenheroen: Geschichte, Mythos, Kult und Darstellungen*. Berlin.
(1981). 'Aglauros, Herse, Pandrosos', in *LIMC I: Aara–Aphlad*. Zürich, 283–98.
(1988). 'Erechtheus', in *LIMC IV: Eros–Herakles*. Zürich, 923–51.
(1996). 'Priesthoods, dedications and euergetism: What part did religion play in the political and social status of women?', in *Religion and power in the ancient Greek world: Proceedings of the Uppsala Symposium of 1993*. P. Hellström, B. Alroth (eds). Boreas 24. Uppsala, 139–82.
Kühr, A. (2006). *Als Kadmos nach Boiotien kam: Polis und Ethnos im Spiegel thebanischer Gründungsmythen*. Stuttgart.
Kymlicka, W. (2002). *Contemporary political philosophy: An introduction* (2nd ed.). Oxford.
Lambert, S.D. (1997a). 'The Attic genos Salaminioi and the island of Salamis', *ZPE* 119, 85–106.
(1997b). *Rationes centesimarum: Sales of public lands in Lykourgan Athens*. Amsterdam.
(1998). *The phratries of Attica (2nd ed.)*. Ann Arbor.
(1999). 'The Attic *genos*', *CQ n.s.* 49, 484–9.
(2000). 'The sacrificial calendar of the Marathonian Tetrapolis: A revised text', *ZPE* 130, 43–70.
(2000a). 'The Erechtheum workers of *IG* II^2 1654', *ZPE* 132, 157–60.
(2000b). 'Two notes on Attic *leges sacrae*', *ZPE* 130, 71–80.
(2001). 'Ten notes on Attic inscriptions', *ZPE* 135, 51–62.
(2002). 'The sacrificial calendar of Athens', *ABSA* 97, 353–99.

(2004a). 'Athenian state laws and decrees 352/1–322/1: I. Decrees honouring Athenians', *ZPE* 150, 85–119.

(2004b). 'Restoring Athenian names', in *Attikai epigraphai praktika symposion eis mnèmèn Adolph Wilhelm (1864–1950)*. A.P. Matthaiou (ed.). Athens, 327–41.

(2006). 'Athenian state laws and decrees, 352/1–322/1: II. Decrees honouring foreigners A. Citizenship, proxeny and euergesy', *ZPE* 158, 115–58.

(2007). 'Athenian State Laws and Decrees, 352/1–322/1: III. Decrees honouring foreigners B. Other awards', *ZPE* 159, 101–54.

(2008a). 'Aglauros, the Euenoridai and the autochthon of Atlantis', *ZPE* 167, 22–6.

(2008b). 'Polis and theatre in Lykourgan Athens: The honorific decrees', in *Mikros hieromnemon: Meletes eis mnemen Michael H. Jameson*. A.P. Matthaiou, I. Polinskaya (eds). Athens, 53–85.

(2010a). 'Connecting with the past in Lykourgan Athens: An epigraphic perspective', in *Intentional history: Spinning time in ancient Greece*. L. Foxhall, H.-J. Gehrke, N. Luraghi (eds). Stuttgart, 225–38.

(2010b). 'A polis and its priests: Athenian priesthoods before and after Pericles' citizenship law', *Historia* 59, 143–75.

(2011). 'What was the point of inscribed honorific decrees in classical Athens?', in *Sociable man: Essays on ancient Greek social behaviour in honour of Nick Fisher*. S.D. Lambert (ed.). Swansea, 193–212.

(2012a). *Inscribed Athenian laws and decrees, 352/1–322/1 BC: Epigraphical essays*. Leiden/Boston.

(2012b). 'The social construction of priests and priestesses in Athenian honorific decrees from the fourth century BC to the Augustan period', in *Civic priests: Cult personnel in Athens from the Hellenistic period to Late Antiquity*. M. Horster, A. Klöckner (eds). Berlin, 67–133.

(2015). 'Aristocracy and the Attic genos: A mythological perspective', in *Aristocracy in antiquity: Redefining Greek and Roman elites*, N. Fisher, H. van Wees (eds). Swansea, 169–202.

(in press). 'Another look at the sacrificial calendar of the Marathonian Tetrapolis', in *Feasting and polis institutions*, F. van den Eijnde, J.H. Blok, R. Strootman (eds). Leiden/ Boston.

Lane Fox, R. (1985). 'Aspects of inheritance in the Greek world', in *Crux: Essays in Greek history presented to G.E.M. de Ste. Croix on his 75th birthday*. P. Cartledge, F.D. Harvey (eds). London, 208–32.

Lanni, A. (1997). 'Spectator sport or serious politics? *Hoi periestekotes* and the Athenian lawcourts', *JHI* 117, 183–9.

(2006). *Law and justice in the courts of Athens*. Cambridge.

Lape, S. (2002–3). 'Solon and the institution of the "democratic" family form', *CJ* 98, 117–39.

(2010). *Race and citizen identity in the classical Athenian democracy*. Cambridge.

Lardinois, A.P.M.H. (2006). 'Have we Solon's verses?', in Blok and Lardinois, 15–35.

Lardinois, A.P.M.H., J.H. Blok, M. van der Poel (eds) (2011). *Sacred words: Orality, literacy and religion*. Orality and literacy in the ancient world, vol. VIII. Leiden/Boston.

Larson, J. (1995). *Greek heroine cults*. Madison/London.

Larson, S.L. (2007). *Tales of epic ancestry: Boiotian collecive identity in the late archaic and early classical periods*. Stuttgart.

Lazzarini, M.L. (1989–90). 'Inscrizioni votive greche', *ScAnt* 3–4, 845–59.

Leduc, C. (1994–5). 'Citoyenneté et parenté dans la cité des Athéniens', *Métis* 9–10, 51–68.

Lévy, E. (1985). 'Astos et politès d'Homére à Hérodote', *Ktèma* 10, 53–66.

Lewis, D.M. (1963). 'Cleisthenes and Attica', *Historia* 12, 23–40.

(1974). 'The Kerameikos ostraka', *ZPE* 14, 1–4.

Liddel, P. (2003). 'The places of publication of Athenian state decrees from the fifth century BC to the third century AD', *ZPE* 143, 79–93.

(2007). *Civic obligation and individual liberty in ancient Athens*. Oxford.

Linders, T. (1975). *The treasurers of the Other Gods in Athens and their functions*. Meisenheim am Glan.

Lohmann, H. (1993). *Atene: Forschungen zu Siedlungs- und Wirtschaftsstruktur des klassischen Attika*. Cologne/Weimar/Vienna.

Loraux, N. (1986). *The invention of Athens: The funeral oration in the classical city*. Cambridge, MA (transl. A. Sheridan; orig. Paris 1981).

(1993). *The children of Athena: Athenian ideas about citizenship and the division between the sexes*. Princeton (transl. C. Levine; orig. Paris 1981).

(2000). *Born of the earth: Myth and politics in Athens*. Ithaca, NY/London. (transl. S. Stewart; orig. Paris 1996).

Low, P. (2007). *Interstate relations in classical Greece: Morality and power*. Cambridge.

Löwisch, I. (2015). *Trauma begets genealogy: Gender and memory in Chronicles*. Sheffield.

Lupu, E. (2005). *Greek sacred law: A collection of new documents*. Leiden/Boston.

Luraghi, N. (2010). 'The demos as narrator: Public honors and the construction of future and past', in *Intentional history: Spinning time in ancient Greece*. L. Foxhall, H.-J. Gehrke, N. Luraghi (eds). Stuttgart, 247–63.

MacDowell, D.M. (1963). *Athenian homicide law in the age of the orators*. Manchester.

(1976). 'Bastards as Athenian citizens'. *CQ n.s.* 26, 88–91.

(1985). 'review of M.J. Osborne, *Naturalization*'. *CR* 35, 317–20.

(1989). 'The *oikos* in Athenian law'. *CQ n.s.* 39(1), 10–21.

(1990). *Demosthenes against Meidias: Edited with introduction, translation and commentary*. Oxford (repr. Bristol 2002).

(2009). *Demosthenes the orator*. Oxford.

Mack, W. (2015). *Proxeny and polis: Institutional networks in the ancient Greek world*. Oxford.

Maffi, A. (1982). '*Ta hiera kai ta hosia*: Contributo alla studio della terminologia giuridico-sacrale greca', in *Symposion 1977*. J. Modrzejewski, D. Liebs (eds). Cologne, 33–53.

Malkin, I. (2003). '"Tradition" in Herodotus: The foundation of Cyrene', in *Herodotus and his world: Essays from a conference in memory of George Forrest.* P. Derow, R. Parker (eds). Oxford, 153–70.
Manin, B. (1997). *The principles of representative government.* Cambridge.
Mann, C. (2008). 'Politische Gleichheit und gesellschaftliche Stratifikation: Die Athenische Demokratie aus der Perspektive der Systemtheorie', *HZ* 286, 1–35.
Manville, P.B. (1990). *The origins of citizenship in ancient Athens.* Princeton.
(1994). 'Toward a new paradigm of Athenian citizenship', in *Athenian identity and civic ideology.* A.L. Boegehold, A.C. Scafuro (eds). Baltimore/London, 21–33.
Markle, M.M. (2004). 'Jury pay and assembly pay at Athens', in *Athenian democracy.* P.J. Rhodes (ed.). Oxford, 95–131. (Orig. 1985).
Martin, G. (2009). *Divine talk: Religious argumentation in Demosthenes.* Oxford.
Martina, A (ed.) (1968). *Solon: Testimonia veterum.* Rome.
Matthaiou, A.P. (2011). 'The Theozotides decree on the sons of those murdered in the oligarchy', in *Ta en tei stelei gegrammena: Six Greek historical inscriptions of the fifth century* B.C. Athens, 71–81.
Maurizio, L. (1998). 'The Panathenaic procession: Athens' participatory democracy on display?', in *Democracy, empire, and the arts in fifth-century Athens.* D. Boedeker, K.A. Raaflaub (eds). Cambridge, MA/London, 297–317.
McCarthy, D.J. (1978). *Treaty and covenant: A study in form in the ancient oriental documents and in the Old Testament (2nd ed.).* Rome.
McInerney, J. (1999). *The folds of Parnassos: Land and ethnicity in ancient Phokis.* Austin.
Meier, C. (1980). *Die Entstehung des Politischen bei den Griechen.* Frankfurt a.M.
Meyer, E.A. (1993). 'Epitaphs and citizenship in classical Athens'. *JHS* 113, 99–121.
(2010). *Metics and the Athenian phialai-inscriptions: A study in Athenian epigraphy and law.* Stuttgart.
(2012). 'Two grants of *politeia* and the Molossians at Dodona', *ZPE* 180, 205–16.
(2013). 'Inscriptions as honors and the Athenian epigraphic habit', *Historia* 62, 453–505.
Migeotte, L. (2006). 'La gestion des biens sacrés dans les cités grecques', in *Symposion 2003: Vorträge zur griechischen und hellenistischen Rechtsgeschichte.* H.A. Rupprecht (ed.). Vienna, 233–46.
Mikalson, J.D. (1975). *The sacred and civil calendar of the Athenian year.* Princeton.
(1977). 'Religion in the Attic demes', *AJPh* 98, 424–35.
(2010). *Greek popular religion in Greek philosophy.* Oxford.
Miles, M.M. (2014). 'Burnt temples in the landscape of the past', in *Valuing the past in the Greco-Roman world. Penn-Leiden Colloquia on Ancient Values*, vol. VII. J. Ker, Chr. Pieper (eds). Leiden/Boston, 111–45.
Miller, M.J. (1983). *The Athenian autochthonous heroes from the classical to the Hellenistic period.* Cambridge, MA.
Mirhady, D.C. (2007). 'The dikasts' oath and the question of fact', in Sommerstein and Fletcher, 48–59.

Morrison, D. (1999). 'Aristotle's definition of citizenship: A problem and some solutions', *History of Philosophy Quarterly* 16, 143–65.
Morrow, G.R. (1960). *Plato's Cretan city: A historical interpretation of the Laws.* Princeton.
Murray, O. (1990). 'Cities of reason', in *The Greek city from Homer to Alexander.* O. Murray, S. Price (eds). Oxford, 1–25.
Neils, J. (2001). *The Parthenon frieze.* Cambridge.
Nielsen, T.H. (2002). *Arkadia and its poleis in the archaic and classical periods.* Göttingen.
Niku, M. (2007). *The official status of the foreign residents in Athens, 322–120 BC.* Helsinki.
North, D.C. (1990). *Institutions, institutional change and economic performance.* New York.
Ober, J. (1993). 'The Athenian revolution of 508/7 BCE: Violence, authority, and the origins of democracy', in *Cultural poetics in archaic Greece: Cult, performance, politics.* C. Dougherty, L. Kurke (eds). Cambridge, 215–32.
(1996). 'The polis as society: Aristotle, John Rawls, and the Athenian social contract', in *The Athenian revolution: Essays on ancient Greek democracy and political theory.* Princeton, 161–87.
(2008). *Democracy and knowledge: Innovation and learning in classical Athens.* Princeton.
Ogden, D. (1996). *Greek bastardy in the classical and Hellenistic periods.* Oxford.
Osborne, R. (1985). *Demos: The discovery of classical Attika.* Cambridge.
(1988). 'Social and economic implications of the leasing of land and property in classical and Hellenistic Greece', *Chiron* 18, 279–323.
(1993). 'Women and sacrifice in classical Greece', *CQ* 43, 392–405.
(1994). 'Archaeology, the Salaminioi, and the politics of sacred space in archaic Attica', in *Placing the gods: Sanctuaries and sacred space in ancient Greece.* S.E. Alcock, R. Osborne (eds). Oxford, 143–60.
(1997). 'Law, the democratic citizen and the representation of women in classical Athens', *Past and Present* 155, 3–33.
(2009). *Greece in the making, 1200–479. 2nd ed.* London/New York.
(2010a). *Athens and Athenian democracy.* Cambridge.
(2010b). 'Competitive festivals and the polis: A context for dramatic festivals at Athens', in Osborne (2010a) 325–40 (orig. 1990).
(2010c). 'The demos and its divisions in classical Athens', in Osborne (2010a) 39–63 (orig. 1990).
(2010d). 'Law in action in classical Athens', in Osborne (2010a) 171–204 (orig. 1985).
(2011). *The history written on the classical Greek body.* Cambridge.
Osborne, R., S. Hornblower (eds) (1994). *Ritual, finance, politics: Athenian democratic accounts presented to David Lewis.* Oxford.
Ostwald, M. (1969). *Nomos and the beginnings of Athenian democracy.* Oxford.
(1996). 'Shares and rights: "Citizenship" Greek style and American style', in *Demokratia: A conversation on democracies ancient and modern.* J. Ober, C.W. Hedrick (eds). Princeton, 49–61.

Palagia, O. (1995). 'Akropolis Museum 581: A family at the Apaturia?', *Hesperia* 64, 493–505.
Papakonstantinou, Z. (2008). *Lawmaking and adjudication in archaic Greece*. London.
Papazarkadas, N. (2011). *Sacred and public lands in ancient Athens*. Oxford.
Parker, R.T.C. (1983). *Miasma: Pollution and purification in early Greek religion*. Oxford.
(1987a). 'Festivals of the attic demes', in *Gifts to the gods*. T. Linders, G. Nordquist (eds). Boreas, 15, Uppsala, 137–48.
(1987b). 'Myths of early Athens', in *Interpretations of Greek mythology*. J.N Bremmer (ed.). London, 187–214.
(1996). *Athenian religion: A history*. Oxford.
(1998). 'Reciprocity in Greek religion', in *Reciprocity in ancient Greece*. D. Gill, N. Postlethwaite, R. Seaford (eds). Oxford, 105–26.
(2000). 'Theophoric names and Greek religion', in *Greek personal names: Their value as evidence*. S. Hornblower, E. Matthews (eds). Oxford, 53–79.
(2003). 'The problem of the Greek cult epithet', *Opuscula Atheniensia* 28, 173–83.
(2004). 'What are sacred laws?', in *The law and the courts in ancient Greece*. E.M. Harris, L. Rubinstein (eds). London, 59–70.
(2011). *On Greek religion*. Ithaca, NY/London.
Parker, R.T.C., D. Obbink (2000). 'Sales of priesthoods on Cos I', *Chiron* 30, 415–49.
Parkin, R., L. Stone (eds) (2004). *Kinship and family: An anthropological reader*. Malden, MA/Oxford.
Patera, I. (2012). *Offrir en Grèce ancienne: Gestes et contextes*. Frankfurt a.M.
Patterson, C. (1981). *Perikles' citizenship law of 451/0*. New York (repr. 1987).
(1986). '*Hai Attikai*: The other Athenians', in *Rescuing Creusa: New methodological approaches to women in antiquity*. M. Skinner (ed.). Helios 13. Austin, 49–68.
(1990). 'Those Athenian bastards', *ClAnt* 9, 40–73.
(1998). *The family in Greek history*. Cambridge, MA/London.
(2005). 'Athenian citizenship law', in *The Cambridge companion to ancient Greek law*. M. Gagarin, D. Cohen (eds). Cambridge, 267–89.
Pavlou, M. (2011). 'Past and present in Pindar's religious poetry', in Lardinois, Blok and van der Poel, 59–78.
Peçirka, J. (1966). *The formula for the grant of enktesis in Attic inscriptions*. Prague.
Peels, S. (2015). *Hosios: A semantic study of Greek piety*. Leiden/Boston.
Peyrou, F. (2006). 'Citizenship and history: Historiographic approaches to citizenship', in *Citizenship in historical perspective*. S.G. Ellis, G. Hálfdanarson, A.K. Isaacs (eds). Pisa, 1–23.
Phillips, D.D. (2008). *Avengers of blood: Homicide in Athenian law and custom from Draco to Demosthenes*. Stuttgart.
(2009). 'Hypereides 3 and the Athenian law of contracts', *TAPhA* 139, 89–122.
Piepenbrink, K. (2001). *Politische Ordnungskonzeptionen in der attischen Demokratie des 4. Jahrhunderts v.Chr.: Eine vergleichende Untersuchung zum philosophischen und rhetorischen Diskurs*. Stuttgart.

Pirenne-Delforge, V. (2005). 'La cité, les *demotele hiera* et les prêtres', in *Idia kai demosia: Les cadres "privés" et "publics" de la religion grecque antique: Actes colloque CIERGA, Fribourg Sept. 2003*. V. Dasen, M. Piérart (eds). Kernos, suppl. 15, Liège, 55–68.

Polignac, F. de (1995a). *Cults, territory, and the origins of the Greek state*. Chicago. (Transl. J. Lloyd; orig. Paris 1984).

(1995b). 'Repenser 'la cité'? Rituels et société en Grèce archaique', in *Studies in the ancient Greek polis*. M.H. Hansen, K.A. Raaflaub (eds). Stuttgart, 7–19.

(2007). 'Ajax l'Athénien: Communautés cultuelles, représentations de l'espace et logique institutionnelle dans un tribu clisthénienne', in *Athènes et le politique: Dans le sillage de Claude Mossé*. P. Schmitt-Pantel, F. de Polignac (eds). Paris, 110–32.

Polinskaya, I. (2010). 'Shared sanctuaries and the gods of others: On the meaning of "common" in Herodotus 8.144', in *Valuing others in classical antiquity. Penn-Leiden Colloquia on Ancient Values, vol.* v. R. Rosen, I. Sluiter (eds). Leiden/Boston/Cologne, 43–70.

Pomeroy, S.B. (1995). 'Women's identity and the family in the classical *polis*', in *Women in antiquity: New assessments*. R. Hawley, B. Levick (eds). London/New York, 111–21.

(1997). *Families in classical and hellenistic Greece: Representations and realities*. Oxford.

Pomeroy, S.B., M. Burstein, W. Donlan, J. Roberts (1999). *Ancient Greece: A political, social and cultural history*. Oxford.

Pouilloux, J. (1951). 'Trois notes Thasiennes', *BCH* 75, 90–100.

Pounder, R.L. (1984). 'The origin of *theoi* as inscription-heading', in *Studies presented to Sterling Dow on his eightieth birthday*. A.L. Boegehold et al. (eds). Duke, NC, 243–50.

Prak, M.R. (1997). 'Burghers into citizens: Urban and national citizenship in the Netherlands during the revolutionary era (c. 1800)', *Theory and society* 26, 403–20.

Pritchard, D.M. (2015). *Public spending and democracy in classical Athens*. Austin.

Pritchett, W.K. (1971). 'Kallias: Fact or fancy?', *CSCA* 4, 219–25.

Pulleyn, S. (1997). *Prayer in Greek religion*. Oxford.

Raaflaub, K.A. (1998). 'The thetes and democracy (a response to Josiah Ober)', in *Democracy 2500? Questions and challenges*. I. Morris, K.A. Raaflaub (eds). Dubuque, 87–103.

(2002). 'Philosophy, science, politics: Herodotus and the intellectual trends of his time', in *Brill's companion to Herodotus*. E.J. Bakker, I.J.F. de Jong, H. van Wees (eds). Leiden/Boston, 149–86.

(2006). 'Athenian and Spartan *eunomia*, or: What to do with Solon's timocracy?', in Blok and Lardinois, 390–428.

Rademaker, A. (2005). *Sophrosyne: Polysemy, prototypicality and persuasive use of an ancient Greek value term*. Leiden/Boston.

Randall, R.H.J. (1953). 'The Erechtheum workmen', *AJA* 57, 199–210.

Reinau, H. (1981). *Die Entstehung des Bürgerbegriffs bei den Griechen*. Basel.
Reinmuth, O.W. (1971). *The ephebic inscriptions of the fourth century* B.C. Leiden.
Rhodes, P.J. (1972). *The Athenian boule*. Oxford.
(1978). 'Bastards as Athenian citizens'. *CQ n.s.* 28, 89–92.
(1981). 'The selection of ephors at Sparta', *Historia* 30, 498–502.
(1991). 'The Athenian code of laws, 410–399 B.C.', *JHS* 111, 87–100.
(2006). 'The reforms and laws of Solon: An optimistic view', in Blok and Lardinois, 248–60.
(2007a). '*Dioikesis*', *Chiron* 37, 349–62.
(2007b). 'Oaths in political life', in Sommerstein and Fletcher, 11–25.
(2009a). 'Civic ideology and citizenship', in *A companion to Greek and Roman political thought*. R. Balot (ed.). Malden, MA/Oxford, 57–69.
(2009b). 'State and religion in Athenian inscriptions', *G&R* 56, 1–13.
Richter, M. (1995). *The history of political and social concepts: A critical introduction*. New York.
Roberts, J.T. (1994). *Athens on trial: The antidemocratic tradition in western thought*. Princeton.
Roccos, L.J. (2000). 'Back-mantle and peplos: The special costume of Greek maidens in 4th-century funerary and votive reliefs', *Hesperia* 69, 235–65.
Roisman, H.M. (2004). 'Women's free speech in Greek tragedy', in *Free speech in classical antiquity*. I. Sluiter, R. Rosen (eds). Mnemosyne Suppl. 254. Leiden/Boston, 91–114.
Rosivach, V. (1987). 'Autochthony and the Athenians', *CQ n.s.* 37, 294–305.
(1994). *The system of public sacrifice in fourth-century Athens*. Atlanta.
Roussel, D. (1976). *Tribu et cité*. Paris.
Rousset, D. (2013). 'Sacred property and public property in the Greek city', *JHS* 133, 113–33.
Rubinstein, L. (1993). *Adoption in* IV. *century Athens*. Copenhagen.
(2009). '*Ateleia* grants and their enforcement in the classical and early Hellenistic periods', in *Greek history and epigraphy: Essays in honour of P.J. Rhodes*. L.G. Mitchell, L. Rubinstein (eds). Swansea, 115–44.
Rudhardt, J. (1962). 'La reconnaissance de la paternité: Sa nature et portée dans la société athénienne', *MusH* 19, 39–64.
(1992). *Notions fondamentales de la pensée religieuse et actes constitutifs du culte dans la Grèce ancienne (2nd ed.)*. Geneva.
(1999). *Thémis et les Horai: Recherche sur les divinités grecques de la justice et de la paix*. Geneva.
Ruschenbusch, E. (1966). *Solonos nomoi: Die Fragmente des Solonischen Gesetzwerkes mit einer Text- und Überlieferungsgeschichte*. Wiesbaden.
(2010). *Solon: Das Gesetzwerk – Fragmente: Übersetzung und Kommentar. Herausgegeben von Klaus Bringmann*. Stuttgart.
Rydberg-Cox, J.A. (2000). 'An unusual exclamation in Aeschines' *Against Timarchus*'. *Mnemosyne* 53, 419–30.
Sakellariou, M.B. (1989). *The polis-state: Definition and origin*. Athens.
Samons, L.J. (2000). *Empire of the owl: Athenian imperial finance*. Stuttgart.

Sarischoulis, E. (2008). *Schicksal, Götter und Handlungsfreiheit in den Epen Homers*. Stuttgart.

Scafuro, A.C. (1994). 'Witnessing and false witnessing: Proving citizenship and kin identity in fourth-century Athens', in *Athenian identity and civic ideology*. A.L. Boegehold, A.C. Scafuro (eds). Baltimore, 156–98.

(1997). *The forensic stage: Settling disputes in greco-roman comedy*. Cambridge.

(2006a). 'Identifying Solonian laws', in Blok and Lardinois, 175–96.

(2006b). 'Magistrates with hegemony in the courts of Athens', in *Symposion 2003: Vorträge zur griechischen und hellenistischen Rechtsgeschichte*. H.A. Rupprecht (ed.). Vienna, 27–52.

Schaps, D.M. (1979). *Economic rights of women in ancient Greece*. Edinburgh.

Schlaifer, R. (1943). 'The cult of Athena Pallenis (Athenaeus VI 234–235)', *HSPh* 54, 35–67.

Schmidt, M. *LfrgrE s.v.* ὁσίη'.

Schmitt-Pantel, P. (1977). 'Athéna Apatouria et la ceinture: Les aspects féminins des Apatouries à Athènes', *Annales ESC* 32, 1059–73.

(1992). *La cité au banquet, histoire des repas publics dans les cités grecques*. Paris/Rome.

Schneider, T. (1991–2). 'Félix Bourriots "Recherches sur la nature du génos" und Denis Roussels "Tribu et cité" in der althistorischen Forschung der Jahre 1977–1989', *Boreas* 14/15, 15–31.

Schuler, C. (2005). 'Die *dioikesis tes poleos* im öffentlichen Finanzwesen der hellenistischen Poleis', *Chiron* 35, 385–403.

Schütrumpf, E. (1991). *Aristoteles, Politik: Buch II–III, übersetzt und erläutert*. Berlin.

Scodel, R. (2008). *Epic facework: Self-presentation and social interaction in Homer*. Swansea.

Scott, J. Wallach (1996). *Only paradoxes to offer: French feminists and the rights of man*. Cambridge.

Scullion, S. (2005). '"Pilgrimage" and Greek religion: Sacred and secular in the pagan polis', in *Pilgrimage in Graeco-Roman and early Christian antiquity: Seeing the gods*. J. Elsner, I. Rutherford (eds). Oxford, 111–30.

Sealey, R. (1983). 'How citizenship and the city began in Athens', *AJAH* 8, 92–129.

Shapiro, H.A. (1998). 'Autochthony and the visual arts in fifth-century Athens', in *Democracy, empire, and the arts in fifth-century Athens*. D. Boedeker, K.A. Raaflaub (eds). Cambridge, MA/London, 127–51.

Shear, J.L. (2001). *Polis and Panathenaia: The history and development of Athena's festival*. Diss. University of Pennsylvania (UMI 3015371).

(2007a). 'Cultural change, space, and the politics of commemoration in Athens', in *Debating the Athenian revolution: Art, literature, philosophy, and politics, 430–380* BC. R. Osborne (ed.). Cambridge, 91–115.

(2007b). 'The oath of Demophantos and the politics of Athenian identity', in Sommerstein and Fletcher, 148–60.

(2007c). 'Reusing statues, rewriting inscriptions', in *Art and inscriptions in the ancient world*. Z. Newby, R. Leader-Newby (eds). Cambridge, 235–8.

(2011). *Polis and revolution: Responding to oligarchy in classical Athens.* Cambridge.
Sickinger, J.P. (1999). *Public records and archives in classical Athens.* Chapel Hill/London.
Siewert, P. (1977). 'The ephebic oath in fifth-century Athens', *JHS* 97, 102–11.
(1982). *Die Trittyen Attikas und die Heeresreform des Kleisthenes.* Munich.
(2002). *Ostrakismos-Testimonien, vol. I: Die Zeugnisse antiker Autoren, der Inschriften und Ostraka über das athenische Scherbengericht aus vorhellenistischer Zeit (487–322 v. Chr.).* Stuttgart.
Sluiter, I. (2015). 'Ancient etymology: A tool for thinking', in *Brill's companion to ancient scholarship.* F. Montanari, S. Matthaios, A. Rengakos (eds). Leiden, 896–922.
Sluiter, I., R. Rosen (2008). 'General introduction', in *KAKOS: Badness and anti-value in classical antiquity. Penn-Leiden Colloquia on Ancient Values, vol.* IV. I. Sluiter, R. Rosen (eds). Leiden/Boston, 1–27.
Smith, C.J. (2006). *The Roman clan: The gens from ancient ideology to modern anthropology.* Cambridge.
Solmsen, F. (1970). *Aristotle's system of the physical world: A comparison with his predecessors.* New York. (Orig. 1960).
Sommerstein, A., J. Fletcher (eds) (2007). *Horkos: The oath in Greek society.* Exeter.
Sourvinou-Inwood, C. (1990). 'What is *polis* religion?', in *The Greek city: From Homer to Alexander.* O. Murray, S. Price (eds). Oxford, 295–322; repr. 2000a.
(1994). 'Something to do with Athens: Tragedy and ritual', in Osborne and Hornblower, 269–90.
(1995). 'Male and female, public and private, ancient and modern', in *Pandora: Women in classical Greece.* E.D. Reeder (ed.). Princeton, 111–20.
(2000a). 'What is *polis* religion?', in *Oxford readings in Greek religion.* R. Buxton (ed.). Oxford, 13–37.
(2000b). 'Further aspects of *polis* religion', in *Oxford readings in Greek religion.* R. Buxton (ed.). Oxford, 38–55.
(2011). *Athenian myths and festivals: Aglauros, Erechtheus, Plynteria, Panathenaia, Dionysia.* R.T.C. Parker (ed.). Oxford.
Stafford, E.J. (1997). 'Themis: Religion and order in the archaic *polis*', in *The development of the polis in archaic Greece.* L.G. Mitchell, P.J. Rhodes (eds). London/New York, 158–67.
Staveley, E.S. (1972). *Greek and Roman voting.* Ithaca, NY.
Ste. Croix, G.E.M. de (1970). 'Some observations on the property rights of women', *CR n.s.* 20, 273–8.
(1972). *The origins of the Peloponnesian War.* Oxford.
(1992). 'Aristotle on history and poetry (Poetics, 9, 1451a36–b11)', in *Essays on Aristotle's Poetics.* A. Oksenberg Rorty (ed.). Princeton, 23–32.
(2004). '*Klerosis ek prokriton* [sortition from pre-selected candidates]: *Ath.Pol.* 8.1', in *Athenian democratic origins and other essays.* D. Harvey, R.T.C. Parker (eds). Oxford, 89–108.

Stehle, E. (2006). 'Solon's self-reflexive political persona and its audience', in Blok and Lardinois, 79–113.

Stone, P. (2011). *The luck of the draw: The role of lotteries in decision making.* Oxford.

Straten, F.T. van (1981). 'Gifts for the gods', in *Faith, hope and worship: Aspects of religious mentality in the ancient world.* H.S. Versnel (ed.). Leiden/Boston, 105–51.

(1995). *Hiera kala: Images of animal sacrifice in archaic and classical Greece.* Leiden/New York/Cologne.

Strauss, B.S. (1986). *Athens after the Peloponnesian War: Class, fiction, and policy 403–386* BC. Ithaca, NY.

Stroud, R.S. (1968). *Drakon's law on homicide.* Berkeley/Los Angeles.

(1979). *The axones and kyrbeis of Drakon and Solon.* Berkeley.

(1998). *The Athenian grain-tax law of 374/3* B.C. Princeton.

Taylor, C. (2007). 'From the whole citizen body? The sociology of election and lot in Athenian democracy', *Hesperia* 76, 323–45.

Taylor, M.C. (1997). *Salamis and the Salaminioi: The history of an unofficial Athenian demos.* Amsterdam.

Themelis, P.G. (1971) *Brauron: Guide to the site and museum.* Athens.

Theodoridis, C. (2002). 'Eine unbeachtete Buchangabe zum Bruchstück des Philochoros über die Attischen Orgeonen', *ZPE* 138, 40–2.

Thomas, R. (1989). *Oral tradition and written record in classical Athens.* Cambridge.

(2000). *Herodotus in context: Ethnography, science and the art of persuasion.* Cambridge.

(2011). '"And you, the demos, made an uproar": Performance, mass audiences and text in the Athenian democracy', in Lardinois, Blok, van der Poel, 161–87.

Tilly, C. (1995). 'Citizenship, identity, and social history', *International Review of Social History* 40, 1–18.

Todd, S.C. (1993). *The shape of Athenian law.* Oxford.

(1996). 'Lysias against Nikomachos: The fate of the expert in Athenian law', in *Greek law in its political setting: Justifications not justice.* L. Foxhall, A.D.E. Lewis (eds). Oxford, 101–31.

Traill, J.S. (1986). *Demos and trittys: Epigraphical and topographical studies in the organization of Attica.* Toronto.

Usher, S. (1999). *Greek oratory: Tradition and originality.* Oxford.

Valk, M.H.A.L.H. van der (1942). 'Zum Worte HOSIOS', *Mnemosyne* 10, 113–40.

(1951). 'Quelques remarques sur le sens du nom "hosia"', *REG* 64, 417–22.

Veligianni-Terzi, C. (1997). *Wertbegriffe in den attischen Ehrendekreten der klassischen Zeit.* Stuttgart.

Vérilhac, A.-M., C. Vial (1998). *Le mariage grec du* VIe *siècle av. J.-C. à l' époque d'Auguste.* Paris.

Vernant, J.-P. (1985) *Mythe et pensée chez les Grecs. Études de psychologie historique. Nouvelle édition revue et augmentée (2nd ed.; orig. 1965).* Paris.

(2006). *Myth and thought among the Greeks.* New York (transl. J. Lloyd, J. Fort; orig. Paris 1965).

Versnel, H.S. (1981). 'Religious mentality in ancient prayer', in *Faith, hope and worship: Studies in Greek and Roman religion*. H.S. Versnel (ed.). Leiden/Boston, 1–64.

(1987). 'Wife and helpmate: Women of ancient Athens in anthropological perspective', in *Sexual asymmetry: Studies in ancient society*. J.H. Blok, P. Mason (eds). Amsterdam, 61–86.

(1990). 'Beyond cursing', in *Magika hiera: Ancient Greek magic and religion*. C.A. Faraone, D. Obbink (eds). New York, 60–106.

(1993). *Inconsistencies in Greek and Roman religion, vol. II: Transition and reversal in myth and ritual*. Leiden/New York.

(2011). *Coping with the gods: Wayward readings in Greek theology*. Leiden/Boston.

Vestergaard, T. (2000). 'Milesian immigrants in late-Hellenistic and Roman Athens', in *The epigraphy of death: Studies in the history and society of Greece and Rome*. G.J. Oliver (ed.). Liverpool, 81–110.

Vidal-Naquet, P. (1986). *The black hunter: Forms of thought and forms of society in the Greek world*. Baltimore (transl. A. Szegedy-Maszak; orig. Paris 1981).

Vlassopoulos, K. (2007). *Unthinking the Greek polis: Ancient Greek history beyond Eurocentrism*. Cambridge/New York.

(2011). 'Greek slavery: From domination to property and back again', *JHS* 131, 115–30.

Wade-Gery, H.T. (1931). 'The financial decrees of Kallias (*IG* I^2 91–92)', *JHS* 51, 57–85.

(1958a). 'Demotionidai', in *Essays in Greek history*. Oxford, 116–34.

(1958b). 'Eupatridai, archons, and Areopagus', in *Essays in Greek history*. Oxford, 86–115.

Wagenvoort, H. (1980). 'Pietas', in *Pietas: Selected studies in Roman religion*. Leiden, 1–20. (Orig. 1924).

Wagner-Hasel, B. (2003). 'Egoistic exchange and altruistic gift: On the roots of Marcel Mauss' theory of the gift', in *Negotiating the gift: Pre-modern figurations of exchange*. G. Algazi, V. Groebner, B. Jussen (eds). Göttingen, 141–71.

Walbank, M.B. (1978). *Athenian proxenies of the fifth century* B.C. Toronto.

Walter, U. (1993). *An der Polis teilhaben: Bürgerstaat und Zugehörigkeit im archaischen Griechenland*. Stuttgart.

Walzer, M. (1988). 'Citizenship', in *Political innovation and conceptual change*. T. Ball, J. Farr, R.L. Hanson (eds). Cambridge, 211–19.

Watson, J. (2010). 'The origin of metic status', *CCJ* 56, 259–78.

Węcowski, M. (2014). *The rise of the aristocratic banquet*. Oxford.

Wees, H. van (1992). *Status warriors: War, violence and society in Homer and history*. Amsterdam.

(1998). 'The law of gratitude: Reciprocity in anthropological theory', in *Reciprocity in ancient Greece*. C. Gill, N. Postlethwaite, R. Seaford (eds). Oxford, 13–49.

(2004). *Greek warfare: Myths and realities*. London.

(2006). 'Mass and elite in Solon's Athens: The property classes revisited', in Blok and Lardinois, 351–89.
(2011). 'Demetrius and Draco: Athens' property classes and population in and before 317 BC', *JHS* 131, 95–114.
(2013). *Ships and silver, taxes and tribute: A fiscal history of Athens*. London.
Weiss, A. (2004). *Sklave der Stadt: Untersuchungen zur öffentlichen Sklaverei in den Städten des Römischen Reiches*. Stuttgart.
Welwei, K.-W. (1967). 'Der "Diapsephismos" nach dem Sturz der Peisistratiden', *Gymnasium* 74, 423–37.
Werlings, M.-J. (2010). *Le dèmos avant la démocratie: Mots, concepts, réalités historiques*. Paris.
West, M.L. (1985). *The Hesiodic Catalogue of Women: Its narrative, structure and origins*. Oxford.
(1997). *The east face of Helicon*. Oxford.
(1999). 'The invention of Homer', *CQ* 49, 364–82.
Whitehead, D. (1977). *The ideology of the Athenian metic*. Cambridge.
(1983). 'Competitive outlay and community profit: *Philotimia* in democratic Athens', *C&M* 34, 55–74.
(1986a). *The demes of Attica, 508/7 – ca. 250 BC: A social and political study*. Princeton.
(1986b). 'Women and naturalisation in fourth-century Athens: The case of Archippe', *CQ* 36, 109–14.
(1991). 'Norms of citizenship in ancient Greece', in *City-states in classical antiquity and medieval Italy*. A. Molho, K.A. Raaflaub, J. Emilen (eds). Stuttgart, 135–54.
(1993). 'Cardinal virtues: The language of public approbation in democratic Athens', *C&M* 44, 37–74.
(2009). '*Andragathia* and *arete*', in *Greek history and epigraphy: Essays in honour of P.J. Rhodes*. L.G. Mitchell, L. Rubinstein (eds). Swansea, 47–58.
Wijma, S.M. (2014). *Embracing the immigrant: The participation of metics in Athenian polis religion (5th–4th century BC)*. HE 233. Stuttgart.
Wilgaux, J. (2000). 'Entre inceste et échange: Réflexions sur le modèle matrimonial athénien', *L'homme* 154–5, 659–76.
(2009). 'De l'exil au partage: La transmission féminine des appartenances parentales et religieuses', in *La religion des femmes en Grèce ancienne: Mythes, cultes et société*. L. Bodiou, V. Mehl (eds). Rennes, 225–37.
Williamson, C.G. (2013). 'As god is my witness: Civic oaths in ritual space as a means towards rational cooperation in the Hellenistic polis', in *Cults, creeds and identities in the Greek city after the classical age*. R. Alston, O.M. van Nijf, C.G. Williamson (eds). Leuven, 119–74.
Willi, A. (2008). '*Nosos* and *hosie*: Etymological and sociocultural observations on the concept of disease and divine (dis)favour in ancient Greece', *JHS* 128, 153–71.
Wilson, P. (2008). 'Costing the Dionysia', in *Performance, iconography, reception: Studies in honour of Oliver Taplin*. P. Wilson, M. Revermann (eds). Oxford, 88–127.

(2010). 'How did the Athenian demes fund their theatre?', in *L'argent dans les concours du monde grec: Théâtres du monde*. B. Le Guen (ed.). Saint-Denis, 37–82.

(2015). 'The festival of Dionysos in Ikarion: A new study of *IG* I³ 254', *Hesperia* 84, 97–147.

Winters, T.F. (1993). 'Kleisthenes and Athenian nomenclature', *JHS* 113, 162–5.

Winton, R. (2004). 'Thucydides 2, 37, 1: Pericles on Athenian democracy', *RhM* 147, 26–34.

Wolff, H.J. (1944). 'Marriage law and family organization in ancient Athens: A study in the interrelation of public and private law in the Greek city', *Traditio* 2, 43–95.

(1952). 'Die Grundlagen des griechischen Eherechts', *RHD* 1–29, 158–81.

Wout, P.E. van 't (2010a). 'Solon's law on *stasis*: Promoting active neutrality', *CQ* 60, 289–301.

(2010b). 'Visibility and social evaluation in Athenian litigation', in *Valuing others in classical antiquity. Penn-Leiden Colloquia on Ancient Values*, vol. VI. I. Sluiter, R. Rosen (eds). Leiden/Boston. 179–204.

(2011a). 'From oath-swearing to entrenchment clause: The introduction of *atimia*-terminology in legal inscriptions', in Lardinois, Blok, van der Poel, 143–60.

(2011b). 'Neglected evidence for the nature of atimia, Agora P 17615 and DTA 107', *ZPE* 176, 126–34.

Wyse, W. (1904). *The speeches of Isaeus: Edited with critical and explanatory notes*. Cambridge.

Yunis, H. (1988). *A new creed: Fundamental religious beliefs in the Athenian polis and Euripidean drama*. Meisenheim.

Zeitlin, F.I. (1970). 'The Argive festival of Hera and Euripides' *Electra*'. *TAPhA* 101, 645–69.

(1996). *Playing the other: Gender and society in classical Greek literature*. Chicago.

Index of Sources

LITERARY TEXTS

INSCRIPTIONS

General Index

Printed in Poland
by Amazon Fulfillment
Poland Sp. z o.o., Wrocław

29961654R00197